P9-DTO-361
THE GREAT SEAL OF THE STATE OF
CALIFORNIA
EUREKA

CALIFORNIA VISTAS

OUR GOLDEN STATE

James A. Banks, Ph.D.
Kevin P. Colleary, Ed.D.
Stephen F. Cunha, Ph.D.
Jana Echevarria, Ph.D.
Walter C. Parker, Ph.D.
James J. Rawls, Ph.D.
Rosalía Salinas
Emily M. Schell, Ed.D.

Macmillan McGraw-Hill

PROGRAM AUTHORS

James A. Banks, Ph.D.
Russell F. Stark University Professor and Director, Center for Multicultural Education
University of Washington
Seattle, Washington

Kevin P. Colleary, Ed.D.
Curriculum and Teaching Department
Graduate School of Education
Fordham University
New York, New York

Stephen F. Cunha, Ph.D.
Professor of Geography
Humboldt State University
Arcata, California

Jana Echevarria, Ph.D.
Professor, College of Education
California State University
Long Beach, California

Walter C. Parker, Ph.D.
Professor of Education and Chair of Social Studies Education
University of Washington
Seattle, Washington

James J. Rawls, Ph.D.
Department of History
Diablo Valley College
Pleasant Hill, California

Rosalía Salinas
Senior Director
Learning Resources and Educational Technology Division (retired)
San Diego County Office of Education
San Diego, California

Emily M. Schell, Ed.D.
Social Studies Education Director,
City Heights Educational Collaborative
Visiting Professor, Teacher Education
San Diego State University
San Diego, California

California Geographic Alliance

California Geographic Alliance
Humboldt State University
Arcata, California

HISTORIANS/SCHOLARS

Steven Aron, Ph.D.
Professor of History and Executive Director, Autry National Center
University of California
Los Angeles, California

Pedro G. Castillo, Ph.D.
Professor of History
Provost, Oakes College
University of California
Santa Cruz, California

Amrik Singh Dua, Ph.D.
Professor and Department Chair
Dept. of Business Administration
Mount San Antonio College
Walnut, California

Eve Kornfeld, Ph.D.
Professor, Department of History
San Diego State University
San Diego, California

Mary Ting Yi Lui, Ph.D.
Assistant Professor of History and American Studies
Yale University
New Haven, Connecticut

Robert Platzner, Ph.D.
Emeritus Professor of Humanities and Religious Studies
California State University
Sacramento, California

Curtis C. Roseman, Ph.D.
Professor Emeritus of Geography
University of Southern California
Los Angeles, California

Kevin Starr, Ph.D.
University Professor and Professor of History
University of Southern California
Los Angeles, California

Quintard Taylor, Ph.D.
Scott and Dorothy Bullitt Professor of American History
University of Washington
Seattle, Washington

Clifford E. Trafzer, Ph.D.
Professor of American Indian History
University of California
Riverside, California

CONSULTANTS

Primary Sources Research

Library of Congress
Publishing Office
Washington, D.C.

Reading and Writing

Adria F. Klein, Ph.D.
Professor Emeritus
California State University
San Bernardino, California

English Learners

Elizabeth Jimenez
Pomona, California

RFB&D learning through listening

Students with print disabilities may be eligible to obtain an accessible, audio version of the pupil edition of this textbook. Please call Recording for the Blind & Dyslexic at 1-800-221-4792 for complete information.

The McGraw·Hill Companies

Macmillan McGraw-Hill

Published by Macmillan/McGraw-Hill, of McGraw-Hill Education, a division of The McGraw-Hill Companies, Inc., Two Penn Plaza, New York, New York 10121.

Printed in the United States of America

ISBN 0-02-150512-8

2 3 4 5 6 7 8 079 10 09 08 07 06

ACKNOWLEDGMENTS

Grateful acknowledgment is given to the following authors and publishers. Every effort has been made to trace the ownership of all copyrighted material and to secure the necessary permissions to reprint these selections. In the case of some selections for which acknowledgment is not given, extensive research has failed to locate the copyright holders.

Sierra, Text by Diane Siebert. Illustrations by Wendell Minor. Text Copyright © 1991 Diane Siebert. Illustrations © 1991 Wendell Minor. Published by HarperCollins Publishers. All Rights Reserved. Used by Permission.

Challenge of the Big Trees, by Lary M. Dilsaver and William C. Tweed. Copyright © 1990 by the Sequoia National History Association. All Rights Reserved. Used by Permission.

Ansel Adams: A Documentary Film, Copyright © 2002 by The Public Broadcasting Society. All Rights Reserved. Used by Permission.

A Frontier Lady, by Sarah Eleanor Royce. Copyright © 1932 by Yale University Press. All Rights Reserved. Used by Permission.

California's Great Central Valley: Finding Its Place in the World, from <http://www.usmayors.org/uscm/us_mayor_newspaper/documents/06_15_98s/documents/sacramento.html Used by Permission.

Northridge Quake Still Stirs Some, by Menaka Fernando. From the UCLA Daily Bruin, January 16, 2004. Copyright by the ASUCLA Communications Board. <http://www.dailybruin.com/news/articles.asp?id=26899> Used by Permission.

Cover permission for **The Ever-Living Tree: The Life and Times of a Coast Redwood**, Text by Linda Vieira. Illustrated by Christopher Canyon. Text Copyright © 1994 by Linda Vieira. Illustrations Copyright © 1994 by Christopher Canyon. Published by Walker and Company. All Rights Reserved.

Cover permission for **Stories in Stone: Rock Art Pictures by Early Americans**, Text by Caroline Arnold. Photographs by Richard Hewett. Text Copyright © 1996 by Caroline Arnold. Illustrations Copyright © 1996 by Richard Hewett. Published by Houghton Mifflin Company. All Rights Reserved.

Cover permission for **John Muir: My Life with Nature**, Text by Joseph Cornell. Illustrated by Elizabeth Ann Kelley and Christopher Canyon. Copyright © 2000 Joseph Cornell. Published by DAWN Publications. All Rights Reserved.

Mountain-Making, from "Back in the Beforetime: Tales of the California Indians." Retold by Jane Louise Curry. Illustrated by James Watts. Text Copyright © 1987 by Jane Louise Curry. Illustrations Copyright © 1987 by James Watts. Published by Margaret K. McElderry Books – Macmillan Publishing Company. All Rights Reserved. Used by Permission.

The Queen of California, by Garci Rodríguez Ordoñez de Montalvo. From Las Sergas de Esplandian in The Literature of California. Copyright © 2000 by the University of California Press. All Rights Reserved. Used by Permission.

The Natural World of the California Indians, by Robert F. Heizer and B. Elasser. Copyright © 1980 by the University of California Press. All Rights Reserved. Used by Permission.

Celebrate American Indian Culture, by Margie Anne Clark. From The Signal. September 27, 2002. Copyright © by The Signal: <http://www.the-signal.com/News/ViewStory.asp?storyID=879> Used by Permission.

Remember Your Relations: The Elsie Allen Baskets, Family, and Friends, by the History Department of the Oakland Museum of California. <http://www.museumca.org/exhibit/exhi_remember_your_relations.html> Used by Permission.

Indians of California: The Changing Image, by James Rawls. Copyright © 1984 by the University of Oklahoma Press. All Rights Reserved. Used by Permission.

The Diary of Sebastián Vízcaino, 1602 – 1603, by The American Journeys Collection. Copyright © 2003 by The Wisconsin Historical Society. <http://content.wisconsinhistory.org/cgi-bin/docviewer.exe?CISOROOT=/aj&CISOPTR=1586> Used by Permission.

(continued on page R49)

★CONTENTS★

The Golden State – Our Home 2

UNIT 2 Early California History 84

Becoming a State 184

UNIT 4 A Growing State 268

Reference Section

Skills and Features

Reading Social Studies

Using Primary Sources

Chart and Graph Skills

Critical Thinking Skills

Map and Globe Skills

Study and Research Skills

Biography

Citizenship
Points of View

Democracy in Action

Literature

Readers' Theater

Field Trip

A Day in the Life

Primary Sources

Music

Datagraphics

At the Same Time

Then and Now

Charts, Graphs, and Diagrams

Time Lines

Maps

Primary Source Quotes

Unit 1 Opener

Chapter 1

Chapter 2

Primary Source Quotes

Unit 2 Opener

Chapter 3

Chapter 4

Chapter 5

Unit 3 Opener

Chapter 6

Chapter 7

Start with Your
CALIFORNIA STANDARDS

You will see California Standards throughout this book. These are topics you are required to learn as a social studies student. Standards will help you focus as you read.

The first page of every lesson lists the standards covered in that lesson. At the end of each lesson, a "What You Learned" box summarizes the lesson and lists its standards. The questions in Lesson Reviews, Chapter Reviews, and Unit Reviews all have standards next to them. You will also find standards next to each chart, graph, and activity.

California standards are listed in blue type on the first page of every lesson.

California standards are explained in black type with page numbers that show where they are taught.

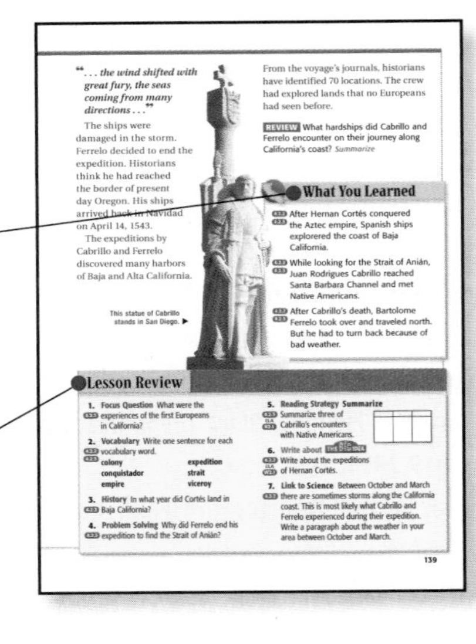

What You Learned reviews the lesson's main ideas and the standards they covered.

Lesson Review questions list History/ Social Science Standards and English-Language Arts Standards.

ABOUT THE BIG IDEA

The Big Ideas in this book are important ideas in social studies. They will help you understand each unit and its California Standards.

The Big Idea question for each unit appears on its opening pages. As you review each lesson, look for the Write about the Big Idea question in the Lesson Review. The question helps you answer the Big Idea question for the unit. When you finish each unit, complete the Big Idea activities. They will help you review what you have learned. Finally, you will find a list of three books that will help you learn more about the Big Idea.

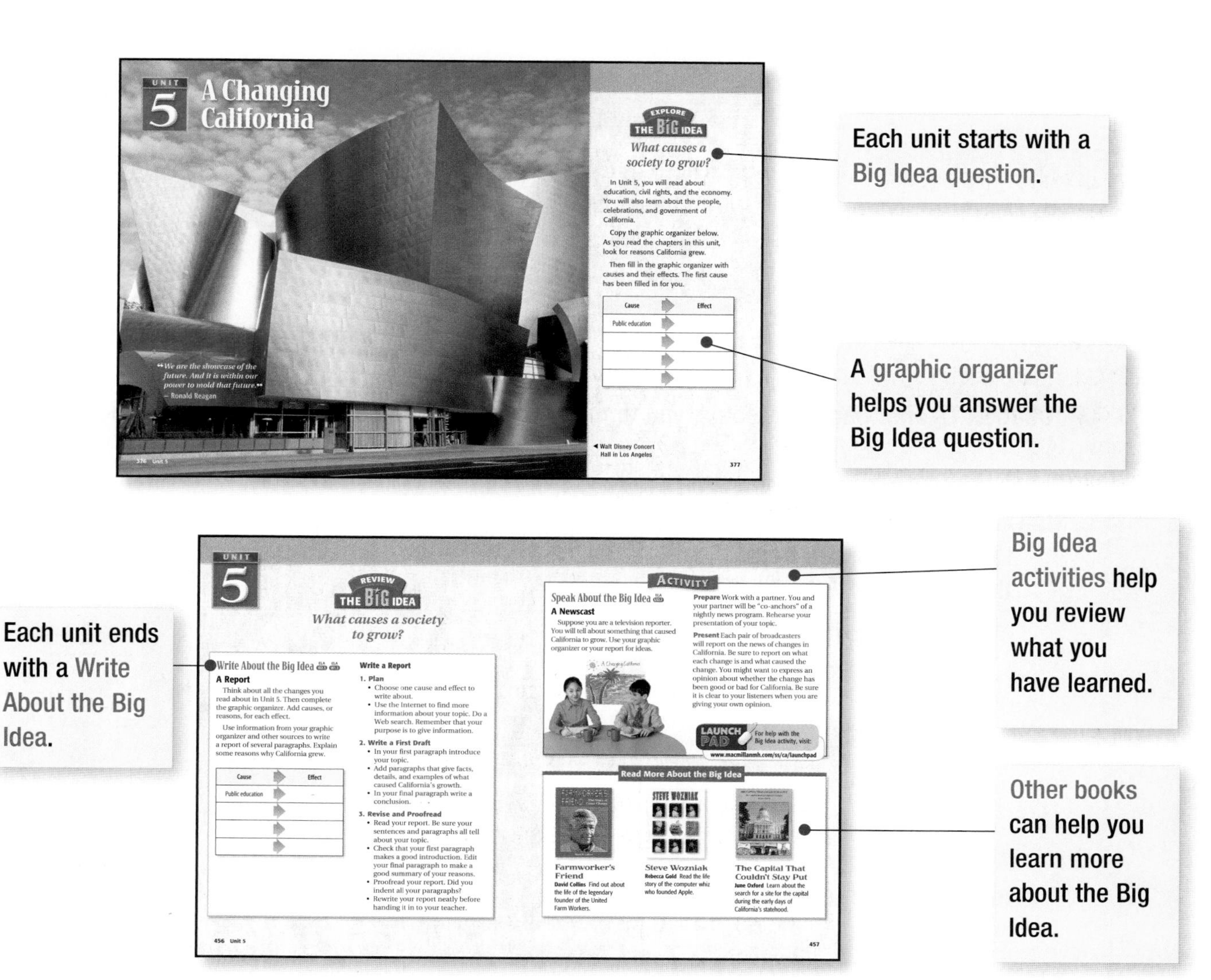

Reading Your Textbook

This book is organized to help you understand and apply social studies content and skills as you read.

Unit Opener and **Unit Closer** pages help you see the big picture.

The Unit Opener photo and quote capture the excitement of the events of the unit.

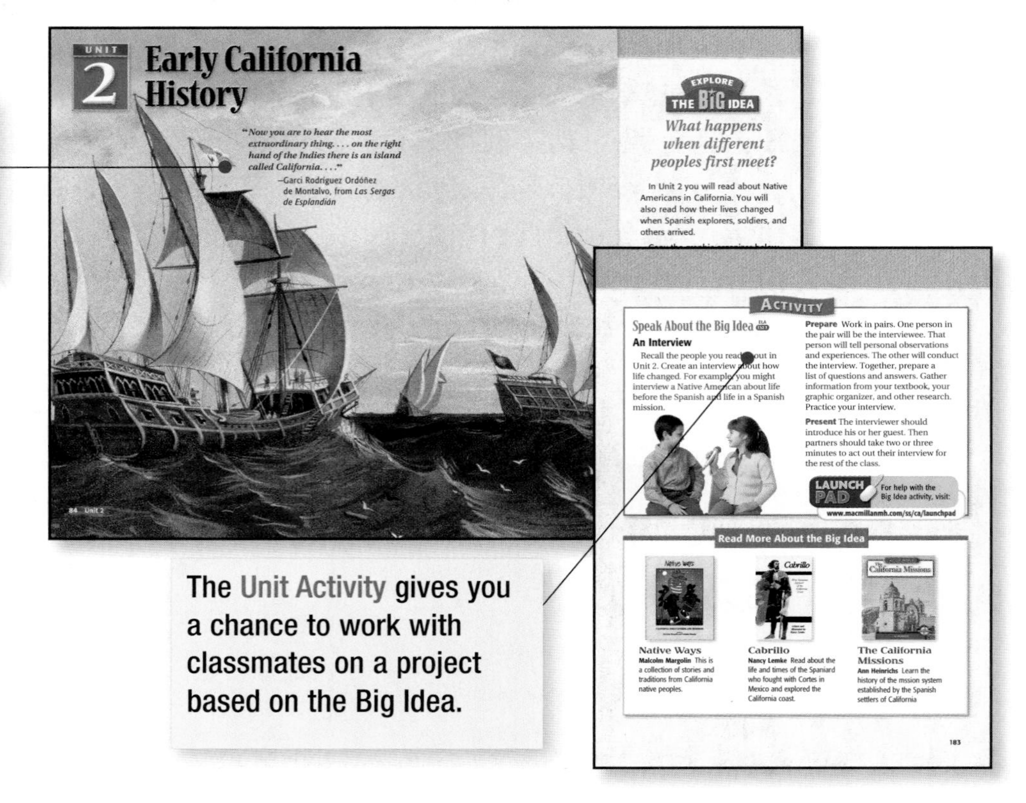

The Unit Activity gives you a chance to work with classmates on a project based on the Big Idea.

Chapter Opener pages introduce you to the time and place of events you will read about.

A map helps you see the locations of places from the chapter.

A time line organizes important chapter events.

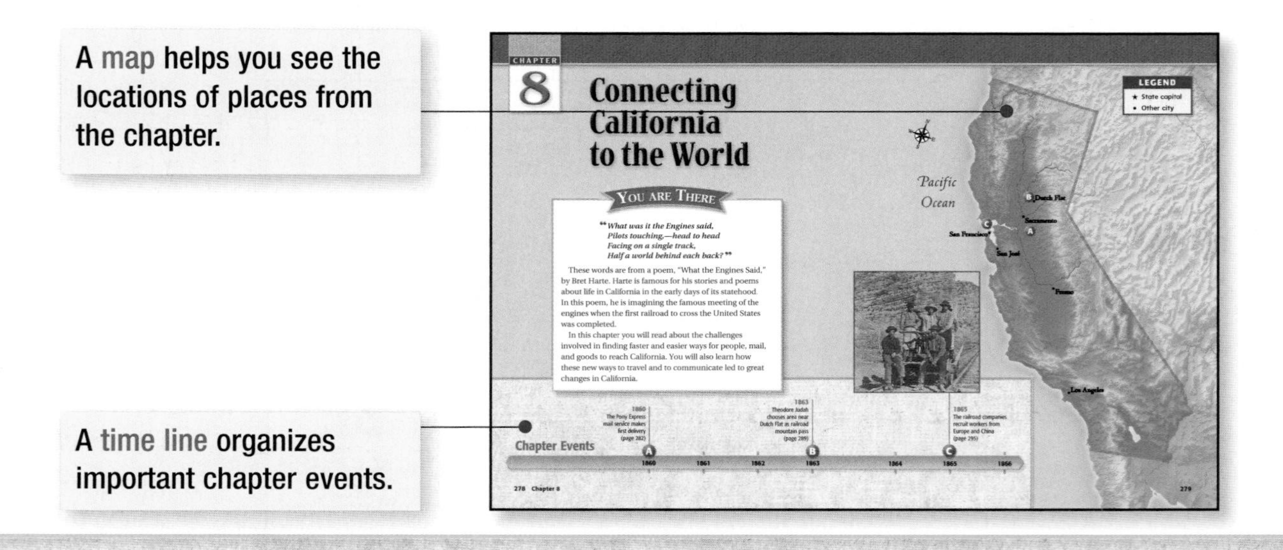

Lesson Opener pages prepare you before you read.

Focus questions set a purpose for reading.

Graphic organizers help you organize information as you read.

Review questions help you know if you understood the section.

LESSON 1

FOCUS QUESTION

How did California become a leader in public education?

VOCABULARY

public education
superintendent
charter
campus

VOCABULARY STRATEGY

PREFIXES A **superintendent** is a person who manages an organization. The prefix **super-** is from the Latin word for **more than.** What other words begin with the prefix **super-**?

READING STRATEGY

Identify Cause and Effect

Use the chart below to list three people whose leadership shaped public school education in our state and tell what impact they had.

Education for All

Start with Your CALIFORNIA STANDARDS

Students explain how California became an agricultural and industrial power, tracing the transformation of the California economy and its political and cultural development since the 1850s.

Describe the history and development of California's public education system, including universities and community colleges.

Learn about the history of the public school system as well as colleges and universities in California. (Begins on page 389)

Californians of all backgrounds benefit from public education. ▼

What are you doing in school today? As you read, write, take tests, or do class projects, you are taking part in something very important. You are preparing not only for your own future, but also for the future of California.

Education in California

Californians know that education is the key to a successful life. In 1849, when representatives met to talk about statehood, education was one of the issues they discussed.

The First Public Schools

A representative named Robert Semple argued for a system of **public education**. He believed that California would be a better place if every Californian could attend school without having to pay. Semple wrote:

> *"If the people are to govern themselves, they should be qualified to do it. They must be educated; they must educate their children."*

In 1850, California's first public school opened in San Francisco. Six years later, the state's first public high school opened in San Francisco. Both schools were paid for by the city. However, California still needed a system for all the students in the state.

In 1863 John Swett became the first **superintendent**, or head, of California's public schools. He set out to make a public education system for all students. In the 1860s, he helped pass laws to create a state tax to support schools.

As a result, all of California's cities were given money to build and run public schools. Money from taxes is still used to pay for our public schools.

REVIEW What happened when John Swett became superintendent of California's public schools? *Cause and Effect*

Lesson Review pages test your understanding of the lesson.

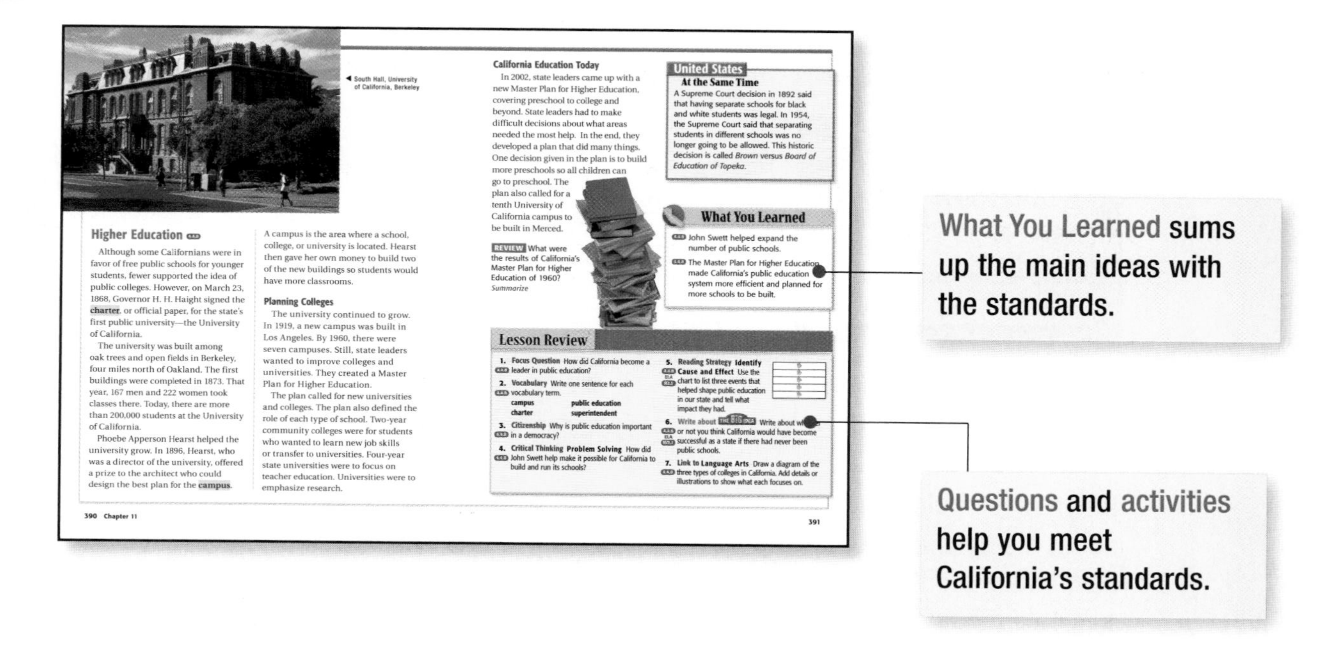

◄ South Hall, University of California, Berkeley

Higher Education

Although some Californians were in favor of free public schools for younger students, fewer supported the idea of public colleges. However, on March 23, 1868, Governor H. H. Haight signed the **charter**, or official paper, for the state's first public university—the University of California.

The university was built among oak trees and open fields in Berkeley, four miles north of Oakland. The first buildings were completed in 1873. That year, 167 men and 222 women took classes there. Today, there are more than 200,000 students at the University of California.

Phoebe Apperson Hearst helped the university grow. In 1896, Hearst, who was a director of the university, offered a prize to the architect who could design the best plan for the **campus**. A campus is the area where a school, college, or university is located. Hearst then gave her own money to build two of the new buildings so students would have more classrooms.

Planning Colleges

The university continued to grow. In 1919, a new campus was built in Los Angeles. By 1960, there were seven campuses. Still, state leaders wanted to improve colleges and universities. They created a Master Plan for Higher Education.

The plan called for new universities and colleges. The plan also defined the role of each type of school. Two-year community colleges were for students who wanted to learn new job skills or transfer to universities. Four-year state universities were to focus on teacher education. Universities were to emphasize research.

California Education Today

In 2002, state leaders came up with a new Master Plan for Higher Education, covering preschool to college and beyond. State leaders had to make difficult decisions about what areas needed the most help. In the end, they developed a plan that did many things. One decision given in the plan is to build more preschools so all children can go to preschool. The plan also called for a tenth University of California campus to be built in Merced.

REVIEW What were the results of California's Master Plan for Higher Education of 1960? *Summarize*

United States — At the Same Time

A Supreme Court decision in 1892 said that having separate schools for black and white students was legal. In 1954, the Supreme Court said that separating students in different schools was no longer going to be allowed. This historic decision is called *Brown* versus *Board of Education of Topeka.*

What You Learned

- John Swett helped expand the number of public schools.
- The Master Plan for Higher Education made California's public education system more efficient and planned for more schools to be built.

Lesson Review

1. **Focus Question** How did California become a leader in public education?
2. **Vocabulary** Write one sentence for each vocabulary term.
   campus **public education**
   charter **superintendent**
3. **Citizenship** Why is public education important in a democracy?
4. **Critical Thinking Problem Solving** How did John Swett help make it possible for California to build and run its schools?
5. **Reading Strategy Identify Cause and Effect** Use the chart to list three events that helped shape public education in our state and tell what impact they had.
6. **Write about THE BIG IDEA** Write about wh[illegible] or not you think California would have become successful as a state if there had never been public schools.
7. **Link to Language Arts** Draw a diagram of the three types of colleges in California. Add details or illustrations to show what each focuses on.

What You Learned sums up the main ideas with the standards.

Questions and activities help you meet California's standards.

Reading Social Studies pages teach reading skills that help you understand social studies content.

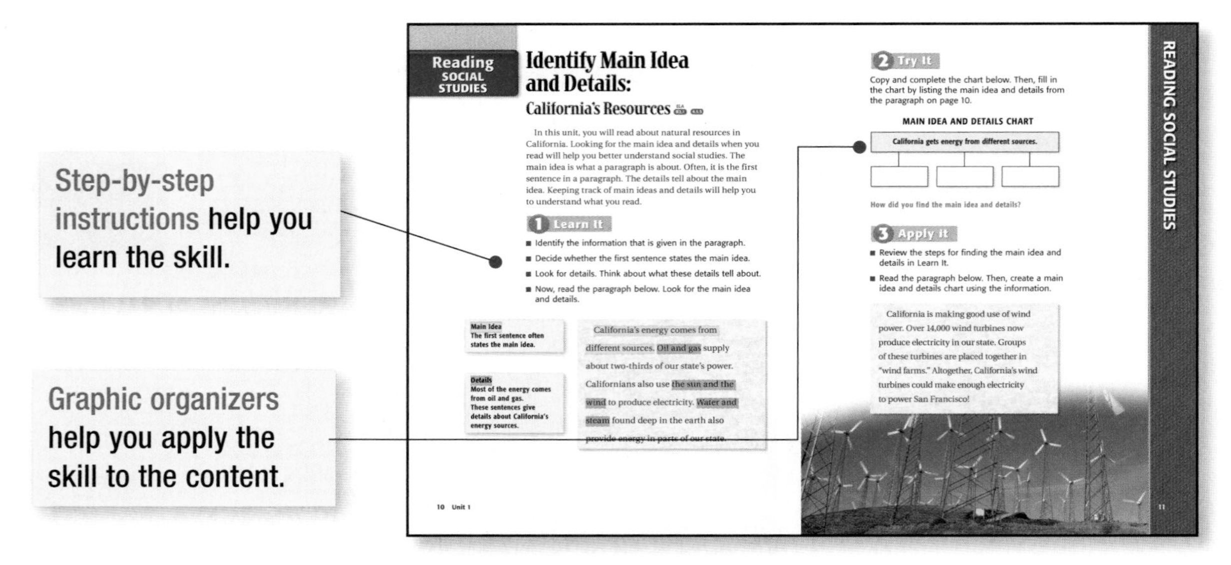

Reading SOCIAL STUDIES

Identify Main Idea and Details:

California's Resources

In this unit, you will read about natural resources in California. Looking for the main idea and details when you read will help you better understand social studies. The main idea is what a paragraph is about. Often, it is the first sentence in a paragraph. The details tell about the main idea. Keeping track of main ideas and details will help you to understand what you read.

1 Learn It

- Identify the information that is given in the paragraph.
- Decide whether the first sentence states the main idea.
- Look for details. Think about what these details tell about.
- Now, read the paragraph below. Look for the main idea and details.

Main Idea
The first sentence often states the main idea.

Details
Most of the energy comes from oil and gas. These sentences give details about California's energy sources.

California's energy comes from different sources. Oil and gas supply about two-thirds of our state's power. Californians also use the sun and the wind to produce electricity. Water and steam found deep in the earth also provide energy in parts of our state.

10 Unit 1

2 Try It

Copy and complete the chart below. Then, fill in the chart by listing the main idea and details from the paragraph on page 10.

MAIN IDEA AND DETAILS CHART

California gets energy from different sources.

How did you find the main idea and details?

3 Apply It

- Review the steps for finding the main idea and details in Learn It.
- Read the paragraph below. Then, create a main idea and details chart using the information.

California is making good use of wind power. Over 14,000 wind turbines now produce electricity in our state. Groups of these turbines are placed together in "wind farms." Altogether, California's wind turbines could make enough electricity to power San Francisco!

READING SOCIAL STUDIES

11

Step-by-step instructions help you learn the skill.

Graphic organizers help you apply the skill to the content.

Biographies and **Primary Sources** bring the past alive.

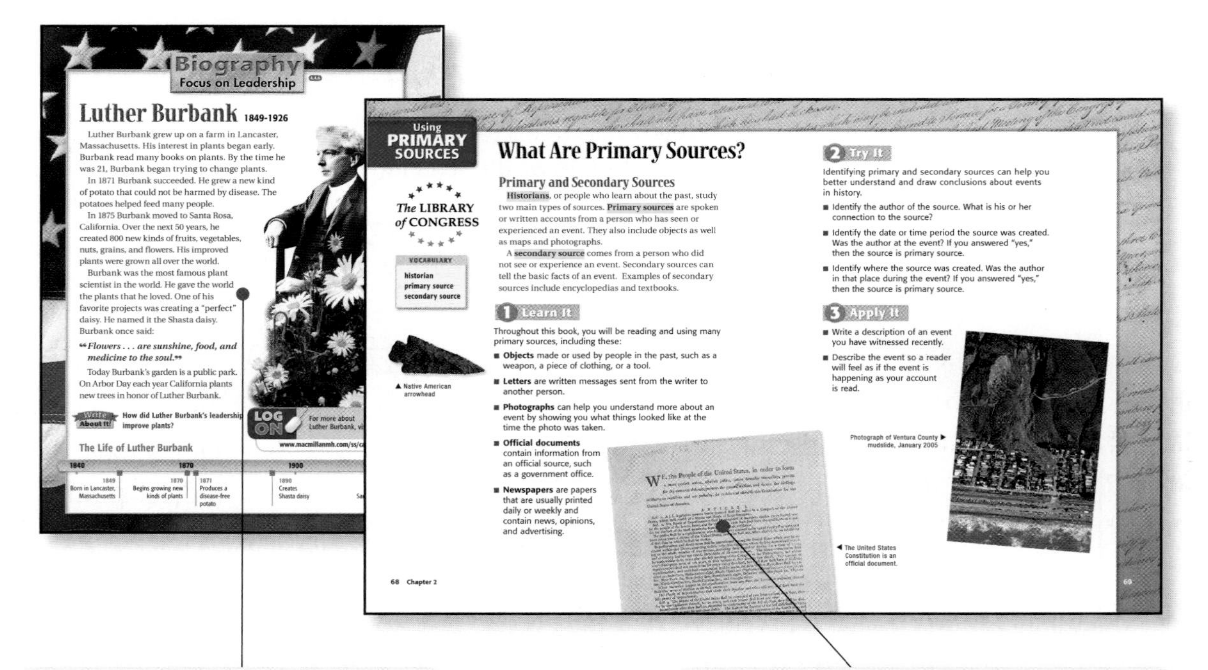

Biography
Focus on Leadership

Luther Burbank 1849-1926

Luther Burbank grew up on a farm in Lancaster, Massachusetts. His interest in plants began early. Burbank read many books on plants. By the time he was 21, Burbank began trying to change plants.

In 1871 Burbank succeeded. He grew a new kind of potato that could not be harmed by disease. The potatoes helped feed many people.

In 1875 Burbank moved to Santa Rosa, California. Over the next 50 years, he created 800 new kinds of fruits, vegetables, nuts, grains, and flowers. His improved plants were grown all over the world.

Burbank was the most famous plant scientist in the world. He gave the world the plants that he loved. One of his favorite projects was creating a "perfect" daisy. He named it the Shasta daisy. Burbank once said:

"Flowers . . . are sunshine, food, and medicine to the soul."

Today Burbank's garden is a public park. On Arbor Day each year California plants new trees in honor of Luther Burbank.

Write About It! How did Luther Burbank's leadership improve plants?

LOG ON For more about Luther Burbank, vi[sit] www.macmillanmh.com/ss/ca

The Life of Luther Burbank

1840 | 1870 | 1900
1849 Born in Lancaster, Massachusetts
1870 Begins growing new kinds of plants
1871 Produces a disease-free potato
1890 Creates Shasta daisy

Using PRIMARY SOURCES

What Are Primary Sources?

The LIBRARY of CONGRESS

VOCABULARY
historian
primary source
secondary source

Primary and Secondary Sources

Historians, or people who learn about the past, study two main types of sources. **Primary sources** are spoken or written accounts from a person who has seen or experienced an event. They also include objects as well as maps and photographs.

A **secondary source** comes from a person who did not see or experience an event. Secondary sources can tell the basic facts of an event. Examples of secondary sources include encyclopedias and textbooks.

1 Learn It

Throughout this book, you will be reading and using many primary sources, including these:

- **Objects** made or used by people in the past, such as a weapon, a piece of clothing, or a tool.
- **Letters** are written messages sent from the writer to another person.
- **Photographs** can help you understand more about an event by showing you what things looked like at the time the photo was taken.
- **Official documents** contain information from an official source, such as a government office.
- **Newspapers** are papers that are usually printed daily or weekly and contain news, opinions, and advertising.

▲ Native American arrowhead

◄ The United States Constitution is an official document.

68 Chapter 2

2 Try It

Identifying primary and secondary sources can help you better understand and draw conclusions about events in history.

- Identify the author of the source. What is his or her connection to the source?
- Identify the date or time period the source was created. Was the author at the event? If you answered "yes," then the source is primary source.
- Identify where the source was created. Was the author in that place during the event? If you answered "yes," then the source is primary source.

3 Apply It

- Write a description of an event you have witnessed recently.
- Describe the event so a reader will feel as if the event is happening as your account is read.

Photograph of Ventura County ► mudslide, January 2005

69

Biographies help you learn about the lives of people who have made a difference.

Primary Sources let you read the words and study the artifacts of people from the past and present.

Citizenship pages show real-life participation in democracy.

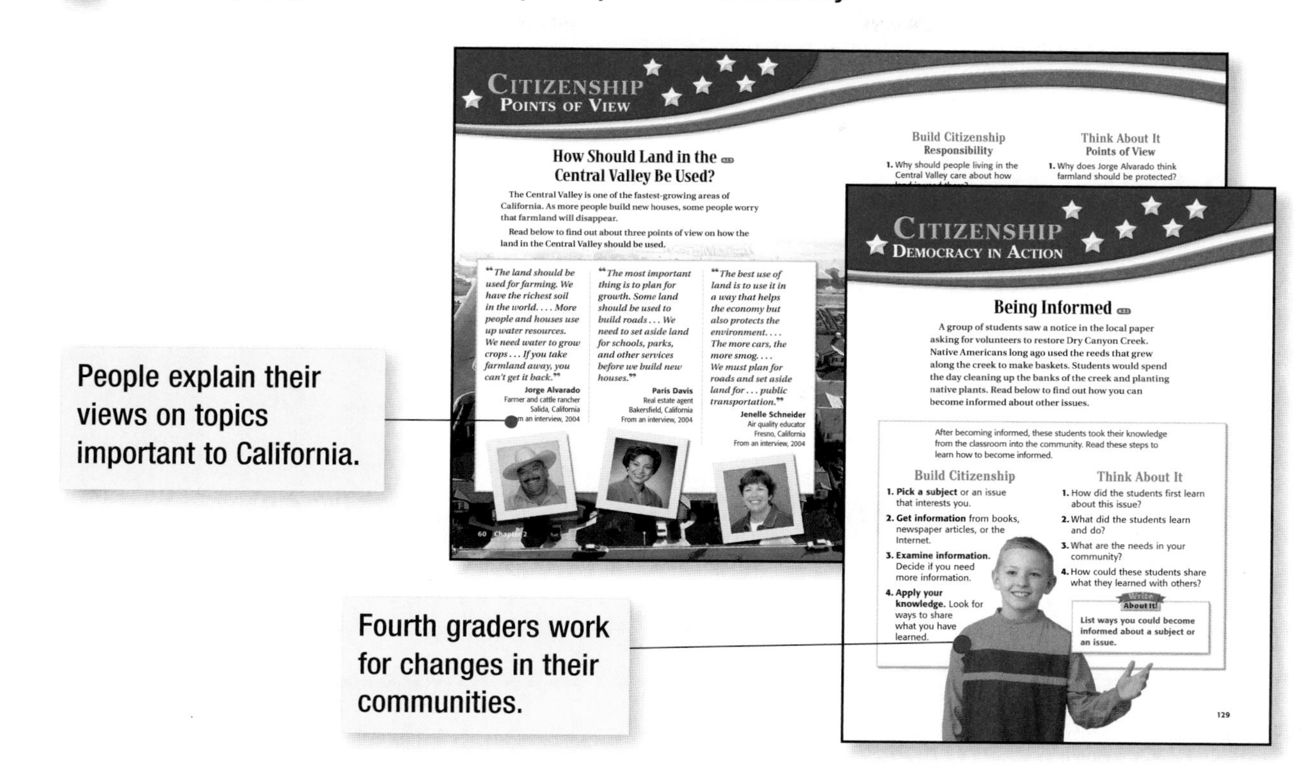
CITIZENSHIP
POINTS OF VIEW

How Should Land in the Central Valley Be Used?

The Central Valley is one of the fastest-growing areas of California. As more people build new houses, some people worry that farmland will disappear.

Read below to find out about three points of view on how the land in the Central Valley should be used.

"The land should be used for farming. We have the richest soil in the world. . . . More people and houses use up water resources. We need water to grow crops . . . If you take farmland away, you can't get it back."
Jorge Alvarado
Farmer and cattle rancher
Salida, California
From an interview, 2004

"The most important thing is to plan for growth. Some land should be used to build roads . . . We need to set aside land for schools, parks, and other services before we build new houses."
Paris Davis
Real estate agent
Bakersfield, California
From an interview, 2004

"The best use of land is to use it in a way that helps the economy but also protects the environment. . . . The more cars, the more smog. . . . We must plan for roads and set aside land for . . . public transportation."
Jenelle Schneider
Air quality educator
Fresno, California
From an interview, 2004

Build Citizenship
Responsibility
1. Why should people living in the Central Valley care about how

Think About It
Points of View
1. Why does Jorge Alvarado think farmland should be protected?

60 Chapter 2

CITIZENSHIP
DEMOCRACY IN ACTION

Being Informed

A group of students saw a notice in the local paper asking for volunteers to restore Dry Canyon Creek. Native Americans long ago used the reeds that grew along the creek to make baskets. Students would spend the day cleaning up the banks of the creek and planting native plants. Read below to find out how you can become informed about other issues.

After becoming informed, these students took their knowledge from the classroom into the community. Read these steps to learn how to become informed.

Build Citizenship
1. **Pick a subject** or an issue that interests you.
2. **Get information** from books, newspaper articles, or the Internet.
3. **Examine information.** Decide if you need more information.
4. **Apply your knowledge.** Look for ways to share what you have learned.

Think About It
1. How did the students first learn about this issue?
2. What did the students learn and do?
3. What are the needs in your community?
4. How could these students share what they learned with others?

Write About It!
List ways you could become informed about a subject or an issue.

129

People explain their views on topics important to California.

Fourth graders work for changes in their communities.

Readers' Theater and Literature bring California history alive.

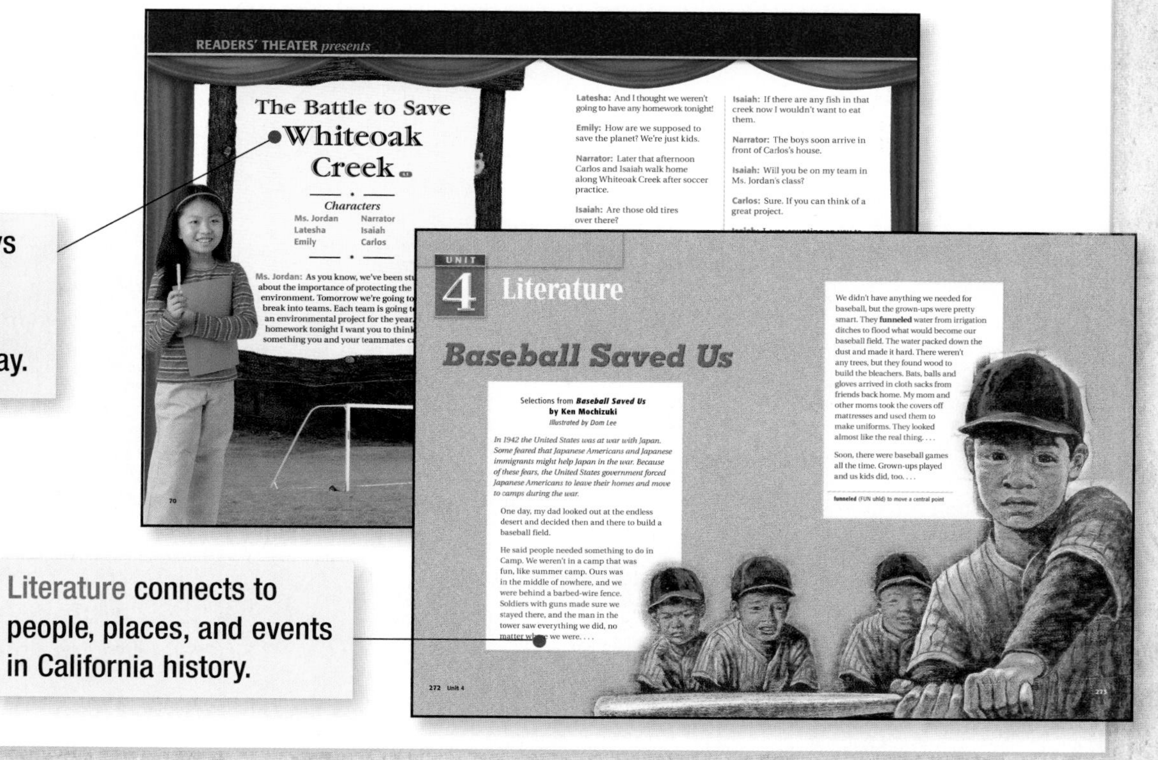
READERS' THEATER presents

The Battle to Save Whiteoak Creek

Characters
Ms. Jordan Narrator
Latesha Isaiah
Emily Carlos

Ms. Jordan: As you know, we've been st... about the importance of protecting the environment. Tomorrow we're going to break into teams. Each team is going to ... an environmental project for the year... homework tonight I want you to think ... something you and your teammates c...

Latesha: And I thought we weren't going to have any homework tonight!

Emily: How are we supposed to save the planet? We're just kids.

Narrator: Later that afternoon Carlos and Isaiah walk home along Whiteoak Creek after soccer practice.

Isaiah: Are those old tires over there?

Isaiah: If there are any fish in that creek now I wouldn't want to eat them.

Narrator: The boys soon arrive in front of Carlos's house.

Isaiah: Will you be on my team in Ms. Jordan's class?

Carlos: Sure. If you can think of a great project.

70

UNIT 4 Literature

Baseball Saved Us

Selections from *Baseball Saved Us*
by Ken Mochizuki
Illustrated by Dom Lee

In 1942 the United States was at war with Japan. Some feared that Japanese Americans and Japanese immigrants might help Japan in the war. Because of these fears, the United States government forced Japanese Americans to leave their homes and move to camps during the war.

One day, my dad looked out at the endless desert and decided then and there to build a baseball field.

He said people needed something to do in Camp. We weren't in a camp that was fun, like summer camp. Ours was in the middle of nowhere, and we were behind a barbed-wire fence. Soldiers with guns made sure we stayed there, and the man in the tower saw everything we did, no matter where we were. . . .

We didn't have anything we needed for baseball, but the grown-ups were pretty smart. They **funneled** water from irrigation ditches to flood what would become our baseball field. The water packed down the dust and made it hard. There weren't any trees, but they found wood to build the bleachers. Bats, balls and gloves arrived in cloth sacks from friends back home. My mom and other moms took the covers off mattresses and used them to make uniforms. They looked almost like the real thing. . . .

Soon, there were baseball games all the time. Grown-ups played and us kids did, too. . . .

272 Unit 4

273

Readers' Theater plays give you a chance to think about events in California in a new way.

Literature connects to people, places, and events in California history.

Geography Handbook

A Letter from Steve Cunha

Dear Student:

Hi, I'm Steve Cunha. I am one of the authors of this book, and I am a geographer. Have you ever wondered why a redwood tree grows in the mountains and a cactus in the desert? Why cities are located near water or major roads? How people have changed the land over time? If so, you are on your way to being a geographer, too.

Geographers are people who study Earth. We look at the land and water, the weather and climate, and the plants and animals on Earth. We also study people—where they live and how they shape where they live.

Knowing about geography helps you study History and Social Sciences. In the following pages, you will review some important ideas about geography. You will also review some key map skills that will help you as you read about California's climates, landforms, and its many regions.

Let's get started. From one geographer to another: Enjoy your travels!

Stephen Cunha

Steve Cunha
The California Geographic Alliance

The Five Themes of Geography

Our world is connected in many ways. Some geographers have broken down the study of geography into five different themes. The themes are location, place, region, movement, and human interaction. Understanding these themes will help you make sense of historical events.

■ Location

In geography, *location* means an exact spot on the planet. A location is usually a street name and number. You write a location when you address a letter.

Hollywood sign in Los Angeles

■ Place

A *place* is described by its features. To name a place, you would describe the physical features of a place, such as rivers, mountains, or valleys. You would also describe the human features of a place. These include the cities, language, and religion that the people in a place share.

Pier at Manhattan Beach in Los Angeles

■ Region

A *region* is bigger than a place or a location. Regions cover large areas of land. The people in a region share physical or human characteristics. For example, the people near California's coast share the Pacific Ocean. They live in the coastal region.

Los Angeles, with the San Gabriel Mountains

■ Movement

Throughout history, people have *moved* from one place to another. They might have moved because the weather changed or because they thought more money could be made in another place. As people moved, they often made changes to a place. Geographers study why these movements occurred. They also look at how people's movement changed an area.

Los Angeles freeway

■ Human Interaction

Geographers are interested in how the environment influences people. For example, hot areas draw people to the beach. Cold areas draw people to the ski slopes. Geographers also study how people *interact*, or affect, the environment. This interaction determines how land is used for factories, houses, farms, or parks.

Griffith Park and Observatory in Los Angeles

Dictionary of Geographic Terms

1 **BASIN** A bowl-shaped landform surrounded by higher land

2 **BAY** Part of an ocean or lake that extends deeply into the land

3 **CANAL** A channel built to carry water for irrigation or transportation

4 **CANYON** A deep, narrow valley with steep sides

5 **COAST** The land along an ocean

6 **DAM** A wall built across a river, creating a lake that stores water

7 **DELTA** Land made of soil left behind as a river drains into a larger body of water

8 **DESERT** A dry environment with few plants and animals

9 **FAULT** The border between two of the plates that make up Earth's crust

10 **GLACIER** A huge sheet of ice that moves slowly across the land

11 **GULF** Part of an ocean that extends into the land; larger than a bay

12 **HARBOR** A sheltered place along a coast where boats dock safely

13 **HILL** A rounded, raised landform; not as high as a mountain

14 **ISLAND** A body of land completely surrounded by water

15 **LAKE** A body of water completely surrounded by land

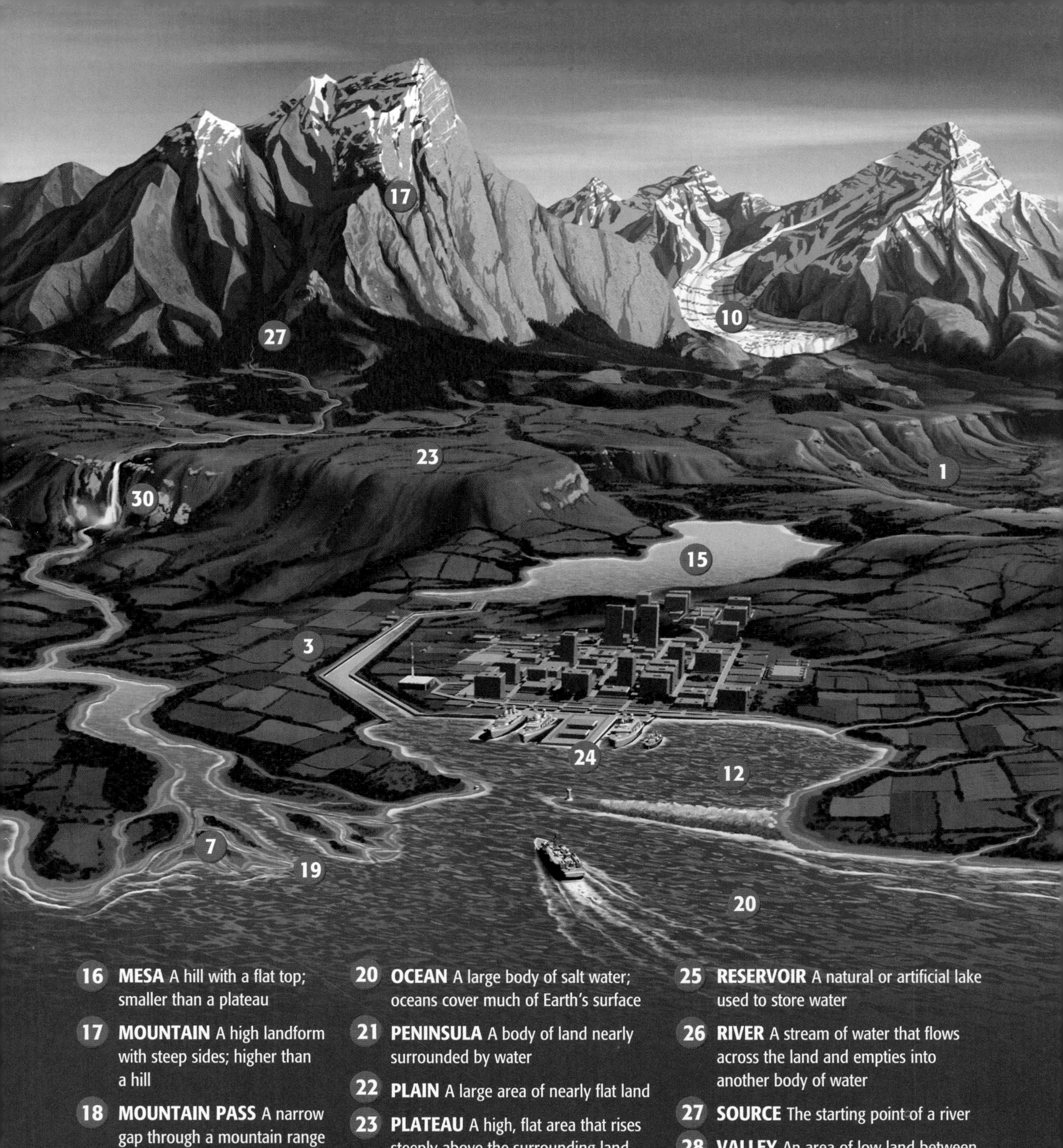

16 MESA A hill with a flat top; smaller than a plateau

17 MOUNTAIN A high landform with steep sides; higher than a hill

18 MOUNTAIN PASS A narrow gap through a mountain range

19 MOUTH The place where a river empties into a larger body of water

20 OCEAN A large body of salt water; oceans cover much of Earth's surface

21 PENINSULA A body of land nearly surrounded by water

22 PLAIN A large area of nearly flat land

23 PLATEAU A high, flat area that rises steeply above the surrounding land

24 PORT A place where ships load and unload their goods

25 RESERVOIR A natural or artificial lake used to store water

26 RIVER A stream of water that flows across the land and empties into another body of water

27 SOURCE The starting point of a river

28 VALLEY An area of low land between hills or mountains

29 VOLCANO An opening in Earth's surface through which hot rock and ash are forced out

30 WATERFALL A flow of water falling vertically

Reviewing Geography Skills

Looking at Earth

Earth and the Globe

From outer space, Earth looks like a big blue ball with brown spots. In order to see a complete view of Earth, we use a globe. A globe is a special map that is shaped like a sphere, or ball. The globe is a model of Earth. It shows what the land and water look like on Earth.

The large areas of land on Earth are called continents. There are seven continents on Earth. Their names are Africa, Antarctica, Asia, Australia, Europe, North America, and South America.

The big bodies of water are called oceans. The names of the four oceans are the Arctic, Atlantic, Indian, and Pacific Oceans.

Hemispheres

The equator is an imaginary line on the Earth. It divides the sphere of Earth in half. A word for half a sphere is hemisphere. The prefix "hemi" means half. Geographers divide the Earth into four hemispheres.

All the land and ocean north of the equator is in the Northern Hemisphere. All the land and ocean south of the equator is in the Southern Hemisphere.

There is another imaginary line on the Earth that runs from the North Pole to the South Pole. It is called the prime meridian. It divides Earth into the Eastern Hemisphere and the Western Hemisphere.

- **What continents are located on the equator?**
- **In which two hemispheres is North America?**

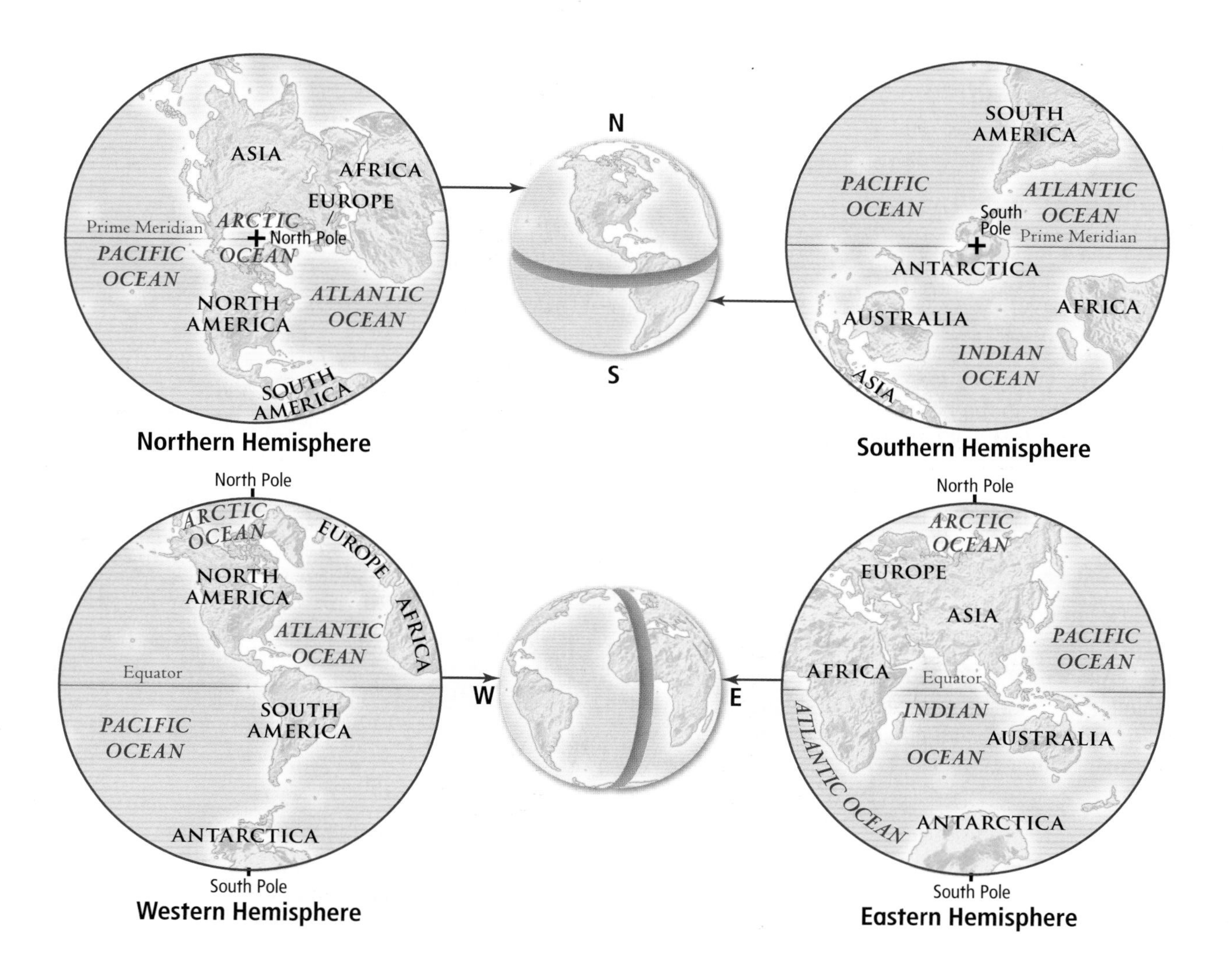

Reading a Map

Maps are drawings of places on Earth. Most maps have standard features to help you read the map. Some important information you get from a map is direction. The main directions are north, south, east, and west. These are called cardinal directions.

The areas between the cardinal directions are called intermediate directions. They show the directions that are in-between the cardinal directions. These are northeast, southeast, southwest, and northwest. You use intermediate directions to describe one place in relation to another. For example, Sacramento, California, is northwest of Phoenix, Arizona.

- **About how far is it from Sacramento to Pierre, South Dakota?**

Map Title

Map titles tell you what information is on the map.

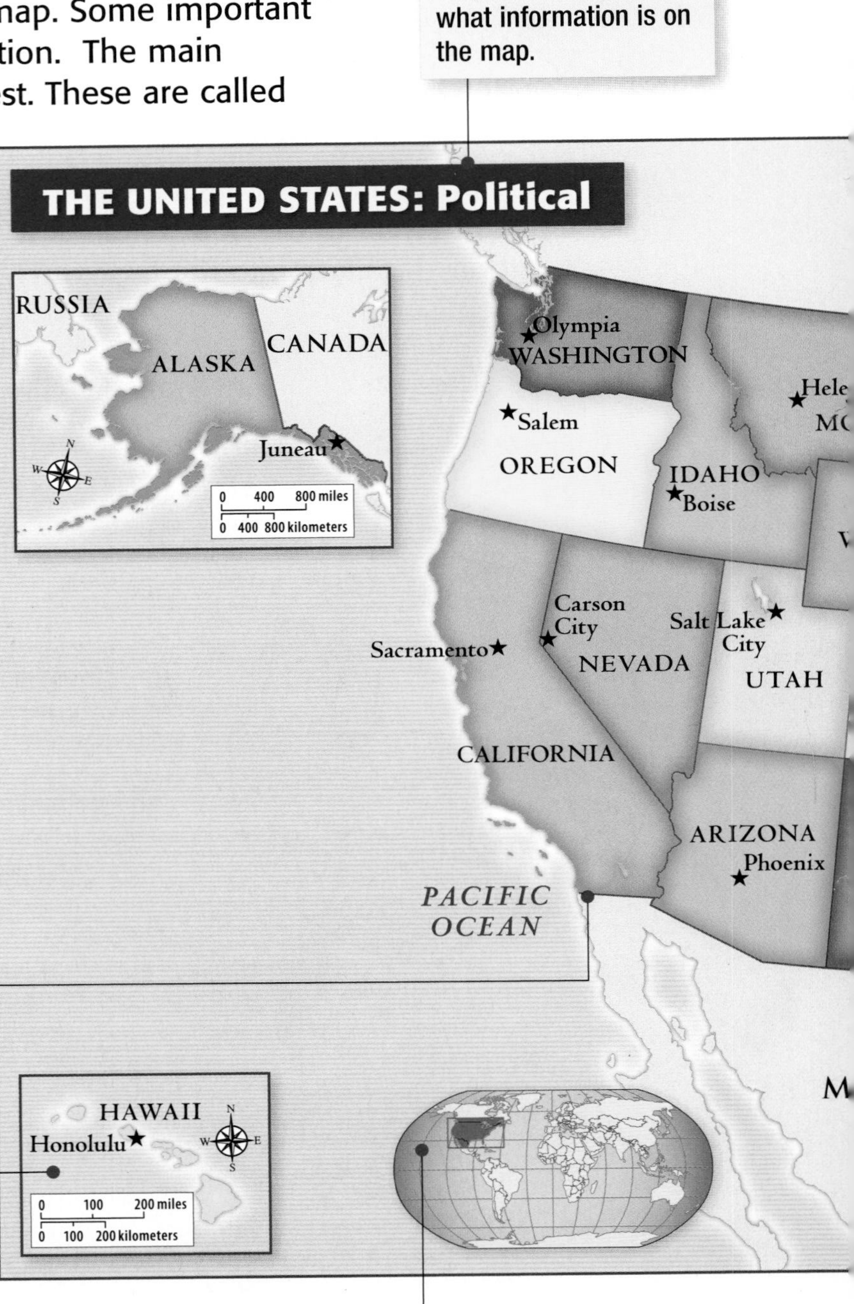

Boundary Lines

The lines on a map are usually shown so the boundary between states looks different than the boundary between nations.

Inset Map

An inset map is a small map set on the main map. An inset map shows an area that is too large, too small, or too far away to be included on the main map. Note that inset maps sometimes use a different scale than the main map.

Locator

A locator map is a small map set into the main map. It shows the location of the main map. Here, the locator map shows where the United States is located in the world.

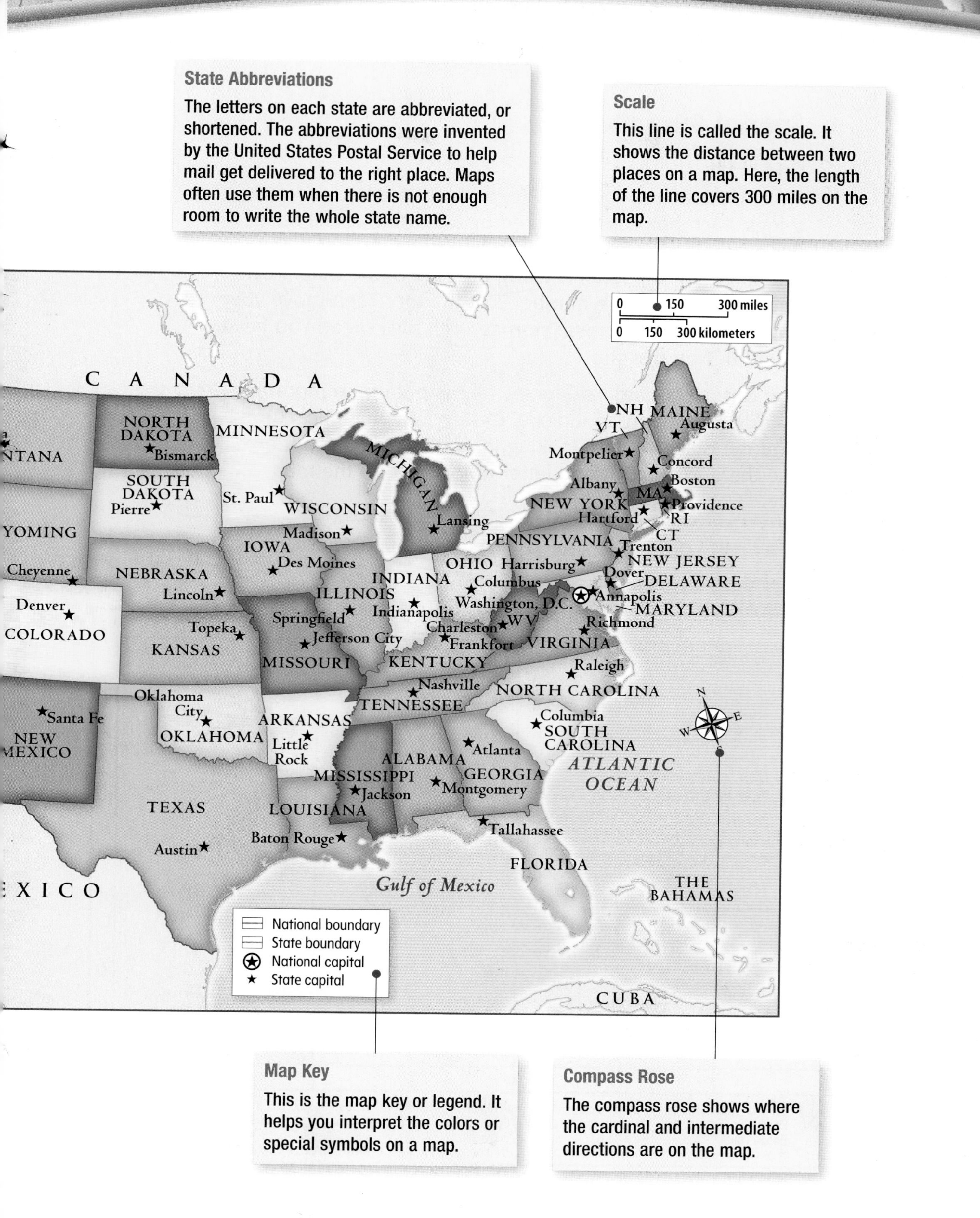
State Abbreviations
The letters on each state are abbreviated, or shortened. The abbreviations were invented by the United States Postal Service to help mail get delivered to the right place. Maps often use them when there is not enough room to write the whole state name.
Scale
This line is called the scale. It shows the distance between two places on a map. Here, the length of the line covers 300 miles on the map.
0 150 300 miles
0 150 300 kilometers
CANADA
NORTH DAKOTA
Bismarck
MINNESOTA
St. Paul
SOUTH DAKOTA
Pierre
WYOMING
Cheyenne
NEBRASKA
Lincoln
Denver
COLORADO
KANSAS
Topeka
IOWA
Des Moines
WISCONSIN
Madison
MICHIGAN
Lansing
ILLINOIS
Springfield
INDIANA
Indianapolis
OHIO
Columbus
MISSOURI
Jefferson City
KENTUCKY
Frankfort
Charleston
WV
PENNSYLVANIA
Harrisburg
NEW YORK
Albany
VT
Montpelier
NH
Concord
MAINE
Augusta
MA
Boston
RI
Providence
CT
Hartford
NEW JERSEY
Trenton
DELAWARE
Dover
MARYLAND
Annapolis
Washington, D.C.
VIRGINIA
Richmond
NORTH CAROLINA
Raleigh
TENNESSEE
Nashville
SOUTH CAROLINA
Columbia
GEORGIA
Atlanta
ALABAMA
Montgomery
MISSISSIPPI
Jackson
ARKANSAS
Little Rock
LOUISIANA
Baton Rouge
OKLAHOMA
Oklahoma City
TEXAS
Austin
NEW MEXICO
Santa Fe
FLORIDA
Tallahassee
ATLANTIC OCEAN
Gulf of Mexico
THE BAHAMAS
CUBA
MEXICO
N
E
W
S
National boundary
State boundary
National capital
State capital
Map Key
This is the map key or legend. It helps you interpret the colors or special symbols on a map.
Compass Rose
The compass rose shows where the cardinal and intermediate directions are on the map.

Special Purpose Maps

Grid Maps

This map has a special grid. A grid map helps you locate things. Each box can be named by a number and a letter. For example, you might want to find Redding in B-3. Put one finger on the letter B along the side of the map. Put another finger on the number 3 at the top. Then move your fingers down and across the map until they meet. You have found B-3 on the grid.

You can use an index to locate places on a map more quickly. Entries on an index are listed in alphabetical order. Find the place you are looking for in the index, and then use the grid number and letter to locate it on the map.

- **Find Crescent City on the map. What grid box is it in?**
- **What are the grid number and letter for Alturas?**

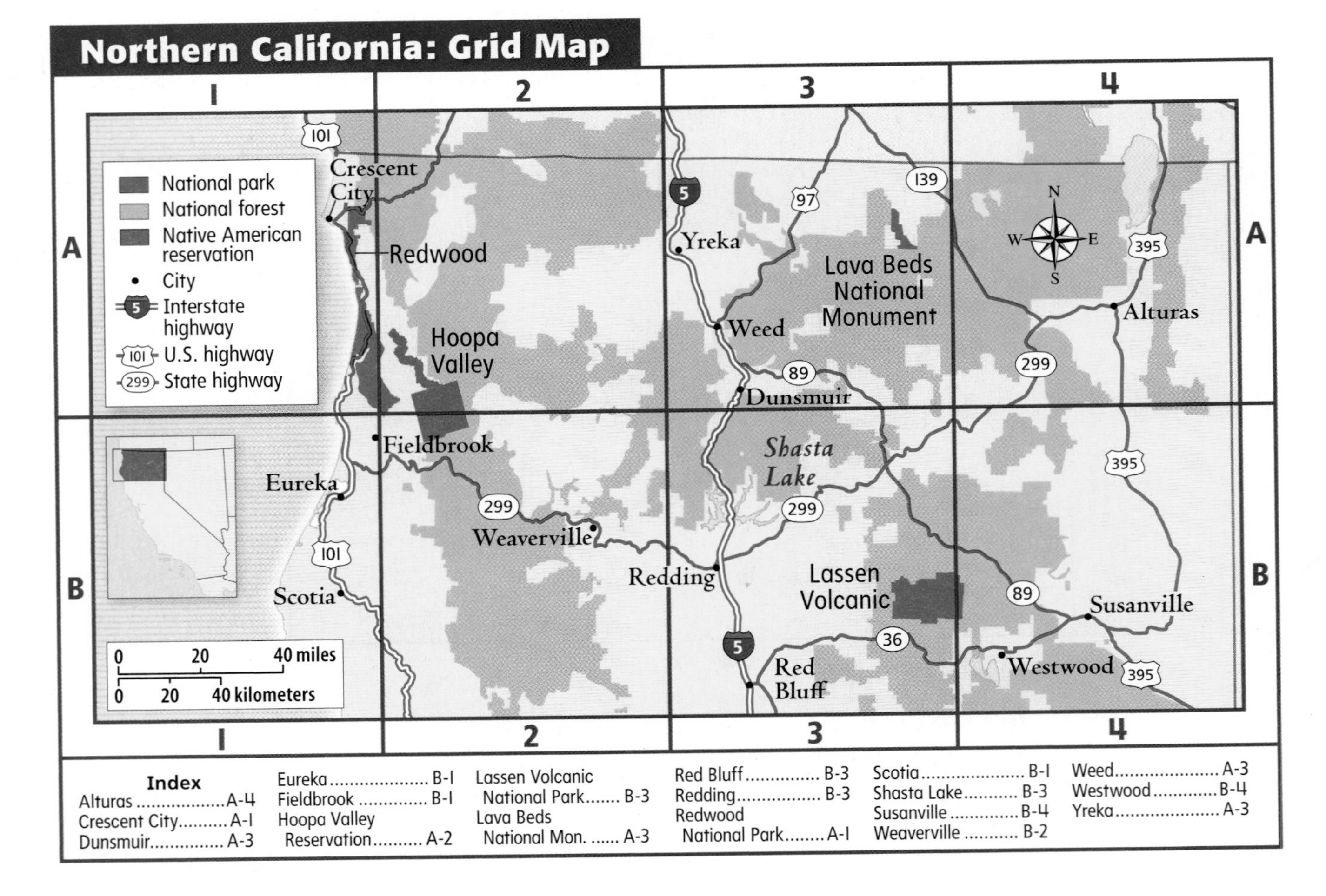

Landform Maps

Some maps are drawn to show one feature of an area. For example, some maps show population. Other maps show the amount of rainfall. Still others show the physical features such as mountains. Each of these maps is called a special purpose map.

One kind of physical map is a landform map. Landforms are the shapes that make up Earth's surface. Mountains, hills, and plains are examples of landforms. You need to use the key to read a landform map.

- **What rivers run through California's Valley region?**
- **What are three mountain peaks shown?**

UNIT 1

The Golden State—Our Home

"Nature's peace will flow into you as sunshine flows into trees."
– John Muir, from *Our National Parks*

How do people adapt to where they live?

Unit 1 tells the story of California's land and how this land is used. You will read about our state's mountains and valleys, the coastal areas, and the dry, desert regions.

Copy the graphic organizer below. As you read the chapters in this unit, think about how the land has influenced and shaped the people who live there.

Then fill in the graphic organizer with the features that most affect the people in each part of the state and some of the ways people adapt. The first one has been started for you.

Regions	Natural Resources	Climate	How People Adapt
1. Mountain 2. 3. 4.			

◀ Ranch in Tehama County

People Who Made a Difference

John Muir
1838–1914

John Muir's love of nature led him to start the Sierra Club, an organization devoted to nature. Muir also helped to start Sequoia National Park and Yosemite National Park. (page 22)

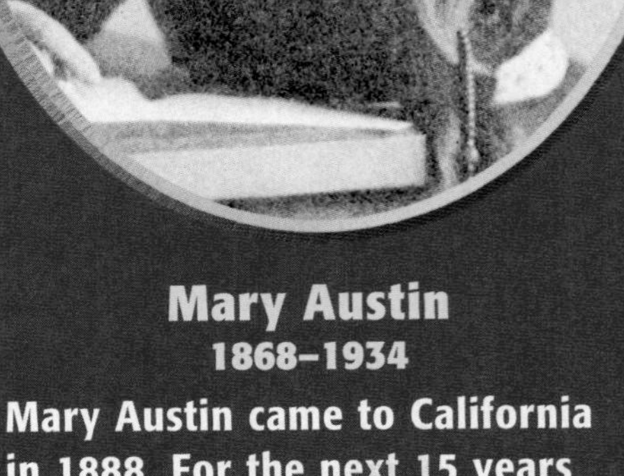

Mary Austin
1868–1934

Mary Austin came to California in 1888. For the next 15 years she moved from one community to another. Her first book, *Land of Little Rain*, tells about her time in California. (page 33)

Unit Events

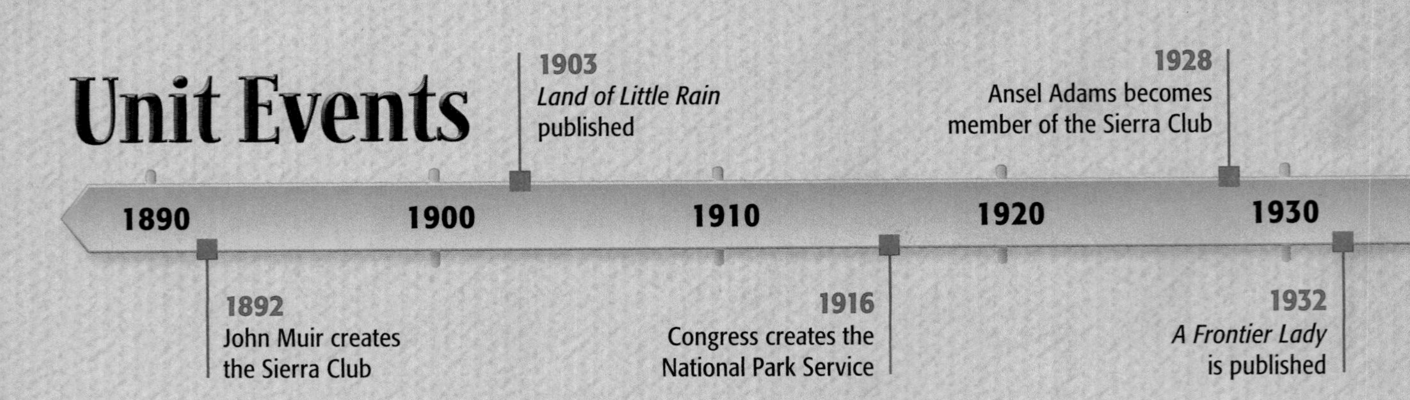

For more about People Who Made a Difference, visit:

www.macmillanmh.com/ss/ca/bios

Ansel Adams
1902–1984

Ansel Adams used photographs to capture beauty in nature. In 1980 Adams was awarded the Presidential Medal of Freedom for his efforts to preserve nature on film and on Earth. (page 51)

Sarah Royce
1819–1891

Sarah Royce and her husband went to California during the Gold Rush. Royce kept a diary of her experiences. Later, the diary was enlarged into a book titled *A Frontier Lady*. (page 56)

1940 | 1950 | 1960 | 1970 | 1980

1980
Ansel Adams awarded the Presidential Medal of Freedom

UNIT 1

Literature

SIERRA

Selection from ***Sierra* by Diane Siebert**

Paintings by Wendell Minor

Sierra *is the Spanish word for "mountain range." California's Sierra Nevada was formed millions of years ago. Its highest mountain is Mt. Whitney at 14,494 feet. The Sierra Nevada runs nearly 400 miles from north to south.*

I am the mountain,
Tall and grand.
And like a **sentinel** I stand.

Surrounding me, my sisters rise
With watchful peaks that pierce the skies;
From north to south we form a chain
Dividing desert, field, and plain.

I am the mountain.
Come and know

Of how, ten million years ago,
Great forces, moving plates of earth,
Brought, to an ancient land, rebirth;
Of how this planet's faulted crust
Was shifted, lifted, tilted, thrust
Toward the sky in waves of change
To form a newborn mountain range . . .

Here stand the pines, so straight and tall,
Whose needles, dry and dying, fall
Upon my sides to slowly form
A natural blanket, soft and warm . . .

---

sentinel (sen tuh nuhl) a person standing guard

And on my western slope I hold
My great sequoias, tall and old;
They've watched three thousand years go by,
And, in their endless quest for sky,
This grove of giants slowly grew
With songs of green on silent blue. . . .

I am the mountain.
From the sea

Come constant winds to **conquer** me—
Pacific winds that touch my face
And bring the storm whose clouds embrace
My **rugged** shoulders, strong and wide;
And in their path, I cannot hide. . . .

By wind and weather, day by day,
I will, in time, be worn away;
For mountains live, and mountains die.
As ages pass, so, too, will I. . . .

---

conquer (kong ker) to overcome or to defeat
rugged (rug id) having a rough and uneven surface

I am the mountain,
Tall and grand,
And like a sentinel I stand.
Yet I, in nature's wonders draped,
Now see this **mantle** being shaped
By something new—a force so real
That every part of me can feel
Its actions changing nature's plan.
Its numbers grow. Its name is MAN.
And what my course of life will be
Depends on how man cares for me.

I am the mountain,
Tall and grand.
And like a sentinel I stand.

---

mantle (man tuhl) a loose cape

Write a poem describing something in nature.

Reading SOCIAL STUDIES

Identify Main Idea and Details:

California's Resources ELA R2.1 4.1.5

In this unit, you will read about natural resources in California. Looking for the main idea and details when you read will help you better understand social studies. The main idea is what a paragraph is about. Often, it is the first sentence in a paragraph. The details tell about the main idea. Keeping track of main ideas and details will help you to understand what you read.

1 Learn It

- Identify the information that is given in the paragraph.
- Decide whether the first sentence states the main idea.
- Look for details. Think about what these details tell about.
- Now, read the paragraph below. Look for the main idea and details.

Main Idea
The first sentence often states the main idea.

Details
Most of the energy comes from oil and gas.
These sentences give details about California's energy sources.

California's energy comes from different sources. Oil and gas supply about two-thirds of our state's power. Californians also use the sun and the wind to produce electricity. Water and steam found deep in the earth also provide energy in parts of our state.

2 Try It

Copy and complete the chart below. Then, fill in the chart by listing the main idea and details from the paragraph on page 10.

MAIN IDEA AND DETAILS CHART

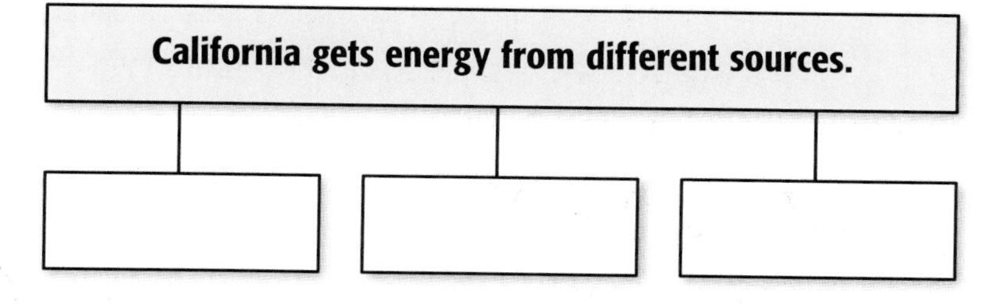

How did you find the main idea and details?

3 Apply It

- Review the steps for finding the main idea and details in Learn It.
- Read the paragraph below. Then, create a main idea and details chart using the information.

California is making good use of wind power. Over 14,000 wind turbines now produce electricity in our state. Groups of these turbines are placed together in "wind farms." Altogether, California's wind turbines could make enough electricity to power San Francisco!

CHAPTER

1 California: Land and People

You Are There

"New immigrants had little more than what they carried with them, yet...with hard work and freedom, they would live a better life and their children even more so."

President Ronald Reagan spoke these words in 1982. Reagan knew that one reason California was a great state was its mix of people from many different places and cultures.

In this chapter you will read about California's location, resources, and climate. You will also learn about the people who call California home.

A California has mountains, deserts, valleys, and coastline. (page 17)

B Wind farms produce some of the electricity used in California. (page 23)

C Owls live in Death Valley, in southeastern California, the hottest place in the United States. (page 31)

D Californians come from more than 90 different countries. (page 37)

LESSON 1

FOCUS QUESTION

Where is California located?

VOCABULARY

hemisphere
relative location
region
geographer
environment
coast
mountain range
plain

VOCABULARY STRATEGY

ROOT WORDS The root of the word **hemisphere** is **-sphere**. A sphere is something round such as a globe. Name another object shaped like a sphere.

READING STRATEGY

Identify Main Idea and Details

Use the chart below to list the main idea and supporting details of this lesson.

Locating California

Start with Your CALIFORNIA STANDARDS

4.1 Students demonstrate an understanding of the physical and human geographic features that define the places and regions in California.

4.1.1 Explain and use the coordinate grid system of latitude and longitude to determine the absolute locations of places in California and on Earth.

Explore latitude and longitude. (Begins on page 18)

4.1.2 Distinguish between the North and South Poles; the equator and the prime meridian; the tropics; and the hemispheres, using coordinates to plot locations.

Locate California in the Western Hemisphere. (page 15)

4.1.5 Use maps, charts, and pictures to describe how communities in California vary in land use, vegetation, wildlife, climate, population density, architecture, services, and transportation.

Explore maps showing the Western Hemisphere and the regions of the United States. (Begins on page 15)

Big Sur is a part of California's 1,264 mile coastline. ▼

The story of California begins where you live. How might you describe the place where you live? Are there trees nearby? Can you see the Sierra Nevada Mountains from your window? Is there a desert outside your door? Can you smell the Pacific Ocean? Can you see the lights of Hollywood?

California in the World 4.1.2

You can describe a place in many ways. You can tell what the weather is like in a place. You can take a photograph of a place. You can even tell a place by its street address.

How might you describe the location of California? You could say that California has a "global address," or address on Earth. California's global address is that it is part of the United States. The United States has a global address, too. It is part of a continent, or large piece of land, called North America. Can you find North America on the map?

Even North America has a global address. It is part of the Western Hemisphere. A **hemisphere** is half of a sphere. Earth is divided into four hemispheres. They are the Northern, Southern, Eastern, and Western hemispheres. The map above shows the Western Hemisphere.

Now, try to locate where you live. You live in the Western Hemisphere, in North America, in the United States, in California.

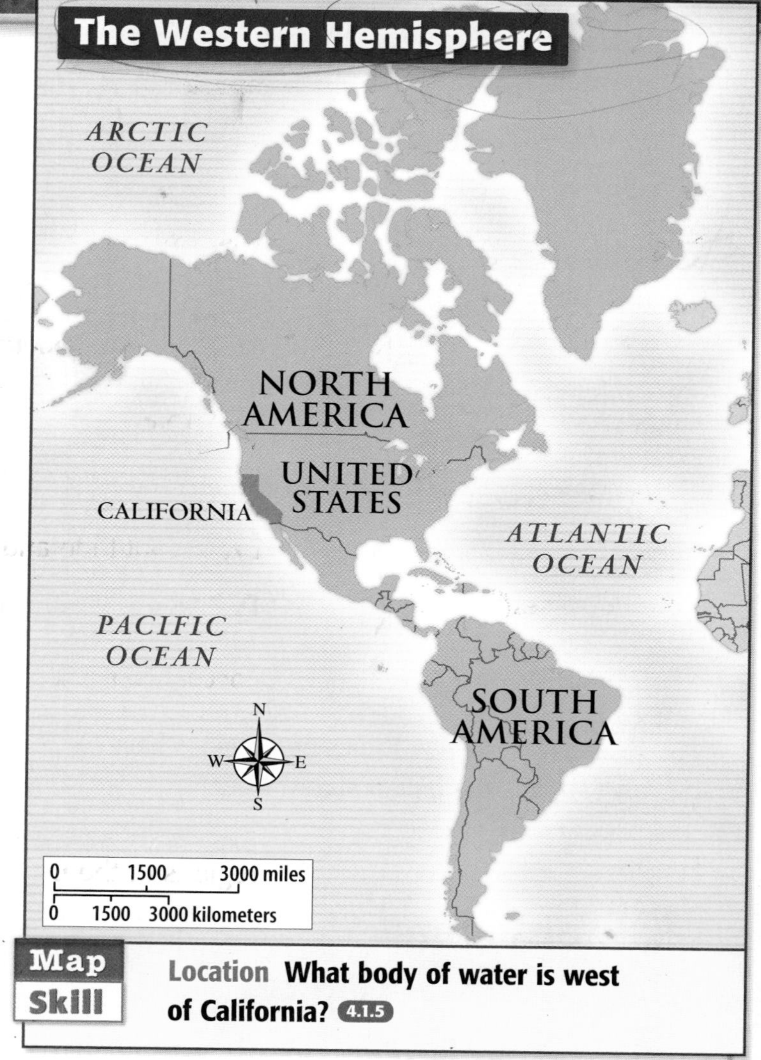

Map Skill Location **What body of water is west of California? 4.1.5**

REVIEW What is the "global address" of California? *Main Idea and Details*

Regions of the United States

Map Skill Region Which two regions have the fewest states? 4.1.5

California and the United States 4.1.5

The **relative location** of California is in the West. The relative location of a place is where it is compared to one or more places on Earth. On the map above, the relative location of New York compared to California is the Northeast.

The West and the Northeast are **regions** of the United States. A region is an area of land with features that set it apart from other areas. **Geographers**, or people who study geography, use different features to define a region. Some geographers use physical features. In this chapter you will learn about population regions.

The United States is divided into six regions. They are the Southwest, Southeast, Northeast, Middle West, Mountain, and the West. Each region is shaped by its **environment**, or the surroundings in which people, plants, and animals live.

California and the West

The West is home to Washington, Oregon, Nevada, California, Hawaii, and Alaska. Oregon, Nevada, and Arizona border, or are next to, California.

The West has many different geographic features. It has snowy mountains, green valleys, hot deserts, and the Pacific **coast**. A coast is land next to an ocean.

Several **mountain ranges** run through the West. A mountain range is a chain of mountains. The Sierra Nevada and Cascade Range are both mountain ranges.

Plains, or large areas of flat land, are not a common feature of the West. However, California has a large plain between two mountain ranges. Plains usually receive enough rainfall for farmers to grow crops.

Unlike plains, deserts do not receive much rain. Deserts cover much of Nevada and parts of southern California. Desert temperatures can be very hot during the day and cool at night. Water is scarce, or hard to find, in a desert.

California's geographic features make it an attractive place for people to live. Native Americans were the first people to live in California. Native Americans shaped California in wonderful ways. Later, people crossed the deserts and mountains to come to California. Others came by ship. Today, people from all over the world live in California.

You will read more about the exciting history of California in the chapters to come. The story of California is a story about its people. You, too, are part of its story.

REVIEW List two mountain ranges in California. *Summarize*

What You Learned

4.1.2 California has a "global address." It is in the United States on the continent of North America. It is in the Western Hemisphere.

4.1.5 The United States is divided into six regions. California's relative location is in the region of the West.

Lesson Review

1. **Focus Question** Where is California located? (4.1)
2. **Vocabulary** Write one sentence for each vocabulary term. (4.1.2, 4.1.5)

coast	**mountain range**
environment	**plain**
geographer	**region**
hemisphere	**relative location**

3. **Geography** What are some of the features of the West region of the United States? (4.1.5)
4. **Critical Thinking** **Problem Solving** Why do you think geographers divide the United States into regions? (4.1.5)
5. **Reading Strategy** **Identify Main Idea and Details** Find the main idea and supporting details about California's location in the United States. (4.1.5, ELA R2.1)
6. **Write about THE BIG IDEA** Describe California's location in the United States. (4.1.5, ELA W1.0)
7. **Link to Science** Suppose your home is in a small country. Write about the regions of your country. Describe one of these regions. How is it different from other regions in your country? (4.1.5)

MAP and GLOBE Skills

Understand Latitude and Longitude 4.1.1 4.1.2

VOCABULARY

grid
latitude
longitude
degree
parallel
meridian

Every place on Earth has a global address based on its location. To describe the address of a place, geographers use maps with **grids**. Grids are lines that cross each other on a map. The grid system is based on two sets of lines called **latitude** and **longitude**.

Lines of latitude measure how far north or south a place is from the equator. Lines of longitude measure distance east or west. Lines of latitude and longitude measure distance in **degrees**. The equator is 0 degrees. The symbol for degrees is °.

1 Learn It

- Lines of latitude are also called **parallels**. Parallels north of the equator are labeled N. Parallels south of the equator are labeled S.
- Lines of longitude are also called **meridians**. The prime meridian is the starting place for measuring distance from east to west. Meridians east of the prime meridian are labeled E. Meridians west of the prime meridian are labeled W.
- Look at Map A on page 19. This is a grid map of the world. It can be used to locate any place on Earth.
- When you locate places on grid maps, give the latitude first and longitude second.

2 Try It

- Use Map A to locate Durban, South Africa. Is Durban east or west of the prime meridian? It is east. Durban is located at about 30°S, 30°E.
- Use Map B to locate the cities closest to the latitude and longitude "addresses" below. Name each city.
  - 34°N, 116°W
  - 36°N, 122°W
- Use Map B to find the latitude and longitude of the following cities in California.
  - Shelter Cove
  - Kettleman City

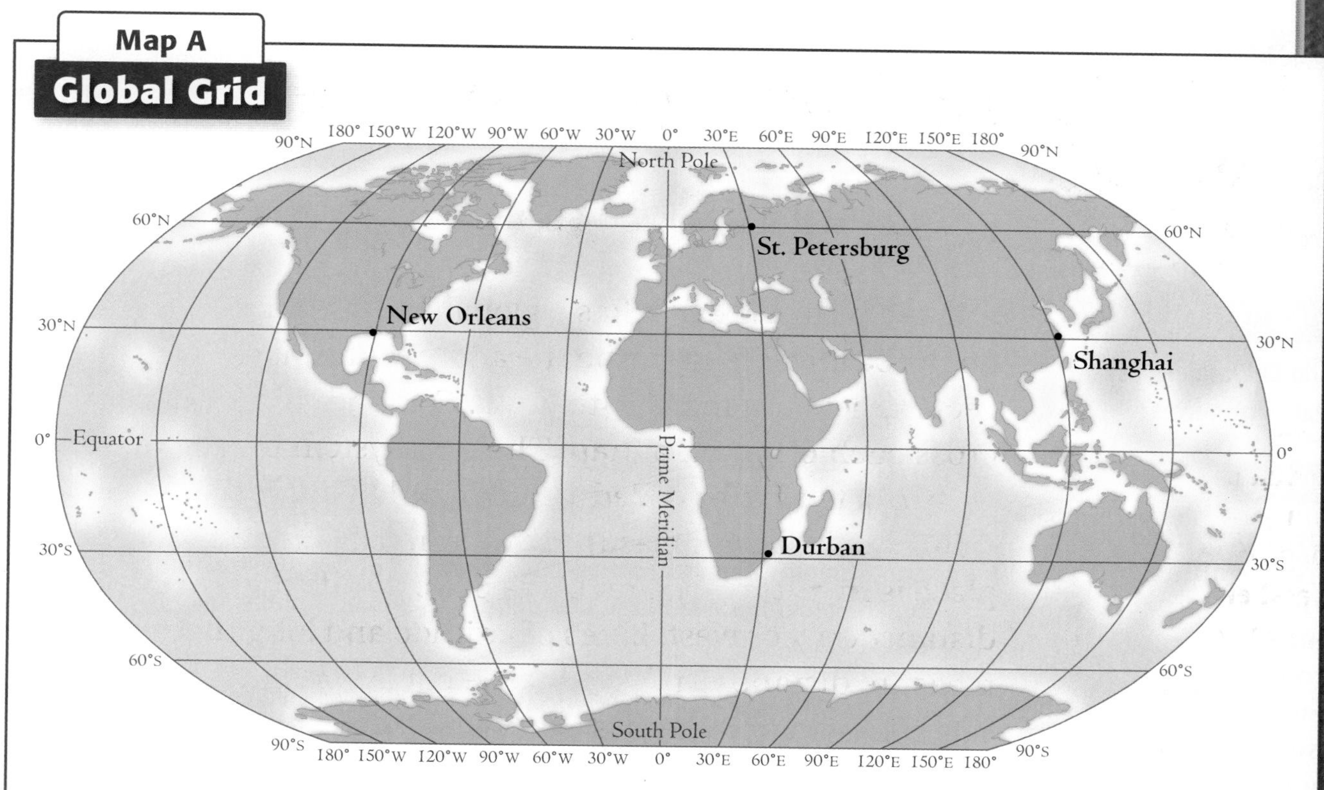

3 Apply It

- Look at Map A. Give the latitude and longitude of the city on the map that is closest to California.
- Look at Map B. Find the longitude and latitude that is closest to where you live.

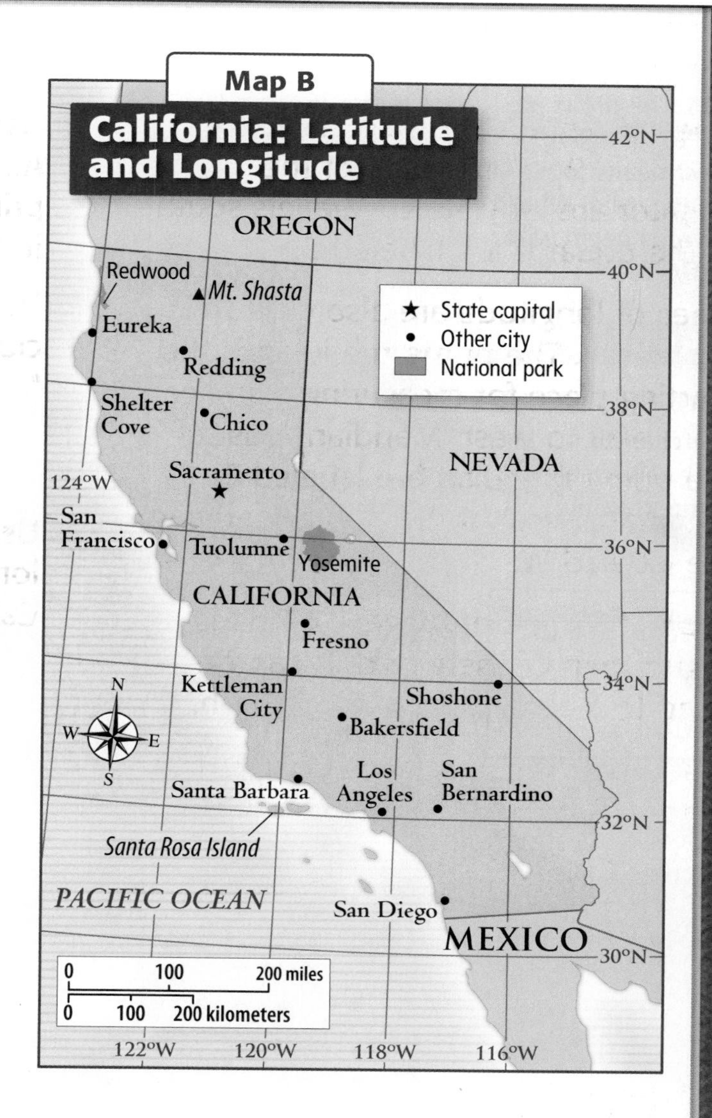

FOCUS QUESTION

How do Californians use the state's resources?

VOCABULARY

natural resource
nonrenewable resource
mineral
petroleum
renewable resource
conservation
recycle
alternative energy

VOCABULARY STRATEGY

PREFIXES The prefix **-re** means "to do again." To **renew** means to make new again. What other words begin with the prefix -re?

READING STRATEGY

Compare and Contrast
Use the chart to compare renewable and nonrenewable resources.

California's Resources

Start with Your
CALIFORNIA STANDARDS

4.1 Students demonstrate an understanding of the physical and human geographic features that define places and regions in California.

4.1.5 Use maps, charts, and pictures to describe how communities in California vary in land use, vegetation, wildlife, climate, population density, architecture, services, and transportation.

Discover how California's resources are used and how to care for California's environment. (Begins on page 21)

Bear Creek Spire, Sequoia National Park ▼

The environment is the surroundings in which we live. It is the mountains and streams, the air and the soil, the animals, and the plants. People, like you, are also part of the environment.

California's Environment 4.1.5

The environment shapes how we live. We also shape the environment. We use trees for wood and paper. We farm rich soil for food.

Trees and soil are only two of the **natural resources** found in California's environment. A natural resource is something found in the environment that people can use. California is rich in natural resources.

Another of our resources is water. Some of our water comes from reservoirs, which are artificial lakes used to store water. Some comes from rivers. Much of it comes from underground.

Limited Resources

Some resources are **nonrenewable resources**. Nonrenewable means there is a limited supply. **Minerals** are nonrenewable resources. Minerals are natural materials found in the earth, such as rocks and metals.

Oil, or **petroleum**, is another mineral. Oil is also a fuel. A fuel is something used to produce energy. Oil is made into gasoline to power the engines of cars and trucks. Oil is a nonrenewable resource, so there is a limited supply.

Unlimited Resources

Some of California's natural resources are **renewable resources**. Renewable means that something can be replaced. Fresh water is a renewable resource. When it rains or snows, fresh water falls to Earth. Soil is another renewable resource. But, soil can wear out if it is overused. Water too, can run out if we use more than the rivers and lakes can hold.

REVIEW Describe one renewable and one nonrenewable resource.
Compare and Contrast

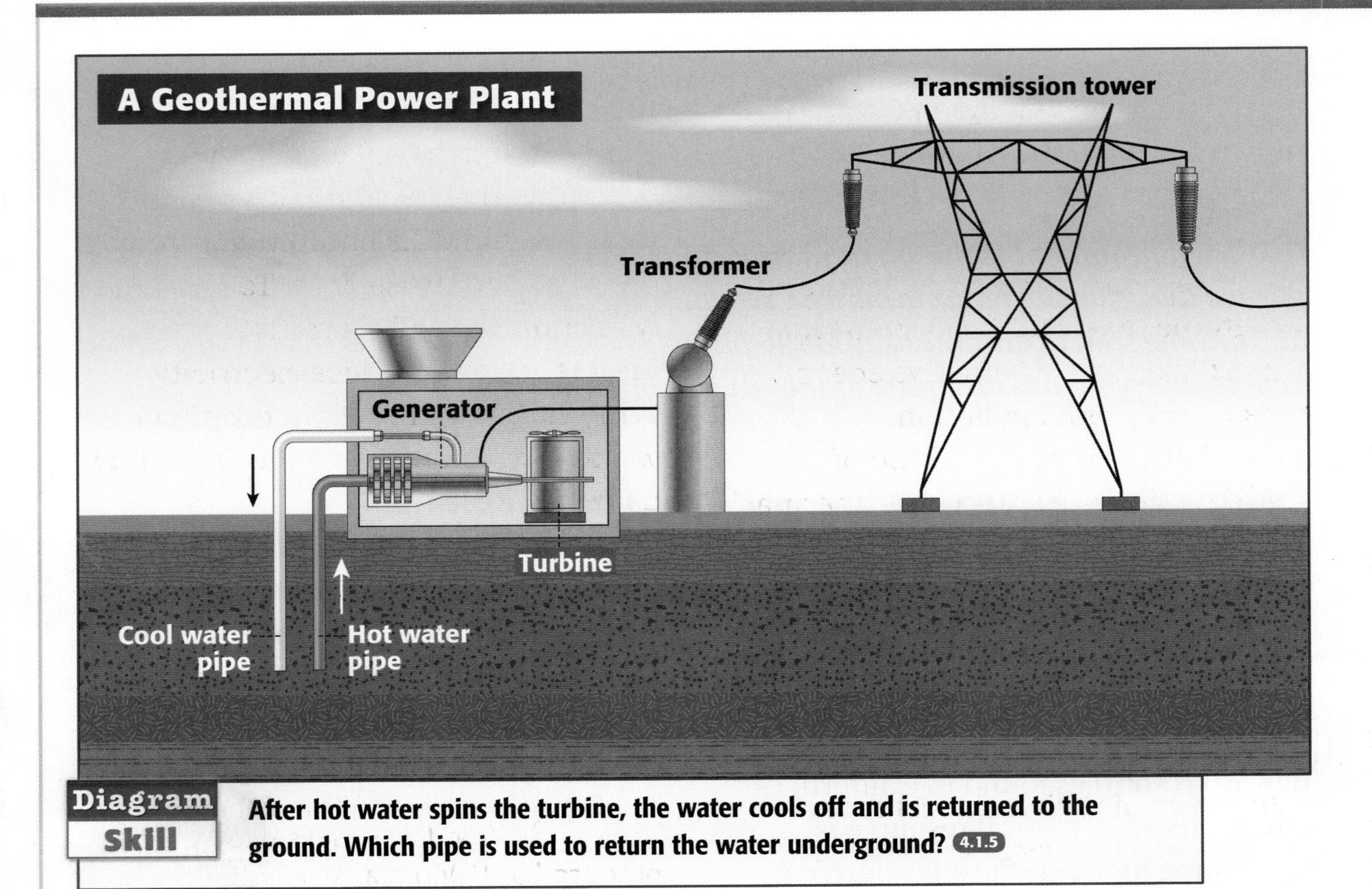

Diagram Skill After hot water spins the turbine, the water cools off and is returned to the ground. Which pipe is used to return the water underground? 4.1.5

Using Resources Wisely 4.1.5

Conservation is the protection of natural resources. You conserve water when you use just enough for what you need. You conserve paper when you use both sides of a sheet. Another way to protect resources is to **recycle**. To recycle means to use something again instead of throwing it away. You can recycle metal cans, glass, plastic, and more.

John Muir recognized the importance of conservation. He wanted to protect California's environment. You will read more about John Muir later in this chapter.

California Energy

With over 35 million people, California has the largest population of any state! Californians use less energy per person than almost any state.

California's energy comes from oil and natural gas. Natural gas is a kind of gas found underground that can be used to make electricity. Oil and natural gas are nonrenewable resources.

To meet rising energy needs, more oil and natural gas power plants are being built. These nonrenewable resources will eventually run out. These fuels, especially oil, pollute the air. These are two reasons why fuel must be used wisely.

Using Energy

More than one quarter of California's energy comes from renewable resources. Energy produced from renewable resources is called **alternative energy**. Alternative means something that is different from what is most common. Alternative energy releases little or no pollution.

Geothermal power is a kind of alternative energy. The word "thermal" means heat, and "geo" means Earth. Geothermal power comes from the hot water or steam beneath Earth's surface. Study the diagram on page 22 to find out how geothermal power is used to make electricity.

Today, 46 of California's 58 counties use geothermal energy in some form. California's geothermal power plants produce about half of the world's geothermal powered electricity.

Wind is another alternative energy source. Windmills pump water from deep wells to the surface. Today, large windmills are called wind turbines. Many turbines produce electricity. Wind turbines are placed together on wind farms in places where the wind is usually strong.

California has about 14,000 wind turbines. One large turbine can produce enough electricity to power a school. If all of California's wind farms were put together, they could produce enough electricity to power San Francisco!

REVIEW Name three ways energy is produced in California. *Summarize*

Wind turbines in Tehachapi turn wind into electricity. ▼

Protecting the Environment 4.1.5

You now know about conserving resources, such as water and fuel, and recycling materials instead of throwing them away. With your help, California's environment can stay strong and healthy.

An easy saying to remember is to *reduce, reuse,* and *recycle. Reduce* the amount of resources you use by buying products packaged in recycled materials. Then, *reuse* what you own instead of throwing it away. Last, *recycle* what you don't reuse. Try to throw away less. A fun game to play is to see how little trash you can throw away each week.

Spread the word that California's environment is worth protecting. Later in life, you will be glad you did.

REVIEW What are three ways you can help protect our environment?
Cause and Effect

What You Learned

4.1.5 California's environment is rich in natural resources. Californians use renewable and nonrenewable resources, such as trees, soil, water, and minerals to help them live.

4.1.5 Conserving resources, such as water and fuel, are important ways you can help protect California's environment. California's energy comes from nonrenewable sources and from alternative sources such as wind and geothermal power.

4.1.5 Reduce, reuse, and recycle, and tell others to do the same.

Lesson Review

1. **Focus Question** How do Californians use the state's resources? 4.1.5
2. **Vocabulary** Write one sentence for each vocabulary term. 4.1.5

   alternative energy **nonrenewable resource**
   conservation **petroleum**
   mineral **recycle**
   natural resource **renewable resource**

3. **Geography** What is geothermal power? 4.1.5
4. **Critical Thinking Cause and Effect** What might happen if we overuse our renewable resources? 4.1.5
5. **Reading Strategy Compare and Contrast** Compare and contrast geothermal power and petroleum. 4.1.5 ELA R2.1

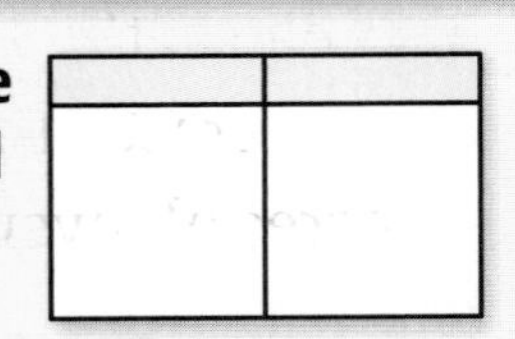

6. **Write about THE BIG IDEA** Write about how Californians can help care for the environment. 4.1.5 ELA W2.1
7. **Link to Art** When John Muir camped in the Sierra Nevada Mountains, he always brought a notebook in which he made drawings and scribbled notes. Visit an environment you love, and make a drawing of it. 4.1.5

Biography
Focus on Responsibility

4.1.5

John Muir 1838–1914

John Muir was born in Dunbar, Scotland in 1838. Muir spent his childhood working on a farm and studying literature and mathematics.

In 1869 Muir took a job as a shepherd in California's Sierra Nevada Mountains. He quickly fell in love with mountains. For twenty years he explored California's forests. Muir wrote,

"Nature's peace will flow into you as sunshine flows into trees."

Muir wanted others to love nature as much as he did. He also wanted to protect nature. In 1892 Muir created the Sierra Club to celebrate the wilderness and work for its preservation. Next, he got the attention of the United States Congress. In 1890 Congress protected two large pieces of California's Sierra Nevada range as Sequoia National Park and Yosemite National Park. In 1916, two years after Muir's death, Congress created the National Park Service. Today, it oversees the protection of millions of acres all over the United States.

▲ El Capitán and the Merced River at Yosemite National Park

Why did John Muir create the Sierra Club?

For more about John Muir, visit:

www.macmillanmh.com/ss/ca/bios

The Life of John Muir

1830 | 1840 | 1850 | 1860 | 1870 | 1880 | 1890 | 1900 | 1910 | 1920

- **1838** Born in Scotland
- **1869** First explores Sierra Nevada Mountains
- **1892** Founds the Sierra Club
- **1914** Dies on December 24

Field Trip to YOSEMITE National Park

4.1

Yosemite National Park

One million years ago large bodies of ice, called glaciers, scraped valleys through the Sierra Nevada. The glaciers left behind wide meadows and towering waterfalls. Both the Sierra Nevada and the valleys are part of an area called Yosemite.

❷ Glacier Point

A short hike leads to Glacier Point, which overlooks Yosemite Valley from the south. You will be eye to eye with Half Dome and face the high Sierras to the east. ▼

❶ Tuolumne Meadows ▲

High up in the mountains is Tuolumne Meadows (TWAWL uh mee). This four-mile long stretch of grass and summer wildflowers offers views of the snow-capped Sierras.

❸ Yosemite Valley ▲

Yosemite Valley is the central attraction of the park. Near the visitor center is the fifth highest waterfall in the world, Yosemite Falls. East of the visitor center is the rock called Half Dome. It rises 4,000 feet above the valley floor. A steep trail leads to the top of the Dome.

▲ ❹ Mariposa Grove

At Mariposa Grove you can stand beside hundreds of the largest living things on Earth. Giant sequoia trees can grow over 300 feet tall and live up to 3,000 years!

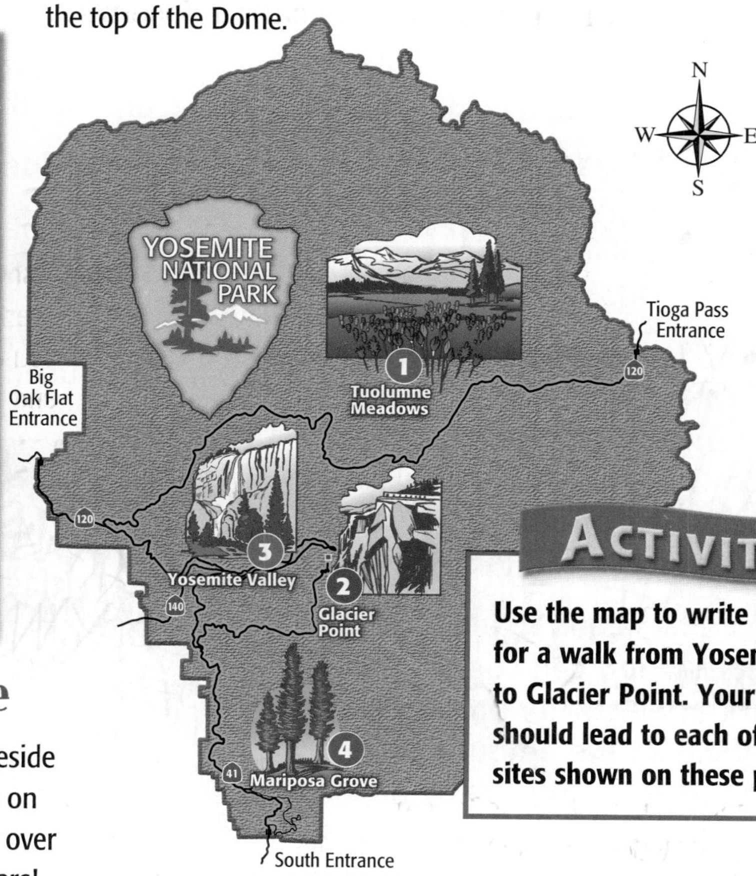

ACTIVITY

Use the map to write directions for a walk from Yosemite Valley to Glacier Point. Your directions should lead to each of the four sites shown on these pages.

LOG ON For more about Yosemite National Park, visit:

www.macmillanmh.com/ss/ca/fieldtrips

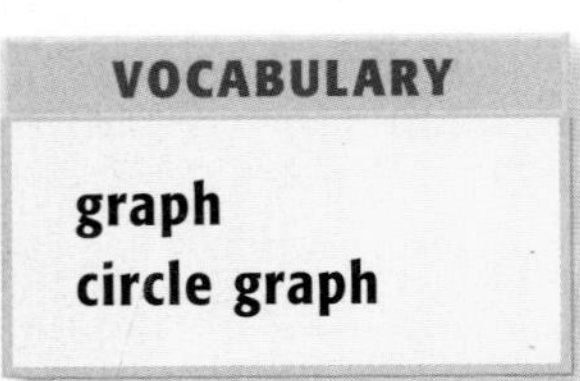

Read Circle Graphs 

Graphs help you compare information. Graphs are diagrams that show information in a clear way. By presenting facts in a picture, they tell you a lot with only a few words.

VOCABULARY

graph
circle graph

1 Learn It

- There are many kinds of graphs. Identify the type of graph. The two graphs on the next page are **circle graphs**. Circle graphs show how parts of something fit into a whole. Because each part looks like a slice of a pie, a circle graph is sometimes called a pie graph.
- Read the graph's title. The title of Graph A is "California: Sources of Electricity, 2003."
- Study the labels on the graph. Labels tell you what the different slices on a graph mean. The labels for each slice on Graph A tell you how much electricity was produced by each energy source.
- Compare facts and figures. Look at Graph A. You can compare the amount of electricity produced by natural gas to the amount produced by other energy sources by looking at the size of the slices. A larger slice means more electricity was produced by that energy source.

2 Try It

- Look at Graph B. From the title, you can see that this circle graph shows the amount of electricity produced by alternative energy sources in California in 2003. Study the labels on the graph and use the graph to answer the following questions.
- What does this circle graph show?
- What does each slice on this circle graph represent?
- Which type of alternative energy produced the most electricity?

3 Apply It

- Look at Graph B. What energy source does this circle graph examine in more detail?
- Make a circle graph of your own that compares how much time you spend sleeping to how much time you spend in school.

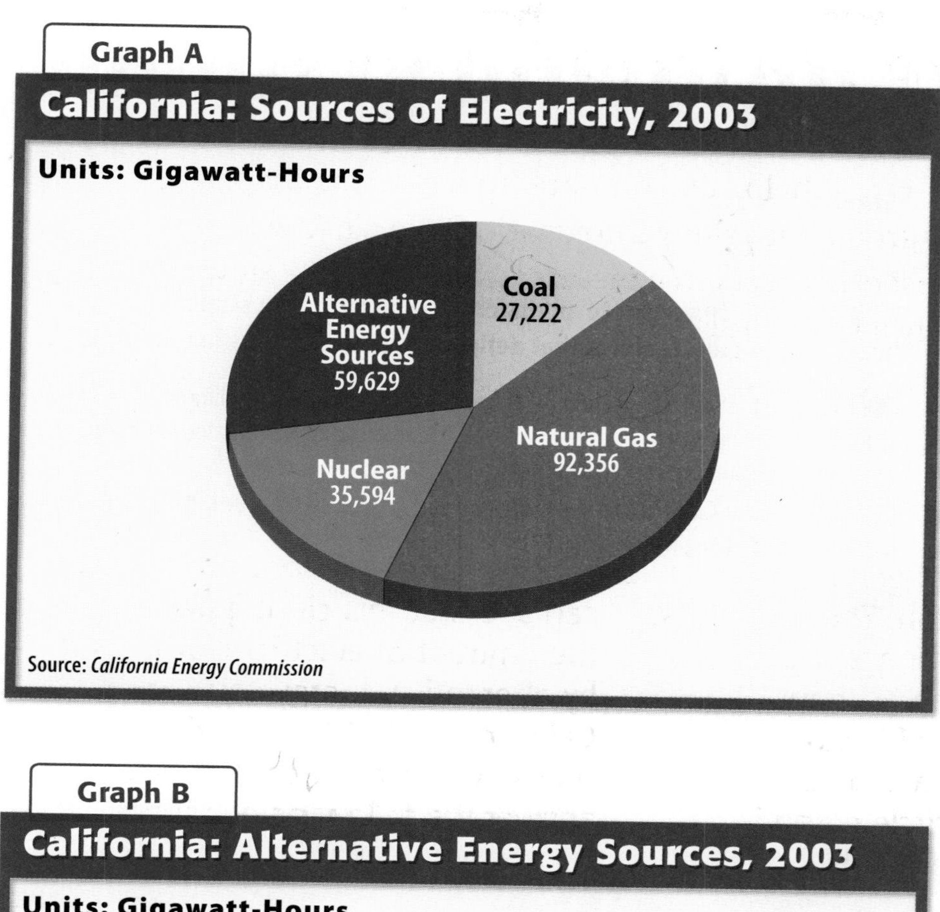
Graph A
California: Sources of Electricity, 2003
Units: Gigawatt-Hours
Alternative Energy Sources
59,629
Coal
27,222
Natural Gas
92,356
Nuclear
35,594
Source: California Energy Commission

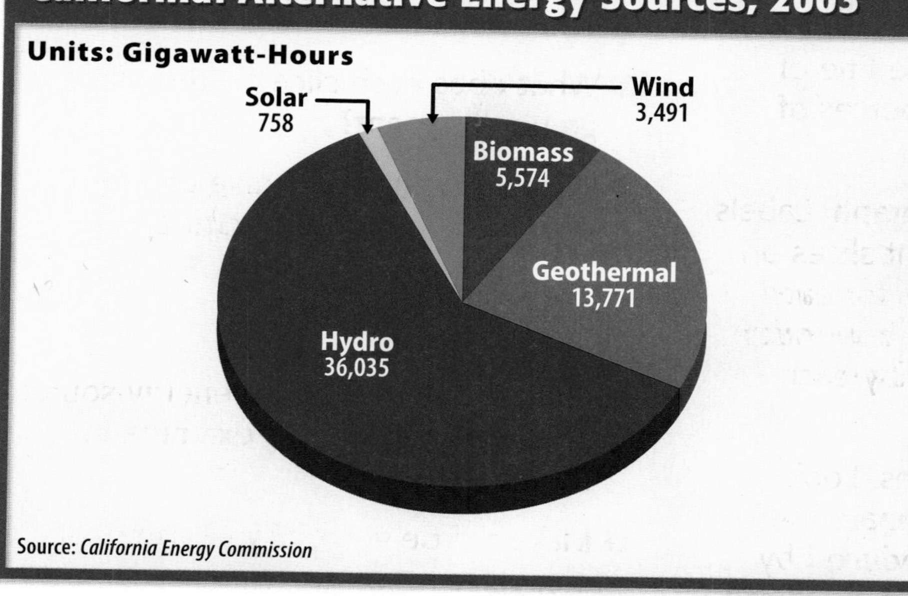
Graph B
California: Alternative Energy Sources, 2003
Units: Gigawatt-Hours
Solar
758
Wind
3,491
Biomass
5,574
Geothermal
13,771
Hydro
36,035
Source: California Energy Commission

LESSON

3

FOCUS QUESTION

Why are there different climates in California?

VOCABULARY

climate
elevation
sea level
precipitation
rain shadow

VOCABULARY STRATEGY

SYNONYMS Elevation describes the height of something. What other words describe height?

READING STRATEGY

Identify Cause and Effect
Use the chart below to list the causes and effects of California's hot and cold climates.

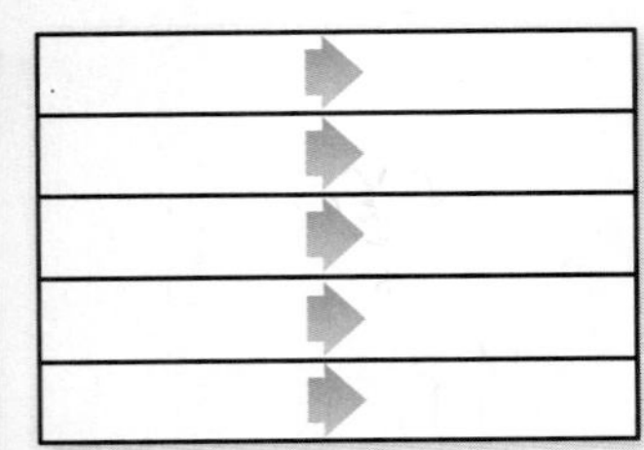

California's Climate

Start with Your
CALIFORNIA STANDARDS

4.1 Students demonstrate an understanding of the physical and human geographic features that define places and regions in California.

4.1.3 Identify the state capital and describe the various regions of California, including how their characteristics and physical environments (e.g., water, landforms, vegetation, climate) affect human activity.

Discover how California's environment affects the lives of Californians. (Begins on page 31)

4.1.5 Use maps, charts, and pictures to describe how communities in California vary in land use, vegetation, wildlife, climate, population density, architecture, services, and transportation.

Find out about California's rain shadow. (Begins on page 31)

Anza-Borrego Desert State Park ▼

In California, one place can have snow, another can have rain, and another can be as dry as a cracker. Within this varied environment are animals such as this burrowing desert owl.

California's Weather 4.1.3 4.1.5

Weather describes the air, dry or rainy, and temperature. Temperature is how hot or cold the air is. Every place has a pattern of weather over time. This is called **climate**. So climate is really a pattern of weather over time.

Temperature

Many things affect the temperature of a place. The farther a place is from the equator, the colder its temperature will be. California is about one third of the way between the equator and the North Pole, so it has generally mild temperatures.

Elevation affects temperature, too. The elevation of a place is how high it is above the ocean. This is called **sea level**. The ocean has an elevation of zero. Places at high elevations are colder than places at low elevations. For example, Mt. Whitney at 14,494 feet above sea level, can get temperatures well below freezing. In contrast, Death Valley is the hottest and lowest place in the United States. Death Valley's lowest elevation is 284 feet *below* sea level. Temperatures can reach to above 100°F.

REVIEW What causes temperatures to vary in California? *Cause and Effect*

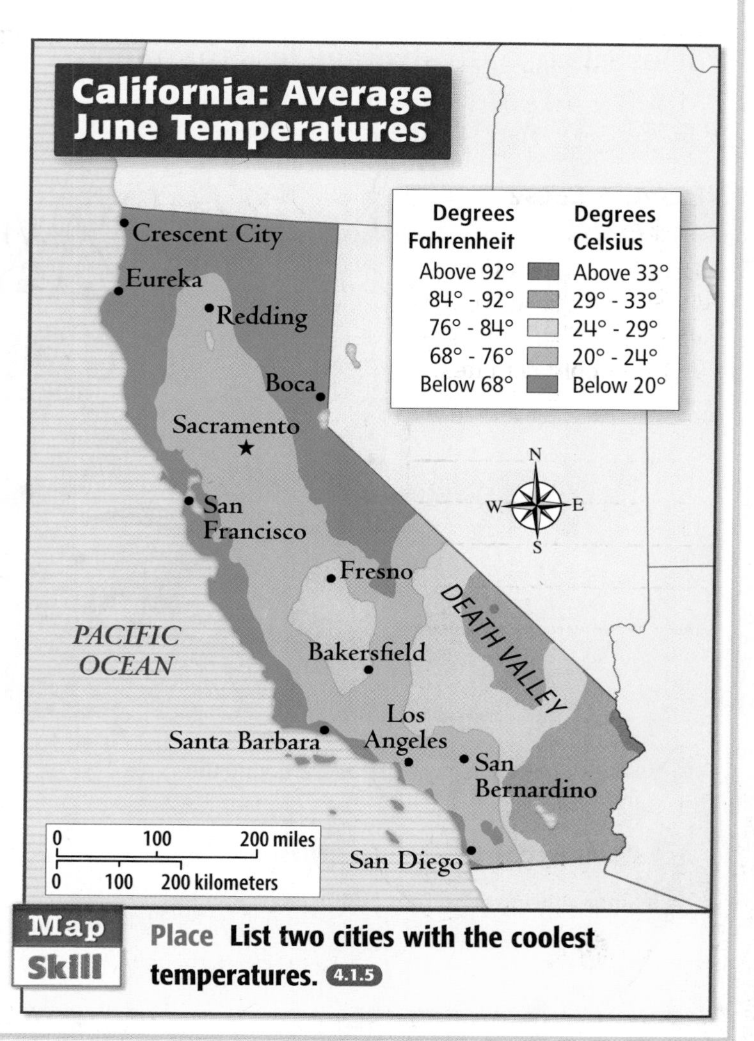

Map Skill Place **List two cities with the coolest temperatures.** 4.1.5

Water in Many Forms 4.1.3 4.1.5

In addition to temperature, climate is also affected by **precipitation**. Precipitation is the amount of water in the air that falls to the ground. Precipitation can fall as rain, snow, sleet, hail, or very slowly as fog. Look at the map on page 33 to see California's average precipitation.

Some places get more precipitation than others. The location of a place affects how much precipitation it will get. It snows a lot in the Sierra Nevada. It rains a lot on the coast. Deserts get almost no rain. Deserts are arid, or dry, for most of the year. Deserts usually average less than ten inches of rain a year.

Wet and Dry Cycles

Why do the deserts of our state get so little rain? California's deserts are in the **rain shadow** of the Sierra Nevada. Land in a rain shadow is land with reduced rainfall on the side of a mountain that is facing away from the wind. Look at the diagram below. As the wet air from the Pacific Ocean moves toward the mountains of the Coast Ranges, it begins to rise. Clouds form. When the clouds rise, the moisture cools and turns into raindrops. Farms in the Central Valley region benefit from this rainfall.

When these same clouds move over the Sierra Nevada, they rise even higher to colder elevations.

The Rain Shadow Effect

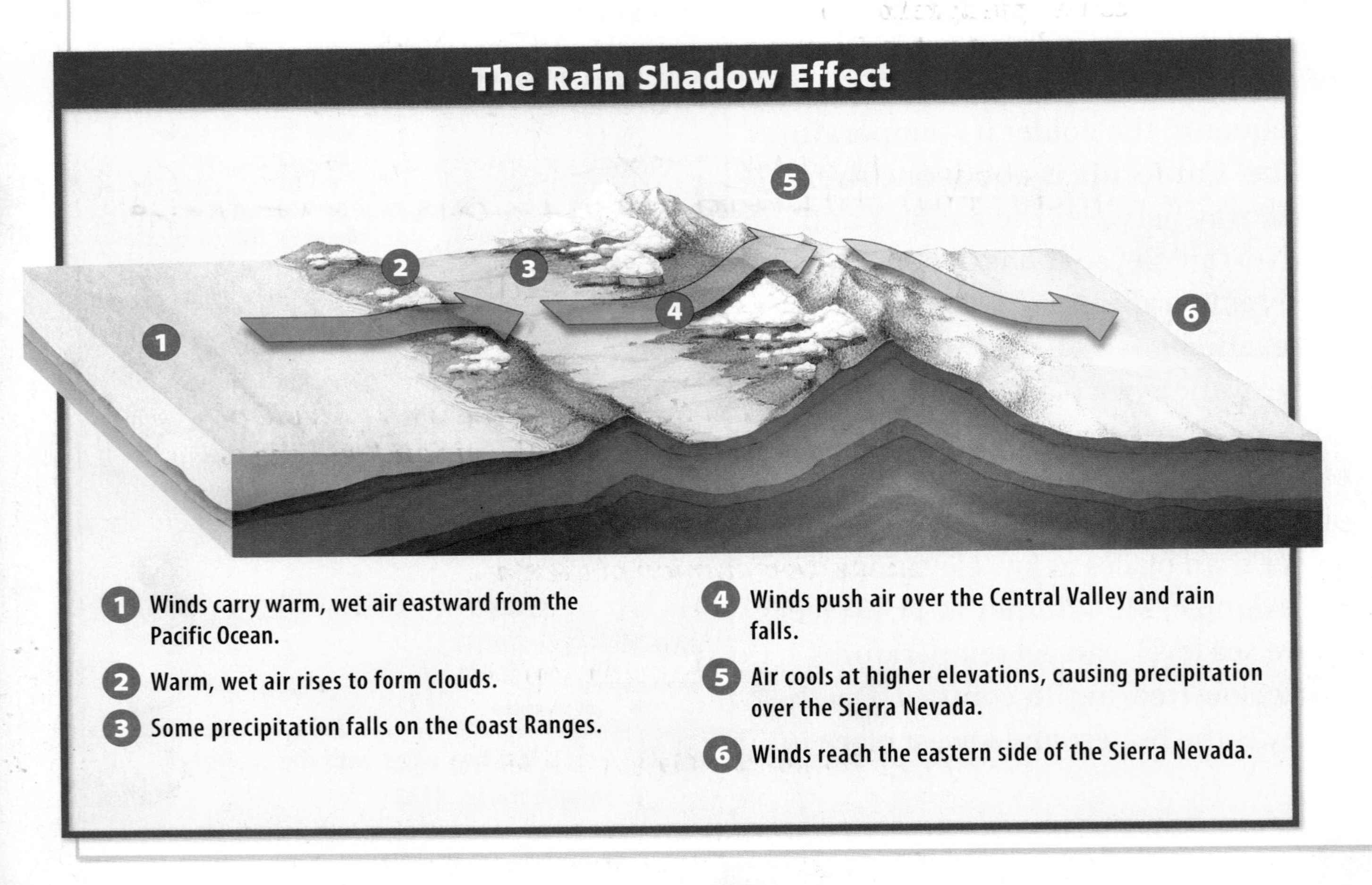

1. Winds carry warm, wet air eastward from the Pacific Ocean.
2. Warm, wet air rises to form clouds.
3. Some precipitation falls on the Coast Ranges.
4. Winds push air over the Central Valley and rain falls.
5. Air cools at higher elevations, causing precipitation over the Sierra Nevada.
6. Winds reach the eastern side of the Sierra Nevada.

The moisture that is left in the clouds turns to ice or snow. That is why it sometimes snows in the mountains when it rains in the valleys. By the time these clouds reach the top of the mountains there is no precipitation left for the other side of the mountains.

Death Valley is in the rain shadow of the Sierra Nevada. By the time air travels from the Pacific Ocean to the eastern side of the Sierra Nevada Range, it is cloudless. This is why Death Valley is so dry all year.

For 17 years Mary Austin lived near Death Valley. She wrote a book about her time there called *Land of Little Rain*. Read the passage below from Austin's book about Death Valley.

REVIEW What causes precipitation to fall in the Sierra Nevada but not in Death Valley? *Cause and Effect*

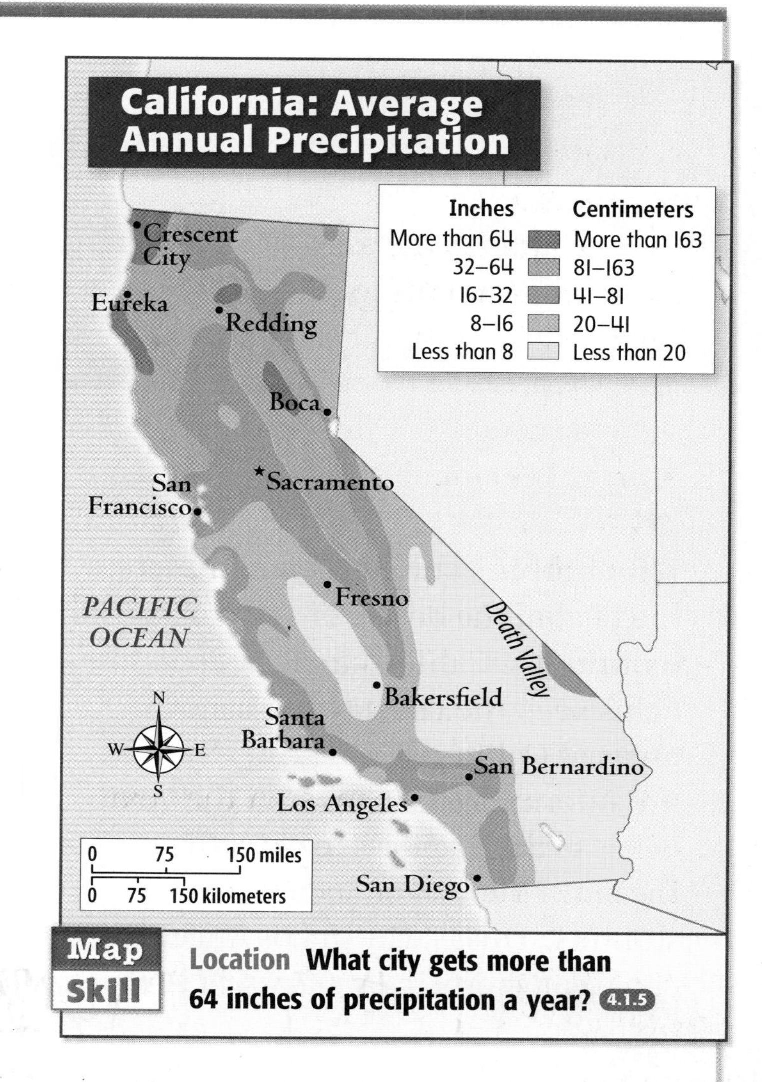

Location What city gets more than 64 inches of precipitation a year? 4.1.5

Primary Sources

Mary Austin

Land of Little Rain

Mary Austin

April 1903

"*Not the law, but the land sets the limit . . . Void of life it never is, however dry the air and villainous the soil. . . . For all the toll the desert takes of a man it gives compensations, deep breaths, deep sleep, and the communion of the stars. . . .*"

void empty
villainous harmful
compensations rewards
communion connection

How did Mary Austin feel about Death Valley?

California's coast in Mendocino ▲

Coastal Climate 4.1.3

California's climate is not limited to the heat of the desert or the cold of the mountains. California's long coastline helps keep the coastal and central areas of California mild.

California's coast has a mild climate because the Pacific Ocean warms the air in the winter. It cools it in the summer. This is why in Los Angeles you can wear shorts in January *and* June.

REVIEW How does the Pacific Ocean affect climate in California? *Cause and Effect*

What You Learned

4.1.3 4.1.5 The hottest temperatures in California are in the desert. The coldest are in the mountains.

4.1.3 4.1.5 Most of the precipitation in California falls along the coast and in the Central Valley. In the Sierra Nevada, snow may fall but the rain shadow keeps Death Valley dry.

4.1.3 Much of the coastal climate is mild because of the cooling or warming effect of the ocean.

Lesson Review

1. **Focus Question** Why are there different climates in California? 4.1.3

2. **Vocabulary** Write one sentence for each vocabulary term. 4.1.3
   climate
   elevation
   precipitation
   rain shadow
   sea level

3. **Geography** How does the rain shadow affect California's climate? 4.1.3

4. **Critical Thinking** **Make Decisions** What kind of clothing would you bring on a trip to the Mojave Desert? 4.1

5. **Reading Strategy** **Identify Cause and Effect** Identify the cause and effect of California's coastal climate. 4.1.3 ELA R2.1

6. **Write about THE BIG IDEA** How does the climate of the Central Valley influence the way people live there? 4.1.3 ELA W2.1

7. **Link to Science** For one week, record the average daily precipitation in the city where you live, and in a California city that is in a different region than yours. Write a report about why the precipitation might be different in the two cities. 4.1.5

CRITICAL THINKING **Skills**

Problem Solving 4.1.5

Problems are part of everyday life. Problem solving is finding answers, or **solutions**. You can use the steps below to solve big problems or to solve small ones.

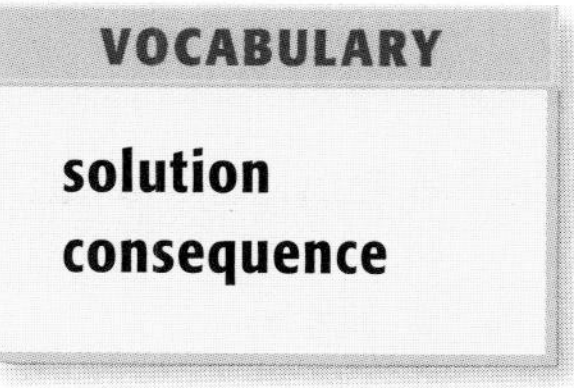

1 Learn It

- Identify the problem. You need to know what the problem is before you can solve it.
- Gather information. Find out as much as you can about the problem.
- Identify the choices. Looking at different choices can help you to solve a problem.
- Think about the **consequences**. Every choice has a consequence, or result. Some consequences are better than others.
- Choose a solution. The best solutions have the best results.

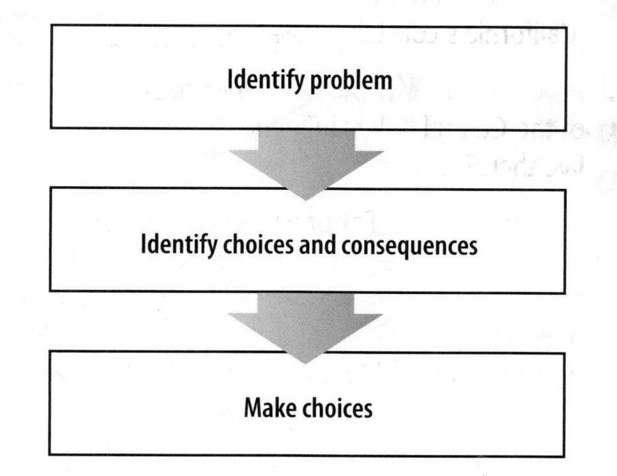

2 Try It

- In Lesson 2, you learned that oil and natural gas are nonrenewable resources. Eventually they will run out in California. Use the steps in Learn It to tell how you might solve this problem. Organize your information in the graphic organizer below to help you.
- Identify an energy problem that is facing our state.
- Gather information about this energy problem.
- Identify the choices California has.
- Think about some consequences of these choices.
- Choose the best solution to this energy problem.

3 Apply It

- Identify a problem in your school or community.
- Use the steps in Learn It to suggest a solution.

LESSON 4

One Land, Many People

FOCUS QUESTION

What makes California so rich in different cultures?

VOCABULARY

- culture
- diverse
- immigrant
- refugee
- ethnic group
- heritage

VOCABULARY STRATEGY

SYNONYMS Diverse is used to describe something that is full of interesting differences. What other words do you know that are similar?

READING STRATEGY

Identify Main Idea and Details

Copy the chart below. Use it to list the main idea and details of this lesson about California's many people.

Start with Your CALIFORNIA STANDARDS

4.1 Students demonstrate an understanding of the physical and human geographic features that define places and regions in California.

4.1.5 Use maps, charts, and pictures to describe how communities in California vary in land use, vegetation, wildlife, climate, population density, architecture, services, and transportation.

Discover where California's most populous cities are. (Begins on page 40)

4.4 Students explain how California became an agricultural and industrial power, tracing the transformation of the California economy and its political and cultural development since the 1850s.

4.4.4 Describe rapid American immigration, internal migration, settlement, and the growth of towns and cities (e.g., Los Angeles).

Find out why people from all over the world come to California. (Begins on page 37)

California has the largest population of any state in the country. About one in every eight Americans lives here, and new people keep arriving. California's population is expected to grow to 39 million by 2010. Why do so many people choose California as their home?

Come to California 4.4.4

Californians come from everywhere. Some were born here. Others came from other parts of the United States. Many come from other countries, such as Japan, Armenia, and Nigeria. People from more than 90 different countries live in California today.

California has always been home to people of many **cultures**. Culture is the way of life of a group of people. Many different cultures live in California. This means that California's population is **diverse**.

For centuries, people have been arriving in California from all over the world. Between 1860 and 1870 as many as 12,000 **immigrants** from China came to California to work on the Central Pacific Railroad. An immigrant is a person who comes to a new country to live.

From about 1920 to 1960, many immigrants from Mexico arrived in California. Many immigrants came to work. Often, immigrants found jobs in California when they could not find work in their home countries.

In the early 1900s people came to California from Great Britain, Germany, Ireland, Japan, and many more countries. These immigrants wanted freedom and a better way of life. They worked hard to make a living.

During the late 1900s many immigrants came to California as **refugees**. A refugee is a person who leaves his or her homeland because of unsafe conditions. Refugees came to California from places such as Vietnam, Laos, and Cambodia, where war made their lives unsafe.

Today, people from all over the world continue to move to California. Many come from Mexico, the Philippines, India, and Vietnam. They come for many different reasons. Immigrants have helped shape California.

◀ Californians recite the Pledge of Allegiance.

REVIEW What are some reasons people come to California? *Main Idea and Details*

A Rich State 4.1 4.1.5

California is home to many **ethnic groups**. An ethnic group is a group of people who share the same culture. Their families have usually come from the same country or area, either recently or long ago. People in an ethnic group also share a common **heritage**. Heritage is something that is passed on from people in one generation to people in another generation, such as holiday customs.

For example, the hula dance is part of the cultural heritage of Hawaiians. Hawaiians have danced hula for many generations. Hula is part of their history. When Hawaiians move to California, they bring their heritage with them.

Festivals of California

One way to learn about California's many cultures is to attend some of the cultural festivals held throughout the year. For example, each July in Los Angeles there is a Lotus Festival. It brings together Asian and Pacific Islanders to celebrate their many cultures. Over 100,000 people attend this weekend

◀ Young dancer at the Lotus Festival in Echo Park, Los Angeles

of music, dancing, singing, and eating. You can see Chinese dancers in colorful costumes twirl on stage. You can also watch as dragon rowboats race across a lake. The air will be filled with the thunder of Japanese drums.

Every June the people of Oakland celebrate Juneteenth. Their festival marks the day of June 19, 1865, when African Americans in Texas learned they had been freed from slavery. Many kinds of African dance, music, and storytelling are the highlights of this festival.

Each August outside Salinas, the Monterey Highland Games and Celtic Festival celebrates Scottish heritage. In San Francisco, the Viva Las Americas Festival celebrates the cultures of Mexico and Central and South America. Thousands of people attend this September festival to look at the diverse artwork on display and to listen to the mariachi bands.

REVIEW What is heritage?
Summarize

▲ A Sikh boy and his sister take part in a festival known as Gurpurab in Pomona.

Drummers in a West African Dance Show, Oakland ▶

DATAGRAPHIC

Where Do Californians Live? 4.1 4.1.5

California has the largest population of any state. In the year 2010, the population of California will likely reach almost 40 million people. Where do all these Californians live? Most Californians live near the coast. Fewer than half of all Californians live in cities with populations of more than 100,000. The map and graph below show information about the 6 largest cities in California. Study them to answer the questions.

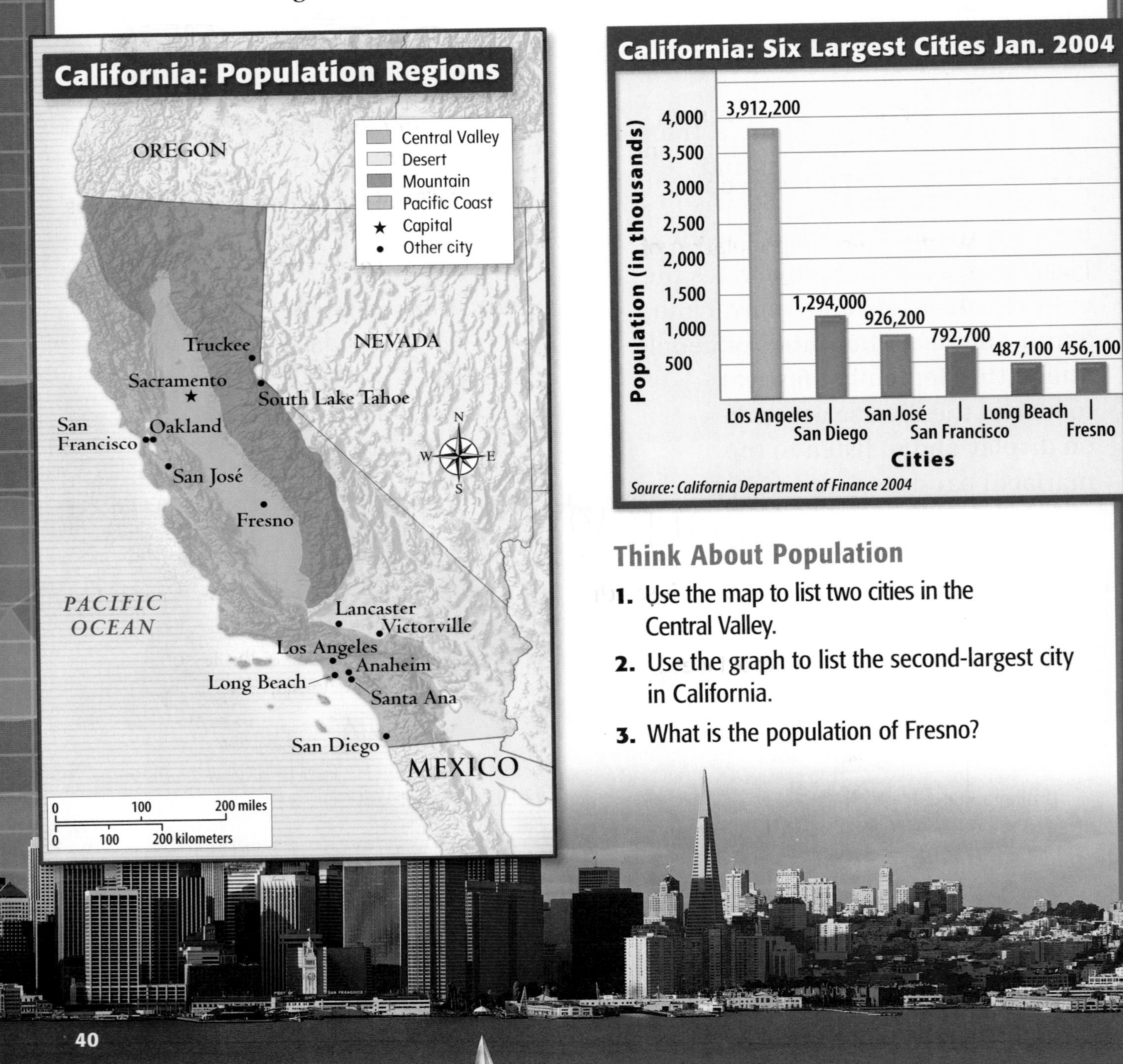

Think About Population

1. Use the map to list two cities in the Central Valley.
2. Use the graph to list the second-largest city in California.
3. What is the population of Fresno?

A Shared Heritage 4.1.5

Californians come from many different ethnic groups. However, we all share the heritage of being Californians. Generation by generation, Californians have shaped our state. As Californians, we share its history and its hopes for the future.

Looking Ahead

Californians want the state to prosper and to offer opportunities for everyone. Californians share important ideas about government, too. We also respect the environment and the freedoms of other people.

REVIEW What makes the population of California diverse? *Summarize*

United States

At the Same Time

While California's population is increasing, so is the population of our country. In 2010 the population of the United States is likely reach 309 million. Like California, the United States is home to diverse ethnic groups.

What You Learned

- 4.4.4 Millions of people from more than 90 countries have come to live in California.
- 4.1, 4.1.5 California is rich in different cultures. Californians of different ethnic groups celebrate many festivals.
- 4.1.5 Californians share ideas about the state's government, environment, people, and its future.

Lesson Review

1. **Focus Question** What makes California so rich in different cultures? 4.4.4
2. **Vocabulary** Write one sentence for each vocabulary term. 4.4.4

culture	**heritage**
diverse	**immigrant**
ethnic group	**refugee**

3. **Culture** What are some of the different ethnic festivals celebrated in California? 4.1, 4.4.4
4. **Critical Thinking** **Problem Solving** How do people escape unsafe conditions they experience in their own countries? 4.4.4
5. **Reading Strategy** **Identify Main Idea and Details** Use the chart to list the main idea and details in the section of this lesson called "Come to California." 4.4.4, ELA R2.1
6. **Write about**  How do people keep their cultural traditions as they adapt to life in a new land? 4.4.4, ELA W2.1
7. **Link to Music** Use the Internet or an encyclopedia to research a musical instrument, such as a bagpipe, Spanish guitar, or Japanese wadaiko drums. Write a short paragraph about it. 4.1

CHAPTER 1

Chapter Review

Vocabulary Review

Copy the sentences below on a separate sheet of paper. Use the list of vocabulary terms to fill in the blanks.

mineral	**conservation**
immigrant	**relative location**

1. ________ is the protection of natural resources so they are not overused. (4.1.5)

2. The ________ of a place explains where it is compared to another place. (4.1.5)

3. A ________ is a natural material found in the earth. (4.1.5)

4. A(n) ________ is a person who moves to a new country to live. (4.4.4)

5. **Test Preparation** Oil is a ________ that can be used to produce energy. (4.1.5)

A. drought **C. fuel**
B. climate **D. renewable resource**

Comprehension Check

6. Which region of the United States does California belong to? (4.1.5)

7. What are three things that can affect temperature? (4.1.3)

8. Why is Death Valley such a dry area? (4.1.3)

9. Where do most Californians come from? (4.4.4)

10. In what region of the state do most people in California live? (4.1.5)

11. **Critical Thinking** Why did railroads make it easier for people to travel to California? (4.1.5)

12. **Critical Thinking** How does reusing and recycling paper help protect trees? (4.1.5)

Using Primary Sources

13. When did Mary Austin publish *Land of Little Rain*, the book she wrote about her time in Death Valley? (4.1.3)

14. What does Mary Austin say the desert gives to a man? (4.1.1)

Skills Check

Write a complete sentence to answer each question.

Understand Latitude and Longitude

15. What do lines of latitude measure? 4.1.1

16. What do lines of longitude measure? 4.1.1

17. Why is it useful to know how to use lines of latitude and longitude? 4.1.1

18. Look at the map of California on this page. Which national park is closest to 32°N, 116°W? 4.1.1

19. Test Preparation The pattern formed by lines of latitude and longitude crossing each other is called the _______ . 4.1.1

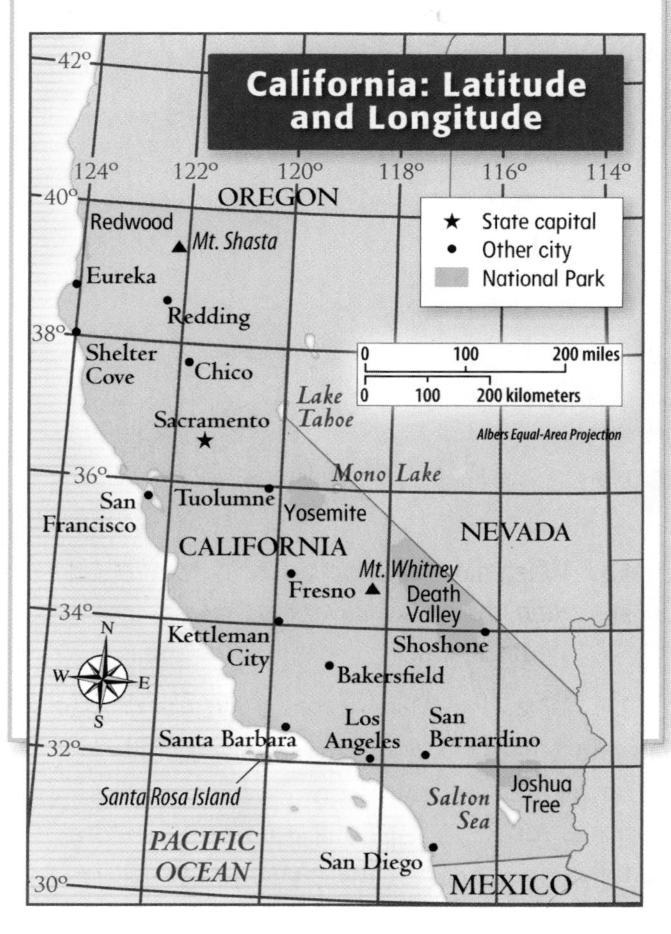

Hands-on Activities

20. Make a Poster Work in groups to create a poster that answers this question: 4.1.5

What is one way that people use three natural resources found in California?

21. Make a Landform Map Use an outline map of California as a base for making a three-dimensional landform map. Trace the shape of the state on heavy cardboard. Then use different colors of clay to model the landforms, such a mountains, on the outline map. 4.1.5

Write About Geography

22. Descriptive Suppose that you have just moved to California from another country. Write a poem to describe your thoughts and feelings about your new home and community. 4.1 ELA W2.1

LOG ON For help with the process of writing, visit:
www.macmillanmh.com/ss/ca/writing

CHAPTER

Geography of California

YOU ARE THERE

"At my feet lay the Great Central Valley of California, level and flowery, like a lake of pure sunshine....And from the eastern boundary of this vast golden flower-bed rose the mighty Sierra, miles in height, and so gloriously colored..."

John Muir saw this sight in 1868. He was standing at Pacheco Pass on the main route from San Francisco to central California and the Sierra Nevada. When Muir looked out over the landscape, he called it the "the most beautiful I have ever beheld."

In this chapter you will read about the four physical regions of California: mountains, valleys, coasts, and deserts.

A Californians enjoy many activities in the state's mountains. (page 50)

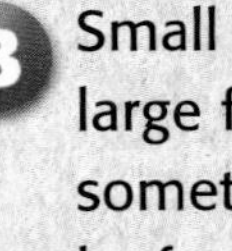

B Small and large farms are sometimes run by families. (page 58)

C Watching for wildlife is one of the activities Californians enjoy along the coast. (page 63)

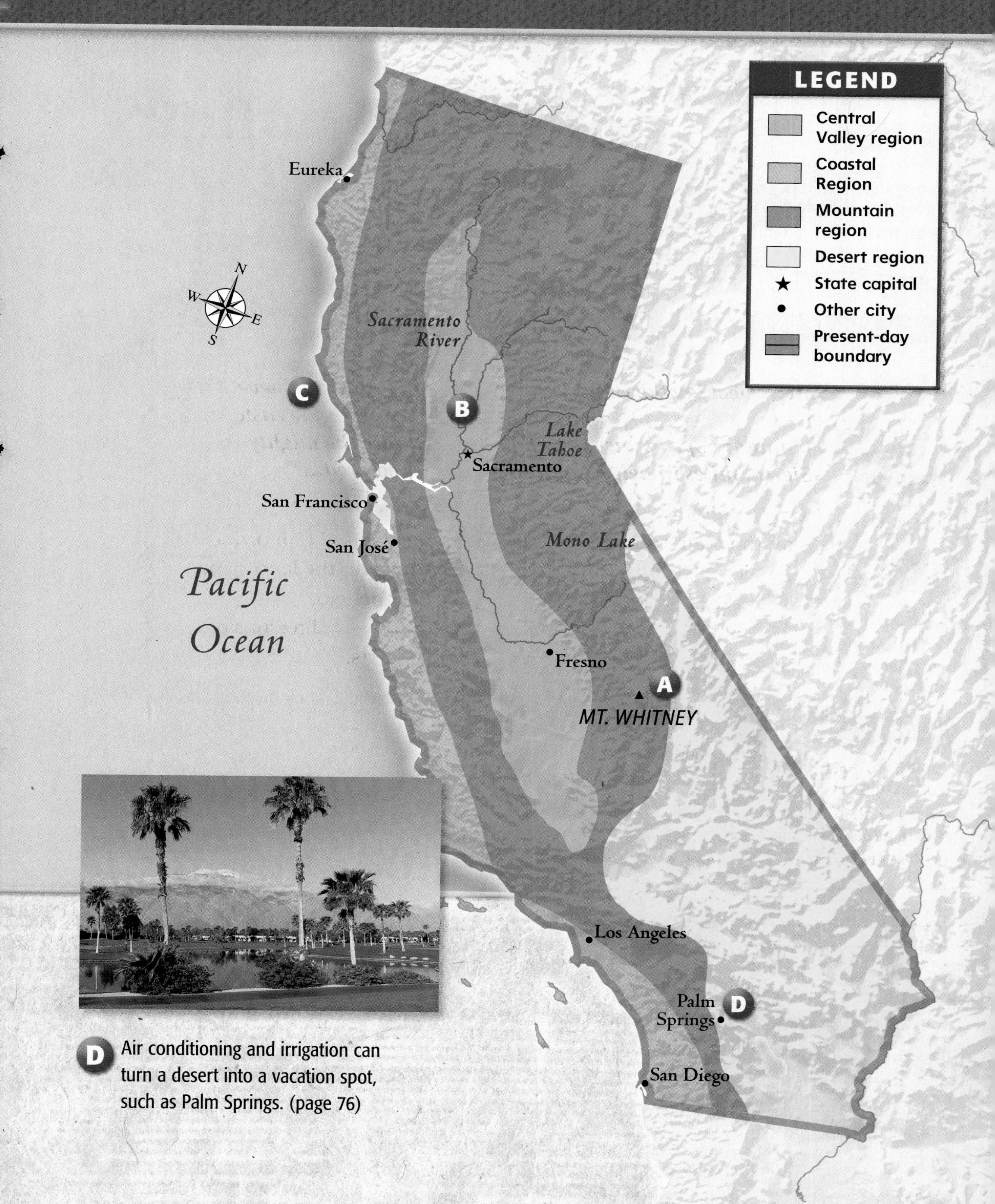

D Air conditioning and irrigation can turn a desert into a vacation spot, such as Palm Springs. (page 76)

LESSON 1

Mountain Ranges of California

FOCUS QUESTION

What makes the mountain regions of California special?

VOCABULARY

- mountain pass
- source
- tributary
- volcano
- erupt
- industry
- tourist

VOCABULARY STRATEGY

SYNONYMS When a thing **erupts** it releases something forcefully. List some other words that describe the act of releasing something forcefully.

READING STRATEGY

Identify Main Idea and Details

Use the chart below to learn about California's mountains.

Start with Your CALIFORNIA STANDARDS

4.1 Students demonstrate an understanding of the physical and human geographic features that define places and regions in California.

4.1.3 Identify the state capital and describe the various regions of California, including how their characteristics and physical environments affect human activity.

Explore the mountain regions of California. Learn how people interact with California's mountains. (Begins on page 47)

4.1.4 Identify the locations of the Pacific Ocean, rivers, valleys, and mountain passes and explain their effects on the growth of towns.

Learn about California's mountains and mountain passes. (Begins on page 48)

4.1.5 Use maps, charts, and pictures to describe how communities in California vary in land use, vegetation, wildlife, climate, population density, architecture, services, and transportation.

Locate California's mountains and volcanoes on maps. (page 49)

In the north, south, east, and west, mountains can be found in every part of California. They are the most common landform in our state and cover more than half the land.

High in the Mountains 4.1.3 4.1.5

There are several mountain ranges, or rows of mountains, in California. The Coast Ranges, the Sierra Nevada, and the Cascade Range are some of the mountain ranges in the state. Can you find them on the map?

California has many of the tallest mountains in the United States. Mt. Whitney is the highest peak in the lower 48 states. Find Mt. Whitney on the map. How tall is it?

Even during the summer, you will find ice and snow at the top of Mt. Whitney. California's tallest mountains are capped with snow during most of the year.

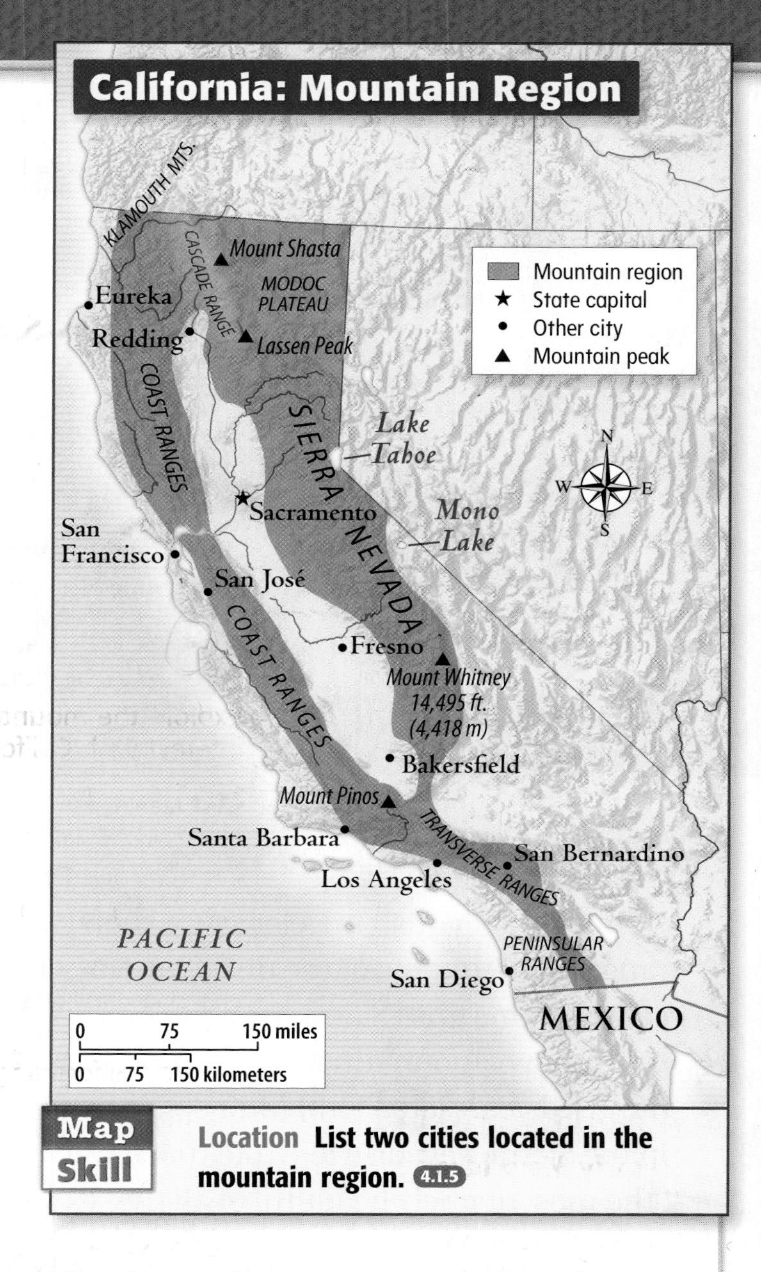

Map Skill **Location** **List two cities located in the mountain region.** 4.1.5

The shorter Coast Ranges, on the other hand, get little snow, and they are warm in the summer.

REVIEW List two of California's mountain ranges. *Main Idea and Details*

◀ Temple Crag is a part of the eastern Sierra Nevada.

Animals, such as this ▶ mountain lion, live in the Sierra Nevada.

The Sierra Nevada 4.1.4 4.1.5

In 1776, a Spanish traveler saw a snowy range of mountains in the distance. He called it "una gran Sierra Nevada," or a great snowy mountain range. Almost one hundred years later, John Muir spent time in the Sierra Nevada. He wrote that it was "the most divinely beautiful of all the mountain-chains I have ever seen."

The Sierra Nevada is 400 miles long and between 40 and 80 miles wide. Only a few **mountain passes** break the chain of peaks, or points. A mountain pass is a narrow gap between mountain peaks. Elsewhere, the Sierra Nevada is nearly impossible to cross.

The Sierra Nevada is the **source** of many of California's rivers. A source is the place where a river begins. You have learned that it snows often in California's mountains. When the snow melts, the water flows downhill, forming **tributaries**. A tributary is a small river that flows into a larger river. These mountain tributaries feed rivers in other regions. The water you drink was once snow in the Sierra Nevada.

Some tributaries empty into mountain lakes such as Lake Tahoe and Mono Lake. Lake Tahoe is the second deepest lake in the United States. It is 1,645 feet deep. It holds enough water to cover the entire state of California to a depth of 14 inches.

Sierra Nevada Animals and Plants

The Sierra Nevada is full of plants and animals. Birds, mammals, reptiles, and fish find perfect homes in the forests, grasslands, and streams. Black bears roam through Yosemite National Park.

The giant sequoias (suh KOY ahs) in Sequoia National Park are the largest living things on Earth. They are also the widest. If you and your classmates stood in a circle around a full-grown sequoia with your arms outstretched, it would take about 20 of you to get around the whole tree.

Giant sequoias are found in Sequoia National Park. ▼

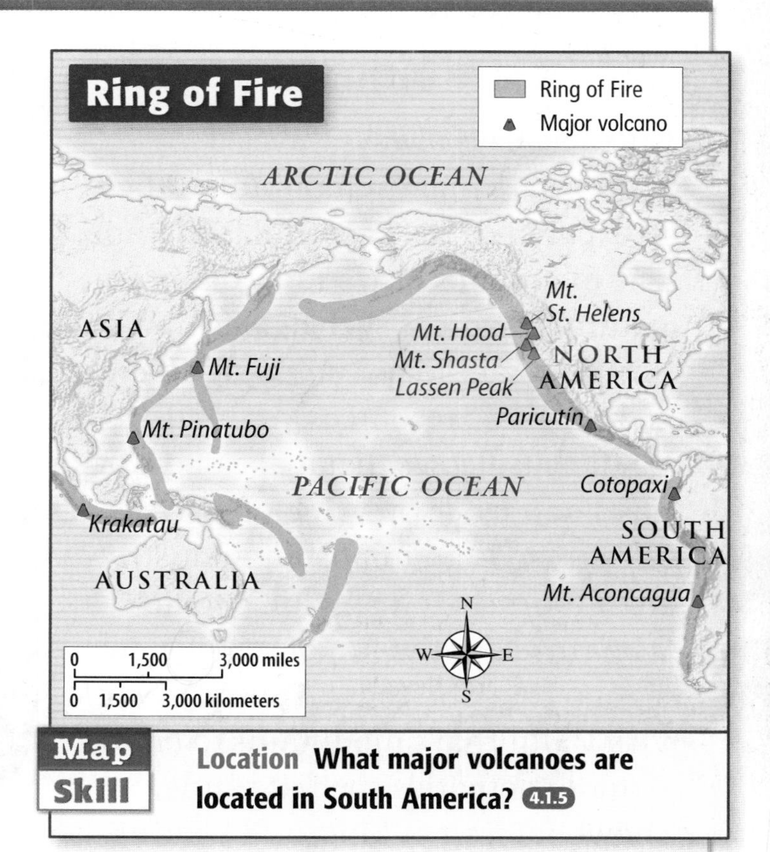

Map Skill **Location** **What major volcanoes are located in South America?** 4.1.5

The Cascade Range

North of the Sierra Nevada, the Cascade Range peaks include **volcanoes**. A volcano is an opening in the earth from which hot liquid rock and ash may pour out.

The Cascade Range is part of a much larger group of volcanoes known as the Ring of Fire. The Ring of Fire circles the edges of the Pacific Ocean. What other volcanoes can you locate on the map?

Most of the volcanoes in the Cascade Range are not active. However, Lassen Peak **erupted**, or released ash and liquid rock, between 1914 and 1917. Ash from the volcano spread more than 300 miles.

REVIEW How did the Sierra Nevada get its name? *Cause and Effect*

Life in the Mountains 4.1.3

People have always traveled to California's highest mountain ranges to experience the beautiful landscape. The mountains also supply important natural resources such as water, wood, and minerals. Major **industries** grew up around these resources. An industry is all the businesses that make one kind of good or provide one kind of service.

Tourism is an important industry in California. **Tourists** are people who travel for the fun of seeing new sights. Tourists from all over the world visit California's mountains to enjoy outdoor activities such as skiing, snowboarding, hiking, and boating.

REVIEW List two reasons why people go to California's mountains.
Main Idea and Details

▲ Snowboarding in California's mountains

What You Learned

4.1.3 4.1.5 More than half of the land in California is covered by mountains.

4.1.4 4.1.5 The Sierra Nevada mountain range is the source of much of California's water.

4.1.3 Natural resources and a beautiful landscape attract people to the mountains.

Lesson Review

1. **Focus Question** What makes the mountain regions of California special? 4.1
2. **Vocabulary** Write one sentence for each vocabulary term. 4.1.3 4.1.4
   - **erupt**
   - **industry**
   - **mountain pass**
   - **source**
   - **tourist**
   - **tributary**
   - **volcano**
3. **Geography** Why are the mountain ranges in California difficult to cross? 4.1.3
4. **Critical Thinking** **Make Decisions** Why do people visit mountains on their vacations? 4.1.3
5. **Reading Strategy** **Identify Main Idea and Details** Use the chart to list details about the Sierra Nevada. 4.1.4 ELA W2.4

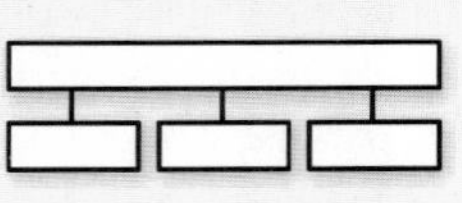

6. **Write about THE BIG IDEA** Write about which mountain range you would want to visit and give some reasons why. 4.1.4 ELA W2.4
7. **Link to Art** Make a collage or painting of California's mountains. 4.1.5

Biography
Focus on Leadership

4.1

Ansel Adams 1902–1984

In 1916, Ansel Adams and his family vacationed in Yosemite National Park, where he took his first pictures.

By the time he was 25, Adams was committed to nature and photography. He said,

"We need a little earth to stand on and feel run through our fingers. Perhaps photography can do this . . . ."

Adams was a member of the conservation group the Sierra Club. In 1928, they gave Adams his first photography show.

For the rest of his life, Adams would photograph nature wherever he could find it. Adams' pictures did more than stand out as works of art. They inspired a country to love nature, and to find a way to protect it.

What did Ansel Adams' photographs inspire in others?

For more about Ansel Adams, visit:

www.macmillanmh.com/ss/ca/bios

The Life of Ansel Adams

1902	Born in San Francisco on February 20
1920	First published photograph in *Sierra Club Bulletin*
1969	Director of the Sierra Club
1980	Receives Presidential Medal of Freedom
1984	Dies on April 22

MAP and GLOBE Skills

Use Elevation Maps 4.1.5

California's mountain ranges run the entire length of the state. How can you tell which mountains are the highest? For this kind of information, you need an **elevation** (el uh VAY shun) map. Elevation is the height of the land above **sea level**. Sea level is the level at the surface of the sea. The elevation at sea level is zero feet.

1 Learn It

To read elevation maps, follow these steps using the map on page 53.

- Read the map title. The title of the map is "California: Elevation."
- Elevation maps use colors to show the height, or elevation, of land. Different colors mean different heights.
- The map key on this page tells you what each color on the map means. For example, all the yellow areas are between 1,650 and 3,300 feet (500 and 1,000 meters) above sea level.

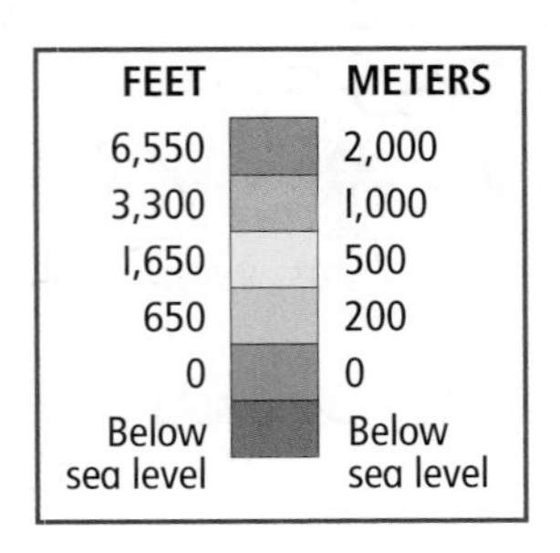

2 Try It

Use the map on page 53 to answer these questions.

- Which mountain range has the highest elevation?
- Are the Coast Ranges lower or higher than the Cascade Range?
- Where is the lowest point in California?

3 Apply It

- What area in California is below sea level?
- How can an elevation map help you learn about geography?

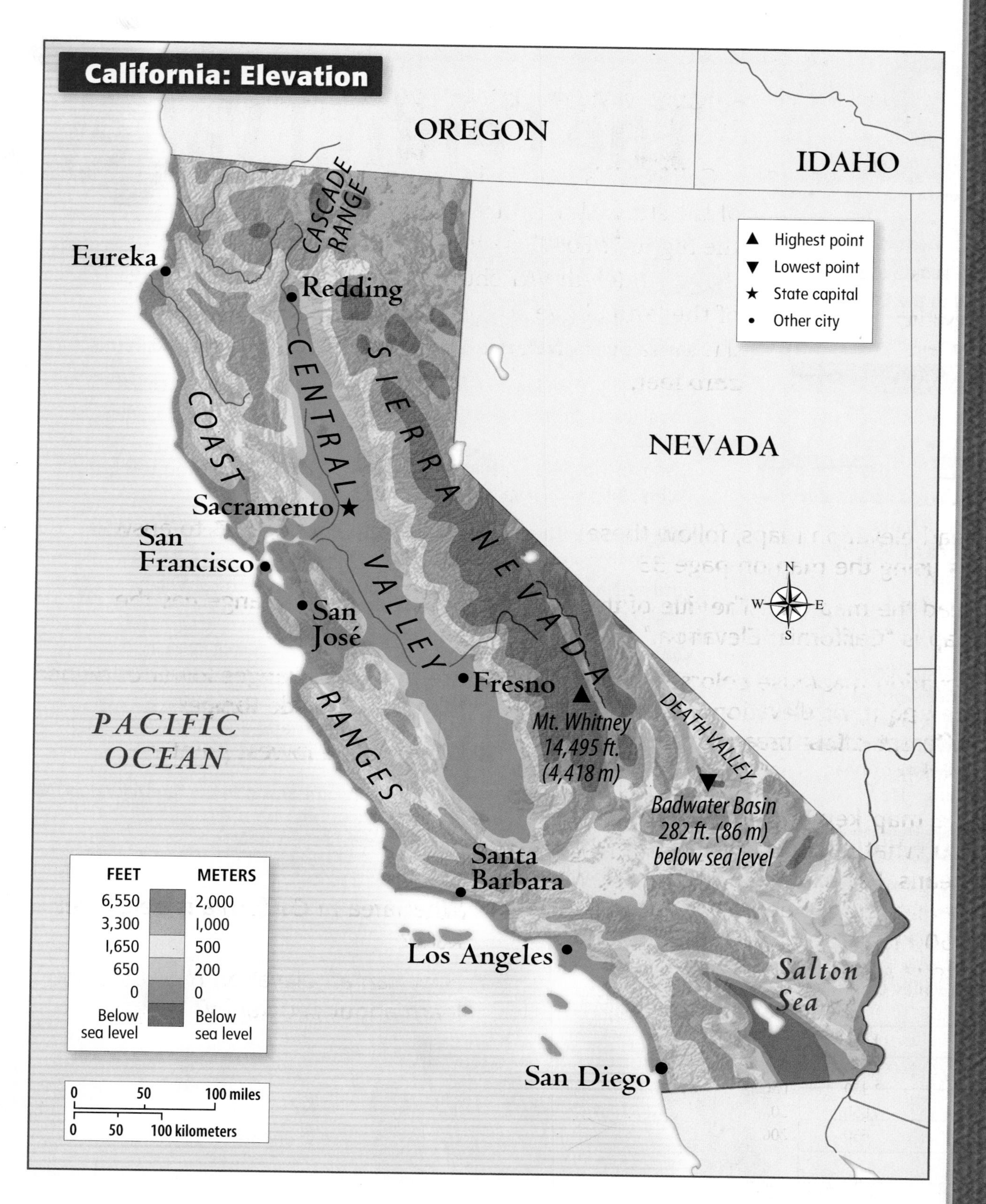
California: Elevation
OREGON
IDAHO
NEVADA
CASCADE RANGE
Eureka
Redding
COAST
CENTRAL
SIERRA NEVADA
Sacramento
San Francisco
San José
VALLEY
Fresno
RANGES
PACIFIC OCEAN
Mt. Whitney 14,495 ft. (4,418 m)
DEATH VALLEY
Badwater Basin 282 ft. (86 m) below sea level
Santa Barbara
Los Angeles
Salton Sea
San Diego
Highest point
Lowest point
State capital
Other city
N
S
E
W
FEET
METERS
6,550
3,300
1,650
650
0
Below sea level
2,000
1,000
500
200
0
Below sea level
0
50
100 miles
0
50
100 kilometers

LESSON 2

The Central Valley

FOCUS QUESTION

How do people use the land in the Central Valley?

VOCABULARY

- valley
- fertile
- delta
- erosion
- agriculture
- migrant worker
- urban
- suburban

VOCABULARY STRATEGY

ROOT WORDS Urban is the root word of **suburban.** It is from the Latin word for city. **Sub** means below or near something else.

READING STRATEGY

Identify Cause and Effect

Use the chart to list reasons why the Central Valley is fertile.

Start with Your CALIFORNIA STANDARDS

4.1 Students demonstrate an understanding of the physical and human geographic features that define places and regions in California.

4.1.3 Identify the state capital and describe the various regions of California, including how their characteristics and physical environments affect human activity.

Discover how Californians use the fertile lands of the Central Valley. (Begins on page 55)

4.1.4 Identify the location of the Pacific Ocean, rivers, valleys, and mountain passes and explain their effects on the growth of towns.

Find out about the population growth in the Central Valley. (Begins on page 58)

4.1.5 Use maps, charts, and pictures to describe how communities in California vary in land use, vegetation, wildlife, climate, population density, architecture, services, and transportation.

Explore California's Central Valley using maps and pictures. (page 55)

Crops are grown in the Central Valley. ▼

In the middle of California is a huge, flat region called the Central Valley. This land, made up mostly of fields and orchards, supplies more than half of America's fruits and vegetables.

A Land Between Mountains 4.1.3 4.1.5

California's Central Valley is one of the biggest **valleys** in the world. A valley is a low area between mountains.

The Central Valley is in the middle of four different mountain ranges. It is formed from two valleys, the Sacramento Valley in the north and the San Joaquin Valley in the south. Together, they are about 450 miles long and about 50 miles wide. In the Central Valley, everywhere you look you will see plains. Before farmers arrived, these plains were mostly grassland.

REVIEW Describe the Central Valley. *Summarize*

Farm Country 4.1.3 4.1.4

Sarah Eleanor Royce traveled across the United States to California in 1849. Her trip took six months. Read about her first sight of the Central Valley.

Today the Central Valley looks very different than when Royce first saw it. In 1849, herds of deer and elk roamed the plains. Now, you can still spot fish, ducks, and geese in parks and nature areas, but the animals you will spot most often are human.

A Rich Land

Many people have come to the Central Valley because of its most valuable natural resource, **fertile** land. Fertile land has rich soil that produces crops easily.

Fertile land requires plenty of water. There are two major rivers that supply the Central Valley with water. The Sacramento River flows south out of the Sacramento Valley and the San Joaquin River flows north from the San Joaquin Valley. Both rivers are fed by tributaries from the mountains.

These tributaries carry mineral-rich soil, sand, and rocks down from the mountains to the Central Valley. As the tributaries then flow into the San Joaquin and Sacramento rivers, some of the soil is deposited, or settles to the bottom, of the rivers.

Farms in the Central Valley ▼

Primary Sources

A selection from
A Frontier Lady
Sarah Eleanor Royce
1849

"... I was rewarded by coming out ... on a rocky height [when] I looked, down, far over ... to where a ... rosy glow that seemed to me a smile of welcome; while beyond ... outlines of other mountains"

How did Sarah Eleanor Royce feel when she first looked down on the Central Valley?

The rivers meet and flow into San Francisco Bay. Where the rivers enter the bay, more sand and soil are deposited. The sand and soil form land called a **delta**. The minerals in the soil that have been deposited make the Central Valley and the delta good places to grow crops.

The flowing water causes **erosion**, or a wearing away of Earth's surface. The surface of the mountains is being worn down each year as some soil is carried away with the melting snow.

Growing Crops

In the middle 1800s, California settlers realized that the Central Valley was a good place for **agriculture** (AG rih kul chur), or the business of growing crops and raising animals. Today, the Central Valley is one of the world's most productive agricultural regions.

Now, farmers grow over 300 different crops in the valley. Some of the major crops are cotton, grapes, tomatoes, almonds, and olives.

REVIEW What makes the land in the Central Valley fertile? *Cause and Effect*

Tractors help farmers prepare the land for planting. ▼

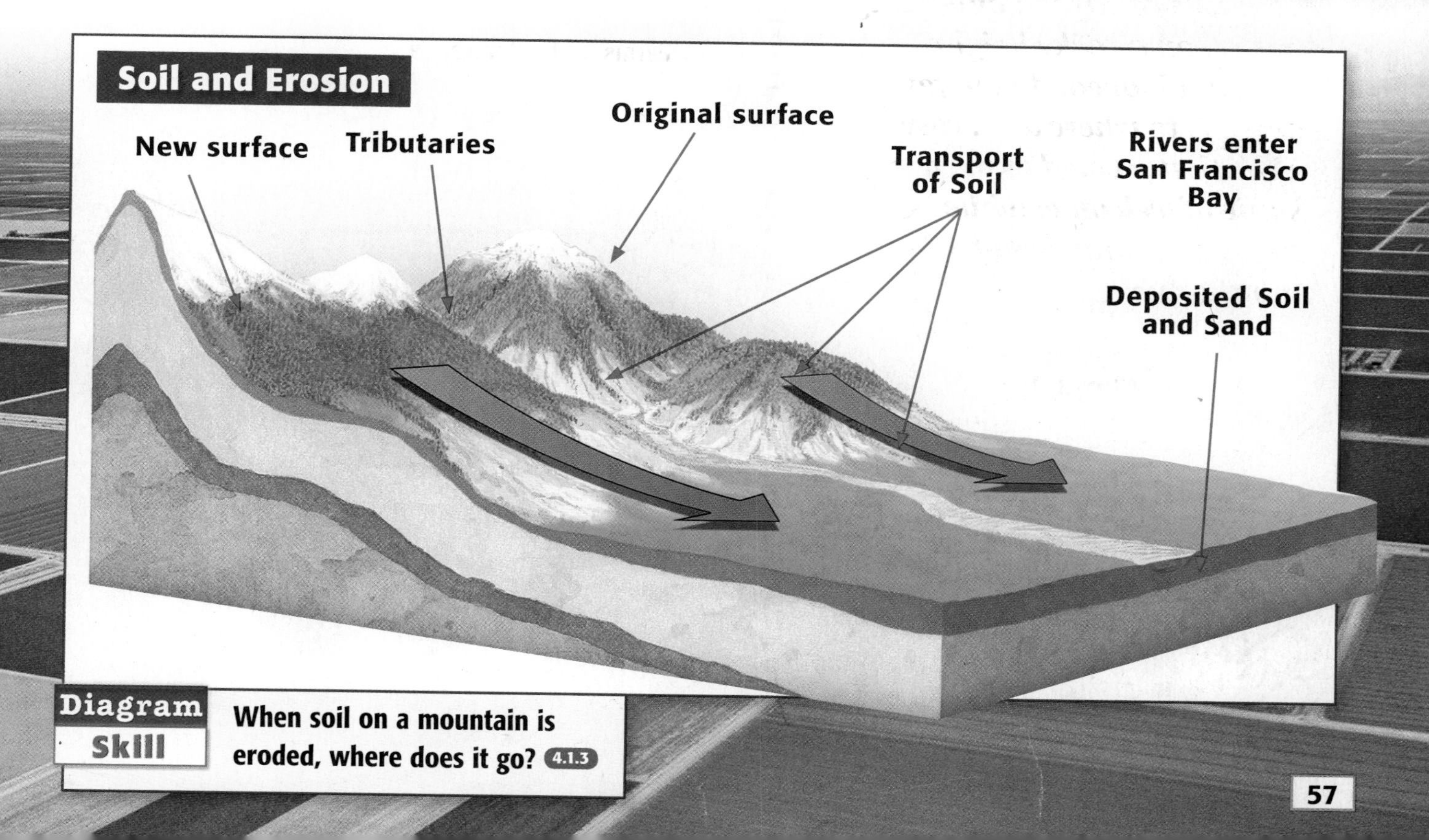

Diagram Skill When soil on a mountain is eroded, where does it go? 4.1.3

Central Valley Life 4.1.4 4.1.5

Agriculture helps shape the lifestyle in the Central Valley. Many people who live here have jobs in the agriculture industry. Most of the farms in the region are owned by families. Often, family members help with the farm work.

Other farm workers move around from farm to farm, following the crops as they are ready to be harvested. They are called **migrant workers**. Most of the migrant workers now in the Central Valley come from Mexico. In earlier times, immigrants from other places, such as India, Portugal, and China, found work in the region as migrant workers.

Not everyone in the Central Valley works on a farm. The region is home to many food processing companies, or factories that package foods. Some people work in the oil and gas industries.

Sacramento is the state capital. There, people work for the state government.

Cities and Surrounding Areas

Urban areas such as Fresno, Bakersfield, Sacramento, and Stockton are growing. Urban areas are cities. **Suburban** areas are communities located just outside cities. These areas are commonly called suburbs.

In fact, the Central Valley is the fastest growing area in California. By 2004 the Central Valley already had a bigger population than most states, with almost 6 million people. By the year 2040, researchers predict that the Central Valley will be home to about 12 million people.

Family members usually help with farm work. ▶

Growth of the Central Valley

As more people move to the Central Valley, they need houses. New houses are being built on farmland. This means there is less room for crops. The population increase has brought other problems for people who live in the region, such as more smog. Smog can cause health and environmental problems.

Hans Johnson works with population figures in the Central Valley. He says, "The question is when will they slow down, and how will [the population rate] slow down." Although they are worried about population growth, Central Valley residents think the Valley is a terrific place to live.

REVIEW What kinds of work do people living in the Central Valley do? *Summarize*

▲ New houses are built on land that was once farmland.

What You Learned

- **4.1.3 4.1.5** The Central Valley is one of the world's largest valleys.
- **4.1.3 4.1.4** Rich soil and plenty of water helped people transform the region into a center of agriculture.
- **4.1.4 4.1.5** The Central Valley's population is growing quickly.

Lesson Review

1. **Focus Question** How do people use the land in the Central Valley? **4.1**
2. **Vocabulary** Write one sentence for each vocabulary term. **4.1**

agriculture	**migrant worker**
delta	**suburban**
erosion	**urban**
fertile	**valley**

3. **Economics** What jobs can people find in the Central Valley? **4.1.3**
4. **Critical Thinking** **Identify Fact and Opinion** Hans Johnson believes the population in the Central Valley is growing very fast. Do you think people should continue to move to the Central Valley? **4.1.3**
5. **Reading Strategy** **Identify Cause and Effect** How do people interact with the land of the Central Valley? **4.1.4** **ELA R2.1**

	➡
	➡
	➡
	➡
	➡

6. **Write about THE BIG IDEA** Write about how Central Valley residents use the region's geography. **4.1.3** **ELA W2.1**
7. **Link to Mathematics** Research a fruit or vegetable grown in the Central Valley. Record how many dollars the crop brings in every year. Present your findings in a bar graph. **4.1.5**

CITIZENSHIP
POINTS OF VIEW

How Should Land in the Central Valley Be Used? 4.1.3

The Central Valley is one of the fastest-growing areas of California. As more people build new houses, some people worry that farmland will disappear.

Read below to find out about three points of view on how the land in the Central Valley should be used.

"The land should be used for farming. We have the richest soil in the world. . . . More people and houses use up water resources. We need water to grow crops . . . If you take farmland away, you can't get it back."

Jorge Alvarado
Farmer and cattle rancher
Salida, California
From an interview, 2004

"The most important thing is to plan for growth. Some land should be used to build roads . . . We need to set aside land for schools, parks, and other services before we build new houses."

Paris Davis
Real estate agent
Bakersfield, California
From an interview, 2004

"The best use of land is to use it in a way that helps the economy but also protects the environment. . . . The more cars, the more smog. . . . We must plan for roads and set aside land for . . . public transportation."

Jenelle Schneider
Air quality educator
Fresno, California
From an interview, 2004

Build Citizenship
Responsibility

1. Why should people living in the Central Valley care about how land is used there?
2. What kind of information would help people in the Central Valley plan for growth?

Think About It
Points of View

1. Why does Jorge Alvarado think farmland should be protected?
2. What reasons does Jenelle Schneider give for her opinion?
3. In what way do Jenelle Schneider and Paris Davis agree?

Think about how you would plan for growth in the Central Valley. Then, write a letter to a newspaper in the area explaining your plan.

LESSON 3

California's Coast

FOCUS QUESTION

Why is California's coastline so important to the people who live there?

VOCABULARY

bay
harbor
earthquake
plate
fault

VOCABULARY STRATEGY

COMPOUND WORDS
Earthquake is a compound word. It is made up of the word **earth** and the word **quake**, which means shaking. What other compound words can you think of?

READING STRATEGY

Identify Cause and Effect

Use the chart to identify the effects of different industries along California's coastline.

Start with Your CALIFORNIA STANDARDS

4.1 Students demonstrate an understanding of the physical and human geographic features that define places and regions in California.

4.1.3 Identify the state capital and describe the various regions of California, including how their characteristics and physical environments affect human activity.

Discover the many different ways the ocean helps Californians.
(Begins on page 64)

4.1.4 Identify the location of the Pacific Ocean, rivers, valleys, and mountain passes and explain their effects on the growth of towns.

Find out how California's geography affects where people live.
(Begins on page 63)

4.1.5 Use maps, charts, and pictures to describe how communities in California vary in land use, vegetation, wildlife, climate, population density, architecture, services, and transportation.

Learn about California's coastline. (Begins on page 63)

Avalon harbor on Santa Catalina island ▼

*C**alifornia's coastline stretches almost 1,300 miles from Oregon in the north to Mexico in the south. Although narrow, this land next to the Pacific Ocean is California's most crowded region.***

Land Meets Water 4.1.3 4.1.5

As you will learn, the first Europeans to explore California sailed along its edge or coast. They found **bays**, or areas where the ocean is partly enclosed by land. The biggest bay in California is San Francisco Bay. Can you find it on the map? Some bays, called **harbors**, are protected. Ships can dock in these harbors. Harbors are like huge parking lots for ships. San Francisco Bay and San Diego Bay are natural harbors. Elsewhere, Californians have built man-made harbors.

Birds, such as this puffin, can be found along California's coast. ▼

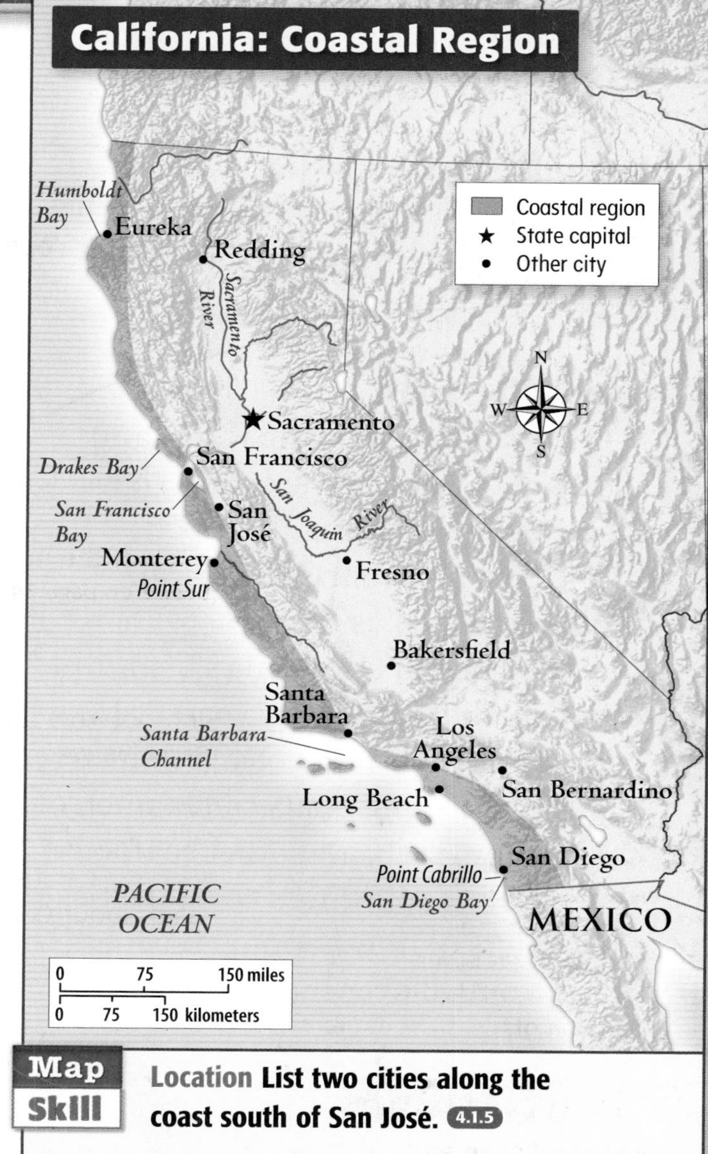

Map Skill Location **List two cities along the coast south of San José.** 4.1.5

The coast in California varies greatly. In Northern California, some of the mountains come straight to the water's edge. The coast is often rocky and the water can be dangerous. In Southern California, the coastal plain is between the mountains and the ocean. This is a place to visit sandy beaches.

REVIEW How is the coast different in the north and the south? *Compare and Contrast*

The Coast 4.1.3 4.1.4

Close to three out of four people who live in California live in the coastal region. Many live near the mountains of the Coast Ranges. Others have settled in the coastal plains of Southern California.

Life On the Coast

Californians enjoy the warm and pleasant climate of the coast. They also enjoy the ocean.

The ocean supports important industries, such as tourism. Millions of tourists flock to California's beautiful coast and beaches every year. Fishing is another important coastal industry. California fishing boats catch much of the salmon, crab, and other seafood that we eat. California's coastal cities are centers of international business. Ships from all over the world dock in their harbors.

The Southern Coast

As you have learned, California is not warm and sunny everywhere. However, Southern California is warm all year round. There is also little rain in the region.

Many Southern Californians spend their free time outside. Surfing, sailing, biking, and beach volleyball are a few of the outdoor activities that residents enjoy.

Southern California is more than just fun in the sun. Two very large cities are located along the southern coast. San Diego and Los Angeles are two of the ten largest cities in the United States by population. These cities have major businesses, restaurants, and museums that make them exciting places to live or visit.

Some Southern Californians enjoy surfing. ▼

◀ The Golden Gate Bridge, in San Francisco, California

Grapes are grown in the valleys north of San Francisco. ▶

The Northern Coast

The Bay Area, or the region around the San Francisco Bay, is home to the largest number of people on the northern coast. There are several large cities in the Bay Area. Can you find the Bay Area on the map on page 63? The Bay Area's Silicon Valley is a famous center for the computer industry.

In the valleys north of San Francisco, the climate is good for growing grapes. Even farther north, the coast is rugged. Thick groves of evergreen forests grow there, and logging, or cutting down trees for their wood, is a major industry.

The tallest evergreen trees are the redwoods. Redwoods can grow to be more than 350 feet tall and 20 feet wide.

Former United States President Theodore Roosevelt once said,

"A grove of giant redwoods . . . should be kept just as we keep a great or beautiful [large church]."

REVIEW How does the ocean support industries? *Main Idea and Details*

Earthquake! 4.1.3 4.1.5

California's coast is not just famous for its natural beauty and relaxing lifestyle. It is also famous for its **earthquakes**. An earthquake is a shaking of the earth.

Do you know what it is that causes earthquakes? The Earth's surface is made up of huge **plates**. These plates are always grinding against each other. Sometimes they slip or slide quickly against each other. If you have ever felt an earthquake, you were feeling the slipping and sliding of these plates.

Two of the Earth's plates meet in California at the San Andreas fault. A **fault** is the crack in the ground where the plates meet. Find the San Andreas fault on the map below.

Earthquakes and Damage

Have there been any earthquakes in California lately? Yes! All the time. Many people are surprised to learn that thousands of earthquakes happen in our state each year. Most are so small that people don't feel them.

The bigger earthquakes can cause damage. In 1994, an earthquake known as the Northridge Quake hit the Los Angeles area. Noelle Shoji remembers the earthquake well.

> ***"Our house was very badly damaged, and an entire room . . . detached from the rest of the house."***

Freeways and buildings collapsed. Many people had to leave their homes because the buildings were no longer safe.

Aerial view of the San Andreas fault ▼

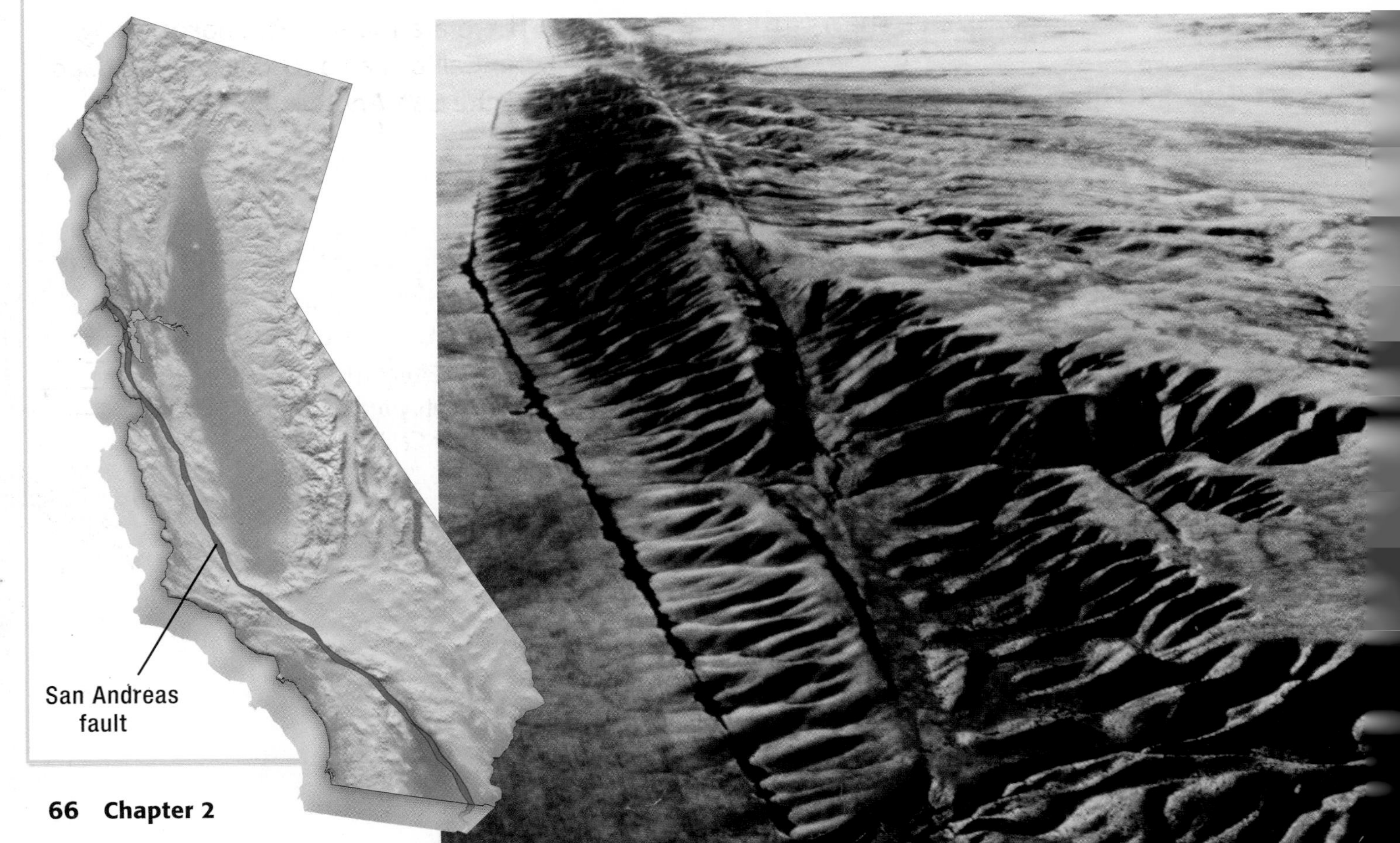

▲ Many buildings were damaged during the Northridge Quake.

Earthquake Safety

California has strict rules about constructing safe buildings. Laws require that buildings, bridges, and roads be made out of materials that can withstand an earthquake. With these laws in place, recent earthquakes have caused less damage than earlier earthquakes.

REVIEW What causes an earthquake? *Cause and Effect*

What You Learned

4.1.3 4.1.5 California's coast includes bays, harbors, mountains, and beaches.

4.1.3 4.1.4 California's coast is a popular tourist region. It is also home to many industries, including fishing, shipping, and international business.

4.1.3 4.1.5 There are many earthquakes along the California coast. Most are caused by the San Andreas fault.

Lesson Review

1. **Focus Question** Why is California's coastline so important to the people who live there? 4.1

2. **Vocabulary** Write one sentence for each vocabulary word. 4.1.3 4.1.4
   bay **fault** **plate**
   earthquake **harbor**

3. **Government** What laws are in place in California because of earthquakes? 4.1.3

4. **Critical Thinking** **Problem Solving** Why do you think many Californians settled near natural harbors? 4.1.3 4.1.4

5. **Reading Strategy** **Identify Cause and Effect** Use the chart to identify the cause and effect of California's earthquakes. 4.1.3 ELA R2.1

6. **Write about THE BIG IDEA** Write about how the residents of the coastal region have adapted to its geography. 4.1.3 ELA W2.1

7. **Link to Science** Find out about recent earthquakes in California. Write a paragraph about what you learn. 4.1.3

Using **PRIMARY SOURCES**

What Are Primary Sources?

VOCABULARY

historian
primary source
secondary source

Primary and Secondary Sources

Historians, or people who learn about the past, study two main types of sources. **Primary sources** are spoken or written accounts from a person who has seen or experienced an event. They also include objects as well as maps and photographs.

A **secondary source** comes from a person who did not see or experience an event. Secondary sources can tell the basic facts of an event. Examples of secondary sources include encyclopedias and textbooks.

1 Learn It

Throughout this book, you will be reading and using many primary sources, including these:

- **Objects** made or used by people in the past, such as a weapon, a piece of clothing, or a tool.
- **Letters** are written messages sent from the writer to another person.
- **Photographs** can help you understand more about an event by showing you what things looked like at the time the photo was taken.
- **Official documents** contain information from an official source, such as a government office.
- **Newspapers** are papers that are usually printed daily or weekly and contain news, opinions, and advertising.

▲ Native American arrowhead

WE, the People of the United States, i
a more perfect union, eſtabliſh juſtice, inſure dome
for the common defence, promote the general welfare, a
of liberty to ourſelves and our poſterity, do ordain and eſtabliſh
United States of America.

ARTICLE I.

Sect. 1. ALL legiſlative powers herein granted ſhall be veſted in
States, which ſhall conſiſt of a Senate and Houſe of Repreſentatives.
Sect. 2. The Houſe of Repreſentatives ſhall be compoſed of membe
by the people of the ſeveral ſtates, and the electors in each ſtate ſhall
ſite for electors of the moſt numerous branch of the ſtate legiſlature.
No perſon ſhall be a repreſentative who ſhall not have attained to th
been ſeven years a citizen of the United States, and who ſhall not, w
of that ſtate in which he ſhall be choſen.
Repreſentatives and direct taxes ſhall be apportioned among the ſe
cluded within this Union, according to their reſpective numbers, whi
ing to the whole number of free perſons, including thoſe bound to
and excluding Indians not taxed, three-fifths of all other perſons.
be made within three years after the firſt meeting of the Congreſs o
every ſubſequent term of ten years, in ſuch manner as they ſhall b
repreſentatives ſhall not exceed one for every thirty thouſand, but
repreſentative; and until ſuch enumeration ſhall be made, the ſtate
titled to chuſe three, Maſſachuſetts eight, Rhode-Iſland and Provide
five, New-York ſix, New-Jerſey four, Pennſylvania eight, Delaw
ten, North-Carolina five, South-Carolina five, and Georgia three.
When vacancies happen in the repreſentation from any ſtate,
ſhall iſſue writs of election to fill ſuch vacancies.
The Houſe of Repreſentatives ſhall chuſe their Speaker and

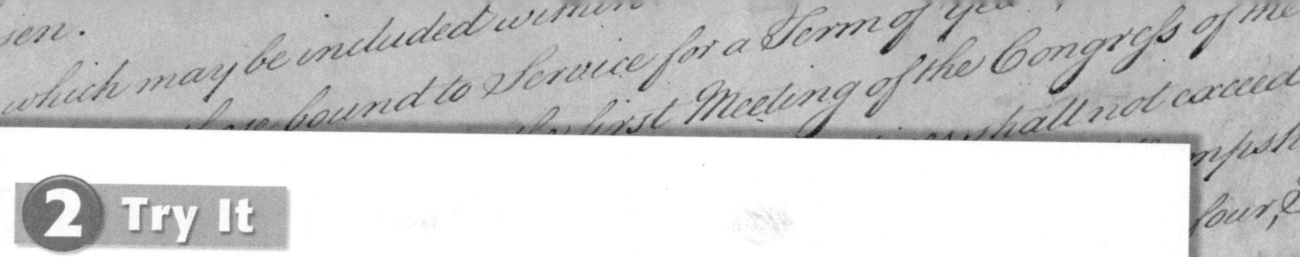

2 Try It

Identifying primary and secondary sources can help you better understand and draw conclusions about events in history.

- Identify the author of the source. What is his or her connection to the source?
- Identify the date or time period the source was created. Was the author at the event? If you answered "yes," then the source is a primary source.
- Identify where the source was created. Was the author in that place during the event? If you answered "yes," then the source is a primary source.

3 Apply It

- Write a description of an event you have witnessed recently.
- Describe the event so a reader will feel as if the event is happening as your account is read.

Photograph of Ventura County ▶ mudslide, January 2005

◀ The United States Constitution is an official document.

The Battle to Save Whiteoak Creek

4.1

*

Characters

Ms. Jordan	Narrator
Latesha	Isaiah
Emily	Carlos

*

Ms. Jordan: As you know, we've been studying about the importance of protecting the environment. Tomorrow we're going to break into teams. Each team is going to do an environmental project for the year. For homework tonight I want you to think of something you and your teammates can do.

Latesha: And I thought we weren't going to have any homework tonight!

Emily: How are we supposed to save the planet? We're just kids.

Narrator: Later that afternoon Carlos and Isaiah walk home along Whiteoak Creek after soccer practice.

Isaiah: Are those old tires over there?

Carlos: Yeah, and check out that mattress and table over there.

Isaiah: How did this stuff get here?

Carlos: People just dump stuff here, and they bring more all the time. My mom says it didn't used to be like this. When my uncle was our age he used to fish here. He'd catch trout and my mom's family would eat them for dinner.

Isaiah: If there are any fish in that creek now I wouldn't want to eat them.

Narrator: The boys soon arrive in front of Carlos's house.

Isaiah: Will you be on my team in Ms. Jordan's class?

Carlos: Sure. If you can think of a great project.

Isaiah: I was counting on you to do that. See you tomorrow.

Narrator: The next day, Ms. Jordan divides the class up into teams. Isaiah, Carlos, Latesha, and Emily are on the same team.

Latesha: Okay, anybody have any brilliant ideas to save the planet?

Carlos: Actually, yes. I think we should clean up Whiteoak Creek. It's near where Isaiah and I live.

Isaiah: That's a big project.

Latesha and Emily: We better see this Whiteoak Creek.

Narrator: After school Carlos, Isaiah, Emily, and Latesha head to the creek. Carlos hands everyone a big garbage bag. The kids start putting bottles, cans, candy wrappers, and other trash into the garbage bags. Soon their bags are almost full.

Latesha: We'll never be able to clean this place up.

Emily: I've got an idea. Why don't we ask if we can make this an entire class project?

Isaiah: That's the best idea I've heard all day!

Narrator: The next day the team tells Ms. Jordan and the rest of the class about Whiteoak Creek and Carlos's idea to clean it up.

Ms. Jordan: What do you think class? All in favor raise your hand.

Narrator: Everyone's hand went up. Soon the entire class was spending time at the creek cleaning up. Parents pitched in on weekends to help. Still, the students would find new garbage on the creek banks. Back in class, the group talked about what to do.

Latesha: This is a creek, not a dump! The people who put their garbage here should be punished!

Emily: We should put up a sign telling people not to dump stuff here.

Ms. Jordan: Both of those ideas are good. Let's write to the city council and ask them to help us.

Narrator: Soon a sign was posted on the road above the creek. It said, "NO DUMPING. MINIMUM FINE $200." But that wasn't the only sign needed to protect the creek.

Ms. Jordan: Class, you've done a great job. But we still need to do something about the garbage in the creek that we can't pick up.

Isaiah: What kind of garbage is that?

Ms. Jordan: When people wash their car or change the oil in their car out in front of their house, sometimes the dirty water or oil goes down the drain in the street. The rain then carries it into Whiteoak Creek.

Emily: Okay, so we have to keep people from dumping stuff in the drains. But how do we do that?

Latesha: Where my grandmother lives, they have signs on the drains to remind people whatever goes down them will end up in a river.

Narrator: The class painted signs on storm drains that led to the creek. "Dump No Waste. Drains to Stream."

Ms. Jordan: Class, we only have a few minutes before the bell rings, but I have an announcement to make. You did an amazing job on this project. You should be very proud.

Write About It!

Write your own Readers' Theater play about an environmental project.

FOCUS QUESTION

How have humans, plants, and animals been able to live in the desert?

VOCABULARY

adapt
technology
irrigation

VOCABULARY STRATEGY

PREFIXES The prefix **ad-** in **adapt** comes from the Latin word for "two" or "toward." Can you think of another word that starts with **ad-** and means the same thing?

READING STRATEGY

Summarize

Use the chart below to summarize important facts about California's three major deserts.

California's Desert Regions

Start with Your CALIFORNIA STANDARDS

4.1 Students demonstrate an understanding of the physical and human geographic features that define places and regions in California.

4.1.3 Identify the state capital and describe the various regions of California, including how their characteristics and physical environments affect human activity.

Find out how people have adapted to the desert environment and also changed it. (Begins on page 74)

4.1.5 Use maps, charts, and pictures to describe how communities in California vary in land use, vegetation, wildlife, climate, population density, architecture, services, and transportation.

Learn about the amazing plants and animals that live in California's deserts. (Begins on page 73)

The Joshua tree can be found throughout California's Mojave Desert. ▼

Crystal clear skies, rolling sand dunes, and twisted trees impress all who see them. Desert cactus flowers add color to the dry land. The deserts of southeastern California are beautiful and fascinating places.

Land of Little Rain 4.1.3 4.1.5

California's desert region is made up of three deserts: the Colorado Desert, the Mojave Desert, and the Great Basin. California's deserts sometimes have no rain for months. Find them on the map on this page.

A desert region can also be very hot. Death Valley, in the Great Basin, got its name in 1849, when 12 people died there while looking for a shortcut to the California gold fields.

Summer temperatures in the desert region are usually over 100 degrees Fahrenheit. However, in the winter the temperature often falls below freezing.

Weird and Wonderful Plants

Have you ever wondered how anything can grow in the desert with so little water? Plants and animals **adapt**. Adapting means changing to suit the environment. For example, most plants in the desert have far-reaching roots. They are searching for water.

California deserts are home to many cactus plants. When it rains, a cactus plant swells up like a sponge to store the water. It doesn't have leaves, but its needles protect it from animals and shade it from the sun. Did you know that a cactus has natural air conditioning? The needles act as a fan when the wind rushes through them.

REVIEW How have cacti adapted to life in the desert? *Cause and Effect*

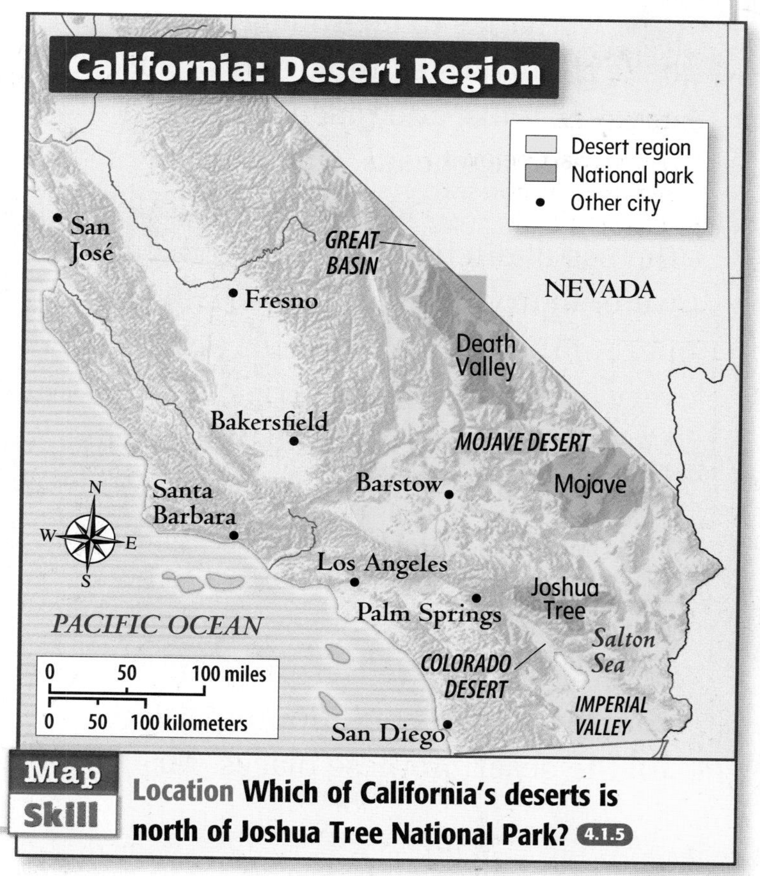

Map Skill Location **Which of California's deserts is north of Joshua Tree National Park?** 4.1.5

▲ Palm Springs, California

Changing the Desert 4.1.3

In 1849, when Death Valley got its name, few people lived in California's deserts. There was little rain and few bodies of water. People struggled to find enough water to survive.

Now, thanks to **technology**, things have changed. Technology is the use of skills, tools, and machinery to meet people's needs. One product of technology is **irrigation**. Irrigation is the use of ditches and pipes to bring water to dry land. The Imperial Valley, part of the Colorado Desert, became very fertile once it was irrigated. Melons, lettuce, corn, and other fruits and vegetables grow there now.

Have you heard of Palm Springs or Borrego Springs? These are two popular vacation spots on the western edge of the Mojave Desert. Golf courses and air conditioning units fill the desert in these places. Air conditioning is another product of technology that makes it possible for people to live, work, and play in very hot places. Today, thousands travel to the California deserts each year to enjoy golf and relaxation.

The California Desert Tortoise

Scientists who study nature have ways to tell how healthy a particular region is. One way is to study animals that live in the region. The California Desert Tortoise is one of these animals.

These tortoises are amazing creatures. They can live where ground temperatures are hotter than 140 degrees Fahrenheit. While humans need water every day to survive, these reptiles can go more than a year without water. Desert tortoises protect themselves from the heat by digging underground holes where they spend most of their time.

Protecting the Desert Tortoise

Over the past 30 years the tortoise population has gotten smaller as humans have moved into the desert. Automobiles have also killed many. Some people have taken them illegally as pets. Diseases are killing the tortoises, too.

People are taking action to protect the tortoises. It is illegal to touch, hurt, or collect wild California Desert Tortoises. At Joshua Tree Tortoise Rescue, people like Rae Packard work hard to protect the tortoises. Packard's organization helps tortoises that have been harmed by car accidents, dog attacks, and disease. The volunteers at Joshua Tree Tortoise Rescue teach people about tortoises. Remember these words of warning: Just look, don't touch!

REVIEW Why do tourists go to the California desert resorts? *Main Idea and Details*

▲ California Desert Tortoise

What You Learned

4.1.3 4.1.5 California's deserts are among the hottest and driest places on Earth. They are home to many interesting plants and animals.

4.1.3 Humans have changed the deserts using irrigation. The increased human population has harmed desert animals, such as the California Desert Tortoise.

Lesson Review

1. **Focus Question** How have people, plants, and animals been able to live in the desert? (4.1.3)
2. **Vocabulary** Write one sentence for each vocabulary word. (4.1)

   adapt **irrigation** **technology**
3. **Culture** How has technology helped humans to live in the desert region? (4.1.3)
4. **Critical Thinking Problem Solving** What is being done to help the California Desert Tortoise survive in the desert? (4.1.3)
5. **Reading Strategy** (4.1.3, ELA R2.1)
   Summarize Use the chart to summarize how humans have changed the desert.

   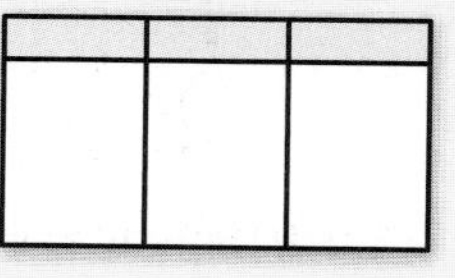
6. **Write about THE BIG IDEA** Find out more about another interesting plant or animal that lives in California's desert regions. Write a paragraph about it. (4.1.3, ELA W2.1)
7. **Link to Mathematics** Look up the weather in two different desert locations. Find the difference between the high and low temperature in each location. (4.1.5)

Chapter Review

Vocabulary Review

Copy the sentences below on a separate sheet of paper. Use the list of vocabulary words to fill in the blanks.

agriculture	**valley**
bay	**volcano**

1. Ash and hot liquid rock might pour out of an opening in the earth called a ________. 4.1.4
2. A ________ is an area where the ocean is partly enclosed by land. 4.1.4
3. A low area between mountains is known as a ________. 4.1.5
4. ________ is the business of growing crops and raising animals. 4.1.5
5. **Test Preparation** A ________ is the place where a river begins. 4.1.4

   A. **delta** C. **tributary**
   B. **source** D. **mountain pass**

Comprehension Check

6. List three mountain ranges that are found in California. 4.1.3
7. What are two important ingredients needed to grow crops easily? 4.1.3
8. How is an urban area different from a suburban area? 4.1.3
9. How are plants able to survive in deserts? 4.1.3
10. Why is it important to protect animals such as the California Desert Tortoise? 4.1.3
11. **Critical Thinking** Why did most people decide to settle in the Central Valley instead of the Sierra Nevada in the 1800s? 4.1.4
12. **Critical Thinking** How do you think building harbors has helped industries in California? 4.1.3

Using Primary Sources

What Are Primary Sources?

13. What event caused the damage seen in the photograph? 4.1.5
14. Who took this photograph? 4.1.5
15. Would this photograph be considered a primary or secondary source? 4.1.5
16. What can you learn by studying this photograph? 4.1.5

Skills Check

Write a complete sentence to answer each question.

Reading Elevation Maps

17. What do the colors on an elevation map key mean? (4.1.5)

18. Is the elevation lower or higher in northeastern California than in southeastern California? How can you tell? (4.1.3)

19. How do you think an elevation map would help people decide where to live? (4.1.5)

20. **Test Preparation** The height of land above sea level is ______ . (4.1.3)

Hands-on Activity

21. **Make a Brochure** Work in groups to create a travel brochure that answers this question: (4.1.3)

What kinds of land and water can tourists explore in California?

Write About Geography

22. **Narrative** Suppose that you are a settler crossing a California desert in the 1800s. Write a letter to a friend that describes the area and any plants or animals. (4.1, ELA W2.1)

LOG ON For help with the process of writing, visit:

www.macmillanmh.com/ss/ca/writing

UNIT 1 Unit Review and Test Prep

Comprehension and Critical Thinking Check

Write one or more sentences to answer each question.

1. How can you find the **relative location** of a place? 4.1.5
2. How are **renewable resources** different from **nonrenewable resources**? 4.1.5
3. Describe the reason for the differences in **temperature** between Mt. Whitney and Death Valley. 4.1.3
4. Why would **refugees** choose to leave their countries and move somewhere else? 4.4.4
5. How do **tributaries** form? 4.1.4
6. How did **erosion** change the soil in the Central Valley over thousands of years? 4.1.3
7. How do Californians protect themselves against **earthquakes**? 4.1.2
8. What is California's global address? 4.1.2
9. Critical Thinking Why do you think farmers would have trouble planting crops within the **rain shadow**? 4.1.3
10. Critical Thinking What made it easier for people to live and grow crops in deserts? 4.1.5

Reading Social Studies Check

Identify Main Idea and Details

Copy this graphic organizer. Reread "California's Environment" on page 21. Use the graphic organizer to identify the main idea and details from this reading selection. Then answer the questions. 4.1.5 ELA R2.1

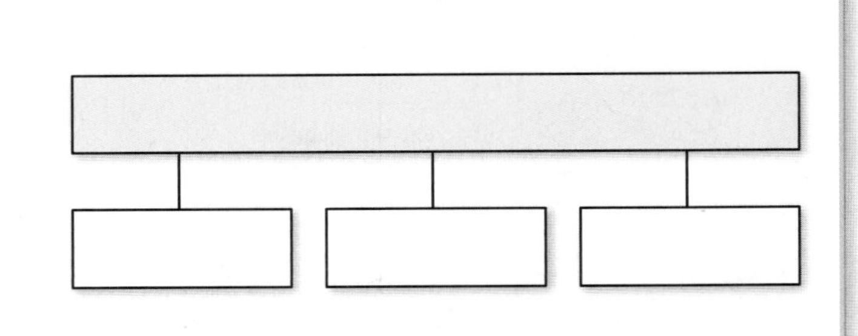

11. How did you identify the main idea? ELA R2.1
12. How did you identify the details? ELA R2.1
13. How are details related to the main idea? ELA R2.1

Test Preparation

Read the paragraphs. Then answer the questions.

John Muir created the Sierra Club in 1892 to honor the beauty of California's environment. Muir also hoped the Sierra Club could help protect the wilderness. That way, wilderness areas would stay beautiful for years to come.

Today about 700,000 people are members of the Sierra Club. They protect land and water not only in California, but also across the entire planet. The organization does many things to save the environment. They have helped set aside land for parks, including Yosemite National Park. Members ask people to conserve and recycle in communities around the country. They also clean garbage from oceans, rivers, and lakes.

14. How was Yosemite National Park created?
4.1.3

A Yosemite National Park began in 1892.

B It was created as a way to help people learn to recycle.

C It is one of several national parks around the country.

D The Sierra Club helped set aside land for the park.

15. What is the main idea of this passage?
4.1.3

A The members of the Sierra Club like to look at wildflowers.

B The Sierra Club works to protect the environment in many different ways.

C The Sierra Club is over 100 years old.

D John Muir believed it was important to protect the wilderness.

Write About History

16. **Narrative** Write a short story that describes a trip through one of California's mountain ranges. Describe what you might see and do along the way.
4.1.3 ELA W2.1

17. **Expository** Write one paragraph about the weather in your area in January and another about what it is like in July. How much precipitation is there? Are temperatures similar or different during those months? Discuss some reasons why the weather in your area is what it is.
4.1.3 ELA W2.3

18. **Letter** Write a one-page letter to people in your neighborhood asking them to reduce, reuse, and recycle more of their garbage.
4.1.5 ELA W2.1

For help with the process of writing, visit:
www.macmillanmh.com/ss/ca/writing

How do people adapt to where they live?

Write about the Big Idea ELA W2.3

Expository Essay

Think about what you learned about California's geography, climate, and natural resources as you read Unit 1. Complete the graphic organizer below by filling in details.

Use your graphic organizer to help you write an essay about one geographic region of California. Your essay should answer the Big Idea question "How do people adapt to where they live?" You might want to describe the geography, people, climate, and resources of the area you chose. Be sure to begin with an introduction. Include one paragraph for each main reason. End with a concluding paragraph.

Regions	Natural Resources	Climate	How People Adapt
1. Mountain 2. 3. 4.			

Write an Expository Essay

1. Plan

- To begin, you will need to decide what your essay topic is. Here it has already been assigned.
- Next, develop a plan. This plan may include researching your topic. Then, organize your information by using an outline or a graphic organizer. For example, you may organize the body of this essay by writing one paragraph for each of the reasons you listed in the graphic organizer.

2. Write a First Draft

- Decide what your readers need to know.
- Focus on getting your thoughts on paper.

3. Revise and Proofread

- Read your essay and make sure that you stated the main idea in the introduction.
- Be sure you included details.
- Proofread your essay, fixing any errors and checking spelling, capitalization, and punctuation.
- Rewrite your essay neatly before you give it to your teacher.

Activity

Speak About the Big Idea ELA LS2.2

Travel Advertisement

Create a television advertisement for a region of California. You will want to explain and describe the positive things that would make people want to come there. You might make a colorful brochure or poster that you can show during the ad to promote the region.

Prepare Work in small groups. Each group should choose a region to promote. Consider including information about your region's climate, natural resources, tourist attractions, cities, or national parks. Use information from Unit 1 and your notes. You may want to gather additional information by using the Internet, your school library, or your local library.

Present Each member of the group should present some information about the area.

For help with the Big Idea activity, visit:

www.macmillanmh.com/ss/ca/launchpad

Read More About the Big Idea

The Ever-Living Tree

by Linda Vieira Important historical events are used to mark the 2,000-year lifetime of a giant redwood tree.

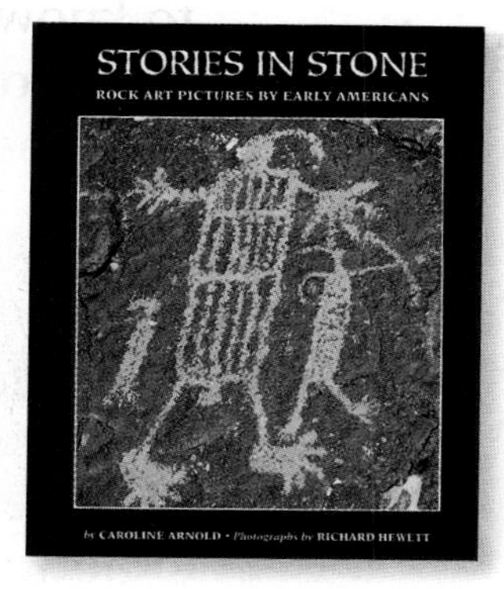

Stories in Stone

by Caroline Arnold Explore the mysterious rock art of the Mojave Desert.

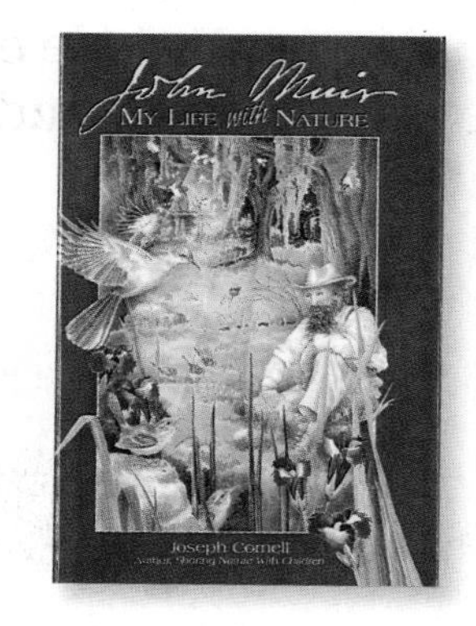

John Muir

by Joseph Cornell A famous nature educator tells the story of Muir's life using Muir's own words.

UNIT 2

Early California History

"Now you are to hear the most extraordinary thing. . . . on the right hand of the Indies there is an island called California. . . ."

—Garci Rodríguez Ordóñez de Montalvo, from *Las Sergas de Esplandián*

What happens when different peoples first meet?

In Unit 2 you will read about Native Americans in California. You will also read how their lives changed when Spanish explorers, soldiers, and others arrived.

Copy the graphic organizer below. As you read the chapters in this unit, look for changes caused by the meeting of Europeans and Native Americans in California.

Then fill in the graphic organizer with details telling how different groups affected Native Americans living in California. The first one has been started for you.

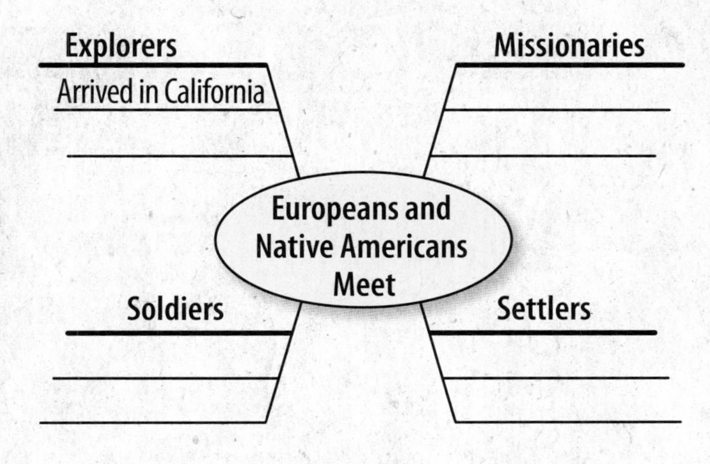

◀ Spanish explorers at sea

UNIT 2

People Who Made a Difference

Elsie Allen
1899–1990

Elsie Allen was a Pomo Native American who wove traditional baskets. Elsie Allen's baskets are exhibited at museums in California. (page 100)

Juan Rodriguez Cabrillo
?–1543

Juan Rodriguez Cabrillo explored California's coast for Spain. He searched for a water passage from the Western Hemisphere to Asia. (page 136)

Sebastián Vizcaíno
about 1550–1616

Sebastián Vizcaíno traveled along the coast of California searching for a safe harbor for Spanish ships. (page 146)

Unit Events

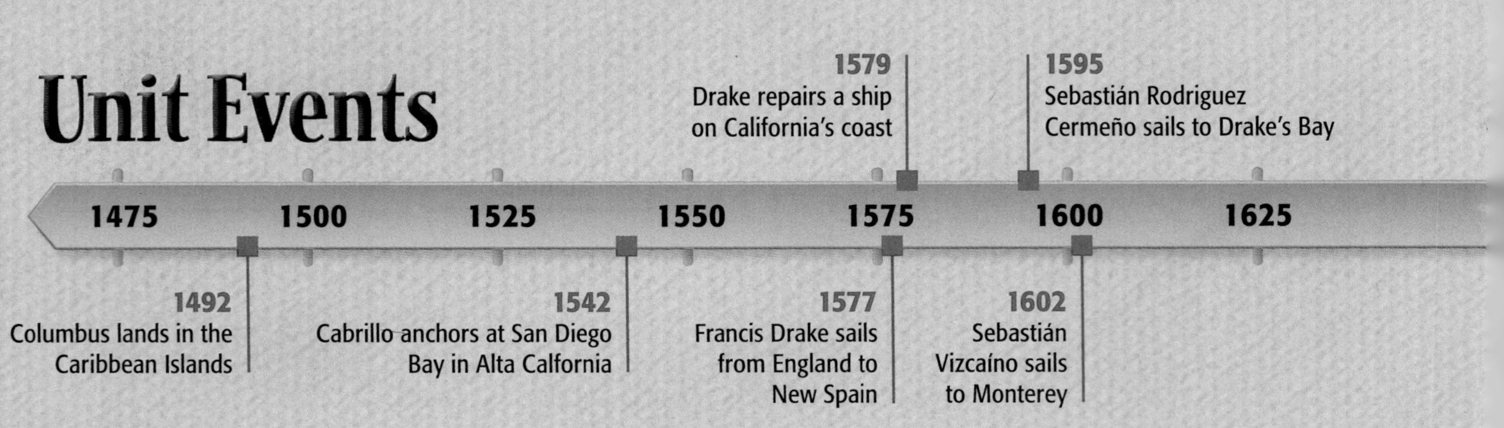

For more about People Who Made a Difference, visit:

www.macmillanmh.com/ss/ca/bios

Junípero Serra
1713–1784

Junípero Serra came to California to establish missions and to convert Native Americans to Christianity. He built nine missions in California. **(page 155)**

Bartolomea
Unknown

Bartolomea was a young girl when missionaries came to her Tongva village. Her husband described Bartolomea's life at the missions in the *Los Angeles Star* in 1852. **(page 166)**

Toypurina
1761–1799

Toypurina was a Gabrielino. She helped lead a revolt against the San Gabriel Mission. **(page 167)**

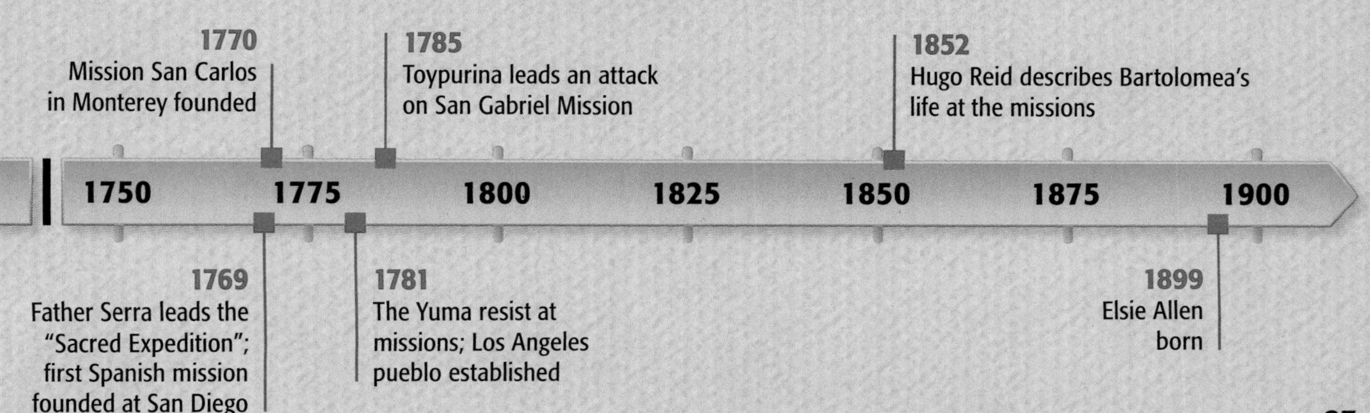

Literature

MOUNTAIN-MAKING

Selections from "Mountain-Making" in
Back in the Beforetime, Tales of the California Indians
retold by Jane Louise Curry
Illustrated by Harriet Peck Taylor

Native American tales, also known as "creation stories," explain how the world began. "Mountain-Making" *tells how some Native Americans of California explained the way in which mountains were created.*

Back in the Beforetime . . . The plains stretched north, south, east, and west to the sky's edge. In all the World there were no landmarks but the white-teepee mountain Shasta and the lake that was called Tulare. On the lake lived all the swimmers and divers among the Beforetime People. The ducks lived there, and the geese. Pelican lived there, and Mud Hen. Coyote and Cuckoo, Prairie Fox and Jackrabbit, Jay and Jumping Mouse, and all the others of the bird and animal people lived together in the villages of the foothills or the plain.

Coyote was . . . full of his own cleverness. . . . For Coyote snooped and gossiped and meddled . . .

"No more!" Eagle shrilled. "I must find somewhere to live where Coyote cannot spread his nonsense." . . .

A mountain!
Now there was an idea, thought Eagle. . . .

"Tell us what to do," said Bear. . . .

Eagle nodded. "Coyote travels the foothills and plains. I must live in the mountains, where he will not go. So you must build me mountains . . . where I can make the highest mountaintop home."

Eagle was a good chief, so the bird and animal people did as he asked. . . .

As the earth was heaped higher and higher, the mountains rose. Bit by bit they grew until at last they were so tall that the snow began to fall on their crests.

"Enough!" called Eagle. "Enough!"

The bird and animal people stopped at the mountain foot and emptied there on the ground the baskets of earth left over. When they looked up at the mountains they had mounded up, they raised a cheer. Such ridges and ranges! Such fine pointed peaks!

And the round mounds you still may see along the foothills of the Sierras? They are the earth from the baskets left over from building Eagle's new home.

Write a paragraph about the ways in which this tale highlights nature.

Reading SOCIAL STUDIES

Summarize:
The First People of California R2.1 4.2.1

In this unit, you will learn about the first people to live in California. Summarizing, or stating the important ideas in a reading selection, will help you understand social studies better. A summary states the main ideas but leaves out minor details. Summarizing will also help you understand and remember what you read.

1 Learn It

- Read a selection and find the main ideas. Restate these ideas briefly in your summary.
- Find important details and combine them in your summary.
- Leave out details that are not important.
- Now, read the selection below and think about how you would summarize the information.

Main Idea
This is a main idea.

Detail
These details can be combined.

Main Idea
This is another main idea.

Detail
These details can be combined.

In Southern California, many Native American groups depended on the ocean for food. Men speared fish and seals from shore. Teenagers dove for shellfish. Children collected clams and mussels along the beaches.

These first Californians were also skilled craftspeople. Women wove beautiful baskets to store supplies and to use for cooking food. Men carved stone knives and bowls. They also created rock paintings of animals and birds.

Copy and complete the summary chart below. Then, fill in the chart by summarizing the two paragraphs on page 90.

SUMMARY CHART

Paragraph 1	Paragraph 2

What information did you look for in the reading selection in order to summarize the paragraphs?

3 Apply It

- Review the steps for summarizing in Learn It.
- Read the passage below. Then, create a summary chart to summarize both paragraphs.

Native Americans in northwestern California built their houses from redwood planks. To split the giant logs, they used elk antlers. They also dug out redwood logs for canoes.

Using their canoes, Native Americans fished and hunted. They caught seals and fish. Salmon was the main part of their diet. In fact, their word for salmon meant "food."

CHAPTER

3 The First People of California

You Are There

"The acorns come down from heaven.
I plant the short acorns in the valley.
I plant the long acorns in the valley.
I sprout, I, the black acorn, sprout, I sprout."

This is part of a Maidu acorn song used in a ceremony asking for the blessings of the spirits. The Maidu lived in the foothills of the Sierra Nevada.

In this chapter, you will read about the Maidu and other Native Americans. The Native Americans were the first people who lived in California.

A Native American artifacts such as this Yokuts basket have been found throughout California. (page 97)

B The Chumash built canoes to fish in the ocean. (page 106)

C The Mohave had great respect for warriors. (page 116)

D The Yurok lived in homes set partially underground. (page 122)

FOCUS QUESTION

How did California's first people develop their different ways of life?

VOCABULARY

Ice Age
glacier
artifact
archaeologist
diversity
culture area

VOCABULARY STRATEGY

SUFFIXES One meaning of the suffix **-ist** is a person who is skilled in something. A scientist is a person who is skilled in science. Can you think of some other words that end in **-ist**?

READING STRATEGY

Summarize

Use the chart to summarize information about California's first people.

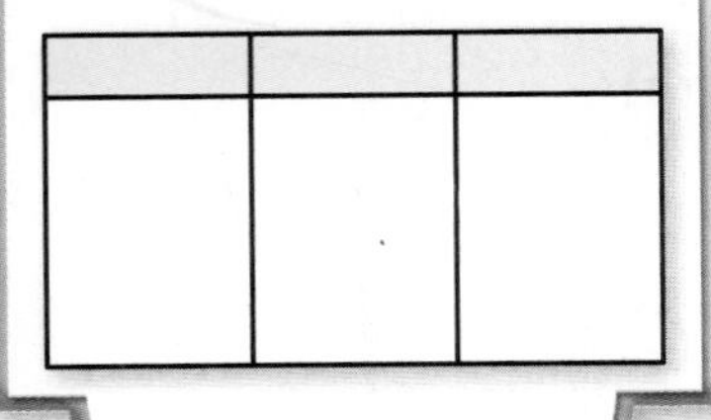

California's First People

Start with Your CALIFORNIA STANDARDS

4.1 Students demonstrate an understanding of the physical and human geographic features that define places and regions in California.

4.1.5 Use maps, charts, and pictures to describe how communities in California vary in land use, vegetation, wildlife, climate, population density, architecture, services, and transportation.

Trace the routes used by the first people to reach North America and learn about the six culture areas. (page 95)

4.2 Students describe the social, political, cultural, and economic life and interactions among people of California from the pre-Columbian societies to the Spanish mission and Mexican rancho periods.

4.2.1 Discuss the major nations of California Indians, including their geographic distribution, economic activities, legends, and religious beliefs; and describe how they depended on, adapted to, and modified the physical environment by cultivation of land and use of sea resources.

Learn how California's first people learned to live in and change their environment. (Begins on page 96)

Early peoples hunted woolly mammoths. ▼

30,000 B.C.	25,000 B.C.	20,000 B.C.	15,000 B.C.	10,000 B.C.

About 30,000 B.C.
Ice Age begins

About 15,000 B.C.
First people arrive in North America

About 15,000–12,000 B.C.
Beringia appears

About 10,000 B.C.
Ice Age ends

Have people always lived in North America? Where did they come from? What brought them here? Scientists and historians believe that the answers to these questions may lie far, far back in time.

Across a Land Bridge 4.1.5 4.2.1

Thousands of years ago, during the **Ice Age**, Earth's climate became very, very cold. Huge sheets of thick ice called **glaciers** (GLAY shurz) slowly covered Canada and northern Europe.

With so much of the Earth's water frozen, the oceans became less deep. Slowly, a strip of dry land appeared between northern Asia and North America. This bridge of land, Beringia (buh RIHN jee uh), joined the continents.

The grasslands in Beringia drew herds of animals from northern Asia. Small groups of people followed. These hunters needed the animals for food, clothing, and bone tools. They were also gatherers, looking for wild nuts and berries.

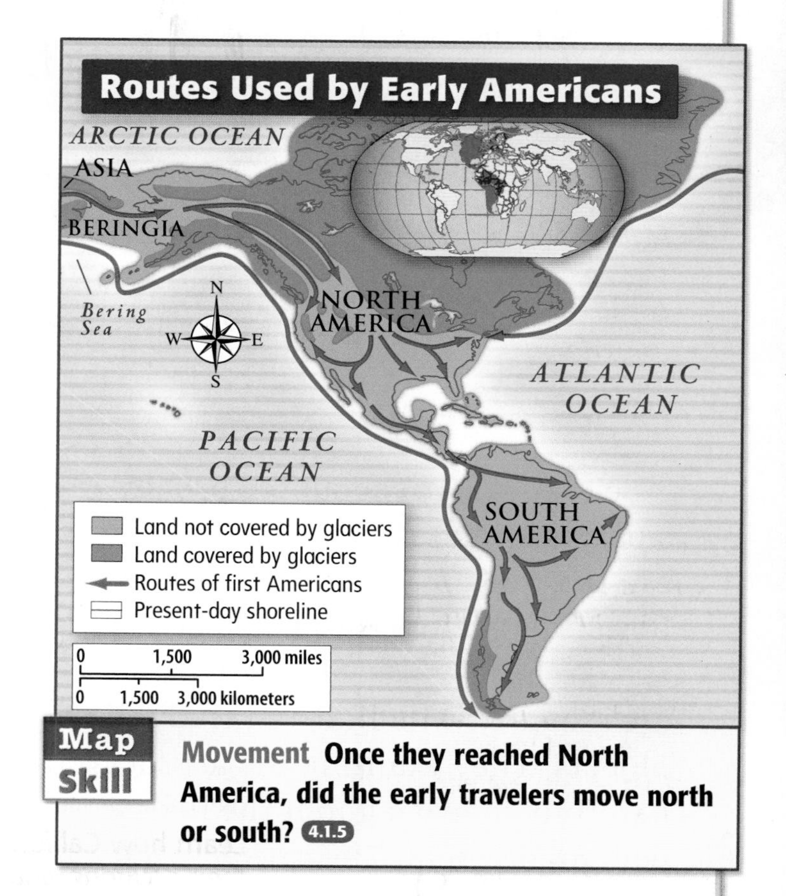

Map Skill Movement **Once they reached North America, did the early travelers move north or south?** 4.1.5

Some scientists believe that, at about the same time, people were reaching North America in small boats. They, too, may have come from northern Asia. Some may even have come from southern Asia or Europe.

REVIEW What made it possible for people to walk from northern Asia to North America during the Ice Age? *Summarize*

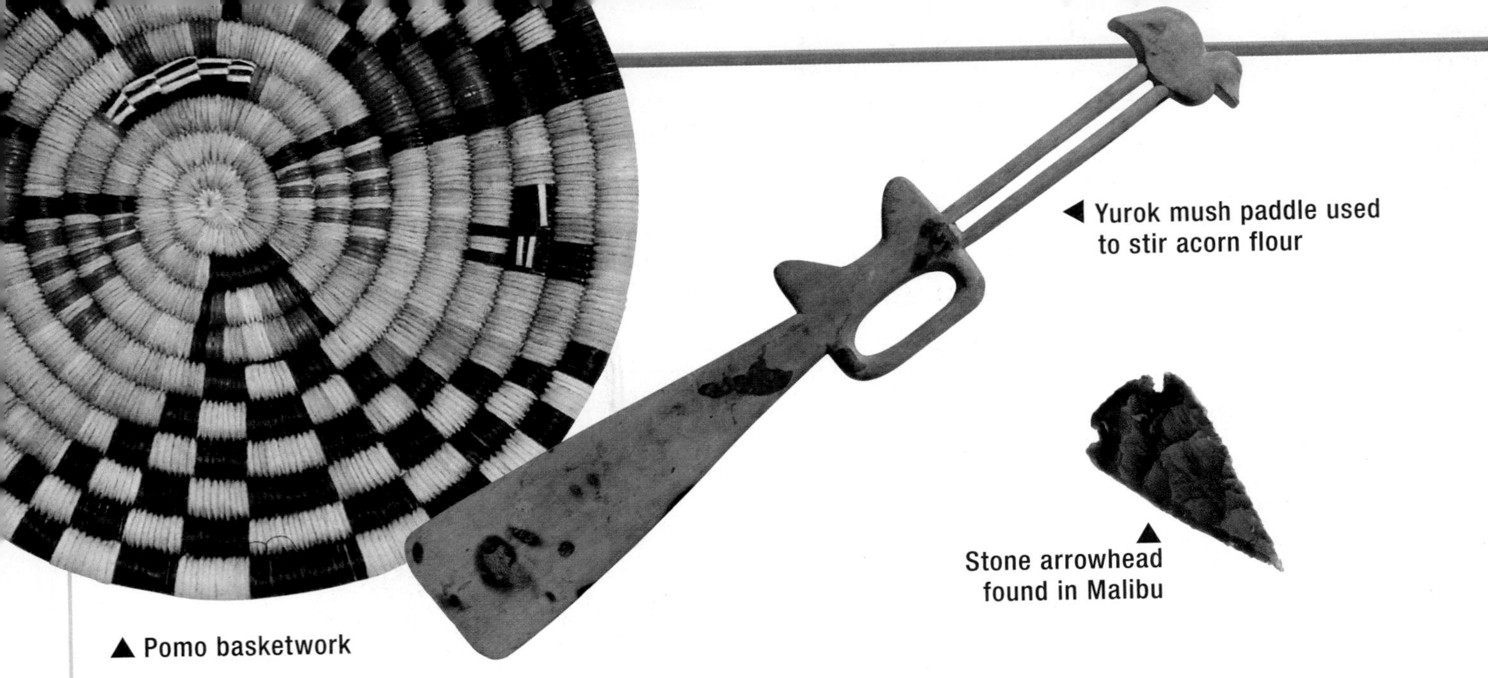

◀ Yurok mush paddle used to stir acorn flour

▲ Stone arrowhead found in Malibu

▲ Pomo basketwork

California's First People 4.1.5 4.2.1

Scientists learn about the past by studying **artifacts** (AR tuh faktz). Artifacts are the tools, weapons, and other objects left behind by people of long ago. **Archaeologists** (ahr kee OL uh jists) are scientists who find and study these objects. They examine the artifacts carefully to learn about the people who made them. The artifacts tell archaeologists that Native Americans have been living in North America for at least 12,000 years. According to Native American legends, they have been living here since the beginning of time.

By the time the first Europeans sailed to North and South America, there were already millions of people living here. A large number of Native Americans, more than 300,000, lived in California.

Different Ways of Life

Over time, California's early people developed a great **diversity**, or range of differences, in the way they did things. This diversity came about as people learned to live with the resources of different climates. Wherever they settled, people used the natural

Archaeologists examine artifacts at a site in San Juan Bautista, California. ▶

◀ Yokuts woven basket

resources around them to make their clothes, tools, and homes.

Groups who lived on the banks of a river or near the ocean developed special tools for catching and drying fish. Those who lived in valleys full of oak trees found ways to turn acorns into flour.

Over time, California's Native American peoples created at least 100 different cultures, or ways of life. Each group had its own crafts, customs, beliefs, and traditions. They also developed 100 different languages.

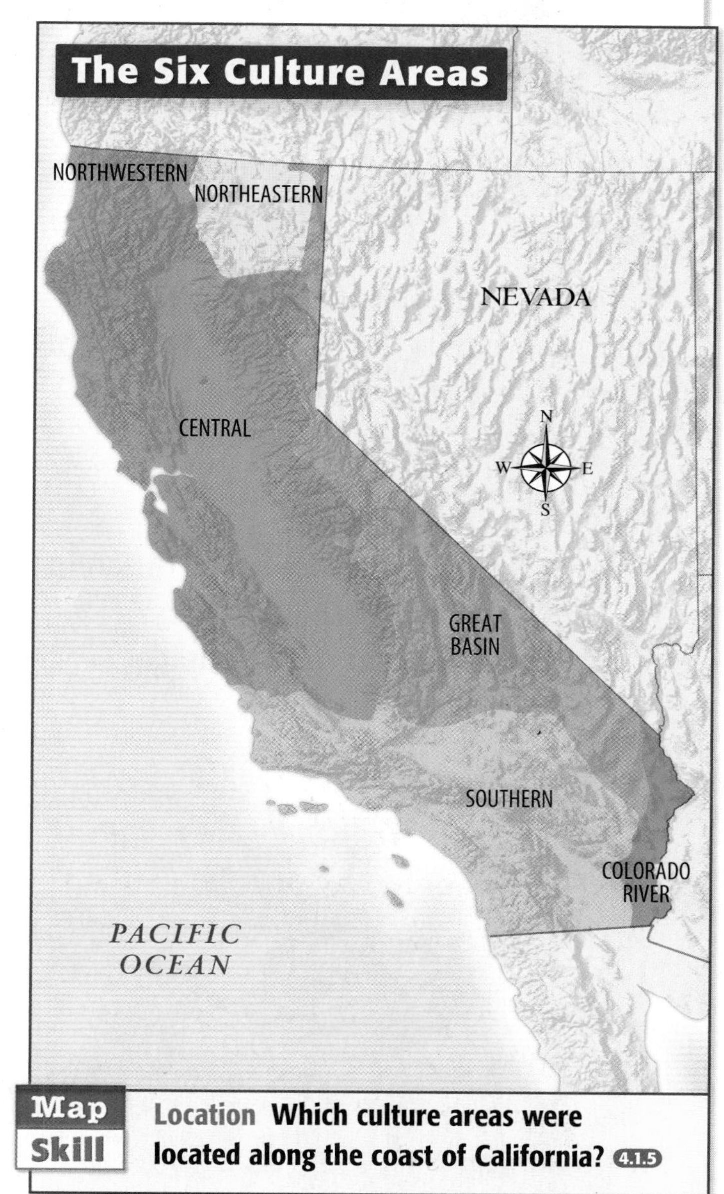

Map Skill Location **Which culture areas were located along the coast of California?** 4.1.5

Six Culture Areas

Geographers divide the 100 groups into six main regions called **culture areas**. That means that all the groups living in each area have cultures that are alike in some important ways. Look at the map to find the six culture areas.

The names of the individual groups came about in different ways. The Washo took their name from a word meaning "people." Several groups came to be known by the names given to them later on by the Spanish.

No one knows for certain how often people traveled beyond their own local areas. We do know that they traded with each other. We also know that most of the Native Americans in California spoke at least two languages.

REVIEW Why are the different groups in California so diverse? *Cause and Effect*

Native Americans Today 4.2.1

California continues to have a larger population of Native Americans than any other state in the United States. In addition to the Native Americans who were born in California, there are many more who have moved here from other parts of the United States and from Central and South America.

History and Traditions

Native Americans from many different backgrounds believe that it is very important to pass on their heritage. Heritage is the history and traditions that a group of people share.

Many Native American groups in California organize gatherings for their members. At these times, special foods are eaten and traditional clothing is worn. The elders of the group tell stories to the younger members. People sing and perform traditional dances.

About 50 years ago, Native Americans began to hold a new kind of gathering which brought together groups from all over the United States.

At these meetings, called powwows, people come together to share and celebrate their different cultures.

Native American dancers are shown at a powwow in Indio. ▼

A Yurok storyteller tells stories to children. ▶

Bill Kimmy is Spirit Elder of one powwow that meets every year in Southern California. As he says,

"*. . . we like to teach [our children] the values of their elders and the traditions of their heritage.*"

REVIEW How do Native Americans celebrate their heritage today? *Summarize*

What You Learned

4.1.5 4.2.1 Scientists believe that people reached North America using several different routes during the Ice Age.

4.1.5 4.2.1 Each group of Native Americans in California learned to live with the climate, land, and resources in its area.

4.2.1 California's Native Americans preserve their heritage.

Lesson Review

1. **Focus Question** How did California's first people develop their different ways of life? 4.2.1
2. **Vocabulary** Write one sentence for each vocabulary term. 4.2.1
   archaeologist **culture area** **glacier**
   artifact **diversity** **Ice Age**
3. **Geography** Which of the Native American culture areas in California border present-day Nevada? 4.1.5 4.2.1
4. **Critical Thinking** **Problem Solving** What problem were the first travelers to North America solving when they crossed Beringia? 4.2.1
5. **Reading Strategy**
   Summarize Use the chart to summarize two ways Native Americans celebrate their heritage today. 4.2.1 ELA R2.1

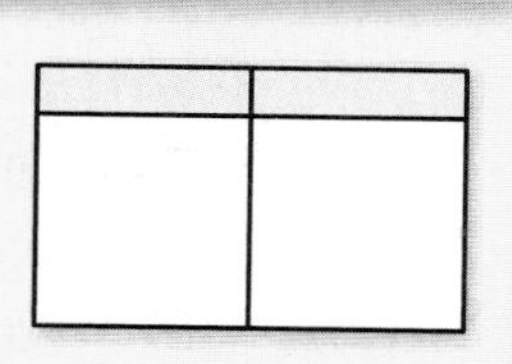

6. **Write about THE BIG IDEA** Write about ways a Native American group living in your area might have adapted to the climate, land, and resources. 4.2.1 ELA W2.1
7. **Link to Science** Write a letter to a friend describing the kinds of artifacts you hope to find as an archaeologist looking for artifacts at an early Native American site. 4.2.1

Biography

Focus on Leadership

4.2.1

Elsie Allen 1899–1990

As a child, Elsie Allen learned the Pomo art of basket weaving from her grandmother. When she was sent to a boarding school, however, she was teased about her Pomo heritage. She began keeping her skill a secret.

In 1962, Allen's mother asked her to start weaving Pomo baskets again. She wanted Allen to keep the art of Pomo basket weaving alive. Over the next 30 years, Allen's skill and her collection of baskets stirred national interest. She wrote a book about Pomo basket weaving and exhibited her baskets at museums in California.

Allen taught her grandniece, Susan Billy, how to weave baskets. Allen told her:

"Basket weaving needs ... love and honor for the great weavers of the past."

Seed beaters were used to knock seeds off of plants into baskets. ▶

How did Elsie Allen's leadership keep the art of Pomo basket weaving alive?

LOG ON For more about Elsie Allen, visit:

www.macmillanmh.com/ss/ca/bios

The Life of Elsie Allen

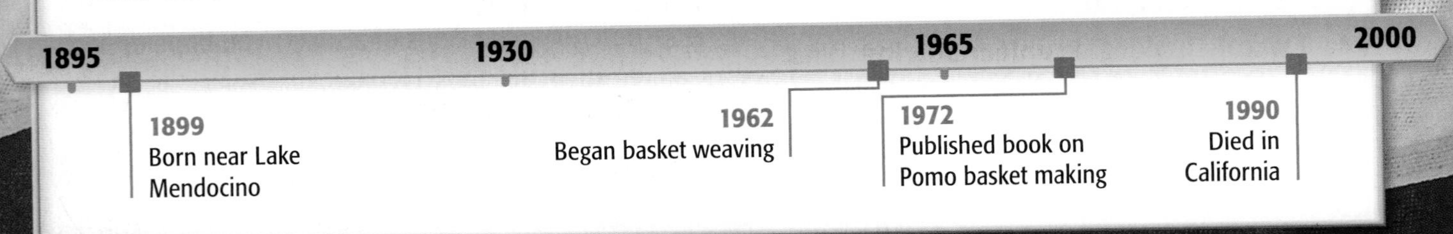

CRITICAL THINKING
Skills

Make Decisions 4.2

Decision making is a skill we all use every day. Decisions may be simple, like deciding what clothes to wear, or more difficult, like deciding where to live. These steps will help you make better decisions.

VOCABULARY

decision
goal
option

1 Learn It

- To make a decision, know your **goal**. Your goal is what you want to happen.
- Identify your **options**, or choices. For any decision, you will have at least two choices.
- Predict the results of each option.
- Choose the option that is most likely to help you reach your goal.

2 Try It

Read the paragraph at the top right and answer these questions.

- What might be Ari's goal?
- What are Ari's options?
- What might happen if Ari acts on his first option?
- Which option will most likely help Ari reach his goal?

Ari's family was hiking in the desert. In a small cave, Ari saw some old clay pots half buried in the sand. "I'd like to learn who made these pots," Ari thought. "Maybe I'll dig them up and take them home."

Then Ari remembered reading about archaeologists, scientists who study artifacts. "Maybe I should leave everything the way it is here and let an archaeologist study it."

3 Apply It

- Think of a decision you have made recently.
- Follow the steps in Learn It to tell about your options.
- Tell whether you reached your goal.

Using
PRIMARY SOURCES

Understanding Artifacts 4.2.1

Artifacts are one kind of primary source. Artifacts are objects made or used by people who lived in the past. Archaeologists examine artifacts such as tools, pottery, and cave paintings to find out about how people lived long ago.

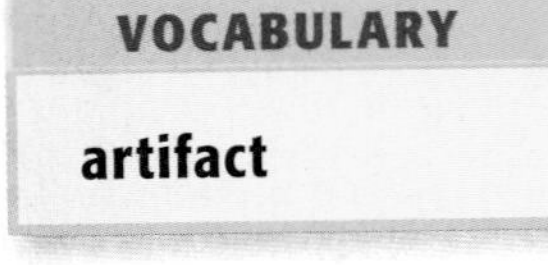

VOCABULARY

artifact

Chumash Artifacts

Images of birds are used widely in Chumash paintings, clothing, traditions, and stories. Stone carvings of birds, such as pelicans, may have been used to bring good luck for fishing.

On cave walls, the Chumash drew pictures of birds, such as condors, and bird-and-humanlike figures. These paintings survived, protected by cave walls from sun and rain. The carvings, found in early Chumash sites, survived because they were made from stone.

▲ Stone carving of a fish

1 Learn It

Read the steps below to help you find information about artifacts.

- Look closely at the artifact to see what it is made of.
- Notice any special skill that the people who made the artifact may have used.
- Try to understand what the artifact was used for.

Arrowheads are artifacts made from stone. ▶

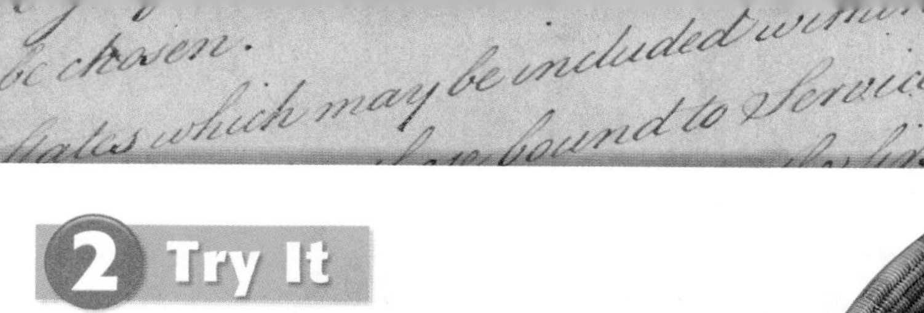

2 Try It

Look at the photograph of the basket.

- What is the basket made of?
- What might it have been used for?
- How might it have been made?
- What can the decorations tell us about the people who made it?

▲ This basket, decorated with birds and butterflies, was made with plant fiber and twigs.

3 Apply It

Look at the photograph of the cave painting below.

- What does the cave painting tell you about the culture of the Chumash?
- What more do you want to know after studying the cave painting?

The cave painting found in Sespe Watershed shows the importance of the condor in Chumash culture. The condor represented the finder of lost objects for the Chumash. ▶

Southern and Central Peoples

FOCUS QUESTION

What natural resources were important to the Chumash and the Yokuts?

VOCABULARY

- religion
- shaman
- tomol
- granary
- pit house
- game
- land management

VOCABULARY STRATEGY

MULTIPLE MEANINGS

The word **game** has two meanings. One is "something you play with." Another is "wild birds or animals." List another word with two meanings.

READING STRATEGY

Compare and Contrast

Use the Venn diagram below to compare and contrast three features of everyday life in a Chumash and a Yokuts village.

Start with Your CALIFORNIA STANDARDS

4.1 Students demonstrate an understanding of the physical and human geographic features that define places and regions in California.

4.1.5 Use maps, charts, and pictures to describe how communities in California vary in land use, vegetation, wildlife, climate, population density, architecture, services, and transportation.

Locate two Native American peoples who were neighbors, but lived very different lives. (Begins on page 106)

4.2 Students describe the social, political, cultural, and economic life and interactions among people of California from the pre-Columbian societies to the Spanish mission and Mexican rancho periods.

4.2.1 Discuss the major nations of California Indians, including their geographic distribution, economic activities, legends, and religious beliefs; and describe how they depended on, adapted to, and modified the physical environment by cultivation of land and use of sea resources.

Discover how Native Americans healed sick people, organized their work, and how they used the land. (Begins on page 105)

The Southern and Central culture areas were home to many Native Americans. Some were skilled basket makers. As seen in the photograph on the right, different colored grasses and decorations, such as feathers, were used in these baskets. Others were expert fishers and hunters.

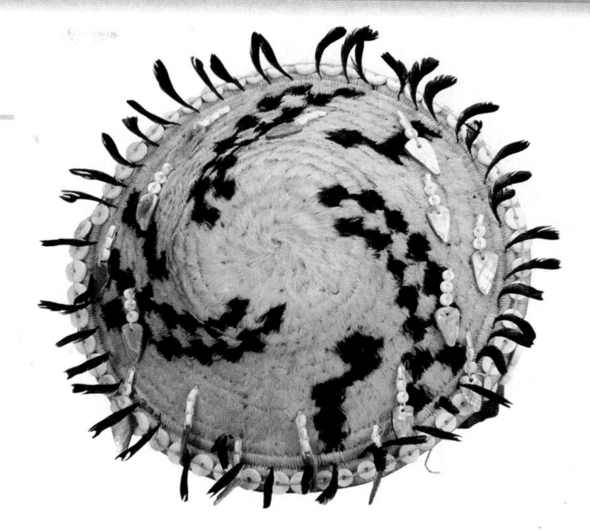

Life in Villages 4.2.1

In all six culture areas, the various Native Americans lived in communities of villages. Many of these communities were located where today's towns and cities now stand.

Some villages had as few as 50 people. Others had as many as 1,000. In most Native American villages, tasks like hunting deer and catching salmon were traditionally done by men. Women usually did the work of gathering and storing plants, preparing meals, and weaving baskets. Women also cared for the children.

Native American Leaders

Three or four neighboring villages usually shared one leader, or chief. People relied on the chiefs to settle quarrels and give advice on how to manage the land wisely.

Native Americans of California followed a **religion**, or a set of beliefs. They believed in a spirit world that was closely linked to themselves and to the natural world.

Most communities had a **shaman**, who was a religious leader and a healer. The shaman would talk to the spirit world. He or she would ask the spirits for things the community needed. This might include asking for rain, for plants to grow, and for sick or hurt people to be healed.

REVIEW What role did the village chiefs play in guiding their people? *Summarize*

◀ Chumash village

Abalone shells

The Seagoing Chumash 4.1.5 4.2.1

Most of the Chumash people of the Southern culture area lived with the sound of the ocean in their ears. Like many other people in their area, they often lived right near the beach.

If you had been a Chumash child, your home might have been anywhere along the coast. You might even have lived on an island. There were Chumash settlements on the islands of San Miguel, Santa Rosa, and Santa Cruz.

The people in your village would have spent their days fishing and hunting sea animals. The ocean was rich in fish, shellfish, seals, sea otters, and porpoises.

Your father and his friends would have used the harpoons they made to spear tuna and other fish. The older boys would have dived into the sea for abalone, which is like a sea snail. You would have helped by digging for clams or pulling mussels from rocks on shore.

Building a Canoe

The Chumash were expert boat builders. They used a type of canoe called a **tomol** (TOH MOHL) for ocean fishing. The tomols were 30 feet long, but very light, strong, and fast. In these canoes, the Chumash were able to travel as far as 65 miles away from the coast.

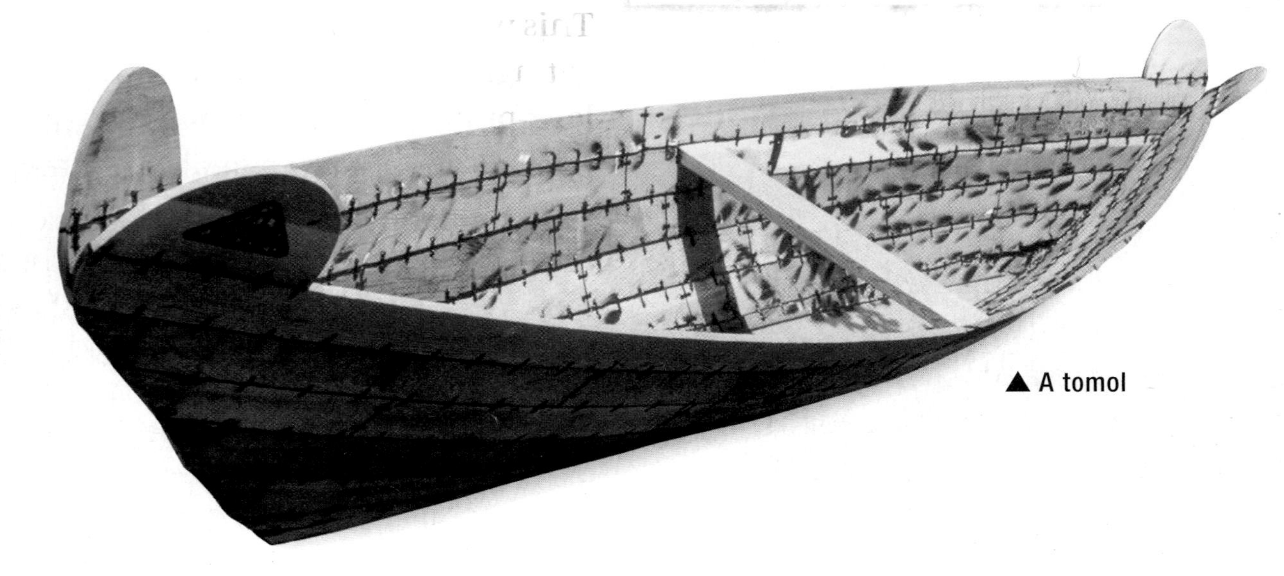
▲ A tomol

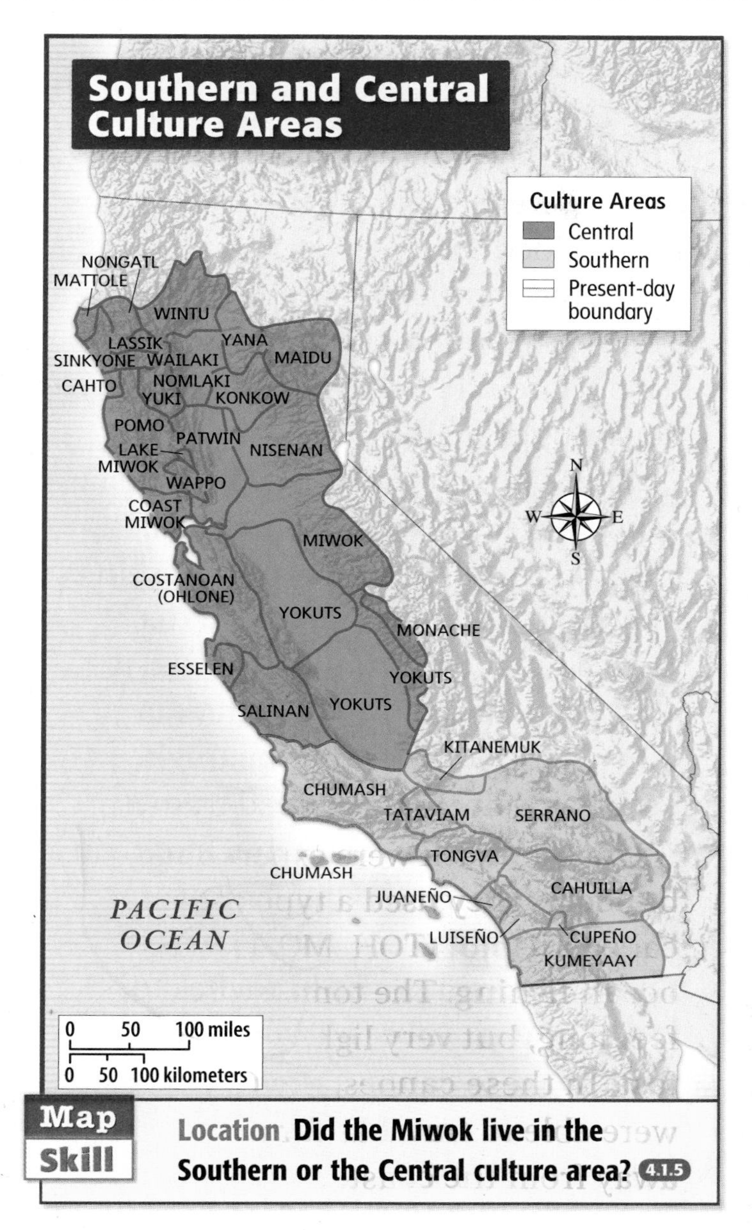

Map Skill Location **Did the Miwok live in the Southern or the Central culture area?** 4.1.5

Life in a Chumash Village

Chumash villages were quite large, with up to 1,000 people living in about 100 homes. Chumash villagers led fairly easy lives in terms of finding food resources and natural materials for boat-building. That is because the coast was so rich in natural resources.

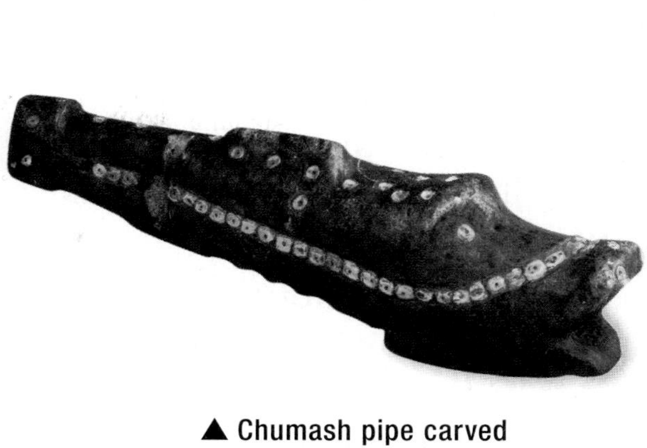

▲ Chumash pipe carved to look like a fish

The Chumash also had time to develop their creative skills. Chumash carvers cut sharp knives, smooth bowls, and little animal figures from stone. Chumash painters left many beautiful pictures of people, animals, birds, fish, and insects on the rock walls of caves and on cliffs in their areas. Chumash weavers wove beautiful baskets for carrying babies, storing supplies, and cooking food.

To prepare a basket for cooking, the women would first soak it in water. This would make the fibers swell and get tighter, so the basket would be leak-proof. Next, they would fill the basket with soup or cereal and place several stones in a fire. When the stones were hot, they would drop them into the basket, one at a time. As they stirred them, the food would boil.

REVIEW How did the Chumash show their creative skills? *Summarize*

The Yokuts of the Central Valley 4.1.5 4.2.1

The Yokuts and numerous other peoples lived in the Central culture area. This was the largest of the six culture areas in California.

The Yokuts's territory, in the San Joaquin Valley and the foothills of the Sierra Nevada, had many natural resources. The most important of these were the towering oak trees that filled the valley and the foothills. Their branches produced tons of acorns every fall.

The Importance of Acorns

Acorns could be ground into flour to make breads, biscuits, puddings, soups, and a kind of hot cereal called weewish. Today, wheat flour is a basic part of the food we eat. We use it to make foods such as bread, pizza crusts, cookies, cakes, and cold cereals. Before the Europeans arrived, Native Americans in California used acorn flour to make their basic foods.

If you were a Yokuts girl, you would have helped shake the acorns from the branches and gather the nuts. Then, with your mother, you would have packed the nuts away in a storage house, or **granary**.

When your mother needed flour, she would have cracked open the shells and taken off the acorns' papery skins. Then she would have pounded the acorns into a fine flour and rinsed it with water to remove the bitter taste. When the flour was dry, you might have helped her make bread from it.

The Yokuts men spent much of their time hunting. In the fall, however, they took part in the acorn harvest. They would shake the branches to loosen the nuts for the women and children to pick up.

◀ A Yokuts woman pounds acorn into flour.

Taking Care of the Land

Some Yokuts lived in homes called **pit houses**, which were built partly underground to keep them cool in hot weather and warm in cold weather.

The Yokuts wanted to make sure there would continue to be a good supply of animal and plant food. So, the Yokuts took special care of their land.

Yokuts communities burned parts of their land each year. The fires made ash, which kept the soil fertile. The fires also cleared away brush, leaving more land for wild **game** such as deer and antelope. This was just one of many ways that Native Americans practiced **land management**, or care of the land.

REVIEW Why were acorns so important to the Yokuts? *Summarize*

▲ Tanoak acorns were used by Native Americans of California to make acorn flour.

What You Learned

- 4.2.1 Chiefs and shamans played an important part in village life.
- 4.1.5 4.2.1 The Chumash lived next to the ocean, in the Southern culture area. In canoes, they caught fish and hunted sea animals.
- 4.1.5 4.2.1 The Yokuts lived in the Central culture area, where they gathered acorns, hunted, and practiced land management.

Lesson Review

1. **Focus Question** What natural resources were important to the Chumash and the Yokuts? (4.2.1)
2. **Vocabulary** Write one sentence for each vocabulary term. (4.2.1)

game	**religion**
granary	**shaman**
land management	**tomol**
pit house	

3. **Geography** Where did the Chumash live? (4.1.5)
4. **Critical Thinking** **Problem Solving** How did the Chumash and other Native Americans solve the problem of cooking hot food in a woven basket? (4.2.1)
5. **Reading Strategy** **Compare and Contrast** Use the chart to compare and contrast the roles of the Native American chiefs and shamans. (4.2.1, ELA R2.1)
6. **Write about THE BIG IDEA** Suppose you were a Yokuts child. Write about a meeting between your family and a Chumash family. What might your two families want to trade with each other? (4.2.1, ELA W2.1)
7. **Link to Art** Suppose you were a Chumash child. Write to explain which creative skill you would like to learn and why. (4.2.1)

CHART and GRAPH Skills

Use Cutaway Diagrams

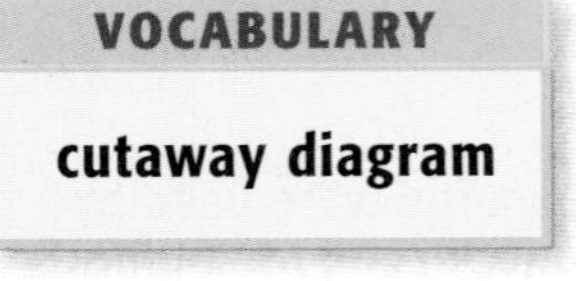

A **cutaway diagram** shows you how the inside of something is arranged. It can show you exactly what you would see if you could look through the middle. A cutaway diagram can show you the inside of a house, a ship, a fort, and many other things.

1 Learn It

Learn how to read a cutaway diagram by following these steps.

- First, learn as much as you can about the subject of the diagram. For example, if you wanted to learn about Chumash houses you would find out that Chumash houses were round, and were made with willow poles that formed the frame. The outside of the frame was covered with layers of brush. There was a hole in the roof and a fire at the center of the floor.
- Compare the cutaway diagram of a Chumash house on the next page with what you know about Chumash houses from reading the text.
- What does the cutaway diagram show you that you would not see by looking at the house from the outside?

2 Try It

- What objects do you see inside of the house?
- What are the people in the house doing?

3 Apply It

- Make a cutaway diagram of your school or classroom.
- Be sure to put in your desks, chairs, your classmates, and teacher.

◀ Chumash basket

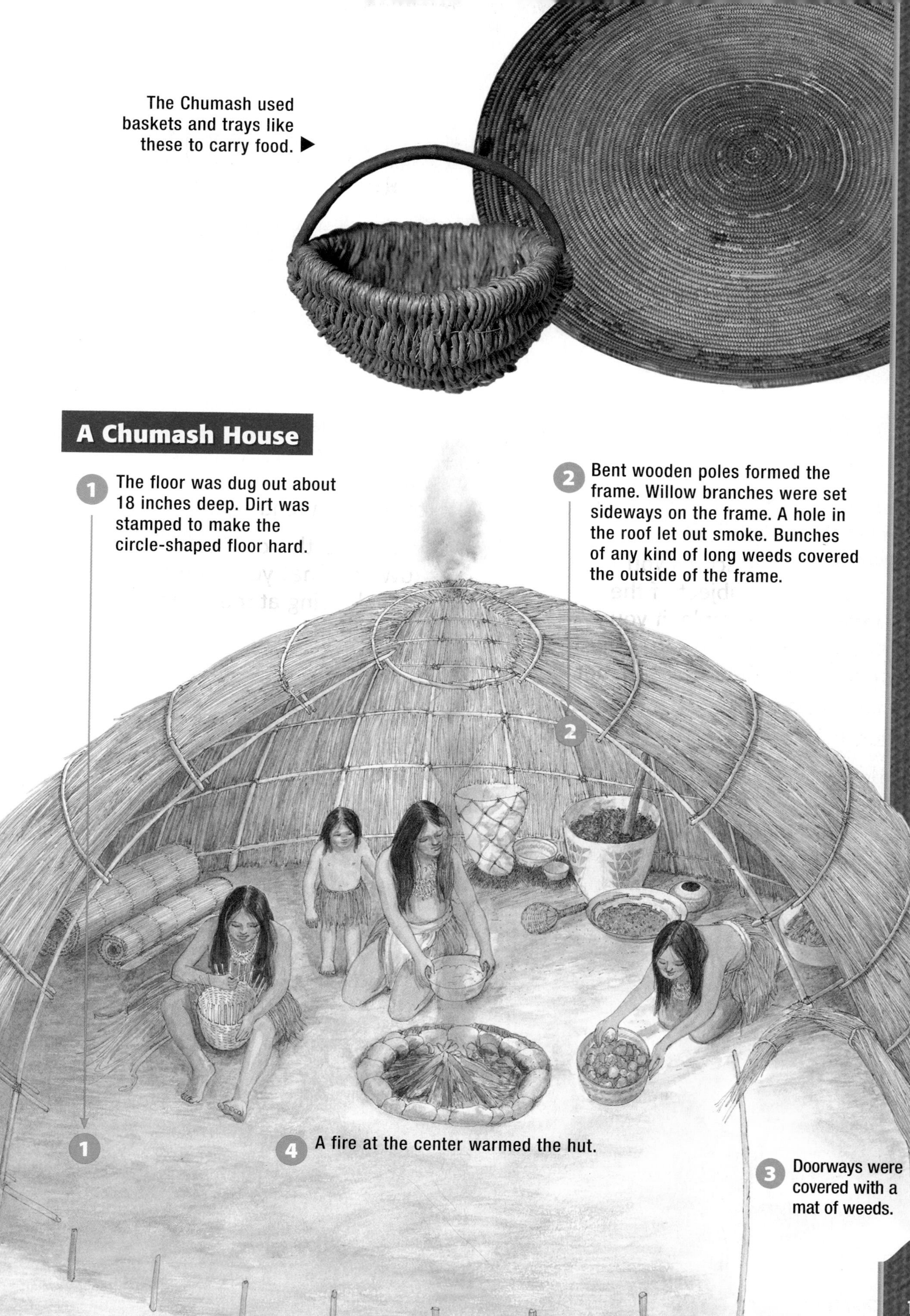

The Chumash used baskets and trays like these to carry food. ▶

A Chumash House

Great Basin and Colorado River

FOCUS QUESTION

How did Native American groups in California use the natural resources in their areas?

VOCABULARY

economy
needs
trade
wants
specialist

VOCABULARY STRATEGY

MULTIPLE MEANINGS
Want can mean both "something you do not have" and "something you wish for." Can you think of other words that have more than one meaning?

READING STRATEGY

Compare and Contrast
Use the Venn diagram to compare and contrast the ways of life of the Northern Paiute and the Mohave people.

Start with Your CALIFORNIA STANDARDS

4.1 Students demonstrate an understanding of the physical and human geographic features that define places and regions in California.

4.1.5 Use maps, charts, and pictures to describe how communities in California vary in land use, vegetation, wildlife, climate, population density, architecture, services, and transportation.

Locate the territories of some of California's most skillful users of natural resources. (page 114)

4.2 Students describe the social, political, cultural, and economic life and interactions among people of California from the pre-Columbian societies to the Spanish mission and Mexican rancho periods.

4.2.1 Discuss the major nations of California Indians, including their geographic distribution, economic activities, legends, and religious beliefs; and describe how they depended on, adapted to, and modified the physical environment by cultivation of land and use of sea resources.

Find out how the Native American groups in the Great Basin and Colorado River culture areas got food and goods. (Begins on page 113)

Anza-Borrego Desert State Park, California ▼

Today, we use paper bills and coins to buy goods. Native Americans of the Colorado River and Great Basin areas sometimes used a string of shells as money. They would trade the shells for goods they needed.

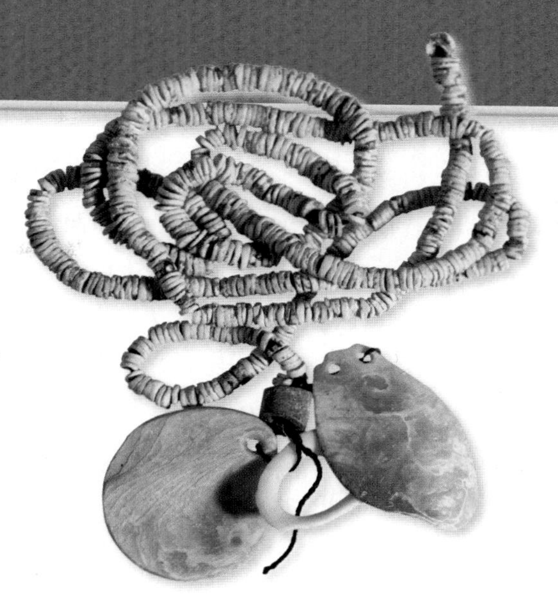

Understanding Economy 4.2.1

The **economy** of a region is the way its people use the natural resources they find there. First, they use those resources to meet their basic **needs**. Needs are the food, shelter, and clothing people must have to live. Then, if they have resources left over, people can **trade**, or exchange, these resources to get things they want but do not have. These things are called **wants**.

When groups traded with each other, they usually exchanged one kind of goods for another. Sometimes, however, they traded goods for strings of shells, which were used as money.

In the larger villages, there were **specialists**. Specialists are people who focus their time on an activity they do well. A few people made all the fishing nets, bows and arrows, or baskets the rest of the village needed. The specialists then traded these things with other villagers for food and other things they needed.

REVIEW How did Native American groups get goods they needed or wanted?
Main Idea and Details

The Northern Paiute of the Great Basin 4.1.5 4.2.1

When we picture the eastern part of California, we think of the Sierra Nevada. We also think of the burning sands of Death Valley.

The groups who lived in this part of California were part of the Great Basin culture area. One of the groups was the Northern Paiute, who lived in a long strip of territory along what is now California's eastern border, next to Nevada.

Finding Sources of Food

How did early people make the most of this challenging land? In these areas, there were no oak trees to supply acorns or green valleys for good hunting. Even so, the Northern Paiute and other groups in the region were able to find sources of food.

These food sources, however, were not to be found all in one place or all at one time. Their availability depended on the time of year. So, people had to stay on the move. They found fish and water birds in the shallow lakes created by water from the

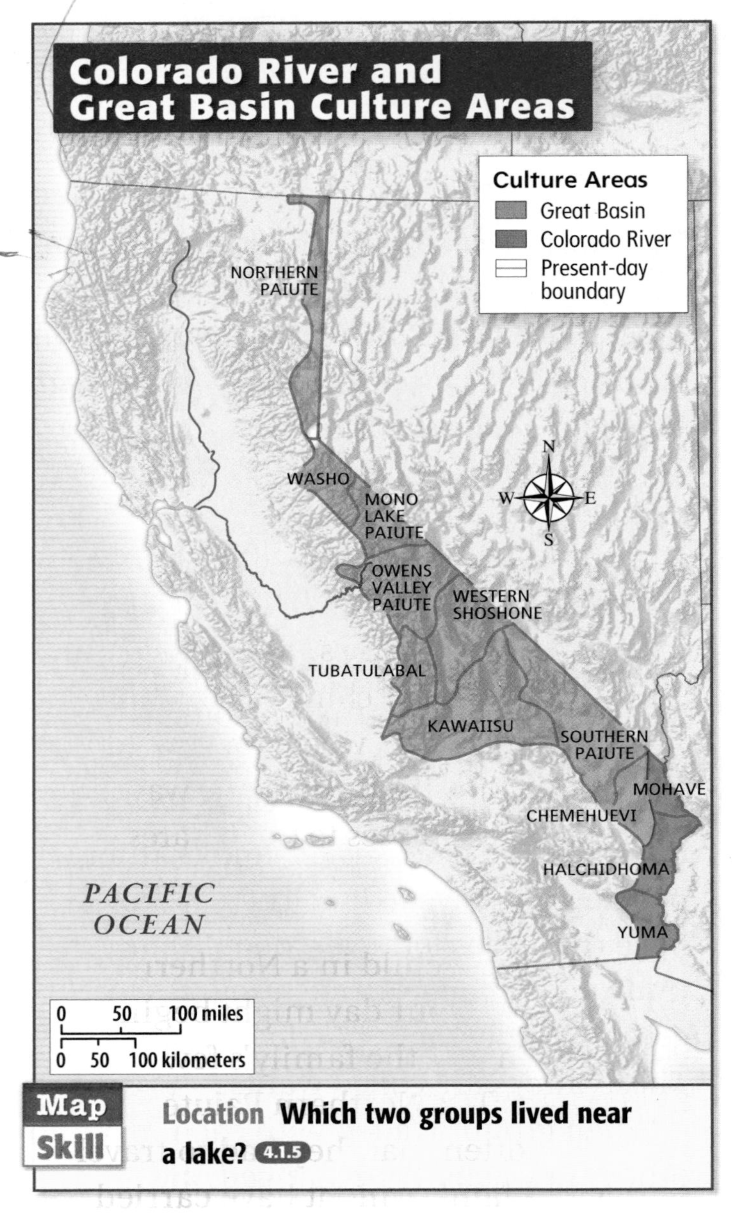

Map Skill Location **Which two groups lived near a lake?** 4.1.5

▼ Snowshoe hares can be found throughout the area that once was the Great Basin culture area.

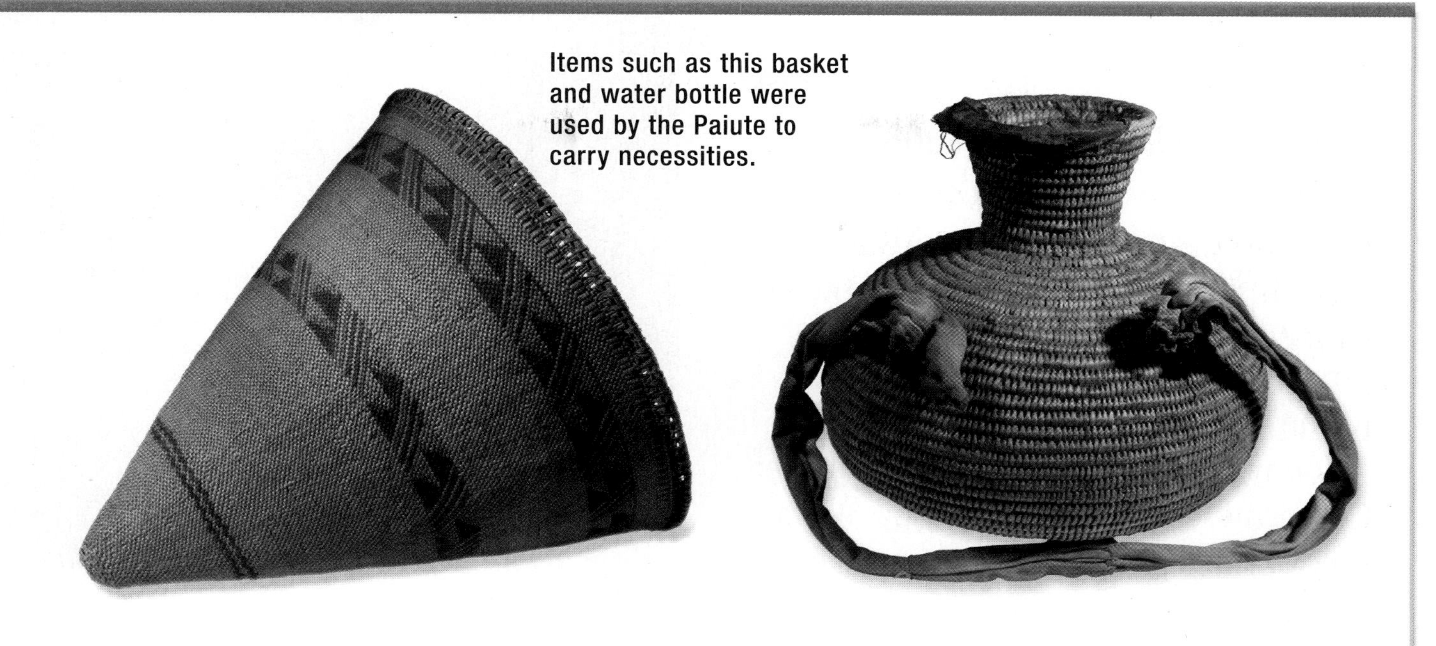
Items such as this basket and water bottle were used by the Paiute to carry necessities.

mountains in the early summer. Later in the year, they would climb the foothills of the Sierra Nevada, where they could hunt mountain sheep. Along the way, they would find places to catch hares.

Life on the Move

If you were a child in a Northern Paiute group, your day might begin with packing up the family's few belongings. The Northern Paiute moved so often that they had to travel light. Your family might have carried some clothing, some rabbitskin blankets for cold nights, a few baskets for gathering seeds, and some bows and arrows for hunting.

As your small group began walking, you would be watching for the plants and animals you needed. When you reached your destination, you might stay there a while. You might even build a home—a round hut covered with grass. Then, when the source of food ran out, you would move on.

Your group might move 20 to 40 times before fall came. Then, your family would gather with other families in the pine groves to harvest pine nuts. The men would beat the pine cones from the tall pine trees. You would help the other children and the women of the group gather the pine cones. Then everyone would put them in a pile and set it on fire to help the cones release the nuts. Your family's share of the harvest would be a large basket of pine nuts. These would be part of your diet during the winter, when you settled down in a village for a few months.

The economy of the Northern Paiute was based on skillful hunting and gathering. To add to their resources, they traded with other groups for foods such as dried fish.

REVIEW How did the Northern Paiute make the most of their environment while traveling? *Main Idea and Details*

The Mohave of the Desert 4.1.5 4.2.1

The Mohave people lived in the southeastern corner of California in an area we now call the Mojave Desert. They lived along the banks of the Colorado River, as did two other groups. These three groups belonged to the Colorado River culture area.

Today, this land is part of three states: California, Nevada, and Arizona. It is a very dry region, without forests, lakes, or large animals.

▲ These Mohave girls stand in front of a Mohave home.

Growing Crops in the Desert

The Mohave caught fish as well as small game like rabbits, lizards, and rattlesnakes for food. However, there was not enough fish and game in the desert for the Mohave to survive. They created other ways of getting food: they learned to grow it, by farming the land.

Farming was mostly the job of the women of the group. If you were a Mohave girl, you would have helped your mother and other women with the spring planting. This was the time when heavy rains would cause the Colorado River to overflow. Its banks would become covered with a deep layer of mud. You would have planted your seeds in this mud. It would have taken only a few days for your seeds to sprout. Soon, squash, beans, corn, and pumpkins would begin to grow.

Your crops would grow quickly over the summer. In the fall, you would help to harvest them. Your mother

▼ The Colorado River flows through California.

would teach you how to cut the fresh vegetables into long, thin strips. These would then be hung to dry so that there would be plenty of food during the winter.

The Mohave were one of the few Native American groups in California that practiced agriculture. By planting seeds and harvesting crops, the Native Americans who did practice farming were using the natural resources available to them in a different way than those groups that gathered wild plants.

Another desert group, the Cahuilla of the Southern culture area, also practiced farming. The Cahuilla created an irrigation system to bring water to dry fields. The Cahuilla dug deep wells in the desert sand. From these wells, they gathered enough water to keep the soil moist for their crops.

Using the Land

Like most of our homes today, the Mohave's houses had straight sides. They covered the roofs with a layer of earth to keep their homes cool in summer and warm in winter.

▲ Pumpkins, squash, and corn were some of the crops the Mohave grew.

The Mohave did not weave baskets. There were not enough reeds and grasses in their region. Instead, they used clay found in their area to make bowls and cooking pots. They decorated these pots and bowls with special designs. Their pottery is known today for the red color they used in making these designs.

REVIEW How did the Mohave use the Colorado River to make farming possible?
Main Idea and Details

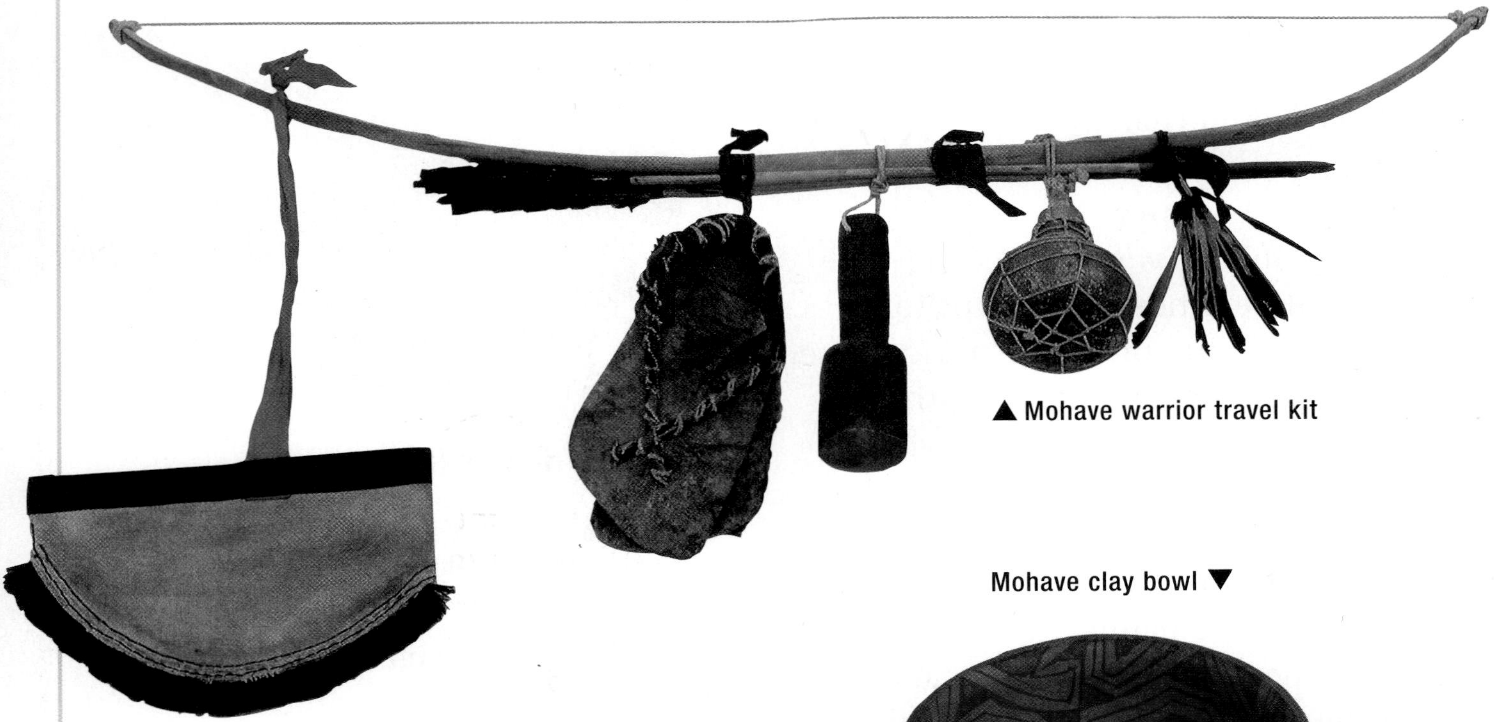

▲ Mohave warrior travel kit

Mohave clay bowl ▼

Warriors and Traders 4.2.1

Most Native American groups in California wished to stay at peace with other groups. For the Mohave, however, and for other groups of the Colorado River area, war was an important part of life.

The Mohave may have learned this attitude toward fighting from other Native American groups who lived to the southeast of California. There were specially trained Mohave warriors who would travel as far as 150 miles to attack their enemies. The Mohave were willing to travel long distances. They often ran all the way to their destinations, as running was a respected practice in their culture.

On these long journeys, Mohave warriors would often carry a travel kit. The travel kit usually included a bow and arrow. They would tie onto the bow other things they needed such as a cap, sandals, a club, a canteen, and a hair ornament usually made of feathers.

Trade

The Mohave also had friendly trading relationships with other groups. Earlier in this lesson, you learned that when people have more of something than they need, they often trade it for what they don't have.

◀ Mohave warrior dolls

The Mohave traded their clay pots and their extra crops for items like wooden bowls, baskets, and shell beads.

REVIEW How were the Mohave different from most other Native American groups in California? *Compare and Contrast*

What You Learned

4.2.1 The economy of a region is the way its people use the natural resources they find there. People trade the resources they do not need themselves for goods they want.

4.1.5 4.2.1 The Northern Paiute lived in the Great Basin culture area. They moved often on a seasonal basis to find the plants and animals they needed.

4.1.5 4.2.1 The Mohave lived in the Colorado River culture area. They grew crops along the Colorado River.

4.2.1 The Mohave traveled far from home to trade and make war.

Lesson Review

1. **Focus Question** How did Native American groups in California use the natural resources in their areas? (4.2.1)

2. **Vocabulary** Write one sentence for each vocabulary word. (4.2.1)
   economy **specialist** **wants**
   needs **trade**

3. **Economics** Why did the Mohave travel so far to trade and fight? (4.2.1)

4. **Critical Thinking** **Problem Solving** How did the Northern Paiute solve the problem of finding food in the desert? (4.2.1)

5. **Reading Strategy** **Compare and Contrast** Use the diagram to compare and contrast lives of the Northern Paiute and the Mohave. (4.2.1, ELA R2.1)

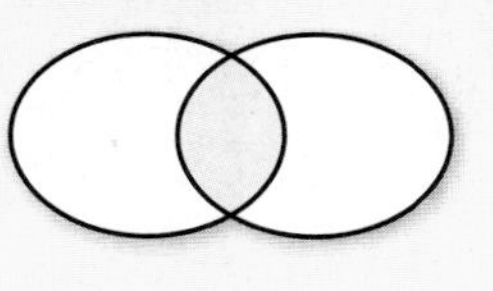

6. **Write about THE BIG IDEA** The Mohave were unusual in making war a regular part of their lives. Write about how you would have reacted if your village were attacked by the Mohave. (4.2.1, ELA W2.1)

7. **Link to Language Arts** Write a journal entry describing a typical day in the life of a Northern Paiute family. (4.2.1)

A Day in the Life

A Young Native American's Life in California 4.2.1

Native American children in California helped their parents from an early age. Boys learned to hunt and fish with their fathers and elder brothers. Girls learned to gather plants with their mothers. They also learned how to weave baskets, turn acorns into flour, and cook the family meals. Just like you, Native American children played games and looked after their younger brothers and sisters.

This Native American boy is shown wearing a popular powwow style of clothing. Powwows have only been part of Native American traditions for about 50 years. ▶

Some Native American children played with toys such as this ring and pin game. ▶

◀ Western Mono girls are playing with leaves. One girl carries her doll in a cradle.

Yurok girl in traditional dress ▶

▲ Many Native Americans wore shoes such as these Yurok moccasins.

▲ This doll in a cradle shows how some Native Americans of California carried their children. The cradle was strapped to a person's back.

Write about how the life of Native Americans may have been similar to your own.

For more about traditional Native American culture, visit:

www.macmillanmh.com/ss/ca/dayinthelife

LESSON 4

FOCUS QUESTION

What did California's Native Americans believe about their relationship to the natural world?

VOCABULARY

creation story
weir
plateau
sweathouse
wickiup

VOCABULARY STRATEGY

WORD ORIGINS Plateau, which means "a high, flat land," comes from a Greek word meaning "flat." Can you think of other words that mean "flat"?

READING STRATEGY

Compare and Contrast
Use the diagram to compare and contrast the ways of life of the Yurok and the Modoc people.

Northwest and Northeast Peoples

Start with Your CALIFORNIA STANDARDS

4.1 Students demonstrate an understanding of the physical and human geographic features that define places and regions in California.

4.1.5 Use maps, charts, and pictures to describe how communities in California vary in land use, vegetation, wildlife, climate, population density, architecture, services, and transportation.

Locate the Native American peoples who lived farthest north in California. (page 124)

4.2 Students describe the social, political, cultural, and economic life and interactions among people of California from the pre-Columbian societies to the Spanish mission and Mexican rancho periods.

4.2.1 Discuss the major nations of California Indians, including their geographic distribution, economic activities, legends, and religious beliefs; and describe how they depended on, adapted to, and modified the physical environment by cultivation of land and use of sea resources.

Find out how Native Americans passed along their religious beliefs. Learn about how the Native Americans in the northern culture areas lived. (Begins on page 123)

Yurok house built from redwood planks ▼

Native Americans shared a deep respect for the environment. The Native Americans of the north passed on their religious beliefs in stories about the natural world. Shamans could heal the sick with their knowledge of the natural world.

Native American Beliefs 4.2.1

Each Native American group passed along its beliefs through stories known as **creation stories**. These were stories that told how the Earth was made and how animals came to look and act the way they do. Above all, they learned how important it was to love, respect, and take good care of the natural world.

Parents and grandparents would tell and retell these creation stories to their children. When the children became adults, they would tell the stories they had heard to their children. Below read a story selection from the Achumawi of northern California.

REVIEW How did Native Americans pass on their beliefs? *Summarize*

Primary Sources

Achumawi Creation Story from

California Indian Nights Entertainments
by Edward Gifford and Gwendolyn Block

"In the beginning all was water. . . . Then one day a cloud formed . . . and turned into Coyote. Next a fog arose . . . and became Silver Fox . . . . [Silver Fox and Coyote] thought about making people. They made little sticks . . . and thrust them all about . . . all became people . . . with the names of birds, animals, and fishes."

Write About It! In what ways is nature a part of this Achumawi story?

The Yurok of the Forests 4.1.5 4.2.1

The Yurok lived in the northwest corner of California. Their territory was along the coast and on the banks of the Klamath River. They belonged to the Northwest culture area.

The Yurok built their villages at the base of towering redwood trees. The forests around them were cool and misty from the winds that blew in from the ocean. Their homes were built of redwood planks and had straight sides. They had slanted roofs to let the rain run off. Each house had a low, round doorway. People had to bend low to step through.

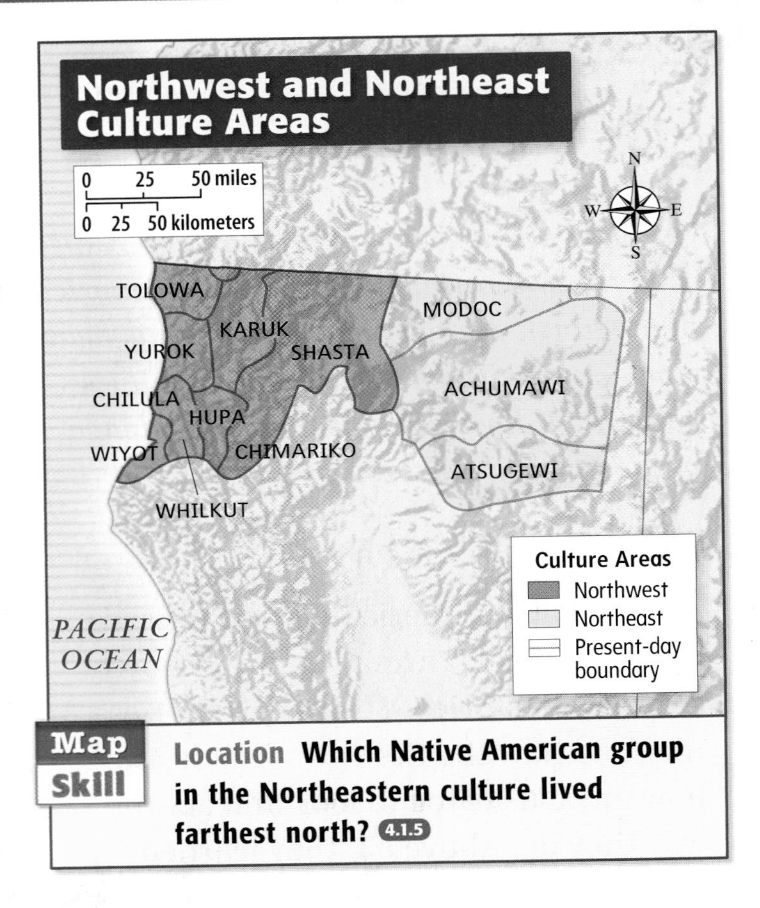

Map Skill **Location** **Which Native American group in the Northeastern culture lived farthest north?** 4.1.5

Canoes and Food

The Yurok were expert boat builders. They made large dugout canoes, carved from hollowed-out redwood logs. The canoes were often decorated with carvings. In these canoes, the Yurok traveled along the coast hunting sea lions and other sea animals, as the Chumash did in the south.

The Yurok gathered acorns, nuts, and berries from the forest. They also hunted deer and other animals in the woods and along the coast. A major

▼ The Yurok built weirs across rivers to catch fish, such as salmon, right.

▲ Yurok woman showing her wealth with shell clothing and jewelry

source of food was salmon. Salmon are large fish that live part of their time in the ocean and part of their time in rivers.

Each spring, the salmon leave the ocean and swim upstream to lay their eggs in the rivers. The rivers become thick with fish. Yurok men and boys would catch the salmon by building **weirs**, or fences, across the rivers. As the fish became trapped behind the fences, the men and boys would spear them. The women and girls of the village would clean the fish. Then they would cook them slowly over a smoky fire to preserve them.

Gaining Wealth and Power

Unlike Native Americans in other parts of California, the Yurok cared about wealth. The Yurok collected shells as a sign of wealth. The richest Yurok people would wear special clothing and jewelry to show off their wealth.

Another sign of Yurok wealth was property. Villagers in other groups shared their land and goods with each other. Yurok men and women, however, gained wealth and power by controlling salmon pools, groves of trees, or stretches of beach. A Yurok man could become the leader of his village by controlling these areas because of the resources they held. He also had to make sure everyone could use them.

REVIEW How did the Yurok show their wealth? *Summarize*

Yurok women wore skirts such as this one. ▶

The Modoc of the Plateau 4.1.5 4.2.1

The Modoc lived in the northeast corner of California. They belonged to the Northeast culture area. This was one of the smallest of the six culture areas.

The Modoc's territory, which was just south of today's eastern Oregon, was on a **plateau**, or an area of high, flat land. The rivers in the northeast of California were smaller than those along the coast. This meant that there were fewer salmon to catch. However, there were many shallow lakes full of otters, beavers, and water birds of all kinds.

The lakes also had many different kinds of plants. The Modoc gathered the plants for food and for use in making baskets. To reach the plants, the Modoc used canoes with squared-off ends. They made their canoes by hollowing out large pine, fir, or cedar logs.

One of their main foods was the seeds of the yellow pond lily. The whole village would help gather the lily pods in the summer, after the lily flowers had bloomed. Then the women and girls would separate the seeds from the lily pods, dry them, and store them in sacks for later use.

Different Hunting Methods

Native American groups in California used the natural resources for food. Many groups hunted with bows and arrows. Others came up with different ways of hunting.

The Modoc were skillful hunters. They trapped large animals by digging deep pits, which they covered with branches. The branches broke when a deer or a bear walked over them. The animal then fell into the pit.

When hunting small game such as rabbits, the Modoc drove the animals

into nets. The Modoc also used nets to catch ducks and other birds that lived in the lakes.

Using the Sweathouse

Before they went hunting, Modoc men would spend time in the village **sweathouse**. This was a heated house that would make the men sweat. The Modoc believed that it helped the hunters cleanse their spirits before the hunt.

If you were an older Modoc boy, you would join the men and other older boys in the sweathouse before a hunt. After soaking in the steam, you would rush out to bathe in the cool river water. Then you would be ready for the hunt.

Some of the sweathouses used by the Modoc were covered with leather to hold the steam inside. They made steam by pouring water over hot stones that had been heated in fires outside.

Most Native American groups in California used some form of a sweathouse. Some groups used ones similar to those the Modoc built. Others built large, earth-covered sweathouses and used dry heat from a small fire.

▼ Modoc sweathouses were sometimes built near the village. Hot stones were needed to produce steam in a sweathouse.

◀ The Modoc used bows similar to this Yurok bow decorated with traditional designs.

Modoc Houses

In winter, Modoc families lived in pit houses with doorways in the roofs. A roof entrance was necessary because the walls of the pit houses were partly underground. In the summer, they lived above ground in bowl-shaped **wickiups**. Wickiups were built using willow frames covered with mats.

REVIEW What were the different hunting methods the Modoc used? *Summarize*

What You Learned

4.2.1 The Native Americans of California used stories to tell about their connections to all living things.

4.1.5 4.2.1 The Yurok lived in the Northwest culture area.

4.1.5 4.2.1 The Modoc lived in the Northeast culture area.

Lesson Review

1. **Focus Question** What did California's Native 4.2.1 Americans believe about their relationship to the natural world?
2. **Vocabulary** Write one sentence for each 4.2.1 vocabulary term.
   creation story **sweathouse** **wickiup**
   plateau **weir**
3. **Culture** How did the Yurok feel about wealth? 4.2.1
4. **Critical Thinking** **Problem Solving** How did 4.2.1 the Yurok trap salmon that swam upstream?
5. **Reading Strategy**
   4.2.1 **Compare and Contrast** ELA R2.1 Use the Venn diagram on the right to compare and contrast types of sweathouses.
6. **Write about THE BIG IDEA** Write about the 4.2.1 similarities and differences between the ways of ELA W2.1 life of the Yurok and the Modoc.
7. **Link to Language Arts** Choose an animal and 4.2.1 write a story about how that animal came to be the way it is. For example, explain how it got its fur or feathers or how it become so shy or noisy.

CITIZENSHIP
DEMOCRACY IN ACTION

Being Informed 4.2.1

A group of students saw a notice in the local paper asking for volunteers to restore Dry Canyon Creek. Native Americans long ago used the reeds that grew along the creek to make baskets. Students would spend the day cleaning up the banks of the creek and planting native plants. Read below to find out how you can become informed about other issues.

After becoming informed, these students took their knowledge from the classroom into the community. Read these steps to learn how to become informed.

Build Citizenship

1. **Pick a subject** or an issue that interests you.
2. **Get information** from books, newspaper articles, or the Internet.
3. **Examine information.** Decide if you need more information.
4. **Apply your knowledge.** Look for ways to share what you have learned.

Think About It

1. How did the students first learn about this issue?
2. What did the students learn and do?
3. What are the needs in your community?
4. How could these students share what they learned with others?

List ways you could become informed about a subject or an issue.

Chapter Review

Vocabulary Review

Copy the sentences below on a separate sheet of paper. Use the list of vocabulary words to fill in the blanks.

economy	**granary**
glacier	**plateau**

1. A ________ is a thick sheet of ice that once covered parts of Earth. (4.2.1)
2. An area of flat, high land is called a ________. (4.2.1)
3. The Yokuts people kept their food in a storage house called a ________. (4.2.1)
4. ________ is the way people use the natural resources of a region. (4.2.1)
5. **Test Preparation** Festivals and other traditions are part of the ________ a group of people can share. (4.2.1)

   A. **heritage** C. **Ice Age**
   B. **prehistory** D. **archaeologist**

Comprehension Check

6. How did Native Americans learn to adapt to their environments? (4.2.1)
7. How did the first people to live in North America reach the continent? (4.2.1)
8. For how long have Native Americans lived in California? (4.2.1)
9. What did some Native American groups use as money? (4.2.1)
10. What kinds of things did the Northern Paiute people take with them when they traveled from place to place? (4.2.1)
11. **Critical Thinking** Compare shamans and chiefs. How were they alike? How were they different? (4.2.1)
12. **Critical Thinking** Why was it important for the Yokuts people to burn parts of their land once a year? (4.2.1)

Using Primary Sources

Artifacts

13. What are some examples of Native American artifacts? (4.2.1)
14. What can you learn by studying Native American artifacts? (4.2.1)

Hands-on Activity

15. **Prepare and Perform a Skit** Work in small groups to write a short skit about finding food in early California. You may want to gather props, such as photos of natural resources, period-style clothing, or other materials. Then, perform your skit for the class. (4.2.1)

Skills Check

Write a complete sentence to answer each question.

Read Cutaway Diagrams

16. How did the Chumash create the frames for their houses? (4.2.1)

17. What natural resource did the Chumash use to cover the frames of their houses and their doors? (4.2.1)

18. **Test Preparation** A diagram that allows you to see how the inside of a place is arranged is a ________. (4.2.1)

19. **Test Preparation** You can see ________ on a cutaway diagram. (4.2.1)

Write About History

20. **Narrative** Write a short story that tells what it might have been like to live in a Chumash village long ago. Describe where the village is located, what it looks like, and some of the things that people do there each day. (4.2.1, ELA W2.1)

For help with the process of writing, visit:

www.macmillanmh.com/ss/ca/writing

A Chumash House

1. The floor was dug out about 18 inches deep. Dirt was stamped to make the circle-shaped floor hard.

2. Bent wooden poles formed the frame. Willow branches were set sideways on the frame. A hole in the roof let out smoke. Bunches of any kind of long weeds covered the outside of the frame.

3. Doorways were covered with a mat of weeds.

4. A fire at the center warmed the hut.

CHAPTER

4 Exploring California

You Are There

"In this place there are great numbers of Indians, and the mainland has signs of being thickly populated. It is fertile [rich], for it has pine groves and oaks, and a fine climate..."

Sebastián Vizcaíno wrote these words in 1602. He was exploring the coast of California for Spain.

In this chapter you will read about Sebastián Vizcaíno and other Europeans who explored California in the 1500s and 1600s. You will also learn about what happened when the explorers met the Native Americans.

1542
Juan Rodriguez Cabrillo anchors at San Miguel Bay (page 136)

1579
Francis Drake repairs his ship on the coast of California (page 143)

Chapter Events

A B

1540 1560 1580

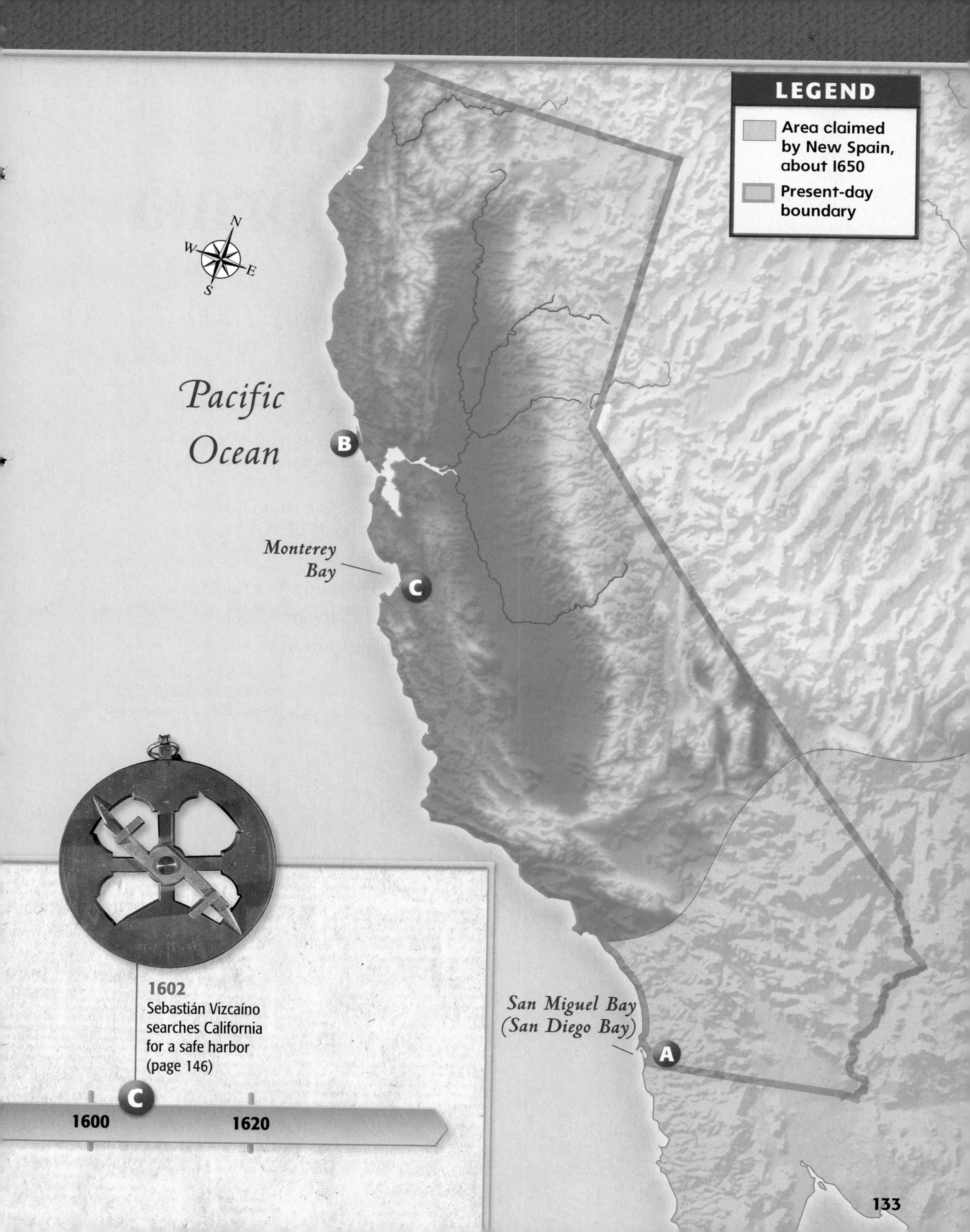
LEGEND
Area claimed by New Spain, about 1650
Present-day boundary
N
W
E
S
Pacific Ocean
B
Monterey Bay
C
San Miguel Bay (San Diego Bay)
A
1602
Sebastián Vizcaíno searches California for a safe harbor (page 146)
C
1600
1620

The Spanish Claim California

FOCUS QUESTION

What were the experiences of the first Europeans in California?

VOCABULARY

- conquistador
- expedition
- empire
- colony
- strait
- viceroy

VOCABULARY STRATEGY

WORD ORIGINS The prefix **vice-** means substitute in Latin. The suffix **-roy** means king. A viceroy then was someone who stands in for a king. List another title using the prefix **vice**.

READING STRATEGY

Summarize

Use the chart below to summarize this lesson.

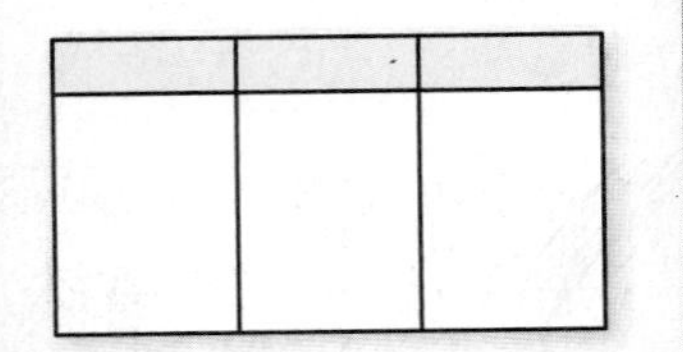

Start with Your CALIFORNIA STANDARDS

4.2 Students describe the social, political, cultural, and economic life and interactions among people of California from the pre-Columbian societies to the Spanish mission and Mexican rancho periods.

4.2.2 Identify the early land and sea routes to, and European settlements in, California with a focus on the exploration of the North Pacific, noting especially the importance of mountains, deserts, ocean currents, and wind patterns.

Find out where Spanish conquerers traveled on their first explorations of California. (Begins on page 135)

4.2.3 Describe the Spanish exploration and colonization of California, including the relationships among soldiers, missionaries, and Indians.

Learn about the first meetings between Europeans and Native Americans. (Begins on page 136)

Spanish explorers sailed north along California's rugged Big Sur coastline. ▼

1490	1510	1530	1550

1492 Columbus lands in the Caribbean

1533 Cortés expedition travels up the coast of Mexico

1542 Cabrillo anchors at San Diego Bay in Alta California

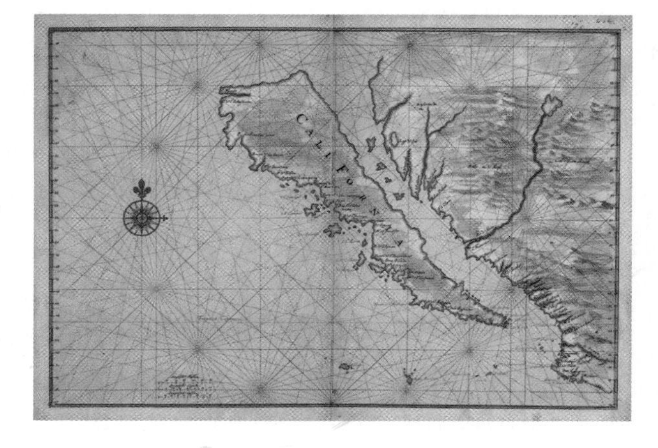

The Native Americans of California would soon have to share their land with newcomers. These newcomers believed California was an island.

The Beginning of New Spain 4.2.2 4.2.3

In 1492 Christopher Columbus set sail from Spain in search of a new route to Asia. After 10 weeks at sea Columbus spotted land. He had arrived at what are now the Caribbean Islands. **Conquistadors** (kon KEES tah dorz), or Spanish soldiers who seized the land by force, would soon follow the sea routes discovered by Columbus.

Baja California

A conquistador named Hernan Cortés left Spain in 1504 to find gold. After many small **expeditions**, Cortés reached the land of Tenochtitlan (te noch tee TLAHN) in November, 1519. An expedition is a journey of exploration. Tenochtitlan was the capital of the Aztec **empire**, a large territory where different groups of people are ruled by a single country or ruler. The leader of the Aztec, Moctezuma II (mahk tuh ZOO muh), greeted Cortés with presents.

The land of the Aztec and other lands captured by the Spanish became the Spanish **colony** of New Spain. A colony is a place ruled by another country.

In 1533 another Cortés expedition traveled up the western coast of Mexico. These explorers landed in an area that came to be known as Baja California, or lower California. Two years later Cortés himself traveled to Baja California and established an outpost at La Paz. The Spanish called this part of New Spain "the Californias."

REVIEW Where did Cortés sail to in 1533? *Summarize*

Explorations of Cabrillo 4.2.2 4.2.3

As you learned, Europeans were searching for a new route to Asia. Instead of finding this new route they found a continent that was new to them. However, they still wanted to find a route to Asia. A legend said that a water route existed from the Western Hemisphere to Asia. It was called the Strait of Anián. A **strait** is a narrow passage of water.

The Search for Anián

Finding the Strait of Anián was an important goal for the **viceroy** of New Spain. A viceroy is a ruler picked by a king. In 1542 the viceroy gave Juan Rodriguez Cabrillo (kah BREE yoh) the job of exploring the coast of California. He was told to go farther north than Cortés' expeditions did. Cabrillo was a conquistador and a sea captain. He left Navidad on the west coast of New Spain on June 27, 1542. Cabrillo set sail with two small ships, the *San Salvador* and the *Victoria*. He had a crew of 250 men.

San Diego

On September 28, 1542, the ships sailed into a bay. Cabrillo named the bay San Miguel. Later explorers would rename the bay San Diego. Cabrillo described the port as "closed and very good." They explored the land and met the local Kumeyaay people. Cabrillo and his men spent six days there before continuing north.

Continuing Journeys

After leaving San Diego, Cabrillo and his crew sailed to what is today known as Santa Catalina Island.

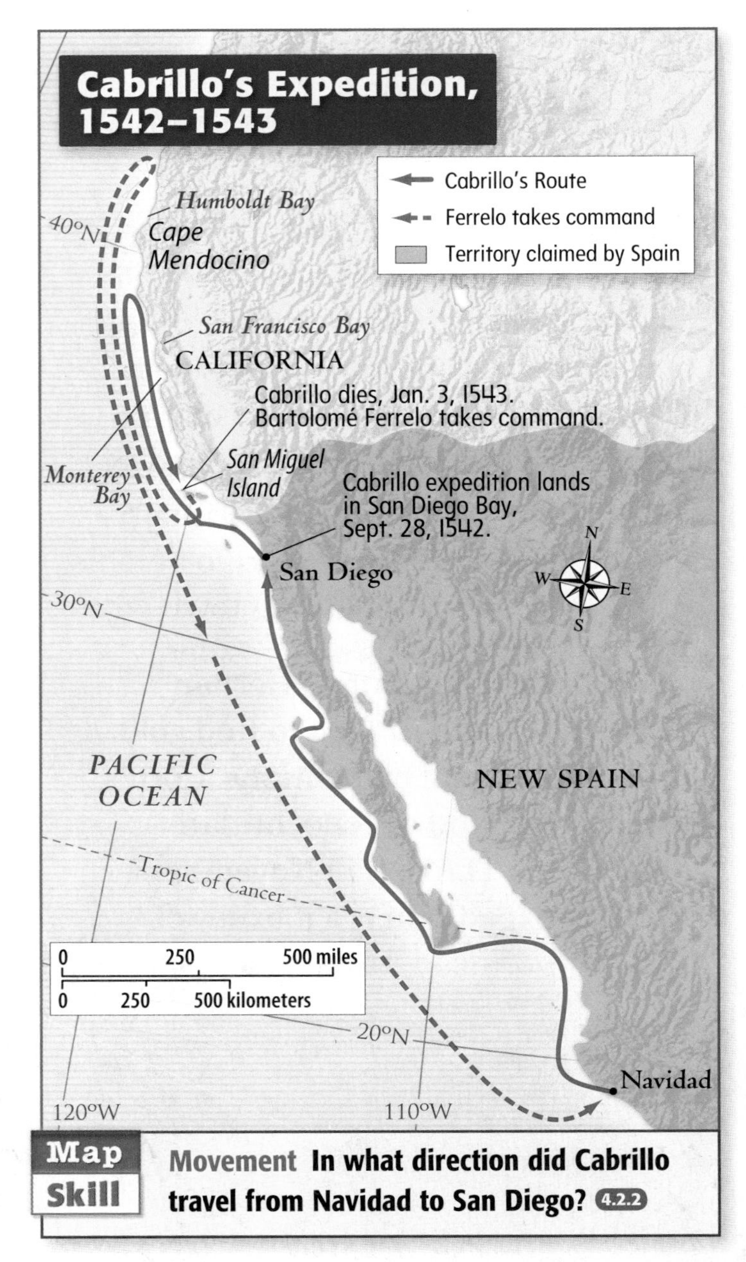

Map Skill Movement **In what direction did Cabrillo travel from Navidad to San Diego?** 4.2.2

In his journal, Cabrillo describes their arrival:

> "*[W]hen the boat came near, a great number of Indians emerged from the bushes and grass, shouting, dancing, and making signs that [we] should land.*"

Cabrillo traveled farther north along the coast. On the islands of San Miguel, Santa Cruz, and Santa Rosa outside the Santa Barbara Channel he and his crew found large populations of Native Americans:

> "*The Indians brought for [us] many sardines. . . . They say that in the interior there are many pueblos and abundant food . . . the country appears to be very fine.*"

The expedition soon passed into the Santa Barbara Channel. On one of the islands in the channel, Cabrillo and his men saw a Native American town with large adobe houses. Some residents rowed out in canoes to greet them. Each canoe held about 13 people.

Cabrillo claimed the land he found for New Spain. He called it "Alta California," or upper California. Cabrillo named the town he found "Pueblo de las Canoas," the Town of the Canoes.

REVIEW Why did the viceroy of New Spain send Cabrillo to the coast of California? *Cause and Effect*

▲ Decorative tiles showing Cabrillo's ship

Spanish soldiers wore suits of armor and helmets such as the ones shown here. ▶

Alta and Baja California 4.2.2 4.2.3

The people Cabrillo met were the Chumash. They told Cabrillo that if he traveled farther north he would find a large river flowing into the sea. Could this be the Strait of Anián? The explorers set sail, but met high winds and rough seas. They turned back after about one month to wait for better weather.

Cabrillo Falls

Cabrillo's dealings with Native Americans had been friendly to this point. However, the Chumash on the Channel Islands were eager for the explorers to leave their land. On December 24, 1542, men from Cabrillo's ships were attacked. While trying to rescue them, Cabrillo broke his arm. He would die from this injury.

Ferrelo Takes Charge

Before dying, Cabrillo asked Bartolomé Ferrelo, his chief pilot, to take charge of the expedition. Cabrillo wanted Ferrelo to continue the search for the Strait of Anián.

Ferrelo ordered the men to bury their leader on the island where he died. Today that island is called San Miguel Island.

Bad weather forced Ferrelo to wait until late February 1543 to leave the Channel Islands and head north. Soon after, the ships ran into another storm:

▼ Cabrillo reached the Channel Islands in 1542.

"... the wind shifted with great fury, the seas coming from many directions ..."

The ships were damaged in the storm. Ferrelo decided to end the expedition. Historians think he had reached the border of present day Oregon. His ships arrived back in Navidad on April 14, 1543.

The expeditions by Cabrillo and Ferrelo discovered many harbors of Baja and Alta California.

This statue of Cabrillo stands in San Diego. ▶

From the voyage's journals, historians have identified 70 locations. The crew had explored lands that no Europeans had seen before.

REVIEW What hardships did Cabrillo and Ferrelo encounter on their journey along California's coast? *Summarize*

What You Learned

4.2.2 4.2.3 After Hernan Cortés conquered the Aztec empire, Spanish ships explorered the coast of Baja California.

4.2.2 4.2.3 While looking for the Strait of Anián, Juan Rodrigues Cabrillo reached Santa Barbara Channel and met Native Americans.

4.2.2 4.2.3 After Cabrillo's death, Bartolomé Ferrelo took over and traveled north. But he had to turn back because of bad weather.

Lesson Review

1. **Focus Question** What were the experiences of the first Europeans in California? 4.2.3
2. **Vocabulary** Write one sentence for each vocabulary word. 4.2.2 4.2.3

   colony **expedition**
   conquistador **strait**
   empire **viceroy**
3. **History** In what year did Cortés land in Baja California? 4.2.3
4. **Problem Solving** Why did Ferrelo end his expedition to find the Strait of Anián? 4.2.3
5. **Reading Strategy** **Summarize** Summarize three of Cabrillo's encounters with Native Americans. 4.2.3 ELA R2.1

6. **Write about THE BIG IDEA** Write about the expeditions of Hernan Cortés. 4.2.2 ELA W2.1
7. **Link to Science** Between October and March there are sometimes storms along the California coast. This is most likely what Cabrillo and Ferrelo experienced during their expedition. Write a paragraph about the weather in your area between October and March. 4.2.2

STUDY and RESEARCH Skills

Use Reference Materials

4.2.3 ELA W1.7

If you want to learn more about the trappers and settlers who came to California, you can use **reference materials** for your research. These are books and other sources that contain facts about many different subjects. Some of them can be found in a part of the library called the reference section, and others are on the computer. If you need help finding something at the library, you can ask a librarian.

VOCABULARY

reference materials
dictionary
guide words
encyclopedia
Internet

1 Learn It

- You might want to learn the exact meaning of the word *conquistador*. To find out, you can use a **dictionary**. A dictionary gives meanings of words. It also shows you how to pronounce and spell them.
- The words in a dictionary are arranged in alphabetical order. The **guide words** at the top of each page can help you find your word quickly. Guide words tell you the first and last words defined on the page.
- Suppose you want to know more about Juan Rodriguez Cabrillo. You can look him up in an **encyclopedia**. This book or set of books gives information about people, places, things, and events. Information in encyclopedias is arranged in alphabetical order. Find the encyclopedia volume, or book, with the letter C on the spine. Then use the guide words at the top of each page to find Cabrillo.
- The **Internet** is another reference source. It is a computer network. Many dictionaries and encyclopedias can be found on the Internet. You will learn more about how to use the Internet to find information on pages 408–409.

2 Try It

Look at the sample dictionary page below.

- Look at the guide words at the top of the page. What is the first word defined on the page? What is the last?
- Would the meaning of the word *elevate* be found on this page? How can you tell?
- Some words have more than one definition. What are the two definitions for the word *exploit*?
- There are often sample sentences that show how a word is used. What is the sample sentence for the second definition of the word *explode*?

3 Apply It

- Choose a person mentioned in the last lesson to research. Use reference sources to find out more information about the person. Write a short report about what you learn.

experimental ➤ explosive 

experimental From or relating to experiments: *The scientists were working on an **experimental** project in the chemistry laboratory.* **ex·per·i·ment·al** (ek sper′ə ment′əl) *adjective.*

expert A person who knows a great deal about some special thing: *One of our teachers is an **expert** on American history. Noun.*
◦ Having or showing a great deal of knowledge: *The swimming coach gave the team **expert** advice on how to dive. Adjective.*
ex·pert (eks′pûrt *for noun;* eks′pûrt *or* ek spûrt′ *for adjective*) *noun, plural* **experts;** *adjective.*

expiration 1. The act of coming to an end or close: *I must get a new library card before the **expiration** of my old one.* **2.** The act of breathing out air: *The sick child's **expirations** were weak.* **ex·pi·ra·tion** (eks′pə rā′shən) *noun, plural* **expirations.**

expire 1. To come to an end: *Your membership at the pool **expires** at the end of the month.* **2.** To breathe out; exhale: *When we **expire**, our bodies let air out of our lungs.* 3. To die. **ex·pire** (ek spīr′) *verb,* **expired, expiring.**

The art teacher is explaining **paintings to the class.**

explanation for why the vase was broken. **ex·pla·na·tion** (eks′plə nā′shən) *noun, plural* **explanations.**

explicit Stated clearly or shown clearly: *Our teacher gave **explicit** instructions on how we should do the work.* **ex·pli·cit** (ek splis′it) *adjective.*

explode 1. To burst or cause to burst suddenly and with a loud noise; blow up: *I pumped too much air into the tire, and it **exploded.*** **2.** To show an emotion noisily or forcefully: *The audience **exploded** with laughter at the funny joke.*
ex·plode (ek splōd′) *verb,* **exploded, exploding.**

exploit A brave deed or act: *The story is about the daring **exploits** of a knight. Noun.*
◦ **1.** To use in an unfair or unjust way for selfish reasons: *The American colonists felt that the British government **exploited** them by taxing the tea they drank.* **2.** To make the fullest possible use of: *This new drill will enable us to **exploit** oil buried far under the ground. Verb.*
ex·ploit (ek′ sploit *for noun;* ek sploit′ *for verb*) *noun, plural* **exploits;** *verb,* **exploited, exploiting.**

exploration The act of exploring: *Sometimes people really mean conquest when they talk about **exploration.*** **ex·plo·ra·tion** (ek′splə rā′shən) *noun, plural* **explorations.**

explore 1. To go to a place that one knows nothing about: *Astronauts **explored** the moon and brought back rocks.* **2.** To try to figure out: *Doctors **explore** the causes of diseases.* **ex·plore** (ek splôr′) *verb,* **explored, exploring.**

explorer A person who explores. **ex·plor·er** (ek splôr′ər) *noun, plural* **explorers.**

explosion 1. The act of bursting or expanding suddenly and noisily: *The **explosion** of the bomb broke windows in the buildings nearby.* **2.** A sudden outburst: *The funny joke caused an **explosion** of*

LESSON 2

Newcomers to California

FOCUS QUESTION

Why did Europeans explore California?

VOCABULARY

Northwest Passage
galleon
financial

VOCABULARY STRATEGY

ROOT WORDS The root of the word **financial** is finance. **Finance** is the money matters of people, businesses, or governments. Can you use the word **finance** in a sentence?

READING STRATEGY

Sequence Events

Use the chart below to sequence the main events discussed in the lesson.

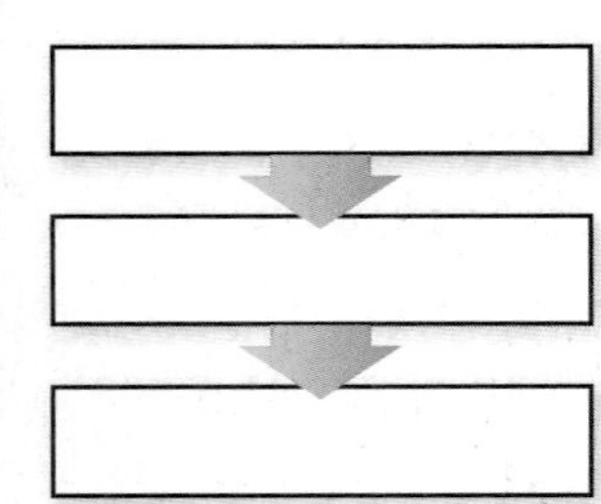

Start with Your CALIFORNIA STANDARDS

4.2 Students describe the social, political, cultural, and economic life and interactions among people of California from the pre-Columbian societies to the Spanish mission and Mexican rancho periods.

4.2.2 Identify the early land and sea routes to, and European settlements in, California with a focus on the exploration of the North Pacific, noting especially the importance of mountains, deserts, ocean currents, and wind patterns.

Discover the routes explored along California's coast by Spanish explorers and by Francis Drake. (Begins on page 143)

4.2.3 Describe the Spanish exploration and colonization of California, including the relationships among soldiers, missionaries, and Indians.

Learn about Sebastián Rodriguez Cermeño's and Sebastián Vizcaíno's search for a safe port for the Manila galleon. (Begins on page 144)

▲ Francis Drake's ship, the *Golden Hind*, robbed Spanish ships of their gold.

1575 | 1585 | 1595 | 1605

1577
Francis Drake sails from England to New Spain

1579
Drake repairs ship on California coast

1595
Sebastián Rodriguez Cermeño sails to Drake's Bay

1602
Sebastián Vizcaíno voyages to Monterey

Cortés, Cabrillo, and Ferrelo were some of the first Europeans to explore the coast of California. Soon others, such as Francis Drake, would follow in their footsteps.

Exploring California 4.2.2

Like the Spanish, the English also wanted to find a sea route from Europe to Asia. They called it the **Northwest Passage**. In 1577 the Queen of England sent a sea captain named Francis Drake to find the Northwest Passage. He was also told to attack Spanish ships and settlements. This meant that Drake should rob the Spanish of their gold.

Nova Albion

Francis Drake and his crew took a huge amount of gold from the Spanish. By June 1579, Drake's ship was loaded with 30 tons of stolen treasure. That is the weight of about 400 people. The *Golden Hind* would sink if Drake did not make some repairs. On June 17, 1579 he found "a convenient and fit harbor." Historians believe Drake landed at what we today call Drake's Bay on the Point Reyes Peninsula. Drake and his crew remained there for 36 days. They repaired their ship, built a small fort, and explored the area.

During their stay, Drake and his crew met the local Native Americans, the Miwok. The Miwok lived along California's coast near present-day Marin County. At first the Miwok were afraid of the strangers. However, after a while the Miwok and the English began to trade. The Miwok also gave food to Drake and his men.

Drake, like the Spanish before him, claimed the land he found for his country, England. Drake named the place Nova Albion, or New England. He put up a brass plate that claimed all the land he found for England.

REVIEW When did Drake find Drake's Bay? *Sequence Events*

The Manila Galleon 4.2.2 4.2.3

The Spanish saw Francis Drake as a pirate. They needed to find a way to protect their gold from others like him.

Every year Spain sent one **galleon** from its New Spain colony to its colony in the Philippines and back. A galleon is a large, heavy ship built to carry goods. The galleon would carry silver and gold across the Pacific Ocean from Acapulco on the west coast of Mexico to Manila, the capital of the Philippines. It became known as the Manila Galleon.

The trip from Acapulco usually took two to three months, as ships followed westward winds. In Manila, the Spanish traded their gold and silver for goods. The more goods the sailors loaded onto the galleon, the greater the profit would be. With all the added weight, sailing against the wind, the trip back to Acapulco could take more than seven months.

The galleon set out with less food and water to make room for more goods. Many sailors got sick from hunger and thirst, and some died.

Sebastián Rodriguez Cermeño

What would make the Manila Galleon's return voyages safer? If the galleon could make port along the coast of California, sailors could go ashore for fresh food and water for the rest of the journey to Acapulco. With this in mind, Spain put the Portuguese explorer Sebastián Rodriguez Cermeño (ser ME nyoh), in charge of the galleons.

Spanish Galleon

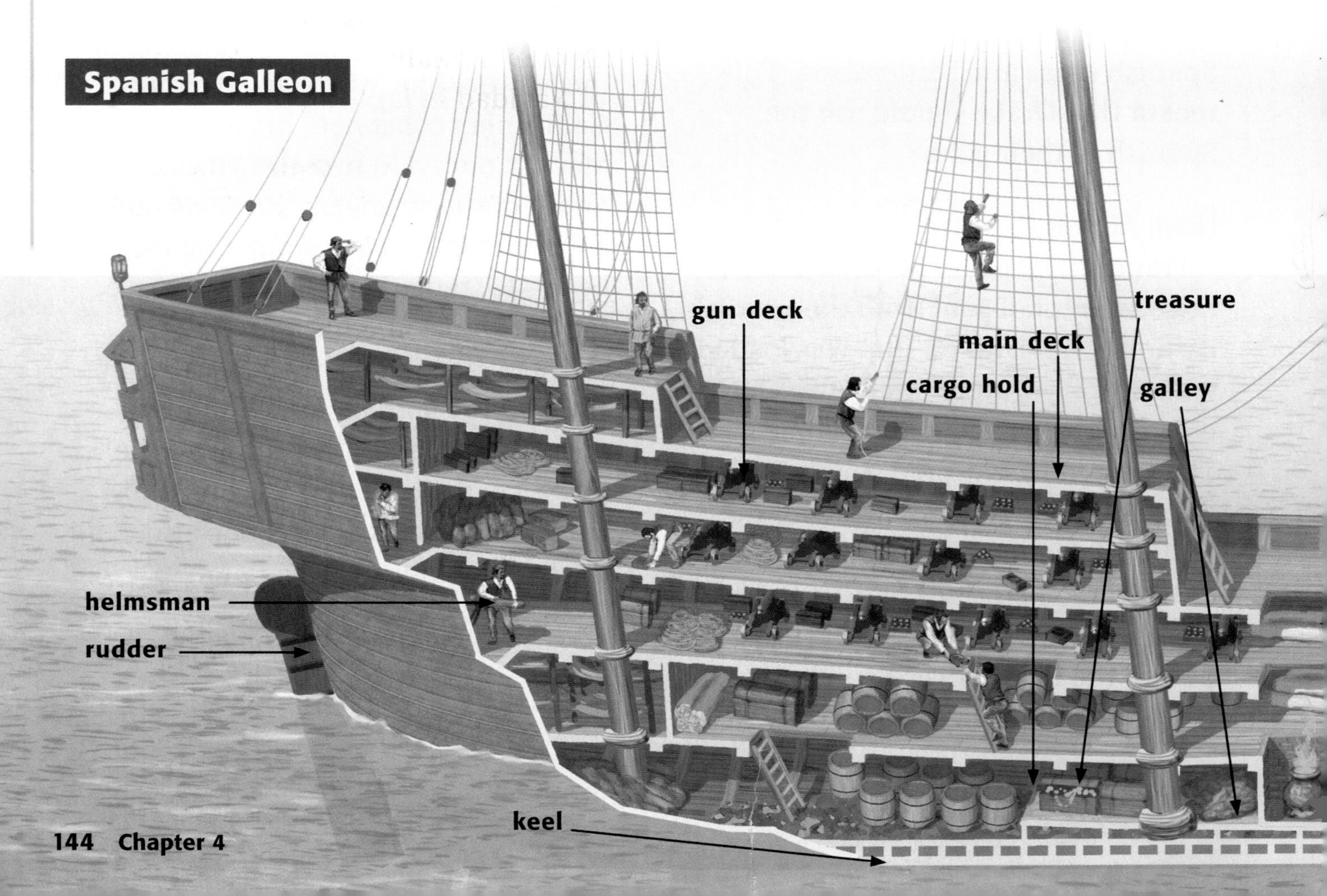

Cermeño left the Philippines on July 5, 1595, headed for California. His ship, the *San Agustín*, was filled with cargo. In early November, Cermeño sighted land around Cape Mendocino. Then a storm hit, and the *San Agustín* was nearly wrecked. Officers on the ship wanted Cermeño to abandon the expedition. On November 6, 1595, they anchored at Drake's Bay, which Cermeño called the Bay of San Francisco. He was at the same place Drake had been 16 years earlier.

On November 30, a violent storm hit the ship and pounded it to pieces. Its cargo was lost. The crew begged Cermeño to return home. Over fifty men squeezed onto one small boat that had survived the storm. But Cermeño refused to give up his exploring.

▲ Sebastián Rodriguez Cermeño carried jewels and gold and silver coins on the galleon.

He made the small boat stop along the coast on their return to New Spain. In his journals he described many points along the California coast. One of these places was Monterey Bay. Cermeño finally reached the port of Navidad in January 1596.

REVIEW What were some of the difficulties the Manila galleons faced on their journeys? *Cause and Effect*

pplies/
od stores
ballast stones
galley fire

Exploring Monterey 4.2.2 4.2.3

Sebastián Rodriguez Cermeño did not find a safe port along California's coast. The loss of gold, silver, and other cargo on his ship was a huge **financial** loss for Spain. Financial is anything having to do with money matters.

In 1602 the viceroy of New Spain sent explorers to search for a safe port, a place where galleons could safely load and unload cargo. The viceroy chose Sebastián Vizcaíno (vees kah EE noh) for the job. If he succeeded, he would become the captain of the next Manila Galleon.

Vizcaíno was told by the viceroy to visit as many places between New Spain and Cape Mendocino as possible. He was told to name all the places where he anchored after Catholic saints. Vizcaíno was also told to mark the entrance to Monterey Bay for future Spanish ships.

Voyage Along the Coast

Vizcaíno set out with three ships. These ships were smaller and quicker than the galleons. He left Acapulco on May 5, 1602. The ships traveled to many of the same places Cabrillo had been to 60 years before.

By November 10, Vizcaíno had reached San Miguel. He renamed San Miguel as San Diego. In his journal below, Vizcaíno described his dealings with the Native Americans he met at San Diego.

Monterey Bay

By December, Vizcaíno had reached the bay which he would name

Sebastián Vizcaíno

A section from
The Diary of Sebastián Vizcaíno
1602-1603

"*. . . In this bay the general, with his men, went ashore . . . a number of Indians appeared with their bows and arrows . . . the Indians came peaceably and took us to their* ***rancherias****, where they were gathering their crops. . . . They had pots in which they cooked their food, and the women were dressed in skins of animals . . .*"

rancheria village

What did Vizcaíno's crew learn about the daily lives of the Native Americans they met?

◀ Astrolabes were used by sailors to find their way at sea.

▲ Vizcaíno exaggerated when he called Monterey Bay "safe from the winds."

Monterey Bay, after the viceroy of New Spain. His descriptions of the bay, however, were so misleading that the next Spaniards to see it, in 1769, did not recognize it.

In his journal Vizcaíno described Monterey as "the best port that one could hope for." He goes on to say that Monterey is "safe from all winds" and has "an abundance [much] of water and . . . game."

On May 23, 1603 Vizcaíno wrote in a letter to the king of Spain that Monterey was "among the most important ports that [he] discovered." He also told the king of Spain that it was a perfect place for the galleons to stop on their way to Acapulco from Manila.

Vizcaíno exaggerated the qualities of Monterey Bay because he wanted to be the captain of the next Manila Galleon. He feared that if he told the king the truth he would not be given the job. The truth was that Monterey was whipped by high winds and was a very dangerous bay for ships.

REVIEW Why did Vizcaíno describe Monterey Bay incorrectly? *Summarize*

DATAGRAPHIC

European Explorers in California

4.2.2

From 1542 to 1603 explorers from Spain and England made voyages along the California coast. They did not settle there. When their journeys ended they returned home. The Native Americans whom they had seen remained the only people in California.

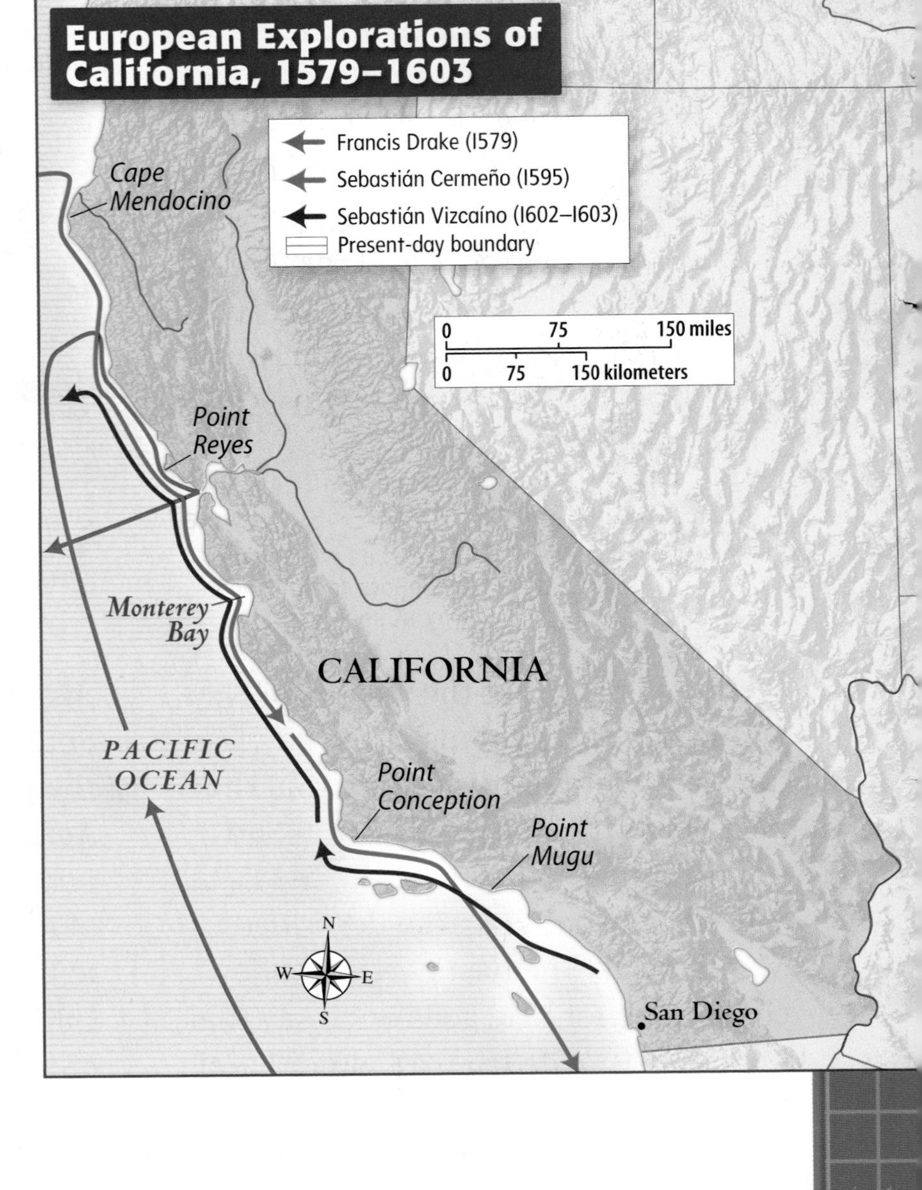

Think About Explorations

1. In what general direction were Sebastián Cermeño's explorations?
2. In what year did Sebastián Vizcaíno lead an expedition up the coast of California?
3. By 1595 how many explorers had sailed past Cape Mendocino?

The Search Ends 4.2.3

After Vizcaíno's expeditions, a new viceroy decided to give up the search for a safe port in California. By the time the galleons reached California, they were just a few days away from Acapulco. The Spanish decided it was not worth building a port there.

On their journeys to California, the Spanish had looked for gold but had found none. They had searched for the Strait of Anián but it was not there. Instead they had found California to have a barren and dangerous coast. It would be 167 years before Spain would send people to California again.

REVIEW Why did the new viceroy decide to end the search for the port in California? *Summarize*

What You Learned

- 4.2.2 Francis Drake named the place where his ship landed Nova Albion, which means New England.
- 4.2.2 4.2.3 The Manila Galleons sailed with silver and gold to the Philippines to trade for goods and return to New Spain.
- 4.2.2 4.2.3 Sebastián Vizcaíno explored the coast of California and declared that Monterey Bay was a safe harbor for the galleons.
- 4.2.3 Spain decided that it would no longer search for a port in California. Spain would not send people to California again for 167 years.

Lesson Review

1. **Focus Question** Why did Europeans explore California? 4.2.3
2. **Vocabulary** Write a summary of this lesson using these vocabulary words. 4.2.3
   financial **galleon**
3. **Geography** Both Drake and Cermeño anchored at the same location along California's coast. What did Cermeño name it? 4.2.2
4. **Critical Thinking** **Cause and Effect** What did Vizcaíno fear would happen if he did not tell the King of Spain that he found a perfect harbor for the galleons? 4.2.3
5. **Reading Strategy** **Sequence** List the sequence of events of Vizcaíno's journey along the coast of California. 4.2.2 ELA R2.1

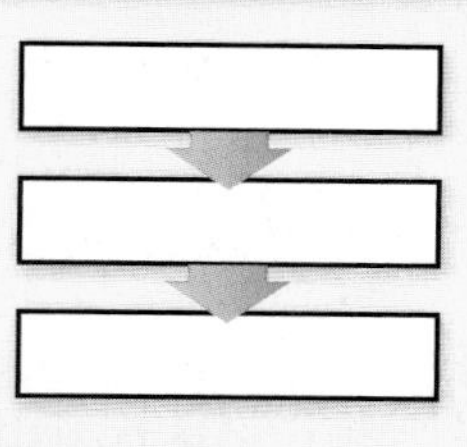

6. **Write about THE BIG IDEA** Write about Francis Drake's search for the Northwest Passage. 4.2.2 ELA W2.1
7. **Link to Math** Cermeño's galleon, the *San Agustín*, was carrying 130 tons of goods when it was destroyed. Suppose a ship today sank with 130 tons of goods and that each ton of its goods was worth $200. How much would the financial loss be if the ship was lost at sea? 4.2.2 4.2.3

CHAPTER

Chapter Review

Vocabulary Review

Copy the sentences below on a separate sheet of paper. Use the list of vocabulary words to fill in the blanks.

colony	**galleon**
expedition	**strait**

1. A ________ is a narrow waterway. 4.2.2
2. The explorer set out on an ________ hoping to find new lands. 4.2.2
3. A heavy ship called a ________ set sail carrying goods. 4.2.2
4. A place ruled by another country is called a ________. 4.2.3
5. Test Preparation A person who is picked by a king to rule is called a ________ . 4.2.3

   A. conquistador **C. empire**
   B. league **D. viceroy**

Comprehension Check

6. What was Cabrillo trying to find as he explored the coast of California? 4.2.3
7. What did Cortés hope to find when he left Spain? 4.2.3
8. Why do many places in California have Spanish names? 4.2.3
9. Why did Francis Drake decide to stop in California in 1579? 4.2.2
10. Why did Cermeño explore the California coast? 4.2.2
11. Critical Thinking How do you think Ferrelo felt when he arrived back in Navidad in 1543? 4.2.2
12. Critical Thinking Why did the Spanish consider finding a safe harbor so important? 4.2.2

Use the Time Line

Use the time line below to answer each question.

13. Did Cabrillo reach California before or after Cortés? 4.2.2
14. How many years after Drake left England did Cermeño reach Drake's Bay? 4.2.2

1480 1500 1520 1540 1560 1580 1600

- 1492 Columbus lands in the Caribbean
- 1533 Cortés sends explorers to Baja California
- 1542 Cabrillo explores the coast of California
- 1577 Drake sails from England to New Spain
- 1595 Cermeño sails to Drake's Bay

Skills Check

Write a complete sentence to answer each question.

Use Reference Materials

15. How would you learn more about Spanish explorers? (4.2.2)

16. How do the guide words on the pages of the open dictionary below help you find the word "explorer"? (4.2.2)

17. **Test Preparation** You would use a ________ to find the meaning of the word "conquistador." (4.2.2)

18. **Test Preparation** A ________ can help you find out more about Hernan Cortés. (4.2.2)

experimental ➤ explosive E

experimental From or relating to experiments: *The scientists were working on an experimental project in the chemistry laboratory.* **ex•per•i•ment•al** (ek sper′ə ment′əl) *adjective.*

expert A person who knows a great deal about some special thing: *One of our teachers is an expert on American history.* Noun.
◦ Having or showing a great deal of knowledge: *The swimming coach gave the team expert advice on how to dive.* Adjective.
ex•pert (eks′pûrt *for noun;* eks′pûrt *or* ek spûrt′ *for adjective*) *noun, plural* **experts;** *adjective.*

expiration 1. The act of coming to an end or close: *I must get a new library card before the expiration of my old one.* 2. The act of breathing out air: *The sick child's expirations were weak.* **ex•pi•ra•tion** (eks′pə rā′shən) *noun, plural* **expirations.**

expire 1. To come to an end: *Your membership at the pool expires at the end of the month.* 2. To breathe out; exhale: *When we expire, our bodies let air out of our lungs.* 3. To die. **ex•pire** (ek spīr′) *verb,* **expired, expiring.**

The art teacher is explaining paintings to the class.

explain 1. To make something plain or clear; tell the meaning of: *Explain how to get the answer to this mathematics problem.* 2. To give or have a reason for: *Can you explain why you were late for school?* **ex•plain** (ek splān′) *verb,* **explained, explaining.**

explanation 1. The act or process of making something plain or clear: *My friend's explanation of how to make a kite helped me understand how to do it.* 2. A reason or meaning: *My parents wanted an explanation for why the vase was broken.* **ex•pla•na•tion** (eks′plə nā′shən) *noun, plural* **explanations.**

explicit Stated clearly or shown clearly: *Our teacher gave explicit instructions on how we should do the work.* **ex•pli•cit** (ek splis′it) *adjective.*

explode 1. To burst or cause to burst suddenly and with a loud noise; blow up: *I pumped too much air into the tire, and it exploded.* 2. To show an emotion noisily or forcefully: *The audience exploded with laughter at the funny joke.*
ex•plode (ek splōd′) *verb,* **exploded, exploding.**

exploit A brave deed or act: *The story is about the daring exploits of a knight.* Noun.
◦ 1. To use in an unfair or unjust way for selfish reasons: *The American colonists felt that the British government exploited them by taxing the tea they drank.* 2. To make the fullest possible use of: *This new drill will enable us to exploit oil buried far under the ground.* Verb.
ex•ploit (ek′ sploit *for noun;* ek sploit′ *for verb*) *noun, plural* **exploits;** *verb,* **exploited, exploiting.**

exploration The act of exploring: *Sometimes people really mean conquest when they talk about exploration.* **ex•plo•ra•tion** (ek′splə rā′shən) *noun, plural* **explorations.**

explore 1. To go to a place that one knows nothing about: *Astronauts explored the moon and brought back rocks.* 2. To try to figure out: *Doctors explore the causes of diseases.* **ex•plore** (ek splôr′) *verb,* **explored, exploring.**

explorer A person who explores. **ex•plor•er** (ek splôr′ər) *noun, plural* **explorers.**

explosion 1. The act of bursting or expanding suddenly and noisily: *The explosion of the bomb broke windows in the buildings nearby.* 2. A sudden outburst: *The funny joke caused an explosion of laughter.* **ex•plo•sion** (ek splō′zhən) *noun, plural* **explosions.**

explosive 1. Likely to explode or cause an explosion: *A bomb is an explosive device.* 2. Likely to cause a lot of trouble: *an explosive political situation.* Adjective.
◦ Something that can explode or cause an explosion: *Dynamite is an explosive.* Noun.
ex•plo•sive (ek splō′siv) *adjective; noun, plural* **explosives.**

PRONUNCIATION KEY:
at āpe fär câre end mē it īce pierce hot ōld sông fôrk
oil out up ūse rüle pull tûrn chin sing shop thin this
hw in white; zh in treasure. The symbol ə stands for the unstressed vowel sound in about, taken, pencil, lemon, and circus.

259

Using Primary Sources

Artifacts

19. What artifacts would show that Spanish explorers reached California? (4.2.2)

20. What are some artifacts that Spanish soldiers left? (4.2.2)

Hands-on Activity

21. **Write a Song** Work in groups to write a song, using a familiar tune, about what it was like to travel on an expedition along the California coast in the 1500s. (4.2.2)

Write About History

22. **Narrative** Write a short story that describes a meeting between a European explorer and a Native American group in California. (4.2.2, ELA W2.1)

LOG ON For help with the process of writing, visit:

www.macmillanmh.com/ss/ca/writing

CHAPTER

5 Spanish Colonial California

YOU ARE THERE

"The King has need of you. Come at once. We are going to found new missions."

These words were written in 1769 by Jóse de Gálvez. He was asking Junípero Serra to join an expedition to establish missions, or religious settlements, in California. Serra wanted to convince Native Americans to become Christians.

In this chapter you will read about how Junípero Serra changed California's history. You will also read about how these changes affected the Native Americans of California.

Chapter Events

A 1769 Father Serra leads "Sacred Expedition" to establish missions (page 155)

B 1770 Gaspar de Portolá finds Monterey Bay (page 159)

C 1776 Juan Batista de Anza builds a fort at San Francisco (page 174)

1765 1770 1775

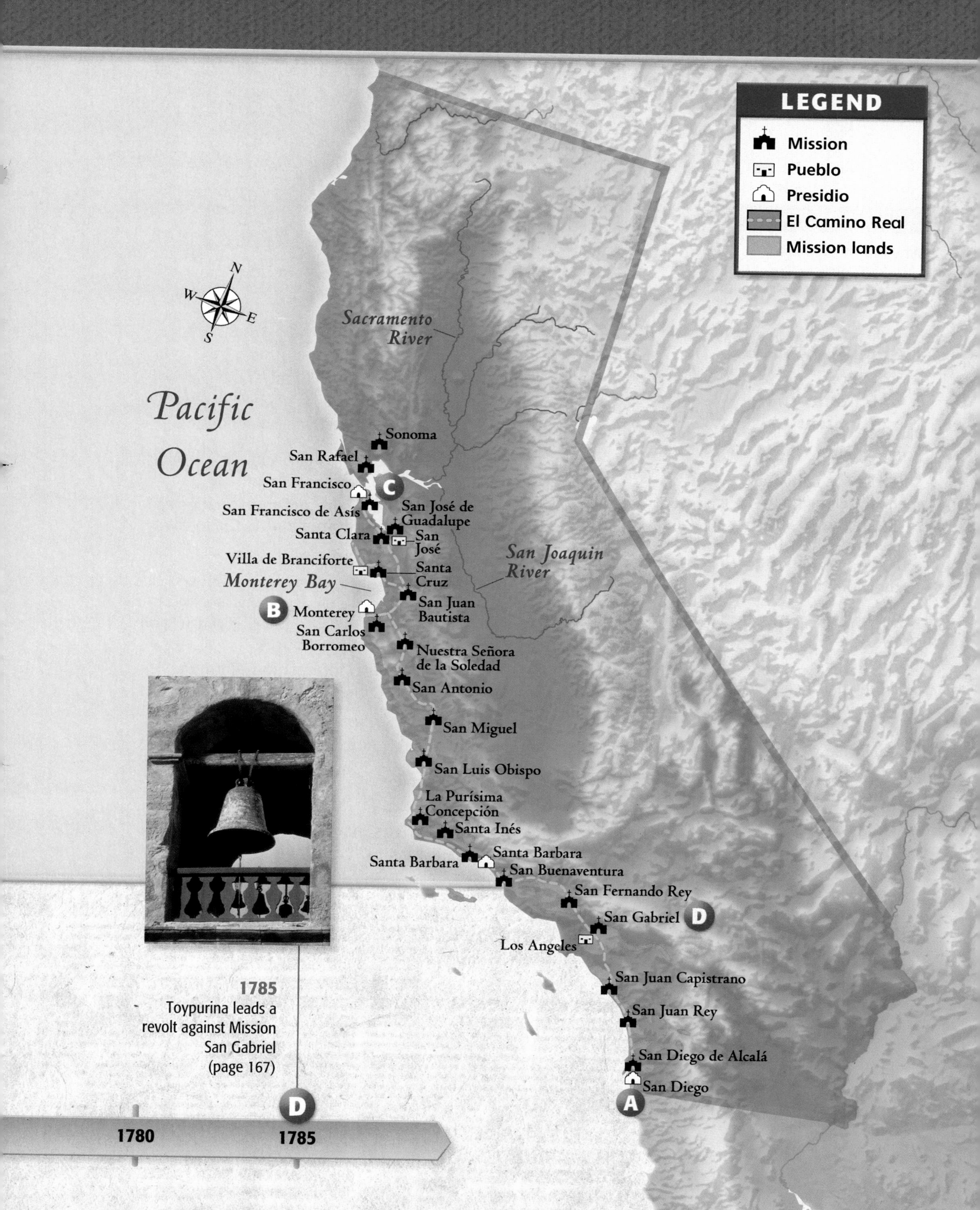

1785
Toypurina leads a revolt against Mission San Gabriel (page 167)

A Plan for Alta California

FOCUS QUESTION

Why did the Spanish want to set up missions in Alta California?

VOCABULARY

mission
missionary
settlement

VOCABULARY STRATEGY

SUFFIXES The suffix **-ary** means "belonging to" or "having to do with." Can you see how the word **missionary** relates to the word **mission**?

READING STRATEGY

Summarize

Use the chart below to summarize this lesson about building missions in California.

Start with Your
CALIFORNIA STANDARDS

4.2 Students describe the social, political, cultural, and economic life and interactions among people of California from the Pre-Columbian societies to the Spanish mission and Mexican rancho periods.

4.2.3 Describe the Spanish exploration and colonization of California, including the relationships among soldiers, missionaries, and Indians.

Trace the routes followed by the soldiers and missionaries as they traveled north through Baja California to Alta California.
(Begins on page 155)

4.2.4 Describe the mapping of, geographic basis of, and economic factors in the placement and function of the Spanish missions; and understand how the mission system expanded the influence of Spain and Catholicism throughout New Spain and Latin America.

Explore the reasons for Spain's new interest in California.
(Begins on page 155)

▼ The Spanish traveled through rugged California lands.

1765 | 1770 | 1775

1769 The Sacred Expedition begins; Mission San Diego founded

1770 Mission San Carlos Borromeo at Monterey founded

After Vizcaíno's journey, the Spanish ignored California for more than 150 years. In the 1700s, Vitus Bering explored Alaska for Russia. Spain began to worry that the Russians would go even farther south—into lands it claimed in California.

The Spanish Return 4.2.3 4.2.4

In 1765 a special officer of the Spanish king named José de Gálvez came up with a plan. He wanted Spain to set up **missions** in Alta, or upper California. A mission is a religious settlement where Spanish priests taught Native Americans the Roman Catholic faith. The priests who worked at the missions were called **missionaries**. A missionary teaches religious beliefs to those who have different beliefs.

Gálvez warned the Spanish government that other countries would soon be interested in California. Russian hunters were already trapping sea otters on lands along the coast north of California. Gálvez insisted that it would not be long before the Russians moved south. Concerned, the Spanish government agreed to Gálvez's plan.

Planning the Expedition

Gálvez quickly organized the ships and supplies for the expedition. He chose Gaspar de Portolá (GAHS pahr de port oh LAH), a captain in the Spanish army, to lead the expedition. Gálvez then asked a Spanish priest named Junípero Serra (hoo NEE per oh SE rah) to set up the missions. Father Serra already headed missions in Baja, or lower, California. He was happy to join what he called a "Sacred Expedition." Sacred means having religious importance.

REVIEW Why did José de Gálvez want to create missions in California? *Summarize*

80 CTS JOSÉ DE GALVEZ CORREOS ESPAÑA F. N. M. T.

Spanish banner from 1765 ▶

The "Sacred Expedition" 4.2.3 4.2.4

Gálvez chose the expedition's route. Three groups would travel by sea. Two groups would go by land. They would all meet in San Diego to build a **settlement** or new community.

Most of the settlers would go on to Monterey Bay. Gálvez had read Vizcaíno's description of Monterey Bay. He believed that it would be the best port to protect Spain's claim to California.

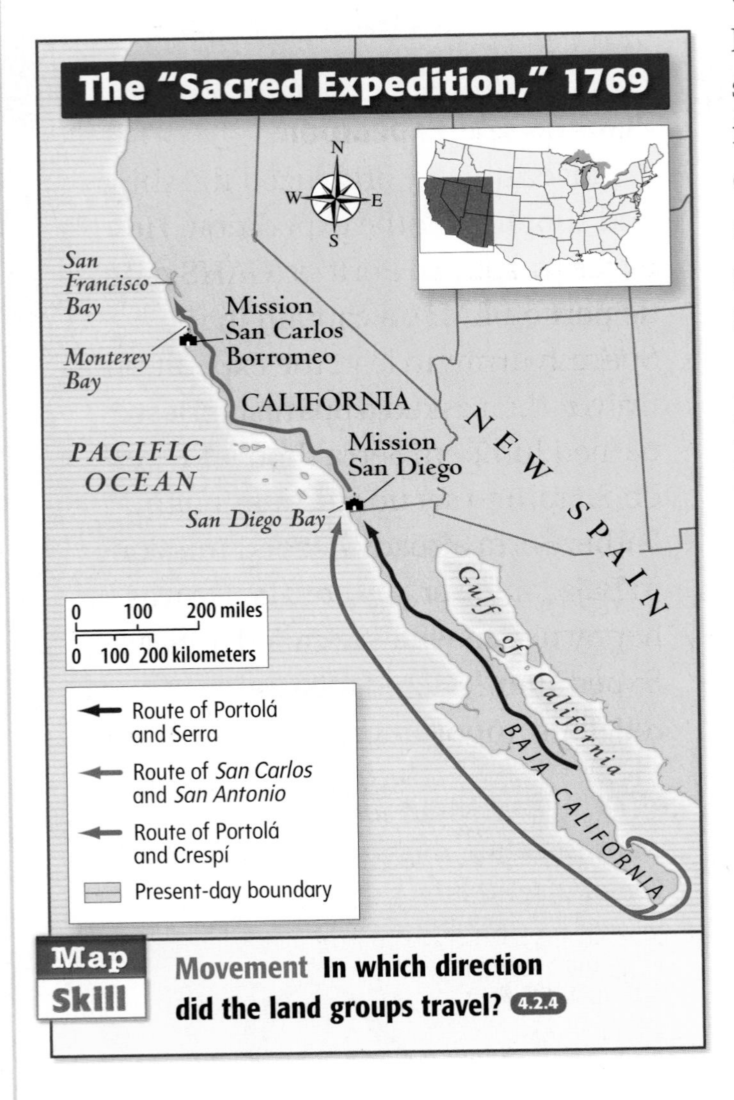

Map Skill **Movement** **In which direction did the land groups travel?** 4.2.4

Gálvez picked many skilled people for the "Sacred Expedition," including missionaries and soldiers to protect them. Many of these people came from Spain. Some were of African ancestry. Native Americans served as guides and translators, mule drivers, and cow herders. Carpenters and blacksmiths also went along. In all, nearly 300 people set out for California.

By Land and Sea

In January 1769 the first ship, the *San Carlos*, set sail from Baja California. More than 60 people shared the small space with supplies, food, and furniture. The ship ran into trouble on its journey. Strong winds swept the ship far out to sea. Many of the sailors got sick. The ship finally arrived in San Diego Bay at the end of April.

The second ship, the *San Antonio*, had already arrived. Its crew, too, had become sick. The final ship was lost at sea.

Meanwhile, the land expeditions were marching north. The first group left Baja California in March. The 70 men included soldiers and Native Americans from Baja California.

Father Juan Crespí (kres PEE), a friend of Father Serra, was also part of the group. His journal of the trip described the difficulty of crossing the dry lands of Baja California.

▲ Ships on Gálvez's expedition experienced rough seas. Astrolabes (right) helped sailors map their routes at sea.

The second land group was led by Gaspar de Portolá. This group brought more supplies and animals. It left Baja California in May. Father Serra traveled with this group. He was in great pain. His leg, which had been infected years before, was swollen and sore. Portolá asked Father Serra to go back, but Serra refused saying:

> ***"Even though I should die on the way, I shall not turn back."***

Arrival at San Diego

The land expeditions arrived in San Diego Bay in the late spring of 1769. Each group had covered nearly 300 miles in about 50 days. The sight of the two ships waiting in the bay filled Father Serra with joy. Soon the work of building a mission could begin.

On July 16, 1769, Serra set up a religious altar sheltered by branches. He held a church service. Then he dedicated the first mission in Alta California, naming it San Diego de Alcalá (san di AY goh de al ca LA).

REVIEW How many groups traveled on the Sacred Expedition?
Main Idea and Details

◀ Gaspar de Portolá did not recognize Monterey Bay when he first marched past it.

Spanish Settlements 4.2.3 4.2.4

Reaching San Diego Bay was the first goal of the "Sacred Expedition." The second goal was to locate Monterey Bay. After two weeks of rest, Portolá set out to find Monterey. Along with Father Crespí and those who were well enough to travel, Portolá marched north.

Father Serra stayed in San Diego to care for the ill. He also started making plans for the mission there. Within a few weeks, Father Serra was able to begin work on the mission.

Looking for Monterey

Portolá's group traveled slowly. Scouts had to go ahead each day to look for paths and water. Along the way, the group saw hills, valleys, mountains, and mesas.

Portolá and his group traveled through what are today Los Angeles, Santa Barbara, and San Simeon. They followed trails used by Native Americans. This route would one day connect all the California missions from San Diego to Sonoma. It would come to be known as "El Camino Real," or the King's Highway.

Continuing north, Portolá's group went right past Monterey Bay. They may have missed it because Vizcaíno described the bay as being much larger than it actually was. Beyond Monterey they came to Point San Pedro. From this place they saw a valley, which they called Santa Clara.

Turning Back

On November 1, 1769, Portolá's group reached San Francisco Bay. This was as far north as Portolá went. Disappointed because he thought he had not found Monterey Bay, Portolá returned to San Diego on January 24, 1770.

A Chain of Missions

With Portolá gone, Father Serra had taken charge of building the settlement at San Diego. The mission had gotten off to a slow start. The group had little food or supplies and many of the men were too sick to work. In the first few months, they managed to build only a few mud buildings and a log fort.

Meanwhile, Portolá remained determined to find Monterey Bay. In April 1770 he, along with Father Serra, again set out to find it. In May the party arrived at Point Pinos. They had found the Monterey Bay Vizcaíno had described.

On June 3, 1770, Father Serra and Portolá founded the second mission of California in Monterey. This mission, San Carlos Borromeo, became Serra's headquarters. Between 1769 and 1782, Serra set up nine missions between San Diego and San Francisco.

After Serra's death other missions were founded. A total of 21 missions stretched from San Diego to Sonoma.

REVIEW On which of Portolá's three trips did he and his group finally find Monterey Bay? *Main Idea and Details*

What You Learned

- 4.2.3 4.2.4 José de Gálvez sent an expedition of soldiers and missionaries to set up Spanish missions in Alta California.
- 4.2.3 4.2.4 Gaspar de Portolá and Father Junípero Serra located San Diego Bay and set up a mission.
- 4.2.3 4.2.4 Gaspar de Portolá continued the expedition to find Monterey Bay; Father Serra founded nine of the 21 missions in California.

Lesson Review

1. **Focus Question** Why did the Spanish want to set up missions in Alta California? 4.2.4
2. **Vocabulary** Write one sentence for each vocabulary word. 4.2.3 4.2.4
   mission **missionary** **settlement**
3. **Geography** Why didn't Portolá find Monterey Bay? 4.2.4
4. **Critical Thinking** **Make Decisions** How do you think the Spanish government's decision to build missions affected the future of California? 4.2.3 4.2.4
5. **Reading Strategy** **Summarize** Reread the section of the lesson called "Spanish Settlements." Use the chart to summarize events in this section. 4.2.4 ELA R2.1

6. **Write about THE BIG IDEA** What prompted the Spanish to return to California? 4.2.3 ELA W2.1
7. **Link to Language Arts** Write a journal entry about a class trip. Be sure to use adjectives in your writing. ELA W2.1

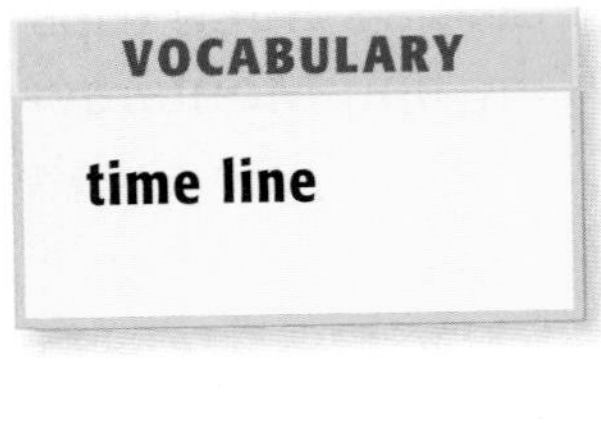

Read Time Lines 4.2.3

To understand history, you need to know when things happened. You also need to know the order in which things happened. A **time line** can help you do this. A time line is a diagram that shows when events took place. You can use this useful tool to figure out the date an event happened, such as the date a mission was founded. A time line also shows whether one event happened before or after another event. You can use the notches on the time line to find out how much time passed between each event.

VOCABULARY

time line

- Read the title of the time line. The title of time line is "Gaspar de Portolá." The title summarizes the main focus of the time line.
- Find out how many years each part on the time line shows. Time lines are usually divided into parts. Each part covers a certain number of years. On Portolá's time line, each part is 10 years.
- Read the captions from left to right. The earliest event on a time line is on the left side. Each event to the right happens after that. The last event on the right side of the time line shows the most recent event. On Portola's time line, you can see the date of Portolá's birth on the left. The date of his death is on the right.

Gaspar de Portolá

2 Try It

Look at the time line on page 160 to answer the questions.

- Did Portolá reach Monterey before or after he became governor of Puebla?
- In what year did Portolá go on the "Sacred Expedition"?
- How many years passed between Portolá's journey on the "Sacred Expedition" and his death?

3 Apply It

Use the time line on this page to answer the questions below.

- When was the first mission founded?
- How many years were there between the founding of the first California mission and Mission San Gabriel?
- When was Mission San Antonio founded?

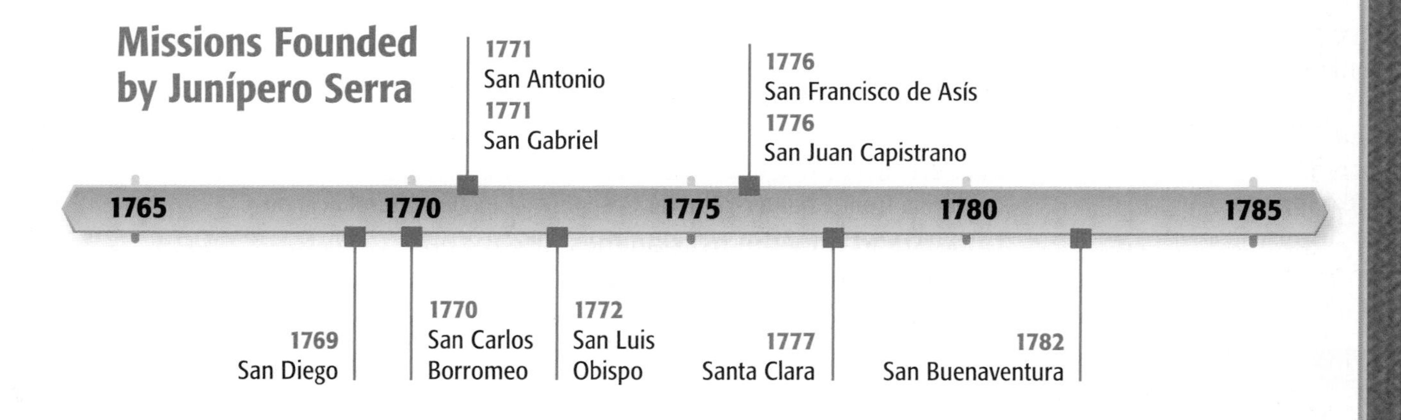

Mission San Carlos Borromeo, Carmel, California ▼

The Impact of the Missions

FOCUS QUESTION

How did mission life affect California's Native Americans?

VOCABULARY

convert
epidemic
neophyte
revolt

VOCABULARY STRATEGY

WORD ORIGINS The word **epidemic** comes from a Greek word that means "among the people." An **epidemic** happens when a disease spreads quickly among a group of people.

READING STRATEGY

Identify Main Idea and Details

Use the chart to list the main idea and details about the impact of the missions.

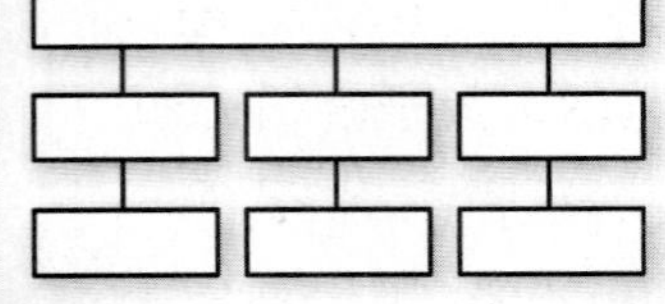

Start with Your CALIFORNIA STANDARDS

4.2 Students describe the social, political, cultural, and economic life and interactions among people of California from the Pre-Columbian societies to the Spanish mission and Mexican rancho periods.

4.2.5 Describe the daily lives of the people, native and nonnative, who occupied the presidios, missions, ranchos, and pueblos.

Learn what a day in a mission might have been like for a Native American. (Begins on page 164)

4.2.6 Discuss the role of the Franciscans in changing the economy of California from a hunter-gatherer economy to an agricultural economy.

Understand how the missionaries' use of land for farming directly affected the traditional ways that Native Americans hunted and gathered their food.
(Begins on page 164)

1765	1770	1775	1780	1785

1769
Kumeyaay attack San Diego mission

1781
Yuma rebel at missions near Colorado River

1785
Toypurina leads a revolt at Mission San Gabriel

Spanish missionaries wanted to teach the Native American people Christianity. The missionaries also wanted to change the Native American way of life—changes that they thought would improve the lives of Native Americans.

Attracting People to the Missions 4.2.5

Native Americans came to live at the missions for different reasons. Curiosity about the Spanish drew some. Others came because they believed the missionaries had a special link to the spirit world. Still others were attracted by the music and ceremony of the Catholic Church services.

Sometimes missionaries went to Native American villages to teach the children about Christianity. They tried to **convert**, or change, the children's beliefs. Then the priests invited the children to come to the missions to learn more about Christianity. Because the parents wanted to be with their children, they too came to live at the missions. At other times, Spanish soldiers used force to bring Native Americans to the missions.

◀ Mission San Luis Rey

As the missions grew, they occupied more and more land that had been Native American hunting grounds. As a result, many Native Americans could no longer hunt and gather enough food for their families. Many hungry families needed food from mission farms to survive.

REVIEW What brought Native Americans to the missions? *Main Idea and Details*

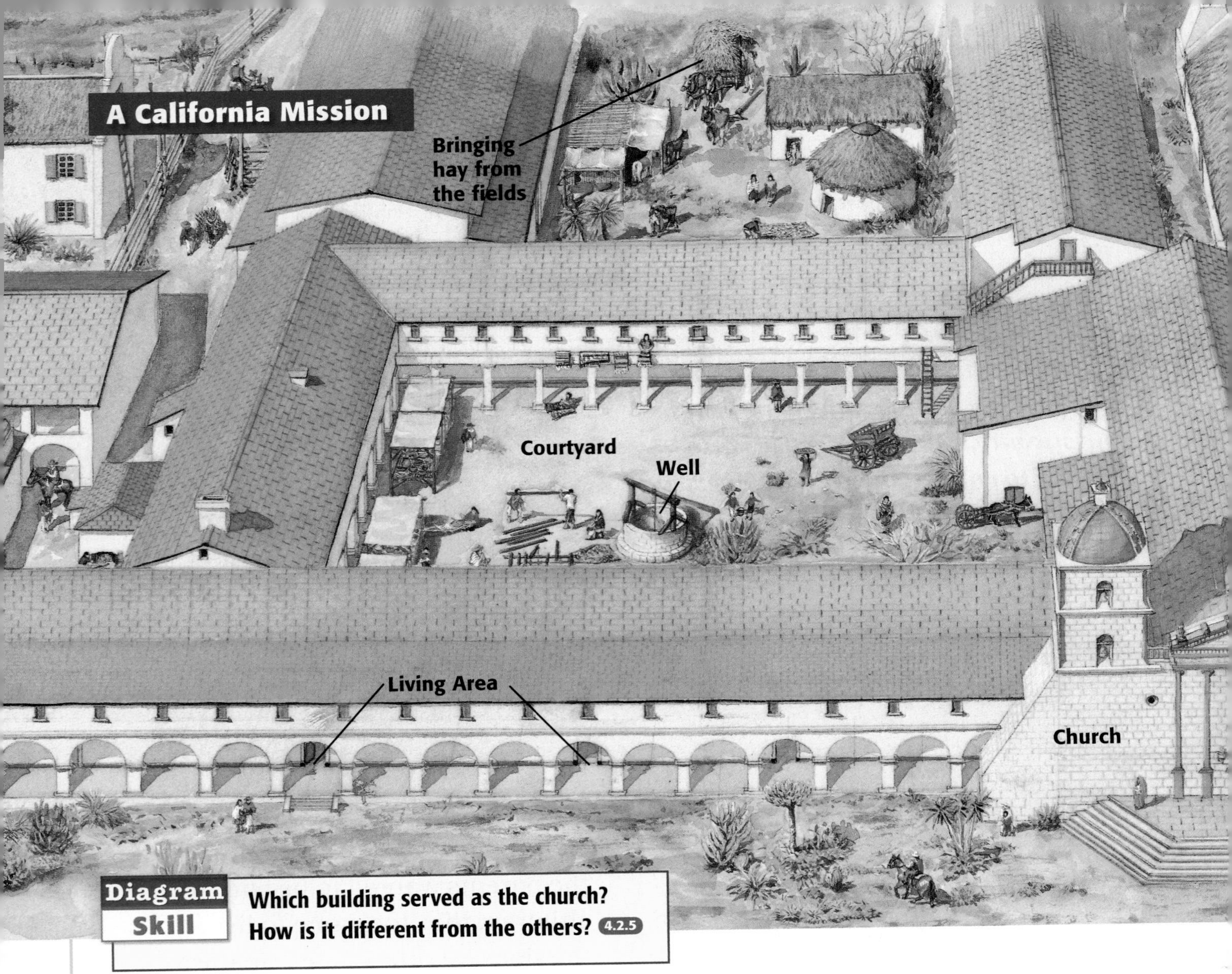

Diagram Skill Which building served as the church? How is it different from the others? 4.2.5

Life at the Missions 4.2.5 4.2.6

Life at a mission involved two main activities—farming and religious services. Native Americans who lived at the missions worked on the mission farms. They planted and harvested crops such as wheat, barley, corn, and squash. Some missions also had fruit orchards and grape vineyards. These were new crops brought by the priests, or padres, to California. The mission farms began California's farming economy.

Daily Life

Native Americans followed a set daily pattern at the missions. After breakfast they went to church and learned about Christianity. In the mornings, some worked in the mission fields or tended the mission animals. Others learned new skills, such as how to be a carpenter or blacksmith. Some made bricks, candles, soap, and other items that the missions needed. At lunchtime, they said more prayers.

Tanning hides

In the evenings, some men returned to work in the fields. The younger men, however, sang and played instruments at choir practice. Girls did not go to choir practice. Those over the age of seven were not allowed to leave their area of the mission.

The missionaries believed that this way of life was better for Native Americans. Father Serra was especially happy to see children thriving at the missions:

> ***"Seeing . . . young children . . . praying . . . hearing them sing . . . playing happily . . . is indeed something moving."***

Still, daily life at a mission could be hard. Often, if the padres thought that someone was doing a poor job or not following the rules, the person would be punished.

No Protection from Diseases

Epidemics of serious diseases killed many Native Americans at the missions. An epidemic occurs when many people catch a disease and pass it along to others in a short period of time. The Spanish had brought many diseases with them. Smallpox, measles, and other diseases were common in Europe, but they were new to Native Americans, who could not fight the diseases off. In addition, crowded conditions in the missions made diseases spread quickly. Mainly because of diseases, the Native American population fell from 300,000 to 100,000 during the mission period.

REVIEW Why did epidemics occur among the Native Americans? *Cause and Effect*

▲ Native Americans at the missions used traditional items, such as these baskets, for their personal use.

Struggles and Hardships 4.2.5

Once Native Americans joined a mission, the missionaries expected them to stay there. They became known as **neophytes** (NEE oh fites), or new believers in Christianity. Native Americans who were born in the missions were also considered neophytes. They were not allowed to leave without permission.

Bartolomea was six years old when Spanish soldiers came to her Tongva village. Years later, Bartolomea's husband, Hugo Reid, described to a Los Angeles newspaper his wife's life as a neophyte. You can read a section from the newspaper article about Bartolomea below.

Native Americans Rebel

Some Native Americans did not like life at the missions. They found ways to keep their traditional ways of life and to practice their own religion in private. They performed native songs and dances.

Other Native Americans resisted learning the Spanish language or pretended not to know it. Still others broke tools or worked slowly on purpose.

Native Americans resisted in other ways, too. Many of them ran away from the missions, while others stole horses and cattle from mission stockyards. Still others attacked the padres physically.

Primary Sources

Bartolomea

A section from

The Los Angeles Star
by Hugo Reid
1852

"The men were instructed to throw their bows and arrows at the feet of the priest. . . . The infants were then baptized, as were also all children under eight years of age. . . . The women ***consented*** *to [be baptized] . . . for the love they* ***bore*** *their children; and finally the males gave away [to be with] wife and family."*

consented agreed **bore** felt for

How were Native American children used to persuade parents to join the missions?

▲ The missions influenced the way Native Americans ate and dressed.

Toypurina ▶

Organizing Attacks

Groups of Native Americans organized **revolts**, or violent attacks. Not long after the Mission San Diego was founded in 1769, hundreds of Kumeyaay tried to drive out the missionaries. Six years later, a more organized attack resulted in the death of a padre. The biggest revolt came in 1781, when the Yuma people destroyed two missions on the Colorado River. Thirty soldiers and four missionaries died in the attack.

In 1785 a Tongva woman named Toypurina helped other Native Americans to plan an attack on Mission San Gabriel. Toypurina was a shaman, or religious leader, who had not joined the Roman Catholic religion. She convinced an important chief to tell Native Americans at the mission to follow her and not the padres.

In October, six Native American villages attacked the mission and tried to destroy the settlement. However, Spanish soldiers captured the rebels. Toypurina was put on trial. At her trial, Toypurina stated that she commanded a chief to attack because

> ***"she was angry with the priests and all the others at the mission, because we (the Spanish) were living on their land."***

Toypurina and the other rebel leaders were found guilty of the plan against the Spanish.

Opposing Views

As you have read, many Native Americans rebelled against living in the missions. However, there were others who enjoyed life there. Pablo Tac was born at the Mission San Luis Rey. He had good memories of mission life. Tac was a good student and was treated well by the padres. In 1833, at the age of 12, Tac was specially chosen to travel to Rome with the missionaries. In Rome, he learned about the practices of the Roman Catholic Church.

While there, Tac taught the people of Rome about his Native American culture. Tac died in Rome in 1841. He never returned to his mission.

REVIEW What are some ways that Native Americans rebelled against the missions? *Summarize*

What You Learned

4.2.5 The missionaries used many methods to draw Native Americans to the missions, including giving them food, instructing their children, and using force.

4.2.5 4.2.6 The missionaries thought that teaching Native Americans Christianity was a good thing. Native Americans often received harsh treatment at the missions, however, and many of them died of diseases.

4.2.5 Some Native Americans revolted against the missions in many ways including running away or attacking the missionaries. Some Native Americans, however, enjoyed their life in missions.

Lesson Review

1. **Focus Question** How did mission life affect California's Native Americans? (4.2.5, 4.2.6)
2. **Vocabulary** Write one sentence for each vocabulary word. (4.2.5, 4.2.6)
   convert **neophyte**
   epidemic **revolt**
3. **Economics** What impact did the missions have on the Native Americans' hunting and gathering economy? (4.2.6)
4. **Critical Thinking** **Problem Solving** In what ways did the Native Americans resist the missionaries? (4.2.5)
5. **Reading Strategy** **Identify Main Idea and Details** Reread the section called "Attracting People to the Missions." Use the chart to list the main idea and details of this section. (4.2.5, ELA R2.1)

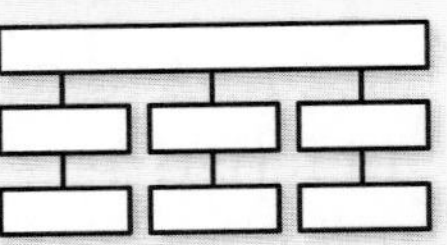

6. **Write about THE BIG IDEA** Write about how your life might be changed by newcomers who come to your area. (4.2.5)
7. **Link to Science** When the Spanish came to California, they used the land in an entirely different way. Write a paragraph pointing out how farming changed the Native Americans' environment. (4.2.5, 4.2.6)

Biography

Focus on Dedication

4.2.3

Junípero Serra 1713–1784

Junípero Serra was born on the Spanish island of Majorca. While still young, he became a Franciscan priest. Eager to be a missionary, he set off for Baja California in 1749.

For the next 15 years, Serra dedicated himself to teaching Native Americans the Roman Catholic religion. Serra was 54 years old when he joined the "Sacred Expedition" in 1767. While he suffered from a breathing disorder called asthma, and limped, Serra took on his work with enthusiasm. In all, he founded a total of nine missions near the California coast. After arriving in 1769, he wrote about the Native American people he met near San Diego:

> ***"They treated us with as much confidence and goodwill as if they had known us all their lives."***

Father Serra's efforts changed California's history. Today, many people believe that Serra and the other missionaries treated the Native Americans too harshly. Yet Serra's leadership helped to give California its rich Spanish heritage.

Write About It! **How did Father Serra affect California's future?**

For more about Junípero Serra, visit:

socialstudies.macmillanmh.com/ss/ca/bios

The Life of Junípero Serra

1710 1720 1730 1740 1750 1760 1770 1780 1790

- **1713** Born in Majorca
- **1749** Travels as a missionary to Mexico
- **1767** Appointed leader of expedition to settle California missions
- **1769** Founds first mission in San Diego
- **1784** Dies on August 28

Mission San Juan Capistrano, halfway between San Diego and Los Angeles, was founded in November 1776. It was the seventh mission founded by Father Serra.

Today, the rebuilt Mission San Juan Capistrano is called the "Jewel of the Missions." You can still see the chapel in which Father Serra held church services. Take a tour of the historic mission.

2 Serra's Chapel

Go through the archway and into the courtyard. From here you can visit the workrooms, the sleeping areas, and the chapel where Father Serra held services 200 years ago. ▼

1 The Great Stone Church ▲

Step into the ruins of the original Great Stone Church. Built with the help of Native Americans, the church was ruined by an earthquake just six years after its completion in 1806.

❸ Mission Bells ▲

Next door to the old church you will see a small garden. Two of the four bells in the wall hung in the building's original bell tower, which collapsed into the church during the earthquake.

The Swallows

Each year, thousands of birds called swallows migrate north from South America. For nearly 200 years, they have arrived in mid-March to build their nests at the mission. Their arrival is celebrated with a festival every March 19. ▼

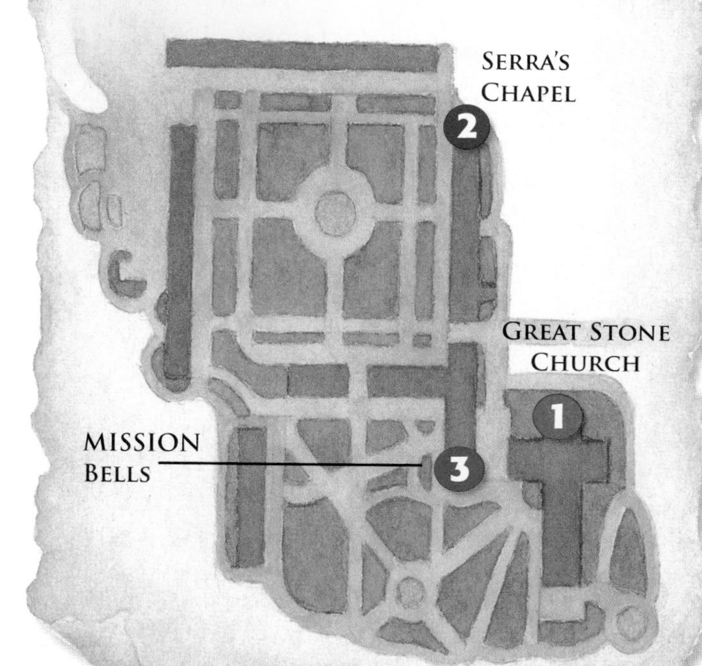

ACTIVITY

Use the map to lead a walking tour from the Great Stone Church to Father Serra's Chapel. Your directions should discuss what visitors can see once they are in the courtyard.

LOG ON For more about Mission San Juan Capistrano, visit:

www.macmillanmh.com/ss/ca/fieldtrips

LESSON 3

Building a Colony

FOCUS QUESTION

How did the Spanish oversee their new settlements in California?

VOCABULARY

presidio
pueblo
tax
pobladores
alcalde

VOCABULARY STRATEGY

WORD ORIGINS Many words that we use today, such as **pueblo** and **presidio,** come from Spanish. Find the Spanish origins of these words: **plaza, canyon.**

READING STRATEGY

Sequence Events
Use the chart to sequence events in this lesson about building a colony.

Start with Your CALIFORNIA STANDARDS

4.2 Students describe the social, political, cultural, and economic life and interactions among people of California from the Pre-Columbian societies to the Spanish mission and Mexican rancho periods.

4.2.3 Describe the Spanish exploration and colonization of California, including the relationships among soldiers, missionaries, and Indians.

Find out about the lives of the Spanish soldiers who manned the forts and guarded the missions. (Begins on page 174)

4.2.4 Describe the mapping of, geographic basis of, and economic factors in the placement and function of the Spanish missions; and understand how the mission system expanded the influence of Spain and Catholicism throughout New Spain and Latin America.

Follow the growth of Spain's colony in California as new missions, forts, and towns were built. (Begins on page 173)

4.2.5 Describe the daily lives of the people, native and nonnative, who occupied the presidios, missions, ranchos, and pueblos.

Learn about new settlers who founded some of California's earliest cities. (Begins on page 176)

Mission Dolores, San Francisco ▼

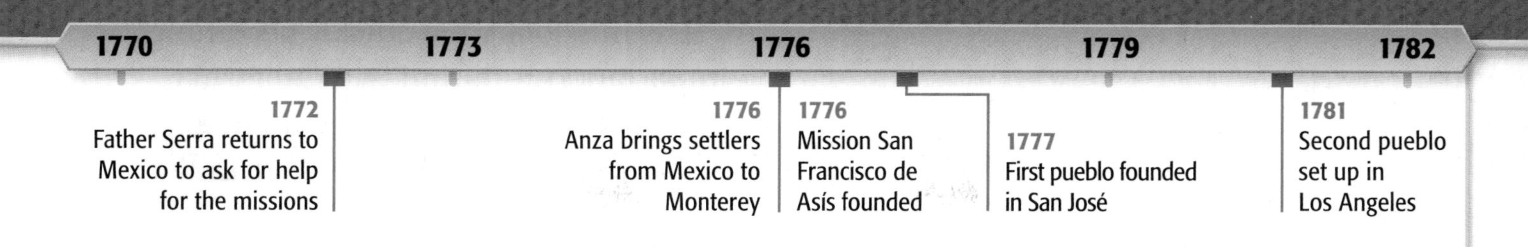

Padres built the missions close to Native American villages. The Spanish soldiers built forts near the missions to guard them. Towns were then built near these forts. Native American trails linked all of these settlements.

Supplies and Settlers 4.2.4

By 1772 Father Serra had already set up five missions in Alta California. Each mission had a few small buildings.

Serra knew he needed help to set up more missions. In 1772 he made a long journey to Mexico City. There, he asked the government to help keep his missions supplied and to help build new ones.

Spain was worried that other countries wanted California. In the late 1760s English sea captain James Cook had sailed to islands in the Pacific. The Spanish king feared Cook's voyage might encourage England to try to claim California. Spain wanted to strengthen its open areas in New Spain to stop such an invasion. These concerns helped Serra get the money and supplies he needed from the Mexican government.

The Trail From Mexico to California

Juan Bautista de Anza was a Spanish captain. He knew that a trail used by Native Americans led to Alta California. The new land route to Alta California started in Tubac in what is today Arizona.

In 1774, Anza led a small group north. With the help of Yuma Indians, the group found its way across the mountains, deserts, and rivers along the trail. After traveling more than 500 miles, they reached Mission San Gabriel in Alta California.

Anza then retraced his route to Tubac. Now that he knew the way, he wanted to take a large group of colonists to Alta California. The Spanish leaders, eager to strengthen Spain's position with more settlements there, gave him their support.

REVIEW What happened when Father Serra went to Mexico City in 1772? *Sequence Events*

Making Missions Strong 4.2.3 4.2.5

Anza convinced 240 settlers—men, women, and children—to leave from Tubac in October 1775. The families who followed Anza's trail endured a tough journey. Fathers carried their children across rivers, deserts, and mountains. After five months, the group arrived in Monterey. They had forged a new trail to California.

Anza's settlers then went to the San Francisco Bay. They founded a fort in September 1776. The next month, Father Francisco Palóu founded Mission San Francisco de Asís, the sixth mission in the chain.

The missions were quickly becoming important communities in California. The **presidios** that protected them were just as important. Presidios were military forts where the Spanish soldiers lived.

The Presidios

Spain built presidios at San Diego, Monterey, San Francisco, and Santa Barbara. All were built near the missions and had sources of fresh water nearby. They were also built where the Spanish could defend the harbors against foreign attack.

They could also defend the missions against attack or revolt by Native

Diagram Skill Why do you think the soldiers' homes were near the guard house? 4.2.5

Americans. If a revolt took place at a mission, soldiers from the nearby presidio would be sent to help. They also served to guide the padres as they traveled to Native American villages and between the missions.

Leather-Jacket Soldiers

The missions relied on the soldiers at the presidios for protection. About 10 soldiers lived and worked at each presidio. In addition to their military duties, the soldiers helped in exploring, hunting, building, and farming. They also delivered letters between the missions.

Commander's house

Leather-jacket soldiers protected the missions. ▶

Soldiers from the presidios were called *soldados de cuera*, or "leather-jacket soldiers." They were called this because of the leather armor they wore. Their long jackets with no sleeves were made of the hides of animals. The leather, which covered the soldiers from shoulders to knees, could stop arrows.

The soldiers carried a variety of weapons. They had a type of gun called a musket. They also used spears and swords. Long spears proved deadly during battles against Native Americans. The soldiers rode on horseback and used the spears against Native Americans who fought on foot.

The leather-jacket soldiers had a reputation for strength and bravery. Miguel Costansó traveled with Portolá's expedition to California. He praised the soldiers on the journey:

> ***"We do not hesitate to say that they are the best horsemen in the world."***

REVIEW What might have happened to the missions without the soldiers in the presidios? *Cause and Effect*

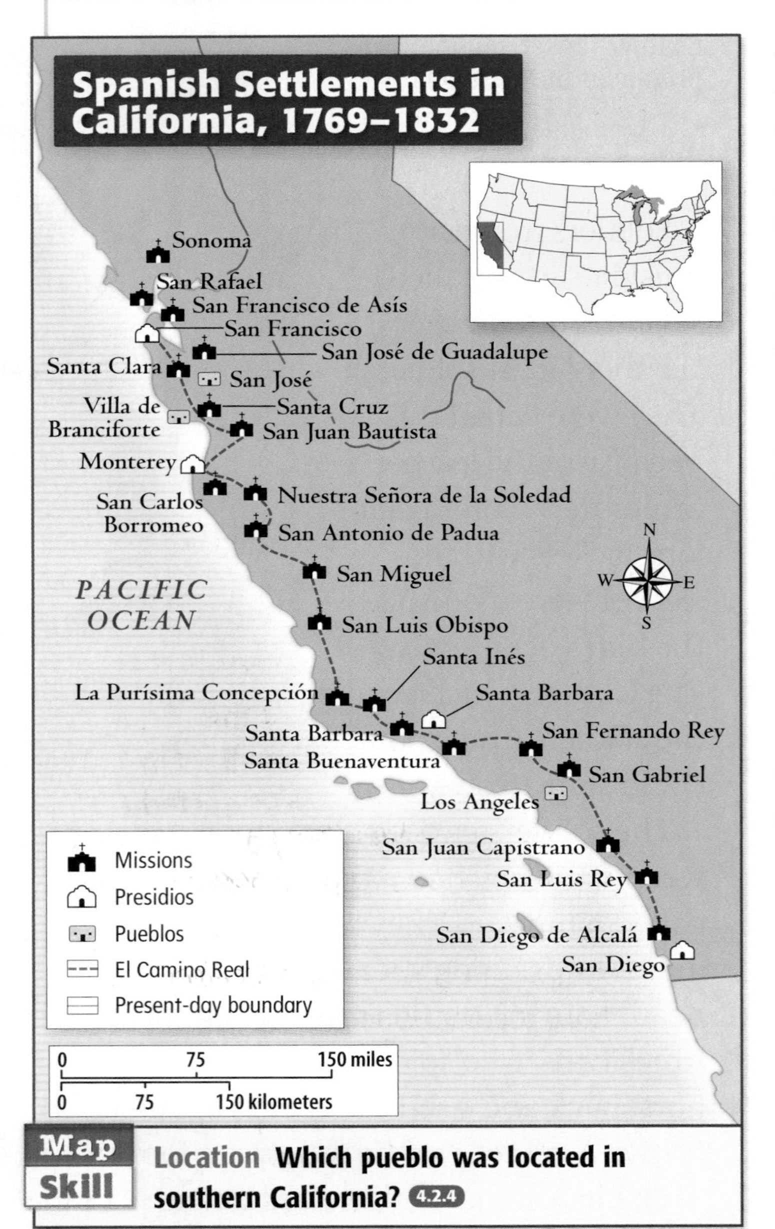

Map Skill **Location** **Which pueblo was located in southern California?** 4.2.4

New Kinds of Settlements 4.2.4 4.2.5

In addition to the missions and presidios, the Spanish started a third type of settlement in California. Spain ordered the founding of **pueblos**. Pueblos were towns that focused on farming.

The Spanish government wanted to attract new settlers to the pueblos. In exchange for agreeing to sell food to the presidios, settlers received land and animals. They were also given tools, clothing, and farming supplies. The government did not require settlers to pay **taxes** for five years. Taxes are the money people pay to a government for public services.

The First Pueblos

Don Felipe de Neve founded the first pueblo in California. De Neve was the governor of both Baja and Alta California. In 1777, he founded the pueblo of San José, south of San Francisco Bay.

Many different kinds of settlers came to San José. Some of the first settlers of San José had come to Alta California with Captain Anza. Some were people with Spanish and Native American parents. Others had a mix of African and Spanish backgrounds.

Governor de Neve built a second pueblo in the south. He called it Nuestra Senõra la Reina de Los Angeles del Río de Porciúncula, which is known today as Los Angeles. He recruited 11 families, who were known as ***pobladores***, or settlers, to live there. Two out of every three of these

Don Felipe de Neve ▶

settlers were of African descent. The third pueblo in California, Villa de Brancifortes, is near today's city of Santa Cruz.

Pueblo Government

The pueblos had a well-organized system of government. Each pueblo had an **alcalde** (ahl CAHL de), or mayor, who was also a judge. There was also a city council, or *ayuntamiento* (ah YUN ta mee en toh). The members of the council were called *regidores* (re hee DOR es). They helped to manage the public affairs of the pueblo.

The residents of the pueblos struggled at first. Farming was difficult, and the pueblo residents were very poor. Over time, however, the tiny pueblos of San José and Los Angeles grew to be large and successful.

REVIEW What helped the pueblos to be successful? *Main Idea and Details*

United States
At the Same Time

At the same time that Spain was settling California, the 13 English colonies along North America's eastern coast were fighting for their independence from England. The English colonists approved the Declaration of Independence in 1776.

What You Learned

4.2.4 Juan Bautista de Anza took settlers to California on a new overland route.

4.2.3 4.2.5 Presidios were built near the missions. The Spanish soldiers in the presidios and missions protected and helped the padres. They also guarded the settlements from attacks by other nations.

4.2.4 4.2.5 Spain set up pueblos in California to help provide food for the presidios.

Lesson Review

1. **Focus Question** How did the Spanish oversee their new settlements in California? 4.2.3 4.2.4
2. **Vocabulary** Write one sentence for each vocabulary word. 4.2.4 4.2.5

alcalde	**presidio**	**tax**
pobladores	**pueblo**	

3. **Government** How was the government of each pueblo organized? 4.2.4
4. **Critical Thinking** **Make Decisions** What decision of Father Serra's was important in getting money and supplies for the California missions? 4.2.5 4.2.6
5. **Reading Strategy** **Sequence Events** Reread the section of this lesson called "New Kinds of Settlements." Use the chart to sequence events in this section. 4.2.4 ELA R2.1

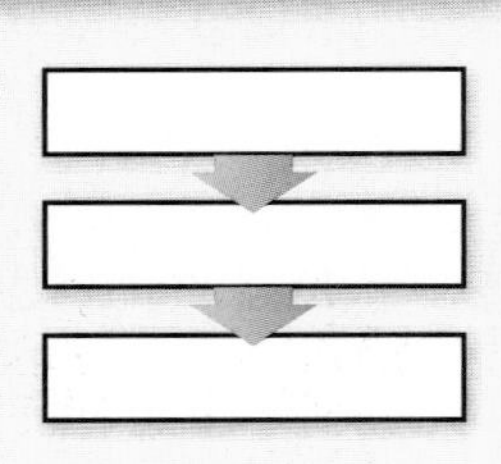

6. **Write about THE BIG IDEA** Why were the pueblos important in the process of building a Spanish colony in California? 4.2.5 ELA W2.1
7. **Link to Art** Suppose you are given the job of making a plan for buildings in a small town. Show the kinds of buildings and places in your plan. Label the buildings and places. 4.2.4

CHAPTER 5

Chapter Review

Vocabulary Review

Copy the sentences below on a separate sheet of paper. Use the list of vocabulary words to fill in the blanks.

missionary	**revolt**
presidio	**tax**

1. (4.2.3) A person who taught the Christian religion to Native Americans of California was a ______.

2. (4.2.5) A fort where Spanish soldiers lived was called a ______.

3. (4.2.3) A ______ is money people pay to the government for public services.

4. (4.2.3) A ______ is a violent attack.

5. (4.2.3) **Test Preparation** The ______, or mayor, also served as a judge.

- **A. pueblo**
- **B. padre**
- **C. alcalde**
- **D. neophyte**

Comprehension Check

6. (4.2.3) How did José de Gálvez prepare for the "Sacred Expedition"?

7. (4.2.3) How many settlers traveled with Anza from Mexico to Monterey?

8. (4.2.5) Why did the soldiers wear armor made of animal skins?

9. (4.2.6) Why did Spain want to set up farming communities in California?

10. (4.2.4) How did settlers attract Native Americans to the missions?

11. (4.2.3) **Critical Thinking** Why do you think Father Serra was chosen to set up the new chain of missions?

12. (4.2.3) **Critical Thinking** Why was it important for Spain to set up many settlements in California?

Use the Time Line

Use the time line below to answer each question.

13. (4.2.4) Which pueblo was founded first, the one in Los Angeles or the one in San José?

14. (4.2.3) How many years after the "Sacred Expedition" was the Monterey Mission founded?

1765 — 1770 — 1775 — 1780 — 1785

- **1769** The "Sacred Expedition" begins
- **1770** A mission was founded in Monterey
- **1777** A pueblo was set up in San José
- **1781** A pueblo was set up in Los Angeles

Skills Check

Write a complete sentence to answer each question.

1540 | 1555 | 1570 | 1585 | 1600 | 1615

1542
Cabrillo anchors at San Diego Bay in Alta California

1577
Francis Drake sails from England to New Spain

1579
Drake repairs the ship on California's coast

1595
Sebastián Rodriguez Cermeño sails to Drake's Bay

1602
Sebastián Vizcaíno sails to Monterey

Read Time Lines

15. (4.2.3) What is the last event that appears on the time line?

16. (4.2.3) Did Francis Drake sail to New Spain before or after Sebastián Rodriguez Cermeño sailed to Drake's Bay?

17. (4.2.3) **Test Preparation** Cabrillo anchored at San Diego Bay in ______.

18. (4.2.3) **Test Preparation** Drake repaired his ship on California's coast _____ years after he sailed from England to New Spain.

Using Primary Sources

Artifacts

19. (4.2) How can artifacts help you understand more about the Spanish influence in California?

20. (4.2) What might you be able to learn from Native American artifacts found at a mission?

Hands-on Activity

21. (4.2.3) **Make a Brochure** Suppose you were working with Anza to convince people to join his mission. Create a poster that answers this question:

Why should settlers move to Alta California?

Write About History

22. (4.2.5, ELA W2.1) **Narrative** Write a short story about a Native American boy or girl who lives near a mission in California in the 1700s. Describe what his or her life is like.

LOG ON For help with the process of writing, visit:

www.macmillanmh.com/ss/ca/writing

Unit Review and Test Prep

Comprehension and Critical Thinking Check

Write one or more sentences to answer each question.

1. How did the **Ice Age** affect where people lived thousands of years ago? 4.2.1
2. Why did the early people of California have such a **diversity** of languages and cultures? 4.2.1
3. Why are the Chumash considered expert boat builders? 4.2.1
4. Why did Modoc hunters spend time in **sweat lodges**? 4.2.1
5. Which areas of California's coast did Cabrillo explore during his **expedition**? 4.2.2
6. Why did Ferrelo stop his search for the **Strait** of Anián? 4.2.2
7. What kind of **settlements** did the Spanish build in New Spain? 4.2.3
8. How were the locations for each **presidio** chosen? 4.2.3
9. **Critical Thinking** Why did the Northern Paiute people often **trade** to get food? 4.2.1
10. **Critical Thinking** Why did the Spanish Conquistadors become interested in Alta California 1765? 4.2.4

Reading Social Studies Check

Summarize

Copy this graphic organizer. Reread "The Sacred Expedition," beginning on page 156. Use the graphic organizer to summarize the passage. Then answer the questions. 4.2.3 ELA R2.1

Paragraph 1	Paragraph 2	Paragraph 3

11. What is a summary? ELA R2.1
12. What did you look for to summarize in the passage? ELA R2.1
13. Would you include the following details: "Strong winds swept the ship far out to sea. Many of the sailors got sick." in your summary? ELA R2.1

Test Preparation

Read the paragraphs. Then answer the questions.

Father Junípero Serra was 50 years old when he started the Alta California missions. During that time he faced many hardships. He was very thin, suffered from asthma, and had an injured leg. But he was determined to build new missions for Spain.

By 1773 Father Serra had set up five missions. He knew he would need help to start others. So he traveled all the way back to Mexico.

Mexican officials gave Father Serra more money. They provided more soldiers to help protect the missions, too. He also asked them to help set up a land route into Alta California. That way new settlers would not have to take the difficult voyage across the sea.

Father Serra died in 1784. By then he had set up nine missions. Other priests continued his work. In the end there were 18 missions, all of which tightened Spain's hold on Alta California.

14. What is the main idea of this passage?
4.2.3

A Father Serra worked hard to set up missions in Alta California.

B In 1773 Father Serra went back to Mexico to ask for money.

C Father Serra was 50 years old when he traveled to Alta California.

D Father Serra died in 1784.

15. Which of these is an opinion from the passage?
4.2.3

A Father Serra's injured leg caused him a lot of problems.

B The sea voyage from Mexico to California was difficult.

C Father Serra constantly argued with Mexican officials.

D Father Serra did not like to travel by boat.

Write About History

16. Expository Write a brief essay that compares the Yokuts and the Modoc.
4.2.1 ELA W2.3

17. Letter Suppose you are a Spanish explorer in the 1500s. You want to sail to North America but need to pay for a ship and supplies. Write a letter to the king to convince him to give you the money.
4.2.2 ELA W2.1

18. Narrative Write a poem that tells what it might have been like to be a soldier working at a presidio in California.
4.2.3 ELA W2.1

LOG ON For help with the process of writing visit:

www.macmillanmh.com/ss/ca/writing

What happens when different peoples first meet?

Write About the Big Idea ELA W2.1

Narrative Essay

Think about what happened as Europeans met the native peoples in California. Then, complete the graphic organizer with details.

Use your graphic organizer below to help you write an essay that answers the Big Idea question "What happens when different peoples first meet?" Describe what happened when Spanish explorers, missionaries, soldiers, and settlers met the Native Americans who lived in California.

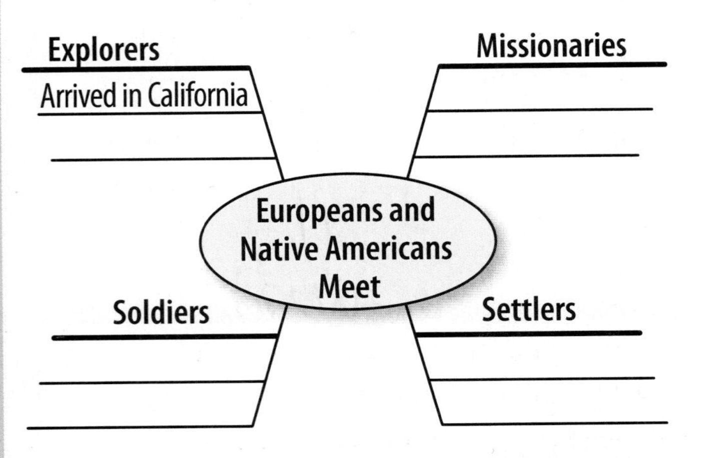

Write a Narrative Essay

1. Plan

- To begin, you will need to decide what your essay topic is. Here it has already been assigned.
- Next, develop a plan. Your narrative should tell a story. You should show the reader why these events are worth remembering.

2. Write a First Draft

- Decide what your readers need to know.
- Focus on getting your thoughts on paper.

3. Revise and Proofread

- Read your narrative essay. Be sure you included the main events and the details that explain them.
- Proofread your narrative essay. Fix any errors in spelling, capitalization, and punctuation.
- Rewrite your essay neatly before you give it to your teacher.

ACTIVITY

Speak About the Big Idea ELA LS2.1

An Interview

Recall the people you read about in Unit 2. Create an interview about how life changed. For example, you might interview a Native American about life before the Spanish and life in a Spanish mission.

Prepare Work in pairs. One person in the pair will be the interviewee. That person will tell personal observations and experiences. The other will conduct the interview. Together, prepare a list of questions and answers. Gather information from your textbook, your graphic organizer, and other research. Practice your interview.

Present The interviewer should introduce his or her guest. Then partners should take two or three minutes to act out their interview for the rest of the class.

For help with the Big Idea activity, visit:

www.macmillanmh.com/ss/ca/launchpad

Read More About the Big Idea

Native Ways

Malcolm Margolin This is a collection of stories and traditions from California native peoples.

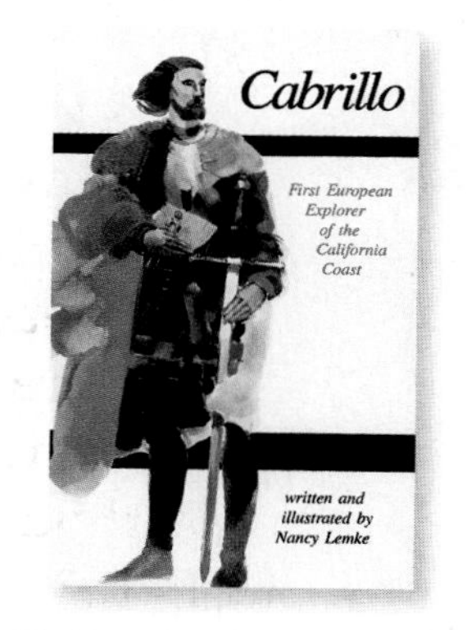

Cabrillo

Nancy Lemke Read about the life and times of the Spaniard who fought with Cortes in Mexico and explored the California coast.

The California Missions

Ann Heinrichs Learn the history of the mission system established by the Spanish settlers of California

Becoming a State

“[P]iles of gold rose up before me at every step. . . .”

– James H. Carson, from *Recollections of the California Mines*

Why do people take great risks?

In Unit 3, you will read about how California grew and became a state. You will also find out about the risks people took to make this happen.

As you read the chapters in this unit, look for the kinds of risks people were willing to take in order to help California grow to statehood. Identify reasons why these people or groups took risks.

As you read, copy and complete the graphic organizer shown below. Think about the events that happened as California grew and became a state. Then complete the graphic organizer. The first one has been started for you.

Mexicans	Californios	Fur Trappers, Settlers, and Gold Miners	Californians
Fought war against Spain			

◀ Miners in the Sierra Nevada

People Who Made a Difference

Juana Briones
1802–1889

Juana Briones was born in California, near present-day Santa Cruz. She was one of the first women to own land in California. (page 199)

Mariano Guadalupe Vallejo
1808–1890

Mariano Guadalupe Vallejo was a Mexican Commander captured during a revolt led by John C. Frémont. Vallejo supported Americans in California. (page 199)

James Beckwourth
1798–1866

James Beckwourth was an African American born into slavery. He became a famous mountain explorer and discovered a safe pass through the Sierra Nevada. (page 213)

Unit Events

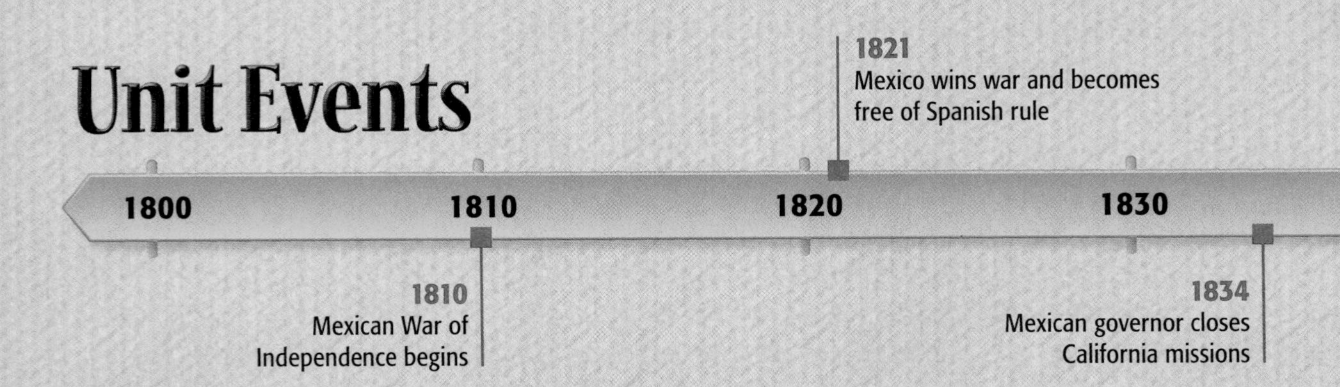

For more about People Who Made a Difference, visit:

www.macmillanmh.com/ss/ca/bios

Johann Sutter
1802–1880

Johann Sutter was a Swiss immigrant who arrived in California in 1834. He founded New Helvetia, near present-day Sacramento. (page 213)

Biddy Mason
1818–1891

Biddy Mason was an enslaved woman brought to California from Georgia. Later, she helped all enslaved persons in California gain freedom. (page 251)

Kintpuash
1837–1873

Kintpuash was a leader of the Modoc during the Modoc War. The war was fought over land the Modoc had lost to the Americans. (page 256)

1840 **1850** **1860** **1870**

1846 Mexican War and the Bear Flag Revolt begin

1848 Mexican War ends; gold is found in California

1849 "Forty Niners" rush to California in search of gold

1850 California becomes 31st state

1854 Sacramento becomes California's state capital

1872 Modoc War begins

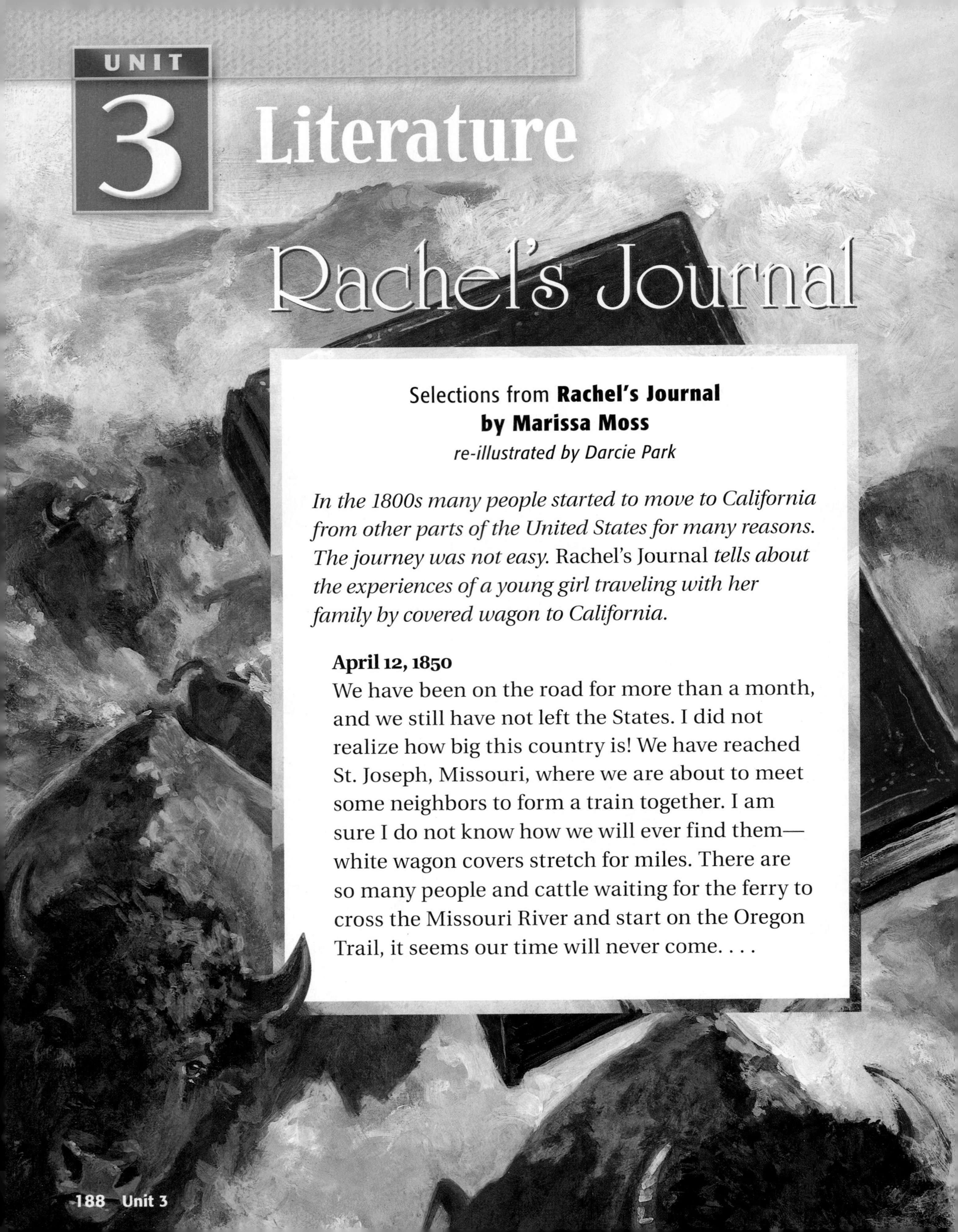

UNIT 3

Literature

Rachel's Journal

Selections from **Rachel's Journal**
by Marissa Moss
re-illustrated by Darcie Park

In the 1800s many people started to move to California from other parts of the United States for many reasons. The journey was not easy. Rachel's Journal *tells about the experiences of a young girl traveling with her family by covered wagon to California.*

April 12, 1850

We have been on the road for more than a month, and we still have not left the States. I did not realize how big this country is! We have reached St. Joseph, Missouri, where we are about to meet some neighbors to form a train together. I am sure I do not know how we will ever find them—white wagon covers stretch for miles. There are so many people and cattle waiting for the ferry to cross the Missouri River and start on the Oregon Trail, it seems our time will never come. . . .

May 3, 1850
I am used to bumping around in the wagon (Pa says I have got my sea legs), but I cannot get used to the mosquitoes. One leg is swollen up and I have a horrid bump over my eye. Prudence has it worse, though. She has a bright red bite on her nose. . . .

June 20, 1850
A different kind of storm passed by us today—a herd of buffalo. It was as if the river had leapt out of its banks and taken solid form to chase us down. A thick cloud of dust **surged** toward us, then there was a tremendous noise, an earthly thunder. We could see their shaggy backs rising and falling like a great wave. . . .

July 5, 1850
Pa says we are not leaving the States, we are going to Opportunity. Besides, California will be a state someday, now that we have won the war with Mexico. Mother says not to count on that. But there is already a **provisional** American government in California, with a governor in charge, so I agree with Pa.

---

surged to move with force, like a wave

provisional (pruh VIZH uhn uhl) temporary

September 30, 1850
We traveled all night through a nightmare landscape. Lee and Daniel led the way with lanterns, but the moon was bright enough to show us the dead cattle, horses, and mules **strewn** everywhere, along with objects left behind by desperate emigrants.

There were whole wagons, trunks, furniture, bedding, tools, a catalogue of goods. Emma and I went on a treasure hunt, pretending we were exploring sunken pirate ships on the sandy sea bottom.

---

strewn (stroon) scattered

October 3, 1850

I thought the Rockies were mountains, but they are just hills compared to the Sierras. Huge granite rocks tower over us, and the tops of the peaks are so high, clouds hide them.

October 23, 1850

This morning we woke up early. The guidebook showed that there were only a dozen or so miles ahead, and no one wanted to sleep. We **descended** the last stretch of 8 miles. The road is smooth and level, dotted with farms and **homesteads**. We are finally, safely here!

---

descended (dee SEND ed) went down

homestead (HOHM sted) a farm with its house and other buildings

Write a journal entry for each day of one month. In each entry, tell about your experiences on that day.

Reading SOCIAL STUDIES

Sequence Events: Exploring California

ELA R2.1 4.3.2

In this unit, you will read about important events in the exploration of California. When you read, think about the order in which these events happened. This order is called the sequence of events. Sequencing events will help you understand and remember what you read.

1 Learn It

- Look for words such as *first, next, then, after, finally,* and *last*. These words show the order of events.
- Look for dates that tell you exactly when events happened.
- Now, read the paragraph below. Look for the sequence of events.

First Event
Fur hunters sail to California.

Second Event
They build Fort Ross.

Third Event
Seals and otters disappear from the area.

Fourth Event
Fort Ross is abandoned.

The first fur hunters from Russia sailed to California in the early 1800s. Fur seal coats and hats were very popular at this time. In 1812, the Russians built a settlement called Fort Ross about 50 miles north of San Francisco. After the fur trappers arrived, seals and otters almost disappeared from the area. Finally, Fort Ross was abandoned.

2 Try It

Copy and complete the chart below. Then, fill in the chart by recording the events in the paragraph on page 192 in the correct sequence.

SEQUENCE OF EVENTS CHART

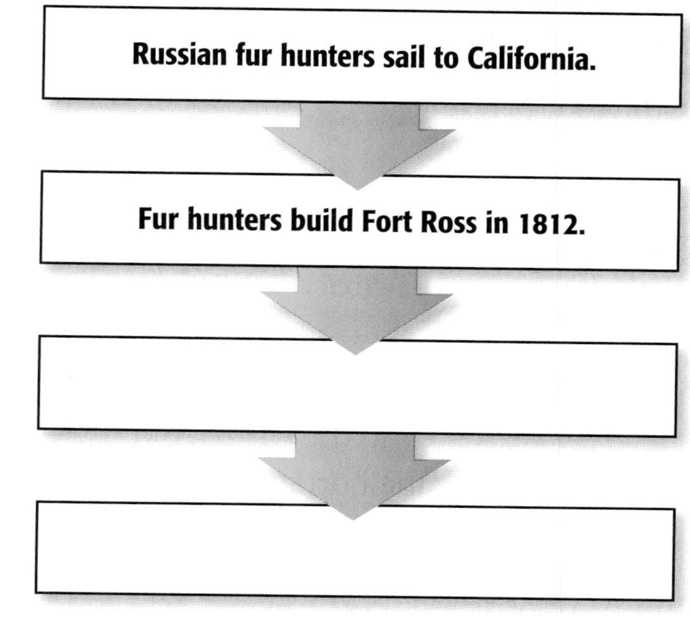

How did you figure out the sequence of events?

3 Apply It

- Review the sequencing steps in Learn It.
- Read the paragraph below. Then, create a sequence of events chart using the information.

Mountain men from the United States were interested in California's furs, too. The first to come was Jedediah Smith. He reached the San Gabriel mission near present-day Los Angeles in November of 1826. Later, Smith and his party collected furs in the San Joaquin Valley. Then, they returned to Utah over the Sierra Nevada. In 1827, Smith made his second and last trip to California in search of furs.

CHAPTER

6 Mexican California

YOU ARE THERE

“I declared my purpose to be to acquire for the United States, California, New Mexico, and perhaps some of the Northern Provinces of Mexico whenever a peace was made.”

President James Polk wrote these words in his diary when war broke out between Mexico and the United States in 1846. The war was fought over the border between Texas and Mexico. However, Polk had already decided to take a great deal of Mexican land, including California, if the United States won the war.

In this chapter you will read about how New Spain became the new nation of Mexico. Later, California and other Mexican lands became part of the United States.

Chapter Events

1821 Mexico becomes free of Spanish rule in War of Independence (page 194)

1826 Jedediah Smith explores routes to California (page 210)

A B

1820 1825 1830

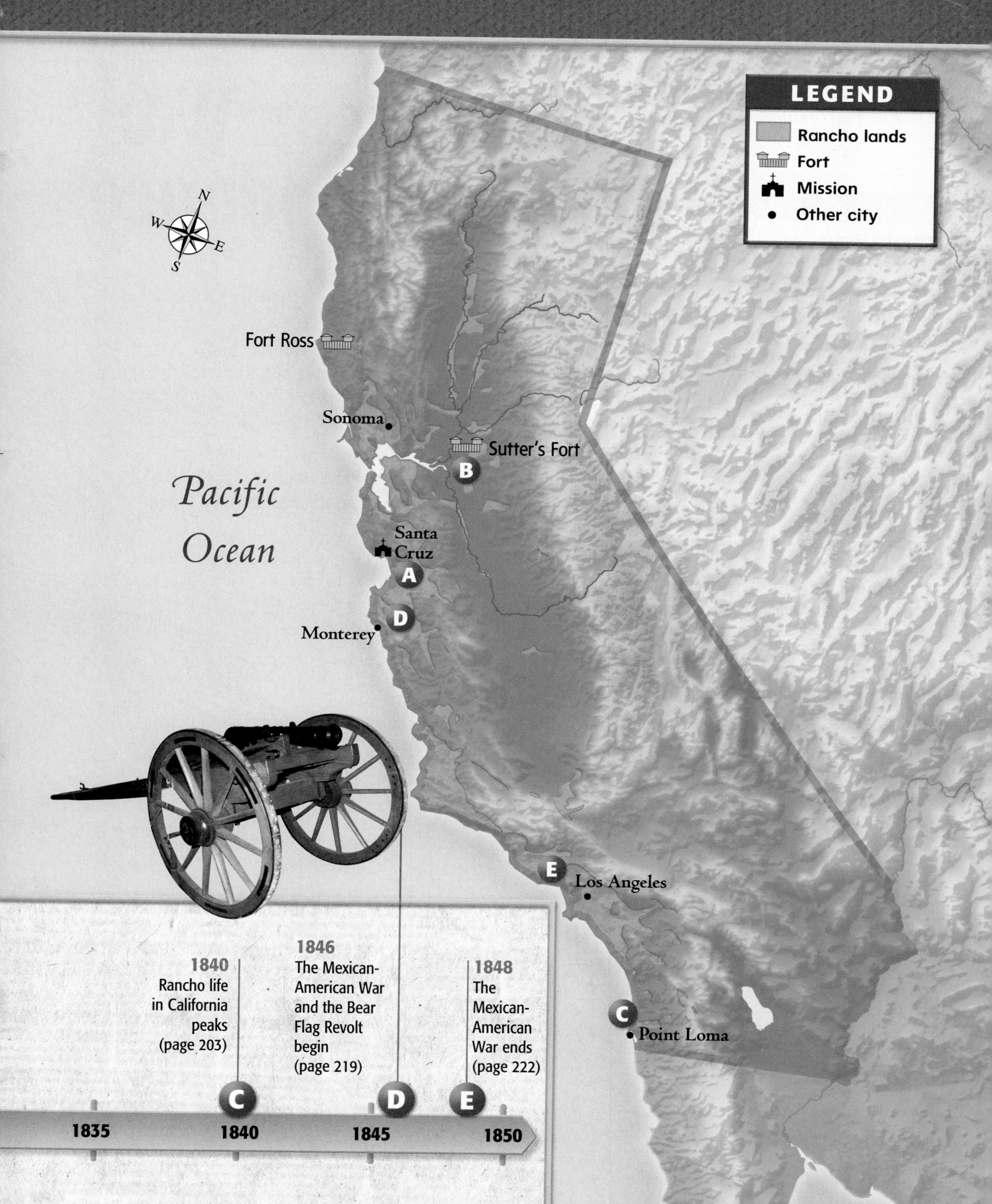
LEGEND
Rancho lands
Fort
Mission
Other city
N
W
E
S
Fort Ross
Sonoma
Sutter's Fort
B
Pacific Ocean
Santa Cruz
A
D
Monterey
E
Los Angeles
C
Point Loma
1840
Rancho life in California peaks (page 203)
1846
The Mexican-American War and the Bear Flag Revolt begin (page 219)
1848
The Mexican-American War ends (page 222)
C
D
E
1835
1840
1845
1850

The Mexican War for Independence

FOCUS QUESTION

Why did Native Americans in California not get their lands back after the missions were closed?

VOCABULARY

Californio
land grant
diseño
rancho

VOCABULARY STRATEGY

WORD ORIGINS The English word **ranch** comes from the Spanish word **rancho**. What English word meaning "ranch owner" comes from the Spanish word **ranchero**?

READING STRATEGY

Sequence Events

Use the chart below to sequence the events in this lesson about the Mexican War for Independence.

Start with Your CALIFORNIA STANDARDS

4.2 Students describe the social, political, cultural, and economic life and interactions among people of California from the Pre-Columbian societies to the Spanish mission and Mexican rancho periods.

4.2.7 Describe the effects of the Mexican War for Independence on Alta California, including its effects on the territorial boundaries of North America.

Find out how Mexico's War for Independence changed life in Alta California. (Begins on page 197)

4.2.8 Discuss the period of Mexican rule in California and its attributes, including land grants, secularization of the missions, and the rise of the rancho economy.

Learn how mission lands, which had once belonged to Native Americans, became ranchos. (Begins on page 198)

In this mural, Miguel Hidalgo calls for a Mexican revolution against Spain. ▼

1810 | 1820 | 1830 | 1840 | 1850 | 1860

1810
The Mexican War for Independence begins

1821
Mexico wins the war and becomes an independent nation

1834
Governor Figueroa announces a plan to end the mission system

1844
Juana Briones buys a rancho

For 300 years Spain sent officials across the Atlantic Ocean to rule New Spain. Mexican colonists grew tired of being ruled by faraway Spain. They learned how the United States had won its freedom from Great Britain. They wanted their freedom, too. In 1810 they went to war with Spain to win independence.

Mexico Wins Independence 4.2.7

Under Spanish rule in Mexico, people born in Spain held all the best jobs in the government and the church. The Mexicans, on the other hand, had little say in the government. They also had fewer job opportunities because they were born in Mexico.

Life under Spanish rule was even harder for Native Americans. As you have read, their land had been taken from them. Laws made it illegal for them to have certain jobs.

Miguel Hidalgo was a Mexican priest who cared deeply about the rights of the Mexican people. By 1810, he had had enough of Spanish rule. He made an inspiring speech to the residents in the town of Dolores. The speech came to be known as the Cry of Dolores.

The Cry of Dolores convinced many people to go to war. A long and bloody war began. The Mexican War for Independence lasted 11 years. When it finally ended in 1821, Mexico was an independent country, free of Spanish rule.

The fighting took place in Mexico, far from California. Many people in California did not find out that Mexico had won the war until 1822. When they heard the news, the **Californios**, as the Mexican people in California called themselves, raised their new flag.

REVIEW What happened after Miguel Hidalgo gave his speech? *Sequence Events*

Missions Become Ranchos 4.2.7 4.2.8

Under Mexico's new government, life changed for the people of California. One big change was that the government decided to close the missions.

Closing the Missions

The Mexican government made this decision for several reasons. The missions were on valuable land. The Californios wanted this land for ranches and farms. Also, many Mexicans believed that Native Americans were not being treated fairly at the missions. Some Native Americans led revolts against the missions. The new government's leaders said that all people were equal.

In 1834, California's new governor, José Figueroa, ordered the missions to be closed. He hoped that closing the missions would stop the revolts. Figueroa also ordered half the mission lands to be given to the Native Americans who had lived and worked there. As you will see, that is not what happened.

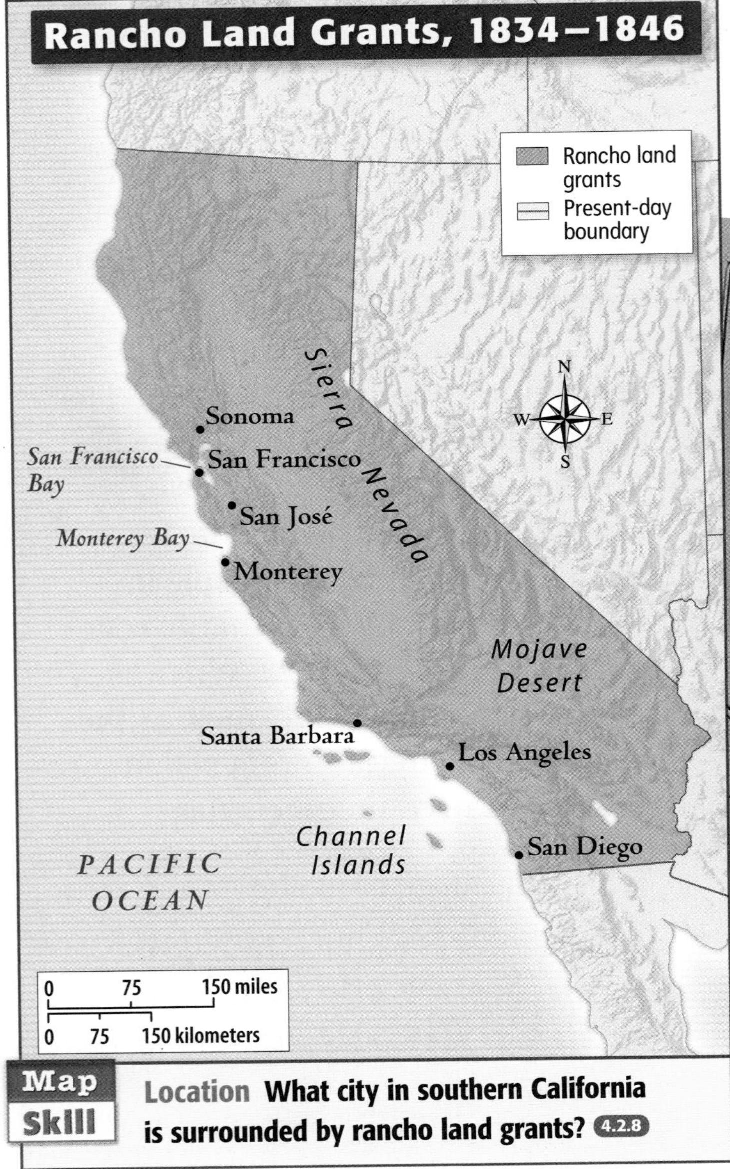

Map Skill **Location** What city in southern California is surrounded by rancho land grants? 4.2.8

▲ This map shows the borders of a California rancho.

▲ Juana Briones (shown right) owned a rancho house that has stood for more than 150 years.

Large Pieces of Land

Many Californios supported Governor Figueroa's plan because they hoped to win some of the mission lands for themselves. The Mexican government began to give out most of the mission lands in very large pieces, known as **land grants**.

Any Mexican citizen could apply for a land grant. However soldiers from the presidios and the Californio land owners received most of the first land grants. Native Americans received very few.

To get a land grant, a person had to make a **diseño** (dee SE nyoh), or a hand-drawn map. This map showed the borders of the land. Often, these borders were marked only by a stone or a few trees. These simple drawings led to later arguments over exact boundaries.

The Californios turned their new land into more than 500 **ranchos**. A rancho was a ranch where cattle, horses, and other animals were raised. Mariano Guadalupe Vallejo became one of the richest rancheros, or ranch owners. He became an army commander and went into politics. As a politician, Vallejo would play an important role in California.

Juana Briones was a ranchera, or woman who owned a rancho. She was a successful businesswoman with a large family. Her house still stands near Palo Alto.

The End of the Missions

Governor Figueroa died before he could complete his plan. After his death, most of the best mission lands went to Californios.

Lorenzo Asisara, a Native American from Mission Santa Cruz, remembered that his Ohlone people did get some land, but "it did not do the Indians any good."

Californios had already taken over many of the lands where the Native Americans' old villages had stood. Other Californios talked the Native Americans into selling their land. Many of the Native Americans who had worked so hard for the missions now had to work just as hard for Californios.

REVIEW Why did the Mexican government close the missions? *Cause and Effect*

▲ Governor José Figueroa was unable to give mission land to Native American groups.

What You Learned

4.2.7 After a war with Spain, Mexico became an independent country in 1821. Mexico now ruled California.

4.2.7 4.2.8 When Mexico closed the missions, most of the land was given to Californios.

Lesson Review

1. **Focus Question** Why did Native Americans in California not get their lands back after the missions were closed? (4.2.8)
2. **Vocabulary** Write one sentence for each vocabulary term. (4.2.7)
   Californio **land grant**
   diseño **rancho**
3. **Government** How did the change in the government of California affect the missions? (4.2.7, 4.2.8)
4. **Critical Thinking** **Problem Solving** The ongoing revolts by Native Americans at the missions were a problem that needed solving. How did the new governor of California plan to solve that problem? (4.2.7, 4.2.8)
5. **Reading Strategy** **Sequence Events** Reread the section called "Missions Become Ranchos." Use the chart to sequence the events in this section. (4.2.7, ELA R2.1)

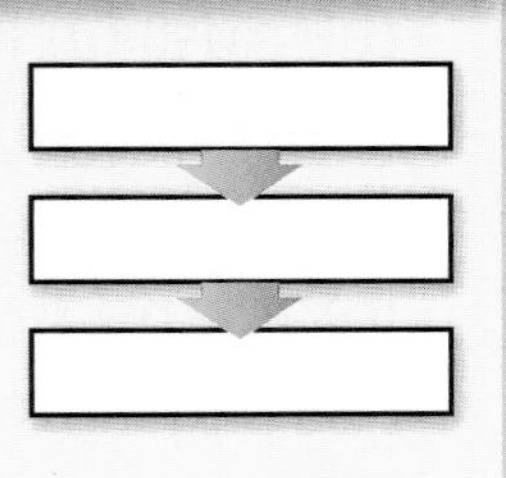

6. **Write about THE BIG IDEA** Why did the Mexicans decide to go to war? (4.2.7, ELA W2.1)
7. **Link to Language Arts** Look at the "Independence Mural" on page 196. Write a poem describing how someone in the mural might have felt at that moment. (4.2)

CRITICAL THINKING
Skills

Identify Fact and Opinion 4.3

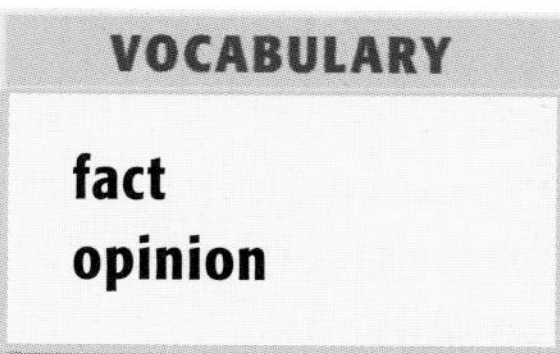

In Lesson 1, you read about Mexico winning independence from Spain. Some of the sentences in the lesson were facts. A **fact** is a statement that can be proven true. You could prove a fact, for example, by checking it in an encyclopedia.

Other statements in the lesson were opinions. An **opinion** tells what someone believes or feels. Opinions cannot be proven true or false.

1 Learn It

- Facts can be proven true. Statements with dates and amounts are often facts.
- Opinions state feelings and beliefs. Words like *better, probably, should, and believe* signal opinions.

Now look for facts and opinions in this paragraph.

> No one cared more about the rights of Native Americans than Miguel Hidalgo! In 1810, he gave a speech against Spanish rule in Mexico. No copies of Hidalgo's speech exist today. The speech probably ended with the words, "Death to bad government!"

2 Try It

Read the paragraph about Miguel Hidalgo again. Then answer the questions.

- Is the first sentence a fact or an opinion? How do you know?
- Is the second sentence a fact or an opinion? How do you know?
- Would you be able to prove the third sentence? Explain.
- Why is the last sentence an opinion?

3 Apply It

Write two statements of fact about your school or classroom. Then write two statements of opinion.

LESSON 2

Rancho Life

FOCUS QUESTION

What made the rancho way of life possible?

VOCABULARY

- fiesta
- vaquero
- rodeo
- hide
- tallow
- export
- California banknote
- import

VOCABULARY STRATEGY

PREFIXES Here's a tip to help you remember the difference between **import** and **export**. The prefix **im-** comes from the Latin word meaning "into." The prefix **ex-** comes from the Latin for "out of."

READING STRATEGY

Summarize

Use the chart below to summarize what you learned about life on a rancho.

Start with Your CALIFORNIA STANDARDS

4.2 Students describe the social, political, cultural, and economic life and interactions among people of California from the Pre-Columbian societies to the Spanish mission and Mexican rancho periods.

4.2.5 Describe the daily lives of the people, native and nonnative, who occupied the presidios, missions, ranchos, and pueblos.

Find out what it was like to live on a rancho and take part in its fiestas and rodeos. (Begins on page 203)

4.2.8 Discuss the period of Mexican rule in California and its attributes, including land grants, secularization of the missions, and the rise of the rancho economy.

Learn about the ways in which ranchos used cattle. (Begins on page 205)

Many rancho families grew wealthy, but they also had to work hard. ▼

The year is 1840, and you are visiting a wealthy rancho. As you arrive, you see people busy setting up tables and hanging up decorations. Today, guests are coming from miles around to have fun at a party.

Rancho Customs 4.2.5

The rancho is always a lively place. The ranchero and his wife, their children and other relatives, as well as many workers, live there. In fact, it takes almost 100 people to run the rancho. They all live together.

Most ranchos are far apart. People have to travel a long way to visit each other. Rancheros and rancheras always reward their guests for coming so far by treating them very well. Today there is a **fiesta**, or party.

Special Celebrations

Today's fiesta is a special treat. Fiestas are a big part of rancho life. Some are held to celebrate weddings. Others are held for religious holidays. Whatever the occasion, fiestas are a time to eat a great meal and have fun.

Everyone dresses up in colorful clothing. Even the horses are dressed up. Their saddles are trimmed in silver today.

You have probably noticed the amazing horseback riding skills of the men, women, and children of the rancho. Californios depend on horses to get around. They take great pride in their ability to ride well. There will be a horseback riding contest later.

There is much singing and dancing at the fiesta. Feel free to join in. The next song is *Cielito lindo,* which means "Beautiful little sky." Follow along with the music on page 204. One of the dances you will see is the *bamba*. To perform it, a dancer must do some difficult moves. Sometimes dancers would even balance a glass of water on his or her head. Would you like to give it a try?

REVIEW What are some things that happen at a fiesta? *Summarize*

Primary Sources
Cielito Lindo
Verse
A E7 A E7
Spanish: De la Sie - rra Mo - re - na, Ci_e - li - to
English: Com - ing down from dark moun-tains, Cie - li - to
A E7
Lin - do vi_e - nen ba - jan - do
Lin - do, you come to cheer us.
E7
Un par de_o - ji - tos ne - gros, Ci_e - li - to
Your dark eyes and your gen - tle voice make us
E7 A
Lin - do, de - con - tra - ban - do.
hap - py when you are near us!
Refrain
A D E7 A
Ay, ay, ay, ay! can - ta_y no llo - res.
Ay, ay, ay, ay! Sing, don't be tear-ful.
A E7
Por - que can - tan - do se_a - le - gran, Ci_e - li - to
For when your sing - ing your heart for - gets all its
E7 A
Lin - do los co - ra - zo - nes.
sad - ness, and can be cheer - ful.
Why do you think this song about the sky was written?

At Work on the Rancho 4.2.5

Children living on ranchos did not go to school. Some were taught by teachers who traveled to ranchos. Others learned from their parents. Still others never got a formal education at all.

Most of the time, children worked along with their parents. Girls helped their mothers cook, garden, and sew. Boys worked with their fathers, many of whom were **vaqueros**, or cowhands.

Most of the hard work on the ranchos was done by Native Americans. After the missions closed, many of them went to work on the ranchos. Some became vaqueros. Others farmed, cared for the animals, cooked, cleaned, and did all the things that made life on the rancho possible.

In exchange for their work, Native Americans received food, clothing, and a place to live. However, they had few rights.

Roundups

For most of the year, cattle roamed freely around the huge rancho lands, grazing on grass. Once a year, the vaqueros gathered them in a **rodeo**, or roundup. Vaqueros branded the new cattle, or calves, and counted the herd.

Rodeos were not just about work. Vaqueros showed off their riding and roping skills in contests. Modern rodeos are based on these old roundups of rancho days.

Once the cattle were rounded up, some of them were killed. First the meat was removed. Then the **hides**, or skins, were stripped from the animals. These were cleaned, stretched, and put in the sun to dry. The hides became the leather for making things like saddles and shoes. The **tallow**, or cattle fat that was scraped off the hides was also used. It would later be boiled and then turned into soap and candles.

REVIEW Why did Californios raise cattle? *Cause and Effect*

Many people were needed to round up cattle. ▼

The Hide and Tallow Trade 4.2.8

Unlike the Spanish government, the Mexican government encouraged trade with other countries. California got rich by trading with the United States. Hides and tallow were California's main **exports**. An export is something that is sold or traded to another country.

Cattle hides were so important that they were called **"California banknotes,"** or money. Californians rarely used money. Instead, they traded hides for the goods they wanted. Each hide was worth two or three dollars.

Ships from the United States sailed to California to trade for hides. Follow the route of the American traders on the map. The journey was thousands of miles long and took many months.

When Californios spotted an American ship arriving, they rushed to the shore. The ships carried **imports**. An import is something brought in from another country for sale or use. The ranchos did not make many of the things people needed, so Californios traded their hides and tallow for the goods on the ship.

Trading Ships

A trading ship was like a floating department store. It carried food like tea, sugar, and spices. There were also items such as dishes, furniture, toys and clothes.

As a young man, Richard Henry Dana sailed from Boston to California on a trading ship. Later he wrote a book about his experiences called

American Trade Routes, 1800s

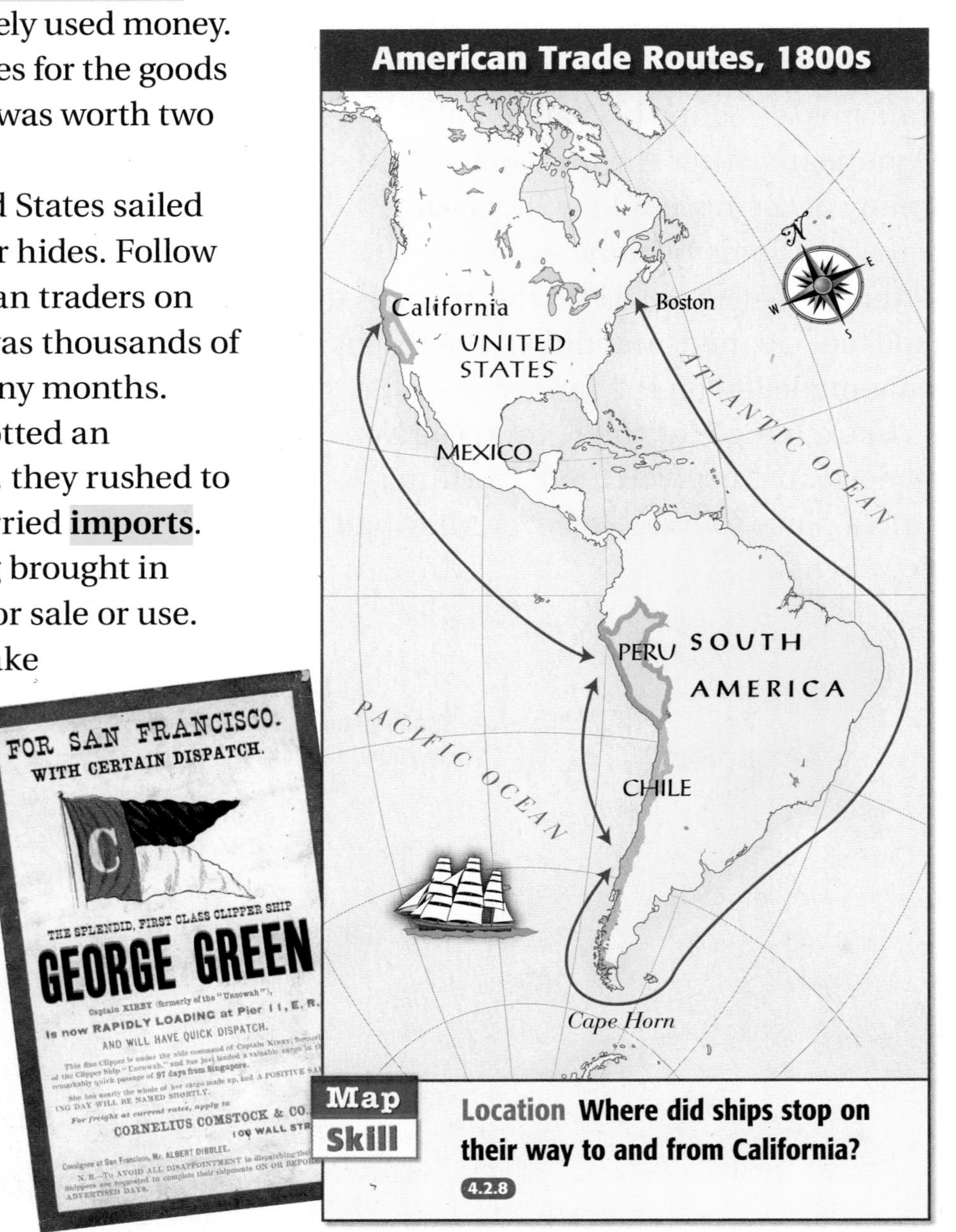

Advertisement for a ship sailing to California ▶

Map Skill **Location** Where did ships stop on their way to and from California? 4.2.8

▲ Clipper ships traveled thousands of miles to trade with California.

Two Years Before the Mast. As Dana described the ships' arrival:

> ***"[People] used to spend whole days on board our vessels, examining the fine clothes and ornaments. . . ."***

REVIEW Why were hides called "California banknotes"? *Cause and Effect*

What You Learned

- **4.2.5** Ranchos were lively places. Fiestas took place on special occasions.
- **4.2.5** It took a lot of work to run a rancho. Everyone, even children, had to help.
- **4.2.8** Californios traded hides and tallow with the United States for goods they did not make on the ranchos.

Lesson Review

1. **Focus Question** What made the rancho way of life possible? (4.2.5, 4.2.8)
2. **Vocabulary** Write one sentence for each vocabulary term. (4.2.5)

California banknote	**hide**	**tallow**
export	**import**	**vaquero**
fiesta	**rodeo**	

3. **Economics** What products did ranchos make? (4.2.8)
4. **Critical Thinking** **Problem Solving** When the missions closed, many Native Americans had nowhere to go because Californios were living on their land. How did they solve this problem? (4.2, 4.2.5)
5. **Reading Strategy** **Summarize** Reread the section "At Work on the Rancho." Use the chart to summarize this section. (4.2, ELA R2.1)

6. **Write about THE BIG IDEA** How did the rancho economy create a link between California and the outside world? (4.2.8, ELA W2.1)
7. **Link to Language Arts** Richard Henry Dana wrote descriptions of the California landscape in his diary. Suppose you have just come to visit a rancho in California. Write a letter home describing it. (4.2.5)

A Day in the Life

A Young Person's Life in the 1840s 4.2.5

Rancho boys and girls helped their parents run the rancho. Girls helped their mothers manage the house. Boys helped their fathers round up the cattle. On fiesta days, boys and girls dressed in their best clothes and watched their family members and guests dance.

▲ Men and boys wore hats like these to shade them from the sun.

From an early age boys were taught skills needed on a rancho. ▼

▲ Rancho homes were usually large. Many family members lived on a rancho.

◀ This saddle once belonged to a rancho family.

Girls spent much of their time learning from their mothers how to cook, sew, knit, and do other things around the house. ▼

Fans were used by women to keep cool on hot days. ▼

Write About It!

Write a paragraph about how a young person's life on a rancho was similar or different from your own.

LOG ON

For more about life in the 1840s, visit:

www.macmillanmh.com/ss/ca/dayinthelife

FOCUS QUESTION

How did fur trappers make it possible for pioneers to travel to California?

VOCABULARY

- pelt
- trapper
- mountain men
- trailblazer
- pioneer
- wagon train

VOCABULARY STRATEGY

COMPOUND WORDS
Trailblazer is a compound word. It is made up of two words, **trail** and **blazer**, that have a different meaning when they are used by themselves. Can you think of any other compound words?

READING STRATEGY

Compare and Contrast
Use the diagram to compare and contrast the different types of people who traveled overland to California.

Trappers and Settlers

Start with Your CALIFORNIA STANDARDS

4.3 Students explain the economic, social, and political life in California from the establishment of the Bear Flag Republic through the Mexican-American War, the Gold Rush, and the granting of statehood.

4.3.1 Identify the locations of Mexican settlements in California and those of other settlements, including Fort Ross and Sutter's Fort.

Learn how the Russians set up a fort just 50 miles north of San Francisco. (Begins on page 211)

4.3.2 Compare how and why people traveled to California and the routes they traveled.

Read about people who were willing and able to walk across our continent in search of what they wanted. (Begins on page 212)

Travelers such as Richard Henry Dana brought back stories of California's rich coastline, animal life, and sunny climate. Their stories sparked people's interest in the land on the far side of the continent.

Far Away California 4.3.2

California, which was still a part of Mexico, was not an easy place to reach in the early 1800s. Endless grassy plains, snow-covered mountains, and hot, dry deserts separated California from the rest of the United States. To Americans back East, California might as well have been on another continent.

It was not easy for Americans to get to California by sea, either. From the east coast of the United States, travelers had to sail south all the way down to the tip of South America and then north all the way up to California. See the map on page 206 to get an idea of what a long journey that was.

◀ Wagon trains crossed the Great Plains on their way to California.

The Fur Trade

In the early 1800s Russian fur hunters sailed down the coast to California from Alaska. In 1812 they built a settlement called Fort Ross about 50 miles north of San Francisco.

Fort Ross was the Russians' base for hunting sea otters and seals, which were valuable for their **pelts**. A pelt is the fur-covered hide of an animal. At the time, fur coats and hats were popular because they were soft, warm, and waterproof.

The Russians weren't the only people interested in fur. American **trappers** soon headed for California in search of beaver pelts. A trapper is someone who traps animals for their fur.

REVIEW Why did Russian and American hunters come to California?
Compare and Contrast

Mountain Trappers 4.3.1 4.3.2

In the early 1800s, trappers known as **mountain men** were living in the Rocky Mountains, and hunting beavers in mountain streams. As they searched for pelts, the mountain men became the explorers of the Far West.

Overland Routes

One famous mountain man was Jedediah Strong Smith. Smith believed there were lots of beavers in California. In 1826, he led a group of 15 trappers there. They were the first people from the United States to journey to California over land.

The group left on August 16, 1826, from what is now Utah. They traveled southwest through mountains and deserts. Follow their route on the map below.

In early October, the group reached the Colorado River near California. With the help of Native American guides, the group made it across the Mojave Desert. On November 27, Smith's group arrived at Mission San Gabriel. There they heard that the San Joaquin Valley was filled with beavers. However, the Mexican governor thought Smith was an American spy and ordered him to leave California.

Smith was an early **trailblazer**, a person who leads the way for others. There were other trailblazers, too, such as Joseph Reddeford Walker

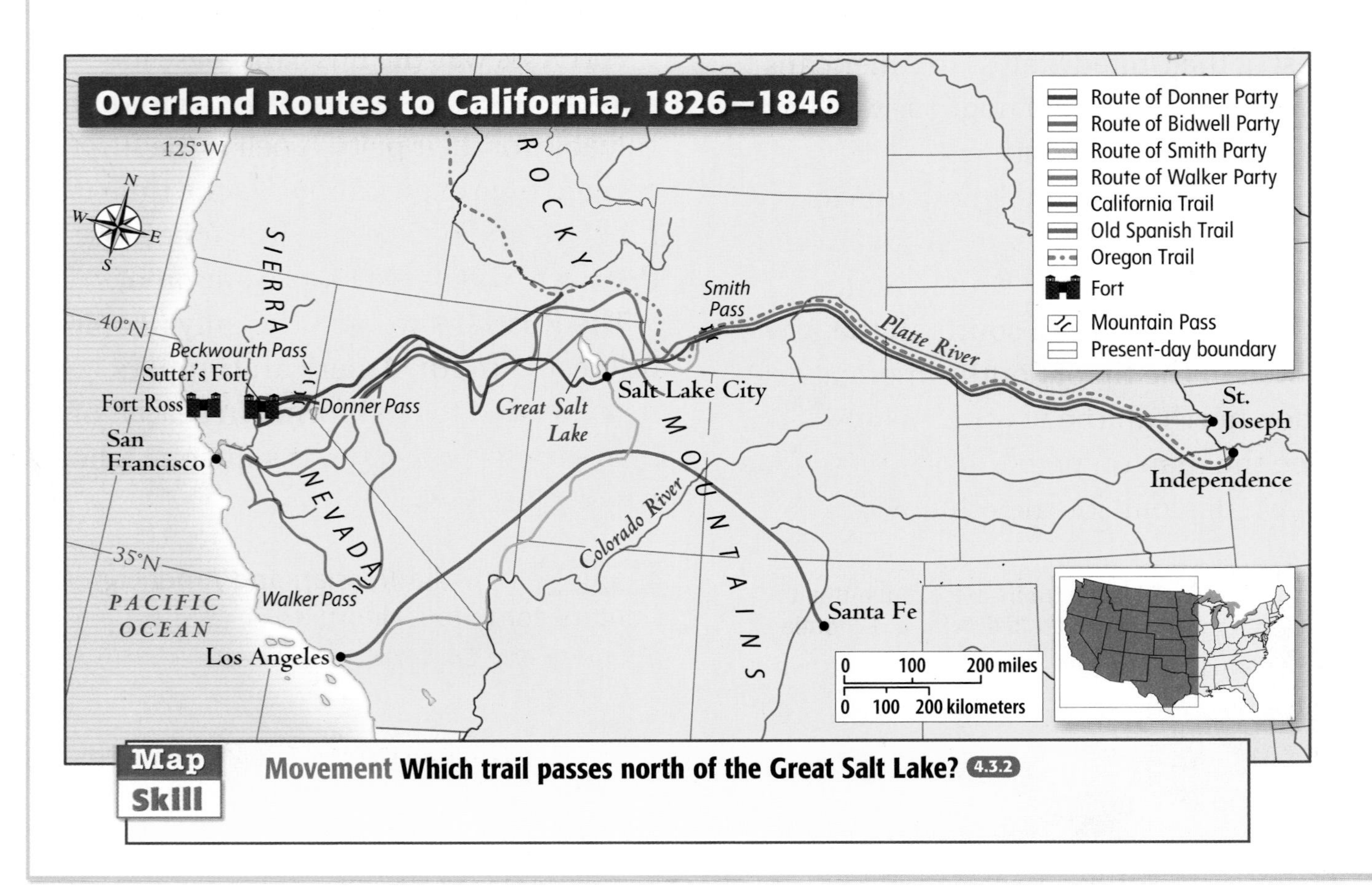

Map Skill Movement **Which trail passes north of the Great Salt Lake?** 4.3.2

▲ Many pioneer families walked beside their covered wagons.

and James Beckwourth, an African American. You can read about Beckwourth on page 215.

Wagon Trains

One day in 1839, a man named Johann Sutter arrived in California. He would play an important part in California's history. Sutter was a businessman from Switzerland. After landing in Monterey in 1839, he received a land grant in the Sacramento Valley. He built a large settlement there, including a fort. Find Sutter's Fort on the map on page 212.

New settlers to California often stopped at Sutter's Fort. These settlers came mostly from Eastern states. They were called **pioneers**.

The pioneers heard about California's fertile land and wonderful climate. They left their old lives behind to follow the routes found by the trailblazers.

They traveled in groups of wagons called **wagon trains**. Each family had to bring everything it needed for its new life out west. It all had to fit in a wagon about the size of a pick-up truck. Often, there was no room left for the family. Many pioneers walked most of the way.

One of the first groups of pioneers arrived in California in 1841. John Bidwell was its leader. When they reached Sutter's Fort, they were weak and hungry. Sutter greeted them and helped them get settled.

REVIEW What hardships did pioneers face?
Main Idea and Details

The Donner Party 4.3.2

In the spring of 1846, a wagon train left Independence, Missouri, for California. George Donner was the leader of about 90 settlers. They started out on the Oregon Trail and everything went well for a few months.

Then the group decided to take a shortcut. The trail was too rough, however, and it was very slow going.

The settlers reached the Sierra Nevada, but a blinding snowstorm trapped the Donner Party high in a mountain pass. That winter 22 feet of snow fell. The group was stuck until February.

By the time a rescue party from Sutter's Fort arrived, about 40 members of the Donner Party had died of cold and hunger.

REVIEW What mistake did the Donner Party make? *Main Idea and Details*

A survivor of the Donner Party was rescued with her doll. ▶

What You Learned

4.3.1 It was very difficult to reach California, but Russian and American hunters and trappers began to arrive.

4.3.1 4.3.2 Mountain men opened up the West. Pioneers traveled to California in wagon trains.

4.3.2 The Donner Party was trapped in the mountains during the winter, and nearly half the group died.

Lesson Review

1. **Focus Question** How did fur trappers make it possible for pioneers to travel to California? 4.3.2
2. **Vocabulary** Write one sentence for each vocabulary term. 4.3.2

mountain men	**trailblazer**
pelt	**trapper**
pioneer	**wagon train**

3. **Economics** Why did the Russians' build Fort Ross? 4.3.1 4.3.2
4. **Critical Thinking** **Make Decisions** What was the result of Jedediah Strong Smith's decision to go to California in search of beaver pelts? 4.3.2
5. **Reading Strategy** **Compare and Contrast** Reread the section called "Mountain Trappers." Use the diagram to compare and contrast the lives of Jedediah Strong Smith and Johann Sutter. 4.3.2 ELA R2.1

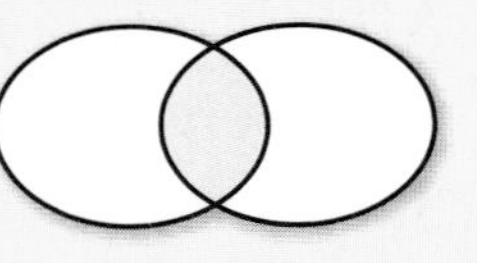

6. **Write about THE BIG IDEA** Why were the pioneers willing to give up their old lives to move to California? 4.3.2 ELA W2.1
7. **Link to Language Arts** The pioneers could not take too many things on their journey. Suppose you are going to a faraway place. What five things would you bring, and why? 4.3.2

Biography
Focus on Courage

4.3.2

James Beckwourth 1798–1866

James Beckwourth was born into slavery in 1798 in the state of Virginia. His father was white and his mother was an enslaved African American woman. The family moved to Missouri when Beckwourth was a boy.

Growing up in Missouri, Beckwourth spent time hunting with his father. He loved adventure and dreamed about being an explorer. As an adult, he made that dream come true.

In 1823, Beckwourth joined a group of fur trappers and set off to explore the West. He was captured by Crow Native Americans in 1828. Beckwourth became friends with the Crow, who taught him how to survive in the wilderness. He later used that knowledge to guide others to California.

In 1850, Beckwourth discovered an important pass through the Sierra Nevada to California. It is now named the Beckwourth Pass.

How did James Beckwourth's actions show his courage?

For more about James Beckwourth, visit:

www.macmillanmh.com/ss/ca/bios

The Life of James Beckwourth

1790 | 1810 | 1830 | 1850 | 1870 | 1890

- **1798** Born into slavery in Virginia
- **1823** Becomes a trapper for Rocky Mountain Fur Company
- **1828** Captured by Crow Native Americans
- **1850** Discovers Beckwourth Pass
- **1866** Dies while visiting with the Crow

MAP and GLOBE Skills

Compare Maps at Different Scales

4.1.5

VOCABULARY

map scale
small-scale map
large-scale map

All maps are drawn to scale. A **map scale** uses a unit of measure, such as an inch, to represent a real distance on earth. A map scale like the one below will tell you the size of an area on the map.

0 10 20 miles

0 10 20 kilometers

A **small-scale map** such as Map A covers a large area but cannot include many details. A **large-scale map** such as Map B shows many details of a smaller area.

1 Learn It

- If you want to find out the routes used to get to Sutter's Fort, use a small-scale map, or Map A. This map will give you the information you need without many details.
- If you want to know about the area immediately surrounding Sutter's Fort, you would need the large-scale map, or Map B. It shows a smaller area with many more details and more information.
- Compare the map scales of both maps.
- Map A has a scale of 200 miles. It shows a large area.
- Map B has a scale of 20 miles. It shows a small area.

2 Try It

- Which map would you use to find the distance between Los Angeles and Sutter's Fort in California?
- Which map would you use to determine the distance between Sutter's Fort and Nicolaus?

3 Apply It

- Using the map scale, find out about how many miles pioneers traveled on the part of the California Trail that was in California.
- When might you need to compare maps of different scales in your own life?

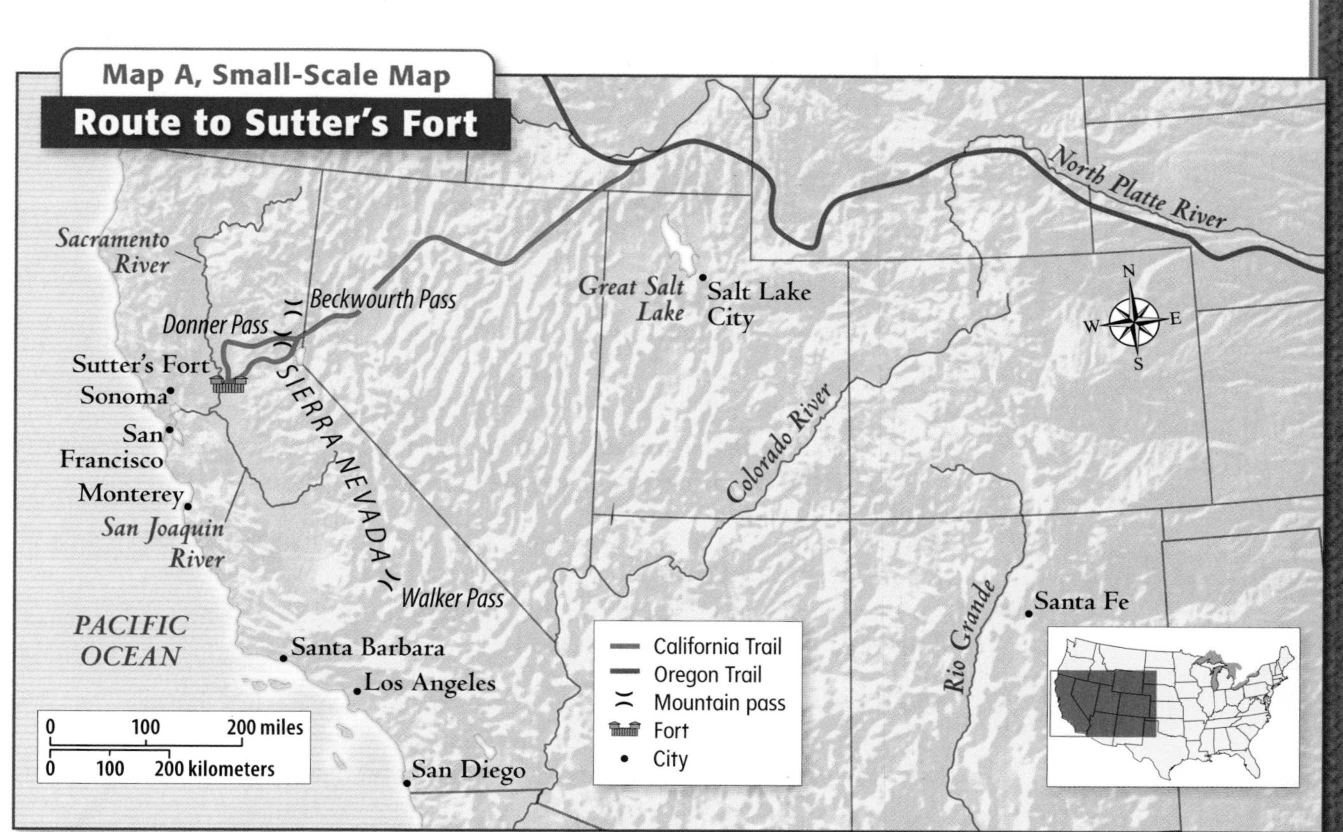
Map A, Small-Scale Map
Route to Sutter's Fort
Sacramento River
Beckwourth Pass
Donner Pass
Sutter's Fort
Sonoma
San Francisco
Monterey
San Joaquin River
SIERRA NEVADA
Walker Pass
PACIFIC OCEAN
Santa Barbara
Los Angeles
San Diego
Great Salt Lake
Salt Lake City
Colorado River
North Platte River
Rio Grande
Santa Fe
California Trail
Oregon Trail
Mountain pass
Fort
City
0 100 200 miles
0 100 200 kilometers

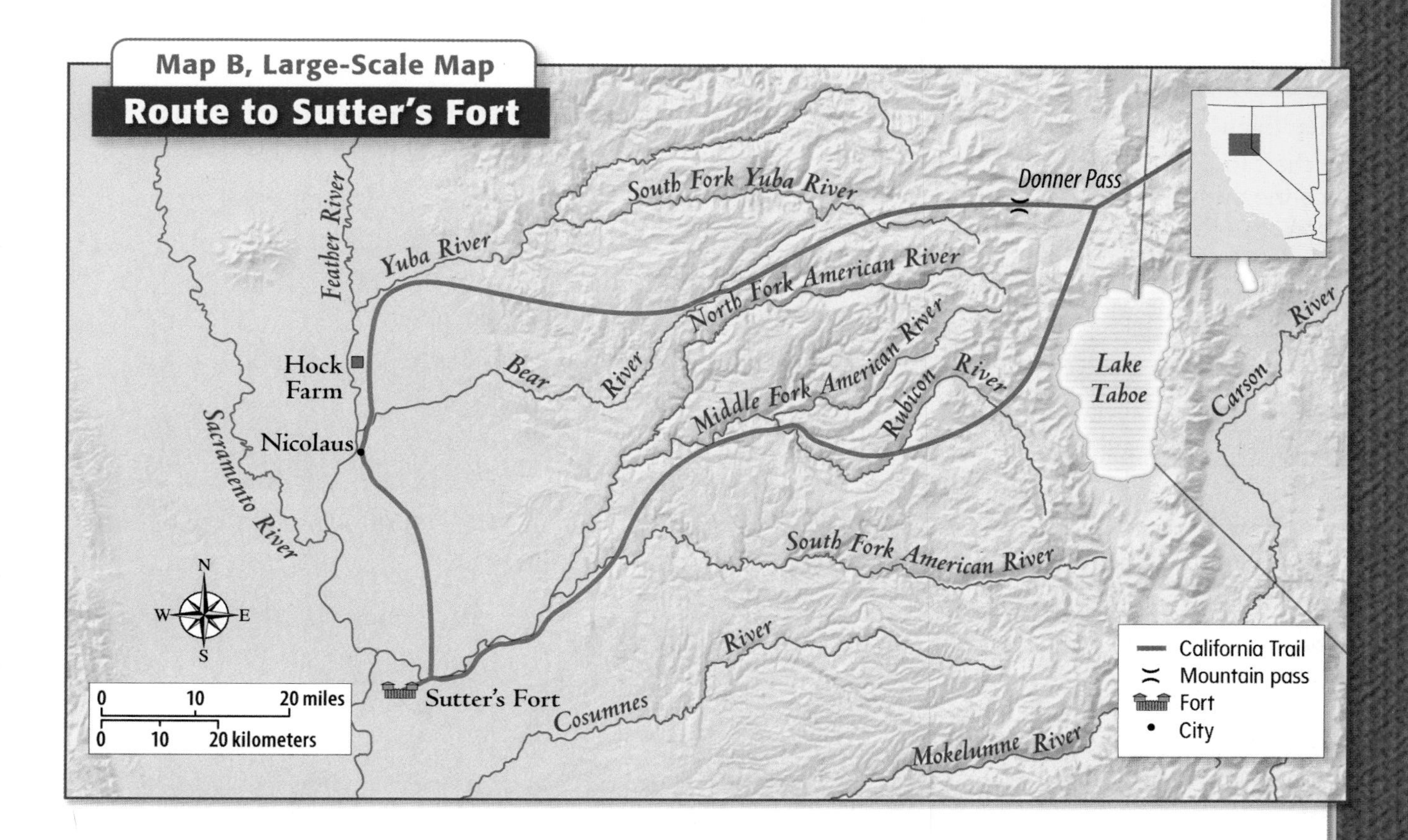
Map B, Large-Scale Map
Route to Sutter's Fort
Feather River
Yuba River
South Fork Yuba River
Donner Pass
North Fork American River
Bear River
Hock Farm
Nicolaus
Middle Fork American River
Rubicon River
Lake Tahoe
Carson River
Sacramento River
South Fork American River
Cosumnes River
Mokelumne River
Sutter's Fort
California Trail
Mountain pass
Fort
City
0 10 20 miles
0 10 20 kilometers

LESSON 4

The Bear Flag Revolt

FOCUS QUESTION

How did an idea called "Manifest Destiny" lead to a war that made California part of the United States?

VOCABULARY

Manifest Destiny
republic
treaty

VOCABULARY STRATEGY

ROOT WORDS The word **treaty** has the root word **treat** in it. Can you think of another word that contains this root?

READING STRATEGY

Sequence Events

Use the chart to sequence the events in this lesson.

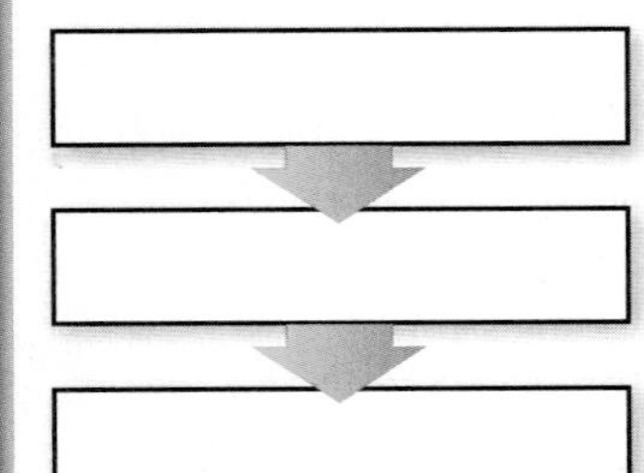

Start with Your CALIFORNIA STANDARDS

4.2 Students describe the social, political, cultural, and economic life and interactions among people of California from the Pre-Columbian societies to the Spanish mission and Mexican rancho periods.

4.2.8 Discuss the period of Mexican rule in California and its attributes, including land grants, secularization of the missions, and the rise of the rancho economy.

Learn how the Californios fought and lost the battle to keep California a part of Mexico. (Begins on page 220)

4.3 Students explain the economic, social, and political life in California from the establishment of the Bear Flag Republic through the Mexican-American War, the Gold Rush, and the granting of statehood.

4.3.2 Compare how and why people traveled to California and the routes they traveled.

Find out how a young American army officer became involved in California politics and started a revolt. (Begins on page 219)

United States settlers held Mexican prisoners at Sutter's Fort during the Bear Flag revolt. ▼

1845	1846	1847	1848	1849
1845 John Frémont is ordered to leave California	**1846** United States declares war on Mexico; Bear Flag Republic lasts one month	**1847** Mexican War in California ends at Cahuenga Pass	**1848** Mexican War ends with Treaty of Guadalupe Hidalgo	

John C. Frémont was a young explorer and mapmaker in the United States Army. He traveled widely through unexplored western territories. In 1845 and 1846, he played an important part in some exciting events that changed California's history.

America's Future 4.3 4.3.2

In the mid-1800s, many Americans were moving west to California. Others settled in the areas that are now Oregon, Washington, New Mexico, and Texas.

Many Americans felt that the United States should control all the land between the Atlantic Ocean and the Pacific Ocean. They believed that American citizens had a right to this land—that the United States was somehow meant to have it. This belief was called **Manifest Destiny**. For Americans, Manifest Destiny meant that the "obvious fate" of this vast area was to belong to the United States.

In 1845, James K. Polk became President of the United States. Polk was a great believer in Manifest Destiny.

Frémont Comes to California

John C. Frémont was an officer in the United States Army. He traveled around the American West, exploring the region for the army. Like Polk, Frémont believed in Manifest Destiny.

In December 1845, Frémont arrived in California to make a map for the army. He brought 60 armed men with him. When Frémont and his men went to Monterey, a Mexican Army officer named José Castro ordered Frémont to leave California.

Frémont crossed the border into Oregon. From there he spread rumors that Colonel Castro was going to force all American settlers to leave California. Many of the settlers were in California without the Mexican government's permission. The rumors made them very afraid.

REVIEW What happened when John Frémont arrived in California with 60 armed men? *Sequence Events*

California Goes to War 4.3

While Frémont was heading toward Oregon, important events were taking place on the other side of the country. On May 13, 1846, President Polk asked the United States Congress to declare war on Mexico. He hoped for a quick war that would bring the United States all of Texas and California. News traveled slowly, however. No one in California knew that there was a war.

The Bear Flag Revolt

Frémont and his men returned to California in June. His return encouraged a group of United States settlers to rebel, or revolt against the Mexican government.

On June 14, 1846, a band of 30 American settlers surrounded the Sonoma home of Commander Mariano Guadalupe Vallejo. Vallejo was one of California's most important citizens. The settlers told him that they could not live with a government that "did not respect the rights of American citizens." Even though Commander Vallejo had always supported the rights of American settlers, he was captured by the rebels.

After Vallejo's arrest, the rebels declared California to be a **republic**,

THEN and NOW

The Bear Flag 4.2.8 4.3

THEN The original Bear Flag was made in a hurry. One settler offered a piece of white cotton, and another painted it with paint that was lying around. The rebels put a grizzly bear on the flag because it was a strong animal. Later, Vallejo remembered that "the bear was so badly painted . . . that it looked more like pig than a bear."

NOW In 1911, the Bear Flag became the official state flag of California. As you can see, no one would mistake the bear for a pig now. Sadly, there are no longer any grizzly bears in California. However, the Bear Flag continues to remind Californians of their history.

What is the difference between the two flags?

independent of Mexico. A republic is a government in which the people choose their own leaders. The rebels raised a new flag over Sonoma. On the flag was a drawing of a grizzly bear, the fiercest animal in California.

The War in California

The Bear Flag Republic did not last long. Less than a month later, the Mexican War reached California. On July 7, 1846, United States Navy ships, led by Commodore John D. Sloat, landed at Monterey. Sloat declared that California was now part of the United States.

When the Bear Flaggers heard the news, they joined Sloat's soldiers. The Bear Flag was replaced by the Stars and Stripes of the United States.

Other United States troops landed in Los Angeles in August. They quickly captured the area. On October 8, a handful of Californio soldiers, led by José Carrillo, fought back.

Carrillo ordered his soldiers to ride their horses back and forth across the dusty hills. They churned up dust that made it hard to see what was going on. Then they dragged a single cannon around to different places and fired. These actions fooled the United States troops into thinking that they were fighting a very large force. The Americans retreated.

Soon United States General Stephen Watts Kearny arrived with more soldiers. At dawn on December 6, Kearny led an attack on Californio troops near the village of San Pasqual. The Californio leader was Andrés Pico, the brother of California Governor Pío Pico. The Californios easily won the battle.

REVIEW Why did no one in California know that the United States and Mexico were at war? *Main Idea and Details*

Primary Sources

An account of the

Battle of San Pasqual

by Felicita Panto

"Early one rainy morning we saw soldiers that were not Mexicans. . . . They looked like ghosts coming through the mist, and then the fighting began. The Indians fled in fear to the mountains on the north side of the Valley, from where they looked down and watched the battle. All day long they fought. We saw some Americans killed and knew they were in a bad way."

Write About It! **How does Panto describe the United States soldiers?**

The War Ends 4.2.7

Although the Californios won some battles, American troops had more soldiers and more weapons. The United States won the war.

Bernarda Ruiz, a woman in Santa Barbara, helped to end the fighting. She was tired of all the bloodshed. She set up a meeting between Frémont and Andrés Pico at Cahuenga Pass, near Los Angeles. There, on January 13, 1847, the Californios surrendered. The two men signed a **treaty**, an agreement to make peace.

Although the Mexican War had ended in California it continued elsewhere for more than a year. The war finally ended on February 2, 1848. The United States and Mexico signed the Treaty of Guadalupe Hidalgo. In this treaty, Mexico gave nearly half its territory to the United States.

Look at the map. You can see that now the United States reached from the Atlantic Ocean to the Pacific Ocean. For many Americans, this meant that Manifest Destiny had been achieved. For Californians, it meant that they were now citizens of the United States.

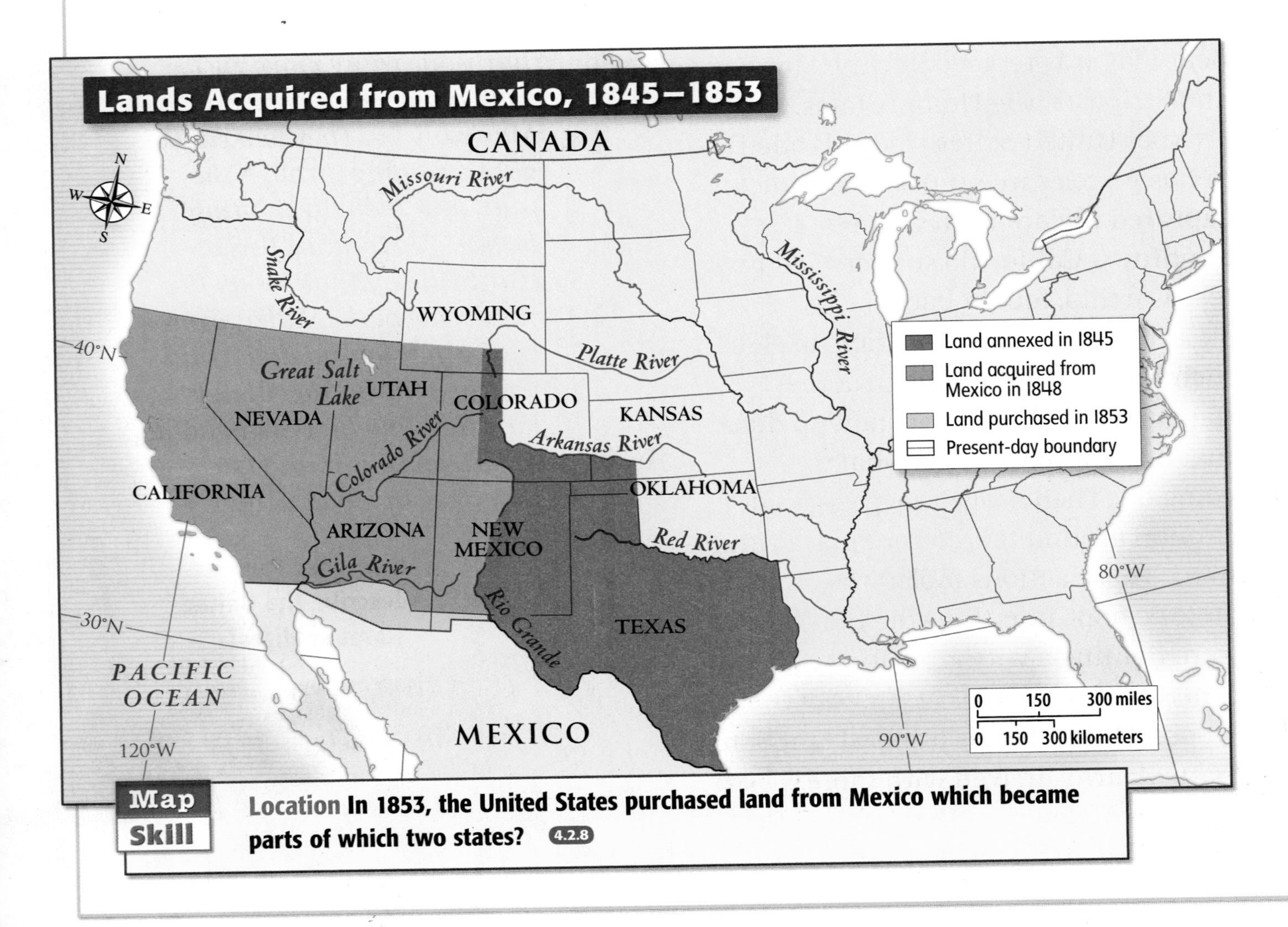

Map Skill **Location** In 1853, the United States purchased land from Mexico which became parts of which two states? 4.2.8

After the War

At the end of the war, the United States had gained the present-day states of California, Nevada, and Utah. Large parts of present-day Arizona, New Mexico, Colorado, and Wyoming became part of the country as well.

California was the greatest prize. It was a rich and varied territory with a sunny climate, fertile soil, and a long coastline. California also had something that only a few people knew about. Just nine days before the signing of the Treaty of Guadalupe Hidalgo, gold was discovered in the foothills of the Sierra Nevada. From now on, California would be even more valuable than anyone imagined.

REVIEW What made California such a valuable addition to the United States? *Main Idea and Details*

The treaty of Guadalupe Hidalgo added more than 1 million square miles of land to the United States. ▶

What You Learned

4.3 4.3.2 Many Americans believed that the United States had a right to the entire American West.

4.3 In the Bear Flag revolt, American settlers declared California to be a republic. Soon, the Mexican War began.

4.2.8 Mexico signed a treaty giving the United States much of its land. The United States now stretched from the Atlantic coast to the Pacific.

Lesson Review

1. **Focus Question** How did an idea called "Manifest Destiny" lead to a war that made California part of the United States? (4.2, 4.3)

2. **Vocabulary** Write one sentence for each vocabulary term. (4.2.8, 4.3)
   Manifest Destiny **republic** **treaty**

3. **Geography** How much of its territory did Mexico hand over to the United States in the Treaty of Guadalupe Hidalgo? (4.3)

4. **Critical Thinking** **Problem Solving** How did Bernarda Ruiz solve the problem of continued fighting between Californios and Americans in California? (4.2.8, 4.3)

5. **Reading Strategy** **Sequence Events** Reread the section of this lesson called "The War Ends." Use the chart to sequence the events in this section. (4.2.8, 4.3, ELA R2.1)

6. **Write about THE BIG IDEA** How did the Mexican War change the boundaries of the United States? (4.3, ELA W2.1)

7. **Link to Language Arts** Suppose you lived in the United States in the 1840s. Write a letter to the President explaining why you are for or against the idea of Manifest Destiny. (4.2, 4.3)

Citizenship
Points of View

What Did People in California Think About the Mexican War? 4.2

In California, people were divided about the war between Mexico and the United States. Some wanted California to become part of the United States. Others wanted to continue being governed by Mexico.

Read below to find out about three different points of view on the Mexican War.

"To rely any longer upon Mexico... would be... absurd. ... [The United States] is our adjoining neighbor... [and] we shall not become subjects, but fellow citizens..."

Mariano Guadalupe Vallejo
Mexican Military Commander
Excerpt from a speech, 1846

"North American adventurers [have invaded]. ... The North Americans can never be our friends [because] they have laws, religion, language, and dress totally the opposite of ours."

Pío Pico
Governor of California
Excerpt from a proclamation from Santa Barbara, 1846

"What... folly it is... to attempt to check the emigration from the United States to this country. They might as well attempt to... resist the mighty water's flow."

Lansford Hasting
United States settler
Excerpt from a letter, 1846

Build Citizenship
Leadership

1. How did the leaders in the Mexican War influence the way Californians felt about the conflict?
2. Which of these speakers seems to believe most strongly in Manifest Destiny?
3. Why do you think American settlers and Californios had different opinions about the Mexican War?

Think About It
Points of View

1. Why does Governor Pico favor fighting against the United States?
2. What reasons does Commander Vallejo give for his opinion?
3. What other opinions might Californians have had about the Mexican War?

Suppose that you owned a local newspaper in California. Write an editorial telling your readers whether you oppose or support the war.

Chapter Review

Vocabulary Review

Copy the sentences below on a separate sheet of paper. Use the list of vocabulary words to fill in the blanks.

diseño	**rancho**
fiesta	**republic**

1. A ________ is a ranch where animals are raised. (4.2.8)
2. The people pick their own leaders in a kind of government called a ________ . (4.2.7)
3. Guests came from miles around to attend the ________ , or party. (4.2.5)
4. A ________ is a hand-drawn map that showed the borders of a land area long ago. (4.2.8)
5. **Test Preparation** An ________ is a good that is sold or traded to another country. (4.2.8)

   A. **import** C. **pelt**
   B. **export** D. **treaty**

Comprehension Check

6. Why was life difficult for Native Americans in New Spain? (4.2.5)
7. How did Miguel Hidalgo inspire the Mexicans to go to fight for freedom? (4.2.7)
8. What effect did Manifest Destiny have on Californios? (4.2.8)
9. How did José Carillo and his soldiers fool the United States troops during the Mexican War? (4.3)
10. How did the war between Mexico and the United States end in California? (4.3)
11. **Critical Thinking** Why do you think the government believed it was more important to build ranchos than missions in California? (4.2.8)
12. **Critical Thinking** Why do you think the rebels decided to put Mariano Vallejo in prison during the Bear Flag Revolt? (4.3)

Use the Time Line

Use the time line below to answer each question.

13. Did the Mexican War for Independence begin before or after James Polk became President? (4.2.7)
14. How long did the war between Mexico and the United States last? (4.3)

1810 · 1820 · 1830 · 1840 · 1850

- **1810** The Mexican War for Independence begins
- **1821** The Mexican War for Independence ends
- **1845** James Polk elected President of the United States
- **1846** President Polk declares war against Mexico
- **1848** The war between Mexico and the United States ends

Skills Check

Write a complete sentence to answer each question.

Compare Maps at Different Scales

15. What is a map scale?
4.1.2

16. What is the scale in miles of the map below?
4.2.2

17. Test Preparation A _______ map could help you learn more about the San Pedro rancho of Los Angeles.
4.2.2

18. Test Preparation A _______ is a map that shows a small area, but a lot of details.
4.1.5

Using Primary Sources

Literature

19. What kind of information can you learn from a story about the 1800s?
4.2

20. Can fiction stories still tell us some facts about a different place and time?
4.2

Hands-on Activity

21. Create a Brochure Work in groups to create a brochure that answers this question:
4.3.2

Why did pioneers from the East want to come live in California?

Write About History

22. Narrative Suppose that you own a rancho in California during the 1800s. Write a short story that describes the kind of work you do there.
4.2.5
ELA W2.1

LOG ON For help with the process of writing, visit:

www.macmillanmh.com/ss/ca/writing

CHAPTER

7 Destination California

You Are There

"The whole country, from San Francisco to Los Angeles...resounds with the sordid [ugly] cry of "Gold! Gold! Gold!" while the field is left half-planted, the house half-built, and everything neglected but the manufacture [making] of pick and shovels."

These words are from the last edition of a San Francisco newspaper in 1849. Only two weeks earlier, the paper had printed the first story about the discovery of gold in the area around Sutter's Mill. Now the paper had to shut down because all the workers left their jobs to hunt for gold.

In this chapter you will learn about the excitement of the search for gold in California. You will also read about how California became a state.

CONSTITUTION of the STATE of CALIFORNIA.

Chapter Events

A 1848 — **1848** Gold is found (page 231)

B 1849 — **1849** Nearly 80,000 people come to California in search of gold (page 237)

C 1850 — **1850** California becomes the 31st state (page 247)

D 1851 — **1851** Towns and gold mining camps grow quickly (page 254)

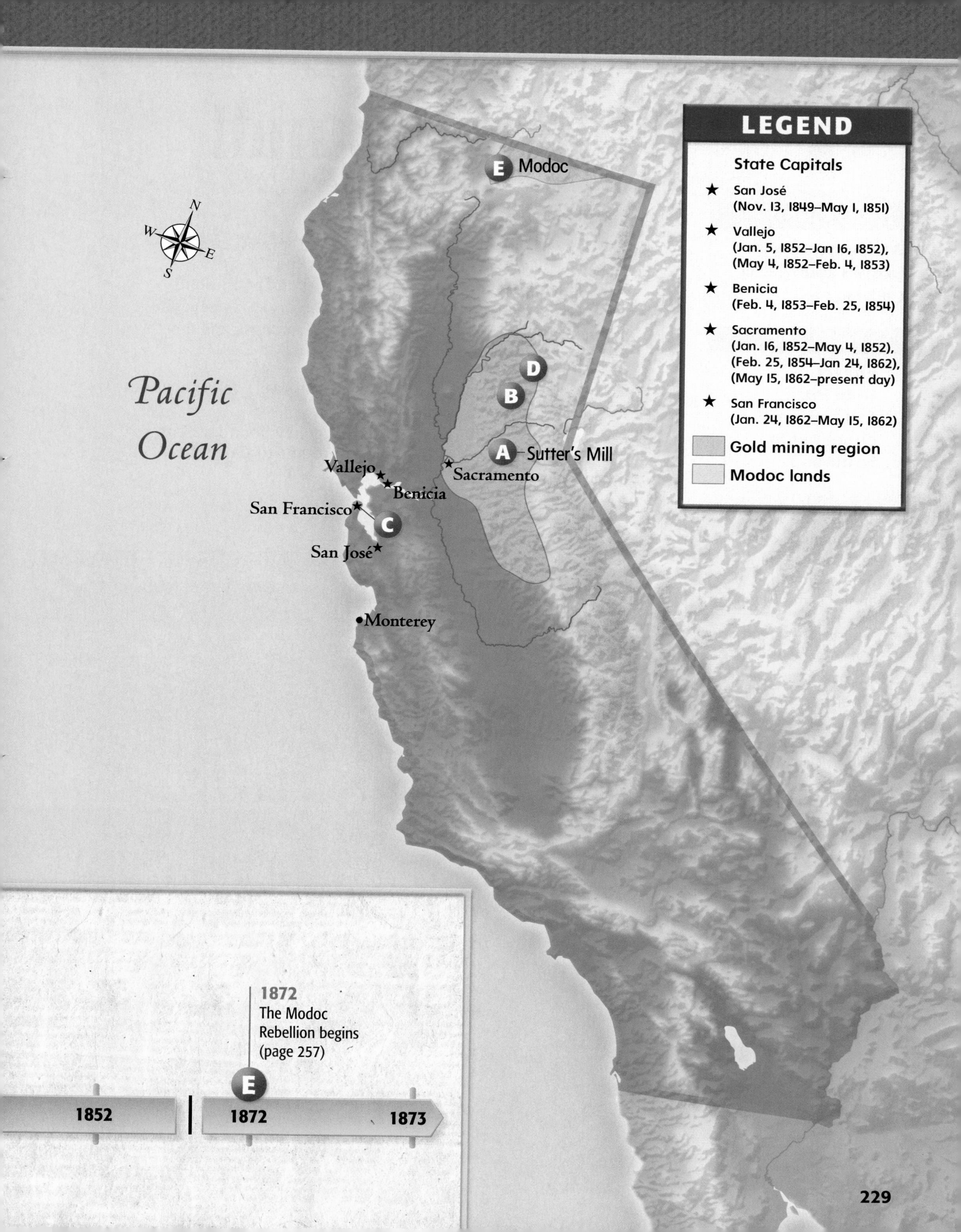

LEGEND
State Capitals
San José
(Nov. 13, 1849–May 1, 1851)
Vallejo
(Jan. 5, 1852–Jan 16, 1852),
(May 4, 1852–Feb. 4, 1853)
Benicia
(Feb. 4, 1853–Feb. 25, 1854)
Sacramento
(Jan. 16, 1852–May 4, 1852),
(Feb. 25, 1854–Jan 24, 1862),
(May 15, 1862–present day)
San Francisco
(Jan. 24, 1862–May 15, 1862)
Gold mining region
Modoc lands
Pacific Ocean
N
S
E
W
E Modoc
D
B
A Sutter's Mill
Sacramento
Vallejo
Benicia
San Francisco
C
San José
Monterey
1872
The Modoc
Rebellion begins
(page 257)
E
1852
1872
1873

Gold Is Found!

FOCUS QUESTION

What happened when gold was discovered in California?

VOCABULARY

nugget
Gold Rush
forty-niner
clipper ship
isthmus

VOCABULARY STRATEGY

SYNONYMS The word **nugget** means "a small piece." Can you think of other words that mean the same thing?

READING STRATEGY

Sequence Events

Use the chart to sequence events related to the discovery of gold in California.

Start with Your CALIFORNIA STANDARDS

4.3 Students explain the economic, social, and political life in California from the establishment of the Bear Flag Republic through the Mexican-American War, the Gold Rush, and the granting of statehood.

4.3.3 Analyze the effects of the Gold Rush on settlements, daily life, politics, and the physical environment.

Experience the excitement as the first gold is found at Sutter's Mill. Explore the risks of the different routes to California.
(Begins on page 231)

◀ Sutter's Mill, where gold was first found in California

1847	1848	1849
1847 Johann Sutter hires James Marshall to build a saw mill on the American River	1848 James Marshall finds gold at Sutter's Mill	1849 The Gold Rush begins

***O**n January 24, 1849, a crew of men was hard at work on a project for Johann Sutter. Standing knee-deep in the American River, they were clearing large stones from the riverbed. Suddenly, one of them let out a cry. He had spotted something shiny, "about the size of a pea." The minute he touched it, he said later, "It made my heart thump, for I was certain it was gold."*

Gold Is Found! 4.3.3

Johann Sutter had hired James Marshall to build a saw mill for cutting logs some distance up the river from Sutter's Fort. Now, with the lump of gold in his pocket, Marshall rode off to show his boss and get his opinion. Behind closed doors, the two men excitedly examined the **nugget**, or piece of metal. There was no doubt about it: It was high-quality gold.

Though a rumor about the gold spread quickly, many people did not believe it. Then, on May 12, 1848, a merchant named Sam Brannan had an idea. First, he bought up all the mining equipment he could find. Then he walked through San Francisco with a bottle of gold dust shouting "Gold! Gold! Gold! Gold from the American River!"

Heading To California

Now, everyone believed there was gold. All over California, people began heading for the gold fields. Ships in San Francisco harbor suddenly emptied as sailors heard the news and left. Everyone needed Brannan's mining equipment, and he became rich.

As the news of the discovery of gold spread around the world, people left everything behind and headed to California. This rapid movement of people in search of gold is known as the **Gold Rush**. Nearly 80,000 gold seekers from around the world came to California during 1849. They were called **forty-niners**.

REVIEW How did Sam Brannan make money from the discovery of gold?
Sequence Events

A poster advertising a clipper ship going to San Francisco ▼

▲ A clipper ship in a storm off Cape Horn in South America

Three Routes to California 4.3.2

People in the eastern United States were not sure what to think about the tales of gold. That changed on December 5, 1848, when President James Polk told Congress that the reports were true. Easterners' doubts turned to excitement.

By the spring of 1849, thousands of people were ready to leave for California. They could choose from three different routes.

Around Cape Horn

The first route was entirely by sea, and as you can see on page 234, went all the way around South America. The trip took four to eight months by cargo ship. Some travelers shortened this time by paying more to travel by **clipper ship**. The clipper ships were sleek and slim, with many more sails than ordinary ships.

Life on board any ship was hard. The ships were usually crowded. The food was often stale or moldy. There was little fresh water to drink. However, the worst part of the journey was getting around Cape Horn at the tip of South America. Terrible storms sank many ships at Cape Horn.

Across Panama

The second route was also by sea, but included a "shortcut." Travelers went by ship to Panama, in Central America. There, they crossed the **Isthmus** of Panama. An isthmus (ISS mus) is a narrow strip of land. You can find the Isthmus of Panama on the map on page 234.

People crossed the Isthmus on foot, by mule, and in small boats. It was a difficult journey through swamps and jungles. One young girl wrote:

> “***With the night came [hundreds] of mosquitoes. . . . Shrieks, growls, and murmurs filled the air, and we were very much afraid. . . .***”

Once they had crossed the Isthmus, travelers had to wait for another ship on Panama's Pacific coast. This ship took them north to San Francisco.

Across the Continent

The third route was overland by wagon train. The largest number of travelers chose this route. It was not only the cheapest way to travel, but allowed them to bring horses, cattle, supplies, and household goods.

The forty-niners in the wagon trains were mostly from farms, towns, and cities in the eastern United States. As you can see on the map on page 234, they gathered at towns in the middle of the United States. There, they waited for the good weather of late spring to start their journey. They were following the trails of the earlier explorers. However, they still had to ride or walk over rough land, wade through roaring rivers, climb steep mountain passes, and cross hot deserts.

Many people and animals died during this journey. Most people were exhausted by the hardships of the trip. However, they were determined to search for gold and start a new life.

REVIEW What were the three main ways of getting to California from the eastern United States? *Summarize*

People crossing the Isthmus of Panama in a small boat ▼

DATAGRAPHIC

Routes to California 4.3.2

Many of the forty-niners came from Europe, South America, and Asia. Europeans first had to get to New York. Once there, they had to choose from the same three routes that people in the eastern United States did.

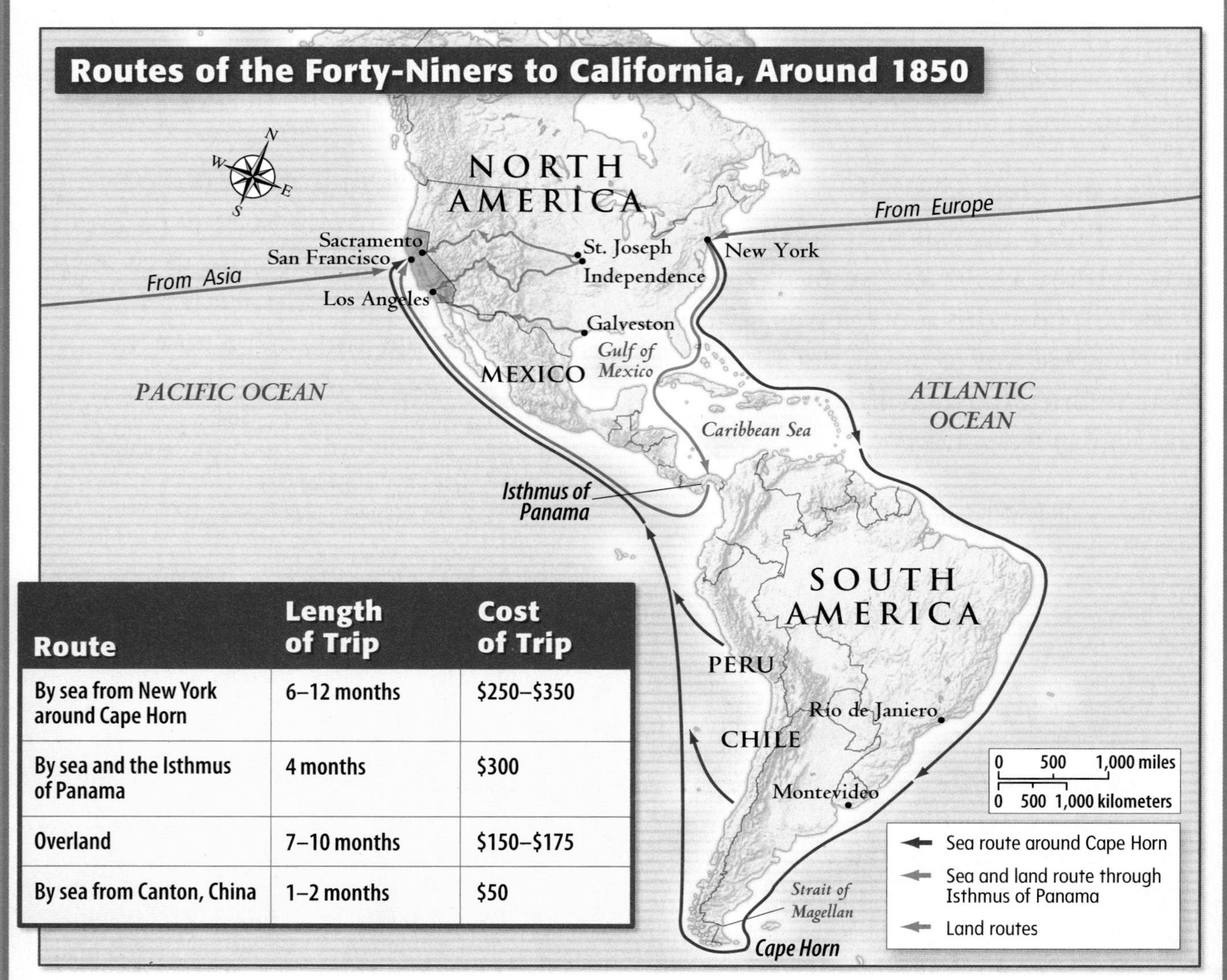

Route	Length of Trip	Cost of Trip
By sea from New York around Cape Horn	6–12 months	$250–$350
By sea and the Isthmus of Panama	4 months	$300
Overland	7–10 months	$150–$175
By sea from Canton, China	1–2 months	$50

Think About Routes to California

1. Looking at the map, which route looks the shortest? Which looks the longest?
2. Looking at the table, which route took the least amount of time?
3. Looking at the map, from which towns did the land routes to California start?

The Forty-Niners 4.3.3

When Bayard Taylor, a forty-niner from New York arrived in San Francisco, he saw:

> *"Hundreds of tents and houses . . . scattered all over the[hills] . . . buildings of all kinds, begun or half-finished . . . covered with all kinds of signs in all languages. . . . goods were piled in the open air. . . . The streets were full of people. . . . One knows not whether he is awake or in some wonderful dream."*

There were so many people that there were not enough hotels or houses for all of them. Stores were opened up everywhere. Some stores were built in the ships sailors had left in the harbor.

REVIEW How did the Gold Rush affect San Francisco? *Summarize*

▲ Ships fill San Francisco Bay in 1851.

What You Learned

- 4.3.3 Gold was discovered at Sutter's Mill in 1848.
- 4.3.3 There were three main routes from the eastern United States to California. All were difficult routes to travel.
- 4.3.3 Towns grew quickly, and finding housing was hard.

Lesson Review

1. **Focus Question** What happened when gold was discovered in California? 4.3.3
2. **Vocabulary** Write one sentence for each vocabulary term. 4.3.3
   clipper ship **Gold Rush** **nugget** **forty-niner** **isthmus**
3. **Economics** How did Sam Brannan profit from the Gold Rush? 4.3.3
4. **Critical Thinking** **Make Decisions** Which route would you have taken to California and why? 4.3.3
5. **Reading Strategy** **Sequence Events** Reread the section called "Gold Is Found!" Use the chart to sequence the events in this section. 4.3.3 ELA R2.1

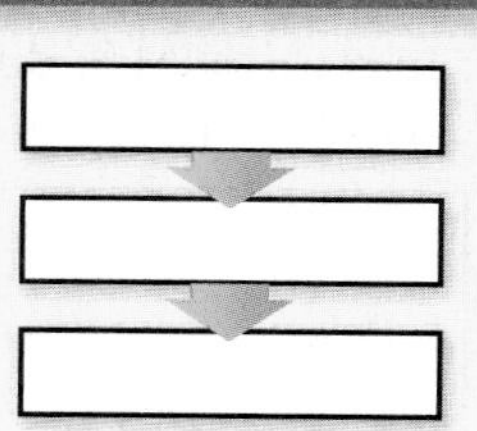

6. **Write about THE BIG IDEA** Write about whether or not you would have gone to California during the Gold Rush. Consider the chances of getting rich and the risks of the journey. 4.3.3 ELA W2.1
7. **Link to Language Arts** Choose one of the three routes to California. Write a letter describing that particular journey. 4.3.3 ELA W2.1

Life During the Gold Rush

FOCUS QUESTION

What was life like for the men and women who came to California in the Gold Rush?

VOCABULARY

- digging
- mother lode
- claim
- entrepreneur
- placer gold
- panning
- cradle
- long tom

VOCABULARY STRATEGY

WORD ORIGINS The word **entrepreneur** comes from a French word meaning "to undertake, organize, and manage."

READING STRATEGY

Summarize
Use the chart to summarize what you learn about life during the Gold Rush.

Start with Your CALIFORNIA STANDARDS

4.3 Students explain the economic, social, and political life in California from the establishment of the Bear Flag Republic through the Mexican-American War, the Gold Rush, and the granting of statehood.

4.3.3 Analyze the effects of the Gold Rush on settlements, daily life, politics, and the physical environment.

Discover what life was like in the gold fields. (Begins on page 238)

4.4 Students explain how California became an agricultural and industrial power, tracing the transformation of the California economy and its political and cultural development since the 1850s.

4.4.2 Explain how the Gold Rush transformed the economy of California, including the types of products produced and consumed, changes in towns, and economic conflicts among the diverse groups of people.

Find out how the struggle for land affected California's Native Americans and rancheros. (page 241)

San Francisco in 1849 ▼

1849	1850	1851	1852
1849 More than 80,000 miners work at the gold fields	**1850** The Foreign Miners' Tax Law is passed		**1852** San Francisco grows to 40,000

The forty-niners arrived with high hopes. As one wrote: "We pitched our tents, shouldered our picks [and] shovels, and with pan in hand headed out to try our fortunes at gold digging."

California Mining 4.3.3

The gold seekers bought mining supplies and recovered from their journeys in towns such as San Francisco. Then, the new miners headed out to a **digging**, as a gold field was called. Most miners went to the **mother lode**. This was the area below the central Sierra Nevada.

At these diggings, streams flowed down from the Sierra Nevada into the Sacramento and San Joaquin rivers. A miner could pick a spot by a stream and stake a **claim**. A claim was the miner's own special mining area.

By the end of 1849, more than 80,000 miners were working the mother lode. Although some miners became very rich, most did not. Only a few gold seekers went home richer than when they arrived.

Wherever gold was discovered, mining camps quickly sprang up. Some of these camps turned into towns. The towns needed stores, hotels, laundries, and places of entertainment. The **entrepreneurs**, or people who started these businesses, often ended up making more money than the miners.

REVIEW What did the miners do after buying supplies? *Summarize*

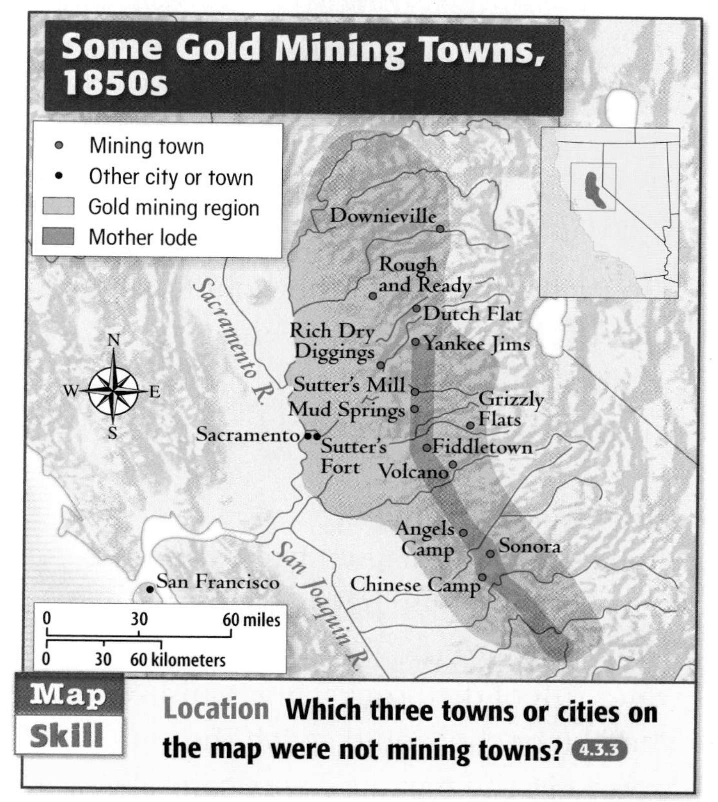

Map Skill Location **Which three towns or cities on the map were not mining towns?** 4.3.3

▲ An African American miner uses a long tom.

A Miner's Life 4.3.3

In the beginning of the Gold Rush, most of the gold in California was found on the banks of sandy streams. This was called **placer gold**.

Three Ways of Mining

The miners took gold from streams in a process called **panning**. A miner would use a round pan to scoop up water full of dirt, rocks, and sand. Then he or she would swish the water around in the pan, and very carefully spill out the water and dirt. Any gold would stay at the bottom of the pan because gold is heavier than dirt.

Another method of separating gold from dirt was to use a **cradle**. A cradle was made of two wooden trays, one on top of another. The upper tray had small holes in the bottom. One miner would shovel dirt into the top tray. A second miner would pour water into it and rock the cradle. Any gold would stay in the upper tray as the muddy water flowed into the lower tray.

Miners also used the **long tom** to separate the gold. The long tom was built on a hillside. It was like a long slide with a type of cradle at the end. Miners shoveled stony dirt and water into the top. The water washed out the dirt and left the gold behind at the bottom.

All three mining methods required long, hard days of work. At night, the miners were often so tired that they fell asleep where they were.

Women in the Gold Rush

A small number of the people who came to the gold fields were women. A few were miners. Other women came to the mining camps to set up businesses to take care of the miners. They cooked, sewed, did laundry, and ran hotels. They could often make more money doing these jobs than miners could make at the diggings.

As one hardworking woman wrote:

> ***"A smart woman can do very well in this country. . . . It is the only country I ever saw where a woman received anything like a [fair price] for work."***

One of the few women among the 1,000 people in the mining camp of Rich Bar was Louise Clappe. She had come out west with her husband. She sent a series of lively letters about her new life back home using the name Dame Shirley.

Dame Shirley complained that the miners sometimes fought and gambled, but she knew how hard it was for them to be so far from their homes and families. In fact, most of the miners lived hard and dangerous lives. One out of every five miners died within the first months of arriving in California.

To keep their spirits up, miners would gather around a fire at the end of the day. They would tell stories and sing songs about the miner's life. One of the best-known of their songs is "My Darling Clementine," which you can read on page 240.

REVIEW What were some of the miners' methods for finding gold? *Summarize*

Mining for gold in California, 1852 ▼

What story does the song tell about Clementine?

Diversity and Conflict 4.3.3 4.4.2

The gold fields drew people from all over the world. California soon became one of the most diverse places in North America. At first, the different groups got along well. However, as the gold fields became more crowded and less gold was found, things changed.

In the early days of the Gold Rush, many Native Americans worked as miners. As more people arrived at the mother lode, Native Americans were chased from their diggings. Some were forced to work for other miners for little pay.

Thousands of Mexicans also came looking for gold. They were skilled and experienced miners, and at first they were allowed to mine without trouble. As more people from the East arrived, however, problems arose. The United States had just finished fighting a war with Mexico. Many of the newly arrived Americans thought of the Mexicans as their enemies.

In order to keep Mexicans and people from other countries from mining, a law was passed. This law was called the Foreign Miners' Tax Law of 1850. Under this law, all miners from other countries had to pay a tax of 20 dollars a month to mine. This was a lot of money at the time. Many Mexican miners were unable to pay this tax and had to leave the gold fields.

Chinese miners also had to pay a tax. Thousands of Chinese immigrants had come to California during the Gold Rush. At first, they were welcomed. They were often willing to work for low pay. But, as the gold started running out, the Americans did not want Chinese miners to get the last gold. In 1852, another tax law was passed that required Chinese miners to pay four dollars a month to mine in California.

REVIEW What was an effect of the Foreign Miners' Tax Law of 1850? *Cause and Effect*

◀ A Chinese miner uses a cradle to look for gold.

A gold mining cradle ▼

Towns and Businesses 4.4.2

Thousands of miners continued to pour into California. As they came, towns and cities sprang up.

The city of Sacramento supplied goods to the northern mining camps. The town that served the miners in the south was Stockton. It was founded in 1848 and quickly grew into a city.

Booming San Francisco

However, the biggest city of all was San Francisco. By 1852, there were nearly 40,000 people living and working there. About 30 new houses were built in San Francisco every day.

The streets of San Francisco rang with the sounds of many languages. In a short time, San Francisco had become the center of banking, business, and society. Miners went to San Francisco to spend their money. They were entertained at music halls and traveling shows. They bought goods at the shops.

Business Opportunities

The miners needed many items. Business owners got rich from selling the miners what they needed. Sam

THEN and NOW

The Popularity of Blue Jeans 4.4.2

16 LEVI STRAUSS & Cº 14

THEN The many workers that had moved to California during the Gold Rush needed sturdy work clothes. In 1873, Levi Strauss got a patent for blue jeans. He used a strong cloth called denim to make pants that would last. His partner, Jacob Davis, fastened the pants pockets with metal rivets to keep them from tearing.

NOW Blue jeans, once popular with miners and cowboys, are now worn by men, women, and children all over the world. Today many different companies make denim jeans. Jeans now come in many colors and styles.

Write About It! Why did Levi Strauss invent denim jeans?

Brannan, the man who had started it all with his cry of "Gold!" continued to make money. By the middle of the 1850s, he was an important businessman in San Francisco.

Levi Strauss had moved to New York from Germany. In 1853, he moved to San Francisco. He began to import goods from New York. By 1873, Strauss and his partner, Jacob Davis, had invented a type of clothing that is popular to this day—blue jeans!

Another success story was Mifflin Gibbs. He was an African American who had worked against slavery. When Gibbs came to San Francisco in 1850, he had only 10 cents in his pocket. Soon he had enough money to open up a shoe store in San Francisco. In 1855, he started the first African American newspaper in California. Later, he became the first African American judge in United States history.

REVIEW What happened to towns in California during the Gold Rush? *Summarize*

What You Learned

- 4.3.3 Miners staked their claims in the gold fields, but few got rich.
- 4.3.3 Miners used panning, cradles, and long toms to separate out the gold. Some women worked in mining camps.
- 4.3.3 4.4.2 The miners from Mexico and China had to pay a tax to mine. Native Americans were driven from their diggings.
- 4.3.3 Towns near the gold fields grew very quickly. Merchants became rich supplying the miners.

Lesson Review

1. **Focus Question** What was life like for the men and women who came to California in the Gold Rush? (4.3.3)
2. **Vocabulary** Write one sentence for each vocabulary term. (4.3.3)

claim	**entrepreneur**	**panning**
cradle	**long tom**	**placer gold**
digging	**mother lode**	

3. **Geography** Why was mining for gold such hard work? (4.3.3)
4. **Critical Thinking** **Problem Solving** How did the miners solve the problem of separating gold from dirt, sand, and rocks? (4.3.3)
5. **Reading Strategy** **Summarize** Reread the section called "Towns and Businesses." Use the chart to summarize this section. (4.3.3, ELA R2.1)

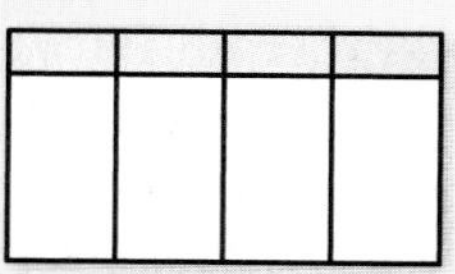

6. **Write about THE BIG IDEA** Write about the people who came to California during the Gold Rush and what their lives were like. (4.3.3, ELA W2.1)
7. **Link to Math** In San Francisco in 1852, about 30 houses were built each day. At that rate, how many houses could be built in a week? (4.3.3)

Using PRIMARY SOURCES

Understanding Letters 4.3.4

VOCABULARY

letter

A **letter** is a written message from the writer to another person. Letters are an important primary source. Letters tell historians how people felt and what they thought at the time an event occurred.

The Letters of Dame Shirley

Louise Clappe and her husband left New England and arrived in San Francisco in 1849. They lived in mining camps. Her husband, a doctor, looked for work and for gold. Clappe wrote a series of letters about her experiences to her sister Molly, who lived in Massachusetts. Dame Shirley was the name Louise Clappe used when signing her letters.

1 Learn It

Read the steps below to help you find information in letters.

- Look for the *date* and *place* the letter was written.
- Scan the letter to see if any events are mentioned or to find *background information.*
- Read to find out *why the letter was written.*
- Look up any unfamiliar words as you read.
- Review what you know about the *letter writer.* Predict the kind of information that the writer might include in a letter.

THE PIONEER;

OR,

CALIFORNIA

MONTHLY MAGAZINE,

EDITED BY F. C. EWER.

VOL. I. JAN. TO JUNE, 1854.

SAN FRANCISCO, CAL.:
PUBLISHED BY W. H. BROOKS & COMPANY.
Monson & Valentine, Book and Job Printers, 121 Sacramento Street.

1854.

2 Try It

■ Read the letter below. What information can you learn from it?

Date and Place — Rich Bar, East Branch of North Fork of Feather River
September 20, 1851.

Background information — On arriving at Rich Bar, part of the adventurers camped there, but many went a few miles further down the river. The next morning, two men turned over a large stone, beneath which they found quite a sizeable piece of gold. . . . Encouraged by this success, they commenced staking off the legal amount of ground allowed to each person for mining purposes . . . and before night the entire bar was "claimed." In a fortnight from that time, the two men who found the first bit of gold had each taken out six thousand dollars . . . .

Letter writer — Dame Shirley

Letter *the* Third
...nd FORTUNE *at the* BAR-DIGGINGS
...AR, EAST BRANCH *of the* NORTH FORK *of* FEATHER RIVER,
September 20, 1851.

I INTEND, to-day, dear M., to be as disagreeably statistical and as praiseworthily matter-of-factish as the most dogged utilitarian could desire. I shall give you a full, true, and particular account of the discovery, rise, and progress of this place, with a religious adherence to *dates* which will rather astonish your unmathematical mind. But let me first ...cribe the spot as it looked to my wondering ...l unaccustomed eyes. Remember, I had never ...en a mining district before, and had just left ...n Francisco, amid whose flashy-looking shops ...d showy houses the most of my time had been ...pent since my arrival in the Golden State. Of ...ourse, to me, the *coup d'œil* of Rich Bar was ...harmingly fresh and original. Imagine a tiny

45

3 Apply It

■ Write a letter to a friend in which you describe finding something valuable or important to you. Describe how you felt and what you did. Use descriptive language, just as Louise Clappe did to describe the discovery of gold by the miners at Rich Bar.

FOCUS QUESTION

How did California become a state?

VOCABULARY

delegate
convention
constitution
compromise
capital

VOCABULARY STRATEGY

PREFIXES Prefixes can help you understand the meaning of a word. The prefix **con-** or **com-** usually means "with" or "together." Which three words in the list above begin with this prefix?

READING STRATEGY

Sequence Events
Use the chart to sequence the events that led to California becoming a state.

The Thirty-First State

Start with Your CALIFORNIA STANDARDS

4.3 Students explain the economic, social, and political life in California from the establishment of the Bear Flag Republic through the Mexican-American War, the Gold Rush, and the granting of statehood.

4.3.3 Analyze the effects of the Gold Rush on settlements, daily life, politics, and the physical environment.

Find out how the effects of the Gold Rush increased the need for a state constitution. (page 247)

4.3.4 Study the lives of women who helped build early California.

Discover how a courageous woman stood up for her rights and won her freedom. (page 251)

4.3.5 Discuss how California became a state and how its new government differed from those during the Spanish and Mexican periods.

Explore the process by which California won its statehood. (Begins on page 247)

Colton Hall, Monterey, California ▼

1849 | 1850 | 1851 | 1852 | 1853 | 1854 | 1855 | 1856

1849
A meeting is held to decide on a constitution for California

1850
California becomes the 31st state in the United States

1856
Biddy Mason goes to court to keep her freedom

The moment had come. California needed to become a state. Delegates such as José Antonio Carrillo, to the right, had heated discussions, and made important decisions about a constitution. Actual statehood, however, would remain out of California's reach until an agreement was made in Washington, D.C.

The Need for Government 4.3.3 4.3.5

California was part of the United States, but it was not a state. Since the end of the Mexican War, it had military governors. They were chosen by the United States government in Washington, D.C. The people of California could not vote or choose their leaders. The old Mexican laws were still used, and there was no court system.

This system had worked as long as California remained a rancho economy. Once gold was discovered, however, everything changed.

The Gold Rush brought thousands of people from all over the world. Mining camps and towns were forming. The new arrivals in California wanted to make their own laws. Each mining area was making and enforcing its own rules. These different rules were confusing and often unfair.

Writing a Constitution

The last military governor, General Bennett F. Riley, knew that he must act. Otherwise, he might soon have trouble on his hands. He called for Californians to choose **delegates**, or people who would represent them. The delegates would come to a **convention**, or meeting, at Colton Hall in Monterey. This meeting would be the first step in writing a **constitution**. A constitution is a plan of government. The constitution would decide the size of California and the rights of its citizens.

REVIEW What were the steps in General Riley's plan? *Sequence Events*

Major Decisions 4.3.3 4.3.5

The convention began on September 1, 1849. Most of the 48 delegates were Americans who had been in California before the Gold Rush. Eight of them were Californios, including Mariano Guadalupe Vallejo and José Antonio Carillo.

The delegates made some important decisions. They had to choose whether to ask the United States Congress to make California a state or a territory. They decided to ask for statehood. Further, they decided that California would be a free state. This meant that California would not allow slavery. The delegates also decided that the Sierra Nevada and the Colorado River would be the eastern boundaries of California.

The Rights of Individuals

The delegates decided that married women should be allowed to control and keep their own property. No state in the nation had such a law. Yet the delegates also decided that only white male citizens could vote.

It would take a long time for all the citizens of California to gain the right to vote. African American men would win the right to vote in 1870. Women would be given voting rights in 1911. Native Americans would finally win the right to vote in 1924.

Following the convention, voters chose lawyer Peter H. Burnett as their first governor. Read the Primary Source below to see how Governor Burnett greeted the new California state legislature in his first speech.

Primary Sources

From the **Inaugural Address of Peter H. Burnett**
December 20, 1849

*"You compose the first Legislature of the first free American State organized upon the distant shores of the Pacific. How rapid [and] astonishing . . . have been the changes in California! . . . and amidst all this . . . excitement, the energetic, **intrepid**, and sensible people of California have **framed** a constitution for our new State."*

intrepid fearless **framed** created

What is Governor Burnett congratulating the California people for doing?

The Compromise of 1850

California's new senators went to Washington D.C. to seek California's admission as a state. At this time, the country was divided over slavery. Half the states were free states, which did not allow slavery. The other states were slave states. If California joined as a free state, there would be 16 free states to 15 slave states. The southern states did not want to let California join as a free state. The northern states wanted another free state.

Finally, a **compromise** was reached. A compromise is an agreement in which each side gives up something. In the Compromise of 1850, California could join the nation as a free state. In exchange, a new law would require the police in free states to return all enslaved people who had escaped from slave states.

◀ General Bennett F. Riley, last military governor of California.

Enslaved people were still brought to California. The question arose whether enslaved people brought to a free state could be returned to a slave state. A remarkable woman named Biddy Mason put this issue to the test in 1856. You will read her story on page 251.

REVIEW Why was California's request to be admitted as a free state a problem?
Main Idea and Details

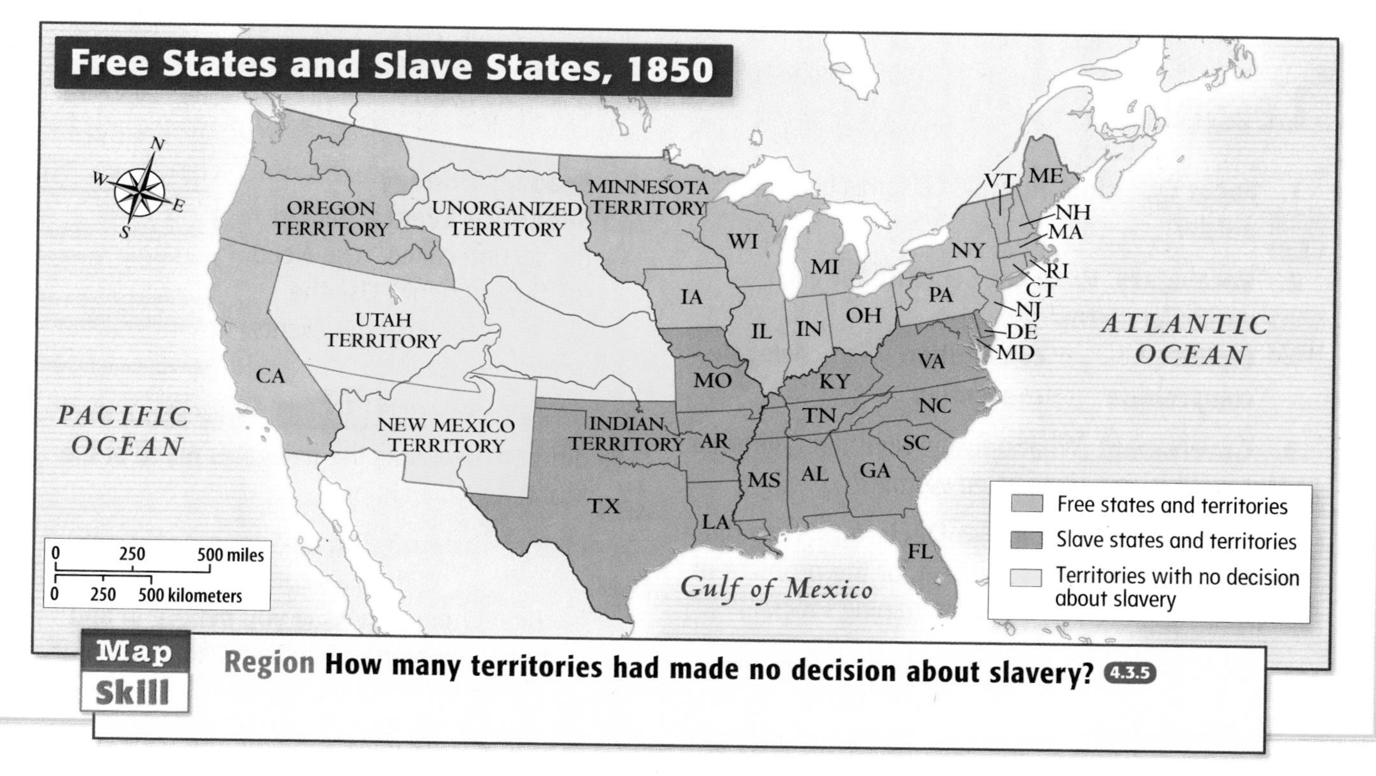

Map Skill Region **How many territories had made no decision about slavery?** 4.3.5

California Becomes a State 4.3.5

On September 9, 1850, California became the 31st state in the nation. That date is now celebrated each year as "Admission Day."

The new state government chose the city of San José as its **capital**, or government center. However, the capital would move to three other cities before Sacramento became the permanent capital in 1954.

There were important differences between the new state government and those of the Spanish and Mexican periods. Under Spanish and Mexican rule, the governor of California was appointed. The governor of the state of California was elected.

REVIEW How did the different governments choose governors for California? *Compare and Contrast*

▲ Room in Colton Hall, Monterey, where delegates met to discuss California's constitution

What You Learned

4.3.3 4.3.5 A convention was held to write a constitution for California.

4.3.3 4.3.5 The delegates to the convention made important decisions about the future of California.

4.3.5 California was admitted as a free state on September 9, 1850.

Lesson Review

1. **Focus Question** How did California become a state? 4.3 4.3.5
2. **Vocabulary** Write one sentence for each vocabulary term. 4.3.3 4.3.5
   capital **constitution** **delegate** **compromise** **convention**
3. **Government** What unusual right did California's constitution give married women? 4.3.3 4.3.5
4. **Critical Thinking** **Make Decisions** How did General Riley find a solution for the problem of having different laws in the mining town? 4.3.3 4.3.5
5. **Reading Strategy** **Sequence Events** Reread the section called "The Need for Government." Use the chart to sequence the events in this section. 4.3.5 ELA R2.1
6. **Write about THE BIG IDEA** Write about the different decisions the delegates made at the Monterey convention. 4.3.5 ELA W2.1
7. **Link to Language Arts** Suppose you were a delegate to California's constitutional convention in 1849. Choose an issue you believe in and write a paragraph to persuade others of your position on it. 4.3.5

4.3.4

Biddy Mason 1818–1891

Biddy Mason was born into slavery on a large farm in Georgia. In 1851, she and her three daughters were brought to California by her owner, Robert Smith.

California was a free state by the time they got there. Slavery was not allowed. Soon, Smith decided to move to Texas, a slave state. Mason and her children would not be free there, so she refused to leave. With the help of the sheriff of Los Angeles County, her case went to court. In 1856, a judge ruled that Mason and her children were "entitled to their freedom and are free forever."

Over the next 10 years, Mason worked very hard as a nurse and midwife in Los Angeles. She saved her money and was able to buy land in 1866. She became known for her kindness and for giving freely to those in need. She said,

"If you hold your hand closed . . . nothing good can come in. The open hand is blessed, for it gives . . . even as it receives."

How did Biddy Mason show courage?

For more about Biddy Mason, visit:

www.macmillanmh.com/ss/ca/bios

The Life of Biddy Mason

1815 · 1835 · 1855 · 1875 · 1895

- **1818** Born in Georgia
- **1851** Brought to California
- **1856** Is declared a free woman
- **1866** Buys her first land
- **1891** Dies in Los Angeles

MAP and GLOBE Skills

Use Special Purpose Maps: Population Maps 4.3.3

VOCABULARY

population map

A **population map** gives you information about where people live in a particular region and how many people live there.

Map A on the next page shows you where most people were living when California achieved statehood in 1850. Map B shows you where most people live in California today. Both maps show how the population was spread out across the state.

1 Learn It

- Suppose you wanted to find out where most of the people in California were living at the time statehood was granted. Map A's title tells you that this map will answer your question.
- Suppose you now wanted to find out where most people in California are living today. Map B's title tells you that this map will show you that information.
- Read the title of the map. Map A shows California's population in 1850.
- Population maps use different colors to stand for different amounts. On these maps, each color stands for a certain number of people. For example, yellow means that there are between 0 and 500 people living in each area that is shaded yellow on the map. Purple stands for areas with the most people, more than 5,000.
- Read the maps to see which areas have more or less of an amount. On Map A you can see that the red-shaded areas are in the middle of California. These were the areas where the Gold Rush took place. In 1850, during the Gold Rush, more people lived in that part of California than in other parts of the state.

2 Try It

Read Map B below and answer the questions.

- What does the color yellow mean on this map?
- How many people are living in the area around Los Angeles?
- Compare the population of the area around San Diego with the population of the area around Eureka. Which area has a larger population?

3 Apply It

- Make a population map of your grade school.
- Give each population group a different color. Use these four categories: 30 – 40 students; 40 – 50 students; 50 – 60 students; 60 – 70 students.

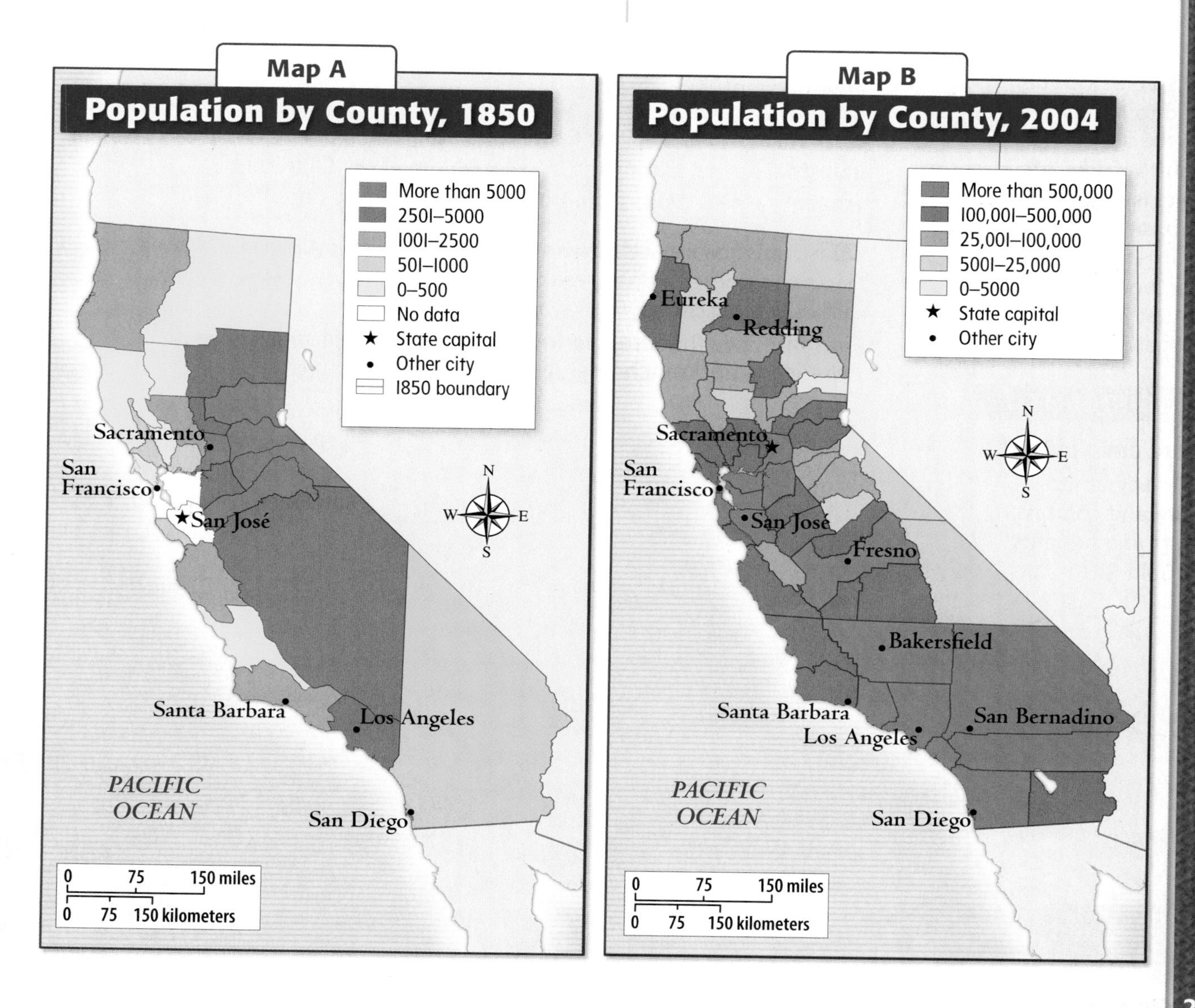

FOCUS QUESTION

How did the Gold Rush change California?

VOCABULARY

cost
benefit
vigilante
reservation
squatter
hydraulic mining

VOCABULARY STRATEGY

SUFFIXES Verbs can be changed to nouns by adding the suffix **-tion.** The noun **vacation**, for example, is made from the verb **vacate** plus the suffix **-tion**. Find another word in the list above that has been made this way.

READING STRATEGY

Compare and Contrast

Use the diagram to compare and contrast the costs and benefits of the Gold Rush.

Impact of the Gold Rush

Start with Your CALIFORNIA STANDARDS

4.3 Students explain the economic, social, and political life in California from the establishment of the Bear Flag Republic through the Mexican-American War, the Gold Rush, and the granting of statehood.

4.3.3 Analyze the effects of the Gold Rush on settlements, daily life, politics, and the physical environment.

Learn how the Gold Rush affected California's natural environment. (page 259)

4.4 Students explain how California became an agricultural and industrial power, tracing the transformation of the California economy and its political and cultural development since the 1850s.

4.4.2 Explain how the Gold Rush transformed the economy of California, including the types of products produced and consumed, changes in towns, and economic conflicts between diverse groups of people.

Find out how the struggle for land affected California's Native Americans and rancheros. (Begins on page 256)

San Francisco in 1860 ▼

1850 | 1855 | 1860 | 1865 | 1870 | 1875

1851 The United States government promises land to Native American groups

1853 Hydraulic mining is invented

1872 The Modoc return to their land

1875 Helen Hunt Jackson writes *A Century of Dishonor*

The Gold Rush was a time of tremendous excitement. New people kept arriving, and most of them believed their luck would change overnight. For many, just being there was amazing. They called it "seeing the elephant."

Costs and Benefits of the Gold Rush 4.3.3 4.4.2

The early years of the Gold Rush were both exciting and scary. No other part of the United States had ever experienced such sudden change on such a large scale.

Some of the effects of the Gold Rush were good. Others were bad. All together, these good and bad effects of the Gold Rush are called its **costs** and **benefits**.

The Benefits

The Gold Rush caused a booming economy. Mining camps grew into towns, and towns grew into cities, sometimes in a matter of months.

Another benefit was the arrival of people from places all over the world. They gave California a rich mix of experience, talent, and culture.

California's rapid achievement of statehood was an indirect benefit of the Gold Rush. Without the huge number of people who came at this time, California might not have applied for statehood so soon.

The Costs

On the cost side, various groups found themselves in conflict. Those in the majority, who were usually white Americans, often used their greater numbers to drive out other groups. Among those who suffered the most in this struggle for resources were Native Americans and Californios. During the same period, the Foreign Miners' Tax Laws of 1850 and 1852 drove away many Mexican and Chinese miner's.

Another cost of the Gold Rush was the environment. New mining methods badly damaged California's mountains, leaving effects that are still being felt today.

REVIEW What law drove many Mexican and Chinese miners away? *Cause and Effect*

▲ Kintpuash, or Captain Jack

Trouble in California 4.4.2

California in the 1850s was a dangerous place. Some new laws were meant to help. Some new laws were unfair. The laws did not protect Native Americans, Mexicans, African Americans, Asians, or Californios.

The towns and mining camps of California were rough places. They had grown so quickly that there wasn't much law or order. No one was in charge. Miners often made their own laws to protect their claims and to settle arguments.

Miners formed groups, called **vigilantes**, to punish people who broke the laws. Often, the vigilantes punished people they considered enemies, even if no laws were broken.

Native Americans Leave Their Lands

The Native Americans suffered during the Gold Rush. In 1846, there were about 150,000 Native Americans in California. By 1870, there were only 30,000.

Many Native Americans died from diseases brought by the miners and settlers. Some Native Americans starved for lack of hunting grounds because mining had damaged their land and water. A great many Native Americans were killed by miners, ranchers, and settlers who wanted to take their land.

▼ A newspaper article about Captain Jack and the Modoc hiding in lava beds

HARPER'S WEEKLY
A JOURNAL OF CIVILIZATION
Vol. XVII.—No. 861.] NEW YORK, SATURDAY, JUNE 28, 1873.
CAPTAIN JACK'S CAVE.
THE MODOC WAR—CAPTAIN JACK'S CAVE IN THE LAVA BEDS.

In 1851 and 1852, the United States government made 18 treaties with the Native Americans. These treaties promised to put aside large **reservations**, or lands, for the Native Americans.

However, this land was never legally set aside. Instead, Native Americans were sent to places where there was little water or food. Different groups of Native Americans were forced to live in the same area. Settlers ignored Native Americans' rights to this land. Settlers, often with the help of United States soldiers, forced Native Americans off their land.

◀ Helen Hunt Jackson's book, *A Century of Dishonor.*

▲ Helen Hunt Jackson

The Modoc Return

In 1872, some 150 Modoc tried to return to their land in northern California. They were led by a man named Kintpuash, also known as Captain Jack. They were attacked by soldiers with guns and cannons. There were more soldiers than there were Modoc, but the Modoc fought hard.

The Modoc War lasted almost a year. In the end, the Modoc lost. Their leader, Kintpuash, was hanged. The Modoc were forced back to land in southern Oregon and in Oklahoma.

After the war, a journalist named Helen Hunt Jackson wrote a book called *A Century of Dishonor.* In it she wrote about the poor treatment of Native Americans in California.

Jackson hoped it would change the way the United States government treated Native Americans. She sent a copy of the book to every member of Congress.

REVIEW What happened to the Native Americans of California during the Gold Rush? *Summarize*

▲ A Californio family

The End of the Ranchos 4.3.3 4.4.2

The Treaty of Guadalupe Hidalgo promised that the Mexican people would be allowed to keep and own their land. This included millions of acres of land owned by the Californios.

However, American settlers and miners believed that all of California belonged to the United States. They felt this allowed them to claim and settle on the Mexican–Americans' ranches.

They took the Californios' land without buying it. These settlers were known as **squatters**. When the Californios tried to remove them, the squatters often fought back.

In 1851, the United States government named a group called the Land Commission to settle the problem of land ownership. The Mexican–American ranchers met with the Land Commission. They hired lawyers to prove they owned their lands. In the end, the rancheros won 600 of their cases and lost 200.

However, it often took as long as 17 years before the Land Commission made a decision. The cases took so long that most of the rancheros had to sell their lands to pay their lawyers.

Apolinaria Lorenzano, once the proud owner of three ranchos, lost all of her lands. She wrote:

> ***"I find myself in the greatest poverty, living . . . from handouts."***

Mariano Guadalupe Vallejo, a Californio, was one of those who lost almost all of his land to the squatters. You will learn more about his life in the biography on page 261.

New Faces in California

The Gold Rush had huge effects on California's population. Earlier, California's population had been made up mostly of Californios and Native Americans.

Suddenly there were thousands of people coming in from all over the world. These people brought their customs and experiences with them. They made California a different place.

It took courage and determination to cross the plains or the ocean to make a new life. It took talent and daring to start a new business. The newcomers had all these qualities.

These same people did a lot of damage, however. They harmed the Native Americans and other groups of people who had been living in California when they arrived.

Mining Changes the Land and Water

In their search for gold, the miners damaged California's natural environment. With so many miners searching for gold, it wasn't long before all the placer gold was gone. When this was gone, miners had to dig deeper into the ground. In 1853, **hydraulic mining** was invented. Miners used hoses to blast water at hillsides to find gold. This newer technology destroyed hills, muddied streams, and killed fish.

The effects of hydraulic mining can still be seen today. The miners dug up tons of dirt and sand. This destroyed parts of the land that used to hold back floods. During heavy rains these areas often experience floods and mudslides today.

Hydraulic mining caused environmental damage that now causes mudslides and landslides. ▼

New Wealth and People

Suddenly there were new towns, cities, and businesses. There were also new ways of doing things. With so many Americans coming to California, the road to statehood was a short one. California became an important place very quickly.

New farms were started to feed all the people who now lived in California. The paths of rivers and streams were changed to bring water to these farms. The land changed forever.

The California Gold Rush became the symbol of taking risks and winning against the odds. It offered a chance to make dreams come true.

REVIEW How did the arrival of so many people affect California's road to statehood? *Cause and Effect*

What You Learned

4.3.3 4.4.2 The Gold Rush had costs, which included damage to the environment and conflict between ethnic groups. It also had benefits such as a boom in the economy and the arrival of new people.

4.4.2 Vigilantes took the law into their own hands. New settlers and miners drove some of the Native Americans off their land. Other Native Americans died of disease and starvation. Native Americans had to move to reservations because treaties were not honored.

4.3.3 4.4.2 Squatters took the land of many Californios without paying for it. Once the placer gold ran out, miners needed new technologies. Their methods caused damage to the environment that is still felt today.

4.4.2 The growth of California because of the Gold Rush caused changes to the land and the culture.

Lesson Review

1. **Focus** How did the Gold Rush change California? 4.3.3 4.4.2
2. **Vocabulary** Write one sentence for each vocabulary term. 4.3.3 4.4.2

benefit	**reservation**
cost	**squatter**
hydraulic mining	**vigilante**

3. **Technology** How did the change in mining methods affect the environment? 4.3.3
4. **Critical Thinking** **Problem Solving** Why did the miners turn to hydraulic mining? 4.3.3
5. **Reading Strategy** **Compare and Contrast** Use the chart to show what happened to Californios and Native Americans during the Gold Rush. How were their experiences similar? 4.4.2 ELA R2.1

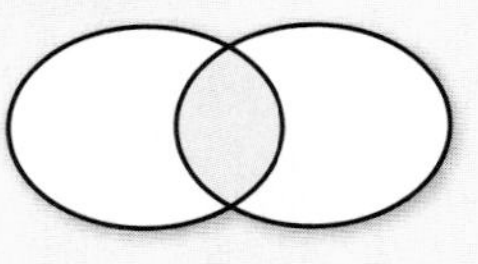

6. **Write about THE BIG IDEA** Write about the costs and benefits of the Gold Rush. 4.3.3 ELA W2.1
7. **Link to Language Arts** Suppose you are a reporter in California during the Gold Rush. Write a paragraph describing a development that especially interests you. 4.3.3

Biography
Focus on Leadership

4.3.3

Mariano Guadalupe Vallejo

1808–1890

Mariano Guadalupe Vallejo was born to a wealthy family in Alta California. At the age of 15, Vallejo became a soldier in the Mexican army. At 22, he defeated a Native American uprising. He was soon made military commander of the Mexican army in Northern California.

Vallejo was not happy with the government of Mexico. He thought that many of its laws were unfair. He believed that the government of the United States would make a good model for an independent California.

Despite his views, Vallejo was briefly arrested during the Bear Flag Revolt, and later lost most of his land to squatters. Still, he had confidence in the new California. In 1849, he became a delegate to its first convention and helped write its constitution. He also became a state senator.

Write About It! **How did Vallejo show his leadership?**

For more about Mariano Guadalupe Vallejo, visit:
www.macmillanmh.com/ss/ca/bios

The Life of Mariano Guadalupe Vallejo

1800 — 1825 — 1850 — 1875 — 1900

- **1808** Born in Monterey
- **1835** Becomes military commander of Northern California
- **1846** Arrested during Bear Flag Revolt
- **1849** Serves as delegate to California's constitutional convention
- **1875** Publishes his memoirs
- **1890** Dies in Sonoma

CHAPTER 7

Chapter Review

Vocabulary Review

Copy the sentences below on a separate sheet of paper. Use the list of vocabulary terms to fill in the blanks.

capital **forty-niner**
constitution **nugget**

1. A ______ is a small lump of gold. 4.3.3
2. A ______ is the center of government. 4.3.5
3. A ______ is a person who came to California in 1849 in search of gold. 4.3.3
4. A ______ is a plan that explains how a government should be set up and run. 4.5.4
5. Test Preparation The ______ was an area that was rich in gold located in the central Sierra Nevada foothills. 4.3.3

   A. **mother lode** C. **claim**
   B. **panning** D. **sluice**

Comprehension Check

6. Name the two sea routes that travelers took to reach California from the East. 4.3.2
7. What was the Foreign Miners' Tax Law of 1850? 4.3.3
8. Which town had the biggest population boom during the Gold Rush? 4.3.3
9. How many delegates attended the 1849 convention to start writing a constitution? 4.3.5
10. How was the new California government different from the old Mexican government? 4.3.5
11. Critical Thinking Why do you think hotel and shop owners often made more money than the miners during the Gold Rush? 4.3.3
12. Critical Thinking Do you think the benefits of the Gold Rush were greater than the costs? Why or why not? 4.3.3

Use the Time Line

Use the time line below to answer each question.

13. How many years does this time line show? 4.4.2
14. Did California become a state before or after gold was discovered? 4.3.5

1845 1855 1865 1875

1848 James Marshall discovers gold at Sutter's Mill

1850 California becomes a state

1851 Native Americans move onto reservations

1872 The Modoc go to war against the United States

Skills Check

Write a complete sentence to answer each question.

Use Special Purpose Maps: Population Maps

15. What do population maps show?
4.1.5

16. Today, about 750,000 people live in San Francisco. Look at the map on this page. Do more people live north or south of the city?
4.1.5

Bay Area: Population Map, 2004

Sonoma
Napa
Petaluma
0 5 10 miles
0 5 10 kilometers
Vallejo
N
W
E
S
Walnut Creek
Berkeley
San Francisco
Oakland
Hayward
San Mateo
Fremont
Palo Alto
Santa Clara
San José

People per Square Mile

- More than 30,000
- 15,000–30,000
- 7,000–15,000
- 2,000–7,000
- Less than 2,000
- • City

Using Primary Sources

Letters

17. Why is a letter an example of a primary source?
4.3.3

18. What kind of information can you learn from a letter written during the Gold Rush?
4.3.3

Hands-on Activity

19. **Make a Poster** Work in groups to make a poster that answers this question:
4.3.3

What is one way that miners searched for gold?

Decorate your poster with drawings or magazine pictures to make it more visually attractive.

Write About History

20. **Expository** Write a brief essay that describes what life was like in a mining camp during the Gold Rush. Be sure to include facts and details.
4.3.3 ELA W2.3

For help with the process of writing, visit:

www.macmillanmh.com/ss/ca/writing

Unit Review and Test Prep

Comprehension and Critical Thinking Check

Write one or more sentences to answer each question.

1. What did most Californios do with the **land grants** they received from the Mexican government? 4.2.8
2. How did Californians use cattle **hides** in the 1800s? 4.2.8
3. Why did Californios need to **import** goods from other places? 4.2.8
4. Why did Jedidiah Strong Smith cross the Rocky Mountains with other **trappers**? 4.3.2
5. Name some of the difficulties people faced on **clipper ships** headed to California. 4.3.2
6. How many **forty-niners** arrived in California in 1849? 4.3.3
7. During the **convention** in 1849, where did the **delegates** decide to set California's border? 4.3.5
8. How did many **entrepreneurs** benefit from the **Gold Rush**? 4.3.3
9. **Critical Thinking** How did California become a state? 4.3.3
10. **Critical Thinking** Why do you think the Modoc people decided to go to war instead of agreeing to live on a **reservation**? 4.4.2

Reading Social Studies Check

Sequence Events

Copy this graphic organizer. Reread "Mexico Wins Its Independence" on page 197. Use the graphic organizer to help you order the sequence of events. Then answer the questions. 4.2.7 ELA R2.1

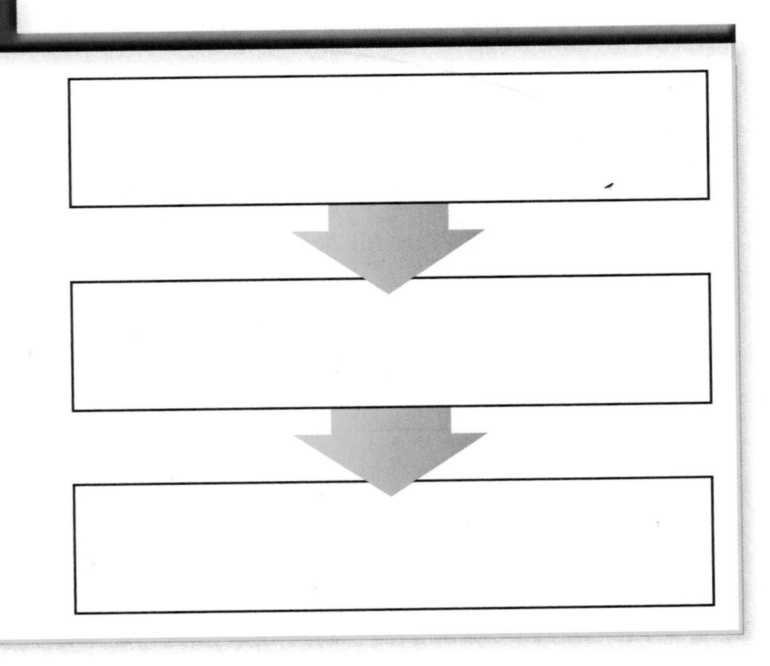

11. What is a sequence of events? ELA R2.1
12. How did you figure out the sequence of events? ELA R2.1
13. How did you know what to put in the second box? ELA R2.1

Test Preparation

Read the paragraphs. Then answer the questions.

In the 1800s, not many women ran a business or owned land. Juana Briones, however, needed to feed her family. So she started her own business. She grew food and sold it to people in San Francisco, and she opened an inn.

With the money she made, Briones bought land near San Francisco Bay. She started a rancho there to raise horses and cattle. She made a great deal of money selling cattle hides.

14. Which of these is a detail from the passage? 4.2.5

A Running a rancho is hard work.

B Juana Briones needed to start a business to take care of her family.

C Women enjoy working with animals.

D Ships often sail in and out of San Francisco.

15. What is the main idea of the passage? 4.2.5

A Juana Briones sold food to people on ships that sailed into San Francisco.

B Juana Briones had twelve children.

C Juana Briones was a success in a time when not many women owned land or a business.

D San Francisco created a plaque in honor of Juana Briones.

Write About History

16. **Expository** Write a brief essay to describe what a rodeo is like today. You will need to use reference sources from the school library or the Internet for research. 4.4.9 ELA W.2.3

17. **Narrative** Suppose you are traveling on a ship to California in the 1840s. Write a diary entry to describe what the trip is like. 4.3.3 ELA W.2.1

18. **Summary** Suppose you are a delegate attending the 1849 convention. Write a summary of the discussions about California's statehood. 4.3.5 ELA W.2.4

For help with the process of writing, visit:

www.macmillanmh.com/ss/ca/writing

Why do people take great risks?

Write About the Big Idea ELA W.1.1 ELA W.1.3

Journal Entry

Think about the events that happened as California grew and became a state. Then, complete the graphic organizer.

Imagine that you live on a rancho, with fur trappers, with settlers, in a gold mining camp, or in a group traveling to California from the east coast. Use information from the graphic organizer and from your textbook. Write a journal entry about your life. Describe what your life is like. Explain why you are willing to take risks.

Mexicans	Californios	Fur Trappers, Settlers, and Gold Miners	Californians
Fought war against Spain			

Write a Journal Entry

1. Plan

- Choose one group from the graphic organizer. Pretend that you live with them.
- List details about what your life is like, including the risks you face.

2. Write a First Draft

- Tell the story of a day in your life in early California. Include details that will be interesting and important to others.
- Use the word "I" as you tell about your life.

3. Revise and Proofread

- Read your journal entry. Did you write about a typical day in your life?
- Proofread your entry. Be sure you spelled words correctly. Check capitalization and punctuation.
- Rewrite your journal entry neatly before handing it in.

ACTIVITY

Speak About the Big Idea

ELA LS2.1

Stories of Experience

Tell stories about the dangers of life in early California.

Prepare Work in groups organized by the journal entries you wrote. All the people who wrote about the same group should be together. Use your journal entries, information from Unit 3, and other sources. Practice telling stories of your lives. Your stories should be brief and interesting.

Present First, each member of the group should tell his or her story. Then, one person from the group should summarize the information from your group.

For help with the Big Idea activity, visit:

www.macmillanmh.com/ss/ca/launchpad

Read More About the Big Idea

A Covered Wagon Girl

Sallie Hester Actual journal entries tell the true story of a 14-year-old girl who made the trip west in a wagon train with her family.

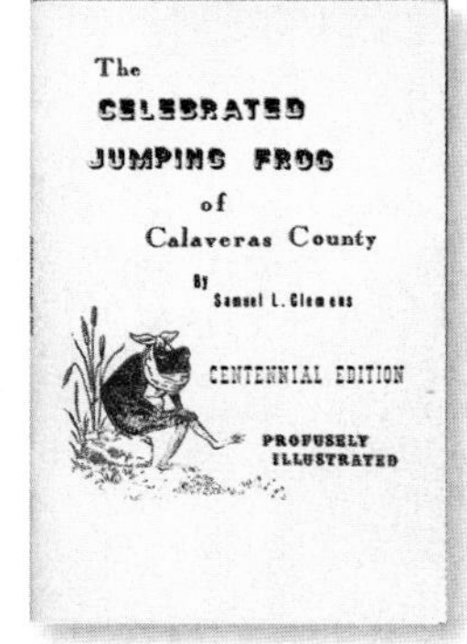

The Celebrated Jumping Frog of Calaveras County

Samuel L. Clemens Enjoy this humorous story of Gold Rush life by one of America's greatest writers.

UNIT 4

A Growing State

"The last rail is laid, the last spike driven, the Pacific railroad is completed."

– Leland Stanford and Thomas C. Durant, from *Golden Spike*

How does technology change people's lives?

In Unit 4, you will read about new inventions and technologies that changed lives. You will also read about many people who helped bring these changes to California.

Copy the graphic organizer below. As you read the chapters in this unit, look for information about improvements in transportation, communication, farming, and industry.

Then fill in details about the information you found. The first one has been started for you.

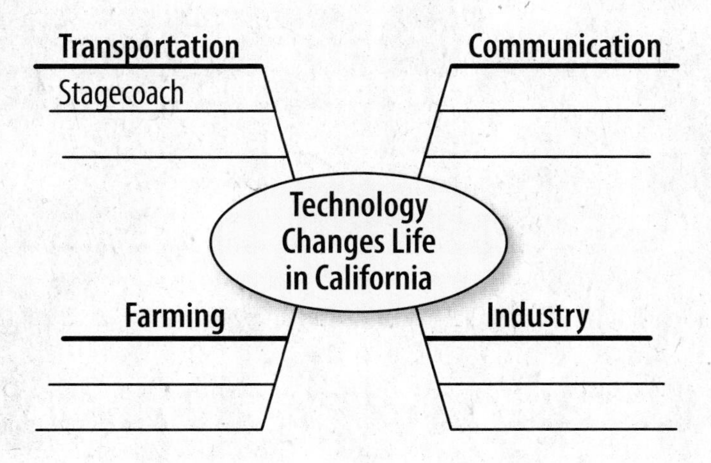

◀ Railroads opened California to more settlement.

UNIT 4

People Who Made a Difference

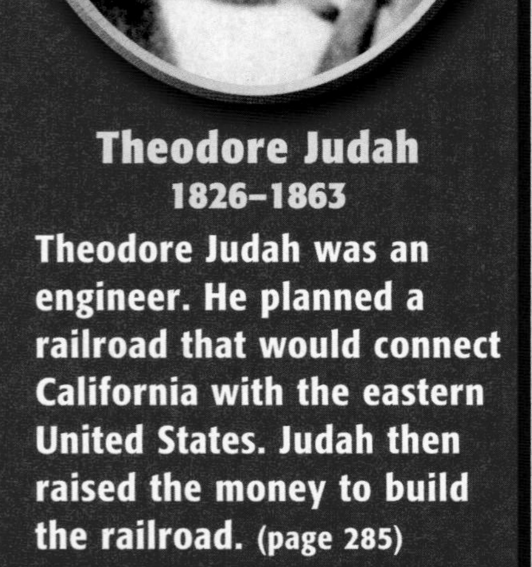

Theodore Judah
1826–1863

Theodore Judah was an engineer. He planned a railroad that would connect California with the eastern United States. Judah then raised the money to build the railroad. (page 285)

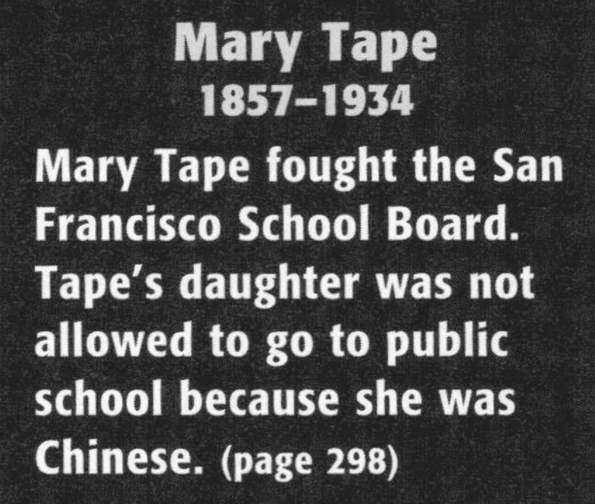

Mary Tape
1857–1934

Mary Tape fought the San Francisco School Board. Tape's daughter was not allowed to go to public school because she was Chinese. (page 298)

Luther Burbank
1849–1926

Luther Burbank was a farmer who used science to develop nearly 800 new kinds of plants on his farm in Santa Rosa in the late 1800s. (page 309)

Unit Events

1850 — 1860 — 1870 — 1880 — 1890 — 1900

- **1861** Coast-to-coast telegraph system is completed
- **1868** Transcontinental railroad is completed
- **1873** First oranges are planted in California
- **1882** Chinese Exclusion Act becomes law

For more about People Who Made a Difference, visit:

www.macmillanmh.com/ss/ca/bios

Allen Allensworth
1842–1914

Allen Allensworth escaped from slavery. At his retirement, he was the highest-ranking African American soldier in the United States. He founded a town in California. (page 320)

Hiram Johnson
1866–1945

Hiram Johnson was the governor of California from 1911 to 1919. He was a leader of the movement to reform California's government. (page 341)

Josefina Fierro de Bright
1920–1998

Josefina Fierro de Bright was a defender of immigrant rights and the first president of the Congress of Spanish Speaking People. (page 350)

1908 Work begins on the Los Angeles Aqueduct

1911 Women gain the right to vote

1913 Los Angeles Aqueduct is finished

1929 Great Depression begins

1941 America enters World War II

1942 Japanese Americans are sent to relocation camps

1950 California's population reaches 10 million

1910 1920 1930 1940 1950 1960

UNIT 4 Literature

Baseball Saved Us

Selections from ***Baseball Saved Us***
by Ken Mochizuki
Illustrated by Dom Lee

In 1942 the United States was at war with Japan. Some feared that Japanese Americans and Japanese immigrants might help Japan in the war. Because of these fears, the United States government forced Japanese Americans to leave their homes and move to camps during the war.

One day, my dad looked out at the endless desert and decided then and there to build a baseball field.

He said people needed something to do in Camp. We weren't in a camp that was fun, like summer camp. Ours was in the middle of nowhere, and we were behind a barbed-wire fence. Soldiers with guns made sure we stayed there, and the man in the tower saw everything we did, no matter where we were. . . .

We didn't have anything we needed for baseball, but the grown-ups were pretty smart. They **funneled** water from irrigation ditches to flood what would become our baseball field. The water packed down the dust and made it hard. There weren't any trees, but they found wood to build the bleachers. Bats, balls and gloves arrived in cloth sacks from friends back home. My mom and other moms took the covers off mattresses and used them to make uniforms. They looked almost like the real thing. . . .

Soon, there were baseball games all the time. Grown-ups played and us kids did, too. . . .

---

funneled (FUN uhld) to move a central point

Then came one of our last games of the year to decide on the championship. It was the bottom of the ninth inning and the other team was winning, 3 to 2. . . . The crowd was getting loud. "You can do it!" "Strike out!" "No hitter, no hitter!". . .

I gripped the bat harder and took a couple of practice swings. I was gonna hit the ball past the **guardhouse** even if it killed me. Everyone got quiet and the pitcher threw.

guardhouse a building used by guards or soldiers on duty

I stepped into my swing and pulled the bat around hard. I'd never heard a crack like that before. . . . The ball went over the head of the **left fielder**.

Before I knew it, I was up in the air on the shoulders of my teammates. I looked up at the tower and the man, with a grin on his face, gave me the thumbs-up sign.

---

left fielder the player defending the left side of the outfield

Write About It!

Write about a group of people who have helped others in very difficult and unfair situations.

Reading SOCIAL STUDIES

Compare and Contrast: Transportation in California

ELA R2.1 4.4.1

In this unit, you will learn about faster travel between the east and west coasts of the United States. Learning how to compare and contrast will help you understand the people and events that caused transportation to change and improve.

1 Learn It

- To compare two or more things, note how they are similar, or alike.
- To contrast two or more things, note how they are different.
- Now, read the passage below. Think about how you would compare and contrast work on the Central Pacific Railroad and Union Pacific Railroad.

Find Similarities
Both railroad companies were formed in 1862.

Find Differences
The railroads hired workers from different countries.

Find Similarities
Both railroads were completed in 1869.

The Central Pacific Railroad and Union Pacific Railroad companies were formed in 1862 to connect the east and west coasts of the United States. Work on the Central Pacific began in Sacramento and moved east. Many of its workers were Chinese immigrants. They built tracks across the Sierra Nevada and the desert.

The Union Pacific headed west from Omaha, Nebraska. Its workers, mainly Irish immigrants, built tracks across the plains. In 1869, the two railroads met at Promontory Summit, Utah. The east and west coasts of the United States were now joined.

Copy and complete the diagram below. Then, fill in the diagram with details from the passage on page 276.

COMPARE AND CONTRAST DIAGRAM

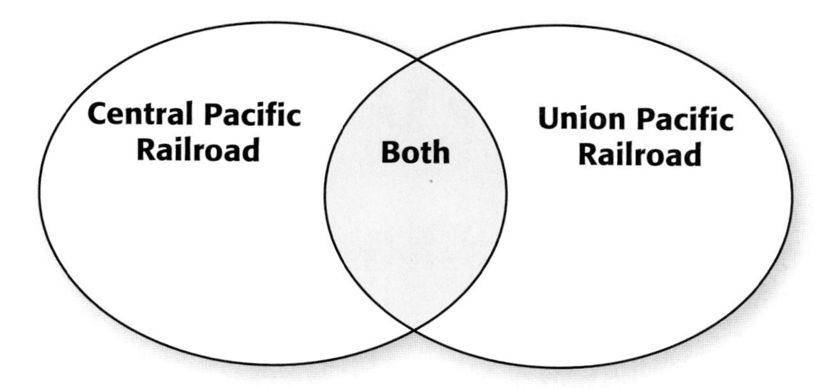

What information did you look for in the reading selection to compare and contrast?

- Review the steps for comparing and contrasting in Learn It.
- Read the passage below. Then, create a compare and contrast diagram using the information.

Before the railroad, travel to California was very difficult. Traveling west by stagecoach, for example, took five or six months. The cost could be $1,000 or more. Also, the trip was dangerous and uncomfortable.

Things got easier once the railroad was built. The train trip from Omaha took about nine days. Railroads provided a smoother, safer ride than stagecoaches. The cost was lower, too—about $150 for a first-class ticket in a sleeper car.

CHAPTER 8

Connecting California to the World

You Are There

"What was it the Engines said,
Pilots touching,—head to head
Facing on a single track,
Half a world behind each back?"

These words are from a poem, "What the Engines Said," by Bret Harte. Harte is famous for his stories and poems about life in California in the early days of its statehood. In this poem, he is imagining the famous meeting of the engines when the first railroad to cross the United States was completed.

In this chapter you will read about the challenges involved in finding faster and easier ways for people, mail, and goods to reach California. You will also learn how these new ways to travel and to communicate led to great changes in California.

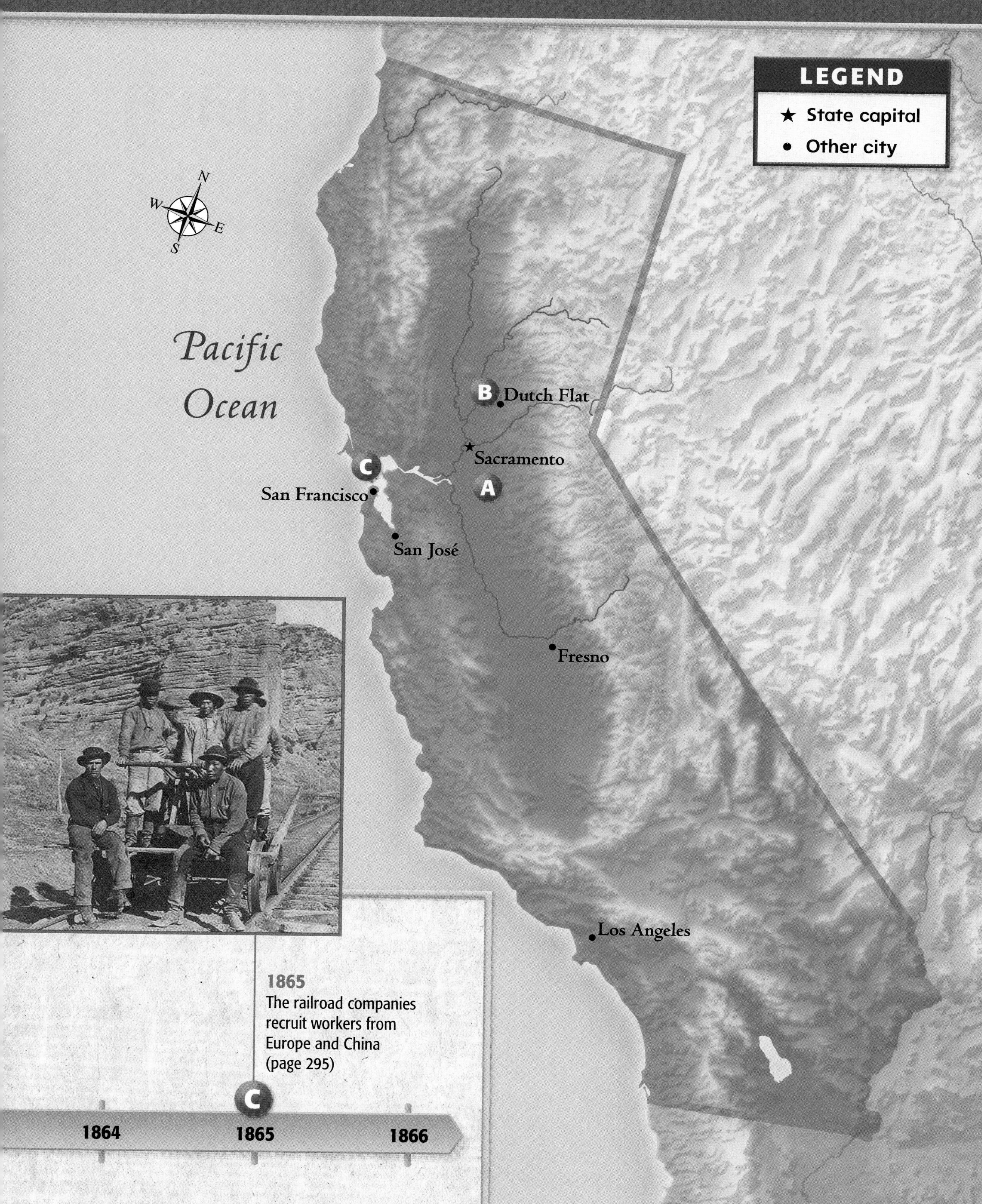
LEGEND
★ State capital
● Other city
N
W
E
S
Pacific Ocean
B
Dutch Flat
Sacramento
C
A
San Francisco
San José
Fresno
Los Angeles
1865
The railroad companies recruit workers from Europe and China
(page 295)
C
1864
1865
1866

From Stagecoach to Railroad

FOCUS QUESTION

How did people communicate between California and the East Coast?

VOCABULARY

communication
stagecoach
transportation
telegraph
transcontinental

VOCABULARY STRATEGY

PREFIXES Tele- is from a Greek word that means **distant**. Think of other words beginning with the prefix **tele-** whose definitions involve distance.

READING STRATEGY

Compare and Contrast
Use the diagram to compare and contrast sending messages by stagecoach and by Pony Express.

Start with Your
CALIFORNIA STANDARDS

4.4 Students explain how California became an agricultural and industrial power, tracing the transformation of the California economy and its political and cultural development since the 1850s.

4.4.1 Understand the story and lasting influence of the Pony Express, Overland Mail Service, Western Union, and the building of the transcontinental railroad, including the contributions of Chinese workers to its construction.

Find out about the different ways that goods, people, and information could be moved between California and the East Coast. (Begins on page 281)

Stagecoaches traveled long distances to deliver mail. ▼

Taking a stagecoach across country was not easy. Mark Twain wrote about his experience, "First we would all be down in a pile at the forward end of the stage . . . and in a second we would shoot to the other end, and stand on our heads." Stagecoach drivers such as "Charley" Parkhurst had to take danger in stride.

Early Transportation 4.4.1

In the 1850s, California's population was growing rapidly, but great distances separated it from the eastern United States. It took months for news, mail, supplies, and people to reach the West Coast. California needed better **communication** with the rest of the country. Communication is the exchange of information between people.

To speed communication, the United States government hired **stagecoach** companies to deliver the mail. A stagecoach was a carriage pulled by horses. Stagecoaches stopped at stations along their routes to change horses. They provided faster **transportation** than wagon trains. Transportation is the movement of people and goods.

Overland Mail Service

It took a stagecoach from the Overland Mail Service three weeks to travel the 2,800 miles from Missouri to San Francisco. Each coach carried about 170 pounds of letters and 140 pounds of newspapers.

Passengers also traveled in the coaches. A stagecoach ride was an exciting but difficult way to travel. Passengers were squeezed together on hard benches as they bumped over rough dirt roads.

"Charley" Parkhurst worked for Wells Fargo & Co., the major stagecoach company of the day. Parkhurst wore an eye patch and was known as a tough, fearless driver. Later, people found out that Parkhurst was really a woman named Charlotte Parkhurst. Stagecoach companies only hired men, so Parkhurst dressed as a man to get the job.

REVIEW What are the differences between the stagecoaches and wagon trains? *Compare and Contrast*

The Need for Speed 4.4.1

When you think about how quickly we can communicate on the Internet today, you can understand that Californians wanted faster ways to send and receive news. Sending a letter to Missouri by stagecoach took three weeks. It was still a long wait.

The Pony Express

On April 13, 1860, Billy Hamilton galloped into the town of Sacramento, California, on a horse. Crowds waved from balconies and rooftops. What had happened? Hamilton was carrying a bag of mail that had been sent only 10 days before from St. Joseph, Missouri. The Pony Express mail service had made its first delivery.

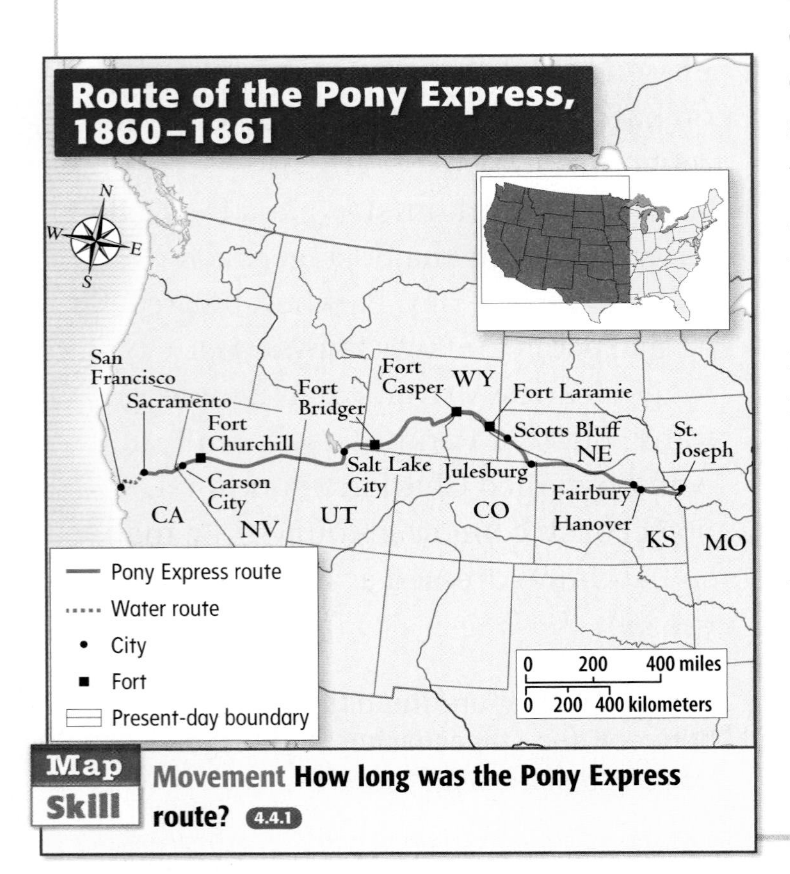

Map Skill Movement **How long was the Pony Express route?** 4.4.1

The Pony Express was the fastest mail service to California at the time. As the map on this page shows, the Pony Express route was almost 2,000 miles long. There were about 160 stations on the route, with about 18 of them in California.

The Pony Express was set up like a relay race. Each rider passed a bag of mail to the rider ahead of him. The riders traveled day and night. A young settler girl who saw them dash past said,

> ***"It seemed almost like the wind racing over the prairie."***

Each rider had a regular run, or route, separated by a number of stations. A rider set off from a station with a mail bag and galloped 10 or 15 miles to the next station. There the rider would quickly change to a fresh horse and ride on to the next station. After about eight stations, or 80 to 100 miles, a new rider took over. At the end of a run, a rider ate and slept at the station house until it was time to make the return trip.

It cost about $5.00 to send a letter, so most of the mail was important. The fastest ride ever made took less than eight days.

As fast as it was, the Pony Express mail service only lasted eighteen months. It was replaced by new technology.

California Camels

The United States Army thought of a different way to solve a transportation

Posters such as these were used to hire Pony Express riders. ▼

▲ Mail carried by a Pony Express rider

A Pony Express rider ▲

problem. The army needed to find a better way to carry military supplies across the western deserts to California. Desert travel was hard on horses and mules. There was very little food or water for them, and it was too hot.

In 1855, Jefferson Davis was the United States Secretary of War. Davis decided to try using camels to transport goods. The camels of Africa and the Middle East could travel long distances in the dry desert without needing much water. They could also carry heavy loads. Davis sent government agents to northern Africa to buy a herd of camels.

The first camel train to California was in 1857. The camels did well, traveling 1,200 miles in 50 days. However, the soldiers said the camels smelled bad and were hard to ride.

The army soon gave up on the camel project. They sold some of the camels in California and others in Texas. For years afterward, people claimed they saw camels wandering around in the desert.

REVIEW How did the Pony Express make communication between California and the East Coast faster? *Summarize*

Camels were used to cross the western deserts to reach California. ▶

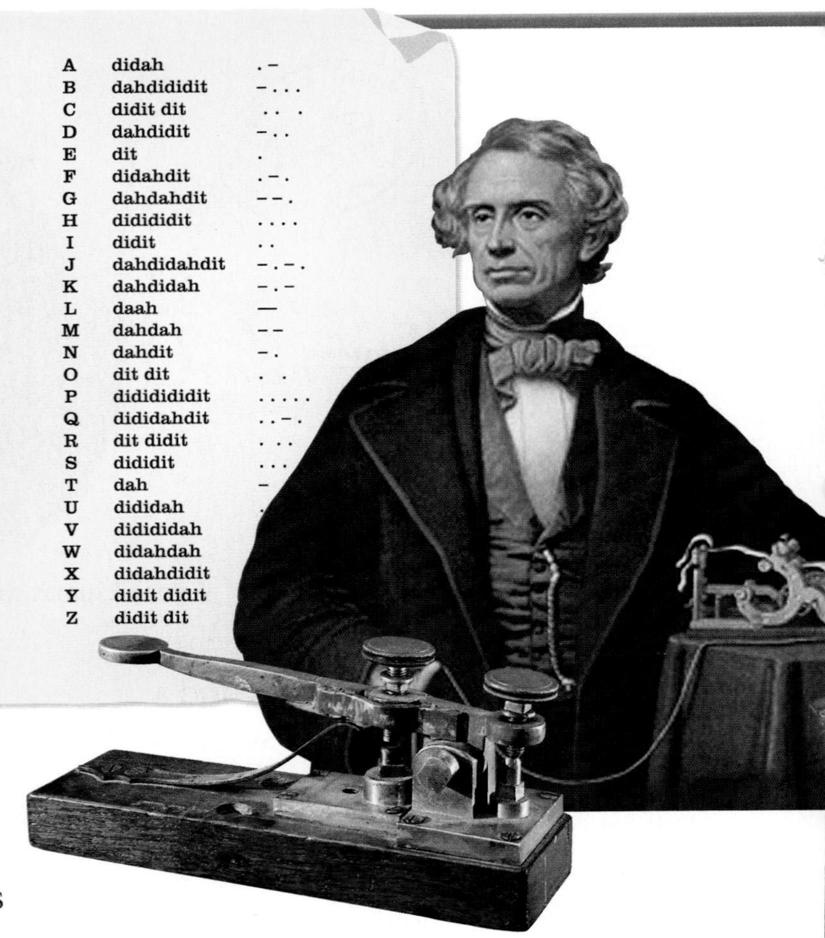

Morse code ▶

▲ Samuel F. B. Morse with his first telegraph machine, 1837

Faster Communication 4.4.1

A new technology soon allowed Californians to communicate in seconds, instead of weeks or days. The **telegraph** could send messages to distant places almost instantly by using electricity. The inventor and artist Samuel F. B. Morse developed the first telegraph in 1836. He also helped design the code that is known as "Morse code." As you can see on the chart, Morse code uses patterns of dots and dashes to stand for each letter of the alphabet. Morse code was used to send telegraph messages.

How the Telegraph Worked

A telegraph operator sent a message on a machine called a telegraph key. The operator moved a lever on the key to tap short and long beats. The beats represented the dots and dashes of Morse code. The electricity traveled along a telegraph line made of wire. At the other end of the line, another operator had a receiving machine called a sounder. The sounder made a click that represented a dot or a dash and marked the code on a strip of paper. Then, the operator used Morse code to translate the message into words.

By 1861 telegraph lines stretched from coast to coast. The lines were strung from poles that ran along the railroad tracks. Most of the lines belonged to the Western Union Telegraph Company.

A coast-to-coast telegraph system was completed on October 24, 1861. Soon after, the Pony Express went out of business. Technology replaced the horse in the communication race. Many people were disappointed to see the end of the Pony Express.

Railroad Dreams

By 1850 railroads were operating in most of the states east of the Mississippi River. The government hoped to build a railroad from coast to coast. People dreamed of a railroad that would be **transcontinental**, meaning that it would cross the continent.

Theodore Judah was a young engineer who shared that dream. Judah came west to help build California's first railroad. As he worked, Judah kept thinking about the possibility of a transcontinental railroad.

The biggest problem would be getting railroad tracks through the Sierra Nevada. Workers would have to build many bridges and dig long tunnels through rock. Still, Judah and other people all over the country were determined to do it.

REVIEW What technology allowed people to communicate almost instantly? *Main Idea and Details*

What You Learned

4.4.1 The stagecoach allowed mail and people from the East to reach California in three weeks.

4.4.1 The Pony Express reduced the time it took mail to reach California to ten days.

4.4.1 The telegraph made it possible to send a message across the country in less than a minute.

Lesson Review

1. **Focus Question** How did people communicate between California and the East Coast? (4.4.1)
2. **Vocabulary** Write one sentence for each vocabulary word. (4.4.1)
   communication **transcontinental**
   stagecoach **transportation**
   telegraph
3. **Technology** What are some other early technologies that used electricity? (4.4.1)
4. **Critical Thinking** **Problem Solving** Messages sent by telegraph could be read by every operator. Think of ways the person sending the message could keep the operators from understanding the message. (4.4.1)
5. **Reading Strategy** **Compare and Contrast** Use the diagram to compare and contrast sending messages by Pony Express and by telegraph. (4.4.1, ELA R2.1)

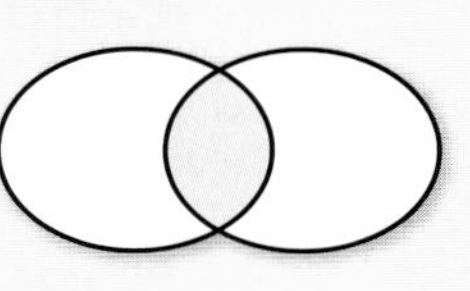

6. **Write about THE BIG IDEA** New technology let people send messages across the United States almost instantly. Write about reasons it was important for people to be able to send messages to each other so quickly. (4.4.1, ELA W2.3)
7. **Link to Language Arts** Suppose that the telegraph line has just been completed in California. Write a short message to a relative in the East about how exciting it is to be able to send a message that a person across the country can receive on the same day. (4.4.1)

Using PRIMARY SOURCES

Understanding Newspapers 4.4.1

VOCABULARY

newspaper

A **newspaper** is a paper that is usually printed daily or weekly and contains news, opinions, and advertising. Newspapers report on current events, or things that happen every day. Before televisions and computers, people relied on newspapers to find out what was happening in their town, city, or country, as well as in the world.

Newspaper Accounts of Track Laying

In the last lesson, you learned about the transcontinental railroad. The newspaper account on page 287 will help you understand what it was like to lay thousands of miles of railroad track across mountains, rivers, and valleys.

1 Learn It

Read the steps below to help you find information in newspapers.

- Identify the name of the newspaper.
- Identify the kind of article you are reading. A news article, or story, describes an important event that has recently taken place. An editorial offers a personal opinion about a topic.
- Identify the parts of the article you are reading. The article's headline is usually printed in larger letters and sums up the main idea of the story. The byline tells the reader who wrote the story. The dateline tells you when and where the story was written.

Laying track for the transcontinental railroad ▼

2 Try It

Read the newspaper account below to understand important parts of what people say in newspapers.

- A news article should answer five questions. They are: Who was involved? What took place? When did the event happen? Where did it happen? Why did it happen?

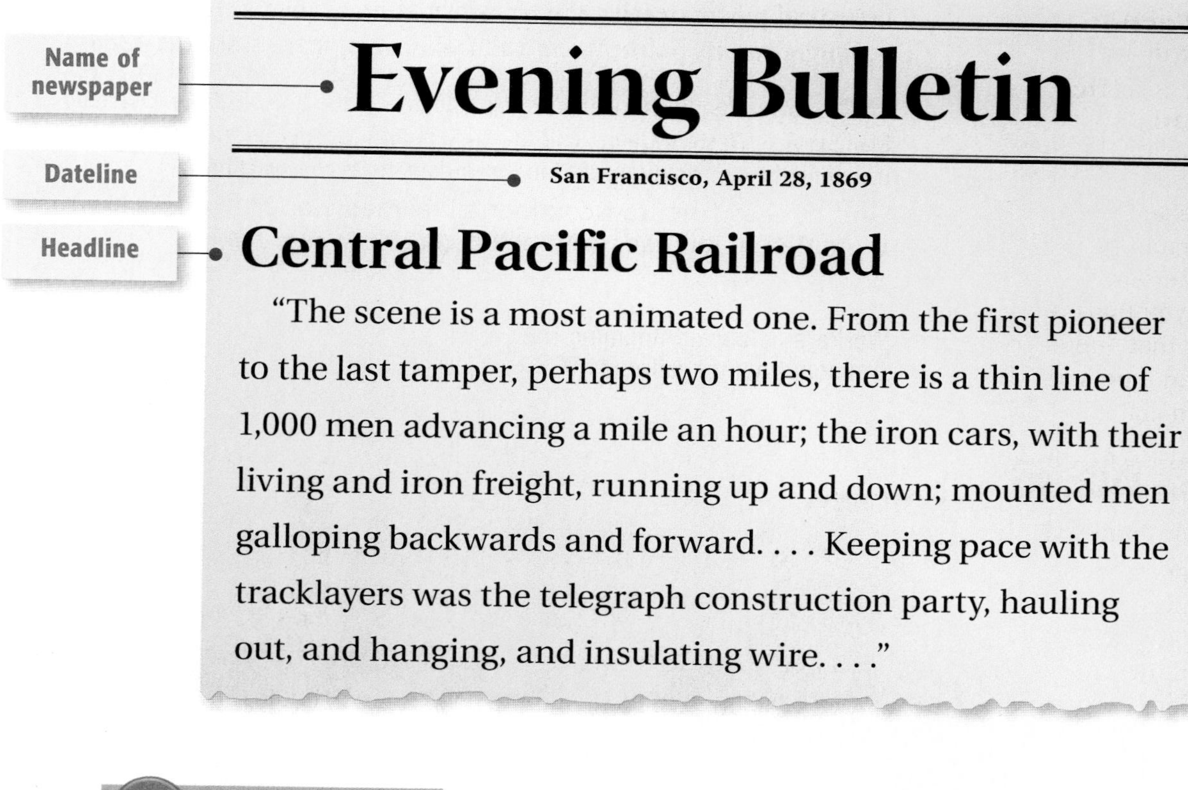

Evening Bulletin

San Francisco, April 28, 1869

Central Pacific Railroad

"The scene is a most animated one. From the first pioneer to the last tamper, perhaps two miles, there is a thin line of 1,000 men advancing a mile an hour; the iron cars, with their living and iron freight, running up and down; mounted men galloping backwards and forward. . . . Keeping pace with the tracklayers was the telegraph construction party, hauling out, and hanging, and insulating wire. . . ."

3 Apply It

- Read an article from a local newspaper. Does it answer the five questions?
- Does the newspaper have a headline or byline?

LESSON 2

Planning the Railroad

FOCUS QUESTION

How was the transcontinental railroad built?

VOCABULARY

- **investor**
- **Union Pacific Railroad**
- **Central Pacific Railroad**

VOCABULARY STRATEGY

SUFFIXES The suffix **-or** means a person that performs a certain action. Can you think of other words that end in **-or** and mean a person who does an action?

READING STRATEGY

Compare and Contrast
Use the diagram to compare and contrast the Union Pacific Railroad and the Central Pacific Railroad.

Start with Your CALIFORNIA STANDARDS

4.4 Students explain how California became an agricultural and industrial power, tracing the transformation of the California economy and its political and cultural development since the 1850s.

4.4.1 Understand the story and lasting influence of the Pony Express, Overland Mail Service, Western Union, and the building of the transcontinental railroad, including the contributions of Chinese workers to its construction.

Find out how the transcontinental railroad was built and where the different railroads connected. (Begins on page 289)

Workers celebrate finishing the transcontinental railroad. ▼

1862 1863 1864 1865 1866 1867

1862
The Pacific Railroad Act is signed

1863
Work begins on transcontinental railroad

1867
The transcontinental railroad is completed

Building a transcontinental railroad was Theodore Judah's great dream. He told his wife, Anna, "It will be built, and I'm going to have something to do with it."

The Beginning of the Railroad 4.4.1

Theodore Judah needed to find a place where a transcontinental railroad could cross the Sierra Nevada. Near Dutch Flat, Judah found land that rose slowly up to Donner Pass. He thought that he could build a railroad on this land.

Next, Judah needed to find wealthy men who could afford to invest in the railroad. An **investor** is a person who puts money into a business in hopes of making money from it later. Four people agreed to invest in the railroad. Leland Stanford, Charles Crocker, Collins Huntington, and Mark Hopkins soon became known as the Big Four.

The project still needed more money. Judah rolled up his 90-foot long map of the route and went to Congress. Judah convinced the government that the railroad could be built. In 1862 President Abraham Lincoln signed the Pacific Railroad Act. This act loaned money to two companies, the **Union Pacific Railroad** and the **Central Pacific Railroad**. It also gave the companies ten square miles of land on both sides of the railroad. Having this land meant that the Big Four could build towns along the railroad line or rent or sell the land. The Big Four would make a fortune.

Work Begins

Work on the transcontinental railroad began in January 1863. As the map on the next page shows, the Union Pacific Railroad went west from Omaha. The Central Pacific Railroad headed east from Sacramento. It took thousands of workers to build the railroad.

REVIEW How were the routes of the Central Pacific and the Union Pacific railroads different? *Compare and Contrast*

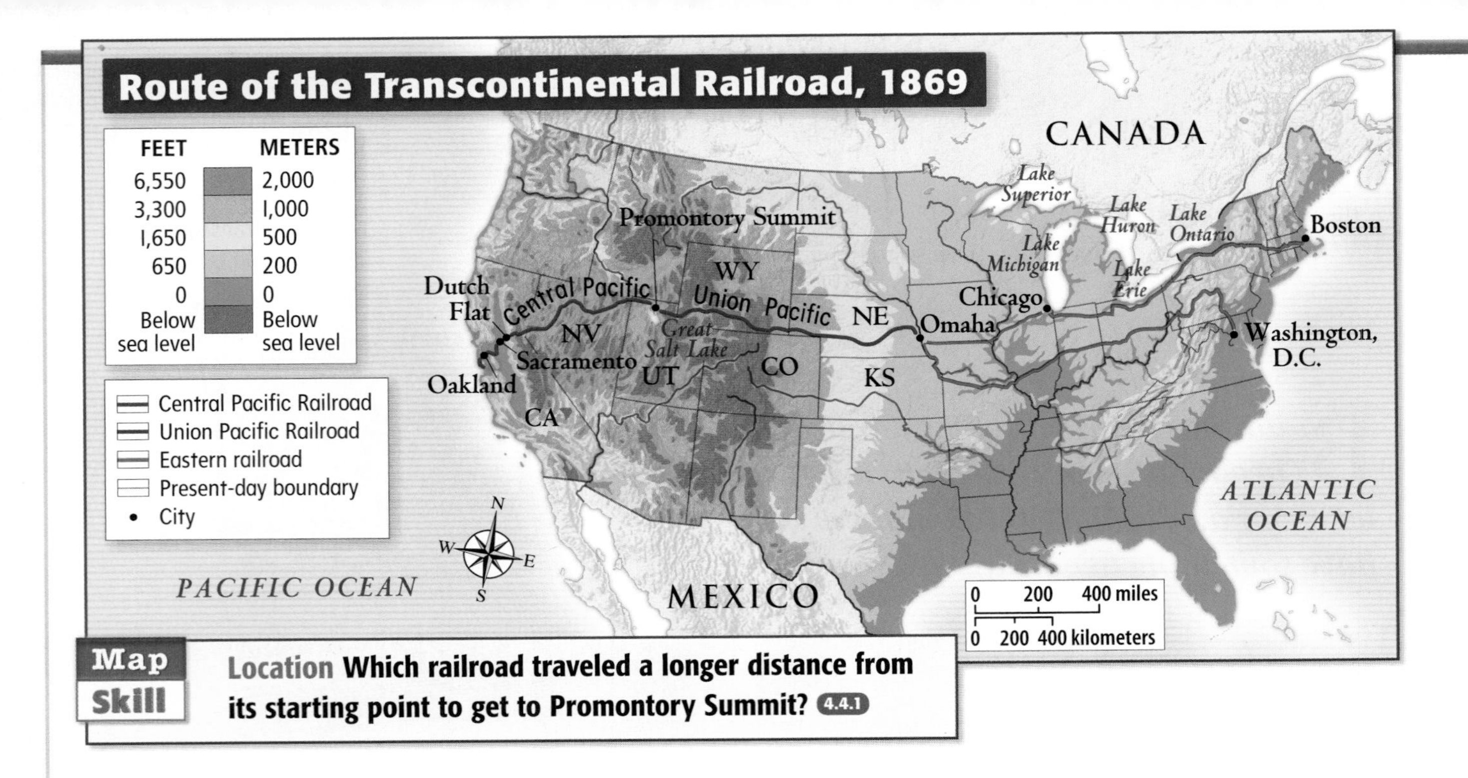

Map Skill **Location** **Which railroad traveled a longer distance from its starting point to get to Promontory Summit?** 4.4.1

Race to the Finish 4.4.1

By 1868, the Central Pacific Railroad had crossed the Sierra Nevada and reached northern Utah. The Union Pacific Railroad had reached as far as Wyoming. However, no one had decided where the two railroads should meet.

On April 8, 1869, it was decided that the meeting point would be at Promontory Summit, Utah. The workers of both railroad companies began to race to get there first. One soldier who was there said,

"It was like an army marching over the ground and leaving a track built behind them."

On May 10, 1869, a crowd gathered for a celebration at Promontory Summit. The crowd cheered as Central Pacific Railroad president Leland Stanford placed the last spike into a railroad tie.

A train from the 1860s ▶

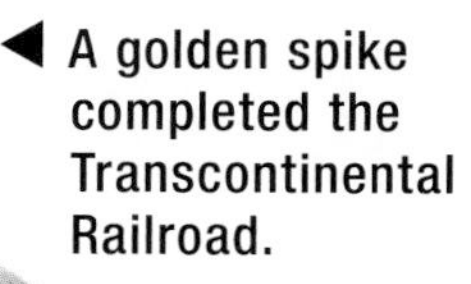

◀ A golden spike completed the Transcontinental Railroad.

The spike was made of gold. The news that the transcontinental railroad was complete went out by telegraph.

Riding the Rails

The coast-to-coast trip on the transcontinental railroad took about a week. A second-class seat from Omaha to Sacramento cost about $80. Second-class cars had wooden seats, and passengers ate at the railroad stations. For about $100, you could buy a first-class ticket. People with first-class tickets had padded seats and ate in fancy restaurant cars.

REVIEW How was the transcontinental railroad finished? *Summarize*

United States At the Same Time

During the 1860s, Northern states had laws that did not allow slavery. Many people in the Southern states believed that they needed enslaved workers to help run large farms. In 1861, the struggle over slavery led to the Civil War. In 1865 the North won, and slavery was no longer allowed in the United States.

What You Learned

4.4.1 A group of four investors, known as the Big Four, and the Railroad Act of 1862 provided the money to begin the transcontinental railroad.

4.4.1 The benefits of gaining more land and competition between the two railroads led to a race to complete the transcontinental railroad.

Lesson Review

1. **Focus Question** How was the transcontinental railroad built? (4.4.1)
2. **Vocabulary** Write one sentence for each vocabulary term. (4.4.1)
   Central Pacific Railroad
   investor
   Union Pacific Railroad
3. **Government** What role did the United States government play in the building of the transcontinental railroad? (4.4.1)
4. **Critical Thinking Problem Solving** How did Theodore Judah solve the problem of getting the railroad tracks to cross the Sierra Nevada? (4.4.1)
5. **Reading Strategy Compare and Contrast** Use the diagram to compare and contrast first and second class railroad seats. (4.4.1, ELA R2.5)
6. **Write about THE BIG IDEA** Write about ways that the transcontinental railroad might have changed life for Californians. (4.4.1, ELA W2.1)
7. **Link to Mathematics** Railroad workers used 100 rails to build one mile of railroad. To hammer the rails into place, workers used ten spikes for each rail. How many spikes were needed to build one mile of railroad tracks? (4.4.1)

CRITICAL THINKING Skills

Identify Stereotypes 4.4.3

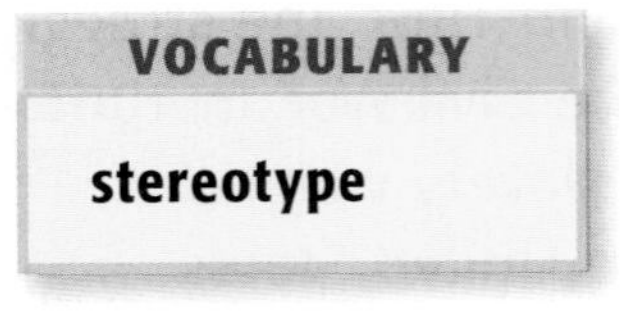

A **stereotype** is an idea that all the people in a group are the same in some way. Stereotypes often, but not always, express dislike for a group.

It is important to think of people as individuals, not just members of a group. So we try to identify stereotypes. By identifying stereotypes, we can treat all people fairly.

1 Learn It

Read the steps below to help you identify stereotypes.

- Look for general statements about whole groups. You can sometimes recognize a stereotype by words such as *all, every,* and *always*.
- Not all stereotypes will use these words, however. The statement: "Americans love peanut butter" is a stereotype. It is a general statement about *all* people in America. However, there are people in America who do not like peanut butter.
- Another example of a stereotype is: "All fourth graders are very noisy." If a statement seems to be a stereotype, try to think of examples that do not agree with it. For example, you probably know lots of fourth graders who are not noisy. So saying "All fourth graders are very noisy" is not fair.
- Copy the chart below. In the left-hand column, the two stereotypes that have been discussed are filled in for you. In the right-hand column, explain why these two statements are stereotypes.

Stereotype	Why It Is a Stereotype
Americans love peanut butter.	
All fourth graders are very noisy.	

2 Try It

■ Read the selection below about Chinese immigrants. Copy the chart from page 292. Fill in the left-hand column with the stereotypes that you find. In the right-hand column, explain why these statements are stereotypes.

Between 1850 and 1860, more than 60,000 Chinese immigrants made their way across the Pacific Ocean. Many had seen flyers about America in China. The flyers said, "All Americans are very rich."

Once in California, the Chinese immigrants always were excellent workers. The Chinese newcomers worked very hard, even for low pay.

This sentence says *all* the people in America are rich.

The word *always* makes a general statement about this group.

This sentence says *all* the members of this group worked very hard.

3 Apply It

■ Now, read this selection. Again, look for stereotypes. Then use a chart to identify any stereotypes you find and explain why they are stereotypes.

As less and less gold was discovered in California, many white miners left the gold fields. They went to cities to find work. Suddenly, there were more workers than jobs. "The Chinese workers are greedy," the white workers claimed. "They all take jobs from American citizens."

At this time, the Chinese immigrants were not allowed to become American citizens. Nevertheless, the state government charged Chinese workers high taxes for not being citizens. So all Americans were unfair to the Chinese immigrants.

Immigrants Build the Railroad

FOCUS QUESTION

What was life like for immigrants who worked on the railroads?

VOCABULARY

recruiter
railbed
discrimination
Chinese Exclusion Act

VOCABULARY STRATEGY

ROOT WORDS The word **recruit** is from the Latin phrase for "to grow." Can you think of other words that mean to grow or to make bigger?

READING STRATEGY

Identify Main Idea and Details

Use the chart below to show what working on the Central Pacific Railroad was like for the Chinese immigrants.

Start with Your CALIFORNIA STANDARDS

4.4 Students explain how California became an agricultural and industrial power, tracing the transformation of the California economy and its political and cultural development since the 1850s.

4.4.1 Understand the story and lasting influence of the Pony Express, Overland Mail Service, Western Union, and the building of the transcontinental railroad, including the contributions of Chinese workers to its construction.

Discover what life was like for the workers who built the transcontinental railroad, and the challenges they faced to complete it. (Begins on page 295)

4.4.3 Discuss immigration and migration to California between 1850 and 1900, including the diverse composition of those who came; the countries of origin and their relative locations; and conflicts and accords among the diverse groups.

Find out about the people who came to the United States from other lands to work on the railroad. (Begins on page 295)

4.4.4 Describe rapid American immigration, internal migration, settlement, and the growth of towns and cities.

Learn where the immigrants lived and what they did after the railroad was finished. (Begins on page 297)

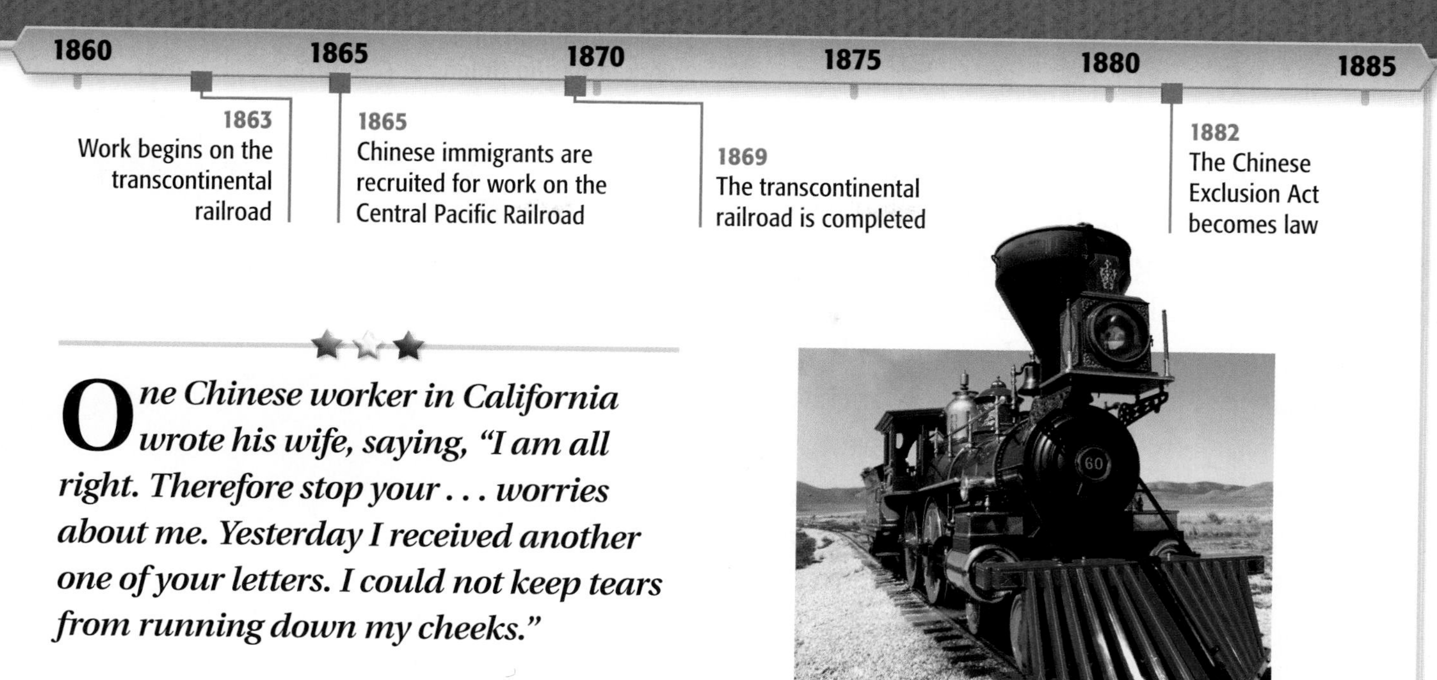

One Chinese worker in California wrote his wife, saying, "I am all right. Therefore stop your . . . worries about me. Yesterday I received another one of your letters. I could not keep tears from running down my cheeks."

Workers from Across the Ocean 4.4.3

The many workers who built the transcontinental railroad were mostly immigrants. Many Irish immigrants from the East Coast worked on the Union Pacific Railroad. About 10,000 Chinese immigrants worked on the Central Pacific Railroad.

Hiring Workers

In 1865 there was work for 4,000 men on the Central Pacific Railroad, but only about 800 jobs were filled. The chief of construction, Charles Crocker, badly needed people to work. He hired 50 Chinese men. He liked their work and decided to hire more Chinese workers. So, Crocker sent **recruiters** to Guangdong Province in southeast China. A recruiter finds workers for employers. The recruiters put up ads that encouraged Chinese workers to come over and help. Times had been hard in China. People wanted and needed to work.

In California, some people were against the idea of foreign workers. However, Crocker told his workers,

> ***"If you can't get along with [the Chinese workers] we'll let you go and hire nobody but them."***

REVIEW Why did Charles Crocker decide to send recruiters to China to hire workers?
Main Idea and Details

◀ Chinese workers building the railroad

Chinese Immigrants 4.4.1 4.4.4

Many thousands of Chinese immigrants made the journey to California to work on the railroad. One Chinese immigrant, Lee Chew, made the two-month trip across the Pacific Ocean when he was only sixteen. In San Francisco, Chew worked in a laundry. After two years, he had enough money to start his own business. Chew ran a laundry for the Central Pacific Railroad. Read below Chew's description of his journey to California.

Chinese immigrants worked on the Union Pacific Railroad. ▶

Difficult Work

Chinese immigrants faced many hardships working on the Central Pacific Railroad. Most workers made $27 a month, for working 12 hours a day, 6 days a week. They also paid for their own food and tents. Irish workers were paid more for the same work and did not have to pay for their housing or meals.

Chinese workers built the railroad beds by hand, using pickaxes, hammers, and crowbars. **Railbeds** are the flat surfaces over which the railroad tracks are laid. To make the ground flat, workers cleared trees,

Primary Sources

Lee Chew

A section from an article from
Independent Magazine
by Lee Chew
February 1903

*"My father gave me $100, and I . . . got **steerage** passage on a **steamer**, paying $50. . . . Everything was new to me. All my life I had been used to sleeping on a board bed with a wooden pillow, and I found the steamer's **bunk** very uncomfortable, because it was so soft. . . ."*

steerage the space on a ship that costs the least money **steamer** steamship
bunk built-in bed

Write About It! **Why did Lee Chew find the steamer's bunk to be uncomfortable?**

pulled up stumps, and hauled dirt and rocks away on carts.

One big challenge was to build railroad tracks on Cape Horn in the Sierra Nevada. A cliff rose 1,400 feet high, and the railroad had to go around it near the top. Workers had to remove rock on the face of the cliff where there was nowhere to stand.

To solve this problem, workers were lowered over the cliff in baskets. Men on top of the cliff held ropes and lowered the baskets down. At the point where the railbed should be, Chinese workers chipped holes into the rock. Then they put gunpowder in the holes and lit a fuse. The fuse would make the gunpowder explode. At a signal from the "basketman," the men at the top quickly pulled him up before the gunpowder blew up.

The workers also faced terrible weather. Between 1865 and 1866, there were 44 blizzards in the Sierra Nevada. The men had to dig tunnels in the snow between the camps where they lived and the places where they worked. It took the Chinese work crews more than two years of hard work to finish the railroad tracks through the Sierra Nevada.

Chinatown

After the railroad was finished, many Chinese workers moved on to find other work. Some stayed in California. Some areas of California had more Chinese residents than others. For example, one area of San Francisco became known as Chinatown. By the 1870s San Francisco's Chinatown was a thriving community, with shops, schools, local newspapers, theaters, and festivals such as Chinese New Year. Because Chinatown was surrounded by buildings, the neighborhood could not expand. Instead it became very crowded. There were other Chinese communities in cities such as Dutch Flat, Fresno, San José, and Los Angeles.

REVIEW How did the Chinese workers build the railbeds? *Main Idea and Details*

Workers had to build railroad tracks through the Sierra Nevadas. ▼

The Fight Against Discrimination 4.4.3

People thought that the railroad would bring good times to California in the 1870s. Instead, it was a difficult period. Neither new immigrants nor people who had worked on the railroad could find work. Many Californians blamed Chinese people for taking "their" jobs.

Local and state governments passed laws that discriminated against Chinese people. **Discrimination** is the unfair treatment of a group of people.

The toughest anti-Chinese law was the **Chinese Exclusion Act** of 1882. Congress voted that no new Chinese workers could come to the United States for the next ten years.

Some Chinese people fought the discrimination laws. Mary Tape, a Chinese American who lived in San Francisco, went to court so her daughter could attend public school. As a result, San Francisco created separate public schools for Chinese students. Although Mary Tape won the right for public education for Chinese children, Chinese immigrants would continue to fight for fair and equal treatment.

REVIEW Why do you think the Chinese Exclusion Act was passed? *Cause and Effect*

What You Learned

- 4.4.3 Immigrants from China and Ireland worked on the transcontinental railroad.
- 4.4.1 4.4.4 Chinese immigrants helped build the Central Pacific Railroad. When the railroad was finished, they moved to other places to find work.
- 4.4.3 Discrimination against the Chinese people led to the Chinese Exclusion Act.

Lesson Review

1. **Focus Question** What was life like for immigrants who worked on the railroads? 4.4.1
2. **Vocabulary** Write one sentence for each vocabulary term. 4.4.1 4.4.3
   Chinese Exclusion Act **railbed**
   discrimination **recruiter**
3. **Culture** Why do you think Chinese immigrants wanted to live near each other? 4.4.4
4. **Critical Thinking** **Problem Solving** How did the workers build the railroad on Cape Horn? 4.4.3
5. **Reading Strategy** **Identify Main Idea and Details** 4.4.1 ELA R2.1 Use the chart to show what happened to the Chinese immigrants after the railroad was completed.
6. **Write about THE BIG IDEA** Write about how the number of workers needed to finish the Central Pacific Railroad changed life in California. 4.4.1 ELA W2.4
7. **Link to Language Arts** Write a letter from the point of view of a Chinese worker who celebrated finishing the railroad at Promontory Summit. Write to a relative in China, and mention how you feel about what you have accomplished. 4.4.3

CITIZENSHIP
DEMOCRACY IN ACTION

Expressing Your Opinion 4.4.3

By expressing your opinion, you let other people know that you are concerned about an issue or a problem. In 1884 Chinese immigrant Mary Tape tried to send her daughter to a public school. The San Francisco school board refused to let Chinese American children go to public schools. Tape asked the courts to decide if the school board's decision was against the law. Tape also wrote letters to the school board protesting its decision. Read below to learn how you can express your opinion.

Mary Tape expressed her opinion about the school board's decision. Read these steps to learn about how to express your opinion.

Build Citizenship

1. **Identify the problem** or the issue you are concerned about.
2. **Get information** from books, newspapers, or the Internet.
3. **Look for solutions.** Decide what you want to accomplish.
4. **Express your opinion.** State clearly what the problem is and how you think it might be solved.

Think About It

1. What was the issue for Mary Tape and her family?
2. What were two ways Tape expressed her opinion?
3. What did Tape hope to achieve by expressing her opinion?

Write About It!

Write a letter to your local newspaper expressing your opinion about an issue.

Field Trip to San Francisco's Chinatown

4.4.4

San Francisco

San Francisco's Chinatown is the largest and oldest Chinatown in America. It grew rapidly in the mid-1800s, when Chinese immigrants came to California.

◀ 1 Gateway to Chinatown

Entering Chinatown from the south, you will pass under this colorful gate. It is inscribed with the words, "All under heaven is for the good of the people."

2 Golden Gate Fortune Cookie Factory ▶

What could be better on a trip to Chinatown than to stop at the Golden Gate Cookie Factory? You will be able to see how fortune cookies are made. Fortune cookies are a Chinese American tradition.

Lunar New Year's Parade

If you visit Chinatown during the Lunar New Year (the first full moon of the new year), be sure to see the dragon parade. About fifty people hold up a paper dragon on poles and make it dance. The dragon is a symbol of spring and brings good luck. ▼

❸ Portsmouth Square ▲

This square is known as the "Heart of Chinatown." The Chinatown Night Market Fair takes place here from July through October, where you might see performers in martial arts, Chinese opera, and traditional Chinese music.

Chinatown

Stockton Street
O'Farrell Street
Post Street
Gateway 1
Grant Avenue
Cookie Factory 2
3 Portsmouth Square
Kearney Street
Market Street

Activity

Use the map to take a walking tour from the gateway to Chinatown to Portsmouth Square. Then write a letter describing what you saw, and what you liked the best.

LOG ON For more about San Francisco's Chinatown, visit:

www.macmillanmh.com/ss/ca/fieldtrips

Chapter Review

Vocabulary Review

Copy the sentences below on a separate sheet of paper. Use the list of vocabulary words to fill in the blanks.

discrimination **railbed**
investor **transcontinental**

1. The ________ railroad traveled from one end of the country to the other. (4.4.1)
2. An ________ is a person who puts money into a business. (4.4.1)
3. A ________ is flat surface over which the railroad tracks are laid. (4.4.1)
4. ________ is the unfair treatment of a group of people (4.4.3)
5. **Test Preparation** ________ is the movement of people and goods. (4.4.1)

   A. **transportation** C. **recruiter**
   B. **communication** D. **steerage**

Comprehension Check

6. How long was the entire Pony Express route? (4.4.1)
7. How does "Morse Code" work? (4.4.1)
8. Name the two companies that received money from the Pacific Railroad Act. (4.4.1)
9. What kind of work did recruiters do in China? (4.4.3)
10. What important right did Mary Tape win? (4.4.3)
11. **Critical Thinking** Why do you think many Chinese immigrants continued to move into Chinatown after it became crowded? (4.4.4)
12. **Critical Thinking** How did the transcontinental railroad affect businesses in California? (4.4.1)

Use the Time Line

Use the time line below to answer each question.

13. How many years does this time line show? (4.4.1)
14. What was finished first, a coast-to-coast telegraph line or railroad line? (4.4.1)

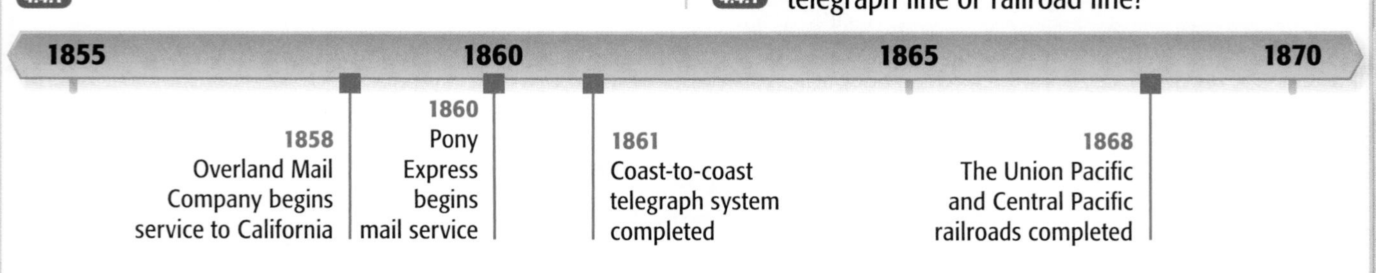

1870 | 1871 | 1872 | 1873

1870
John Wesley North uses irrigation to water his orange groves

1873
Eliza and Luther Tibbets plant two navel orange trees

In the first half of the 1800s, California was cattle country. At one time, nearly four times as many cows lived in the state as did people. Then, in the 1860s, there was a period with almost no rain. The cattle died, and many ranchers became poor.

From Cattle to Wheat 4.4.6

When California became a state in 1850, raising cattle was an important part of its economy. Then came two **droughts**, or periods of little rain. The first drought was in 1856. The second one lasted from 1862 to 1864.

By the time the droughts were over, many ranchers had gone out of business. The land was ready to be used for something else. Soon farming began to take the place of ranching.

Farmers already knew that the soil of the Central Valley and the long dry summers were just right for growing wheat. Wheat had already started to be a **cash crop**. A cash crop is a crop that is grown to be sold.

New Farm Machines

From 1860 to 1890, several new machines were made for planting and harvesting crops. One of these was the huge, steam-powered **combine**, which could cut and bind wheat at the same time. Another machine was the steam-powered tractor, which made it much easier to pull farm machinery.

These were just two of many **inventions**, or new tools for doing things, that improved farming. It now took less time and fewer people to plant and harvest crops.

From 1860 to 1890 wheat was an important crop for California. One of the largest wheat farms was owned by a doctor. He owned 55,000 acres of land. That's about the size of Bakersfield. So much wheat was produced in California that it was shipped all over the world.

REVIEW What did the tractor have in common with the combine? *Compare and Contrast*

▲ Label from a crate of California oranges

▲ Workers load ice into a refrigerated railcar.

New Crops for California 4.4.6

Today California grows billions of dollars of food products that are sold around the world. However, farming in California has not always been easy. In some places, the land has been too dry for farming, in others, too wet.

Working with Water

Many crops are grown in California's delta region, a triangle of land located between Sacramento, Stockton, and San Francisco. The delta is below sea level and many rivers run through it, so the soil is wet. The soil is also very rich and good for farming.

In the middle of the 1800s people tried to farm the delta. However, floods from the Sacramento River often ruined their crops. Some farmers worried that the delta was too wet to farm.

Other farmers decided to dry the land out. These farmers built **levees** (LEH veez), or high walls of earth that kept flood water from overflowing onto the land. Many Chinese workers who had helped build the railroads also found work building levees in the delta.

While some land was too wet to farm, other land was too dry. In 1870, John Wesley North used irrigation to water his land in Riverside. North irrigated his grove of orange trees by digging a long canal from the Santa Ana River to his farm. Soon farmers in southern California were using irrigation to turn thousands of acres of dry land into fertile farmland.

California Oranges

In 1873 Eliza Tibbets and Luther Tibbets planted two navel orange trees at their home near Riverside. The navel orange had never been grown in California. It is juicier and sweeter than other oranges and has no seeds.

Other farmers heard about these two orange trees and paid the Tibbets a visit. They clipped off pieces of the navel orange trees, went home, and planted their own. Twenty years later, navel oranges were being grown all over southern California.

The navel orange wasn't California's only new fruit. Many California farmers began introducing new fruits and vegetables. In Santa Rosa, plant scientist Luther Burbank grew more than 800 new plants, including new kinds of plums and apples.

Helped by inventions like the combine and the tractor, California became an agricultural giant. By 1900, for example, the farms in Riverside produced a total of two million boxes of oranges and 24,000 boxes of lemons. Providing so much of the food supply greatly increased California's importance to the nation.

Today California farmers grow many fruits and vegetables, including beets, tomatoes, lettuce, avocados, peaches, melons, and strawberries. Our state has also become a leader in growing grapes, dates, and olives, as well as almonds and walnuts. Every year California sells about $30 billion worth of farm food.

Eliza Tibbets ▲

REVIEW How did John Wesley North bring water to his orange grove? *Cause and Effect*

Many types of fruit are now grown in California. ▼

California Feeds the Country 4.4.6

Railroads made it possible to deliver products across the country in just a few days. However, even this was too long for fruits and vegetables to stay fresh.

In the 1800s the refrigerated railroad car was invented. **Refrigeration** is the process of keeping food fresh by keeping it cool. From the 1880s California farmers used refrigerated railroad cars to ship their fruits and vegetables across the country.

Many of the large cities in the Central Valley began as stations along the San Joaquin Valley railroad. This railroad was built in the 1870s and connected Los Angeles with Sacramento. Towns along this route such as Modesto, Merced, Fresno, Tulare, and Bakersfield all began this way. As the railroad came through, these cities grew in size.

REVIEW What made it possible for California farmers to ship their food across the country? *Summarize*

What You Learned

- 4.4.6 Droughts in the 1850s and 1860s caused California's cattle-ranching industry to fail. Wheat became the region's cash crop.
- 4.4.6 California farmers increased the amount of land they could farm by building levees and irrigating dry land.
- 4.4.6 In the late 1800s Californians began shipping their fruits and vegetables east in refrigerated trains.

Lesson Review

1. **Focus Question** How did farming become big business in California? (4.4.6)
2. **Vocabulary** Write one sentence for each vocabulary term. (4.4.6)

cash crop	**invention**
combine	**levee**
drought	**refrigeration**

3. **Economics** Why did California cattle ranchers go out of business in the 1860s? (4.4.6)
4. **Critical Thinking** **Cause and Effect** How did new inventions affect the farming industry in California? (4.4.6)
5. **Reading Strategy** **Compare and Contrast** Compare and contrast the different ways farmers watered their crops in the middle 1800s in California. (4.4.6, ELA R2.1)

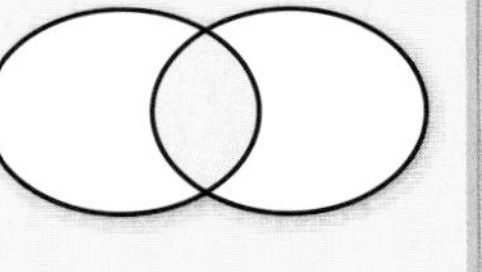

6. **Write about THE BIG IDEA** Write about the new technology that helped California's agricultural industry in the late 1800s. (4.4.6, ELA W2.3)
7. **Link to Science** Use a library or the Internet to find out more about droughts. Why do they happen? Write a paragraph about droughts. (4.4.6)

Biography
Focus on Leadership

4.4.6

Luther Burbank 1849-1926

Luther Burbank grew up on a farm in Lancaster, Massachusetts. His interest in plants began early. Burbank read many books on plants. By the time he was 21, Burbank began trying to change plants.

In 1871 Burbank succeeded. He grew a new kind of potato that could not be harmed by disease. The potatoes helped feed many people.

In 1875 Burbank moved to Santa Rosa, California. Over the next 50 years, he created 800 new kinds of fruits, vegetables, nuts, grains, and flowers. His improved plants were grown all over the world.

Burbank was the most famous plant scientist in the world. He gave the world the plants that he loved. One of his favorite projects was creating a "perfect" daisy. He named it the Shasta daisy. Burbank once said:

"Flowers . . . are sunshine, food, and medicine to the soul."

Today Burbank's garden is a public park. On Arbor Day each year California plants new trees in honor of Luther Burbank.

How did Luther Burbank's leadership improve plants?

LOG ON For more about Luther Burbank, visit:
www.macmillanmh.com/ss/ca/bios

The Life of Luther Burbank

1840 — 1870 — 1900 — 1930

- **1849** Born in Lancaster, Massachusetts
- **1870** Begins growing new kinds of plants
- **1871** Produces a disease-free potato
- **1890** Creates Shasta daisy
- **1926** Dies in Santa Rosa

CHART and GRAPH Skills

Read Line Graphs

4.4

You have learned how farming became big business in California. Suppose you wanted to know how many fruits and vegetables California has produced over the years. You can find out by looking at a **graph**. Graphs are special diagrams that show information in a clear way. Different types of graphs can teach you different things.

VOCABULARY

graph
line graph

1 Learn It

Use the graph on this page to learn the skill.

- The graph on this page is a **line graph**. A line graph shows how something has changed over time. A line graph often shows an increase or decrease in number.
- The title of the line graph on this page is "California: Grapes Produced, 1994–2002." The title tells you what the graph is about.
- The numbers and labels on the left side of the line graph represent the amount of grapes. The labels at the bottom of the graph show the years that the graph covers.
- The yellow line in the graph shows either an increase or a decrease in the amount of grapes produced over these years.
- Each red dot on the line stands for the amount of grape supply during a particular year. You can see from the graph that California produced the most grapes in the year 2000. California produced about 4 million tons of grapes in that year.

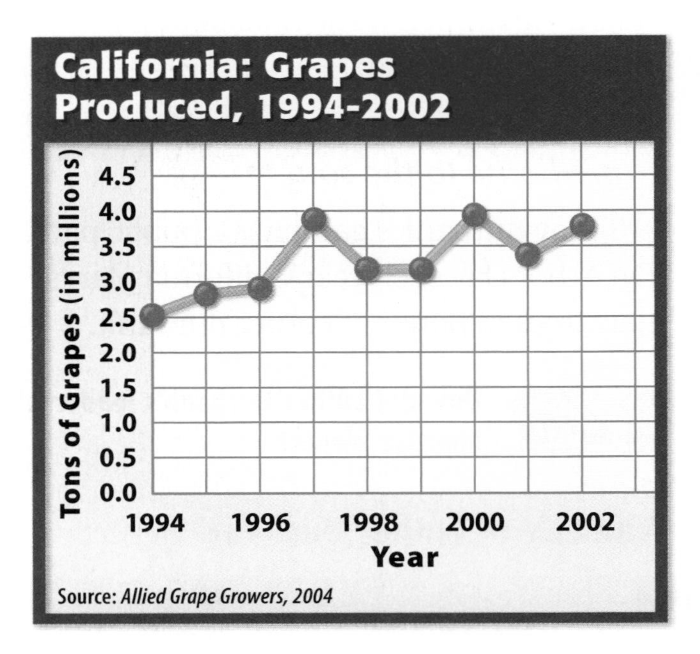

2 Try It

Use the graph below to answer these questions.

- What kind of graph is this?
- What does the graph show?
- What do the labels on the left side of the graph represent?
- In which year were the largest amount of strawberries produced?

3 Apply It

- Write a summary about California's grape supply based on information on the line graph on page 312.
- What can you conclude from the line graph shown on this page about California's strawberry production?
- How can line graphs help you to compare and contrast information?

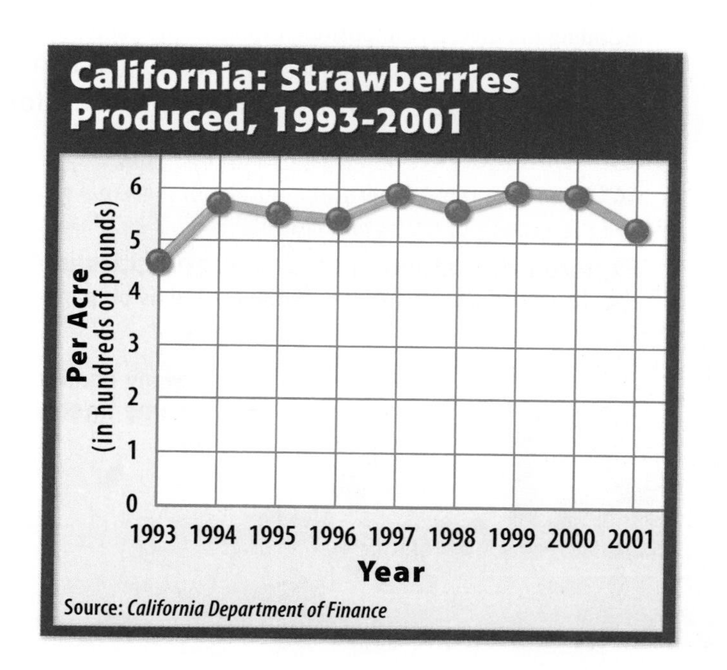

CHART AND GRAPH SKILLS

FOCUS QUESTION

Why did immigrants leave their homelands to come to California?

VOCABULARY

migration
barrio
mutual aid society
mutualista
prejudice

VOCABULARY STRATEGY

PREFIXES The prefix **pre-** means before. The word **prejudice** means judging before knowing. What other words use this prefix?

READING STRATEGY

Summarize

Use the chart below to summarize the lesson.

Coming to California

Start with Your CALIFORNIA STANDARDS

4.4 Students explain how California became an agricultural and industrial power, tracing the transformation of the California economy and its political and cultural development since the 1850s.

4.4.3 Discuss immigration and migration to California between 1850 and 1900, including the diverse composition of those who came; the countries of origin and relative locations; and conflicts and accords among the diverse groups.

Learn about the origins of newcomers to California.
(Begins on page 314)

4.4.4 Describe rapid American immigration, internal migration, settlement, and the growth of towns and cities.

Explore new settlements, towns, and cities in California during the late 1800s and early 1900s. (Begins on page 314)

Many immigrants to California came through Angel Island. ▼

1880	1890	1900	1910	1920	1930
1880 About 850,000 people live in California		1900 Over 1 million people in California	1910 Over 2 million people in California	1920 Over 3 million people in California	1930 Over 5 million people in California

In the late 1800s and early 1900s California experienced a population explosion. California's population grew to more than five-and-one-half million from 1880 to 1930. Many people were drawn to California because of advertisements.

Land of Opportunity 4.4.3 4.4.4

At the end of the 1800s, many people came to California seeking a new life. Some came to escape harsh conditions back home. Others came looking for gold or jobs on railroads and farms. All were seeking a chance to build a better life for their families.

When large numbers of newcomers move to a place it is called **migration**. People who lived in other parts of the United States moved to California. Others came from all over the world. As you learned in Chapter 1, people who move to a new country are known as immigrants.

Immigrants came for many reasons. Some came to escape poverty or wars at home. Others were drawn by newspaper ads. In 1913, a farmer advertised for people to help with a harvest. His ad brought workers from 27 different countries.

In 1898 the Philippines became part of the United States. Many people from the Philippines moved to the United States, including Carlos Bulosan who came here in 1930. Bulosan read that it was easy to earn a living and get an education in America. Everyone was treated fairly and equally. Life in America sounded so good that he moved here.

Bulosan found work in California picking fruit. He did not find life easy. Bulosan found that most immigrants were treated unfairly. He also found that they were often paid less than others for the same work.

Many immigrants remained poor after moving to California. Many others did succeed, however. Today immigrants continue to come to California.

REVIEW Why did people choose to migrate to California? *Summarize*

DATAGRAPHIC

Immigration to California: 1880-1930

4.4.3

From 1880 to 1930, immigrants from many different countries came to California. Where did these new Californians come from? The map below shows the countries which were the homelands of the most immigrants.

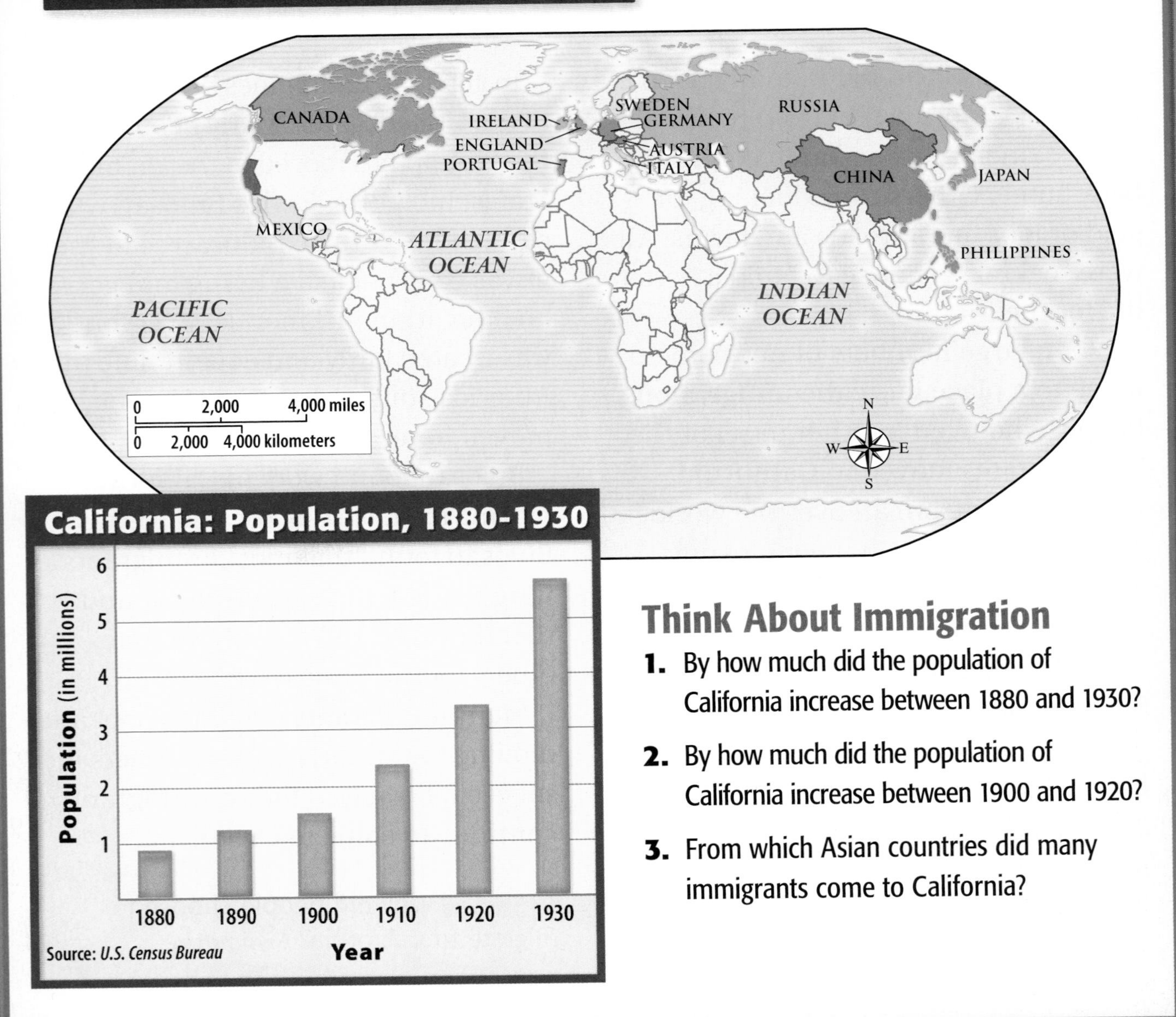

Think About Immigration

1. By how much did the population of California increase between 1880 and 1930?
2. By how much did the population of California increase between 1900 and 1920?
3. From which Asian countries did many immigrants come to California?

Traveling to California 4.4.3 4.4.4

European immigrants usually arrived at eastern ports such as New York. Once in the United States, many continued their journey west by train. However, most immigrants from Asia and some from Latin America came directly to San Francisco by ship.

Angel Island

The Chinese Exclusion Act of 1882 was meant to prevent most Chinese immigrants from entering the country. However, many Chinese immigrants continued to come to California.

Between 1910 and 1940, Chinese immigrants were stopped at Angel Island in San Francisco Bay. They had to stay on the island until immigration officials decided whether they could enter the United States.

Chinese immigrants were allowed to enter the state if they had an immediate family member who was already a United States citizen. Some Chinese immigrants arrived at Angel Island with fake papers that said they were the children of United States citizens. Many, however, came legally to California.

Immigration officials could take weeks, months, or even years to check these documents. Meanwhile, the immigrants were not allowed to leave Angel Island. Read about one immigrant's experiences below.

REVIEW What law was meant to prevent Chinese immigrants from entering the United States? *Cause and Effect*

Primary Sources

Poem
Author Unknown

During the long wait at Angel Island, some people wrote poetry on the walls.

> "*Imprisoned in the wooden building day after day, My freedom is withheld; how can I bear to talk about it? I look to see who is happy but they only sit quietly. I am **anxious** and depressed and cannot fall asleep. . . .Why not just return home and learn to plow the fields?*"

anxious worried

Write About It! **How do you think the author felt about being at Angel Island?**

Living and Working in a New Land 4.4.3 4.4.4

The land, climate, and economic growth in California gave many immigrants the chance to earn a living by farming. Some newcomers were able to buy their own land. Others made a life for themselves in California's cities.

Immigrants from Russia, Poland, and Korea settled in places like Los Angeles, San Francisco, and San Diego. They worked in factories, and restaurants, and on boats as fishermen.

Immigrants also started one of the most important companies in Hollywood. In the mid-1920s, two young immigrants—Samuel Goldwyn from Poland and Louis B. Mayer from Russia—created a new film company. The company was called Metro-Goldwyn-Mayer (MGM) and it went on to become one of Hollywood's biggest film studios.

Building Communities

Immigrants who came from the same country were drawn together by their common cultures. Members of some immigrant groups settled together in neighborhoods in large cities.

Like the Chinese, Mexican immigrants created their own communities within cities. In these neighborhoods, called **barrios**, Spanish was spoken.

Immigrant communities also supported new arrivals from their homelands by forming **mutual aid societies**. These organizations helped new immigrants find housing and jobs. The Mexican mutual aid societies were called **mutualistas**.

Some immigrant groups founded their own towns. The city of Anaheim was founded by German immigrants in 1857. They worked together on farms and shared the profits. Look at the map on page 319 to see where other immigrant groups lived.

Samuel Goldwyn (left) and Louis B. Mayer created MGM. ▼

▲ Many immigrants worked as blacksmiths or carpenters.

Competition for jobs and differences in culture often led to feelings of dislike, or **prejudice**, against immigrants. Often, people acted on these feelings by treating immigrants unfairly. This kind of unfair treatment is called discrimination. Many immigrant communities in California worked to defend their members from discrimination and prejudice.

Immigrant Contributions

Immigrants soon became a large part of the California work force. Immigrants brought more than their labor to California, however. They also brought new kinds of music, dance, food, and celebrations. Immigrants have made California a richer and more diverse place to live. Japanese immigrant Kenju Ikuta showed that rice could be a California cash crop. As a result, many rice farms were started in Northern California. Gaetano Merola came to California from Italy in 1921. Two years later he started the San Francisco Opera.

Swiss conductor and musician Ernest Bloch arrived in the United States in 1916. By 1925 he was the director of the San Francisco Conservatory of Music.

REVIEW What are some ways that immigrants have made California richer and more diverse? *Summarize*

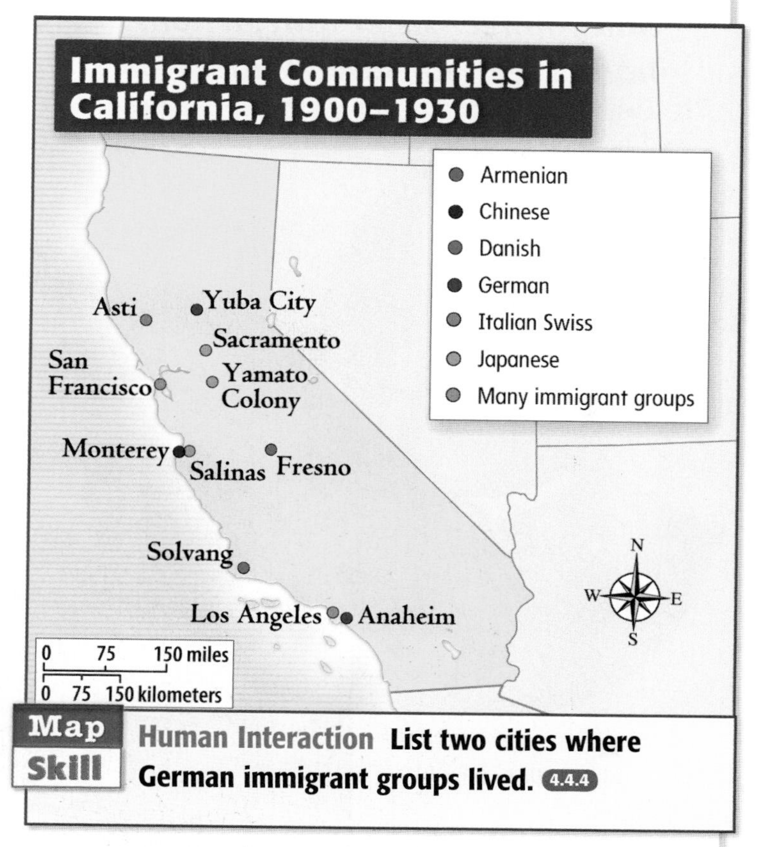

Map Skill **Human Interaction** **List two cities where German immigrant groups lived.** 4.4.4

Migration to California 4.4.4

California's population grew by almost two million between 1920 and 1930. Many of these new arrivals were Americans from other states who migrated west to California. People came from every region of the country. They no longer had to travel by ship or covered wagon. Many, like young Thomas Fleming, an African American, simply took the train.

Fleming later wrote about his experience for the San Francisco *Sun-Reporter,* a newspaper he founded in 1944. He wrote:

> **"*In the spring of 1919, when I was 11, I boarded the train in Jacksonville, Florida for Chico, California, to rejoin my mother and younger sister Kate, whom I hadn't seen for seven years. . . .*"**

Allen Allensworth

Between 1900 and 1930, many African Americans migrated to California. They came to escape the discrimination and prejudice they experienced in the South. California promised a life free from prejudice.

A man named Allen Allensworth understood how much African Americans felt the need for a place of their own. Allensworth was born in Kentucky in 1842. During the Civil War he escaped slavery and joined the Union Army. In 1906, Allensworth retired from the military as the nation's highest-ranking African American soldier. Two years later, Allensworth and William Payne founded the town of Allensworth in the San Joaquin Valley.

▲ Allen Allensworth

Many African Americans moved to Allensworth. ▼

The Town of Allensworth

Allensworth was the first town of its kind in California. The residents were all African American. The town had a school, library, and hotel. Many residents farmed grain or cotton, or raised cattle or chickens.

However, the town grew too quickly. By 1925 there was not enough water to grow crops. The town of Allensworth could not survive. By the late 1930s, most residents had left.

For 10 years however, the residents of Allensworth had achieved their dream. They had lived in freedom, owned homes, held good jobs, and they gave their children a better life. Each spring, Californians celebrate the history of Allensworth, which is now a historical park.

REVIEW Why did many African Americans choose to settle in California? *Summarize*

What You Learned

4.4.3 4.4.4 California's population boomed in the late 1800s and early 1900s, when immigrants from around the world came to the state.

4.4.3 4.4.4 Immigrants arrived in California by ship or train. Some Asian immigrants, such as the Chinese, were stopped and questioned at Angel Island.

4.4.3 4.4.4 Many immigrants settled together in communities and formed mutual aid societies to help newcomers find jobs and deal with discrimination.

4.4.4 Many Americans migrated to California from other states. Many African Americans settled in the new town of Allensworth.

Lesson Review

1. **Focus Question** Why did immigrants leave their homelands to come to California? 4.4.3 4.4.4
2. **Vocabulary** Write one sentence for each vocabulary term. 4.4.3 4.4.4
   barrio **mutualista**
   migration **prejudice**
   mutual aid society
3. **Economics** What was one important reason why immigrants came to California? 4.4.3 4.4.4
4. **Critical Thinking** **Draw Conclusions** Why did many people leave the town of Allensworth? 4.4.4
5. **Reading Strategy** **Summarize** Summarize the contributions made by new immigrant communities in California. 4.4.3 ELA R2.4

6. **Write about THE BIG IDEA** Write about how the railroad made it easier for people to come to California. 4.4.3 ELA W2.3
7. **Link to Language Arts** Suppose you are an immigrant who hopes to make a new life in California. Write a descriptive paragraph about why you have come to the state. 4.4.3 4.4.4

FOCUS QUESTION

What new industries brought growth to Southern California?

VOCABULARY

competition
derrick
refined

VOCABULARY STRATEGY

RELATED WORDS
A **competition** is a contest between two parties. Can you think of a similar verb?

READING STRATEGY

Identify Cause and Effect
Use the chart below to list the causes and effects of Los Angeles's economic boom.

The Rise of Southern California

Start with Your CALIFORNIA STANDARDS

4.4 Students explain how California became an agricultural and industrial power, tracing the transformation of the California economy and its political and cultural development since the 1850s.

4.4.4 Describe rapid American immigration, internal migration, settlement, and the growth of towns and cities.

Learn about the many people who settled in Southern California.
(Begins on page 323)

4.4.6 Describe the development and locations of new industries since the nineteenth century, such as the aerospace industry, electronics industry, large-scale commercial agriculture and irrigation projects, the oil and automobile industries, communications and defense industries, and important trade links with the Pacific Basin.

Explore the new industries that helped Southern California to grow.
(Begins on page 323)

In 1923 Hollywood was called "Hollywoodland." The sign was changed in 1949. ▼

HOLLYWOODLAND

1880	1890	1900	1910	1920
1880 The population of Los Angeles is 11,000	1890 More people migrate to Los Angeles after the completion of the railroad	1900 The population of Los Angeles grows to about 100,000	1910 Oil becomes a big industry and the filmmaking industry begins	1920 The population of Los Angeles is almost 600,000

The population boom of the 1800s mainly affected the gold rich areas of Northern California. Southern California's boom was not far behind. Railroads, industry, oil, and Hollywood were about to bring millions of newcomers to the south.

Southern California Grows

4.4.4

In 1876, the Southern Pacific Railroad connected Los Angeles to cities in Northern California. Another railroad line was built to San Diego. A line was also built from Los Angeles to cities in Texas. The Santa Fe Railroad connected Los Angeles to cities in the East. By 1883, a passenger from Chicago could take a train directly to Southern California.

Soon the railroad companies began a **competition**. A competition is an effort to win or gain something from others. Companies began lowering the price of train tickets. If it cost less to go to Los Angeles than to San Francisco, people would go to Los Angeles. For a short while, a ticket between Kansas City and Los Angeles cost just $1. Many people chose Los Angeles over San Francisco for this reason.

Railroad companies printed ads in newspapers and magazines. Many of these ads focused on the sunny climate of Southern California. According to some of these ads, Southern California's climate—and its oranges—could cure any sickness. As one ad put it: "*Oranges for Health—California for Wealth.*"

Soon people began coming to Southern California. Most settled in Los Angeles and San Diego. Between 1880 and 1920, the population of Los Angeles grew from 11,000 to over one-half million. By 1920, the population of Los Angeles had passed that of San Francisco. Los Angeles had become California's largest city.

REVIEW Why did people come to Southern California? *Cause and Effect*

New Industries 4.4.6

At the turn of the nineteenth century, Los Angeles was not prepared for a population boom. It needed to be able to ship supplies in and ship products out. Los Angeles needed a port.

The Port of Los Angeles

Construction of Los Angeles Harbor began in 1899. The Port of Los Angeles opened in 1907. New rail lines were built to connect the port to the main railroads.

The Panama Canal opened in 1914. It cut a path for ships to travel through Central America. Now, ships no longer had to sail around the continent to reach California. The Panama Canal increased the amount of cargo that passed through California ports.

The Port of Los Angeles became the first stop in California for all ships coming from Europe, the eastern United States, and Central and South America. By the mid-1920s, Los Angeles was the busiest port in the western United States. Los Angeles was becoming an important new center of trade and industry.

The Oil Boom

In 1893, Edward Doheny noticed that the back of a wagon which passed by him was filled with a sticky dark soil. The driver told him it came from a hole at a street corner in Los Angeles.

Los Angeles Harbor in the early 1930s ▼

▲ Oil derricks were sometimes built near schools.

Diagram Skill What layer is directly above oil? 4.4.6

At the time, coal was the main source of fuel in the country. Doheny knew that oil could also be used for fuel.

Doheny and a partner bought the land and drilled down until they struck oil. Then they built an oil **derrick** above the source. A derrick is a tower built over a drill site to support a drill and bring oil to the surface. The diagram on this page shows the layers of Earth between a derrick and oil.

Word of Doheny's discovery soon spread. People began to build derricks in their front and back yards. By 1900, there were more than 1,000 oil derricks in the city. Soon people from around the country moved to Southern California to find oil and strike it rich.

At the same time, railroads began using oil for fuel instead of coal. Cars powered by gasoline (an oil product) were becoming popular too. This made the price of oil increase. Oil became so valuable it was known as "black gold."

For cars to use oil, the fuel needed to be **refined**, or improved. In the 1920s, petroleum refining became California's biggest industry. More oil was exported out of Los Angeles than from any other port in the world.

REVIEW Between 1900 and 1930, what important changes occurred in Los Angeles? *Summarize*

Hollywood 4.4.6

In the early 1900s, movies were short and silent. Movies were made mainly in New York and New Jersey. Film companies there controlled the small filmmaking industry. They also owned all the equipment. However, Thomas Edison, who had invented the equipment, often took filmmakers to court. So, many went far away. Their new home was a small suburb of Los Angeles called Hollywood.

Southern California was a perfect place to make movies. Its climate allowed the filmmakers to film year-round. In addition, California had every kind of landscape filmmakers needed.

In 1914, Cecil B. DeMille made Hollywood's first long film. It was a hit. DeMille and others made many more. Within 10 years, the movie business had become an important industry in California. Thousands of actors moved to Los Angeles to work in movies.

Early Hollywood Stars

One of Hollywood's biggest stars, Charlie Chaplin, was an immigrant who moved to California to work in the film industry. Charlie Chaplin was born in England. He was about 10 years old when he began performing

Movies 4.4.6

THEN The first full-length movies made in Hollywood were silent, black and white, and shown in small theaters. Moviegoers found them amazing. Most Americans had not seen actors and actresses on screen.

NOW Today, movies have sound, dialogue, color, and are often shown in large cinemas with big screens. Filmmakers still use movie cameras to "shoot" films, but they are now easier to use.

How were the movies of the early 1900s different from the movies of today?

in the theater. In 1910, he went on tour in the United States.

Chaplin's comedy was done with his body, not his voice, because the films did not have sound. He became known all over the world.

In the 1920s, Hollywood became the movie capital of the world. In every town across the nation, going to the movies became a popular pastime. In the years to come Hollywood stars like John Wayne and Katharine Hepburn became popular figures throughout the world.

REVIEW Why was Southern California a good place to make movies? *Summarize*

Film reels come in different sizes. ▶

United States
At the Same Time

The United States entered World War I in 1917. Navy ships were built at Los Angeles Harbor. California shipped cotton overseas to make soldiers' uniforms.

What You Learned

4.4.4 In the late 1800s, railroad competition and advertising helped cause a boom in the population of Southern California.

4.4.6 In the 1920s, Los Angeles Harbor became the biggest port in the West. The oil boom brought new people and wealth to Southern California.

4.4.6 Filmmakers moved to Hollywood, California.

Lesson Review

1. **Focus Question** What new industries brought growth to Southern California? (4.4.6)
2. **Vocabulary** Write one sentence for each vocabulary word. (4.4.6)
   competition **derrick** **refined**
3. **Geography** How did changes to the geography of Central America affect Los Angeles? (4.4.4)
4. **Critical Thinking** **Problem Solving** How did railroad companies attract passengers? (4.4.6)
5. **Reading Strategy** **Identify Cause and Effect** List three causes and effects of the rise of Hollywood. (4.4.4, ELA R2.1)

	▶	
	▶	
	▶	
	▶	
	▶	

6. **Write about THE BIG IDEA** Write about how the technological developments that occurred in the late 1800s and early 1900s helped Southern California grow. (4.4.6, ELA W2.4)
7. **Link to Science** Research today's new technologies. Choose one and write a paragraph explaining how you think it will change your community. (4.4.6)

A Thirsty State

FOCUS QUESTION

How does California move its water to places that need it?

VOCABULARY

canal
aqueduct
dam
reservoir
hydroelectric power
aquifer

VOCABULARY STRATEGY

ROOT WORDS Aqueduct and **aquifer** both come from the Latin word for water, *aqua*. Can you think of another word that starts with aqua and has to do with water?

READING STRATEGY

Compare and Contrast
Use the diagram below to compare the benefits and costs of California's statewide water system.

Start with Your CALIFORNIA STANDARDS

4.4 Students explain how California became an agricultural and industrial power, tracing the transformation of the California economy and its political and cultural development since the 1850s.

4.4.7 Trace the evolution of California's water system into a network of dams, aqueducts, and reservoirs.

Find out about the development of California's water system.
(Begins on page 329)

Crops growing by the Salton Sea ▼

1900	1908	1916	1924	1932	1940

1901
Canals bring water from the Colorado River to the desert

1913
The Los Angeles Aqueduct is built

1934
Hetch Hetchy Aqueduct brings water to San Francisco

The farmers and others watched with horror as their beautiful Imperial Valley was pounded with fierce rain. What had once been lush, green farmland was now lost underwater.

The Need for Water 4.4.7

The story of California's population growth is also partly a story about water. For example, a city full of people needs huge amounts of water every day for drinking, cooking, washing, and bathing. People and animals are not the only living things that need water. Crops also cannot grow without water.

California gets much of its water from the northern Sierra Nevada. In the north, the average rainfall is 56 inches a year. The average annual rainfall in parts of the south is just a few inches. Yet Southern California uses most of the state's water.

From Desert to Farmland

Do you remember reading about the irrigation system John Wesley North used for his orange groves? In 1885 North went one step further. He built a **canal**, or waterway, to bring water to Riverside's orange groves.

In 1901, engineer George Chaffey built a 70-mile canal from the Colorado River to bring water to the Colorado Desert in southeastern California. Then, he renamed the area "Imperial Valley" and sold the newly irrigated land to farmers.

The climate in the Imperial Valley was so good that crops could grow there all year long. The area was advertised as "the Winter Garden of the World." In 1905, after heavy rains, the Imperial Valley flooded, and the farms there sat underwater for two years. The floodwaters were drained, but a huge inland lake called the Salton Sea was left. Today, much of the Salton Sea is used for fishing and boating.

REVIEW Compare the Colorado Desert before and after 1905. *Compare and Contrast*

Thirsty Cities 4.4.7

Between 1850 and 1920, the cities of Los Angeles and San Francisco outgrew their water supply. Solving the need for water became an urgent challenge for both cities.

Water for Los Angeles

Before 1900, the Los Angeles River gave Los Angeles all the water it needed. It was clear, however, that the river could not meet the growing city's needs forever.

In the 1890s, an Irish immigrant, William Mulholland, became head of the Los Angeles water department. Mulholland's answer to Los Angeles's water needs was to build an **aqueduct** to bring water to the city. An aqueduct is a large pipe or other channel that carries water over a long distance. The Los Angeles Aqueduct would run from the Owens River to Los Angeles, a distance of 200 miles.

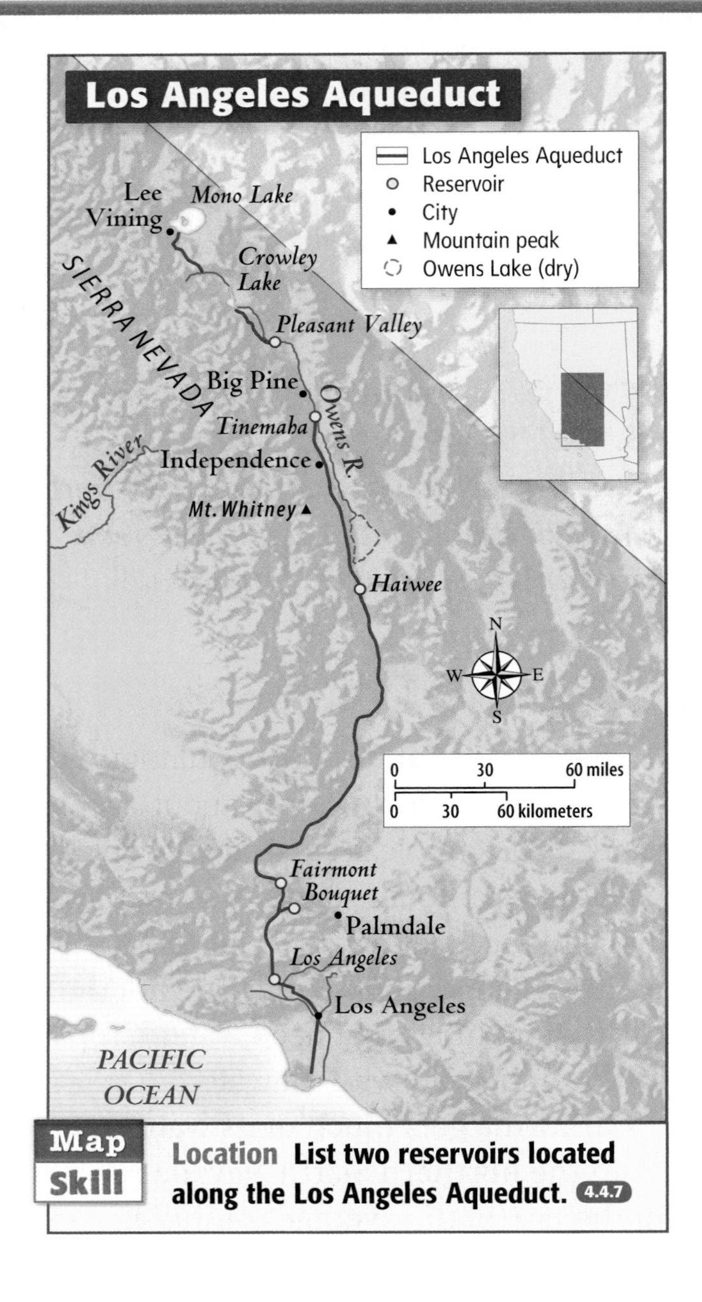

Map Skill Location **List two reservoirs located along the Los Angeles Aqueduct.** 4.4.7

The Los Angeles Aqueduct opened on November 5, 1913. ▼

Some people were against building the aqueduct. However, in 1908, construction of the aqueduct began.

Five years later the Los Angeles Aqueduct was competed. Its water source was the Owens River. The aqueduct irrigated farms and supplied water to the people of Los Angeles. Meanwhile, without a river flowing into it any longer, Owens Lake dried up and the Owens Valley farmlands suffered. By 1930, most of the farmers and ranchers in the Owens Valley sold their land and water rights to the city and rented the land back to ranchers.

Water for San Francisco

San Francisco also needed more water for its own growing population. To meet this need, the city's engineers drew up a plan to build a **dam** across the Tuolumne River. A dam is a wall built across a river to create a **reservoir** (REZ ur vwahr). A reservoir is a natural or man-made lake used to store water.

The reservoir at Hetch Hetchy would supply San Francisco with water through a new aqueduct. However, building the dam would flood the beautiful Hetch Hetchy Valley inside Yosemite National Park. Many people were upset by this idea, including John Muir.

Among those in favor of building the reservoir was James Phelan, mayor of San Francisco from 1897–1902. Phelan thought having a water supply was more important than the beautiful scenery.

In 1913, the United States Congress approved the flooding of Hetch Hetchy Valley. It took nine years to build the dam. The 150-mile aqueduct was completed in 1934.

REVIEW How did Los Angeles and San Francisco bring water to their cities? *Summarize*

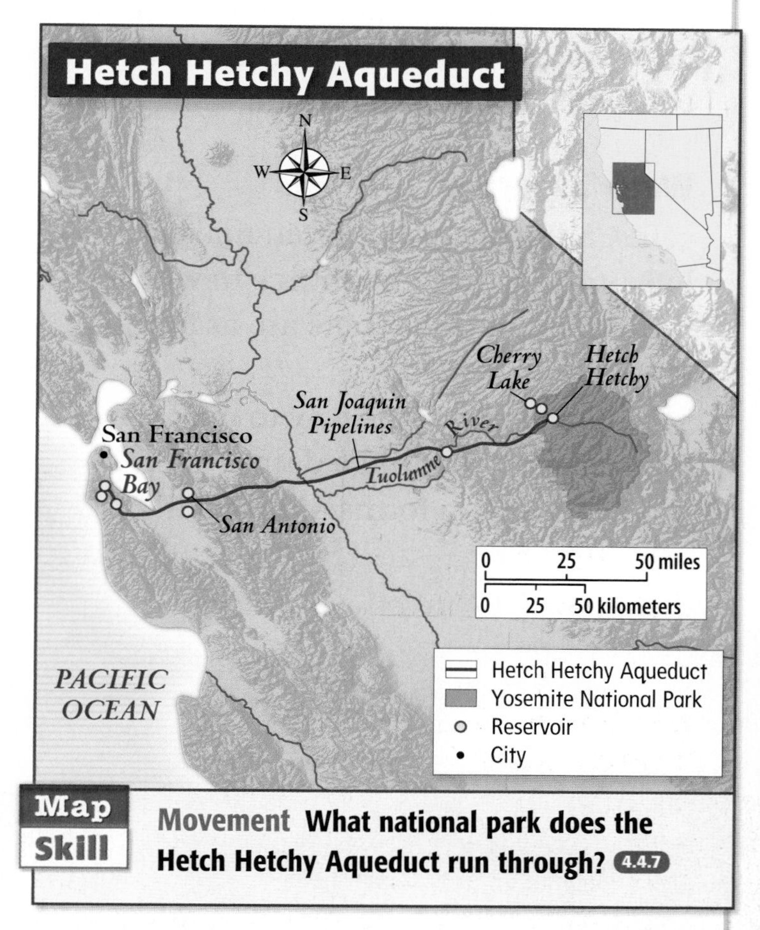

Map Skill Movement **What national park does the Hetch Hetchy Aqueduct run through?** 4.4.7

A Statewide System 4.4.7

After the Los Angeles and Hetch Hetchy aqueducts were built, California continued to find ways to deliver water to its cities and its farms. A system of dams, reservoirs, and aqueducts was planned. Look at the map of the California water system on the next page to see the result of the statewide plan.

The Central Valley Project was one part of that plan. Its main purpose was to bring water from the rainy Sacramento Valley to the drier San Joaquin Valley.

Water's Journey

In California, water often makes a long journey from its source to where it is used. Some aqueducts are as long as 300 miles.

As you've read, one way to make a reservoir is to build a dam. Water behind the dam forms a reservoir. When water is needed, the dam releases water into an aqueduct. From the aqueduct, water is run through additional pipes to provide irrigation. It is then made pure for residential use.

Dams are also used to make **hydroelectric power**. Hydroelectric power is electricity made by falling water. The water behind a dam can be released through pipes low in the dam. As it falls, it turns wheels inside the dam. These wheels are connected to a machine called a generator. A generator changes the moving power of the wheel into electricity.

California's vast water system has helped the state become a leader in many industries and in agriculture. It has also made it possible for the population of its cities to keep growing.

REVIEW Why does California need such a large water system? *Main Idea and Details*

All Californians appreciate the water available to us. ▼

DATAGRAPHIC

California's Water System

4.4.7

California's many water projects provide water to its residents. Billions of gallons of water are brought from one end of the state to the other to meet the needs of cities and farms. The Central Valley Project and the State Water Project are two of California's largest water projects.

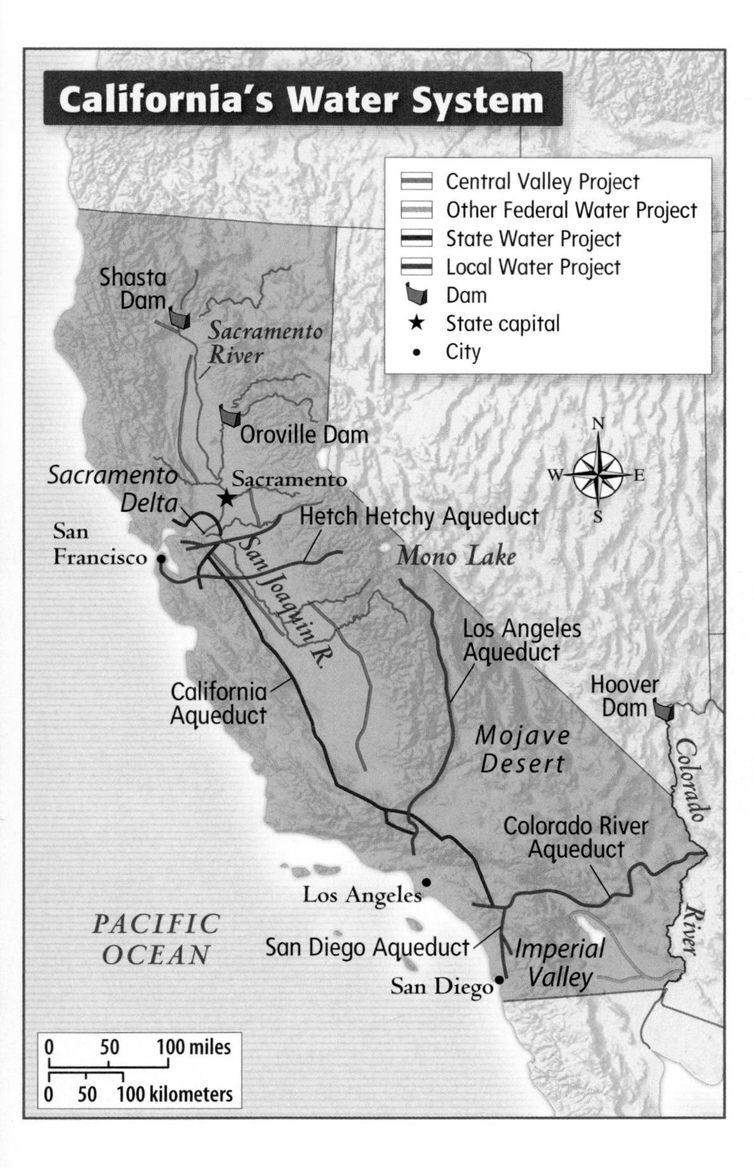

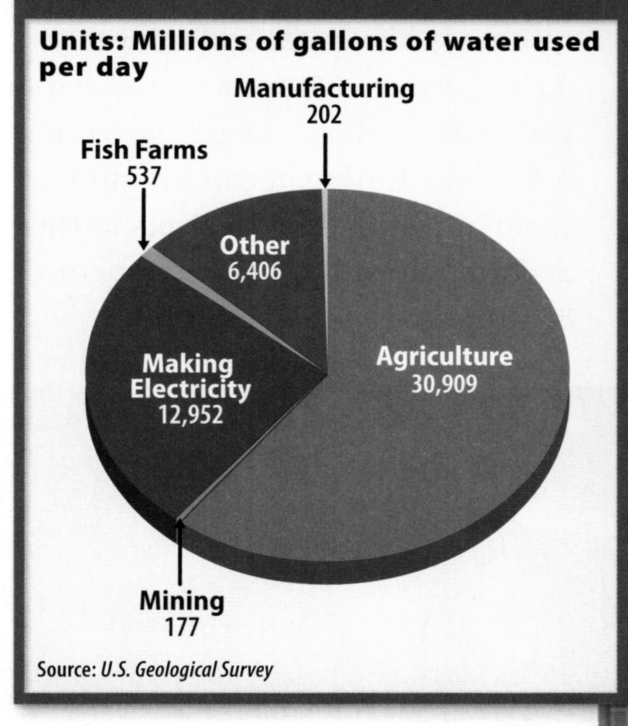

Think About Water

1. Which aqueduct is the longest?
2. What used the most water in California in 2000?
3. How much water did fish farms use in 2000?

Issues About Water 4.4.7

California's many water projects have done much to help the state grow. Dry plains and deserts have become rich farmlands. Agriculture has become one of the state's leading industries. However, some believe that the creation of California's water system has also harmed plants and animals.

Environmental Changes

Often, using large amounts of natural resources like water and minerals damages the environment. In Chapter 7, you learned about the damage done by hydraulic mining. It caused mud to wash into streams and rivers in the Sacramento Valley and clog them.

In this lesson you have learned about how water is sometimes taken from a source so that this same water can be used in a different place, often far away.

When water is taken away from a place where it has always been, the plants and animals that depend on it can no longer survive.

In rivers such as the Trinity River in Northern California, a dam blocks fish from swimming upriver to lay their eggs. Fish are now raised in a hatchery below the dam.

Another way in which Californians get water is from underground lakes called **aquifers**. If more water is taken out of an aquifer than goes into it, an aquifer may someday dry out.

Trinity River Dam ▼

Northern pintails were once a common sight in Mono Lake. ▶

Water Rights

Ever since California became a state, industries, cities, and individuals have argued over water rights. Water rights are the rights to use a source of water.

As you have read in this lesson, having enough water can be the difference between success and failure in California.

How and where California uses its water may continue to be argued about for years to come. The state's population is likely to grow, and so will the state's need for water.

REVIEW In what ways has California delivered water to areas around the state? *Summarize*

What You Learned

- 4.4.7 Most of California's water is located in the north but is needed in the south. Projects like the Imperial Valley irrigated dry land.
- 4.4.7 Los Angeles and San Francisco built aqueducts to bring water to their growing populations.
- 4.4.7 California's water system includes reservoirs and dams that deliver water to dry areas of the state and create electricity.
- 4.4.7 California's vast water system has affected the environment and may continue to affect it in the future.

Lesson Review

1. **Focus Question** How does California move its water to places that need it? (4.4.7)
2. **Vocabulary** Write one sentence for each vocabulary term. (4.4.7)

aqueduct	**dam**
aquifer	**hydroelectric power**
canal	**reservoir**

3. **Geography** Which part of California supplies most of its water? (4.4.7)
4. **Critical Thinking** **Problem Solving** How might Californians help conserve water? (4.4.7)
5. **Reading Strategy** **Compare and Contrast** Copy the diagram and use it to compare the benefits and costs of the Los Angeles Aqueduct. (4.4.7, ELA R2.1)

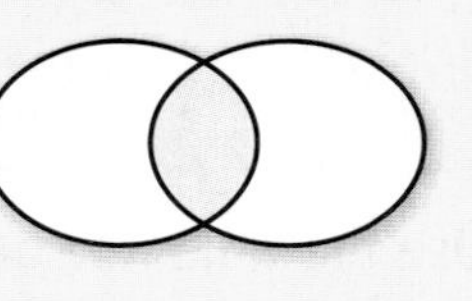

6. **Write about THE BIG IDEA** Use the library or the Internet to find out more about a dam, aqueduct, or reservoir in your area. Write a paragraph about what you learned. (4.4.7, ELA W2.4)
7. **Link to Science** Suppose you are following a drop of water in the Owens River. Write a paragraph about the route it would travel on its way to Los Angeles. (4.4.7)

Chapter Review

Vocabulary Review

Copy the sentences below on a separate sheet of paper. Use the list of vocabulary words to fill in the blanks.

aqueduct	**migration**
levee	**reservoir**

1. The farmer built a ________ , or a high wall made out of earth, to keep water from flooding his field. 4.4.6

2. A ________ is a lake created by a dam and used to store water. 4.4.7

3. A ________ occurs when a large group moves from one place to another. 4.4.3

4. A large pipe that carries water over a long distance is an ________ . 4.4.7

5. Test Preparation A tower built over a drill site that helps to support a drill and bring oil to the surface is a ________ . 4.4.6

A. **combine**
B. **canal**
C. **barrio**
D. **derrick**

Comprehension Check

6. What did immigrants from the same country do once they arrived in California? 4.4.4

7. Why is the delta region a big farming area? 4.4.6

8. Why were some Chinese immigrants held at Angel Island when they arrived? 4.4.3

9. How did railroads affect the price of oil? 4.4.6

10. What did farmers in California build to help irrigate their fields? 4.4.7

11. Critical Thinking How did the railroad affect the Central Valley? 4.4.6

12. Critical Thinking What did farmers do if their land was too dry to grow crops? 4.4.6

Use the Time Line

Use the time line below to answer each question.

13. How many years after the droughts did the Tibbets plant an orange tree? 4.4.6

14. Which industry was established in California after 1900? 4.4.6

1860 | 1870 | 1880 | 1890 | 1900 | 1910

1860 Droughts begin to hurt cattle ranching

1873 Luther and Eliza Tibbets plant a navel orange tree

1893 The oil industry begins in California

1908 The film industry begins in California

Skills Check

Write a complete sentence to answer each question.

Read Line Graphs

15. (4.4.4) How has the population of Los Angeles changed?

16. (4.4.4) What period does the line graph on this page show?

17. (4.1.5) Test Preparation What does each dot stand for?

18. (4.1.5) Test Preparation A graph that shows how information, such as the population of Los Angeles, changes over time is a ________ .

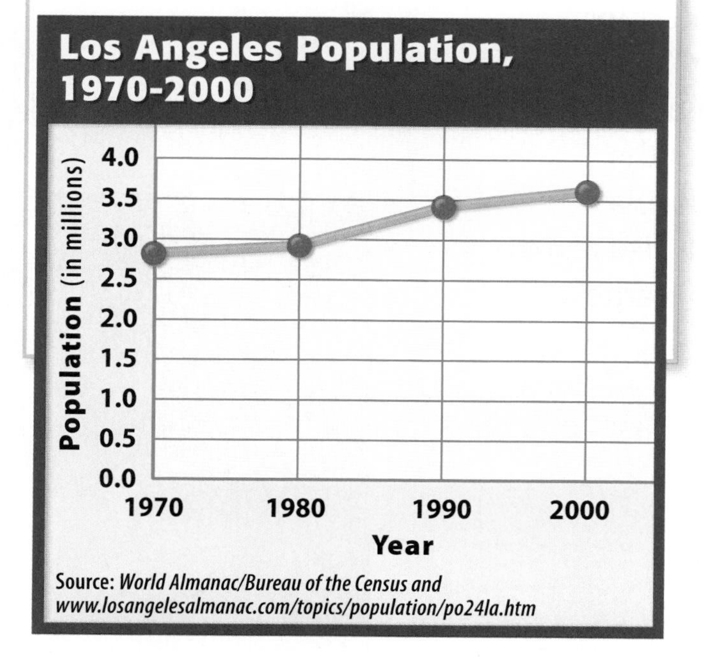

Source: *World Almanac/Bureau of the Census and www.losangelesalmanac.com/topics/population/po24la.htm*

Using Primary Sources

Newspapers

19. (4.5) What would a newspaper from September 1, 1849, explain about California's constitution?

20. (4.5) How can newspapers help us to learn more about our state?

Hands-on Activity

21. (4.4.6) Make a Poster Work in groups to make a poster that answers this question:

What are five fruits or vegetables grown in California?

Illustrate your poster with magazine pictures and drawings as well as writing captions and labels.

Write About History

22. (4.4.4, ELA W2.3) Expository Choose one of the famous immigrants mentioned in Lesson 2. Write two paragraphs that explain how he or she changed California. You may need to use reference sources.

For help with the process of writing, visit:

www.macmillanmh.com/ss/ca/writing

CHAPTER

10 Changing Times

You Are There

"All the day long,
Whether rain or shine,
She's a part of the assembly line.
She's making history,
Working for victory,
Rosie the Riveter."

In the early 1940s the United States entered a war in Europe. Since many men were fighting in Europe, women were needed to work in factories making planes and ships. Women workers became known as "Rosie the Riveter" because of a song popular at the time.

In this chapter you will read about the war in Europe and changes in California's government and economy. You will also learn how cars, highways, and suburbs became a major part of life in California.

Chapter Events

1906 San Francisco is destroyed by earthquake and fires (page 341)

1910 Hiram Johnson runs for governor (page 342)

A B

1905 1920

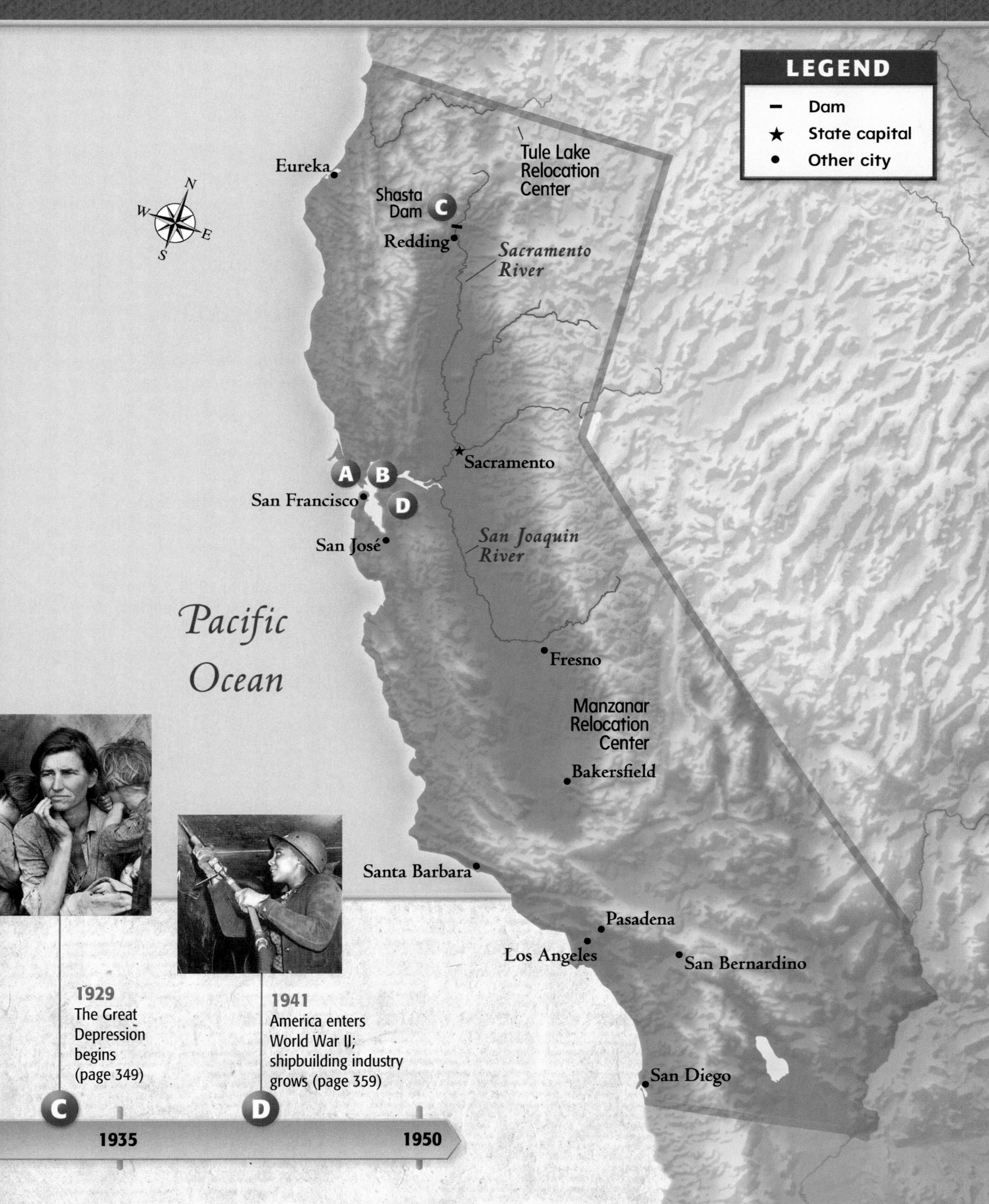
LEGEND
Dam
State capital
Other city
N
S
E
W
Eureka
Shasta Dam
C
Redding
Tule Lake Relocation Center
Sacramento River
Sacramento
A
B
D
San Francisco
San José
San Joaquin River
Pacific Ocean
Fresno
Manzanar Relocation Center
Bakersfield
Santa Barbara
Pasadena
Los Angeles
San Bernardino
San Diego
1929
The Great Depression begins (page 349)
1941
America enters World War II; shipbuilding industry grows (page 359)
C
D
1935
1950

LESSON 1

The Need for Reform

FOCUS QUESTION

How did people work to change California's government?

VOCABULARY

- reformer
- bribe
- amendment
- initiative
- referendum
- recall
- suffrage
- minimum wage

VOCABULARY STRATEGY

SYNONYMS Amend means to change for the better. Can you think of other words that have similar meanings?

READING STRATEGY

Compare and Contrast Use the chart below to explain the differences between San Francisco's city government before and after the 1906 earthquake. Label each side of the chart.

Start with Your CALIFORNIA STANDARDS

4.5 Students understand the structures, functions, and powers of the local, state, and federal governments as described in the U.S. Constitution.

4.5.4 Explain the structures and functions of state governments, including the roles and responsibilities of their elected officials.

Find out how Californians work to make changes in their state and local governments. (Begins on page 341)

The earthquake of 1906 destroyed many buildings in San Francisco. ▼

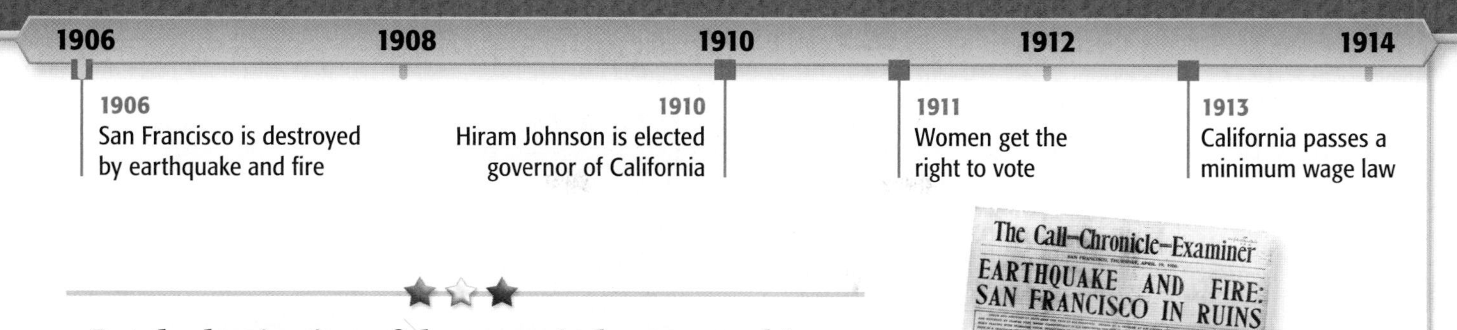

The Call–Chronicle–Examiner

EARTHQUAKE AND FIRE: SAN FRANCISCO IN RUINS

At the beginning of the twentieth century, big businesses controlled the government in California. Women could not vote. Workers worked long hours for little pay. The San Francisco earthquake of 1906 sparked a reform movement that would change all of this.

Renewal and Reform 4.5.4

In the early morning on April 18, 1906, a strong earthquake was felt along the coast of California. In San Francisco, many buildings collapsed, and more than 50 fires started burning.

San Francisco burned for three days. The city was almost completely destroyed. As many as 3,000 people were killed and 350,000 people were left homeless.

Reform in San Francisco

With the rebuilding of the city came changes. Many people were unhappy with the way the city was run. They felt that large businesses were controlling the government. These people wanted things to change. They were called **reformers**.

One of the people the reformers wanted to get rid of was Abraham Ruef. He was a political "boss" who ran the city as if he owned it. He used **bribes** to get what he wanted. A bribe is the money, gifts, or favors one person gives another to do something.

Ruef got paid by many big businesses to bribe the people in government. After they received a bribe, the city officials would pass laws or make decisions that would help the businesses that gave Ruef money. This was not fair to the people who lived in San Francisco.

The reformers turned to a lawyer named Hiram Johnson for help. He presented the court case against Ruef and the city officials. Hiram Johnson soon became a leader of the reform movement.

REVIEW How did bribes to city officials help businesses? *Summarize*

Giving Citizens Power 4.5.4

Shipping products by railroad greatly helped California's economy. The railroad was now owned by the Southern Pacific Company. The company owned most of California's transportation system and the waterfront in San Francisco.

Farmers and merchants had to pay very high fees to ship their goods. Since there was no other system, most people had no choice but to do what the company wanted. Because of the high prices they charged, the owners of the railroad were making a lot of money.

The Octopus Loses Power

The Southern Pacific Company became known as the Octopus. The company got this nickname because people thought of it as a huge creature that squeezed all the money out of hard-working citizens.

Farmers tried complaining to the government but it did no good. The Southern Pacific Company was giving bribes to government officials. In return for the bribes, these officials made laws that helped the railroad.

Many people in California thought the Southern Pacific Company was too involved with the government. In 1910, the leaders of the reform movement asked Hiram Johnson to run for governor. Johnson agreed to run.

▲ The Southern Pacific Company was known as the Octopus.

He was angry that the government took bribes from the company. In his speeches Johnson promised

> ***"to kick the Southern Pacific Railroad out of [government]."***

Hiram Johnson won the race and became governor. He helped pass laws that controlled what businesses could do. One of these laws controlled how much the railroads could charge for shipping goods.

▲ Hiram Johnson was a leader in the reform movement.

▲ Gray Davis was the first governor to be recalled in California.

New Laws

The reformers in California wanted to give voters a way to have more say in what the government did. Governor Johnson helped pass an **amendment**, or change, to the state constitution. This new law was called the **initiative**. It gave voters a way to create laws directly.

The second part of the new law passed under Governor Johnson was called the **referendum**. This law made it possible for voters to say "no" to laws already passed by the legislature.

Another change in the law was called the **recall**. Under this law, citizens could vote someone out of office if they did not like what that person was doing. This law was used in 2003 to remove a governor from office. California citizens did not approve of the way Governor Gray Davis handled taxes and the state budgets. A special vote was called, and Davis was voted out of office. Out of 135 candidates, nearly half of all Californians chose Arnold Schwarzenegger to be the new governor of California.

REVIEW Why was the Southern Pacific Company called "the Octopus"? *Summarize*

▲ Caroline Severance

▲ Women march for the right to vote.

Women Reformers 4.5.4

Many reformers worked hard to improve life for the people of California. One of these reformers was Katherine Philips Edson. Edson saw that children in Los Angeles were getting sick from drinking bad milk. She and other women demanded that the government test the milk supply to see that it was safe. As a result, the city government hired inspectors to test all the milk sold in Los Angeles.

In the early 1900s, women in California could be elected to school boards. They could have many different jobs. But women could not vote.

Edson became one of the leaders in the fight for women's **suffrage**, or right to vote. Caroline Maria Severance was another woman who worked for women's suffrage.

In 1911, California became the sixth state to give women the right to vote. At the age of 91, Severance became the first woman in California to register to vote.

Improving Life for Workers

Governor Johnson was very impressed by Edson's work with reform issues. Johnson asked Edson to study working conditions in California. Edson found that women were often paid less than 15 cents an hour.

▲ Katherine Edson

In 1913, thanks to Edson's work, the state legislature passed a **minimum wage** law for women and children. A minimum wage is the lowest amount of money that a company can pay its workers. Today there are minimum wage laws for all workers.

Delilah Beasley

Delilah Beasley also helped improve the lives of Californians. She studied the history of African Americans who had come to California. She wrote a book called *The Negro Trailblazers of California*. Beasley convinced other writers to be more respectful when writing about African Americans.

REVIEW Katherine Philips Edson worked on what three reforms? *Summarize*

What You Learned

4.5.4 Many people in San Francisco did not want businesses bribing government officials.

4.5.4 New laws were passed that controlled big businesses and improved the lives of working people.

4.5.4 Reformers worked to give women the right to vote, to protect children, and to improve the lives of workers.

Lesson Review

1. **Focus Question** How did people work to change California's government? (4.5.4)
2. **Vocabulary** Write one sentence for each vocabulary term. (4.5.4)
   amendment **minimum wage** **reformer**
   bribe **recall** **suffrage**
   initiative **referendum**
3. **History** How did Katherine Philips Edson help make life better for Californians? (4.5.4)
4. **Critical Thinking** **Problem Solving** What did the laws do that Hiram Johnson passed when he became governor of California? (4.5.4)
5. **Reading Strategy** **Compare and Contrast** Describe people's lives before and after the reforms Katherine Edson worked for. (4.5.4, ELA R2.1)

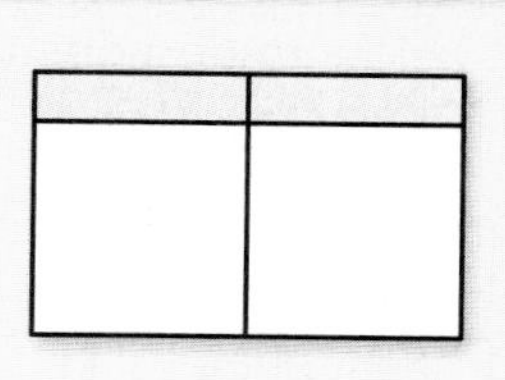

6. **Write about** THE BIG IDEA Write about how you would feel if you were working in a factory for 10 hours a day. (4.5.4, ELA W2.1)
7. **Link to Art** Think of a rule or law that you do not like. Draw a cartoon or poster that would convince others to change the rule. (4.5)

LESSON 2

FOCUS QUESTION

How did the Great Depression affect California?

VOCABULARY

Great Depression
shares of stock
stock market
stock market crash
Dust Bowl
New Deal
deport

VOCABULARY STRATEGY

RELATED WORDS The word **migrate** means to move around from one place to another. Can you think of other words that mean to move around?

READING STRATEGY

Identify Main Idea and Details
Use the chart below to describe the Great Depression.

Hard Times Hit Home

Start with Your
CALIFORNIA STANDARDS

4.4 Students explain how California became an agricultural and industrial power, tracing the transformation of the California economy and its political and cultural development since the 1850s.

4.4.5 Discuss the effects of the Great Depression, the Dust Bowl, and World War II on California.

Learn about what happened in California during the Great Depression and World War II, and what happened as people came to California from the Dust Bowl. (Begins on page 347)

▲ Many unemployed Californians waited in long lines for free soup and bread during the Great Depression.

During the 1920s, the economy of the United States was growing. President Calvin Coolidge said "the chief business of the American people is business." Unfortunately, hard times were ahead.

OUT OF WORK
BUY APPLES
5¢ EACH

The Great Depression 4.4.5

In 1929, ten years after World War I ended, the **Great Depression** began. An economic depression happens when people lose their jobs and have less money to buy things.

One of the causes of the Great Depression was that companies started making more products than they could sell. When a company cannot sell the goods it makes, it loses money. When companies continue to lose money, they usually close. Then workers lose their jobs.

The Stock Market Crashes

Another cause was that many people were buying **shares of stock**. When people buy a share of stock, they become part owner of a business. If the business grows, the people who own the shares of stock make money.

However, some businesses did not grow. Instead, these companies did worse, and their shares were soon worth less than what they had cost to buy.

Then, on October 29, 1929, the stock market crashed. The **stock market** is where shares of stock are bought and sold. A **stock market crash** happens when the prices of many different shares suddenly become very low. People who owned stock wanted to sell their shares so that they would not lose all of their money.

Banks Close

Many banks lost the money they had invested in the stock market. Many businesses closed and could not pay back money they had borrowed from banks. So these banks also closed. People lost their jobs and their life savings. Many people lost their homes and farms.

REVIEW What are shares of stock?
Main Idea and Details

Dorothea Lange took this photo of a migrant mother during the Dust Bowl.

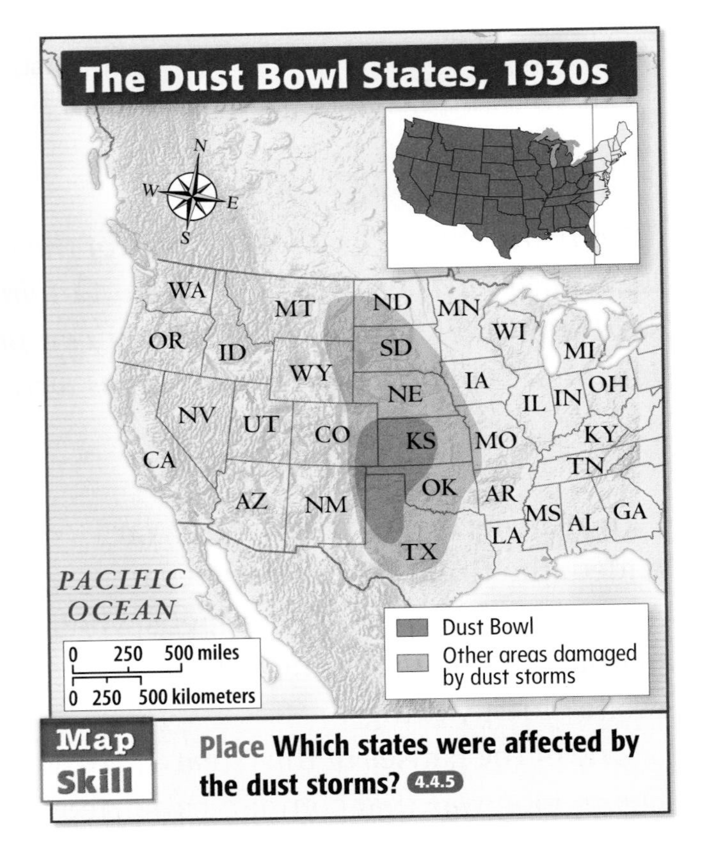

Map Skill Place **Which states were affected by the dust storms?** 4.4.5

Soil Turned to Dust 4.4.5

During the 1930s, many states were affected by a drought. A drought is when little or no rain falls. This drought lasted for so many years that the soil turned to dust.

Look at the map to see where the drought occurred. This area became known as the **Dust Bowl**.

Many of the people who lived in the Dust Bowl had to leave. Many of them migrated, or moved, to California, where they believed they could find good jobs and a better life.

Many Californians were also looking for work. They were afraid that the migrants would take the few jobs that there were. Some Californians tried to pass a law to keep the migrants out. The law did not pass.

Many of the people who came to California became migrant workers who usually moved from place to place to harvest crops. Often the migrant workers were not paid much and lived in bad conditions.

A photographer, Dorothea Lange, was hired by the government to take photographs of how the Great Depression was affecting people. One of her well-known photos is called *Migrant Mother*. Lange said about the photo,

"... the hungry and desperate mother ... had just sold the tires from the car to buy food."

Below you can read about the experiences of a Dust Bowl family from a novel called *The Grapes of Wrath*, written by John Steinbeck. Steinbeck describes in the novel what it was like to live in the Dust Bowl.

Primary Sources

A section from
The Grapes of Wrath
by John Steinbeck
Published 1939

"... Women and men huddled in their houses, and they tied handkerchiefs over their noses when they went out, and wore ***goggles*** *to protect their eyes. . . .*

When the night came again, it was black night, for the stars could not pierce the dust to get down, and the window lights could not even spread beyond their own yards."

goggles glasses to protect the eyes

What was Steinbeck trying to explain to the reader?

New Projects Provide New Jobs

In 1933, Franklin Delano Roosevelt became President of the United States. To bring the country out of the Great Depression, he started programs that put people back to work. These programs were known as the **New Deal**.

Among the projects completed under the New Deal were the construction of the Hoover Dam on the Colorado River and the Shasta Dam in Central Valley.

The Golden Gate Bridge

Another construction project during the Great Depression was the Golden Gate Bridge, which connects Marin County and San Francisco. The Golden Gate Bridge took four years to build and was finished in 1937.

REVIEW How did the New Deal help people? *Main Idea and Details*

Golden Gate Bridge, San Francisco ▼

Fair Treatment for Mexican Workers 4.4.5

During the Great Depression, a large number of Californians feared that Mexican immigrants were taking the jobs of Americans. The government began to **deport**, or send back to their country, Mexicans and Mexican Americans. Between 1931 and 1934, 100,000 Mexicans were forced to leave California and return to Mexico.

The Mexican American community fought back against this discrimination. As you read in Chapter 9, one way the Mexican community fought was by forming groups called mutualistas. These groups struggled for immigrants' rights. The mutualistas demanded better working conditions and fairer treatment.

Another organization that was formed was the Congress of Spanish Speaking People. It was founded in 1938 by Luisa Moreno. Its first president was Josefina Fierro de Bright. You can learn more about her on page 351.

REVIEW How did Mexicans work for fair treatment in California? *Cause and Effect*

What You Learned

- 4.4.5 During the Great Depression, many people lost their jobs, life savings, homes, or farms.
- 4.4.5 Many states were affected by a drought in the 1930s. People had to move to find work.
- 4.4.5 The Mexican American community formed groups to fight discrimination and get better working conditions.

Lesson Review

1. **Focus Question** How did the Great Depression affect California? 4.4.5
2. **Vocabulary** Write one sentence for each vocabulary term. 4.4.5
   - **deport**
   - **Dust Bowl**
   - **Great Depression**
   - **New Deal**
   - **shares of stock**
   - **stock market**
   - **stock market crash**
3. **Economics** What brought about the Great Depression? 4.4.5
4. **Critical Thinking** **Problem Solving** How did President Roosevelt create more jobs during the Great Depression? 4.4.5
5. **Reading Strategy** **Identify Main Idea and Details** Use the chart to discuss the Dust Bowl. 4.4.5 ELA R2.1

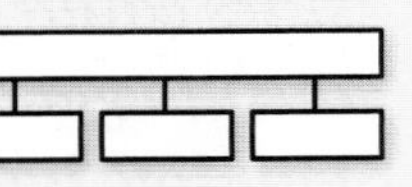

6. **Write about THE BIG IDEA** Write about how Californians managed during these economic difficulties. 4.4.5 ELA W2.3
7. **Link to Technology** Research how farming practices in the 1930s helped cause the Dust Bowl. Write a paragraph describing the causes of the Dust Bowl and how it led to improvements in the way people farmed. 4.4.5

Biography
Focus on Justice

4.4.5

Josefina Fierro de Bright 1920–1998

Josefina Fierro de Bright was born in Mexico in 1920. As a child, she moved to California and lived in farm camps where her mother served meals to the workers. At the camps, de Bright experienced the poor living and working conditions of migrant workers.

After high school de Bright went to the University of California at Los Angeles. She soon left school to try and help migrant workers. De Bright organized the workers into groups to demand better working conditions.

In 1938, de Bright became the first president of the Congress of Spanish Speaking People. Under her leadership, the Congress fought for better housing and healthcare for Mexican immigrants.

From 1939 to 1940, de Bright organized protests to end discrimination in schools and in the legal system. She also supported the struggle for fair wages and better working conditions for Spanish speaking people.

Josefina Fierro de Bright gave her time and energy to help others improve their lives. She focused on trying to achieve justice for all.

Write About It! In what ways did Josefina Fierro de Bright help bring justice to Mexican workers?

For more about Josefina Fierro de Bright, visit:
www.macmillanmh.com/ca/ss/bios

Life of Josefina Fierro de Bright

1920 · 1935 · 1950 · 1965 · 1980 · 2005

- **1920** Born in Mexico
- **1938** Became the first president of the Congress of Spanish Speaking People
- **1939-40** Works to end discrimination in schools, legal system, and the workplace
- **1998** Dies in Mexico

A School of Their Own

4.4.5

*

Characters

Narrator	Alice	Mabel
Mr. Jenkins	Bill	Florence
Mrs. Jenkins	Teacher	Cody

*

Narrator: It is 1940 in Weedpatch, California. We are near a tent on the side of a road where the Jenkins family lives. The Jenkins used to be farmers in Oklahoma. Then the rains stopped. The Dust Bowl spread across the land. Without rain, the Jenkins could not farm. Finally, they moved to California. So far, life in California has not been easy. Still, they hope that their children will get a good education.

Narrator: Mrs. Jenkins calls out to her husband.

Mrs. Jenkins: Lunch will be ready soon!

Alice: You better make lunch for us, too.

Mrs. Jenkins: Why are you back so early? You're supposed to be in school!

Alice: Oh, Mom, it was terrible. The school turned us away.

Bill: They called us Okies. They said no Okies could go to their school.

Mrs. Jenkins: What will we do?

Mr. Jenkins: I heard someone say a man named Leo Hart is starting a school for people like us.

Narrator: That very morning, they went down to the school…except there was no school building.

Mr. Jenkins: Excuse me, we're looking for the school that Mr. Hart is starting.

Teacher: You've found it.

Alice: Where is it?

Mabel: We have to build it.

Bill: Build it?!

Florence: With our bare hands.

Teacher: It's true. We don't have a building but we have lots of land.

Cody: Mr. Hart thinks that we can learn a lot from building the school ourselves.

Teacher: Our students will learn how to lay bricks, plaster walls, install electrical wiring, and even plumbing.

Teacher: We'll spend half the day building and the other half studying.

Mr. Jenkins: Our kids are strong, but they've grown weak from hunger. It takes a lot of energy to build a school.

Teacher: See those cows and chickens over there? We're going to have a farm at our school. We're going to grow our own vegetables and make our own food.

Mrs. Jenkins: Well, what are you kids waiting for? Get to work!

Narrator: The students went to work. Brick by brick, they built the school.

Florence: I need some bricks.

Bill: How many do you need?

Alice: Let's see. This space takes 3 bricks across and 10 bricks high. Hmm, 3 x 10 equals 30, I need 30 bricks.

Mabel: Thirty bricks coming right up.

Teacher: Kids, it's time for math class.

Narrator: Every day, the students spent time learning to read, write, and do math.

Teacher: You have all done a great job. Mr. Hart had an idea. What if our school had a science lab?

Mabel: For making experiments?

Teacher: Exactly.

Bill: Could we really do it?

Alice: We've built a school already. We can do anything!

Narrator: And so the students began work on a science lab.

Alice: I went to the orchard and picked us some peaches.

Cody: Thanks. It sure is hot in here.

Alice: I wish I could dive into a pool.

Bill: Wouldn't it be great if we had a swimming pool?

Florence: Pass me some nails and quit dreaming.

Bill: I'm serious.

Mabel: Are you thinking what I'm thinking?

Bill, Mabel, Florence, Alice and Cody: Let's ask Mr. Hart!

Narrator: Soon the students were building a swimming pool.

Narrator: Before they knew it, the Weedpatch School became famous. People said it was the finest school for miles around. It was all thanks to one man named Leo Hart, who wanted to make a difference.

Write About It!

If you could build your own school, what would it have? Describe the school that you would build and tell why you would build it that way.

World War II Changes California

FOCUS QUESTION

How did World War II change California?

VOCABULARY

- World War II
- Axis
- Allies
- Liberty ship
- relocation camp

VOCABULARY STRATEGY

RELATED WORDS An **ally** is someone who takes your side. The word comes from the Latin word **alligare**, which means to bind to or to unite. Think of other words that describe the act of putting things together.

READING STRATEGY

Identify Main Idea and Details

Use the chart below to identify how California helped the war effort.

Start with Your CALIFORNIA STANDARDS

4.4 Students explain how California became an agricultural and industrial power, tracing the transformation of the California economy and its political and cultural development since the 1850s.

4.4.5 Discuss the effects of the Great Depression, the Dust Bowl, and World War II on California.

Find out about how California helped the United States during World War II. Read about the role of African Americans and Japanese Americans during the war. (Begins on page 357)

4.4.6 Describe the development and locations of new industries since the nineteenth century, such as the aerospace industry, the electronics industry, large-scale commercial agriculture and irrigation projects, the oil and automobile industries, the communications and defense industries, and important trade links with the Pacific Basin.

Learn about the men and women who built planes and ships during World War II. (Begins on page 358)

Pearl Harbor in Hawaii was attacked by the Japanese on December 7, 1941. ▶

1939	1941	1943	1945

1939 World War II begins in Europe

1941 Pearl Harbor is bombed; America enters the war

1942 Japanese Americans sent to relocation camps

1945 World War II ends

"Yesterday, December 7, 1941 . . . the United States of America was . . . attacked by . . . the Empire of Japan." These words were part of a speech given by President Franklin D. Roosevelt as the United States entered World War II. After the war many soldiers received the Purple Heart for bravery.

The World at War 4.4.5

In 1939 the leader of Germany wanted to control Europe. He forced many European countries to become part of Germany. His actions started **World War II**. Germany, Italy, and Japan became partners. These countries were called the **Axis**. The Axis powers fought against the **Allies**. As the war progressed, the Allies included Australia, Great Britain, China, France, New Zealand, the Soviet Union, and the United States.

The United States Joins the War

At first, the United States tried to stay out of the war. However, on December 7, 1941, Japanese planes bombed the United States Naval Base at Pearl Harbor in Hawaii. Almost 2,400 people were killed. After the bombing of Pearl Harbor, the United States entered the war on the side of the Allies.

Many people from California fought in World War II. California made many supplies for the war. However, with so many Californians fighting in Europe and Asia, more workers were needed to make equipment, such as weapons, ships, and planes, for the war. People who had been looking for jobs during the Great Depression could now find work. People came from all over the country to work in California. The state's population grew by three and a half million people between 1940 and 1950.

REVIEW How did World War II help California's economy? *Main Idea and Details*

▲ During World War II women did jobs that up until then only men had done.

California Workers 4.4.5 4.4.6

President Roosevelt asked the ship building industry to build ships faster than the enemy could sink them. California businessman Henry J. Kaiser accepted the challenge. He developed new ways to build ships quickly. These ships were called **Liberty ships**.

By 1942 there were five new shipyards in California. These shipyards employed almost 300,000 workers. The shipyard workers made one out of every four American ships.

Ships were not the only vessels needed in the war. There was also a huge demand for planes. Six companies in Southern California began making almost 100,000 airplanes a year. These companies made their old factories larger and built many new ones. Many of these companies continue to make airplanes today.

New Workers

Since so many men were away from home fighting the war, women were able to get jobs they had never had before. Nearly half of California's aircraft workers were women. At the Richmond Kaiser shipyards, women made up over one quarter of the workers. A national historic park is being built in Richmond, California, to honor the many women who served the war effort at home.

African American Workers

Many of the new factory and shipyard workers were African American. Before World War I, the African American population of California was 125,000. By 1950, that number had risen to 450,000.

During World II, African Americans faced discrimination in the armed forces. African Americans and other Americans were not allowed to work together in the same units of the armed forces. African Americans often did not get training that was as good as other Americans in the armed forces.

In 1944, in the harbor at Port Chicago, California, weapons were being loaded onto ships. The men had not been properly trained about how to move the weapons safely. When two ships and a train that were carrying weapons exploded, 320 men were killed. Of those killed, 202 were African American sailors.

The explosion made people more aware of the problems of discrimination in the armed forces. By 1948, the armed forces allowed everyone to work together and gave everyone the same training.

REVIEW Why were so many women hired to fill factory jobs during World War II?
Main Idea and Details

African Americans became a large part of California's workforce in the 1940s. ▼

Japanese Americans in World War II 4.4.5

After Japan bombed Pearl Harbor, many people became afraid that Japan might also attack California. They were also afraid that Japanese Americans living in California and other states in the west might help Japan fight the United States. In 1942 the government decided to send Japanese Americans to **relocation camps**. These camps were places where people were held during the war.

More than 110,000 people of Japanese descent were sent to these camps. Two thirds of the people sent away were American citizens. Over one half were children. Many of the people who were sent to the camps had their homes and businesses taken from them.

There were ten relocation camps throughout the west. Two of these camps, Manzanar and Tule Lake, were in California. Manzanar is located in the desert in eastern California's Owens Valley. Tule Lake is in the Klamath Falls Basin in northern California.

Life at the Camps

Life was often difficult at the camps. They were built in remote areas, or places where there were no towns nearby.

Many of the buildings had no running water and there was no heat in the winter. Everyone had to share bathrooms.

The families at the camps did whatever they could to make the camps feel like a home. They started schools and baseball teams for their children. Japanese Americans were forced to stay at the relocation camps until World War II ended in 1945.

Joining the Armed Forces

Even though their families remained in camps, many Japanese Americans joined the armed forces. The 442nd regiment, or troop, was made up entirely

Japanese Americans of all ages were forced to live at relocation camps during World War II.

Many Japanese Americans joined the armed forces during World War II.

of Japanese Americans. The men in this regiment won more medals for bravery than any other unit in the army.

An Official Apology

In 1988, the United States government apologized for its treatment of Japanese American citizens during World War II. Each person who had been at the camps was given $20,000 to try to make up for their experience in the camps.

REVIEW What effect did World War II have on Japanese Americans? *Main Idea and Details*

What You Learned

4.4.5 The Axis and Allies fought during World War II. The United States entered the war after Japan bombed Pearl Harbor.

4.4.5 4.4.6 Many new workers were needed in California to make ships and planes.

4.4.5 Japanese Americans were sent to relocation camps. Many Japanese Americans joined the armed forces.

Lesson Review

1. **Focus Question** How did World War II change California? 4.4.5
2. **Vocabulary** Write one sentence for each vocabulary term. 4.4.5 4.4.6
   Allies **Liberty ship** **World War II**
   Axis **relocation camp**
3. **History** California's African American population was 125,000 before World War I. How many more African Americans had come to California by 1950? 4.4.5
4. **Critical Thinking** **Identify Stereotypes** What did many people think Japanese Americans were going to do after Japan bombed Pearl Harbor? 4.4.5
5. **Reading Strategy** **Identify Main Idea and Details** Use the chart to identify what happened to Japanese Americans during World War II. 4.4.5 ELA R2.1
6. **Write about** THE BIG IDEA Write about what you think it would be like to be a worker making ships or planes for the war. 4.4.6 ELA W2.1
7. **Link to Art** Suppose that you are living during World War II. Design a poster that will convince people to come to California and work for the defense industry. 4.4.5

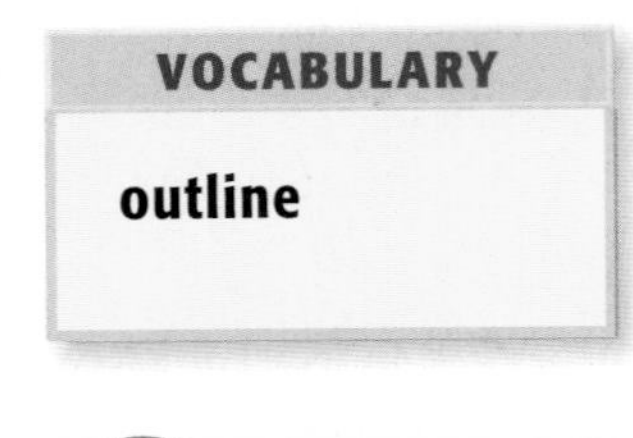

Write an Outline 4.4.5

You have just read about the effects of World War II on Japanese Americans. It might seem difficult at first to organize all the information you read. Writing an **outline** will help you group facts and see how they are related. An outline is a plan that presents ideas about a subject in an organized way. It helps you to better understand what you read.

VOCABULARY

outline

1 Learn It

Use the following steps when you create an outline:

- Identify the topic. Look back at pages 360–361. The topic is "Japanese Americans in World War II."
- Identify the main ideas. The main ideas of the topic are:
  - People begin to fear Japanese Americans.
  - Japanese Americans are sent to relocation camps.
  - Life at the relocation camps is difficult.
- Include supporting details and facts. Look back at pages 360–361. There are several details that support the main idea. The first idea is "People begin to fear Japanese Americans." A supporting detail would be "After the Japanese bombed Pearl Harbor, many people started to be afraid that the Japanese might also attack California."

  Supporting details should be included in the outline.
- Organize the information. When you create an outline, start with Roman Numerals to show the sequence of the main ideas. Then, under each of your main ideas, group the facts that support it. Place a capital letter beside each fact.

The effects of World War II on Japanese Americans

I. People begin to fear Japanese Americans.
   A. People begin to fear that the Japanese would attack California.
   B. People feared that Japanese Americans might help the Japanese in the war.

II. Japanese Americans are sent to relocation camps.
   A. Over 110,000 people were sent to camps.
   B. Many lost their homes and businesses.

III. Life at the relocation camps is difficult.
   A. Living conditions were hard.
   B. People tried to improve conditions.

Try It

Another group of people you read about in the last lesson were women. Read the following article about their experience working during the war. Take notes as you read.

Women and the War Effort

Many American women worked hard during World War Two. They did this by helping with the war effort here in the United States.

Women who worked during the war often had two jobs. One might be working in the defense industry, hospitals, or driving streetcars. The other job was working at home.

During the war many women worked six days a week at their paying job. In the evenings and on whatever free day they had, most of these women had the job of taking care of their children and homes.

Now, create an outline organizing the information found in the article. Include a topic and supporting facts for each of the main ideas. Then use your outline to answer the following questions.

- What is the topic of the article?
- In your outline, are taking care of children and homes main ideas or supporting facts?
- How did you decide which statements were main ideas and which were supporting facts?

3 Apply It

- How can writing outlines help you better understand what you read?
- Reread pages 348–349. Write an outline about what you've read. Use the outline to write a report about the Dust Bowl.

LESSON 4

FOCUS QUESTION

What happened in California after the end of World War II?

VOCABULARY

- baby boom
- commuter
- freeway
- Cold War
- defense industry
- aerospace
- Space Race
- astronaut

VOCABULARY STRATEGY

SYNONYMS The root word **way** means road or path. Can you think of other words that have a similar meaning?

READING STRATEGY

Identify Cause and Effect

Use the chart below to describe where people lived when the population grew.

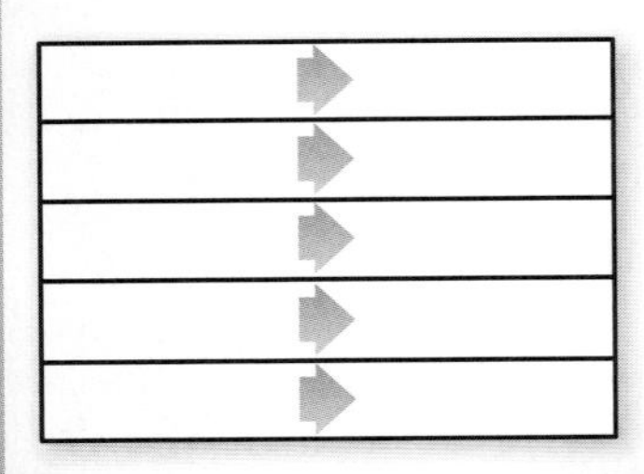

California After World War II

Start with Your CALIFORNIA STANDARDS

4.4 Students explain how California became an agricultural and industrial power, tracing the transformation of the California economy and its political and cultural development since the 1850s.

4.4.4 Describe rapid American immigration, internal migration, settlement, and the growth of towns and cities.

Find out where and how people lived as California's population grew. (page 365)

4.4.6 Describe the development and locations of new industries since the nineteenth century, such as the aerospace industry, electronics industry, large-scale commercial agriculture and irrigation projects, the oil and automobile industries, communications and defense industries, and important trade links with the Pacific Basin.

Learn about how different kinds of airplanes and spaceships have been built and tested in California. (pages 366–367)

During the 1950s many people wanted to live in homes like the one below. ▼

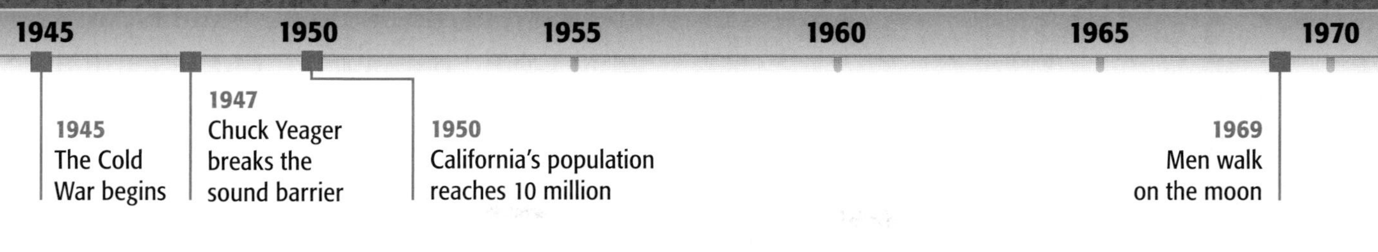

The end of World War II brought a time of growth to California. New communities, new roads, and new technologies, such as TV sets, changed the way Californians lived.

Growth After the War 4.4.4

If you look at the chart, you will see that by 1950 over 10 million people lived in California. The population of California grew because new people were moving into the state. It also grew because many people had decided to start families. This growth in population was called the **baby boom**. The baby boom lasted from the late 1940s through the early 1960s.

All the new people and new families needed somewhere to live. Communities called suburbs were quickly built on land near large cities.

People in the suburbs needed cars to travel from their homes to their jobs in the cities. These people were called **commuters**. To make traveling easier for the commuters, fast roads, called **freeways**, were built. As more people moved to suburbs and bought cars, more roads were needed. This helped bring about a new way of life.

REVIEW Why were freeways built?
Cause and Effect

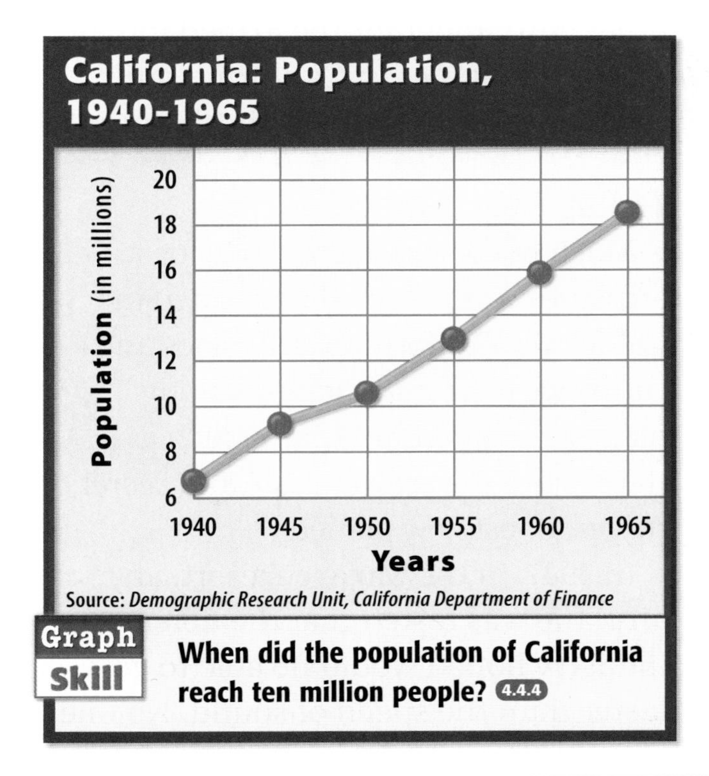

Graph Skill **When did the population of California reach ten million people?** 4.4.4

The Airplane Industry 4.4.6

During World War II, California's aircraft industry created jobs for many people. The United States and the Soviet Union were both on the side of the Allies during World War II. However, the government of the United States and the government of the Soviet Union had different ideas about how a country should be run. Both countries were concerned that they would wind up in a war over these differences. The period of time during which the United States and the Soviet Union were concerned that a war might start was called the **Cold War**.

Because the United States government was concerned that a war might start, it gave millions of dollars to the **defense industry**. The defense industry builds weapons and other equipment for the armed forces. Many companies in California built airplanes for the defense industry.

Testing New Planes

Much of the new technology for airplanes was invented and tested in California. California's clear skies and sunny weather made it easier to fly planes. Large, empty spaces such as the Mojave Desert were safe and secret places to test new planes.

In 1947, in the Mojave Desert, an airplane was tested that the defense industry hoped would be able to go faster than the speed of sound. No one knew if a plane could go that fast, or what would happen if it did. The pilot of that plane was Chuck Yeager. Yeager said about the flight,

> ***"I had flown at supersonic speeds for 18 seconds . . . [and] . . . I was [still] alive."***

In the 1950s and 1960s, California's **aerospace**, or flight, industry continued to grow. By 1965, many Californians were working in the aerospace industry.

The Space Race

The United States and the Soviet Union each wanted to be the first to put a person on the moon. This became known as the **Space Race**. Both nations started space programs. In California, the Jet Propulsion Laboratory in Pasadena supplied many of the rockets used to send

Chuck Yeager ▶

American **astronauts** into space. Astronauts are people trained to fly a spacecraft. Several different types of spacecraft were built and tested in southern California.

On July 16, 1969, the Apollo 11 spacecraft was launched on a trip to the moon. On July 20, 1969, American astronauts Neil Armstrong and Edwin Aldrin became the first people to walk on the moon.

Today, the United States uses space shuttles and robots to explore space. Companies in California continue to improve the technology used by our nation's space program.

Blast-off of the first American space flight.

The Cassini spacecraft was built at the Jet Propulsion Laboratory. This spacecraft carries a probe called Huygens. It is part of an international project to explore the planet Saturn and its moons. On July 1, 2004 the Cassini spacecraft reached Saturn and sent back the first close up pictures of Saturn's rings.

REVIEW How did California become a leader in the aerospace industry? *Main Idea and Details*

What You Learned

4.4.4 After the war, California's population grew. New communities were built.

4.4.6 California became a leader in the aerospace industry.

Lesson Review

1. **Focus Question** What happened in California after the end of World War II? 4.4.4 4.4.6
2. **Vocabulary** Write one sentence for each vocabulary term. 4.4.4 4.4.6

aerospace	**commuter**
astronaut	**defense industry**
baby boom	**freeway**
Cold War	**Space Race**

3. **Geography** Why was California an ideal location for the aerospace industry? 4.4.6
4. **Critical Thinking** **Problem Solving** What did Californians do as the population grew? 4.4.4
5. **Reading Strategy** **Identify Cause and Effect** Use the chart to list the things the United States did when it became concerned about a possible war with the Soviet Union. 4.4.6 ELA R2.1

6. **Write about THE BIG IDEA** Neil Armstrong's first steps on the moon were shown on television. Write about how you would have felt watching a man walk on the moon for the first time. 4.4.6 ELA W2.1
7. **Link to Science** The Cassini spacecraft has reached Saturn. Use your research skills to find pictures of Saturn that have been taken on this mission and to learn more about the Huygens probe. 4.4.6

A Day in the Life

Suburban Life in the 1950s 4.4.4

The car helped bring about a new way of life in the 1950s. For many activities people didn't even need to get out of their cars. You could go to a movie, bank, and even stores and never needed to get out of the car. The spirit of innovation was fast making California the nation's leader in everything from technology to recreation.

Drive-in diners grew popular. ▼

Families watched the newest invention, television. Grocery stores soon began selling TV dinners. ▶

◀ Teenagers took up fads.

Diners often had jukeboxes playing the latest songs. ▶

Write About It!

Choose one invention or trend from the 1950s. Write a paragraph comparing it to a similar invention or trend today.

LOG ON For more about life in the 1950s visit:

www.macmillanmh.com/ss/ca/dayinthelife

Chapter Review

Vocabulary Review

Copy the sentences below on a separate sheet of paper. Use the list of vocabulary terms to fill in the blanks.

aerospace **relocation camp**
commuter **suffrage**

1. A ________ was where Japanese Americans were held during World War II. (4.4.5)
2. ________ is the right to vote. (4.4)
3. California's ________, or flight, industry grew during the 1950s and 1960s. (4.4.6)
4. A person who travels to a city each day to go to work is a ________. (4.4.4)
5. Test Preparation An ________ is a change made to a constitution. (4.5.2)

   A. **reformer** C. **amendment**
   B. **initiative** D. **recall**

Comprehension Check

6. How did the earthquake of 1906 affect San Francisco's economy? (4.5.4)
7. What caused the Great Depression? (4.4.5)
8. How were African American soldiers discriminated against during World War II? (4.4.5)
9. What happened to many Japanese Americans during World War II? (4.4.5)
10. By 1950, how many people lived in California? (4.4.4)
11. Critical Thinking Do you think it was fair that the Southern Pacific Company owned most of California's transportation? Why or why not? (4.5.4)
12. Critical Thinking Why were freeways built in the years after World War II? (4.4.4)

Use the Time Line

Use the time line to answer each question.

13. How long did the Great Depression last? (4.4.5)
14. Was the minimum wage law passed before or after women got the right to vote? (4.5.4)

1900 1910 1920 1930 1940

1906 An earthquake hits San Francisco

1911 Women gain the right to vote in California

1929 The Great Depression begins

1933 The minimum wage law is passed

1939 The Great Depression ends

Skills Check

Write a complete sentence to answer each question.

Write an Outline

Read the selection below and use it to answer the following questions.

The San Francisco earthquake of 1906 lasted for 70 seconds. During that time, the city was almost destroyed. Buildings fell down and large cracks split the streets. Gas pipes and water pipes broke. Pieces of brick, glass, wood, and metal were everywhere. People's stoves fell over, and their houses started burning.

More damage was done because of the fires. Within an hour after the earthquake, over fifty fires were burning out of control. Smoke and dust filled the air. The streets and hills were filled with people leaving the city.

15. What is the topic of this passage? (4.4.4)

16. What are the main ideas in this passage? (4.4.4)

17. Test Preparation Write an outline of this passage. (4.4.4)

18. Test Preparation An ________ is a plan that presents ideas about a subject in an organized way. (4.4.4)

Hands-on Activity

19. Make a Newspaper Work in groups to write a newspaper article that answers this question: (4.4)

What is one way that reformers helped improve life in California?

Using Primary Sources

Letters

April 23, 1906

Dear Mother,

I hope you have not been worrying about me. As you might have heard, five days ago San Francisco was hit by a dreadful earthquake. The house I was living in made it through the earthquake.

However, terrible fires swept the streets afterward. I fled the city with Uncle Mark. We walked to the hills, where we have been staying since. Although we are hungry, we are both fine.

We hope to return to San Francisco tomorrow to see what is left of the city. With luck, we will not need to rebuild. I will write again soon.

Your son,
William

20. Who wrote this letter? (4.4.4)

21. From the background information in this letter, can you tell where William lived? (4.4.4)

Write About History

22. Narrative Suppose your family lived in one of the states that was hit by the dust storms. Write about how your family's life changed once the storms occurred. Include your family's decision whether or not to move to California. (4.4.5, ELA W2.3)

LOG ON

For help with the process of writing, visit:

www.macmillanmh.com/ss/ca/writing

Unit Review and Test Prep

Comprehension and Critical Thinking Check

Write one or more sentences to answer each question.

1. Why was it difficult to build the **transcontinental** railroad across the Sierra Nevada? 4.4.1
2. How did the **Chinese Exclusion Act** of 1882 discriminate against Chinese people? 4.4.3
3. Why did wheat become an important **cash crop** for farmers in California? 4.4.6
4. How did **mutual aid societies** help new immigrants from Mexico? 4.4.3
5. Why did many people build towers called **derricks** in their yards during the early 1900s? 4.4.6
6. Why did the Hetch Hetchy **reservoir** upset John Muir and others? 4.4.7
7. How did the **referendum** give California voters more of a say in the government? 4.5.4
8. Name some of the **New Deal** programs created by President Roosevelt. 4.4.4
9. **Critical Thinking** Why did the **telegraph** cause the Pony Express to go out of business? 4.4.1
10. **Critical Thinking** How did changes in the **stock market** contribute to the **Great Depression**? 4.4.5

Reading Social Studies Check

Compare and Contrast

Copy this graphic organizer. Recall what you have read in this unit about changes in the California economy. Use the graphic organizer to help you compare and contrast the economy before and after World War II. 4.4.5 ELA R2.1

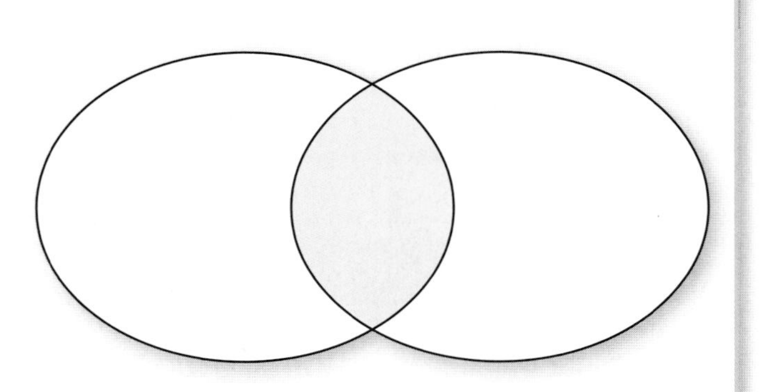

11. What was the California economy like before World War II? ELA R2.1
12. How did the California economy change after the United States entered World War II? ELA R2.1
13. How did you decide which events to include in each section? ELA R2.1

Test Preparation

Read the paragraphs. Then answer the questions.

Each year, visitors come to San Francisco to see the Golden Gate Bridge. The bridge has been part of the city's skyline for about 70 years. It is one of the most famous bridges in the world.

However, the Golden Gate Bridge is more than just famous. Commuters rely on it. Every day, thousands of people travel over the bridge in and out of the city. Over 45 million cars and trucks cross the bridge each year.

The people of the Bay Area depend on the Golden Gate Bridge. In fact, the city of San Francisco would be very different without it.

14. What is the main idea of this passage?
4.4.6 ELA R2.1

A The Golden Gate Bridge is famous.

B The Golden Gate Bridge was built about 70 years ago.

C People in the Bay Area depend on the Golden Gate Bridge.

D People are not allowed to roller blade over the bridge.

15. Based on the passage, which generalization can you make?
4.4.6 ELA R2.1

A The bridge makes it possible for people who live outside San Francisco to work in the city.

B More people travel across it each year than any other bridge.

C It is difficult to ride a bicycle across the bridge.

D Not many people drive across the Golden Gate Bridge.

Write About History

16. Letter Suppose that you are Theodore Judah. Write a letter to a businessperson explaining why he or she should give money to help build the transcontinental railroad.
4.4.1 ELA W2.4

17. Narrative Suppose that you are a Chinese immigrant living in California in the 1800s. Write a diary entry. Describe how your life is different in America.
4.4.3 ELA W2.1

18. Expository Create an outline of the life of Katherine Philips Edson. Remember to include main ideas and details. You may need to use the school library or the Internet for research.

For help with the process of writing visit:

www.macmillanmh.com/ss/ca/writing

How does technology change people's lives?

Write About the Big Idea ELA W1.0 ELA W1.3

A Letter of Request

Recall the aspects of technology you read about in Unit 4. Then, complete the graphic organizer. Add details about each type of technology.

Use information from your graphic organizer. Choose one type of technology. Write a letter to an organization or to a professional person. Request information about someone who brought that type of technology to California. Mail your letter.

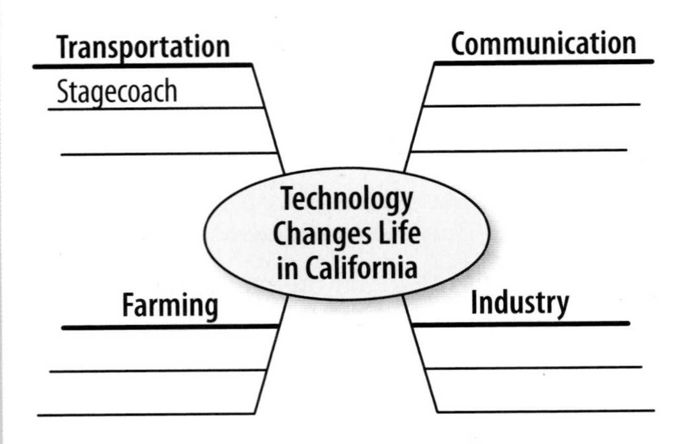

Steps for Writing a Letter of Request

1. Plan
- Decide what you want to know.
- Think about the body of your letter. Specify exactly what information you are requesting. Tell when you need it.

2. Write a First Draft
- Include your address, and a greeting. Remember your signature.
- Use language that is friendly, yet formal. State your request clearly in simple language.

3. Revise and Proofread
- Be sure the information you are requesting is clear.
- Check the tone of your language. Remember to thank the person who will receive your letter for his or her help.
- Combine related sentences.
- Proofread your letter. Be sure you have all the parts of a letter. Be sure you have used correct punctuation.
- Ask your teacher to review your letter. Rewrite it neatly before you mail it.

ACTIVITY

Speak About the Big Idea ELA LS2.1 4.4

Role-Play

Choose a person you read about in Unit 4. Think about that person's contribution to California. The person may have invented a new technology. The person may have contributed to reforms for people who live and work in California.

Prepare Take the role of a person and explain what you contributed to California. Give details and examples. You can dress in clothing similar to what the person would have worn. Use information from Unit 4, your graphic organizer, and information you received in response to your letter of request.

Present Act out the person. Explain his or her contribution to technology that changed California.

For help with the Big Idea activity, visit:

www.macmillanmh.com/ss/ca/launchpad

Read More About the Big Idea

Riding Freedom

Pam Muñoz Ryan This is a novel about Charley Parkhurst, the real-life teen-age girl who ran away from an orphanage and made her way to California during the Gold Rush.

Nature Art with Chiura Obata

Michael Elsohn Ross Read the biography of the Japanese American artist who sketched the San Francisco earthquake, Yosemite, and the Japanese relocation camps.

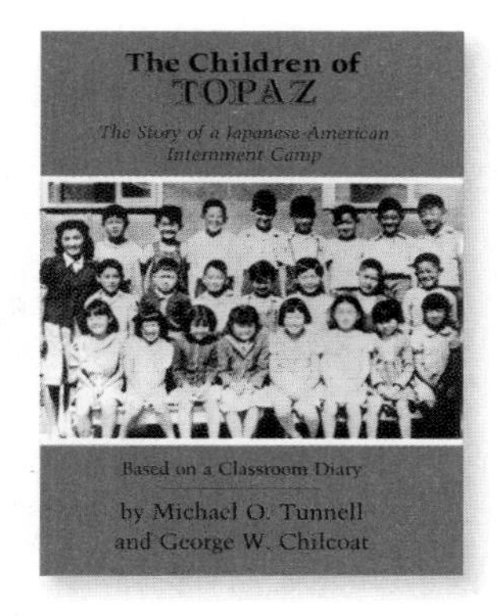

The Children of Topaz

Michael O. Tunnell Learn about the experience of some Japanese American third graders in a relocation camp during World War II.

UNIT 5

A Changing California

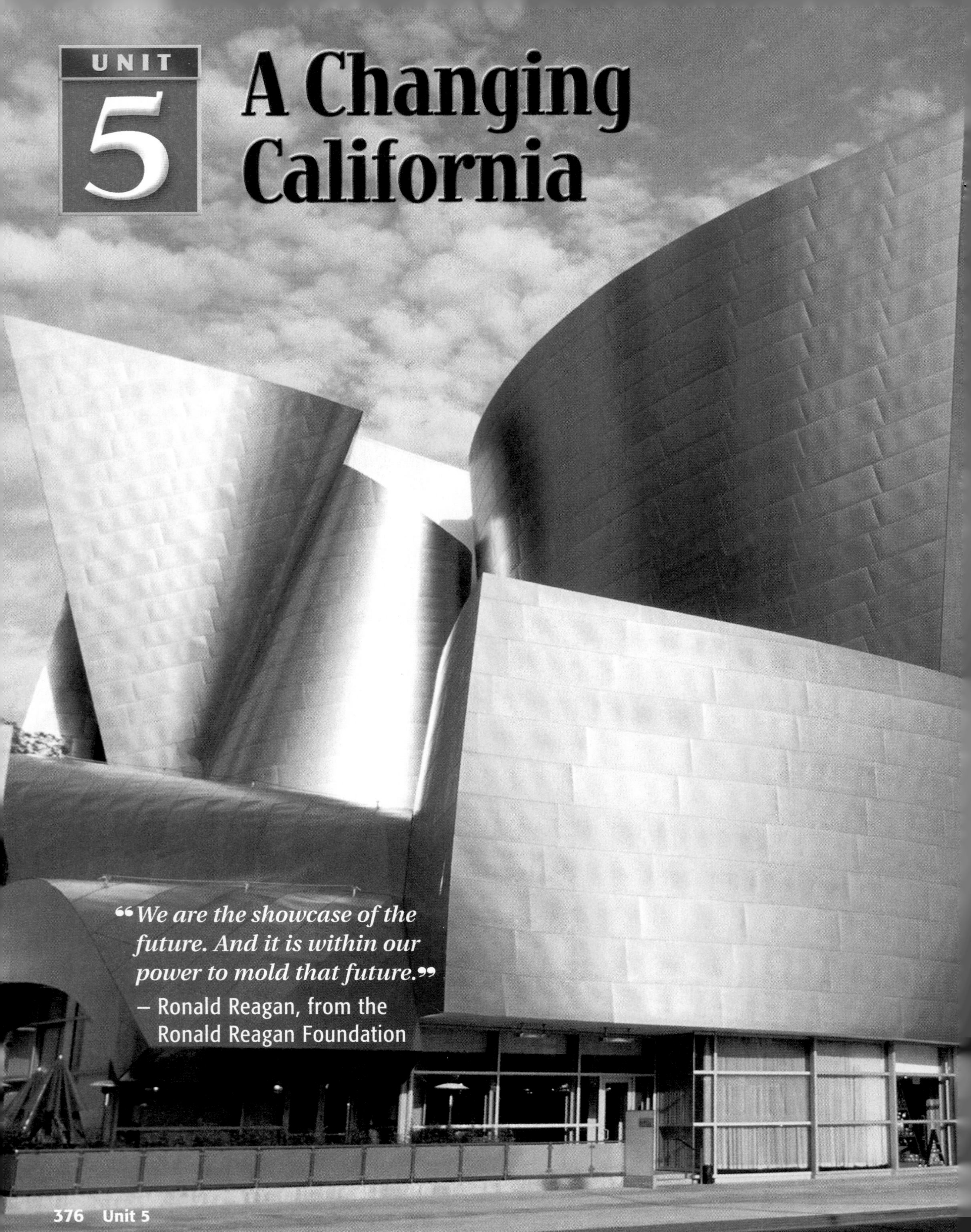

"We are the showcase of the future. And it is within our power to mold that future."

– Ronald Reagan, from the Ronald Reagan Foundation

What causes a society to grow?

In Unit 5, you will read about education, civil rights, and the economy. You will also learn about the people, celebrations, and government of California.

Copy the graphic organizer below. As you read the chapters in this unit, look for reasons California grew.

Then fill in the graphic organizer with causes and their effects. The first cause has been filled in for you.

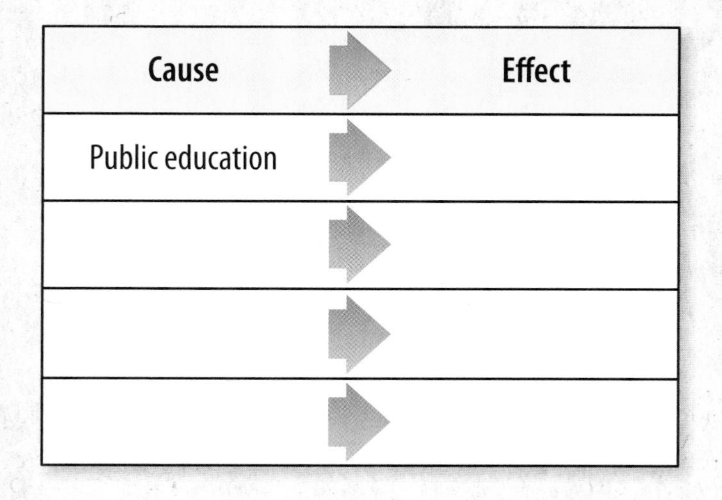

Cause	Effect
Public education	

◀ Walt Disney Concert Hall in Los Angeles

UNIT 5

People Who Made a Difference

Phoebe Apperson Hearst
1842–1919

Phoebe Hearst was a supporter of the University of California. She served on the governing board of the university from 1897 to 1919. (page 390)

William Byron Rumford
1908–1986

William Rumford helped pass the Rumford Act. This law did not allow discrimination by California property owners and businesses. (page 394)

César Chávez
1927–1993

César Chávez had worked on farms and knew about the poor working conditions. He and the workers joined together to ask for better working conditions. (page 397)

Unit Events

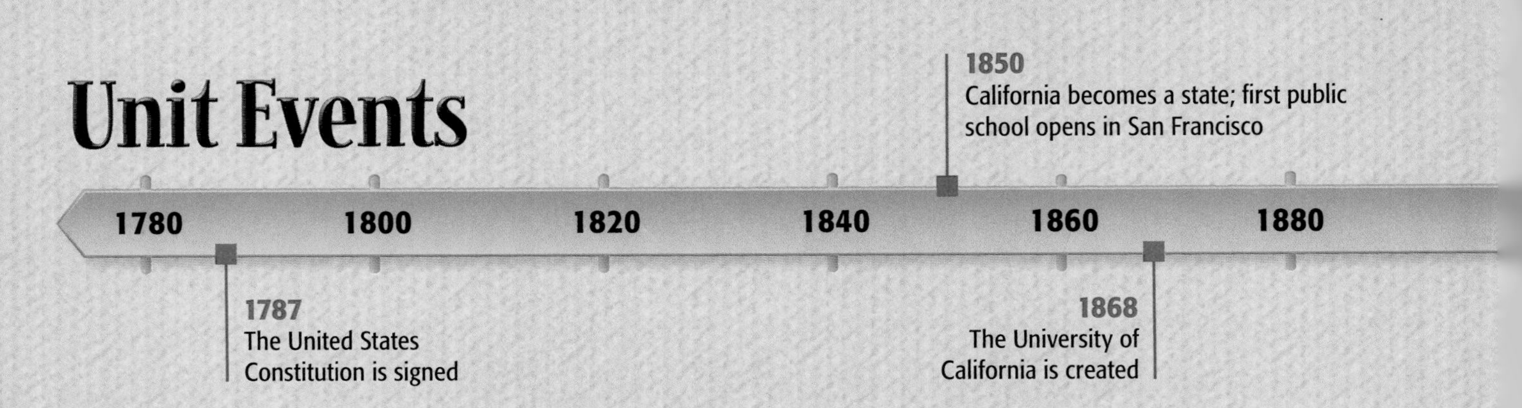

For more about People Who Made a Difference, visit:

www.macmillanmh.com/ss/ca/bios

Dolores Huerta
1929–

Dolores Huerta was a teacher whose students were children of farm workers. She worked to improve the working conditions of her students' parents. (page 397)

Isamu Noguchi
1904–1988

Isamu Noguchi was an artist. He built sculptures, gardens, monuments, and fountains. His work blended his Japanese and American heritage. (page 415)

Heather Fong
1956–

Heather Fong joined the San Francisco police force in 1977. In April 2004, she became the first Asian American woman to become the police chief. (page 448)

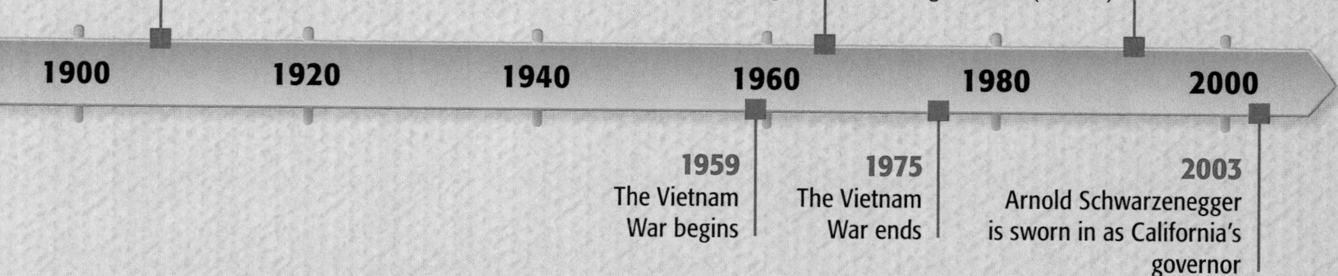

Literature

The Upside Down Boy

Selections from
The Upside Down Boy
by Juan Felipe Herrera
Illustrated by Elizabeth Gómez

Juan Felipe Herrera was a boy when his family moved to the United States from Mexico. He spoke very little English when he first went to his new school. The Upside Down Boy *tells how a teacher helped Herrera adjust to his new surroundings and language. Herrera went on to become a teacher himself.*

When I was little, my family spent years working in the fields. One day, my mama said to my papi, "Let's settle down. It's time that Juanito goes to school." That year we were living in the mountains by Lake Wolfer, a glassy world full of sky colors. . . .

"Don't worry, *chico*," Papi says as he walks me to school. "Everything changes. A new place has new leaves on the trees and blows fresh air into your body. . . ."

I make a clown face, half funny, half scared. "I don't speak English," I say to Papi. "Will my tongue turn into a rock?"

I slow step into school. . . . Mrs. Sampson, the teacher, shows me my desk.

Mrs. Sampson invites me to the front of the class. "Sing, Juanito, sing a song we have been practicing."

I pop up shaking. I am alone facing the class.

"Ready to sing?" Mrs. Sampson asks me. I am frozen, then a deep breath fills me, "Three blind mice, three blind mice," I sing.

My eyes open as big as the ceiling and my hands spread out as if catching rain drops from the sky.

"You have a very beautiful voice, Juanito," Mrs. Sampson says. "What is beautiful?" I ask Amanda after school. . . .

In the morning, as we walk to school Papi turns and says, “You do have a nice voice, Juanito. I never heard you sing until yesterday when you fed the chickens. At first, when we moved here, you looked sad and I didn’t know what to do.”

“I felt funny, upside down,” I say to him. “The city streets aren’t soft with flowers. Buildings don’t have faces. You know, Papi, in the campo I knew all the names, even of those bugs with little wild eyes and shiny noses!”

“Here,” he says. “Here’s my **harmonica**. It has many voices, many beautiful songs just like you. Sing them!”

---

harmonica (har MON ee kah) a small musical instrument played by blowing through slots

On Open House Day, Mama and Papi sit in the front row.

"Our paintings look like the flowery fields back in the Valley," I tell Amanda.

"I have a surprise," I whisper to Mama. "I am '*El Maestro* Juanito,' the **choir** conductor!" Mrs. Sampson smiles wearing a chile **sombrero** and puts on the music.

I blow a "C" with my harmonica—"La la la laaaaah! Ready to sing out your poems?" I ask my choir. "*Uno . . . dos . . .* and three!"

---

choir (kwighr) a group of singers who sing together

sombrero (sohm BRAY roh) a hat with a broad rim

Write About It!

Write about how you would feel as a new student in a school.

Reading SOCIAL STUDIES

Identify Cause and Effect:
California's Economy ELA R2.1 4.4.6

In this unit, you will read about California's economy. New technologies, trading partners, and industries have created new areas of growth. Thinking about causes and effects will help you understand how and why California's economy has changed. A cause is an event that makes something happen. An effect is what happens. When one thing causes another thing to happen, they have a cause-and-effect relationship.

- When you read, ask yourself what happened. This will help you find an effect.
- Also ask yourself why did this effect happen. This will help you find a cause.
- Look for the words *because*, *therefore*, *so*, and *as a result*. These clue words point to causes and effects.
- Now, read the paragraph below. Look for causes and effects as you read.

Effect
The Santa Clara Valley is busy. This is an effect.

Cause
The word *because* helps you know this is a cause.

Effect
The area is called Silicon Valley. This is an effect.

The Santa Clara Valley between Palo Alto and San José is one of California's busiest places. That is because about 4,000 high-technology companies have offices there. Many of these companies use a substance called silicon to make computer chips. As a result, people call this area "Silicon Valley."

2 Try It

Copy and complete the chart below. Then, fill in the chart with causes and effects from the paragraph on page 384.

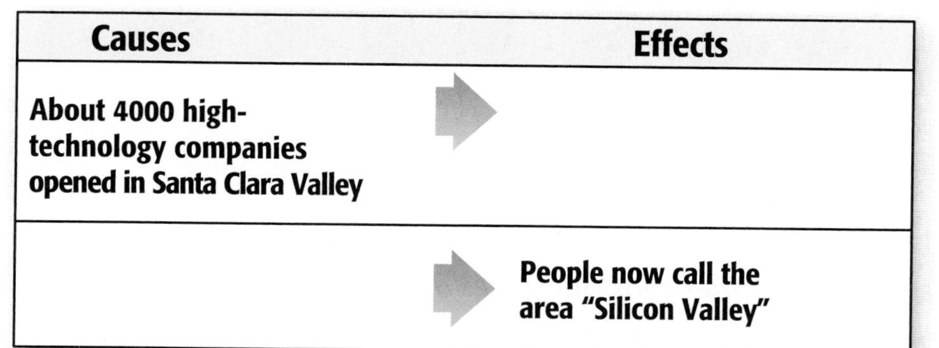

CAUSE AND EFFECT CHART

Causes		Effects
About 4000 high-technology companies opened in Santa Clara Valley	→	
	→	People now call the area "Silicon Valley"

What questions help you identify cause and effect?

3 Apply It

- Review the steps for understanding cause and effect in Learn It.
- Read the paragraphs below. Then, create a cause and effect chart using the information.

In 2004, California's Mojave Desert became part of space history. That is because the first private spacecraft, called SpaceShipOne, was launched there. Once in the air, SpaceShipOne fired its rockets and climbed 71 miles high.

After a few minutes in space, SpaceShipOne headed back to the desert. On the way down, its wings flipped up 90 degrees. So, the craft slowed in order to land. The builders of SpaceShipOne won a $10 million prize. As a result, they can continue their work on private space travel.

CHAPTER 11

The Growth of California

You Are There

“We cannot seek achievement for ourselves and forget about progress and prosperity for our community...”

These words were spoken by César Chávez. He organized farm workers to ask for better working conditions. Chávez also wanted to improve the communities where the farm workers lived.

In this chapter you will learn about modern California. You will read about civil rights activists, educators, business owners, artists, and many other people who have all worked to make California a better place to live.

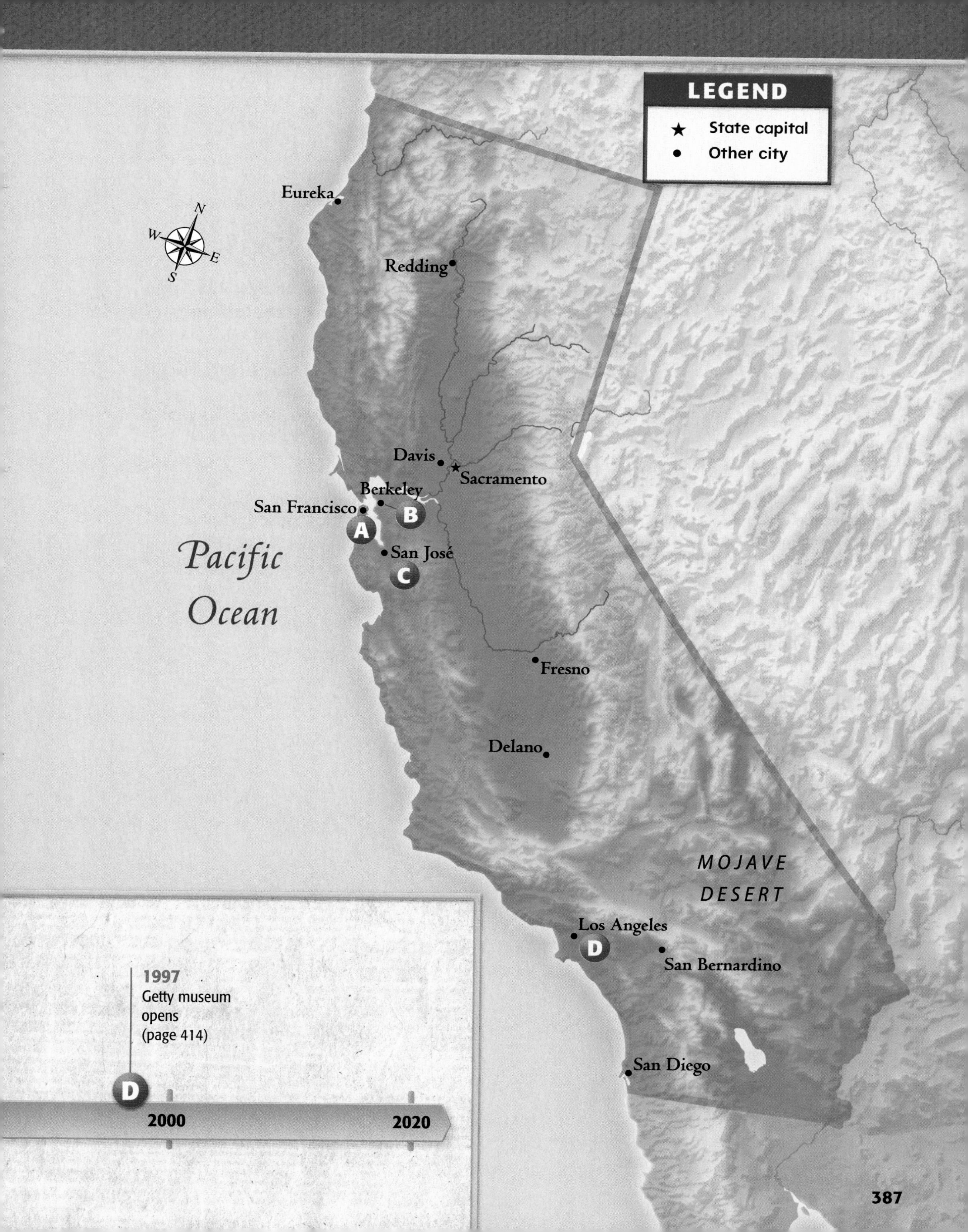
LEGEND
State capital
Other city
N
E
S
W
Eureka
Redding
Davis
Sacramento
Berkeley
San Francisco
A
B
San José
C
Pacific Ocean
Fresno
Delano
MOJAVE DESERT
Los Angeles
D
San Bernardino
San Diego
1997
Getty museum opens
(page 414)
D
2000
2020

FOCUS QUESTION

How did California become a leader in public education?

VOCABULARY

public education
superintendent
charter
campuses

VOCABULARY STRATEGY

PREFIXES A **superintendent** is a person who manages an organization. The prefix **super-** is from the Latin word for **more than**. What other words begin with the prefix **super-**?

READING STRATEGY

Identify Cause and Effect

Use the chart below to list three people whose leadership shaped public school education in our state and tell what impact they had.

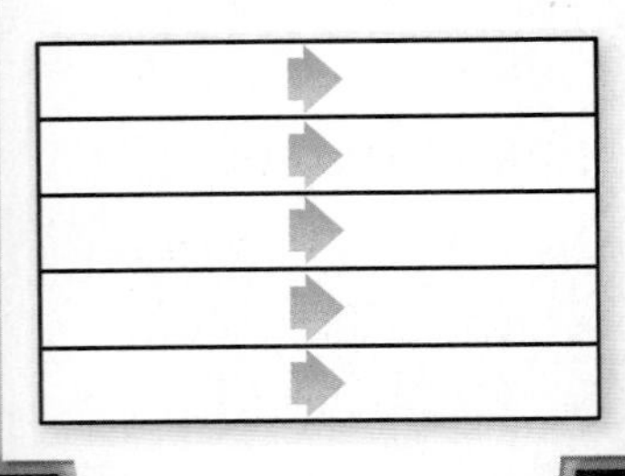

Education for All

Start with Your CALIFORNIA STANDARDS

4.4 Students explain how California became an agricultural and industrial power, tracing the transformation of the California economy and its political and cultural development since the 1850s.

4.4.8 Describe the history and development of California's public education system, including universities and community colleges.

Learn about the history of the public school system as well as colleges and universities in California. (Begins on page 389)

Californians of all backgrounds benefit from public education. ▼

1850 | 1890 | 1930 | 1970 | 2010

1850 California's first public school opens

1860s State law passed to pay for public schools

1868 University of California is created

1960 Master Plan for Higher Education expands

2002 New Master Plan makes public education available from preschool to college and beyond

What are you doing in school today? As you read, write, take tests, or do class projects, you are taking part in something very important. You are preparing not only for your own future, but also for the future of California.

Education in California 4.4.8

Californians know that education is the key to a successful life. In 1849, when representatives met to talk about statehood, education was one of the issues they discussed.

The First Public Schools

A representative named Robert Semple argued for a system of **public education**. He believed that California would be a better place if every Californian could attend school without having to pay. Semple wrote:

> ***"If the people are to govern themselves, they should be qualified to do it. They must be educated; they must educate their children."***

In 1850, California's first public school opened in San Francisco. Six years later, the state's first public high school opened in San Francisco. Both schools were paid for by the city. However, California still needed a system for all the students in the state.

In 1863 John Swett became the first **superintendent**, or head, of California's public schools. He set out to make a public education system for all students. In the 1860s, he helped pass laws to create a state tax to support schools.

As a result, all of California's cities were given money to build and run public schools. Money from taxes is still used to pay for our public schools.

REVIEW What happened when John Swett became superintendent of California's public schools? *Cause and Effect*

South Hall, University of California, Berkeley

Higher Education 4.4.8

Although some Californians were in favor of free public schools for younger students, fewer supported the idea of public colleges. However, on March 23, 1868, Governor H. H. Haight signed the **charter**, or official paper, for the state's first public university—the University of California.

The university was built among oak trees and open fields in Berkeley, four miles north of Oakland. The first buildings were completed in 1873. That year, 167 men and 222 women took classes there. Today, there are more than 200,000 students at the University of California **campuses**.

Phoebe Apperson Hearst helped the university grow. In 1896, Hearst, who was a director of the university, offered a prize to the architect who could design the best plan for the campuses. Campuses are areas where a school, college, or university is located. Hearst then gave her own money to build two of the new buildings so students would have more classrooms.

Planning Colleges

The university continued to grow. In 1919, a new campus was built in Los Angeles. By 1960, there were seven campuses. Still, state leaders wanted to improve colleges and universities. They created a Master Plan for Higher Education.

The plan called for new universities and colleges. The plan also defined the role of each type of school. Two-year community colleges were for students who wanted to learn new job skills or transfer to universities. Four-year state universities were to focus on teacher education. Universities were to emphasize research.

California Education Today

In 2002, state leaders came up with a new Master Plan for Higher Education, covering preschool to college and beyond. State leaders had to make difficult decisions about what areas needed the most help. In the end, they developed a plan that did many things. One decision given in the plan was to build more preschools so all children can go to preschool. The plan also called for a tenth University of California campus to be built in Merced.

REVIEW What were the results of California's Master Plan for Higher Education of 1960? *Summarize*

United States

At the Same Time

A Supreme Court decision in 1892 said that having separate schools for black and white students was legal. In 1954, the Supreme Court said that separating students in different schools was no longer going to be allowed. This historic decision is called *Brown* versus *Board of Education of Topeka.*

What You Learned

4.4.8 John Swett helped expand the number of public schools.

4.4.8 The Master Plan for Higher Education made California's public education system more efficient and planned for more schools to be built.

Lesson Review

1. **Focus Question** How did California become a leader in public education? (4.4.8)
2. **Vocabulary** Write one sentence for each vocabulary term. (4.4.8)
   campus **public education** **charter** **superintendent**
3. **Citizenship** Why is public education important in a democracy? (4.4.8)
4. **Critical Thinking** **Problem Solving** How did John Swett help make it possible for California to build and run its schools? (4.4.8)
5. **Reading Strategy** **Identify Cause and Effect** Use the chart to list three events that helped shape public education in our state and tell what impact they had. (4.4.8, ELA R2.1)

6. **Write about THE BIG IDEA** Write about whether or not you think California would have become successful as a state if there had never been public schools. (4.4.8, ELA W2.1)
7. **Link to Language Arts** Draw a diagram of the three types of colleges in California. Add details or illustrations to show what each focuses on. (4.4.8)

Working for Change

FOCUS QUESTION

What causes did Californians protest?

VOCABULARY

- segregation
- civil rights
- demonstration
- labor union
- boycott
- Vietnam War

VOCABULARY STRATEGY

WORD ORIGINS Civil comes from the Latin word for citizen. **Civil rights** are the rights of every citizen in a country. Can you think of other terms that start with **civil?**

READING STRATEGY

Sequence Events
Use the chart to list three major movements of the 1950s, 1960s, and 1970s in order.

Start with Your
CALIFORNIA STANDARDS

4.4 Students explain how California became an agricultural and industrial power, tracing the transformation of the California economy and its political and cultural development since the 1850s.

Learn about how Californians worked for change during the 1950s, 1960s, and 1970s. (Begins on page 393)

César Chávez speaks to farm workers in Salinas. ▼

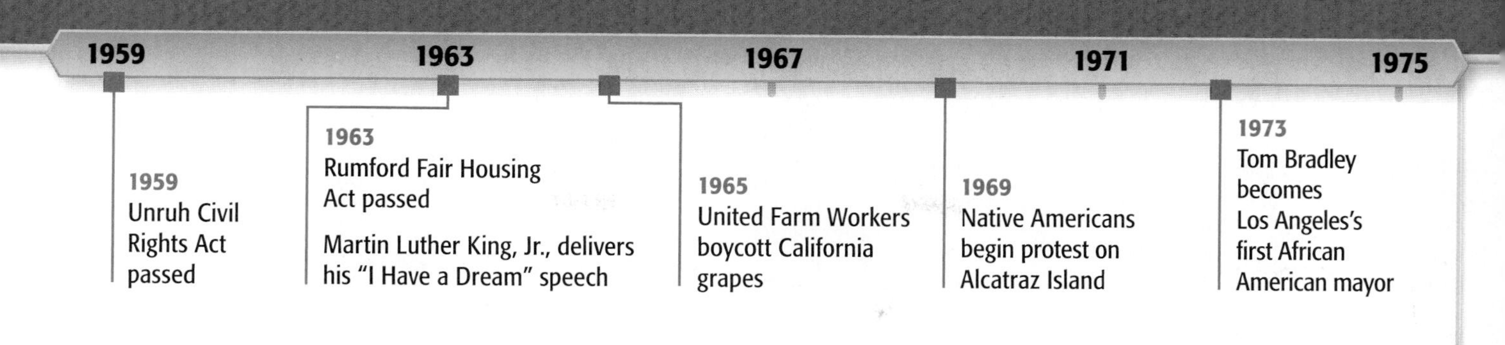

Martin Luther King, Jr., gave his most famous speech on the steps of the Lincoln Memorial in Washington, D.C. He said: "I have a dream that . . . children will one day live in a nation where they will not be judged by the color of their skin but by the content of their character."

The Need for Change 4.4

In the last chapter, you read about California's economic boom after World War II. However, many African Americans, Hispanic Americans, Asian Americans, and Native Americans did not share equally in this success.

They faced **segregation**, a policy of keeping different groups of people separate. In the 1950s, people all over the United States began fighting against segregation and other forms of discrimination.

Martin Luther King, Jr., led the movement to gain **civil rights** for African Americans in the 1950s and 1960s. Civil rights are the rights granted to every citizen by the United States Constitution.

African Americans were denied the right to vote. To fight for this right and other rights, King organized peaceful **demonstrations**. A demonstration is a large gathering of people who want to call attention to a problem.

REVIEW How did people fight segregation? *Summarize*

Martin Luther King, Jr. ▶

▲ California workers protest their low pay.

Jesse Unruh ▲

Tom Bradley ▶

Civil Rights in California 4.4

Jesse Unruh was born on a farm in Kansas. Following World War II, he moved to California, went to college, and entered politics. As a member of the State Assembly, he wrote the Unruh Civil Rights Act of 1959. This important law made it illegal for restaurants, hotels, and other businesses to refuse to serve African Americans and other minorities. It also made it illegal for landlords to choose their renters based on race.

Slow Gains for African Americans

Despite the new law, progress in civil rights came slowly. Some landlords still refused to rent to minority families.

Then in 1963, state assemblyman William Byron Rumford helped pass the Rumford Fair Housing Act. This law made it illegal to discriminate against home buyers based on a person's skin color.

Meanwhile, the United States Congress passed a series of civil rights laws. These laws guaranteed equal opportunity in housing, jobs, schools, and public services.

By the 1970s, African Americans had won important leadership positions in California. In 1966, Yvonne Braithwaite Burke became the first African American woman elected to the legislature. In 1973, Tom Bradley became the first African American mayor of Los Angeles.

Native Americans protested on Alcatraz Island for 18 months. ▶

Native Americans Protest

In the 1960s thousands of Native Americans moved to California from other states. Here they faced discrimination in jobs, schools, and housing.

In November 1969, a group called Indians of All Nations began a protest. They took a boat to Alcatraz Island in San Francisco Bay and set up a kitchen and a school. They refused to leave.

Richard Oakes, a leader of the group, called for the government to set up a Native American museum and educational center on the island.

The government would not agree to meet their demands. After 18 months, police forced the last protesters from the island. However, the group did raise awareness of Native American rights. Read the primary source interview of a protester who was at Alcatraz Island.

REVIEW Which two California civil rights laws were passed in the 1950s and 1960s? *Summarize*

Primary Sources

Adam Fortunate Eagle

From the San Francisco Chronicle
Interview with Adam Fortunate Eagle

Adam Fortunate Eagle was among the protesters on Alcatraz Island. In a later interview with the *San Francisco Chronicle,* he summed up the success of the protest.

> ***"The purpose of occupying Alcatraz was to start an Indian movement and call attention to Indian problems. . . . It has served its purpose."***

Write About It! **What were the Native American protesters trying to do by taking over Alcatraz Island?**

Boycotts and Protests 4.4

César Chávez had worked on farms since he was a boy. He knew that workers spent long days picking crops for little money. He thought they could ask for better wages and working conditions if they formed a **labor union**. A labor union is a group of workers who make agreements with their employers to improve their working conditions.

In 1962, Chávez and Dolores Huerta organized the National Farm Workers Association. Huerta had been a teacher. Many of her students were the children of farm workers.

In 1965 their union joined another union. The two groups refused to work for grape growers until wages were raised. The workers marched 340 miles from Delano to Sacramento to bring attention to their cause. Finally, the growers agreed to raise wages.

▲ César Chávez

Some farm owners used violence to try to stop the union. But Chávez refused to answer violence with violence. In 1968, his union, now called the United Farm Workers, called for a worldwide **boycott** of California grapes. A boycott is when people refuse to buy a certain product. This boycott ended in 1970, when 26 grape growers agreed to improve working conditions for grape pickers.

Chávez died in 1993. Today, Californians remember him every March 31 on the César Chávez Day of Service and Learning.

◀ Farm workers harvest lettuce in El Centro, California.

▲ Women in California and the nation continued to fight for women's rights after the 1970s. Some wore the ERA pin to show support for the women's movement.

Students Speak Out

In the late 1960s and early 1970s, students at Berkeley and other California campuses protested United States involvement in the **Vietnam War**. This war, between North Vietnam and South Vietnam, lasted from 1954 to 1975. The United States entered the war in 1964 on the side of South Vietnam. Students and other people called for the United States to end its support of South Vietnam. In addition, many young people did not believe they should serve as soldiers during the war when they could not even vote. The United States left Vietnam in 1973.

As a result of the powerful voice of the student protests, changes to voting rights were made. On July 5, 1971 the Twenty-Sixth Amendment to the Constitution was passed. It lowered the voting age from 21 to 18. It added 11 million possible voters. Half of these voters cast their ballots in the 1972 presidential election.

The Women's Movement

In the 1960s, women working the same jobs as men earned less than half of what men earned. Women were also kept out of many types of jobs. Many people thought this was unfair. They started a movement for equal rights for women. It became known as the "women's movement."

The women's movement led to the passage of national laws that banned discrimination against women. The laws called for women to receive equal pay for similar jobs. The laws also made sure that women could not be kept from taking jobs of any kind.

REVIEW Which Americans benefited from the boycotts and protests of the 1960s and 1970s? *Summarize*

Many Californians protested the cuts to public services made by Proposition 13. ▶

A Revolt Against Taxes 4.4

In the 1970s, California voters took part in a protest of a different kind. Many Californians believed that their taxes were too high and that their state government was too big. They thought the state was spending too much of their money.

In June 1978, voters passed a law called Proposition 13. It cut taxes on property such as homes and office buildings by more than half. Proposition 13 forced the state to spend less money on public services.

REVIEW How did many Californians protest their high taxes? *Summarize*

What You Learned

- 4.4 Martin Luther King, Jr., fought to end discrimination against African Americans.
- 4.4 California passed civil rights laws to end racial discrimination in services and housing.
- 4.4 Farm workers boycotted, students protested, and women started a movement to have their voices heard.
- 4.4 In the 1970s Californians protested how the state spent money. Proposition 13 was passed to cut taxes.

Lesson Review

1. **Focus Question** What causes did Californians protest? 4.4
2. **Vocabulary** Write one sentence for each vocabulary term. 4.4

   boycott **labor union**
   civil rights **segregation**
   demonstration **Vietnam War**
3. **Government** How did demonstrations affect state and national laws? 4.4
4. **Critical Thinking** **Make Decisions** What important decision did César Chávez and Dolores Huerta make in 1965? 4.4
5. **Reading Strategy** **Sequence Events** Use the chart to list things Berkeley students protested against in the 1960s and 1970s. 4.4 ELA R2.1

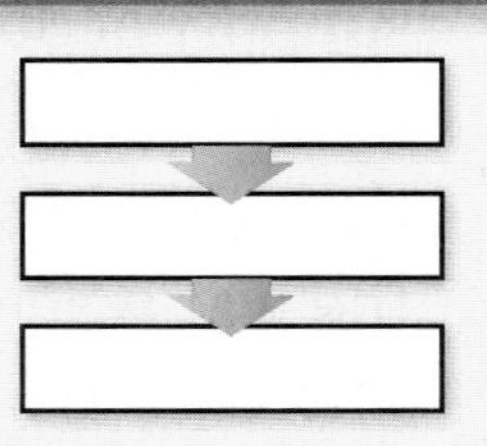

6. **Write about THE BIG IDEA** Write about what it might have been like to be a protester at one of the protests discussed in this lesson. 4.4 ELA W2.1
7. **Link to Music** "We Shall Overcome" was a song that civil rights workers sang for inspiration. You can find the words to this song online. Write a title and words for another song that tells about the need for equal rights for everyone. 4.4

Biography

Focus on Courage

4.4

Dolores Huerta 1930–

Dolores Huerta was born on April 10, 1930, in Dawson, New Mexico. When Huerta was three, she moved to Stockton. There, she met farm worker families. She saw how hard it was to live on the small amount of money the workers earned.

Huerta became a teacher so that she could help farm workers' children, but she soon left her job. As she said,

"I couldn't stand seeing kids come to class hungry and needing shoes. I thought I could do more by organizing farm workers."

Huerta started an organization to help farm workers. She urged lawmakers to pass laws that would treat farm workers more fairly. In 1962, she joined César Chávez to start a labor union called the National Farm Workers Association. Their union won higher wages and better working conditions for California's grape workers.

Today, Dolores Huerta continues to fight for farm workers' rights. She remains actively involved in the struggle to make sure farm workers receive justice.

Write About It! **How did Dolores Huerta's courage help improve the lives of farm workers?**

For more about Dolores Huerta, visit:

www.macmillanmh.com/ss/ca/bios

The Life of Dolores Huerta

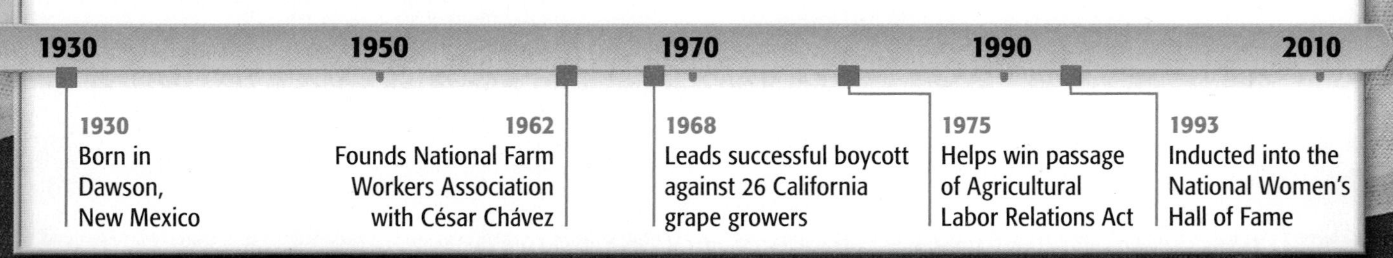

LESSON 3

California's Economy

FOCUS QUESTION

How do different industries support California's economy?

VOCABULARY

microchip
software
nanotechnology
biotechnology
Pacific Rim
NAFTA
free trade

VOCABULARY STRATEGY

PREFIXES The prefix **micro-** comes from the Greek word for small. Can you think of other words that begin with the prefix **micro-**?

READING STRATEGY

Compare and Contrast

Use the diagram below to compare two industries, including details about the way the industries work.

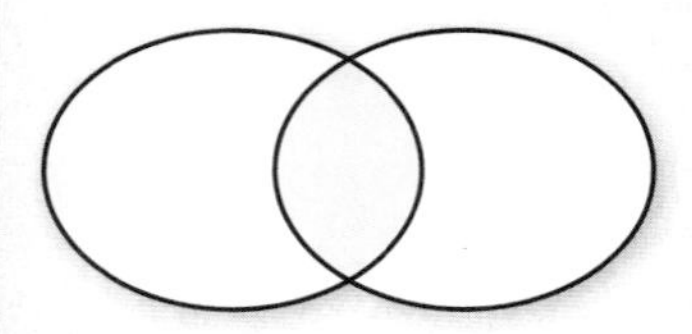

Start with Your CALIFORNIA STANDARDS

4.4 Students explain how California became an agricultural and industrial power, tracing the transformation of the California economy and its political and cultural development since the 1850s.

4.4.6 Describe the development and locations of new industries since the nineteenth century, such as the aerospace industry, electronics industries, large-scale commercial agriculture and irrigation projects, the oil and automobile industries, communications and defense industries, and important trade links with the Pacific Basin.

Learn about California's economy, the industries in California, and California's trade with other countries. (Begins on page 401)

1975	1980	1985	1990	1995

1976 Californians start the world's first biotechnology company

1977 Apple II computer is sold

1992 The United States, Mexico, and Canada sign NAFTA

1994 David Filo and Jerry Yang design a way to search the Internet

The goods made in California range from movies to milk, from grapes to guitars, from skateboards to spacecraft, and from cheese to chocolate. The invention of a very tiny computer chip, shown on the right in the ant's mouth, sparked a revolution in computers in California. Go to nearly any country in the world, and chances are you will find a product that was made in our state.

Parts of the Economy 4.4

The service industries make up the biggest part of California's economy. Workers in these industries help people and businesses. These workers include nurses, doctors, teachers, builders, cooks, waiters, hair dressers, shop keepers, lawyers, car mechanics, and many others.

Other Industries

Manufacturing is an important part of California's economy. California businesses manufacture goods such as furniture, books, clothes, cars, toys, computers, and satellites.

Several other areas of the economy are important in California. California is known as a top producer of movies. Many tourists also visit California every year. The agricultural industry produces crops that are sold in California, in the United States, and around the world.

Trade is a large part of California's economy. California sells the goods that all of its different industries make to countries around the world.

REVIEW What kinds of jobs do people in the service industry have? *Main Idea and Details*

◀ A communication satellite

A Computer Revolution 4.4.6

The computer industry started in the 1950s. At that time, a computer filled a room and took a long time to process information. These computers were expensive, and only a few places had them.

Faster and Smaller Computers

This changed with the invention of the **microchip**. This tiny computer part can process information quickly. By using microchips, companies could build smaller, faster computers called personal computers.

In 1977 two Californians from San José, Steve Wozniak and Steven Jobs, built and sold a computer that fit on top of a desk. It was the first popular and affordable "personal" computer. By 2003, two out of every three people said they have computers in their homes.

Personal computers need **software**, or computer instructions, to tell them what to do. These instructions allow you to write papers, listen to music, add numbers, draw and edit pictures, and play games.

The California companies that design, make, and sell computers and computer software are an important part of the state's economy. Many of these companies are located in the Santa Clara Valley in Northern California. After the invention of the

This room-sized computer took two years to build. ▼

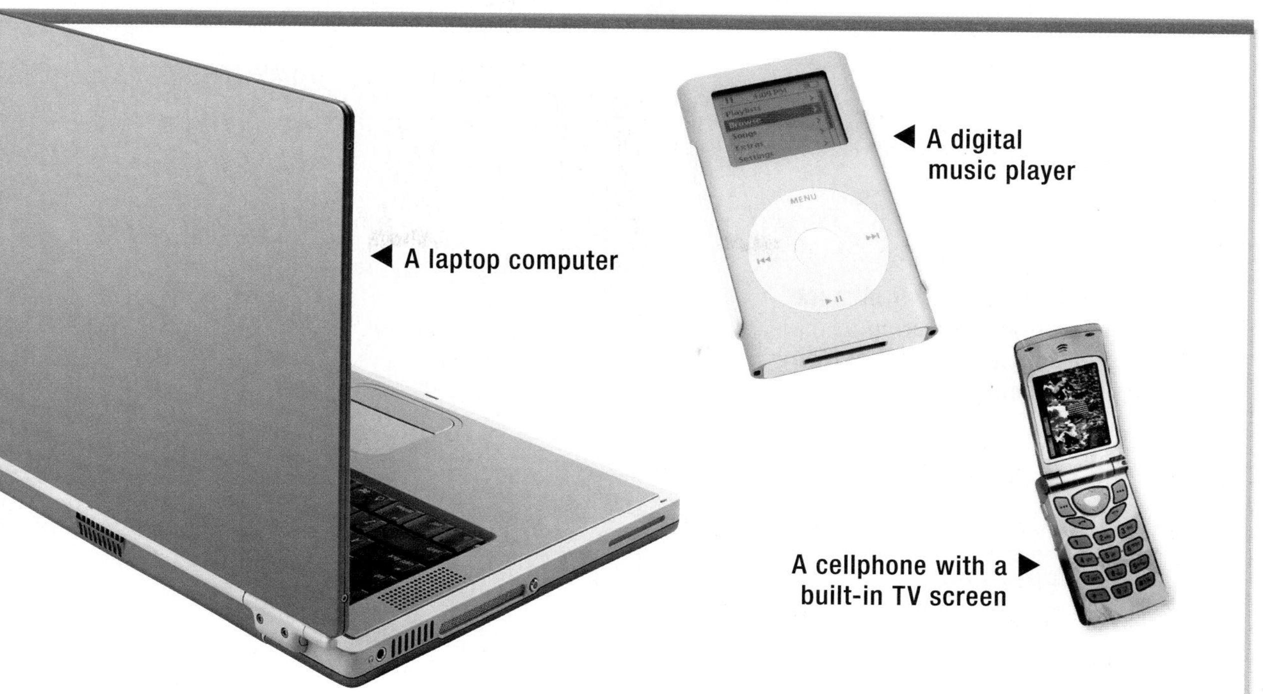

personal computer, this area became known as Silicon Valley.

One of the first companies in Silicon Valley was founded by William Hewlett and David Packard. Their company now makes computers and the equipment that can be used with them. This equipment includes printers, speakers, and digital cameras.

Connecting Computers

The development of the Internet, a way of connecting computers all over the world, has created new uses for computers. The Internet has given people new ways of communicating and finding information.

Electronic mail, or e-mail, was the first software that let people communicate using the Internet. With e-mail, you can send messages from one computer to another.

Instant messaging is another way of communicating through the Internet. Instant messaging software lets users of computers that are connected to the Internet type messages back and forth, so both users can see the messages almost instantly.

As the Internet grew, computer users were able to find information from libraries, companies, universities, and the government. In fact, so much information was available on the Internet that it was often hard to find specific information.

In 1994 Californians David Filo and Jerry Yang designed software that provides an easy way to search for information on the Internet. Later in this chapter, you will learn how to use this kind of software.

REVIEW What can people do using computers? *Main Idea and Details*

This tiny nanoguitar is much smaller than the period at the end of this sentence. It can be played using beams of light. ▶

▲ This robot insect will chase any moving object near it.

Future Technologies 4.4.6

One new technology that California companies are exploring is **nanotechnology**. This technology uses atoms—the tiniest parts of matter—to make structures that are about a million times smaller than the head of a pin.

Such small structures do amazing things. One college built a nanoguitar that can be played by hitting it with beams of light.

Companies continue to look at ways to apply nanotechnology in other areas, including making energy, making medicines, and even making better sunscreen lotions. Using nanotechnology, scientists hope to build tiny machines that can enter the body and repair damaged organs. Putting "nanowhiskers" on clothing keeps clothes from getting stained. When a liquid hits the nanowhiskers, it rolls off, instead of soaking into the fabric.

Another field being studied in California is **biotechnology**. This industry works with living cells to make new drugs. In fact, in 1976 Californians started the first biotechnology company in the world. The industry grew quickly. Today, there are about 2,500 biotechnology companies in California, including the world's largest.

Biotechnology also changes plants to make them grow better. For example, a California company has developed tomatoes that can grow in very salty soil. Some people are against changing plants this way, however. They worry that these plants might harm people or the environment.

REVIEW Describe nanotechnology and biotechnology. *Main Idea and Details*

DATAGRAPHIC

California's Economy

4.4

Many kinds of products are made in California. These products are important to California's economy. Another important part of California's economy is the service industry. Look at the map and graph below to learn more about California's economy.

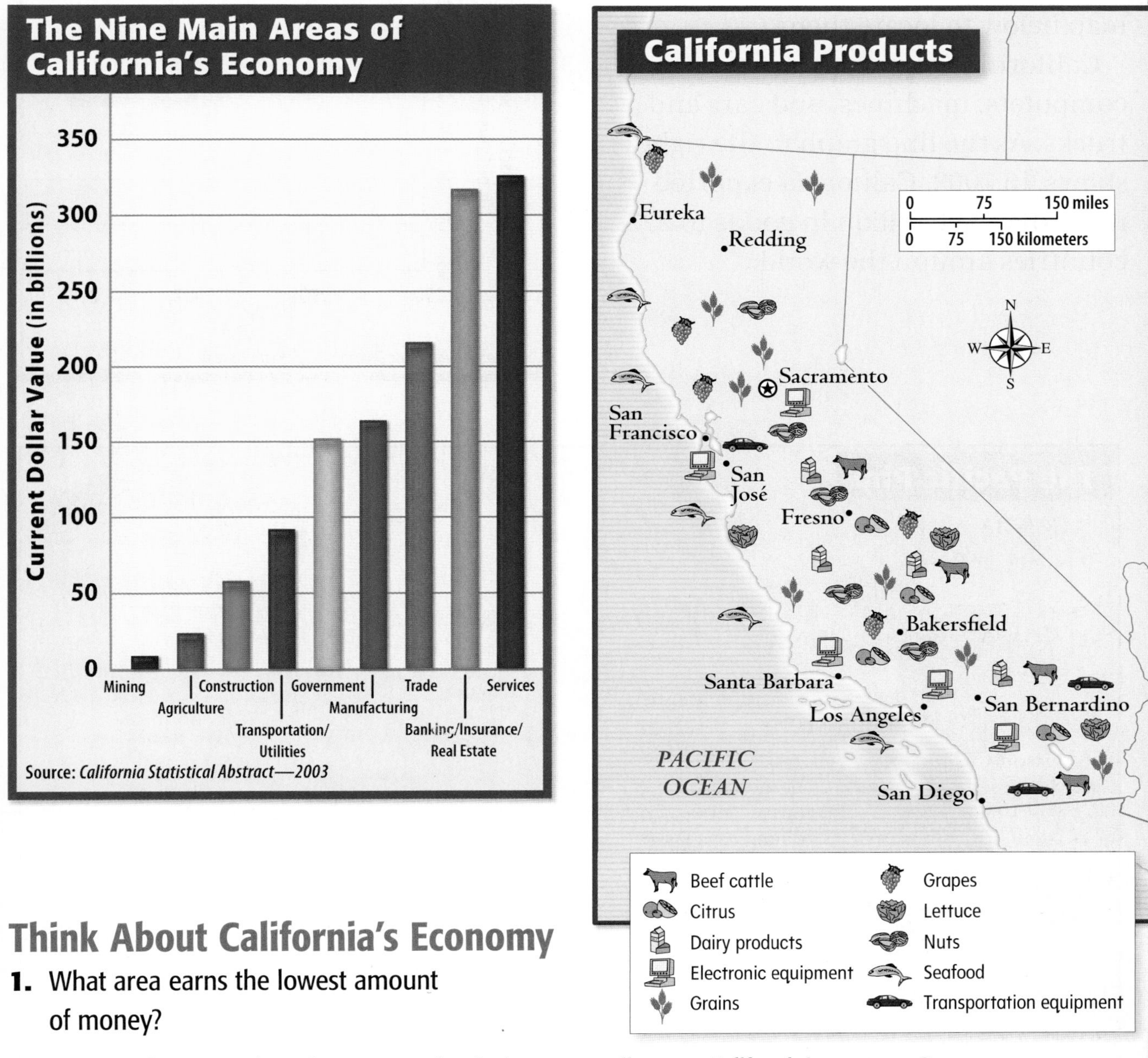

Think About California's Economy

1. What area earns the lowest amount of money?
2. How much money does the construction industry contribute to California's economy?
3. What goods are produced near Fresno?

Trade Across an Ocean 4.4.6

California's many ports make it easy to trade with countries on the shores of the Pacific Ocean. These nations are known as **Pacific Rim** countries. California's top six trading partners are all countries in the Pacific Rim. They are Mexico, Japan, Canada, Taiwan, South Korea, and China. Look at the map below to locate them.

California's top exports are computers, machines, and cars and trucks. As the line graph to the right shows, in 2002, California exported more than $90 billion in goods to 222 countries around the world.

Trade Agreements

California's trade with Mexico and Canada is especially strong. In 1992, the United States, Mexico, and Canada signed a special trade agreement called **NAFTA**, or the North American

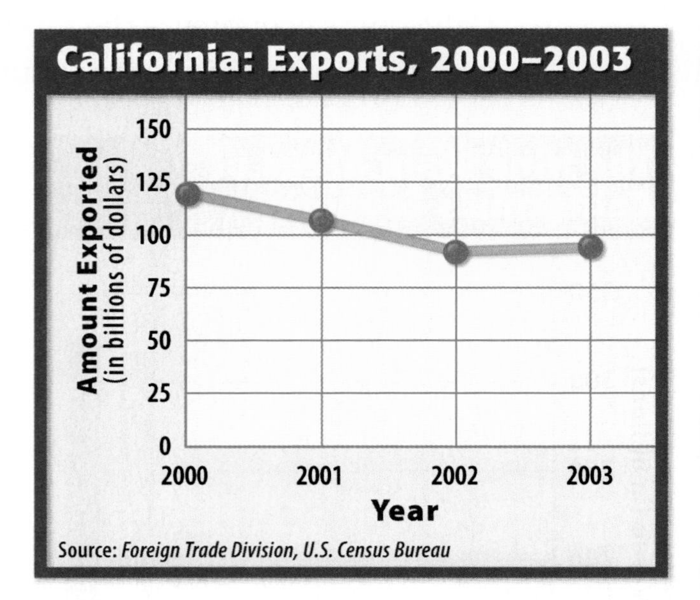

Source: *Foreign Trade Division, U.S. Census Bureau*

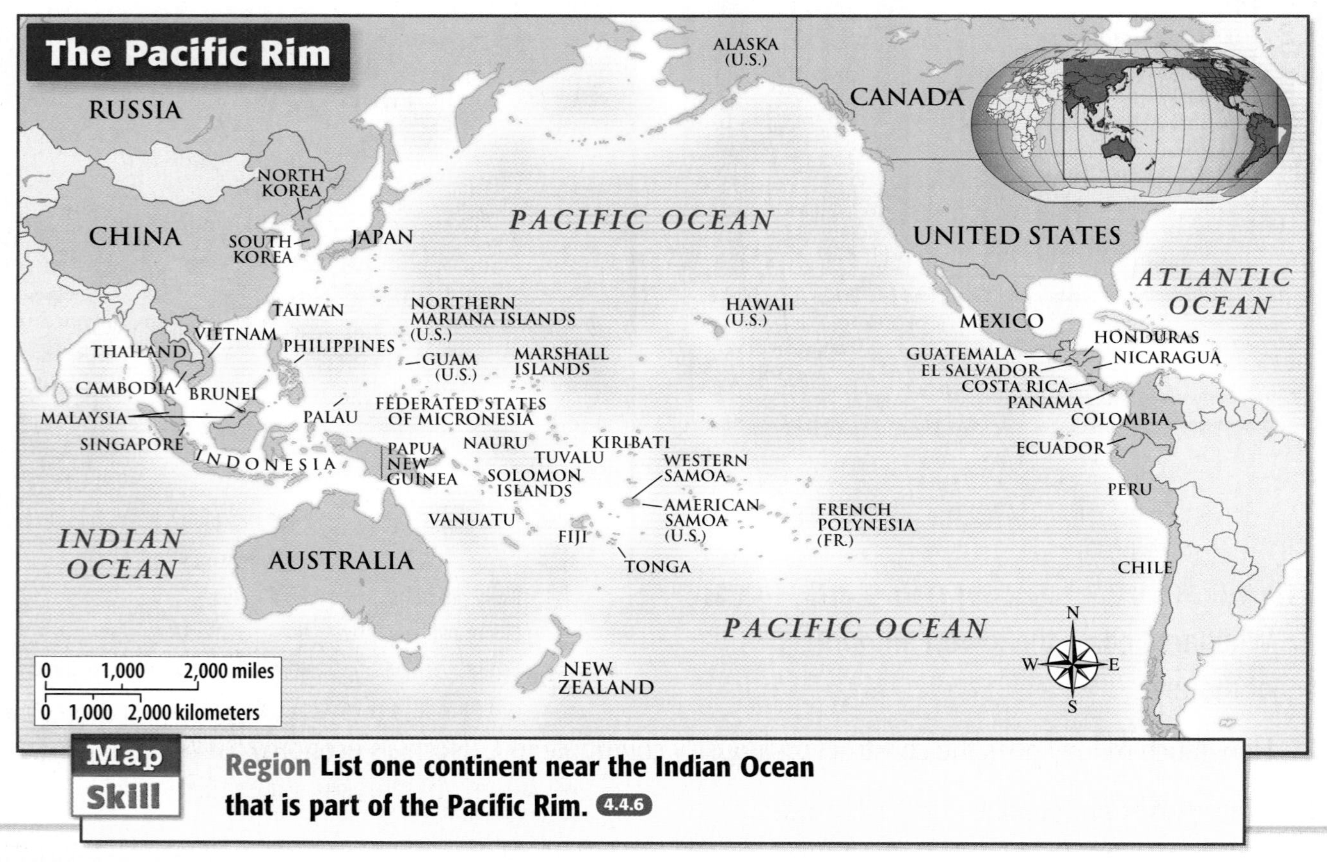

Map Skill Region List one continent near the Indian Ocean that is part of the Pacific Rim. 4.4.6

Free Trade Agreement. The three nations agreed to practice **free trade** with each other. Free trade means they will not use extra costs or rules to limit trade. The agreement makes North America the largest free trade area in the world.

Some people were unhappy about NAFTA. Farmers worried that cheap imports would lower their profits and force them out of business. Factory workers said that factories would move to Mexico, where workers are paid less money. On the other hand, people in favor of NAFTA pointed out that it would add to California's exports and jobs.

More Trade Partners

The discussion continues as other countries consider signing NAFTA and joining the free trade area. In 2005 the Dominican Republic and six countries of Central America formed CAFTA, or the Central American Free Trade Agreement. It unites them as one free trade area.

REVIEW What do California's most important trading partners have in common? *Main Idea and Details*

What You Learned

- 4.4 California's economy is supported by many different industries.
- 4.4.6 Companies in California make computers and computer equipment.
- 4.4.6 California companies are exploring biotechnology and nanotechnology.
- 4.4.6 California trades with countries around the Pacific Rim. The United States has a free trade agreement with Canada and Mexico.

Lesson Review

1. **Focus Question** How do different industries support California's economy? (4.4)
2. **Vocabulary** Write one sentence for each vocabulary term. (4.4.6)
   biotechnology **NAFTA** **Pacific Rim**
   free trade **nanotechnology** **software**
   microchip
3. **Economics** Name one industry in California and describe what it does. (4.4.6)
4. **Critical Thinking** **Problem Solving** With what invention can companies make smaller, faster computers? (4.4.6)
5. **Reading Strategy** **Compare and Contrast** Compare California's trade with Canada and Mexico to California's trade with the other countries in the Pacific Rim. (4.4.6, ELA R2.1)

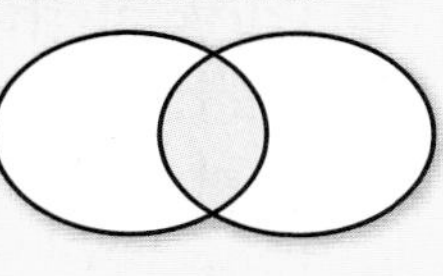

6. **Write about THE BIG IDEA** Write about which part of California's economy you would want to work in and why. (4.4.6, ELA W2.1)
7. **Link to Science** Biotechnology is used to make crops grow better. Write a paragraph discussing which plant you would want to change and what you would want to do. Explain why you would want to make changes to this plant.

STUDY and RESEARCH Skills

Use the Internet 4.4

The **World Wide Web** is a collection of information on the Internet. The Web has about three billion **Web sites**, or locations where you can find information. The California government has its own Web site. So do most California companies, cities, and schools.

You can use a search engine to help you sort through the sites. A search engine is a computer program that finds information on the Web.

VOCABULARY

World Wide Web
Web site
keyword
URL

1 Learn It

- Type in a **keyword** in a search engine to start a search. A keyword is a topic word that helps you find information. For example, the keyword "nanotechnology" helps you find information about high-tech inventions.
- Your search engine will then give you a list of Web sites that match your search. Read the Web sites' titles and description to see if they have information you might want.
- Look at the **URL**, or address, for each site. The last three letters in each URL give you an idea of the type and quality of the information on each site. For example, the URL for government sites will always be ".gov." The URL for private companies is ".com." Schools use ".edu," and research organizations and charity groups are listed as ".org."
- Don't simply trust the information you find. Always find at least two sources for your information. That allows you to compare what one site says against what the other says.

2 Try It

Compare the sample search engine pages to answer the following questions.

- What are the keywords for the two searches? Which keyword would you choose to find out how to get a job in high-technology?
- What is the URL for Nanotechnology for Kids in Search 1?
- Which site would you trust to offer the most scientific information about nanotechnology? Explain your answer.

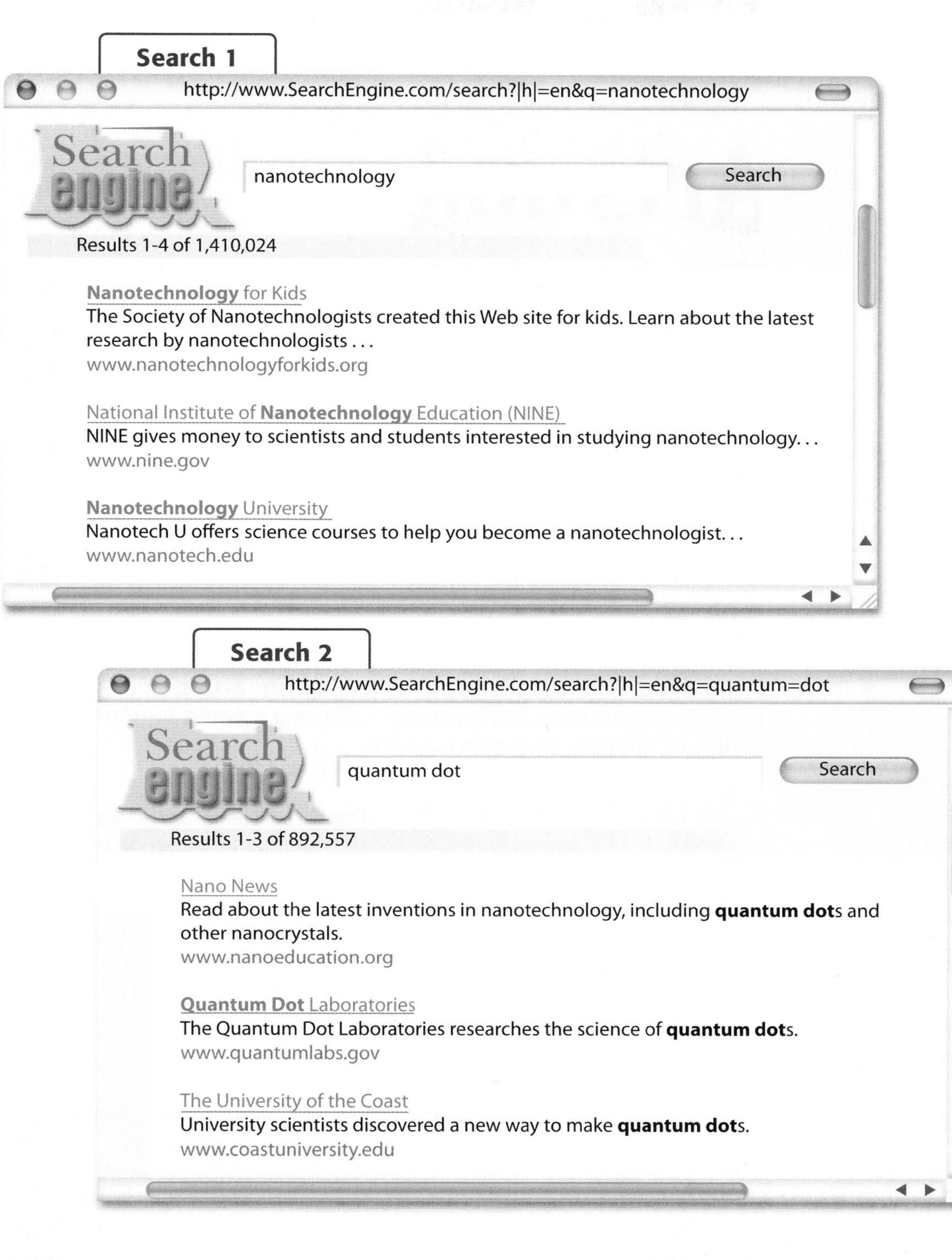

3 Apply It

Compare the two sample searches on this page to answer these questions.

- Do an Internet search to find out about California's products.
- What keywords will help you find information?
- Start with more general keywords such as "California Products." You may also choose to search for specific products.

LESSON 4

FOCUS QUESTION

How do the arts in California reflect the history of California?

VOCABULARY

composer
visual arts

VOCABULARY STRATEGY

SUFFIXES To **compose** means "to put together." When we add the suffix **-er** to *compose*, we get *composer*, which means someone who writes music. What other words for artists can you think of that follow this pattern?

READING STRATEGY

Summarize

Use the chart to summarize this lesson about the arts in California.

Arts and Entertainment

Start with Your CALIFORNIA STANDARDS

4.4 Students explain how California became an agricultural and industrial power, tracing the transformation of the California economy and its political and cultural development since the 1850s.

4.4.9 Analyze the impact of twentieth-century Californians on the nation's artistic and cultural development, including the rise of the entertainment industry.

Learn about some of the many writers, artists, actors, and musicians who have helped make California a world famous center of the arts. (Begins on page 411)

The Yerba Buena Center for the Arts and The San Francisco Museum of Modern Art ▼

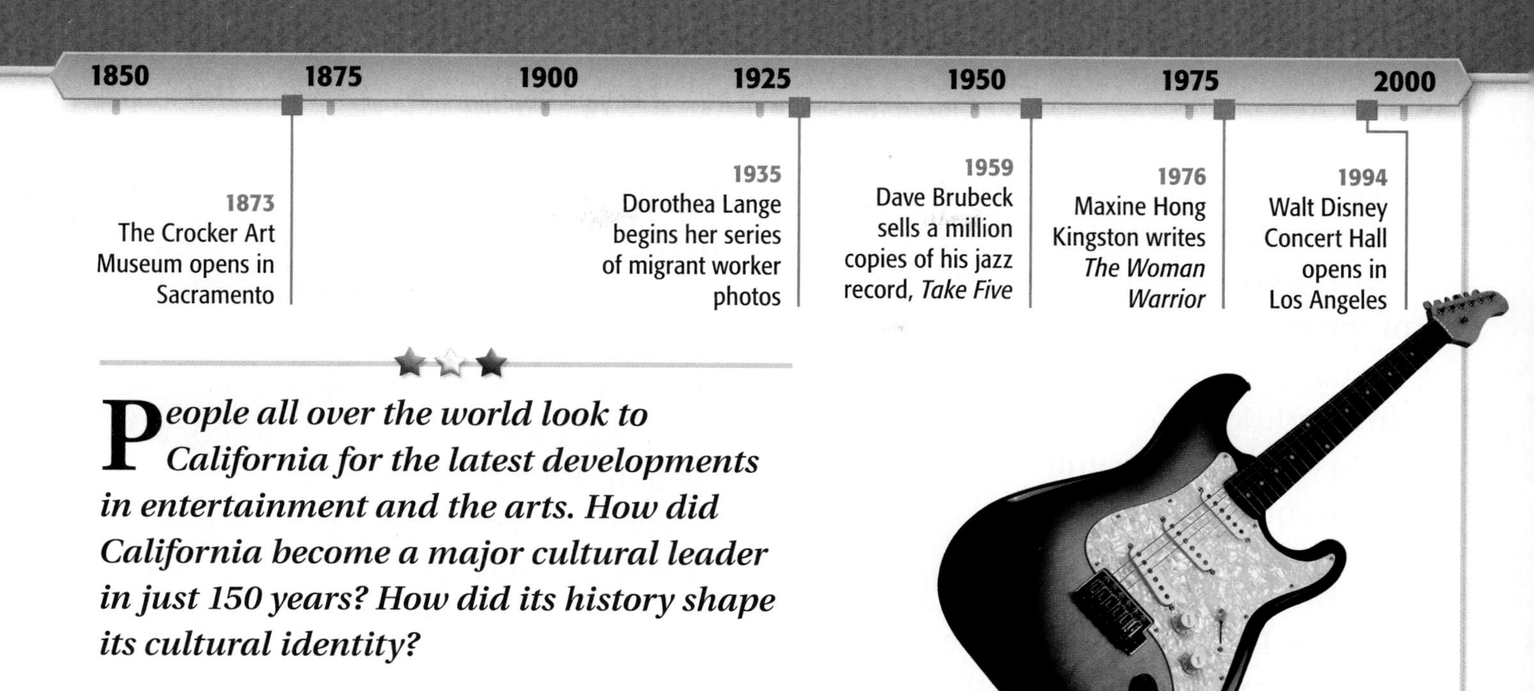

People all over the world look to California for the latest developments in entertainment and the arts. How did California become a major cultural leader in just 150 years? How did its history shape its cultural identity?

Sounds of California 4.4.9

The story of music in California goes back to the songs sung by Native Americans. Rancheros and miners celebrated their lives in song. In the first half of the twentieth century, the music created for Hollywood films became very popular. People all over the country began humming songs they first heard in films. The tradition of writing film music continues today. California **composer**, or music writer, John Williams has written the music for *Star Wars* as well as for the *Harry Potter* movies.

From Rock to Rap

By the 1960s, rock music had become the most popular music in America. The Beach Boys sang about surfing and fun in Southern California. With their song "California Dreamin'," the Mamas and the Papas celebrated the dream of endless sunshine and freedom. By the end of the 1960s there were many rock bands in California.

In the 1970s and 1980s Hispanic artists like Santana and Los Lobos blended Latin music with rock and roll. Since the 1980s, California has also been a lively center of rap and hip hop music. Today, Gwen Stefani from Anaheim is part of the popular band No Doubt.

REVIEW What groups of people made music in early California?
Main Idea and Details

Picturing California 4.4.9

Every period of change in California has produced important writers. The Gold Rush inspired Dame Shirley, Bret Harte, and Mark Twain to write stories of the miners and their pastimes. In the early 1900s, Jack London carried on this tradition. He wrote stories based on his adventurous life as a sailor and a gold miner.

Twentieth Century Writers

In the Depression, John Steinbeck wrote about people struggling to overcome poverty in a land of plenty. Steinbeck was born and raised in the Salinas Valley, where he learned about farm workers' poverty and hardship. In 1962 he won the Nobel Prize in literature.

Writers in the second half of the twentieth century wrote of California's great ethnic diversity. Novelist Alice Walker, poet Maya Angelou, and mystery writer Walter Mosley wrote powerfully about the African American experience.

Richard Rodriguez ▶

Vivid descriptions of the Mexican American experience came from writers like Gary Soto and Richard Rodriguez.

Asian American authors have written gripping stories about the immigrant experience. In *Farewell to Manzanar*, for example, Jeanne Wakatsuki Houston tells the story of her Japanese American family's internment during World War II. In her award-winning 1976 book, *The Woman Warrior*, Chinese American Maxine Hong Kingston described what it is like to grow up torn between two cultures. Novelist Bharati Mukherjee writes about the same theme in her novels about the Indian American community.

◀ Walter Mosley

◀ Maxine Hong Kingston

The Visual Arts in California

The **visual arts** include painting, drawing, sculpture, architecture, photography, film, and television. California's first visual artists were its Native American painters, sculptors, and basket-weavers.

In more recent times, California's visual artists have bridged the gap between the old and new traditions they grew up with. In the 1970s, young artists began painting huge, colorful murals on the walls of public places in Los Angeles and San Francisco. Many of the murals celebrated life in immigrant communities. Some of the most famous murals were painted by a group of Hispanic artists called Los Four.

Simon Rodia became famous for his Watts Towers, built with the simplest of tools and materials. Mexican American Richard Serra's sculptures are massive works of stone and metal.

California women have made contributions in many artistic fields. Dorothea Lange took photographs of migrant workers in 1935, which helped change government policy toward helping the poor. African American artist Kara Walker shows African American history by using light and shapes made from cut paper.

Beatrice Wood ▶

Beatrice Wood's pottery became known around the world. ▶

Pottery maker Beatrice Wood, who lived to be 105, became so well known for her stylish and humorous pottery that she was declared a California Living Treasure in 1994. Judy Chicago has worked with hundreds of volunteers to create art projects that celebrated women around the world.

REVIEW What contributions have California women made to the visual arts?
Main Idea and Details

Where to Enjoy Music and Art in California 4.4.9

California's first museum was the Crocker Art Museum, built in Sacramento in 1873. Today, California boasts many extraordinary places to see art. One of these is the San Francisco Museum of Modern Art. One of the best places to learn about California's natural history is the Oakland Museum of California.

Today, you can hear classical music in many locations. In 1994, Walt Disney Concert Hall, named after the California filmmaker Walt Disney, became the home of the Los Angeles Philharmonic. The San Francisco Symphony plays at the city's Performing Arts Center. You can listen to jazz or see modern dance at the Mondavi Center in Davis.

REVIEW Where can you go to see exhibits about California's natural history? *Main Idea and Details*

▲ The Getty Museum, which opened in 1997, sits on a hilltop overlooking Los Angeles.

What You Learned

- 4.4.9 In the twentieth century, music in California has taken several forms: film music, rock, rap, Latin music, and hip hop.
- 4.4.9 Each period of change in California has produced its own writers and visual artists. Today's writers and artists come from many backgrounds.
- 4.4.9 California has numerous outstanding art museums and concert halls.

Lesson Review

1. **Focus Question** How do the arts in California reflect the history of California? 4.4.9
2. **Vocabulary** Write one sentence for each vocabulary term. 4.4.9
   composer **visual arts**
3. **Culture** How has California's history of immigration enriched its visual arts and literature? 4.4.9
4. **Critical Thinking** **Problem Solving** What are some ways that citizens of other states can experience the work of California's creative artists? 4.4.9
5. **Reading Strategy** **Summarize** Reread the section called "Sounds of California" and use the chart to summarize it. 4.4.9 ELA R2.1

6. **Write about THE BIG IDEA** Which of the visual arts in California do you think has convinced the most people to move there? 4.4.9 ELA W2.1
7. **Link to Art** Briefly research a California musician, visual artist, or writer online or in the library. Then write a paragraph or two describing the main events of his or her life. 4.4.9

Biography

Focus on Courage

4.4.9

Isamu Noguchi 1904–1988

Isamu Noguchi was born in Los Angeles in 1904. His mother was from the United States. His father was from Japan. Isamu went to elementary school in Japan and high school in the United States. This experience helped him to understand both cultures.

When he grew up, Noguchi wanted to be a sculptor—someone who carves things from wood or stone. A famous sculptor, however, told him he was not good enough. Isamu was disappointed, and for a while he studied to be a doctor. Before long, though, he returned to art. Noguchi became world-famous for his sculptures, fountains, and gardens. The beautiful things he created have been used and loved by people in many different cultures.

In 1942 Noguchi spent time in an internment camp for Japanese Americans. He later said about his time there:

"I realized I was . . . not just American but Japanese American."

How did Isamu Noguchi's early life and travels affect his art?

For more about Isamu Noguchi, visit:

www.macmillanmh.com/ss/ca/bios

The Life of Isamu Noguchi

1900 | 1930 | 1960 | 1990

- **1904** Born in Los Angeles
- **1929** First art gallery exhibit devoted to his work
- **1949** Awarded travel fellowship for study in Europe and Asia
- **1987** Awarded National Medal of Arts

Read Road Maps 4.4

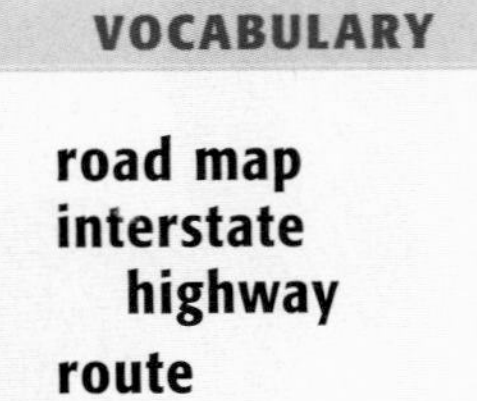

VOCABULARY

road map
interstate highway
route

Throughout California's history, thousands of roads have been built. Today, roads can take you to almost every place in the state.

Suppose you want to go somewhere you have never been before. How do you know what road to take? You use a **road map**. Road maps show where the roads in a certain area go. By reading a road map you can figure out how to get from one place to another.

1 Learn It

- Map A has several different kinds of roads. The thick green lines are **interstate highways**. An interstate highway connects two or more states.
- Interstate highways run through states and major cities across the United States. They usually have at least two lanes running in each direction.
- Study the map key on Road Map A. A purple line identifies a state highway. State highways are those that run within a state.
- The "name" of each interstate and state highway is a number. Notice the different symbols for each of the three kinds of highways. Which highway runs from Inglewood to Torrance?
- Remember this fact: Odd-numbered highways usually run in the general direction of north and south. Even-numbered highways usually run east and west. This helps lost drivers figure out what direction they are going in.

2 Try It

- Look at Road Map A. How is Interstate Highway 5 different from State Highway 57?
- What **route** would you take to get from Glendale to Anaheim? A route is the course you take to get somewhere.

3 Apply It

Road maps can also be useful for smaller areas. Smaller area road maps show how different streets connect.

- Look at Road Map B, it shows a section of downtown Los Angeles.
- What are two routes you could take to get from the Staples Center to Walt Disney Concert Hall?
- What kind of roads would you find on a map of the area where you live?

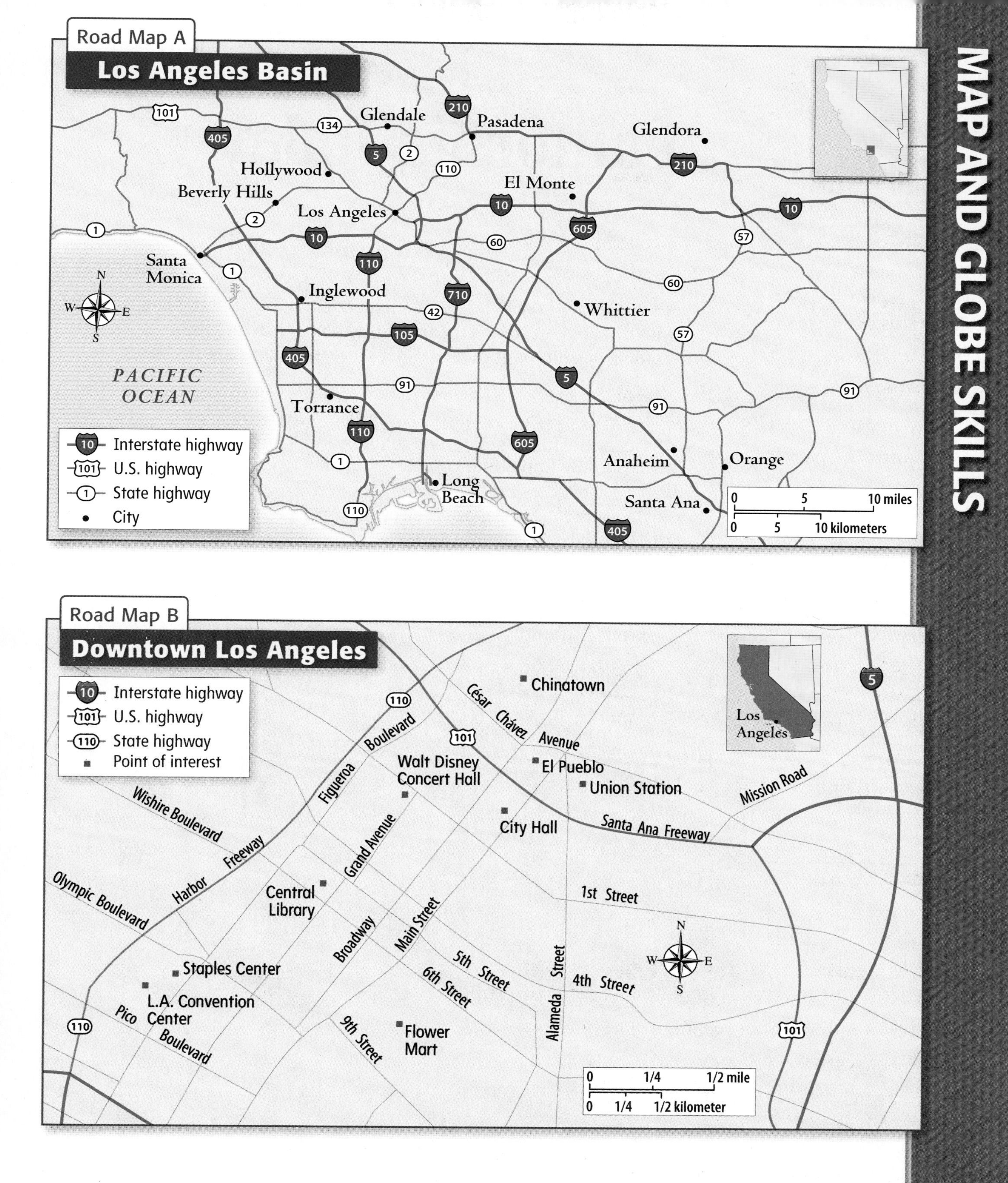

Road Map A
Los Angeles Basin
Glendale
Pasadena
Glendora
Hollywood
Beverly Hills
Los Angeles
El Monte
Santa Monica
Inglewood
Whittier
PACIFIC OCEAN
Torrance
Long Beach
Anaheim
Orange
Santa Ana
Interstate highway
U.S. highway
State highway
City
0 5 10 miles
0 5 10 kilometers
Road Map B
Downtown Los Angeles
Interstate highway
U.S. highway
State highway
Point of interest
Chinatown
César Chávez Avenue
Figueroa Boulevard
Walt Disney Concert Hall
El Pueblo
Union Station
City Hall
Santa Ana Freeway
Mission Road
Wishire Boulevard
Harbor Freeway
Grand Avenue
Olympic Boulevard
Central Library
1st Street
Broadway
Main Street
5th Street
6th Street
4th Street
Alameda Street
Staples Center
L.A. Convention Center
Pico Boulevard
9th Street
Flower Mart
Los Angeles
0 1/4 1/2 mile
0 1/4 1/2 kilometer

California Today

FOCUS QUESTION

What are some ways you can experience California's diversity and history?

VOCABULARY

multicultural
landmark

VOCABULARY STRATEGY

WORD ORIGINS Landmark used to mean "an object used to mark the boundaries of a kingdom." In 1859 its meaning changed to "marking a historical place."

READING STRATEGY

Summarize

Use the chart to summarize life in California today.

Start with Your CALIFORNIA STANDARDS

4.4 Students explain how California became an agricultural and industrial power, tracing the transformation of the California economy and its political and cultural development since the 1850s.

4.4.9 Analyze the impact of twentieth-century Californians on the nation's artistic and cultural development, including the rise of the entertainment industry.

Discover California's different cultures and learn historical places in California that you can visit. (Begins on page 419)

Californians of all backgrounds enjoy the Fourth of July at Fisherman's Wharf. ▼

How many languages would you guess are spoken in the state of California? The answer is more than 200 different languages! Many of these languages are spoken by immigrants who bring the culture of their homelands with them.

A Blend of Cultures 4.4.9

In 2004 California's population was about 36 million. The state's blend of immigrants from many countries made it the most culturally diverse state in the United States. It is truly **multicultural**. Multicultural means having many different cultures.

California's Immigrants

People from all over the world already call California home, and more are coming all the time. One out of every four immigrants to the United States chooses to settle here.

In 2002 almost half of these immigrants came from Latin America and the Caribbean. The largest number of Latin American immigrants came from Mexico. Two out of every five immigrants in California are Asian. They came mostly from China, Japan, South Korea, the Philippines, Vietnam, Cambodia, and Laos.

California's diversity is one of its greatest strengths. The mix of traditions from other countries enriches people's lives. Traditions are customs and beliefs passed from parents to their children.

REVIEW How has immigration affected California? *Summarize*

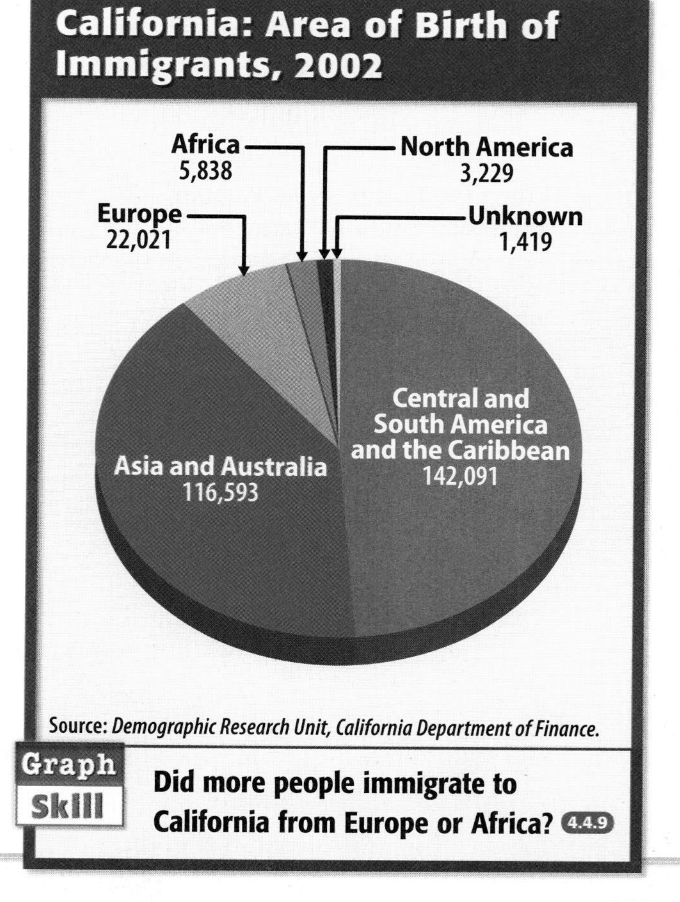

California: Area of Birth of Immigrants, 2002

Source: *Demographic Research Unit, California Department of Finance.*

Graph Skill **Did more people immigrate to California from Europe or Africa?** 4.4.9

One State, Many Cultures 4.4.9

Californians come from many different cultures, and each culture has its own holidays to celebrate. These celebrations are important because they remind Californians of their heritage and teach others about their cultures.

▲ A traditional Chinese American gift given in honor of the Lunar New Year, containing money

The César Chávez Day of Service and Learning honors the labor union organizer and his work. Chávez believed that:

> ***“The end of all education should surely be service to others.”***

As a result, on March 31 of every year, Californians work on projects that help others. Volunteers have cleaned up parks and even picked crops.

Mexican Americans in California celebrate “Cinco de Mayo,” on May 5. Cinco de Mayo commemorates the Mexican victory in a battle with France in 1862. Californians celebrate this patriotic Mexican holiday with parades and parties.

Asian Californians celebrate the Lunar New Year. Dragons wind their way through the streets of Chinatown. Firecrackers pop as the dragons pass by. During the holiday, people in the community exchange wishes for a healthy and prosperous year.

February is also Black History Month. Storytellers, dance groups, and musicians celebrate the contributions of African Americans since California’s earliest days.

Artists at the I Madonnari Street Painting Festival at Mission Santa Barbara. ▼

◀ Traditional Irish step dancers often wear colorful outfits.

Each June the Palace of Fine Arts comes alive with the sounds of World Music, in San Francisco. Hundreds of dancers perform to the music at the San Francisco Ethnic Dance Festival. Inuit dancers take turns on the stage with Middle Eastern belly dancers, Irish step dancers, Hawaiian hula groups, and traditional dancers from Mexico and Peru. In Little Tokyo in Los Angeles, Japanese Californians sponsor a Tofu Festival in July. People sample many dishes made of tofu. At the I Madonnari Italian Street Painting Festival, artists create large chalk drawings on the streets.

Other festivals bring Native American traditions to life. In Indian Grinding Rock State Historic Park, the Miwok Indians celebrate the Acorn Harvest Thanksgiving every September. During the celebration, singers and storytellers recreate Miwok traditions from before the Gold Rush. Dancers chant and play clappers and foot drums in a traditional Miwok roundhouse.

REVIEW What are some celebrations held in California? *Summarize*

A young dancer at Cinco de Mayo festival in Los Angeles. ▶

California Fun 4.4.9

In addition to celebrating the heritages of the many places they come from, Californians also celebrate the state's colorful history. There are many places in California where you can walk through historical buildings and see historical artifacts.

Indoor Adventures

The California State Indian Museum records the lives of the earliest Californians. Built at Sutter's Fort in Sacramento, the museum shows full-size models of different kinds of Native American houses.

Along the old Camino Real, signs with a mission bell point to the Spanish missions that still exist today. These missions preserve an important part of California's past.

Landmark buildings trace the growth of California's government. A landmark is an important building, structure, or place. The state capitol building in Sacramento took 14 years to build, and was finished in 1874. It combines the spirit of the past with the energy of the present. You can tour the California capitol building today. Portraits of past governors look down at you from an upstairs hallway. From a balcony in the senate you can watch as senators debate bills that may become laws.

You can watch humpback whales play near Monterey. ▼

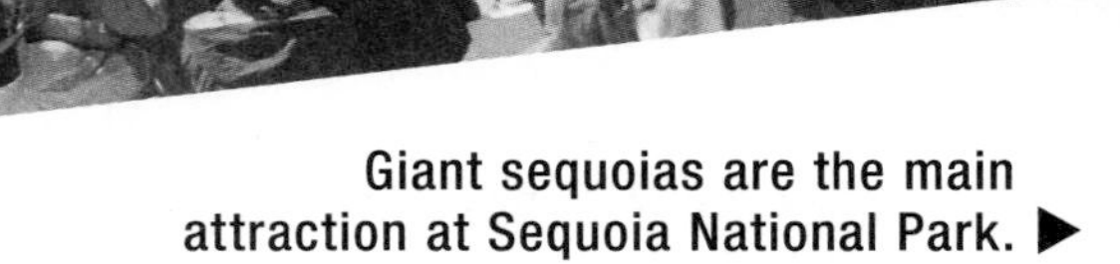

Giant sequoias are the main attraction at Sequoia National Park. ▶

Outdoor Adventures

The Gold Rush still lives in several parks and towns. At the Marshall Gold Discovery State Historic Park in Coloma, you can pan for gold in the American River, where the first gold nugget was found. Just north of Barstow is a ghost town called Calico. It used to be a booming mining town. Today, you can walk through its deserted streets and abandoned silver mine.

California has a network of state and national parks open for all to explore and enjoy. John Muir felt that maintaining California's natural lands was important for us all. He wrote:

> ***"Everybody needs beauty as well as bread, places to play in and pray in, where nature may heal and give strength to body and soul alike."***

Today many people hike through Muir Woods National Monument in the San Francisco Bay Area. You can also wander among the towering redwoods or marvel at the state's lowest point at Death Valley National Park. You can even imagine that you are back in the time of the dinosaurs as you pass through the multicolored cliffs of Red Rock Canyon State Park.

REVIEW How does California preserve its history and natural resources? *Summarize*

What You Learned

- 4.4.9 Immigrants have helped make California the most populated and diverse state in the United States.
- 4.4.9 Holidays and festivals from many cultures reflect and celebrate the diversity of Californians.
- 4.4.9 Museums, historic buildings, and parks preserve California's history.

Lesson Review

1. **Focus Question** What are some ways you can experience California's diversity and history? (4.4.9)
2. **Vocabulary** Write one sentence for each vocabulary term. (4.4.9)
   landmark **multicultural**
3. **Culture** List three different cultural holidays celebrated in California each year and name the country or culture they come from. (4.4.9)
4. **Critical Thinking** **Identify Fact and Opinion** Tell if the following statement is fact or opinion: "May 5 is an important date in Mexican culture." (4.4.9)
5. **Summarize** Use the chart to write down the different places you can go to see California's history. (4.4.9, ELA R2.1)

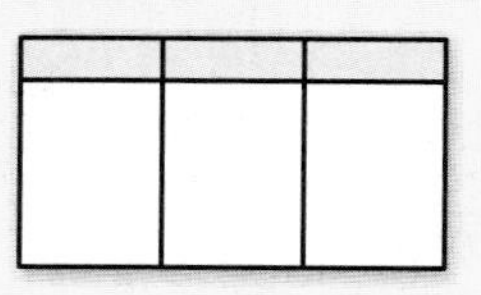

6. **Write about THE BIG IDEA** Write about a park, museum, or ethnic festival you would want to visit. (4.4.9, ELA W2.1)
7. **Link to Geography** You are part of California's rich mosaic of people. When did you or your family come to California? Draw a map that shows the route that brought you or your family to California. (4.4.9)

Chapter Review

Vocabulary Review

Copy the sentences below on a separate sheet of paper. Use the list of vocabulary terms to fill in the blanks.

boycott	**labor union**
civil rights	**nanotechnology**

1. A ________ is a group of workers who make agreements with their employer for fair wages and work conditions. 4.4

2. ________ are the rights that the Constitution gives to all Americans. 4.5.1

3. ________ is a technology that uses atoms to make tiny structures. 4.4.6

4. A ________ is when people refuse to buy a certain product. 4.4

5. **Test Preparation** The policy of keeping groups of people separate is called ________ . 4.4

A. **segregation**
B. **demonstration**
C. **manufacturing**
D. **public education**

Comprehension Check

6. When did the first public school open in San Francisco? 4.4.8

7. Who was the first African American mayor of Los Angeles? 4.4

8. What did the Twenty-Sixth Amendment do to the voting age? 4.4

9. What are some of the industries in California? 4.4.6

10. What type of music become popular in the first half of the twentieth century? 4.4.9

11. **Critical Thinking** Why is public education important? 4.4.8

12. **Critical Thinking** How do people feel about NAFTA? 4.4

Use the Time Line

Use the time line below to answer each question.

13. When did Tom Bradley become mayor of Los Angeles? 4.4

14. Did the farm workers union begin before or after the Unruh Civil Rights Act? 4.4

1955 — 1960 — 1965 — 1970 — 1975

1959 The Unruh Civil Rights Act helps stop discrimination

1962 Dolores Huerta and César Chávez form union for farm workers

1973 Tom Bradley becomes first African American mayor of Los Angeles

1975 War in Vietnam ends

Skills Check

Write a complete sentence to answer each question.

Reading Road Maps

15. What does the road map below show? 4.1.5

16. Which interstate highway runs through Redding? 4.1.5

17. **Test Preparation** U.S. highway ______ runs through Bishop. 4.1.5

18. **Test Preparation** State highway ______ runs to Alturas. 4.1.5

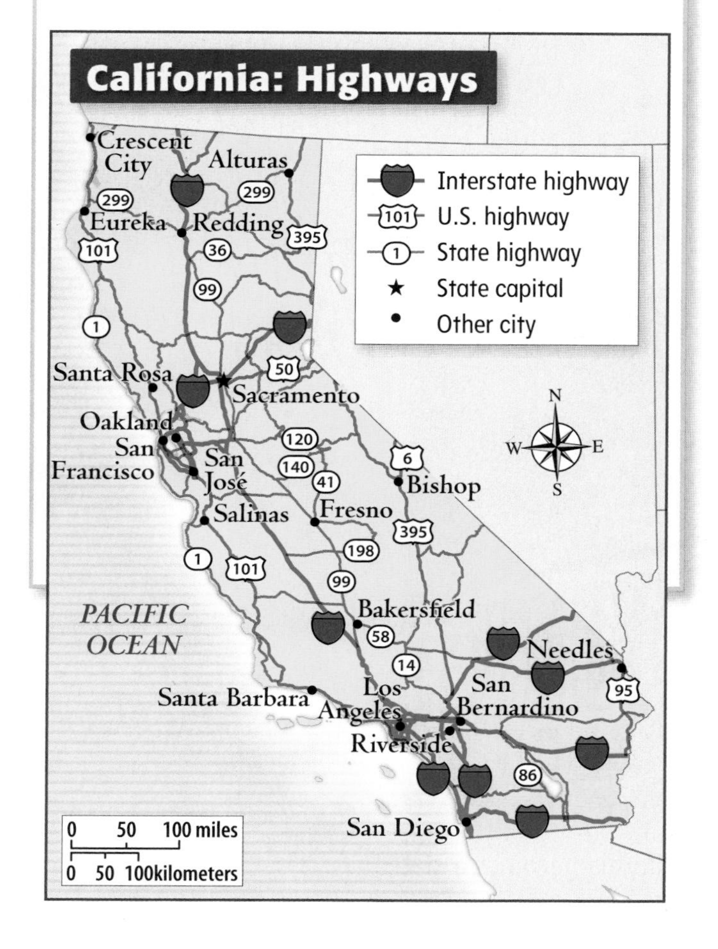

Using Primary Sources

Artifacts

19. What kind of artifacts might be found at California's museums? 4.4

20. What might we learn from artifacts? 4.4

Hands-on Activity

21. **Make a Brochure** Work in groups to create a brochure that answers the following question: 4.4

What are fun things to do and see in California?

Write About History

22. **Expository** Write a paragraph that explains how the civil rights movement changed life for people in California. 4.4 ELA 2.1

For help with the process of writing, visit:

www.macmillanmh.com/ss/ca/writing

Government

You Are There

"...I always dream[ed] about coming to California, because it was always known as the place of great opportunities, the place where you can chase your dreams."

California Governor Arnold Schwarzenegger spoke these words during a speech. He was encouraging people and businesses to come to California.

In this chapter you will read about the three levels of government. You will learn that people living in California have national, state, and local governments.

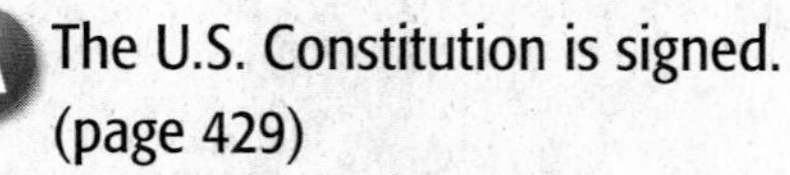

A The U.S. Constitution is signed. (page 429)

B California becomes a state. (page 439)

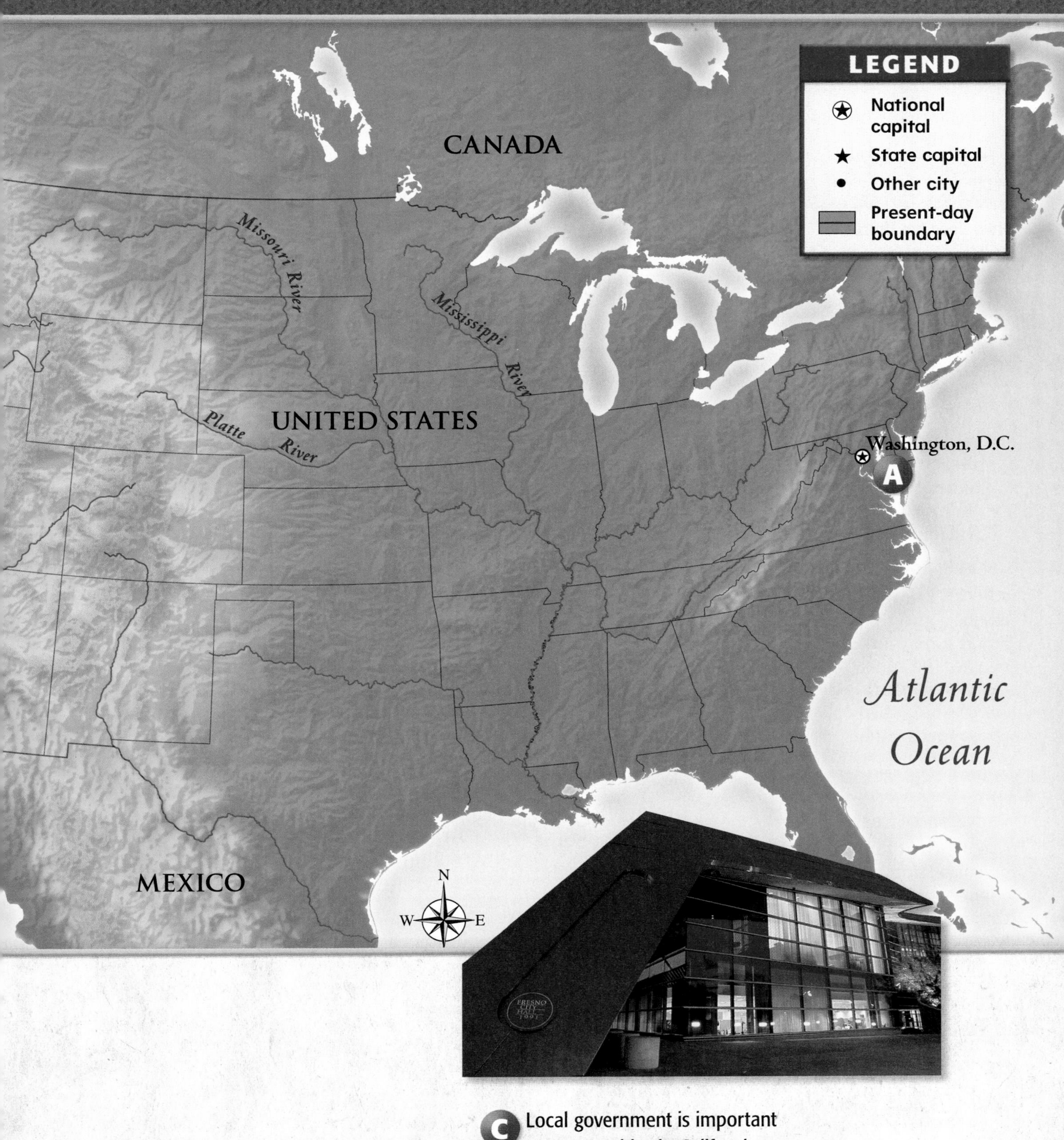

C Local government is important to communities in California. (page 446)

FOCUS QUESTION

How does the United States government work?

VOCABULARY

- democracy
- citizen
- jury
- federal
- legislative branch
- executive branch
- judicial branch

VOCABULARY STRATEGY

SUFFIXES Democracy means a government that is run by its people. The suffix **-cracy** is from a Greek word which means government or rule.

READING STRATEGY

Cause and Effect

Use the chart to organize information about how laws are carried out in the three levels of government.

Our Nation's Government

Start with Your CALIFORNIA STANDARDS

4.5 Students understand the structures, functions, and powers of the local, state, and federal governments as described in the U.S. Constitution.

4.5.1 Discuss what the United States Constitution is and why it is important.

Learn about how the United States Constitution separates the jobs of the three branches of government. (pages 430–431)

4.5.3 Describe the similarities and differences among federal, state, and local governments.

Understand the United States Constitution as a plan for how government works in our country, with powers shared by three levels of government. (pages 432–433)

▼ The United States government is located in Washington, D.C.

We the People

The United States is home to almost 300 million people. How can so many people work together to make our country strong? We follow a plan. The United States Constitution is our plan. It is a set of rights and laws that explain how our nation's government should work.

The People's Government 4.5

The United States has a "government of the people, by the people, and for the people." This is how Abraham Lincoln, the sixteenth President of the United States, described **democracy**. The United States government is a democracy, or a government that is run by its people. The **citizens** of the United States elect those who run our government. A citizen is someone who is a member of a country, either by birth or by law.

Citizens of the United States have many rights. At age 18, all citizens have the right to vote in elections. In a democracy people vote for their leaders. If the citizens do not like a leader, they can try to replace that leader by voting for someone else in the next election.

Everyone in the United States has certain rights, such as freedom of speech and freedom of religion. This means people can say what they think and practice any religion they want.

With Rights Come Responsibilities

With these rights come responsibilities. People must pay taxes and follow laws. In addition, citizens are asked to vote in every election. At times they must serve on a **jury**. A jury is a group of citizens in a court of law who decides if someone accused of a crime is innocent or guilty. By being a good citizen, a person can help protect his or her rights, as well as the rights of others.

REVIEW How does having a democracy affect citizens of the United States?
Cause and Effect

VOTE

National Government 4.5.1

▲ Former California Governor Ronald Reagan served eight years as President.

The United States Constitution was written over 200 years ago. It explains the role of the **federal**, or national, government in our country. The Constitution says that the government shall have three branches, or parts. Each branch has its own job to do. Each branch also has some power over the other branches. This prevents any single branch from gaining too much power. The Constitution also limits the responsibility of the federal government by giving a lot of responsibility to each of our country's 50 states.

The Constitution includes a part called the Bill of Rights. This explains some of the rights held by everyone in the United States. You read about some of these rights at the beginning of this lesson, such as the right to freedom of speech and religion.

Branches of Government

The **legislative branch**, or Congress, is the law-making part of government.

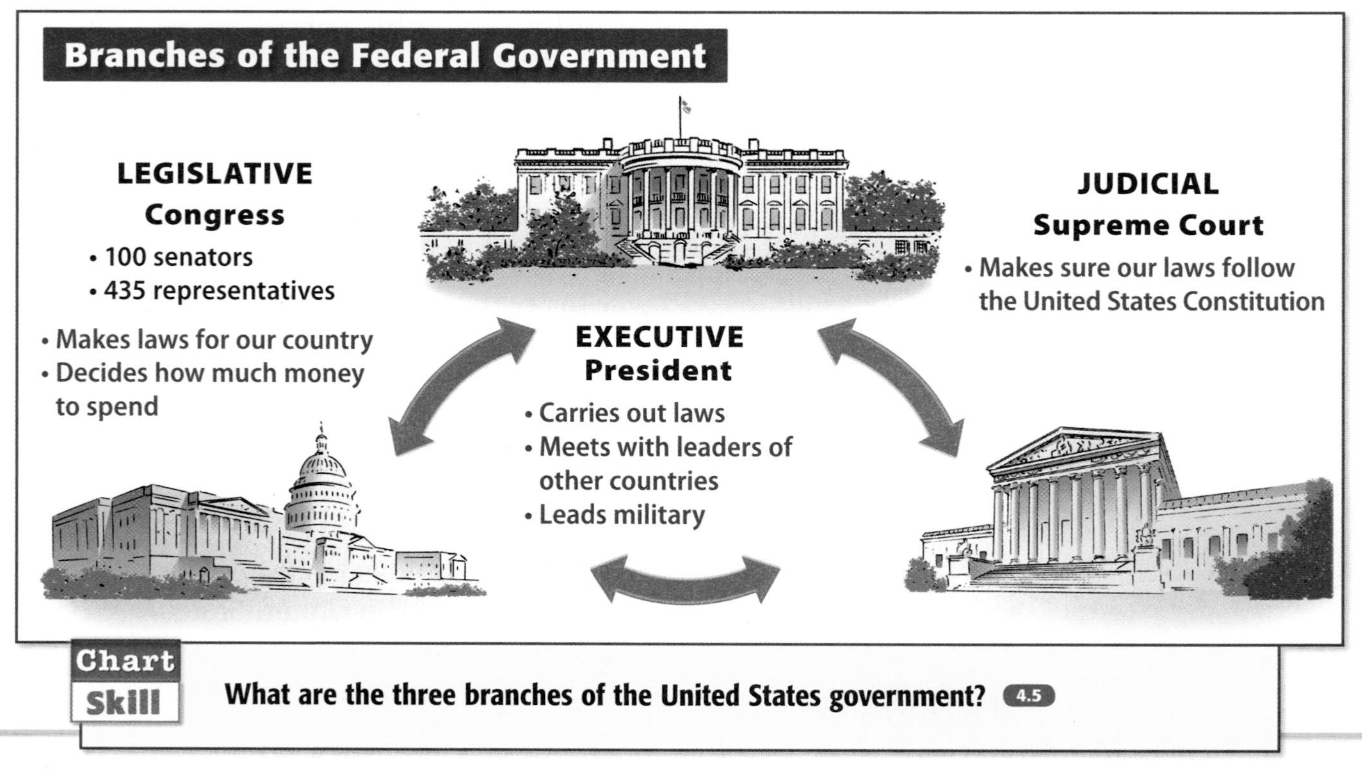

Chart Skill What are the three branches of the United States government? 4.5

It includes the Senate and the House of Representatives. Citizens elect senators and representatives to serve terms in Congress. Every state sends two senators to Congress. The number of representatives for each state depends on the state's population. The larger the state's population, the more representatives it may have. California has 53 representatives, more than any other state.

Each year members of Congress meet in the Capitol to discuss issues and make new laws. They also help decide how the government will spend its money.

The **executive branch** carries out the laws. It is led by the President, who is also Commander in Chief of the United States military. The President meets with leaders of other countries and selects people to head national departments, such as for health and transportation.

The **judicial branch** of the federal government includes all the federal courts. These courts make sure the laws are followed. The Supreme Court is the highest court in the country. It decides if new laws passed by Congress and approved by the President agree with the Constitution. In this way, the judicial branch limits the powers of the legislative and executive branches. The chart on page 430 shows the three branches of the United States government.

Justice David Souter ▶

◀ Representative Diane Watson

REVIEW How is the number of state's senators and representatives determined? *Main Idea and Details*

◀ Senator Dianne Feinstein

▲ Arnold Schwarzenegger is governor of California. Here he is meeting with Santa Monica firefighters.

Los Angeles County pays for lifeguards to patrol its beaches. ▼

Three Levels of Government 4.5.3

There are three levels of government in our country. You have read about the federal level. There are also governments in charge of states and local communities.

The United States Constitution says that the power of the government must be shared between the federal government and state governments. The writers of the Constitution did not want the national government to have too much power. In addition, they believed that it was better to handle some issues at the state level.

California's state government passes laws that only affect Californians. For example, in 2004 the state government passed a new law that made a large area in the Sierra Nevada a conservancy area. This means communities in that area can get money to protect and restore the environment and manage water resources. This law affects only Californians. In Lesson 2, you will read more about state government.

Local Government

In addition to the state government, California also has many smaller local governments that serve communities in the state. For example, the County of Shasta government makes laws only for the people of Shasta County.

These small governments focus on the needs of the community. They are in charge of the local police force and

◀ Fire departments are funded by local government.

fire departments. They perform services like putting up stop signs, streetlights, and picking up garbage and recycling. They also maintain the public schools, the libraries, and the local parks where you play. In Lesson 3, you will read more about local governments.

REVIEW Why doesn't the federal government oversee services like garbage pickup? *Main Idea and Details*

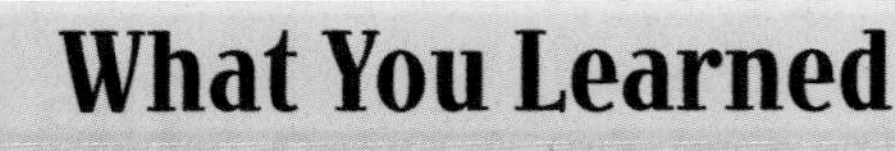

What You Learned

- 4.5 The United States is a democracy, or a government run by its people, as outlined by the United States Constitution.
- 4.5.1 The federal, or national, government has three branches that share power and have different responsibilities.
- 4.5.3 Three levels of government affect every Californian, from the federal to the local level.

Lesson Review

1. **Focus Question** How does the United States government work? (4.5)
2. **Vocabulary** Write one sentence for each vocabulary term. (4.5.1, 4.5.3)
   citizen
   democracy
   executive branch
   federal
   judicial branch
   jury
   legislative branch
3. **Government** Write a short paragraph about the rights of all United States citizens. (4.5.1)
4. **Critical Thinking** **Problem Solving** How does the United States Constitution solve the problem of dividing up the power of government? (4.5.1)
5. **Reading Strategy** **Cause and Effect** Reread the section titled "Three Levels of Government" on page 432. Fill in the chart to show how state and local governments work. (4.5.3, ELA R2.1)

6. **Write about THE BIG IDEA** Write about your area's local government. How does it help the community? (4.5.3, ELA W2.3)

Link to Mathematics To make a law, a majority of both the House of Representatives and the Senate must vote "yes." In the Senate, that makes 51 out of 100 votes. How many of the House's 435 members need to vote "yes"? (4.5.1)

Using PRIMARY SOURCES

Understanding Official Documents 4.5

VOCABULARY

official document

An **official document** contains information that has been agreed upon by one or more people or institutions. Official documents often describe something in detail, such as facts, rules, or directions.

The United States Constitution

The United States Constitution is the official document that states the rules about how our country is governed. Over 200 years ago, members of twelve states, as well as President George Washington, agreed about what it said. They signed it, making the Constitution of the United States an official document. To this day, the Constitution is the official document our government follows to run the United States.

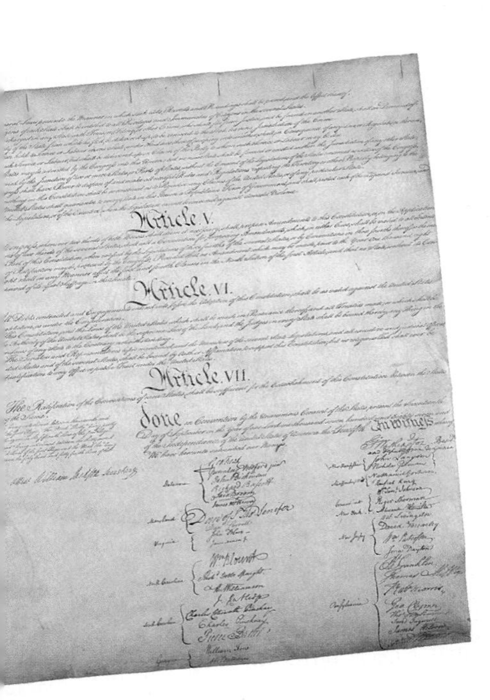

▲ The United States Constitution

1 Learn It

Read the steps below to help you recognize official documents and find information in them.

- Look for a date and a signature. Can you see the date and the signatures on the last page of the Constitution?
- Does the person who signed the document hold a special position of authority? If not, the document is not official.
- Does the document contain any facts, rules, or directions? Some official documents are written to serve as the proof of a fact. Others are written to explain rules or directions.

2 Try It

Read this section from the Bill of Rights of the Constitution. The Bill of Rights was added to the Constitution in 1791.

> *"Congress shall make no law respecting an establishment of religion, or prohibiting the free exercise thereof; or* ***abridging*** *the freedom of speech, or of the press; or the right of the people peaceably to assemble, and to petition the Government for a* ***redress*** *of* ***grievances.****"*

abridge to weaken **redress** to make right **grievance** suffering

- Is the section a collection of facts, rules, or directions?
- How do you know the Constitution of the United States is an official document?

3 Apply It

- Is a textbook or newspaper an official document? Why or why not?
- What can you learn from an official document?

Signing of the Constitution ▼

Citizenship
Points of View

Should There Be Special Rules About Who Can Hold Public Office? 4.5.1

The United States Constitution lists rules about who can hold public office. A person who wants to be elected senator or President must be a United States citizen and have lived in the country for a certain number of years. Read below for three points of view about who can hold public office.

"Experience in having a government job is more important than where a person was born. . . . A person from another country will also have the experience . . . with different rules."

Shona Hemmady
Cupertino, California
From an interview, 2004

"The Constitution sets the rules for who can hold public office . . . for good reasons. . . . These rules have worked very well so far. Citizens who come from other places . . . have many ways to express their opinions."

Adrian Perez
Culver City, California
From an interview, 2004

"A person should have experience in government . . . so they can know this country and learn the rules. You don't need to be born a citizen of the United States to know the rules and laws of the United States."

Arturo Silberstein
San Diego, California
From an interview, 2004

Build Citizenship
Responsibility

1. Do you think requirements for President should be more strict than for a member of Congress?
2. Why do you think the Constitution requires people to be citizens for a certain number of years before they can run for office?
3. What are the qualifications for participating in student government in your school? Are there more qualifications needed if you run for president of the student government?

Think About It
Points of View

1. In what ways do the points of view of Shona Hemmady and Arturo Silberstein agree?
2. What reasons does Adrian Perez give for his opinion?
3. What other points of view might people have on this issue?

Write About It!

Work with a partner to make a list of qualifications you think are needed for a person to run for President. Give reasons for your requirements.

LESSON 2

State Government

FOCUS QUESTION

How does the California state government work?

VOCABULARY

bill
veto

VOCABULARY STRATEGY

MULTIPLE MEANINGS
Bill is a word that has multiple meanings. In this chapter, it means a suggested law. Can you think of two other meanings of the word **bill**?

READING STRATEGY

Sequence Events
Copy the chart below and use it to trace how a bill becomes a law.

Start with Your CALIFORNIA STANDARDS

4.5 Students understand the structures, functions, and powers of the local, state, and federal governments as described in the U.S. Constitution.

4.5.2 Understand the purpose of the California Constitution, its key principles, and its relationship to the U.S. Constitution.
Find out about the California Constitution and its similarities to the United States Constitution. (page 439)

4.5.3 Describe the similarities among federal, state, and local governments.
Learn about the three branches of state government. (pages 440–441)

4.5.4 Explain the structures and functions of state governments, including the roles and responsibilities of their elected officials.
Discover how the state government works and how a bill becomes a law. (pages 440–441)

Senate Chambers in the State Capitol Building ▼

When California became a state in 1850, its constitution had one major difference from the United States Constitution: it outlawed slavery.

California Constitution 4.5.2

The California Constitution, written in 1849, was modeled on the United States Constitution. Both constitutions divide the government into three branches. Both also have a written list of people's rights such as the freedom of speech and religion. Over the years the California Constitution has been slightly modified. Read below Section 1 from the California Constitution.

The United States Constitution applies to all of the citizens of our country. The California Constitution applies only to Californians. Also, the California Constitution is longer. Sections of it explain in detail the specific responsibilities of the state government.

REVIEW Describe the California Constitution. *Main Idea and Details*

Primary Sources

Section 1 of the Declaration of Rights from the California Constitution

"SECTION 1. All people are by nature free and independent and have ***inalienable*** *rights. Among these are enjoying and defending life and* ***liberty, acquiring,*** *possessing, and protecting property, and* ***pursuing*** *and* ***obtaining*** *safety, happiness, and privacy."*

inalienable not surrendered
liberty freedom
acquire to get
pursue to seek
obtain to gain

What are some of the rights that the Declaration of Rights gives Californians?

How State Government Works 4.5.3 4.5.4

California's government is located in Sacramento, the state's capital. Like the United States government, California's government has three branches. Members of the legislative and executive branches work in the state capitol building shown below.

The state legislature consists of the 80-member State Assembly and the 40-member Senate. California citizens elect members of the Assembly for two-year terms and members of the Senate for four-year terms. Assembly members can serve up to three terms and Senators up to two terms.

Making Laws

The United States and California legislatures debate and analyze **bills**. A bill is a suggestion for a new law. For example, in 1996, the state legislature debated a bill limiting the size of many public elementary school classes. Although it would be a costly law to carry out, they voted in favor of the bill.

Once most of the members of both the Assembly and the Senate vote in favor of a bill, it goes to the governor for approval. The governor is the head of the state's executive branch.

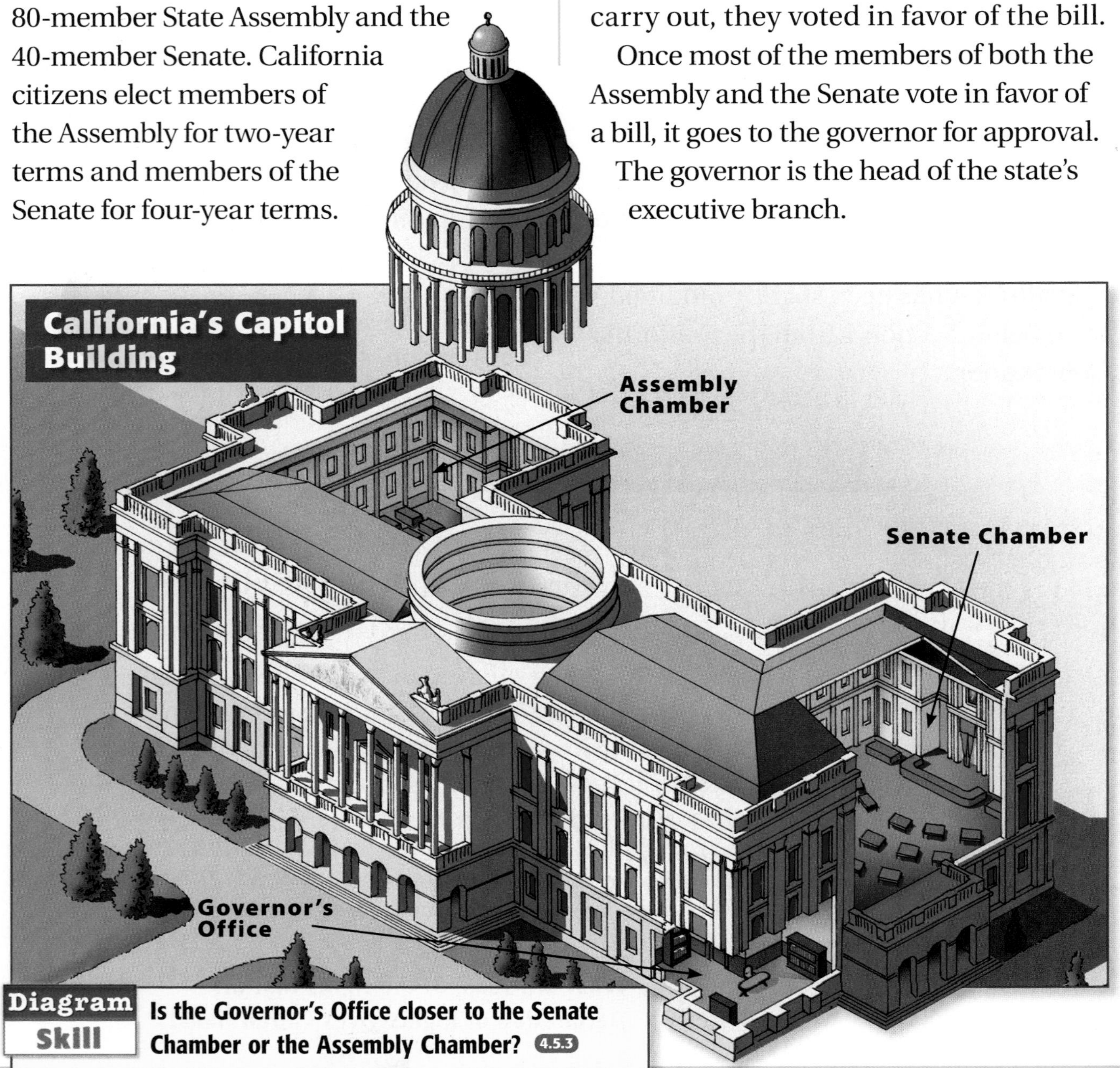

California's Capitol Building

Diagram Skill Is the Governor's Office closer to the Senate Chamber or the Assembly Chamber? 4.5.3

Electing a Governor

California citizens elect governors to serve up to two four-year terms. The governor has the power to approve new laws by signing the bill. The governor can also **veto** the bill. A veto is the power of the executive branch to reject a bill that has been passed by the legislature. A veto sends the bill back to the legislature.

The legislative branch then has the power to call a new vote on the bill. The bill will become a law if two-thirds of the Assembly and Senate vote for it.

In 1996, Governor Pete Wilson signed the Class Size Reduction Program into law. It granted one billion dollars in the first year, and one and a half billion each year after that, to pay for more classrooms and teachers.

In 1951, the legislature voted to make "I Love You, California," our state song. You can sing along with it on page 442.

The judicial branch of the state government runs California's court system. It is similar to the federal judicial branch, except that it is responsible for upholding state law, not federal law.

The highest court in California is the California Supreme Court. The governor appoints each of its seven judges. Citizens then approve the judges in the next general election.

REVIEW How is California's state government similar to the federal government? *Compare and Contrast*

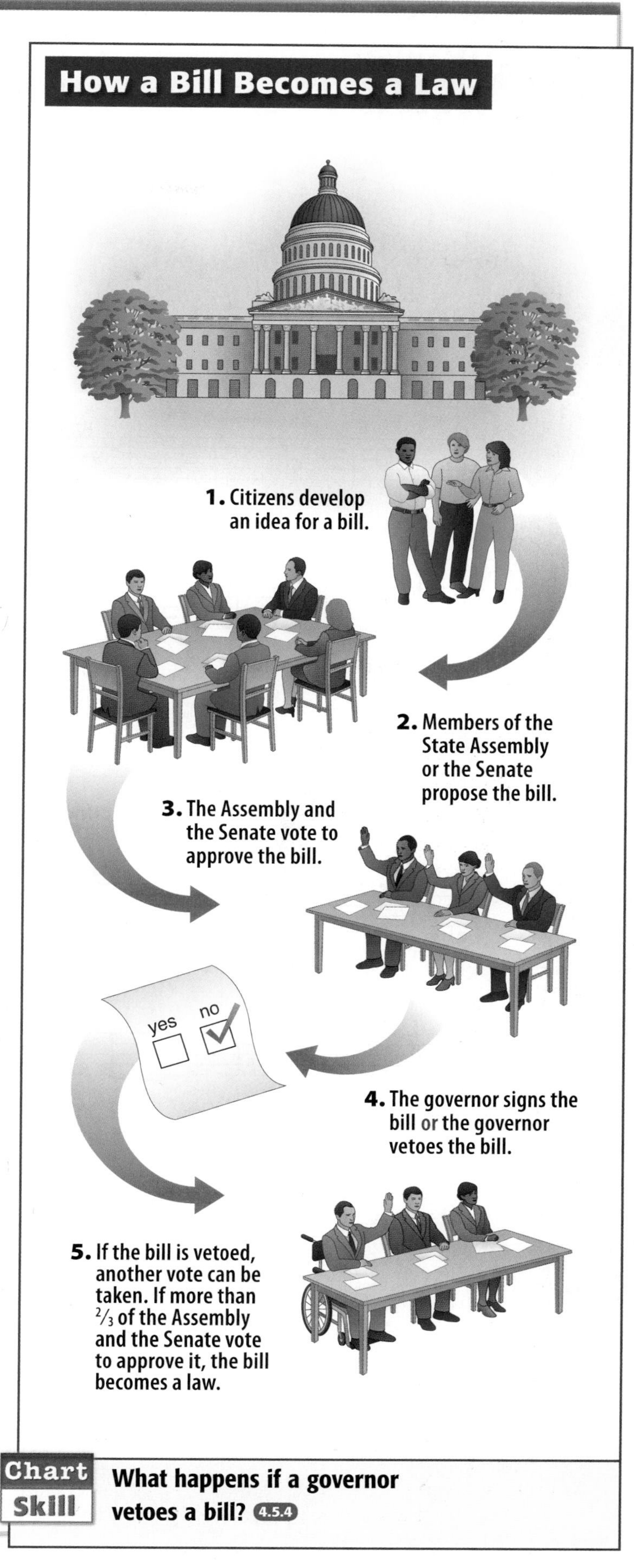

Chart Skill **What happens if a governor vetoes a bill?** 4.5.4

Primary Sources

I Love You, California

Music by A. F. Frankenstein
Words by F. B. Silverwood

Why do you think California chose "I Love You, California" to be the state song?

Recall 2003 4.5.4

As you read in Chapter 10, the California Constitution allows for a recall of elected officials. In 2003, Governor Gray Davis became the first California governor ever to face a recall election. Many voters felt he governed poorly during a time of electricity shortage in 2001. The state government went into heavy debt.

To force a recall election, about a million Californian voters must sign a petition to ask for a recall vote. If this happens, a recall election is held.

On October 7, 2003, voters had two questions to answer. First, should Governor Davis be recalled from office? Second, if he is recalled, who should replace him?

In the end, a majority of voters chose to recall Governor Davis. Arnold Schwarzenegger was elected to replace him. On November 17, 2003, Arnold Schwarzenegger was sworn in as California's new governor.

REVIEW What role did California citizens play in the recall of 2003? *Summarize*

What You Learned

4.5.2 The California Constitution, modeled on the United States Constitution, gives Californians power over the state government. It also includes a written list of citizen's rights.

4.5.3 4.5.4 California's state government has three branches: legislative, executive, and judicial.

4.5.4 In 2003, Californians recalled Governor Gray Davis from office and replaced him with Governor Arnold Schwarzenegger.

Lesson Review

1. **Focus Question** How does the California state government work? (4.5)
2. **Vocabulary** Write one sentence for each vocabulary word. (4.5)
   bill **veto**
3. **Government** Describe the roles of the executive, legislative, and judicial branches in California's government. (4.5.3, 4.5.4)
4. **Critical Thinking** **Compare and Contrast** How are the California Constitution and United States Constitution similar and different? (4.5.2)
5. **Reading Strategy** **Sequence Events** Reread "Recall 2003." What was the sequence of events that led to Arnold Schwarzenegger becoming governor? (4.5.4, ELA R2.1)
6. **Write about THE BIG IDEA** Write about a bill that you want to suggest to the state legislature. Give reasons why you want this bill to become a law. (4.5.3, ELA W2.1)
7. **Link to Music** Research to find the complete lyrics to California's state song, "I Love You, California." Read or sing the lyrics. Then, write a new verse for the song. (4.5.3, 4.5.4)

As California's capital, Sacramento has played an important part in our state history. You can see, hear, and touch much of that history when you visit Sacramento today.

◀ ❶ Sutter's Fort

Visit the spot where Sacramento was born. Johann Sutter built Sutter's Fort in 1839. When gold was discovered in the nearby hills, it caused a rush of settlement.

❷ Governor's Mansion

For more than sixty years, California's governors lived in this home, bought in 1903. It has over 30 rooms, nine bathrooms, fine Persian carpets, and a swimming pool. The last governor to live here, Ronald Reagan, moved out in 1967. ▼

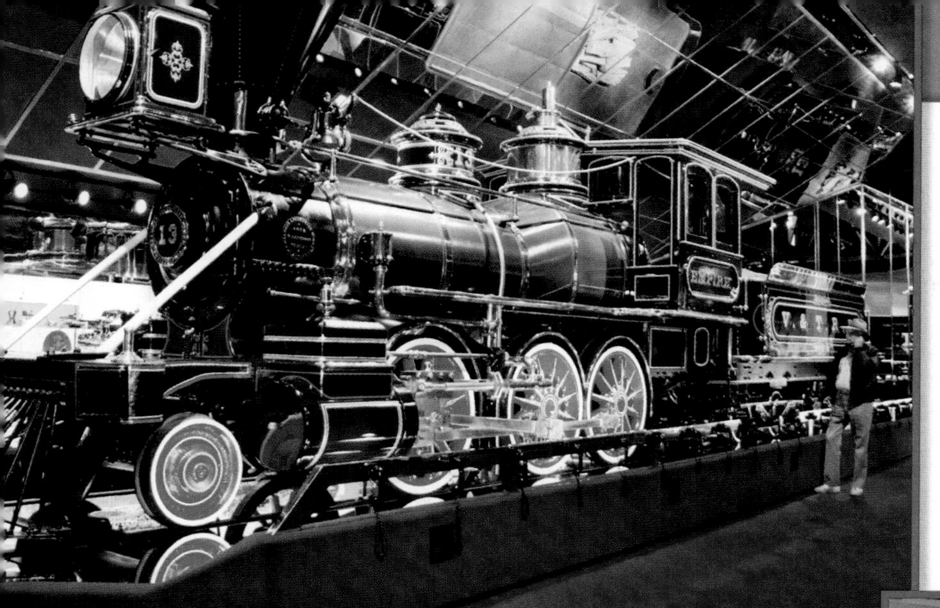

❹ California State History Museum

What did California look like 1,000 years ago? What did immigrants carry in their pockets? What does it feel like to stand under Hollywood's lights? At the museum, you can experience California's history through sight, sound, and touch. ▼

▲ ❸ California State Railroad Museum

All aboard to learn about the history of trains. In the late 1800s through the 1900s, railroads brought millions of people to California. Many came to Sacramento, starting point for the transcontinental railroad. At the Railroad Museum, you can walk through trains, look at huge displays of model trains, and even ride a steam locomotive!

ACTIVITY

Use the Internet to learn more about one of the locations on these pages. Then write a paragraph about which place you would like to visit and why.

LOG ON For more about Sacramento, visit:

www.macmillanmh.com/ss/ca/fieldtrips

FOCUS QUESTION

How do local governments work?

VOCABULARY

budget
city council
mayor
county
tribal government

VOCABULARY STRATEGY

ROOT WORDS The word **council** means to give advice. A **city council** advises the city leaders on how best to run the city. What other people give advice?

READING STRATEGY

Identify Main Idea and Details
Describe the main purpose of local government and give details about what it does.

Local Government

Start with Your CALIFORNIA STANDARDS

4.5 Students understand the structures, functions, and powers of the local, state, and federal governments as described in the U.S. Constitution.

4.5.3 Describe the similarities and differences among federal, state, and local governments.

Learn about the services local governments provide for Californians. (Begins on page 447)

4.5.5 Describe the components of California's governance structure.

Learn about different kinds of local governments. (Begins on page 448)

▼ San Francisco's City Hall

If the hoop falls off the backboard at the local public basketball court, who should you talk to about getting it fixed? Or, if some community members decide to start a local youth club that meets at the town hall, where would they get permission?

Local Government and You 4.5.3

The answer to both of the questions above is local government. It is the job of local government to maintain public property and review public meeting places. Local government will fix the hoop so you can play again, and it will find a place where people might meet.

Local Government Services

Local governments provide services for citizens who live in the area. They run libraries, museums, stadiums, and public parks. Local governments hold fairs and parades. They also run the police and fire departments, public transportation, road maintenance, and garbage and recycling pick up.

Local governments charge a fee for some of these services, but they also collect taxes. Cities decide how to spend this money by making a **budget**. A budget is a plan for spending money.

The chart on this page explains how most local governments spend money.

REVIEW What are some services local governments provide? *Main Idea and Details*

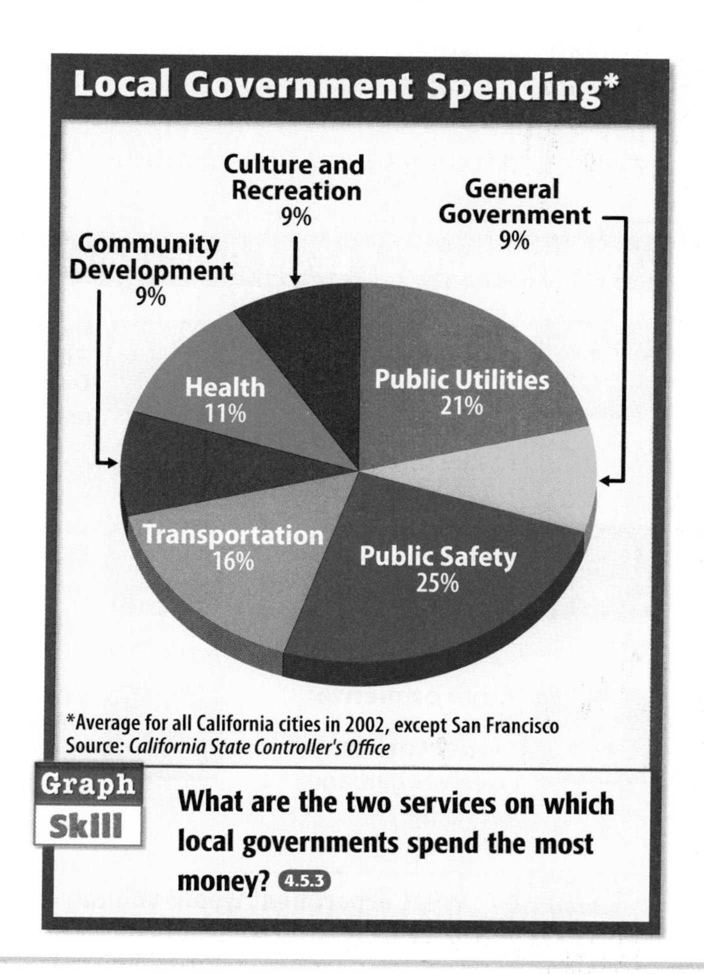

*Average for all California cities in 2002, except San Francisco
Source: *California State Controller's Office*

Graph Skill **What are the two services on which local governments spend the most money?** 4.5.3

How Local Government Works 4.5.3 4.5.5

Most cities and towns are governed by **city councils**. A city council is like the legislative branch of a city. It makes laws for the city. Most city councils have an odd number of members, usually 5, 7, or 9. This is so when a vote is called it will not end in a tie.

Council members are elected by citizens. In most California cities, the city council will usually hire a city manager to run the day-to-day affairs of the city. The city manager's job is to make sure all the city's departments run smoothly. Look at the chart on this page to learn about the many departments of a local government and what they do.

The city council meets about once a week to discuss new laws and new projects. The members will talk about the different departments of the city. The city manager attends these meetings and updates the council about any changes or problems.

▲ Nora Campos, San José Council Member

In many cities, citizens elect a **mayor** to be the head of the local government. In San Francisco, for example, the mayor appoints, or picks, people to run city departments.

In 2004, San Francisco Mayor Gavin Newsom appointed policewoman Heather Fong to be the new chief of San Francisco's police department. Fong is the first Asian American woman to lead a big city police department.

Departments of Local Government

Fire Department
provides ambulance, fire, and rescue services

Parks and Recreation Department
maintains parks

Planning Department
plans for city projects

Police Department
keeps citizens safe

Public Health Department
helps citizens fight disease

Building Inspection Department
grants permits for new buildings, inspects plans

Environmental Services Department
oversees garbage, recycling

Finance Department
collects taxes, handles city money

Maintenance Department
repairs streets, signs, traffic lights

Main St.

Chart Skill **What department would you call if your garbage was not picked up?** 4.5.3

▲ Beverly Hills City Council

Most of California's cities are not as large as San Francisco. In many smaller cities, like Chico, the mayor is not elected directly by voters. Instead, the mayor is chosen by the city council from among its members. The mayor then serves as the head of the city council.

County Government

Every city and town in California is part of a larger **county**. A county is one of the sections into which a state is divided. California has 58 counties. Look at the map on page R15 to see California's counties.

Counties are governed by boards of supervisors. The board usually has five members, each of whom represents a different district in the county.

A county will provide many of the services of a local government. One important difference is that a county is responsible for hospitals and courts. Courts make up the judicial branch of a local government.

Tribal Government

Another kind of local government is **tribal government**. There are over 100 Native American reservations and rancherias in California. Each has its own tribal government.

Like a city government, a tribal government is responsible for a wide range of services. They provide police, fire, and environmental protection. They operate schools, offer health care, and run job assistance programs.

REVIEW How are local governments and tribal governments similar?
Compare and Contrast

Campo Reservation Fire Department ▼

Other Districts

Local governments do not always provide all the services people need. Sometimes a district is formed to manage a service that falls outside a local government's responsibility. There are over 2,000 special districts in California, each run by a board of directors. Special taxes pay for special districts. You are very familiar with one service run by a special district—your school district.

California is divided into hundreds of school districts. Each district is run by a school board. The members of the school board work with the state's education department to make decisions about public education. California has the largest school system of any state in our nation. Nearly 6.5 million students attend public school in California.

REVIEW How does California run its school system? *Main Idea and Details*

What You Learned

4.5.3 Local governments provide many services to citizens. It pays for these services by collecting taxes and fees and making a budget.

4.5.3 4.5.5 School districts, cities and towns with a city council and a mayor, counties, and tribal governments are all different kinds of local governments.

Lesson Review

1. **Focus Question** How do local governments work? 4.5.5
2. **Vocabulary** Write one sentence for each vocabulary term. 4.5.3 4.5.5
   budget
   city council
   county
   mayor
   tribal government
3. **Government** Write a letter to a department of your local government telling how you like or dislike their service. 4.5.5
4. **Critical Thinking** **Problem Solving** What are some things a city council has to pay for when it makes a budget? 4.5.3
5. **Reading Strategy** **Identify Main Idea and Details** Describe the main idea and give supporting details about what each of the following types of governments do: 4.5.3 ELA R2.1
   tribal government
   county
   city council

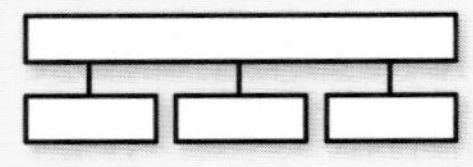

6. **Write about** THE BIG IDEA Write about some of the services your local government provides the community. 4.5.3 ELA W2.1
7. **Link to Health** Local governments work hard to provide a safe and healthy environment for people. Make a list of things that your local government has done to help keep residents healthy. 4.5.5

Biography
Focus on Leadership

4.5.5

Heather Fong 1956–

San Francisco Chief of Police Heather Fong grew up on the edge of San Francisco's Chinatown. At home the family spoke a southern Chinese dialect called Lung Do (YUNG DOW). At school Fong learned to speak Cantonese and English.

An officer from the San Francisco Police Department came to speak to Fong's high school class about police work. Fong was so excited by the talk that she signed up for classes to learn more. Fong was the first Chinese American woman to become an officer with the force.

While still in training, Fong helped solve an important case. She also translated audiotapes from Cantonese into English for the police.

In 1979, Heather Fong became an instructor at the Police Academy. Her ability to stay cool and thoughtful in the middle of difficult situations helped her advance. In 1994, Fong was promoted to lieutenant. In 2004, Fong was appointed Chief of Police. Fong once said:

"I want to assure everyone that . . . the San Francisco Police Department [is] on duty 24 hours a day, seven days a week."

Write About It! **What skills has Heather Fong used as a police officer?**

For more about Heather Fong visit:

www.macmillanmh.com/ca/ss/bios

The Life of Heather Fong

1955 — 1965 — 1975 — 1985 — 1995 — 2005

- **1956** Born in San Francisco
- **1973** Joins cadet academy
- **1977** Graduates from Police Academy
- **1994** Promoted to lieutenant
- **2004** Appointed Chief of the San Francisco Police Department

Chapter Review

Vocabulary Review

Copy the sentences below on a separate sheet of paper. Use the list of vocabulary words to fill in the blanks.

bill	**democracy**
citizen	**mayor**

1. A proposal for a new law is called a ________ .
4.5.3

2. A ________ is a government that is run by its people.
4.5

3. A ________ is a member of a country, either by birth or by law.
4.5

4. A ________ is the head of the local city government.
4.5.5

5. Test Preparation The governor has the power to approve a new law or ________ it.
4.5.4

A. **budget** **C.** **county**
B. **veto** **D.** **tax**

Comprehension Check

6. Name three rights of all Americans.
4.5

7. Name three responsibilities of all Americans over the age of 18.
4.5

8. When was the California constitution written?
4.5.2

9. Where is California's state government located?
4.5.4

10. Name three services that local governments provide.
4.5.3

11. Critical Thinking How is the California Constitution the same as the United States Constitution? How is it different?
4.5.2

12. Critical Thinking Why do you think it is important for citizens to have responsibilities along with their rights?
4.5.1

Use the Time Line

Use the time line below to answer each question.

13. Which event happened in 2003?
4.5.4

14. Did the state government pass a law to help reduce pollution before or after the energy crisis?
4.5.4

2001	2002	2003	2004
2001 California faces an energy crisis	**2002** Law passed to help reduce pollution in California	**2003** Arnold Schwarzenegger elected governor of California	**2004** Heather Fong becomes San Francisco's Chief of Police

Skills Check

Write a complete sentence to answer each question.

Official Documents

15. What do official documents often describe? (4.5)

16. Why is an official document a primary source? (4.5)

17. **Test Preparation** The California constitution is an ________ . (4.5.2)

18. **Test Preparation** A ________ is a type of official document. (4.5)

CONSTITUTION
of the
STATE of CALIFORNIA.
Article I.
Declaration of Rights
Section 1.

Hands-on Activity

19. **Make a Poster** Work in groups to create a poster that answers this question: (4.5.3)

What are the three branches of California's state government?

Write About History

20. **Expository** Write a paragraph that summarizes what happened during the recall election of 2003. (4.5, ELA W2.1)

For help with the process of writing, visit

www.macmillanmh.com/ss/ca/writing

Unit Review and Test Prep

Comprehension and Critical Thinking Check

Write one or more sentences to answer each question.

1. Why did Robert Semple want to create a system of **public education**? (4.4.8)
2. What are some changes that **labor unions** brought about for California workers in the 1960s? (4.4)
3. What are some ways that companies in California use **nanotechnology**? (4.4.6)
4. Who runs the government in a **democracy**? (4.5)
5. Which officials are elected to the **legislative branch** of our state government? (4.5.1)
6. Who runs the **executive** branch of our state government? (4.5.1)
7. What are the responsibilities of the **judicial** branch of our state government? (4.5.1)
8. How are members of a **city council** chosen? (4.5.5)
9. Critical Thinking How did the Unruh **Civil Rights** Act affect life in California? (4.4)
10. Critical Thinking How is a **mayor's** job similar to a governor's job? How is it different? (4.5.3)

Reading Social Studies Check

Identify Cause and Effect

Copy this graphic organizer. Recall what you learned about new technology in Chapter 11. Use the graphic organizer to help you figure out what effects new technologies have. (4.4.8) (ELA W2.1)

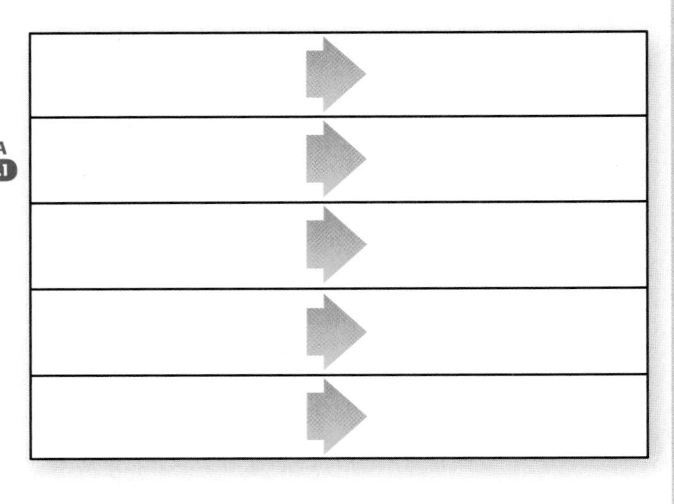

11. How do you know what is a cause and what is an effect? (ELA W2.1)
12. What causes people to develop new technologies? (ELA W2.1)
13. What are some effects of new technologies? (ELA W2.1)

Test Preparation

Read the paragraphs. Then answer the questions.

In the early 1900s the area now known as Silicon Valley was filled with farms and fruit orchards. Today this part of Northern California looks very different. Instead of farm fields you can find offices for several different kinds of technology businesses. Many companies in Silicon Valley manufacture computers and microchips. They also create new kinds of software and other products.

All of these Silicon Valley businesses have completely changed the computer industry. They have helped make computers cheaper, smaller, and easier to use. In the past, computers were giant machines that only big businesses could afford to use. Today you can find computers in homes, libraries, schools, and many other places because of Silicon Valley.

14. Which of the following statements is a detail from the passage?
4.4.6

A It is difficult to find work in Silicon Valley.

B Silicon Valley has several different kinds of technology businesses.

C Companies in Silicon Valley employ about half a million workers.

D Silicon Valley is located near San Francisco.

15. What is the main idea of this passage?
4.4.6

A Silicon Valley used to be a farming area.

B Companies in Silicon Valley have had a big effect on the computer industry.

C Hardly anyone uses computers today.

D Computers used to be much bigger in the past.

Write About History

16. Letter Suppose that you are a member of the state legislature in 1959. Write a letter to your state legislature that explains why you support the Unruh Civil Rights Act.
ELA W2.1

17. Expository Write a short essay that explains how a bill becomes a law in our state government.
ELA W2.3

18. Summary Think about why California has become strong in many kinds of art. Write a one paragraph summary of your ideas.
ELA W2.4

For help with the process of writing, visit:

www.macmillanmh.com/ss/ca/writing

What causes a society to grow?

Write About the Big Idea ELA W2.3 ELA W1.2

A Report

Think about all the changes you read about in Unit 5. Then complete the graphic organizer. Add causes, or reasons, for each effect.

Use information from your graphic organizer and other sources to write a report of several paragraphs. Explain some reasons why California grew.

Cause		Effect
Public education		

Write a Report

1. Plan

- Choose one cause and effect to write about.
- Use the Internet to find more information about your topic. Do a Web search. Remember that your purpose is to give information.

2. Write a First Draft

- In your first paragraph introduce your topic.
- Add paragraphs that give facts, details, and examples of what caused California's growth.
- In your final paragraph write a conclusion.

3. Revise and Proofread

- Read your report. Be sure your sentences and paragraphs all tell about your topic.
- Check that your first paragraph makes a good introduction. Edit your final paragraph to make a good summary of your reasons.
- Proofread your report. Did you indent all your paragraphs?
- Rewrite your report neatly before handing it in to your teacher.

ACTIVITY

Speak About the Big Idea ELA LS2.2

A Newscast

Suppose you are a television reporter. You will tell about something that caused California to grow. Use your graphic organizer or your report for ideas.

Prepare Work with a partner. You and your partner will be "co-anchors" of a nightly news program. Rehearse your presentation of your topic.

Present Each pair of broadcasters will report on the news of changes in California. Be sure to report on what each change is and what caused the change. You might want to express an opinion about whether the change has been good or bad for California. Be sure it is clear to your listeners when you are giving your own opinion.

For help with the Big Idea activity, visit:

www.macmillanmh.com/ss/ca/launchpad

Read More About the Big Idea

Farmworker's Friend

David Collins Find out about the life of the legendary founder of the United Farm Workers.

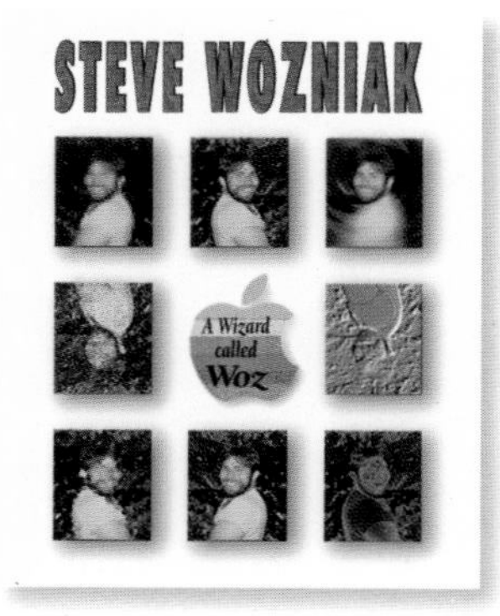

Steve Wozniak

Rebecca Gold Read the life story of the computer whiz who founded Apple.

The Capital That Couldn't Stay Put

June Oxford Learn about the search for a site for the capital during the early days of California's statehood.

Reference Section

The Reference Section has many parts, each with a different type of information. Use this section to look up people, places, and events as you study.

UNITED STATES: Political

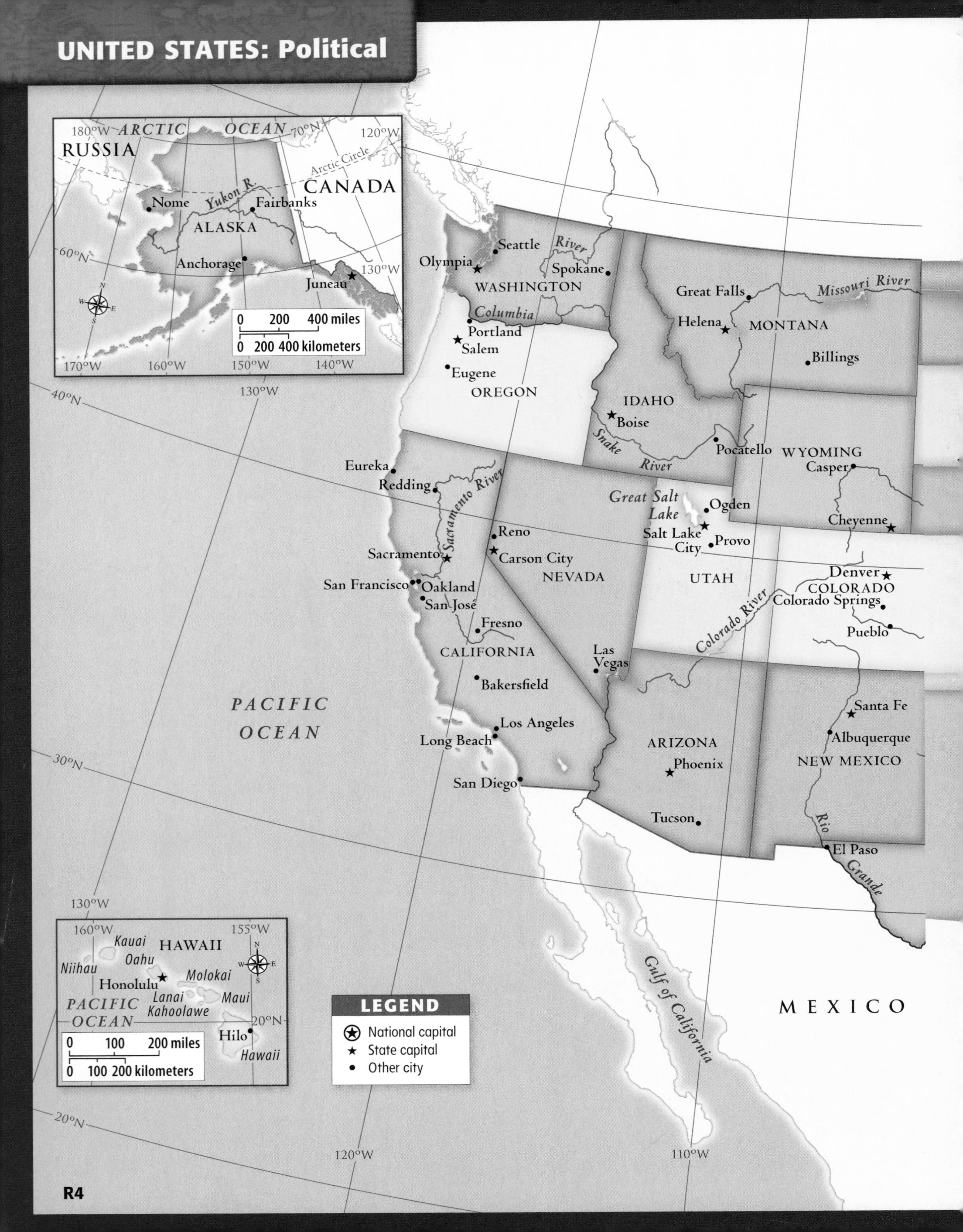

CANADA
Lake Superior
Lake Michigan
Lake Huron
Lake Ontario
Lake Erie
NORTH DAKOTA
Grand Forks
Fargo
Bismarck
MINNESOTA
Duluth
St. Paul
Minneapolis
SOUTH DAKOTA
Pierre
Sioux Falls
WISCONSIN
Green Bay
Milwaukee
Madison
MICHIGAN
Grand Rapids
Lansing
Detroit
NEBRASKA
Omaha
Lincoln
Platte River
Missouri River
IOWA
Cedar Rapids
Des Moines
Davenport
ILLINOIS
Chicago
Springfield
INDIANA
Gary
Indianapolis
OHIO
Toledo
Cleveland
Columbus
Cincinnati
KANSAS
Kansas City
Topeka
Wichita
MISSOURI
Kansas City
St. Louis
Jefferson City
Evansville
Ohio River
KENTUCKY
Louisville
Frankfort
WEST VIRGINIA
Charleston
VIRGINIA
Richmond
Norfolk
NEW YORK
Buffalo
Albany
New York
PENNSYLVANIA
Harrisburg
Pittsburgh
Philadelphia
NEW JERSEY
Newark
Trenton
DELAWARE
Dover
MARYLAND
Baltimore
Annapolis
Washington, D.C.
NEW HAMPSHIRE
VERMONT
Montpelier
Concord
MAINE
Augusta
Portland
MASSACHUSETTS
Boston
RHODE ISLAND
Providence
CONNECTICUT
Hartford
OKLAHOMA
Oklahoma City
Tulsa
Arkansas River
ARKANSAS
Fort Smith
Little Rock
Mississippi River
TENNESSEE
Nashville
Memphis
Knoxville
Tennessee River
NORTH CAROLINA
Raleigh
Charlotte
SOUTH CAROLINA
Columbia
Charleston
GEORGIA
Atlanta
Columbus
Savannah
ALABAMA
Birmingham
Montgomery
Mobile
MISSISSIPPI
Jackson
Biloxi
LOUISIANA
Shreveport
Baton Rouge
New Orleans
TEXAS
Red River
Dallas
Fort Worth
Brazos River
Colorado River
Austin
Houston
San Antonio
Laredo
Corpus Christi
FLORIDA
Jacksonville
Tallahassee
Orlando
Tampa
Miami
Gulf of Mexico
ATLANTIC OCEAN
THE BAHAMAS
CUBA
50°N
40°N
30°N
70°W
80°W
90°W
100°W
0 200 400 miles
0 200 400 kilometers
N
S
E
W

UNITED STATES: Physical

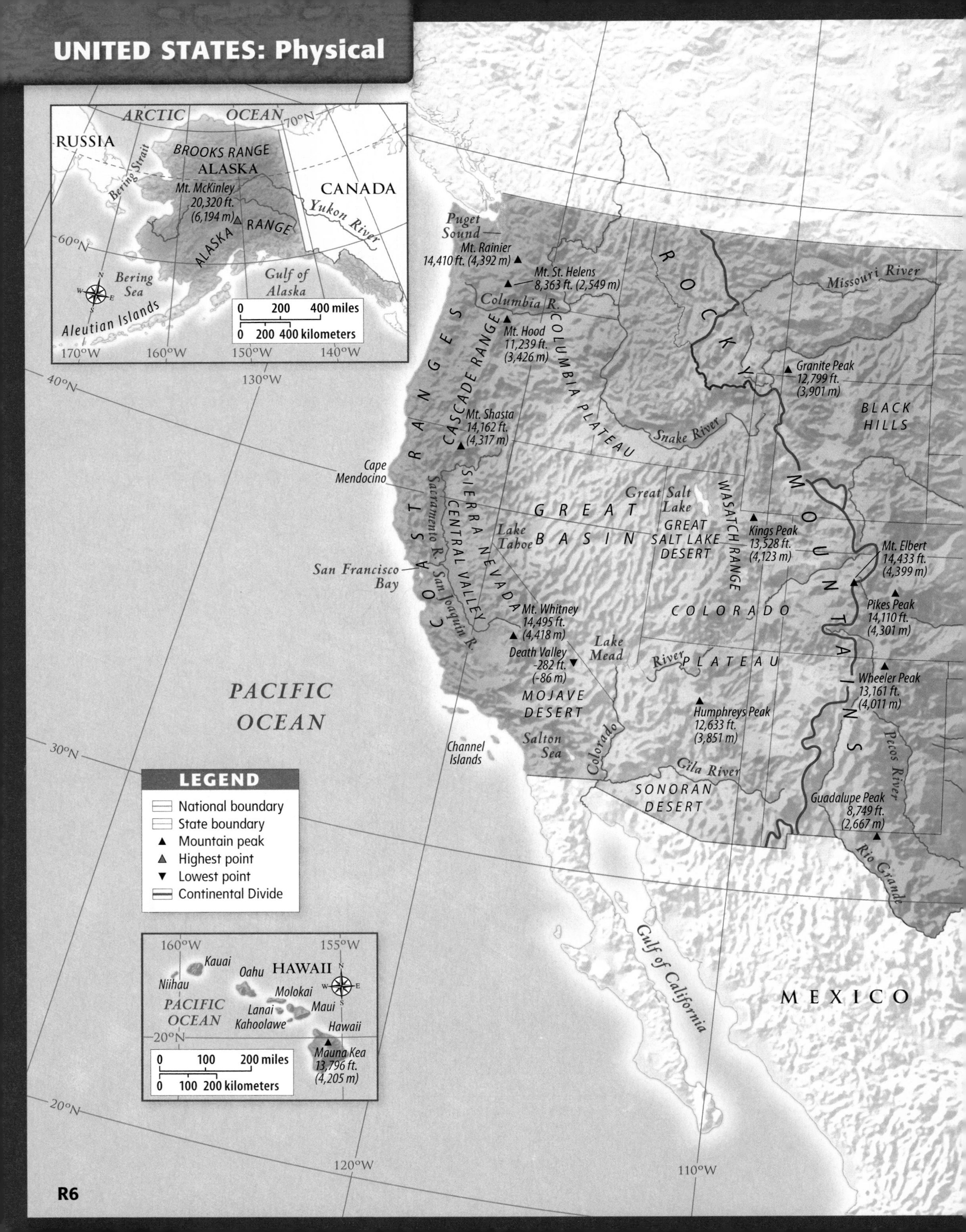

0
200
400 miles
0
200
400 kilometers
CANADA
GREAT PLAINS
GREAT LAKES
Lake Superior
Lake Michigan
Lake Huron
Lake Ontario
Lake Erie
St. Lawrence River
MESABI RANGE
Mississippi River
Missouri River
Platte River
CENTRAL PLAINS
WHITE MTS.
Mt. Washington 6,288 ft. (1,917 m)
GREEN MTS.
ADIRONDACK MTS.
Hudson R.
Susquehanna R.
Cape Cod
Long Island
40°N
ALLEGHENY PLATEAU
ALLEGHENY MTS.
APPALACHIAN MOUNTAINS
Delaware Bay
Potomac River
Chesapeake Bay
Ohio River
Wabash River
Arkansas River
INTERIOR PLAINS
OZARK PLATEAU
Tennessee River
Mt. Mitchell 6,684 ft. (2,037 m)
PIEDMONT
ATLANTIC COASTAL PLAIN
Cape Hatteras
ATLANTIC OCEAN
OUACHITA MOUNTAINS
Red River
Mississippi River
Alabama River
Chattahoochee River
Savannah River
30°N
Brazos River
Colorado River
EDWARDS PLATEAU
GULF COASTAL PLAIN
Mobile Bay
Galveston Bay
Mississippi River Delta
Lake Okeechobee
THE BAHAMAS
Gulf of Mexico
N
W
E
S
Florida Keys
Straits of Florida
CUBA
90°W
80°W
20°N

THE 50 UNITED STATES

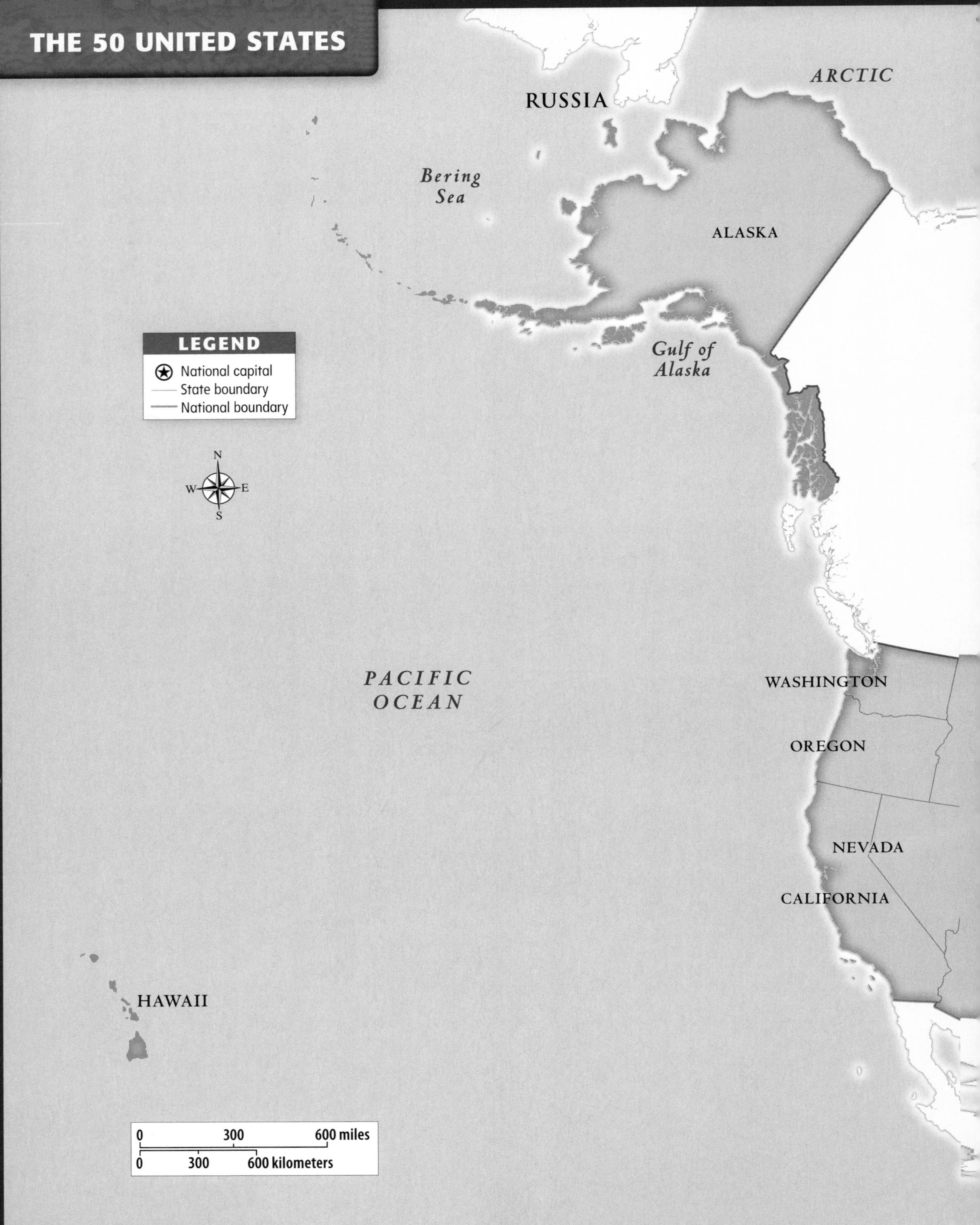

OCEAN
Greenland
(Denmark)
Labrador
Sea
Hudson
Bay
CANADA
Great
Lakes
NEW
HAMPSHIRE
VERMONT
MAINE
MONTANA
NORTH
DAKOTA
MINNESOTA
MICHIGAN
WISCONSIN
NEW
YORK
MASSACHUSETTS
IDAHO
SOUTH
DAKOTA
RHODE ISLAND
CONNECTICUT
WYOMING
PENNSYLVANIA
NEW JERSEY
IOWA
NEBRASKA
OHIO
DELAWARE
INDIANA
MARYLAND
UTAH
ILLINOIS
WEST
VIRGINIA
Washington, D.C.
COLORADO
KANSAS
VIRGINIA
KENTUCKY
MISSOURI
NORTH
CAROLINA
TENNESSEE
ARIZONA
ARKANSAS
OKLAHOMA
SOUTH
CAROLINA
ATLANTIC
OCEAN
NEW
MEXICO
MISSISSIPPI
GEORGIA
ALABAMA
TEXAS
LOUISIANA
FLORIDA
THE
BAHAMAS
Gulf of
Mexico
MEXICO
CUBA

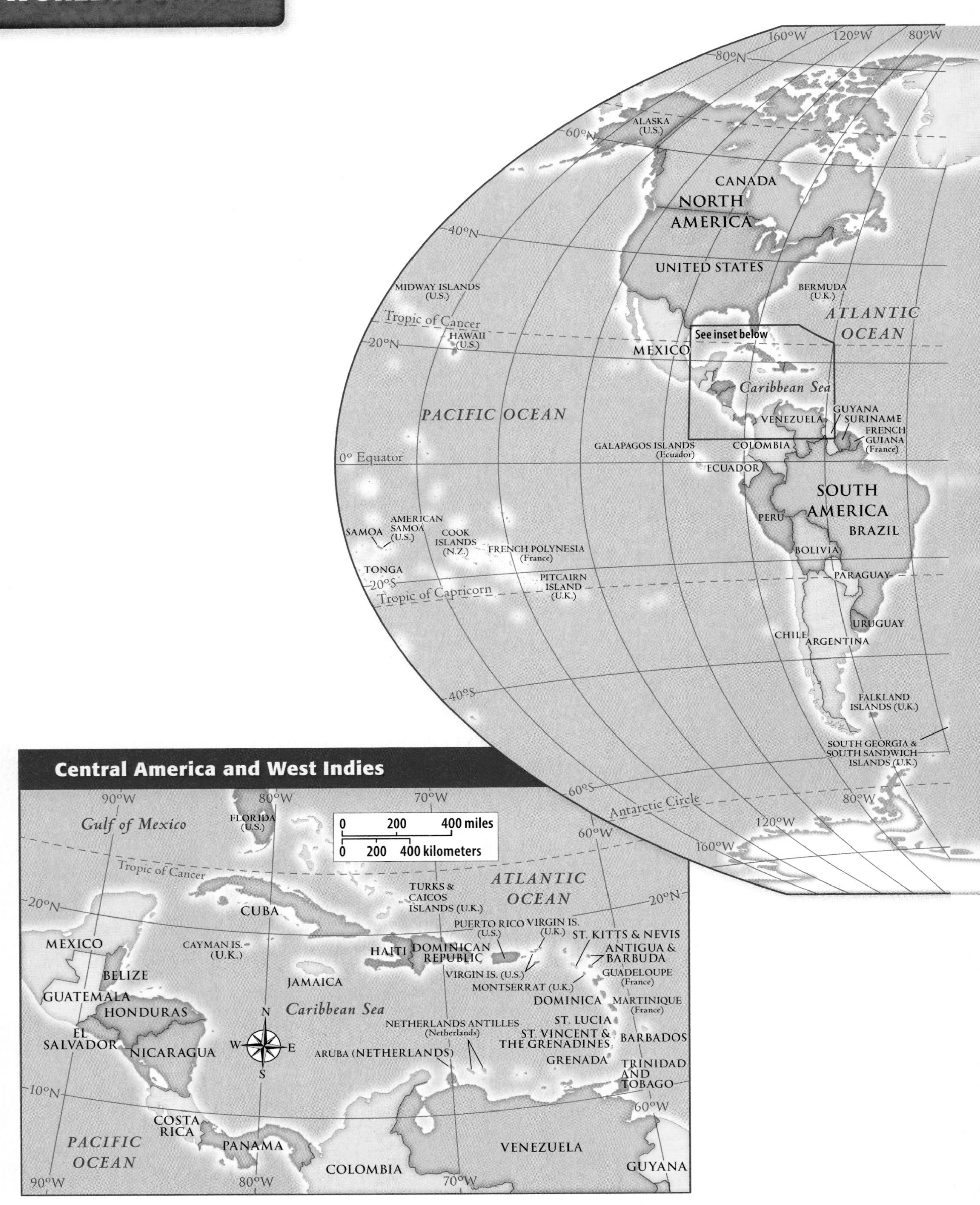
160°W
120°W
80°W
80°N
60°N
40°N
20°N
0° Equator
20°S
40°S
60°S
Tropic of Cancer
Tropic of Capricorn
Antarctic Circle
ALASKA (U.S.)
CANADA
NORTH AMERICA
UNITED STATES
MIDWAY ISLANDS (U.S.)
HAWAII (U.S.)
BERMUDA (U.K.)
ATLANTIC OCEAN
See inset below
MEXICO
Caribbean Sea
PACIFIC OCEAN
GUYANA
SURINAME
FRENCH GUIANA (France)
VENEZUELA
COLOMBIA
GALAPAGOS ISLANDS (Ecuador)
ECUADOR
SOUTH AMERICA
PERU
BRAZIL
BOLIVIA
PARAGUAY
URUGUAY
CHILE
ARGENTINA
FALKLAND ISLANDS (U.K.)
SOUTH GEORGIA & SOUTH SANDWICH ISLANDS (U.K.)
SAMOA
AMERICAN SAMOA (U.S.)
COOK ISLANDS (N.Z.)
FRENCH POLYNESIA (France)
TONGA
PITCAIRN ISLAND (U.K.)
Central America and West Indies
90°W
80°W
70°W
60°W
20°N
10°N
Gulf of Mexico
FLORIDA (U.S.)
0 200 400 miles
0 200 400 kilometers
Tropic of Cancer
ATLANTIC OCEAN
TURKS & CAICOS ISLANDS (U.K.)
CUBA
MEXICO
CAYMAN IS. (U.K.)
HAITI
DOMINICAN REPUBLIC
PUERTO RICO (U.S.)
VIRGIN IS. (U.K.)
VIRGIN IS. (U.S.)
ST. KITTS & NEVIS
ANTIGUA & BARBUDA
GUADELOUPE (France)
MONTSERRAT (U.K.)
BELIZE
GUATEMALA
HONDURAS
JAMAICA
Caribbean Sea
DOMINICA
MARTINIQUE (France)
ST. LUCIA
NETHERLANDS ANTILLES (Netherlands)
ST. VINCENT & THE GRENADINES
BARBADOS
EL SALVADOR
NICARAGUA
ARUBA (NETHERLANDS)
GRENADA
TRINIDAD AND TOBAGO
N
E
S
W
COSTA RICA
PANAMA
PACIFIC OCEAN
VENEZUELA
COLOMBIA
GUYANA

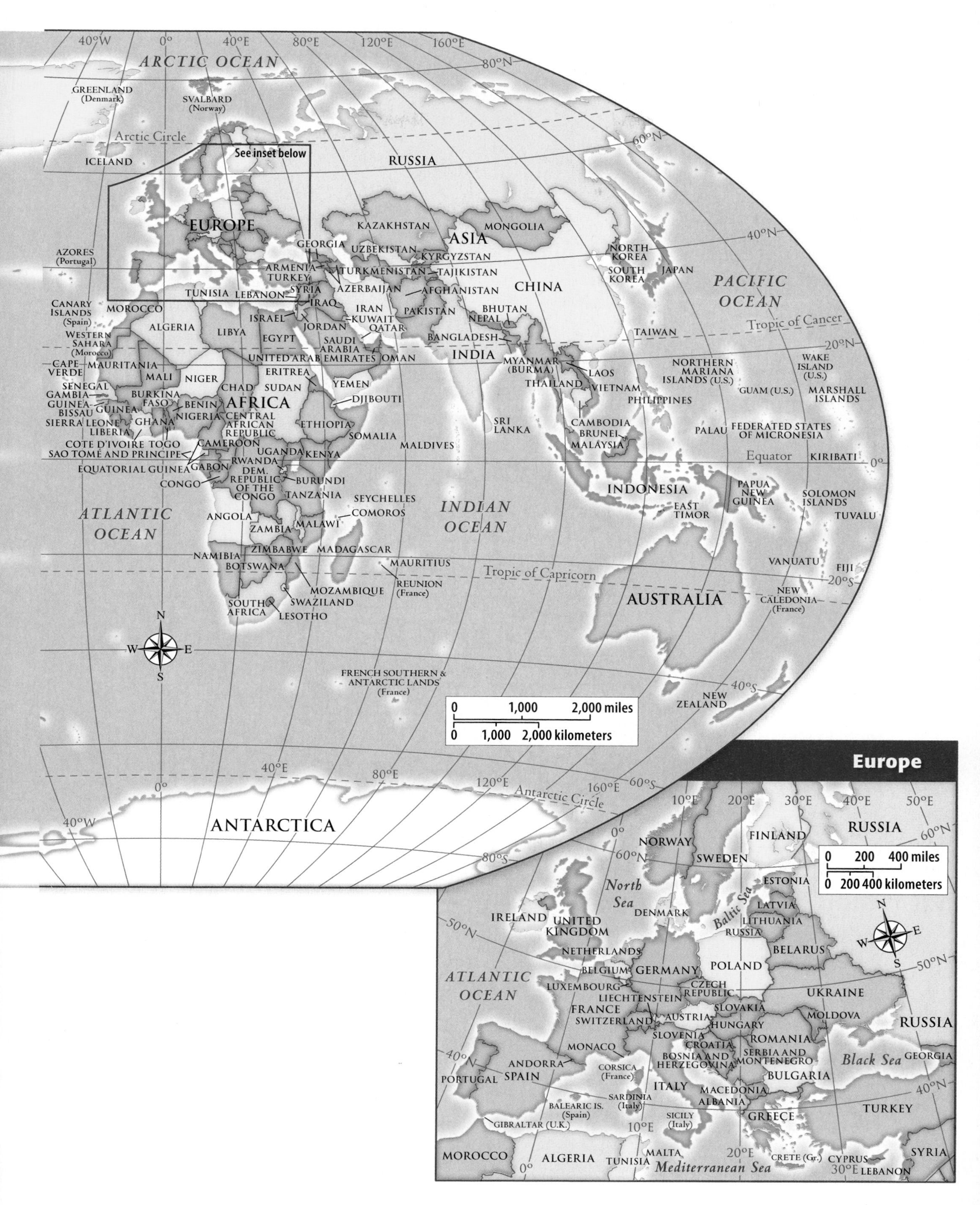

ARCTIC OCEAN
GREENLAND (Denmark)
SVALBARD (Norway)
Arctic Circle
See inset below
ICELAND
RUSSIA
EUROPE
KAZAKHSTAN
ASIA
MONGOLIA
AZORES (Portugal)
GEORGIA
UZBEKISTAN
KYRGYZSTAN
NORTH KOREA
SOUTH KOREA
JAPAN
ARMENIA
TURKEY
TURKMENISTAN
TAJIKISTAN
SYRIA
AZERBAIJAN
AFGHANISTAN
CHINA
PACIFIC OCEAN
TUNISIA
LEBANON
IRAQ
CANARY ISLANDS (Spain)
MOROCCO
IRAN
PAKISTAN
BHUTAN
NEPAL
ISRAEL
KUWAIT
ALGERIA
LIBYA
JORDAN
QATAR
Tropic of Cancer
WESTERN SAHARA (Morocco)
EGYPT
SAUDI ARABIA
BANGLADESH
TAIWAN
UNITED ARAB EMIRATES
OMAN
INDIA
CAPE VERDE
MAURITANIA
MYANMAR (BURMA)
LAOS
NORTHERN MARIANA ISLANDS (U.S.)
WAKE ISLAND (U.S.)
MALI
NIGER
ERITREA
SENEGAL
GAMBIA
GUINEA-BISSAU
CHAD
SUDAN
YEMEN
THAILAND
VIETNAM
GUAM (U.S.)
MARSHALL ISLANDS
BURKINA FASO
BENIN
AFRICA
DJIBOUTI
PHILIPPINES
GUINEA
SIERRA LEONE
GHANA
NIGERIA
CENTRAL AFRICAN REPUBLIC
ETHIOPIA
SRI LANKA
CAMBODIA
PALAU
FEDERATED STATES OF MICRONESIA
LIBERIA
COTE D'IVOIRE
TOGO
SOMALIA
BRUNEI
MALAYSIA
CAMEROON
MALDIVES
SAO TOME AND PRINCIPE
UGANDA
KENYA
Equator
KIRIBATI
EQUATORIAL GUINEA
GABON
RWANDA
DEM. REPUBLIC OF THE CONGO
BURUNDI
CONGO
INDONESIA
PAPUA NEW GUINEA
SOLOMON ISLANDS
TANZANIA
SEYCHELLES
ATLANTIC OCEAN
INDIAN OCEAN
COMOROS
EAST TIMOR
TUVALU
ANGOLA
MALAWI
ZAMBIA
ZIMBABWE
MADAGASCAR
NAMIBIA
BOTSWANA
MAURITIUS
VANUATU
FIJI
Tropic of Capricorn
MOZAMBIQUE
REUNION (France)
NEW CALEDONIA (France)
SOUTH AFRICA
SWAZILAND
LESOTHO
AUSTRALIA
N
W
E
S
FRENCH SOUTHERN & ANTARCTIC LANDS (France)
NEW ZEALAND
0 1,000 2,000 miles
0 1,000 2,000 kilometers
Antarctic Circle
ANTARCTICA
40°W 0° 40°E 80°E 120°E 160°E
80°N 60°N 40°N 20°N 0° 20°S 40°S 60°S 80°S
Europe
NORWAY
FINLAND
RUSSIA
SWEDEN
0 200 400 miles
0 200 400 kilometers
North Sea
ESTONIA
DENMARK
Baltic Sea
LATVIA
LITHUANIA
RUSSIA
IRELAND
UNITED KINGDOM
BELARUS
NETHERLANDS
POLAND
GERMANY
BELGIUM
ATLANTIC OCEAN
LUXEMBOURG
CZECH REPUBLIC
UKRAINE
LIECHTENSTEIN
FRANCE
SLOVAKIA
MOLDOVA
SWITZERLAND
AUSTRIA
HUNGARY
RUSSIA
SLOVENIA
ROMANIA
CROATIA
MONACO
BOSNIA AND HERZEGOVINA
SERBIA AND MONTENEGRO
Black Sea
GEORGIA
ANDORRA
CORSICA (France)
PORTUGAL
SPAIN
BULGARIA
ITALY
MACEDONIA
SARDINIA (Italy)
ALBANIA
BALEARIC IS. (Spain)
TURKEY
GREECE
GIBRALTAR (U.K.)
SICILY (Italy)
MOROCCO
ALGERIA
TUNISIA
MALTA
Mediterranean Sea
CRETE (Gr.)
CYPRUS
SYRIA
LEBANON
10°E 20°E 30°E 40°E 50°E 0°
60°N 50°N 40°N

NORTH AMERICA: Political

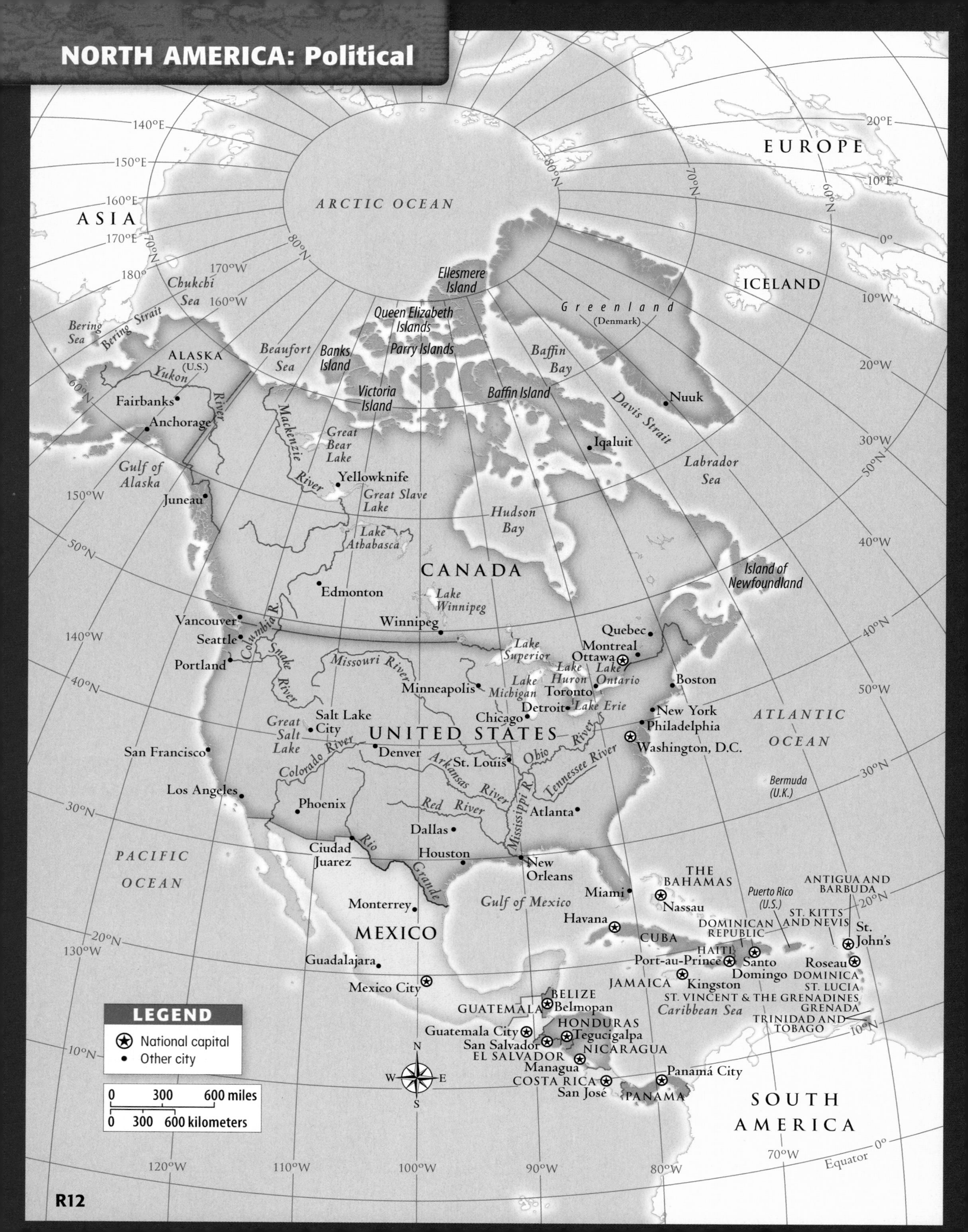

SOUTH AMERICA: Political

CALIFORNIA: Physical

CALIFORNIA: Counties

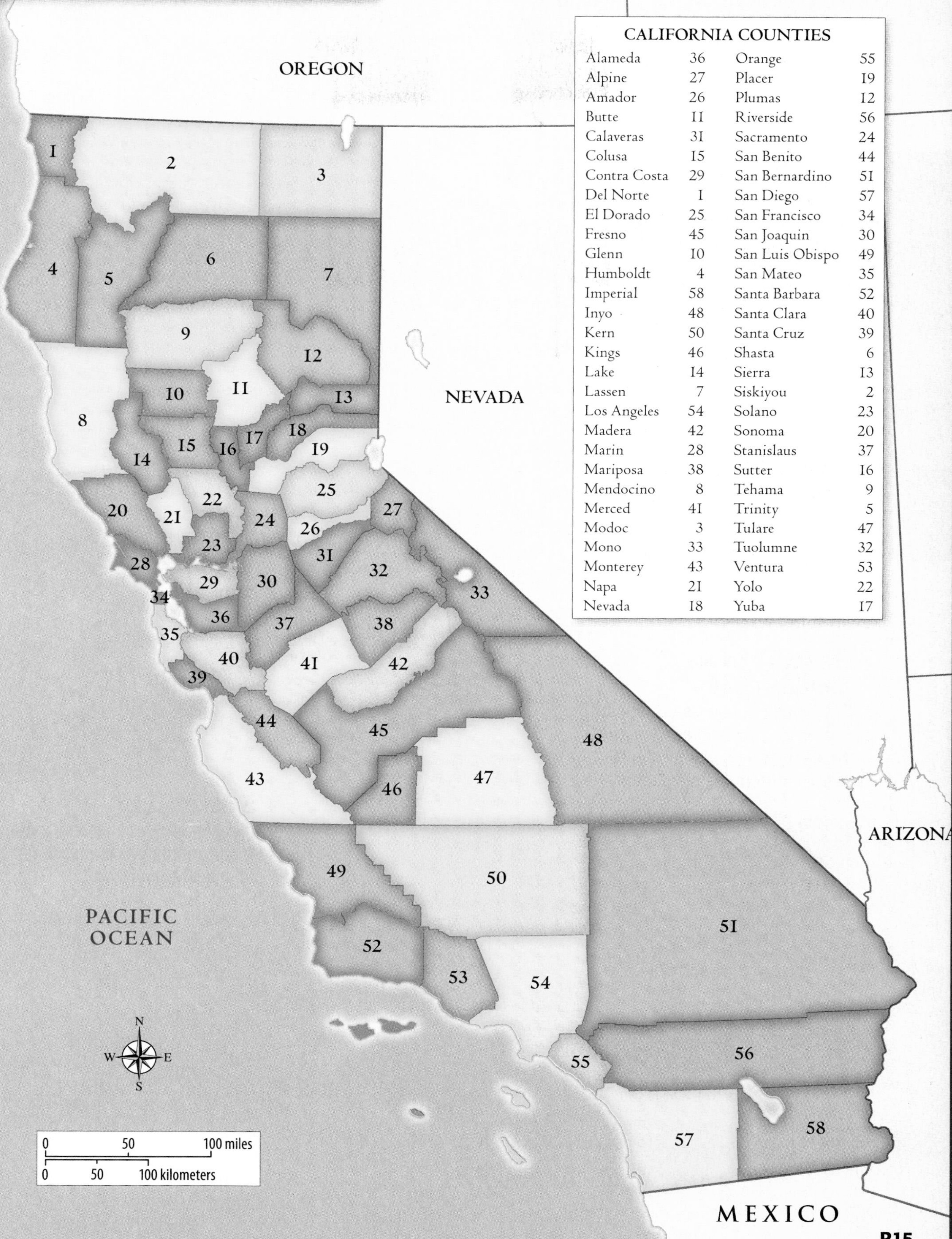

California Symbols

▲ **State Seal**
California is the 31st state. For this reason there are 31 stars on the state seal.

◀ **State Bird**
California quail
The California quail became the state bird in 1931.

CALIFORNIA REPUBLIC

State Flower
Golden Poppy
The Golden Poppy was valued by California Native Americans as a source of food and for the oil extracted from the plant. ▼

▲ **State Flag**
This flag was first used by a group of early settlers who revolted against Mexican rule.

◀ **State Tree**
California Redwood
The California Redwood is found only on the Pacific Coast. It can grow to more than 300 feet tall.

State Motto
"Eureka"
The state motto, Eureka, comes from the Greek word which means "I have found it." The motto is thought to refer to the Gold Rush. ▼

State Animal
California Grizzly Bear
The California Grizzly Bear, related to the more numerous Grizzly Bear (right), once numbered more than 10,000 in California. ▶

Governors of California

Spanish Governors	Term
Gaspar de Portolá	1769–1770
Pedro Fages	1770–1773
Fernando Rivera y Moncada	1773–1775
Felipe de Neve	1775–1782
Pedro Fages	1782–1791
José Antonio Roméu	1791–1792
José Joaquin de Arrillaga	1792–1794
Diego de Borica	1794–1800
José Joaquin de Arrillaga	1800–1814
José Arguello	1814–1815
Pablo Vicente de Solá	1815–1822

Mexican Governors	Term
Luis Arguello	1822–1825
José María Echeandía	1825–1831
Manuel Victoria	1831–1832
Pío Pico	1832
José María Echeandía (South)	1833
Agustin V. Zamorano (North)	1833
José Figueroa	1833–1835
José Castro	1835–1836
Nicholás Gutiérrez	1836
Mariano Chico	1836
Juan Bautista Alvarado	1837–1842
Manuel Micheltorena	1842–1845
Pío Pico	1845–1846
José María Flores	1846

Military Governors	Term
John D. Sloat	1846
Robert F. Stockton	1846–1847
John C. Frémont	1847
Stephen W. Kearny	1847
Richard B. Mason	1847–1849
Persifor F. Smith	1849
Bennett Riley	1849

Interim Governor	Term
Peter H. Burnett	1849–1851

State Governors	Term
John McDougal	1851–1852
John Bigler	1852–1856
J. Neely Johnson	1856–1858
John B. Weller	1858–1860
Milton S. Latham	1860
John G. Downey	1860–1862
Leland Stanford	1862–1863
Frederick F. Low	1863–1867
Henry H. Haight	1867–1871
Newton Booth	1871–1875
Romualdo Pacheco	1875–1876
William Irwin	1876–1880
George C. Perkins	1880–1883
George Stoneman	1883–1887
Washington Bartlett	1887–1888
Robert W. Waterman	1888–1891
Henry H. Markham	1891–1895
James H. Budd	1895–1899
Henry T. Gage	1899–1903
George C. Pardee	1903–1907
James N. Gillett	1907–1911
Hiram W. Johnson	1911–1917
William D. Stephens	1917–1923
Friend W. Richardson	1923–1927
Clement C. Young	1927–1931
James Rolph, Jr.	1931–1934
Frank F. Merriam	1934–1939
Culbert L. Olson	1939–1943
Earl Warren	1943–1953
Goodwin J. Knight	1953–1959
Edmund G. Brown	1959–1967
Ronald Reagan	1967–1975
Edmund G. Brown, Jr.	1975–1983
George Deukmejian	1983–1991
Pete Wilson	1991–1999
Gray Davis	1999–2003
Arnold Schwarzenegger	2003–

Famous Californians

Greg Sarris is a professor at the University of California, Los Angeles. He has written about the lives and stories of Native Americans in California. Sarris is a chief of the Coast Miwok.

Eldrick "Tiger" Woods is a professional golfer. He won his first tournament when he was eight years old. Since then, Woods has won numerous tournaments all over the world. He has broken many golfing records. Woods also founded an organization that offers different programs for children to help them improve their lives through education and sports.

Janice Rogers Brown now serves as an Associate Justice of the California Supreme Court. She has worked for various other government offices, as well as for a private law firm. Justice Brown received her law degree from the University of California School of Law in 1977.

Maxine Hong Kingston is a teacher and award-winning author. Her first two books combined fiction and non-fiction to tell stories about her Chinese heritage.

Sally Kristen Ride was the first American woman to travel into space. On June 18, 1983, she was one of the crew on board the space shuttle *Challenger*. Ride is now an author and professor of physics at the University of California, San Diego.

Famous Californians

Tom Hanks is an actor. He has played roles in movies that have ranged from comedy to voice acting and from romance to horror. Hanks was the voice of one of the characters in "Toy Story," which was the first full-length animated film to be made entirely using computer technology.

Natalie Coughlin swam in the 2004 Olympics. She won two gold medals, two silver medals, and a bronze medal. Coughlin has been swimming competitively since she was six years old. She has won swimming events around the world.

Nancy Pelosi has represented California's Eighth District in the United States House of Representatives since 1987. She is the Democratic leader of the House of Representatives. Pelosi is the first woman in United States history to lead a major party in Congress.

Stephen Gerald Breyer currently serves as an Associate Justice of the Supreme Court of the United States. He has held that position for over 10 years. During this time, he has written several decisions that changed the laws in California.

Landon Donovan is a soccer player. He has competed in the Olympics and in several World Cups. Donovan has been named the United States soccer's team player of the year three times. He led the San José Earthquakes to two Major League Soccer Cup championships in his four seasons with the club.

Congresswoman **Linda Sánchez** was sworn into office on January 7, 2003, to represent the newly created 39th Congressional District of California. Linda Sánchez joins her sister **Loretta Sánchez** in the House of Representatives. Loretta Sánchez represents California's 47th Congressional District of California. They are the first sisters to ever serve in Congress together.

Thomas Fleming is the oldest and longest-published African American journalist. He writes for the *Sun-Reporter*, San Francisco's African American weekly, which he co-founded in 1944. Fleming has used his editorial columns to support civil rights and equality for African Americans.

Lisa Fernandez is a softball player. She has won gold medals at the 1996, 2000, and 2004 Olympic Games. In the 2004 Games, the United States softball team broke several Olympic records.

Leroy Chiao is an astronaut and engineer. He was the first Asian American to walk in space. Chiao has run many different science experiments while in space. He has lived and worked in the International Space Station and flown on three different space shuttles.

Gary Soto is an award-winning author of children's books and poetry, as well as works for adults. He also serves as an ambassador for the United Farm Workers of America, an organization whose goal is to improve the lives and working conditions of farm workers.

California and United States History 1500 – 2005

California Events

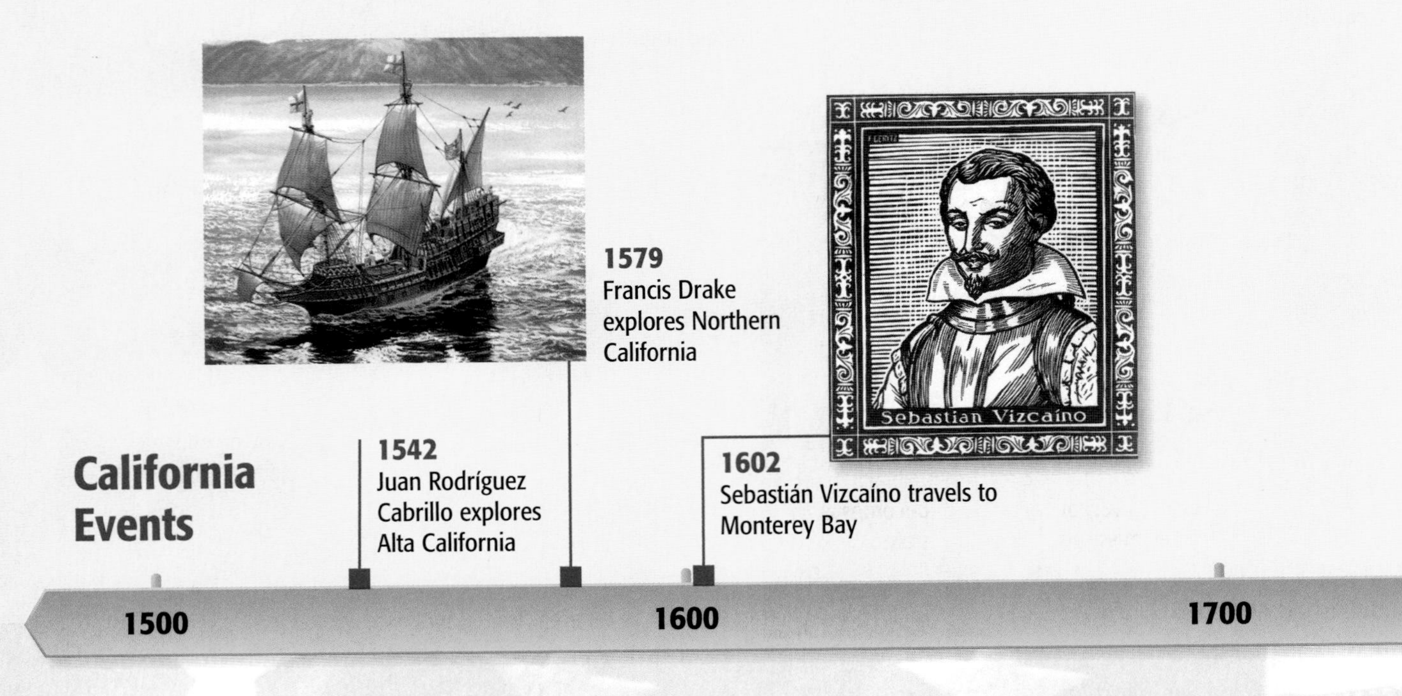

1542
Juan Rodríguez Cabrillo explores Alta California

1579
Francis Drake explores Northern California

1602
Sebastián Vizcaíno travels to Monterey Bay

1500 | 1600 | 1700

United States Events

1607
English settlers start Jamestown, Virginia, colony

1621
English settlers and Native Americans hold the first Thanksgiving

1673
Explorers from France reach the Mississippi River

1500 | 1600 | 1700

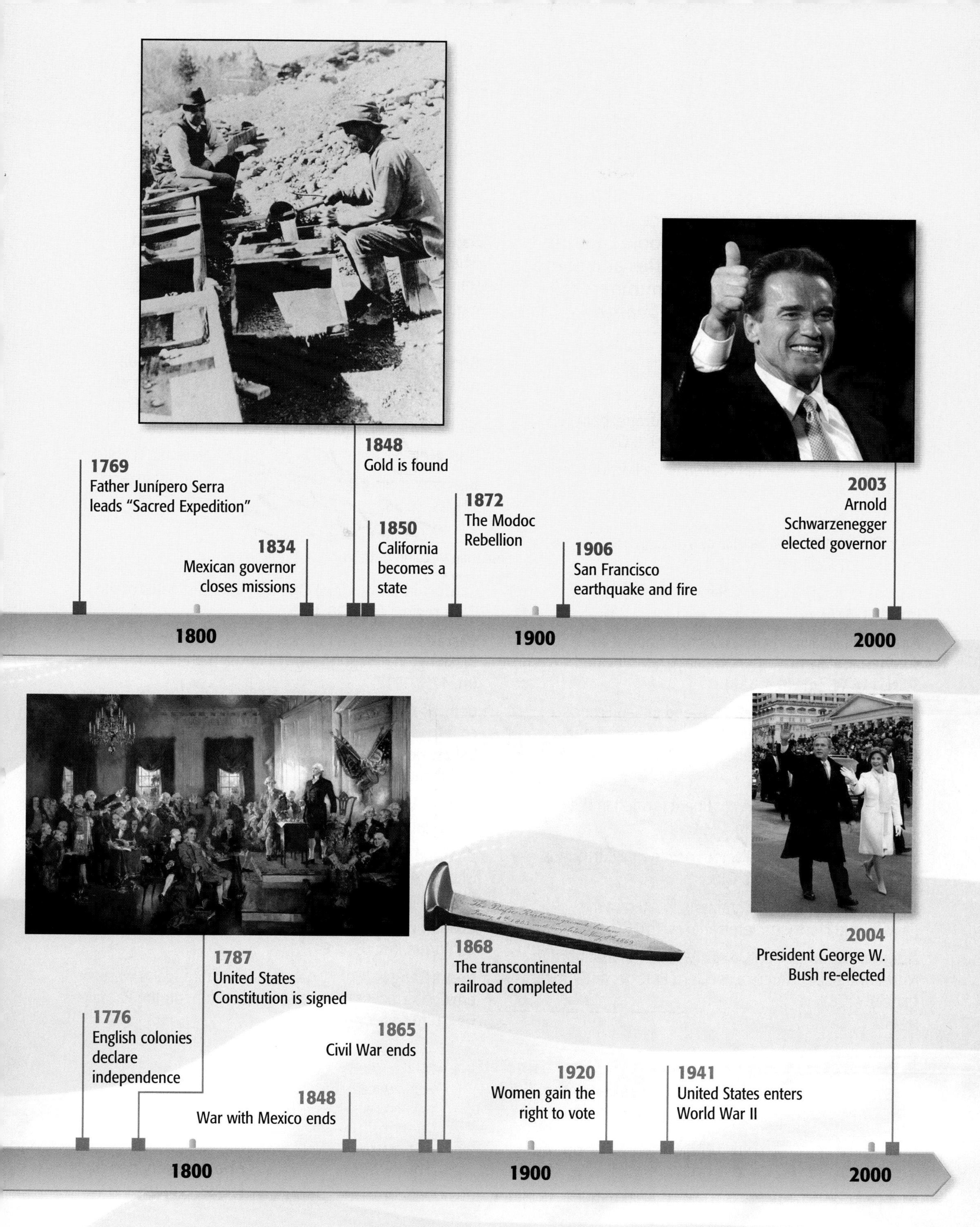
1769
Father Junípero Serra leads “Sacred Expedition”
1834
Mexican governor closes missions
1848
Gold is found
1850
California becomes a state
1872
The Modoc Rebellion
1906
San Francisco earthquake and fire
2003
Arnold Schwarzenegger elected governor
1800
1900
2000
1776
English colonies declare independence
1787
United States Constitution is signed
1848
War with Mexico ends
1865
Civil War ends
1868
The transcontinental railroad completed
1920
Women gain the right to vote
1941
United States enters World War II
2004
President George W. Bush re-elected
1800
1900
2000

Gazetteer

This Gazetteer is a geographical dictionary that will help you to pronounce and locate the places discussed in this book. Latitude and longitude are given for cities and some other places. The letters and numbers tell you where each place first appears on a map (m.) or in the text (t.).

A

Africa (af´ri kə) A continent south of Europe, between the Atlantic and Indian oceans. (m. G9, t. G8)

Allensworth (al´əns worth) A town in California, the first all African American town in the United States; 36°N, 119°W. (t. 320)

Alta California (al´tə kal ə fôr´nyə) The Spanish name for present day California. (t. 137)

Alturas (al tər əs) A city in California; 41°N, 120°W. (m. 12, t. 416)

Anaheim (an'ə hīm) A city in Orange County, in Southern California, where Disneyland is located; 34°N, 118°W. (m. 40, t. 318)

Angel Island (an´jəl ī´lənd) An island in San Francisco Bay where Chinese immigrants waited to find out whether they would be allowed into the United States. (t. 317)

Antarctica (ant ärk´ti kə) A continent located in the Southern Hemisphere. (m. G9, t. G8)

Arctic Ocean (ärk´tik ō´shən) An ocean that surrounds the North Pole. (m. G9, t. G8)

Asia (ā´zhə) The largest continent, located in the Eastern and Northern hemispheres. (m. G9, t. G8)

Atlantic Ocean (at lan´tik ô´shən) An ocean that borders North and South America, western Europe, and Africa. (m. G9, t. G8)

B

Baja California (bä´hä kal ə fôr´nyə) A peninsula in what is now Mexico, Cortes claimed it for Spain. (m. 156, t. 135)

Bakersfield (bā´kərz fēld) A city in the San Joaquin Valley of California; 35°N, 119°W. (m. 19, t. 58)

Beckwourth Pass (bek´wəorth pas) A Sierra Nevada pass discovered in 1851 by James Beckwourth; it was used by some of the gold seekers known as the Forty-Niners. (m. 212, t. 215)

Berkeley (bûr'klē) A city in Northern California. (t. 390)

Burbank (bər bank) A city in southern California; 34°N, 118°W. (t. 357)

C

California (kal ə fôr´nyə) One of the Pacific states of the West region. (m. G10, t. 15)

Cascade Range (kas kād' rānj) Mountain range in Washington, Oregon, and California in the West. (m. 47, t. 17)

Central America (sen'trəl ə mer´i kə) A group of countries in Latin America made up of Guatemala, Belize, Honduras, El Salvador, Nicaragua, Costa Rica, and Panama. (t. 39)

Central Valley region (sen'trəl val´ē rē'jən) One of the four regions of California. (m. 53, t. 32)

Channel Islands (chan'əl ī'ləlndz) A chain of eight islands in the Pacific Ocean off the coast of Southern California. (m. 198, t. 138)

Coastal region (kos'təl rē'jən) One of the four regions of California. (m. 63, t. 64)

Coast Ranges (kôst rān´jəs) A mountain range in western California, Oregon, and Washington, on the Pacific Coast. (m. 11, t. 47)

Pronunciation Key

a	at	ē	me	ō	old	ū	use	ng	song
ā	ape	i	it	ô	fork	ü	rule	th	thin
ä	far	ī	ice	oi	oil	ů	pull	th	this
âr	care	îr	pierce	ou	out	ûr	turn	zh	measure
e	end	o	hot	u	up	hw	white	ə	about, taken, pencil, lemon, circus

Colorado Desert (kol ə rad´ô dez´ərt) A desert in California. (m. 75, t. 75)

Colorado River (kol ə rad´ō ri´vər) A river that flows from the Rocky Mountains to the Gulf of Mexico and provides some drinking water for Southern California. (m. 212, t. 116)

D

Death Valley (deth val´ē) A desert in California; the driest place in the United States. (m. 31, t. 31)

Delano (de´lə nō) A small farming town in the San Joaquin Valley; headquarters of the United Farm Workers union; 36°N, 119°W. (t. 396)

Desert region (dez´ərt rē´jən) One of four regions of California. (m. 9)

Donner Pass (don´ər pas) A pass in the Sierra Nevada where the Donner Party became stranded. (m. 212, t. 289)

Drake's Bay (drāks) A bay on California's coast (m. 148, t. 143)

E

Eastern Hemisphere (ēs´tərn hem´is fir) The half of Earth east of the prime meridian. (m. G9, t. G9)

El Camino Real (el kä mē'nō rä äl') A walking trail that connected Spanish missions in California; it means "The King's Highway." (m. 153, t. 158)

Europe (yur´əp) A continent located in the Eastern and Northern hemispheres. (m. G9, t. G8)

F

Fort Ross (fôrt ros) A Russian settlement in Sonoma County, north of San Francisco, from 1812–1840; a state historic park today. (m. 212, t. 211)

Fresno (frez´nō) A city in California's San Joaquin Valley; 36°N, 119°W. (m. G13, t. 58)

H

Hetch Hetchy Valley (hech hech'ē val'ē) A valley inside Yosemite National Park which was flooded by the Hetch Hetchy reservoir; it is part of the aqueduct system that supplies San Francisco with water. (m. 331, t. 331)

Hoover Dam (hüv'vər) A dam on the Colorado River that supplies water for Southern California, Arizona, and Mexico; it also provides hydroelectric power. (m. 333, t. 349)

Imperial Valley (im pir´ē əl val´ē) A farming area in the Colorado Desert known for its lettuce, cantaloupe, and other crops. (m. 75, t. 76)

Indian Ocean (in'dē ən ô´shən) An ocean between Africa, southern Asia, and Australia. (m. G9, t. G8)

Isthmus of Panama (is´məs əv pan´ə mä) A narrow stretch of land in Central America. (m. 234, t. 233)

Klamath River (kla´məth riv´ər) A river in northwestern California. (t. 124)

L

Lake Tahoe (lāk tä´hô) A mountain lake in the Sierra Nevada known for its deep, blue water. (m. G13, t. 48)

Lassen Peak (las´ən pēk) An active volcano in the Cascade Range. (m. G13, t. 49)

Long Beach (long bēch) A city in Los Angeles County known for its large port; 34°N, 118°W. (m. 63, t. 357)

Los Angeles (lôs an´jə ləs) Founded as a pueblo in 1781, it is today California's largest city; 34°N, 118°W. (m. 19, t. 34)

Manzanar (man'zan ər) A World War II Japanese internment camp located in California. (t. 360)

Merced (mər sed') A town in California; 37°N, 120°W. (t. 391)

Mojave Desert (mō hä´vē dez´ərt) A desert in southeastern California. (m. G13, t. 75)

Modesto (mə des'tō) A town in California; 37°N, 121°W. (t. 310)

Mono Lake (mō'nō lāk) A lake at the northern end of the Owens Valley. (m. 47, t. 48)

Monterey (mon tə rā´) The location of a presidio in 1821, it is now a city in southwestern California; 37°N, 122°W. (m. 63, t. 147)

Monterey Bay (mon tə rā´ bā) An inlet of the Pacific Ocean named by Sebastian Vizcaíno. (m. 136, t. 145)

Mountain region (moun´tən rē´jən) One of four regions of California. (m. 9, t. 9)

Mount Whitney (mount wit´nē) The highest mountain in the United States outside of Alaska; elevation 14,495 feet; located in southeastern California, in the Sierra Nevada range. (m. G13, t. 31)

N

New Spain (nü spān) The Spanish colony in North America, made up of all or parts of the lands now called Mexico, Central America, and the United States. (m. 156, t. 135)

North America (nôrth ə mer´i kə) A continent in the Northern and Western hemispheres. (m. G9, t. G8)

Northern Hemisphere (nôr´thərn hem´i sfir) The half of Earth north of the equator. (m. G9, t. G9)

O

Oakland (ōk´lənd) A city on the east side of San Francisco Bay; a major West Coast shipping port; 37°N, 122°W. (m. 290, t. 39)

Owens River (ō´ənz riv´ər) A river in the Owens Valley whose flow is diverted to provide some of Los Angeles's water supply. (m. 330, t. 330)

Owens Valley (ō´ənz val´ē) A valley 200 miles northeast of Los Angeles. (m. 330, t. 330)

P

Pacific Ocean (pə sif´ik ō´shən) An ocean that borders western North and South America and eastern Asia. (m. G9, t. G8)

Pacific Rim (pə si´fik rim) The edges of the northern Pacific Ocean, countries on the Pacific Rim are: Mexico, Japan, Canada, Taiwan, South Korea, China, and the United States. (m. 406, t. 406)

Palm Springs (pälm springz) A city in the desert region of California; 34°N, 117°W. (m. 75, t. 76)

Palmdale (pälm'dāl) A city in southern California; 34°N, 118°W. (t. 366)

Palo Alto (pal´ō al´tō) A town in Santa Clara County where Stanford University is located. (t. 199)

Panama Canal (pan´ə ma) A canal through Panama that allows ships to cross between the Atlantic and Pacific Oceans (t. 324)

Pasadena (pasə'dē'nə) A city in Southern California; 34°N, 118°W. (t. 367)

Pearl Harbor, Hawaii (pûrl här´bər hə wī´ē) The location of a United States Navy base that was bombed by Japanese planes on December 7, 1941. (t. 357)

Port Chicago (pôrt shi kä gō) A port in California where an explosion killed many people in 1944; 38°N, 122°W. (t. 359)

Promontory Summit (prom´ən tôr ē sum'it) The place, in Utah, where the transcontinental railroad was completed. (m. 290, t. 290)

R

Redding (red'ing) A town in Shasta County, California; 40° N, 122°W. (m. 19, t. 416)

Richmond (rich´mənd) A city in Northern California where many Liberty ships were built in World War II; 38°N, 122°W. (t. 358)

Ring of Fire A group of active volcanoes. (m. 49, t. 49)

Riverside (riv´ər sīd) A large city in Southern California once known for its many orange groves; 34°N, 117°W. (t. 308)

Sacramento (sak rə men´tō) The capital of California, in the central part of the state; 38°N, 121°W. (m. G10, t. 58)

Sacramento River (sak rə men´tô riv´ər) A river that flows 382 miles from the Cascades through Northern California into San Francisco Bay. (m. 9, t. 56)

Sacramento Valley (sak rə men´tō val ē) One of the two valleys that make up the Central Valley of California. (t. 55)

St. Joseph, Missouri (sānt jō´səf mi sûr´ē) A city in the Plains states of the Middle West region; the starting point of the Pony Express. (m. 212, t. 282)

Salinas (sə lē′nəs) A town in central California. (m. 319, t. 39)

Salton Sea (säl′tən sē) An inland lake in the Imperial Valley. (m. 53, t. 329)

San Andreas Fault (san an drā′əs fält) Where two of Earth's plates meet in California; movement of these plates can cause an earthquake. (t. 66)

San Bernardino (san bər´nər dē nō) A city in Southern California; 34°N, 117°W. (m. 19)

San Diego (san dē a′gō) A city in Southern California near the border with Mexico; 33°N, 117°W. (m. G6, t. 64)

San Diego Bay (san dē a′gō bā) An inlet of the Pacific Ocean on the California coastline. (m. 63, t. 63)

San Francisco (san frən sis´kō) A port city in central California, on the Pacific Ocean; 38°N, 122°W. (m. G13, t. 65)

San Francisco Bay (san frən sis´kō bā) A bay off the Pacific Ocean on the California coastline at the city of San Francisco. (m. 66, t. 57)

San Joaquin River (san wä kēn´ riv´ər) A river that flows 350 miles from the Sierra Nevada through central California into San Francisco Bay. (m. 9, t. 56)

San Joaquin Valley (san wä kēn´ val ē) One of two valleys that make up the Central Valley of California. (t. 55)

San José (san hō zā´) First founded as a pueblo in 1777, now a large city in Northern California; 37°N, 122°W. (m. G13, t. 176)

San Luis Obispo County (san lü′əs ə bis´pō koun´tē) A county in southern California, on the Pacific coast. (m. R15, t. 432)

Santa Barbara (san´tə bär´bər ə) A city in Southern California; 34°N, 120°W. (m. 19, t. 74)

Santa Barbara Channel (san´tə bär´bər ə chan´əl) A body of water that lies between the Pacific Coast and the Channel Islands. (m. 63, t. 137)

Santa Clara (san´tə kler´ə) A city in Santa Clara Valley. (m. 76, t. 325)

Santa Clara Valley (san´tə kler´ə val´ē) A valley in California with several cities that make up a key center of the country's computer industry. (t. 158)

Sequoia National Park (sə kou′ə nash´ə nəl park) A park created in the Sierra Nevada. (t. 25)

Shasta Dam (shas´tə) A dam on the Sacramento River (m. 287, t. 349)

Sierra Nevada (sē er´ə nə vad´ə) A mountain range in eastern California. (m. G13, t. 17)

Sonoma A city north of San Francisco where the Bear Flag Revolt took place; 38°N, 122°W. (m. 176, t. 159)

South America (south ə mer´i kə) A continent in the Southern and Western hemispheres. (m. G9, t. G8)

Southern Hemisphere (suth´ərn hem´i sfīr) The half of Earth south of the equator. (m. G9, t. G9)

Sutter's Fort (sut´ərz fôrt) A fort built by John Sutter in 1839. (m. 212, t. 213)

Sutter's Mill (sut´ərz mil) John Sutter's mill, built along the south fork of the American River in 1847. (m. 237, t. 231)

V

Vallejo (vä yā′jō) A city in California, one of the first capitals of the state; 38°N, 122°W. (t. 250)

Washington, D.C. (wä´shing tən dē cē) The home of our country's government. (m. G10, t. 247)

Western Hemisphere (wes´tərn hem´i sfēr) The half of Earth west of the prime meridian. (m. G9, t. G9)

Yosemite National Park (yō sem´i tē nash´ə nəl pärk) A part of the Sierra Nevada range in California that became a park in 1890. (m. 19, t. 25)

Biographical Dictionary

The Biographical Dictionary lists the people you have learned about in this book. The Pronunciation Key tells you how to say their names. The page numbers let you see where each person first appears in the text.

Adams, Ansel (ad'əmz), 1902–1984 A photographer who was awarded the Presidential Medal of Freedom for his efforts to preserve nature on film and on Earth. (p. 15)

Aldrin, Edwin (äl'drin), 1930– A famous astronaut and one of the first people to walk on the Moon. (p. 317)

Allen, Elsie (alən), 1899–1990 A Pomo Native American who began weaving traditional Pomo baskets as a child. Her baskets are exhibited at museums in California. (p. 100)

Allensworth, Allen (al´əns wərth), 1842–1914 Born into slavery, he escaped during the Civil War. He joined the Union army and fought against the south. He became the highest ranked African American officer in American history up to that point. (p. 271)

Anza, Juan Bautista de (än´zə), 1735–1788 A Spanish captain who led an early expedition to northern California coast, and founded what would become San Francisco. (p. 173)

Armstrong, Neil (ärm´strông), 1930– A famous astronaut and the first person ever to walk on the Moon. (p. 317)

Austin, Mary (os´tən), 1868–1934 Author of the 1903 book *The Land of Little Rain*, in which she describes life near Death Valley. (p. 14)

Bartolomea (bär tō lō mā´ə), 1800s Tongva girl who told of missionaries forcing the people of her town to be baptized and live in a Roman Catholic mission. (p. 116)

Beasley, Delilah (bēz´lē), 1872–1934 Woman who studied and wrote about the lives of African Americans. Starting in 1923, her newspaper column in the Oakland *Tribune* discussed laws and customs that were unfair to black people. (p. 345)

Beckwourth, James (bek´wûrth), 1798–1867 African American who was born into slavery and became a famous mountain man. He discovered a safer pass in the Sierra Nevada, making travel easier. (p. 186)

Bering, Vitus (bâr´ing), 1681–1741 A Russian explorer who explored Alaska in 1741. (p. 155)

Bidwell, John (bid´wel), 1819–1900 Leader of the first wagon train of settlers to arrive in California, in 1841. (p. 213)

Bradley, Tom (brad'lē), 1917–1998 The first African American mayor of Los Angeles. (p. 314)

Brannan, Sam (bran'ən), 1819–1889 A businessman in San Francisco who got rich selling equipment to gold miners. (p. 231)

Bright, Josefina Fierro de (brīt), 1920–1998 Defender of immigrant rights and first president of the Congress of Spanish Speaking People. (p. 270)

Briones, Juana (brē ō'nās), 1802–1889 Born in Mexican California, she was one of the first women to own land in California. In 1844 she purchased 4,400 acres of land to raise cattle and horses. (p. 186)

Burbank, Luther (bur´bank), 1849–1926 Farmer who used science to develop about 800 new kinds of plants while living in Santa Rosa in the late 1800s. (p. 270)

Burke, Yvonne Braithwaite (burk), 1932– The first African American woman elected to the United States House of Representatives. (p. 194)

Burnett, Peter (bûr net´), 1807–1895 Chosen in 1849 to be the first governor of the state of California. (p. 248)

Pronunciation Key

a	at	ē	me	ō	old	ū	use	ng	song
ā	ape	i	it	ô	fork	ü	rule	th	thin
ä	far	ī	ice	oi	oil	u̇	pull	th	this
âr	care	îr	pierce	ou	out	ûr	turn	zh	measure
e	end	o	hot	u	up	hw	white	ə	about, taken, pencil, lemon, circus

Cabrillo, Juan Rodríguez (kə brē´yō), ?–1543 Conquistador who led the first European expedition along the coast of California, in 1542. (p. 186)

Carrillo, José Antonio (kə rē´yô), 1796–1862 Led Californio soldiers to victory in a battle with Americans at Dominguez Rancho in 1846. One of eight Californio delegates present at the convention to write the California constitution. (p. 211)

Castro, José (kas´trô), 1810–1860 Mexican colonel who ordered John C. Frémont and his men out of California in 1845. This action led to the Bear Flag Revolt. (p. 219)

Cermeño, Sebastián Rodriguez (sər men´yô), late 1500s–early 1600s ship captain who in 1595 sailed from Manila to California, exploring Monterey Bay and other points along the California coast. (p. 144)

Chaffey, George (cha'fe), 1848–1932 Engineer who built a canal to bring water to the Colorado Desert. He renamed the irrigated land Imperial Valley. (p. 329)

Chávez, César (chä´vez, sâ´zär), 1927–1993 A leader in the drive to improve lives of farmworkers. In 1962, with Dolores Huerta, he formed a union called the National Farm Workers Association. (p. 378)

Chicago, Judy (shi kä'gō), 1939– A contemporary artist whose work celebrates women. (p. 413)

Clay, Henry (klā), 1777–1852 Senator from Kentucky who helped work out the Compromise of 1850, enabling California to become a state. (p. 219)

Clappe, Louise (klap), 1819–1906 She traveled to California with her husband during the Gold Rush. Letters she wrote to her sister, using the name Dame Shirley, about life in a mining camp were published in 1854. (p. 239)

Cook, James (kük), 1728–1779 A British explorer who made the first voyage to Antarctica. (p. 173)

Cortés, Hernan (kôr tez´), 1485–1547 Spanish conquistador who landed in Mexico in 1519 and named the land New Spain. (p. 135)

Crespí, Juan (kres pē´), 1721–1782 Aide to Junípero Serra who traveled with the "Sacred Expedition" and kept a journal describing what he saw. (p. 156)

Crocker, Charles (kro kər) 1822–1888 One of the "Big Four" investors in the Central Pacific Railroad. (p. 289)

Dana, Richard Henry (dā'nə), 1815–1882 A young man who sailed to California. He wrote about life in California before the Gold Rush. (p. 207)

Davis, Gray (dā'vis) 1942– The governor of California from 1999–2003. He was voted out of office in a recall. (p. 343)

DeMille, Cecil B. (də mil´), 1881–1959 Director of the first full-length movie in the United States, in 1913. (p. 326)

Disney, Walt (diz' nē) 1901–1966 Movie producer and creator of Disneyland in Anaheim, CA. (p. 414)

Doheny, Edward L. (dô´nē), 1856–1935 Discovered oil in Los Angeles in 1892, leading to a huge oil boom. (p. 325)

Donner, George (don´ər), 1784–1847 Leader of a group of settlers from Missouri. (p. 214)

Drake, Francis (drāk), 1543?–1596 English explorer sent by the queen of England to find the Northwest Passage. (p. 143)

Echeandía, José (e chē ən dē' ə), ?–1855 Governor of Mexican California during the time the first white Americans arrived overland in California, in 1826. (p. 160)

Edson, Katherine Philips (ed´sən), 1870–1933 California reformer whose efforts led to women's suffrage and a minimum wage law for women and children. (p. 344)

Ferrelo, Bartolomé (fər el´ô), 1499–1550 Spanish ship pilot of the first European expedition along the California coast. He was named commander of the expedition when Juan Rodríguez Cabrillo died in 1543. (p. 138)

Figueroa, José (fig ə rō'ə), 1782–1835 Governor who closed the missions in California in 1834, attempting to divide the land between Native Americans and Mexican settlers. (p. 198)

Fong, Heather (fäng), 1956– Heather Fong was born in San Francisco. She joined the police force in 1977, and worked her way up. On April 14, 2004 she became the first Asian American woman to be Police Chief. (p. 379)

Frémont, Jessie (frē´mont), 1824–1902 Wife of John C. Frémont. She and her husband wrote many exciting books about their travels in the American West. (p. 159)

Frémont, John C. (frē´mont), 1813–1890 United States Army captain who led a band of armed men into California in 1845, declaring California independent from Mexico and starting the Bear Flag Revolt. (p. 219)

Gálvez, José de (gäl´väz), 1729–1787 A special official to the king of Spain. He planned the "Sacred Expedition" to set up the first European settlements in California, in 1768. (p. 155)

Gibbs, Mifflin (gibs), 1823–1915 An African American journalist. He started the first African American newspaper in California. (p. 243)

Goldwyn, Samuel (gōld'win), 1882–1974 One of the founders of Metro Goldwyn-Mayer, a film company in Hollywood. (p. 318)

H

Haight, H.H. (hāt), 1825–1878 Governor of California from 1867-1871, he signed the charter for California's first public college. (p. 390)

Hearst, Phoebe Apperson (hûrst), 1842–1919 A wealthy supporter of the University of California, she served on the governing board from 1897 to 1919. (379)

Herrera, Juan Felipe (her rer'ā), 1948– Latin American poet and author of books for children who lives in Fresno, California. (p. 380)

Hidalgo, Miguel (hi dal'go), 1753–1811 Priest who convinced Mexicans to fight for independence from Spain with a speech known as The Cry of Dolores. (p. 197)

Hopkins, Mark (hop'kəns), 1813–1878 One of the "Big Four" investors in the Central Pacific Railroad. (p. 289)

Houston, Jeanne Wakatsuki (hû´stən), 1934– Japanese American who wrote about her experiences in the Manzanar internment camp in Owens Valley during World War II. (p. 412)

Huerta, Dolores (wer´tä), 1929– Formed a union for farmworkers with Cesar Chavez in 1962 called the National Farm Workers Association. (p. 378)

Huntington, Collins (hunt'ing tən), 1821–1900 One of the "Big Four" investors in the Central Pacific Railroad. (p. 289)

Jackson, Helen Hunt (jak´sən), 1830–1885 Wrote *A Century of Dishonor* in 1881. This book criticized how the government treated Native Americans. (p. 257)

Jobs, Steve (jobz), 1955– Built the first small, easy-to-use computer in 1975, with his friend Steve Wozniak. (p. 402)

Johnson, Hiram (jon´sən), 1866–1945 Governor of California from 1911 to 1919, he was a strong leader of the movement to reform California's government. (p. 271)

Judah, Theodore (jü´də), 1826–1863 Engineer responsible for the building of the first transcontinental railroad. (p. 270)

Kaiser, Henry J. (kī´zər), 1882–1967 California businessman known for building thousands of Liberty ships during World War II. (p. 358)

Kearny, Stephen Watts (kär´nē), 1794–1848 United States general in the Mexican American War. Defeated by Andrés Pico's army of Californios in the Battle of San Pascual. (p. 221)

King, Martin Luther, Jr., (king), 1929–1968 Major civil rights leader from Alabama during the 1960s. He inspired many Californians to fight discrimination. (p. 393)

Kingston, Maxine Hong (kings´tən), 1940– Wrote about her Chinese American heritage in her books like *The Woman Warrior*. (p. 412)

Kintpuash (kint'pwash), 1837–1872 Leader of the Modoc in the Modoc War. (p. 187)

Lange, Dorothea (lang), 1895–1965 A photographer who took pictures of people during the Great Depression. (p. 348)

Lincoln, Abraham (link´ən), 1809–1865 The 16th president of the United States. (p. 429)

Marshall, James (mär´shəl), 1810–1885 Discovered gold while building Sutter's Mill in 1848. (p. 231)

Mason, Biddy (mā´sən), 1818–1891 Enslaved woman brought to California from Georgia by her owner, Robert Smith. Her refusal to go with Smith to Texas led to the freedom of all enslaved persons in California. (p. 187)

Mayer, Louis B. (mā´ər), 1885–1957 One of the founders of Metro Goldwyn-Mayer, a company in Hollywood. (p. 318)

Morse, Samuel F. B. (môrs), 1791–1872 Painter and inventor of the telegraph. (p. 284)

Moreno, Luisa (môr ā'nō), 1907–1992 A Hispanic labor leader who helped found the Congress of Spanish Speaking people. (p. 350)

Muir, John (myər), 1838–1914 California settler who explored and wrote about the Sierra Nevada Mountains and founded the Sierra Club. He also helped create Yosemite National Park. (p. 4)

Mulholland, William (mul hol´ənd), 1855–1935 Built an aqueduct from Owens River, to Los Angeles. (p. 330)

Neve, Felipe de (nev´āy), 1728–1784 Governor who offered supplies to settlers to start farming towns in California to feed soldiers living in presidios. (p. 176)

Newsom, Gavin (nü'səm), 1967– The 42nd mayor of San Francisco. (p. 419)

North, John Wesley (nôrth) 1815–1890 Farmer who used irrigation to bring water to his orange groves in Riverside, California, in 1870. (p. 308)

Noguchi, Isamu (nō gü´chē, ē´sä mü), 1904–1988 A Japanese American artist born in Los Angeles. He created large scale garden and stone sculptures. His worked to make art that represented both the East and the West. (p. 378)

P

Parkhurst, Charlotte (pärk´hurst), 1812?–1879 First woman stagecoach driver, who got her job with Wells, Fargo and Company by dressing as a man and applying for the job as "Charley Parkhurst." (p. 281)

Payne, William (pān), 1877–1954 One of the founders of town of Allensworth. (p. 320)

Pico, Andrés (pē´ko), 1810–1876 Californio leader who won the Battle of San Pasqual in 1846. (p. 220)

Pico, Pío (pē´ō pē kō) 1801–1894 Mexican Governor of California during the Bear Flag Revolt and the Mexican-American War (p. 221)

Phelan, James (fē'lan), 1861–1930 San Francisco mayor who supported building the Hetch-Hetchy Aqueduct to bring water to the city. (p. 331)

Polk, James K. (pōlk), 1795–1849 President of the United States from 1845 to 1849, during the Mexican War. (p. 219)

Portola, Gaspar de (pôr tō'lä), 1734–1784 A captain in the Spanish Army who led an expedition to explore Alta California. (p. 155)

Reagan, Ronald (rā gən), 1911–2004 The 40th president of the United States. He moved to Hollywood to be an actor in 1937. (p. 412)

Reyes, Francisco (rā´əs), 1700s First alcalde of Los Angeles, he was of African and Spanish heritage. (p. 176)

Riley, Bennett (rī´lē), 1787–1853 Last military governor in California. He held a convention in 1849 where Californians took the first steps toward statehood. (p. 247)

Rodriguez, Richard (rod rē'gəz), 1944– A Mexican American author who was born in San Francisco. (p. 412)

Roosevelt, Franklin Delano (rü´zə velt), 1882–1945 The 32nd President of the United States, from 1933 to 1945. He created the New Deal programs to fight the Great Depression and led the country during World War II. (p. 319)

Royce, Sarah (rois),1819–1891 Went to California during the gold rush. Her diary became a book titled *A Frontier Lady*. (p. 15)

Ruef, Abraham (rüf), 1864–1936 Political "boss" who used money from big businesses to bribe city officials. His misuse of power and money led the citizens of San Francisco to reform the way government was run. (p. 341)

Ruiz, Bernarda (rü ēs´), 1800s Woman who set up a meeting between Frémont and Pico at Cahuenga Pass in 1847. At this meeting the Californios surrendered, and the fighting in California ended. (p. 212)

Rumford, William Byron (rum´fərd), 1908–1986 Representative in the California legislature who helped make a law called the Rumford Act, in 1963, that said California property owners could not discriminate because of race. (p. 379)

Schwarzenegger, Arnold (shwôrtz'ə neg ər), 1947– Elected Governor in 2003 in the recall vote to replace Gray Davis. (p. 343)

Semple, Robert (sem'pəl), 1806–1854 A representative in early California government. He argued for public education. (p. 389)

Serra, Junípero (ser´ə, hü nē´pe rə), 1713–1784 Missionary from New Spain who worked with José Gálvez to found and lead the first missions in what is now called California. (p. 187)

Serra, Richard (ser´ə), 1939– American artist who creates massive sculptures out of steel and other materials. (p. 413)

Severance, Caroline Maria (sev'ər ens), 1820–1914 Worked to win women the right to vote. (p. 344)

Sloat, John Drake (slôt), 1713–1784 United States Navy officer during the Mexican War. The war spread to California when he led ships to Monterey in 1846, claiming California as part of the United States. (p. 211)

Smith, Jedediah Strong (smith), 1799–1831 Mountain man who traveled overland from the Great Salt Lake to California in 1826. His party was the first white American group to make this dangerous journey. (p. 212)

Stanford, Leland (stan´fərd), 1824–1893 One of the "Big Four" investors in the Central Pacific Railroad. (p. 289)

Steinbeck, John (stīn´bek), 1902–1968 Author of *The Grapes of Wrath*. (p. 349)

Strauss, Levi (strous), 1829–1902 San Francisco shopkeeper who became successful buying Eastern goods and selling them to businesses in the West. With Jacob Davis he made the world's first blue jeans, in 1872. (p. 212)

Sutter, Johann (su´tər), 1802–1880 Swiss immigrant who arrived in Mexican California in 1834. He founded Sutter's Fort. (p. 186)

Swett, John (swet), 1830–1913 The first superintendent of California's public schools. (p. 389)

T

Tac, Pablo (tac), 1822–1841 Native American who lived on Mission San Luis Rey from birth and thought of the mission as home. He appreciated the European subjects he learned there. (p. 167)

Tape, Mary (tāp), 1857–1934 Chinese woman who won her court case against San Francisco schools. Her daughter had not been allowed to go to school because she was Chinese. (p. 270)

Tibbets, Eliza (tib´əts), ?–1898 Wife of Luther Tibbets. She helped introduce navel oranges to California. (p. 309)

Tibbets, Luther (tib´əts), 1820–1902 Farmer near Riverside who helped make orange growing a big business in California by introducing navel oranges from South America. (p. 309)

Toypurina (toi pər īn'ə), 1761–1799 Tongva woman who helped organize an unsuccessful revolt at Mission San Gabriel in 1785. (p. 187)

Twain, Mark (twān), 1835–1910 Famous American author, born Samuel Clemens, who wrote several short stories about life in California. (p. 411)

Unruh, Jesse (un rü), 1922–1987 A politician in California who passed the Unruh Civil Rights act in 1959. The act made it illegal for landlords to choose their renters based on race. (p. 394)

Vallejo, Mariano Guadalupe (vä yā´hō), 1808–1890 Mexican colonel captured and held prisoner during a revolt led by John C. Frémont in 1846. (p. 187)

Vizcaíno, Sebastián (viz kī ē'nō), 1550?–1616? Explorer who led an expedition from New Spain in search of a safe harbor along the coast of California in 1602. (p. 87)

Walker, Alice (wô' kər), 1944– African American author who has written books including The Color Purple. (p. 412)

Wayne, John (wān), 1907–1979 American actor famous for his work in movies about California and the West. (p. 327)

Williams, John (wil' yəmz), 1932– Composer of music for movies including the Star Wars series, and a symphony conductor. (p. 411)

Wilson, Pete (wil´sən), 1933– Governor of California from 1991 to 1999. He also served as mayor of San Diego and as United States senator from California. (p. 441)

Yeager, Chuck (yā'gər) 1923– A fighter pilot during World War II, and the first person to fly faster than the speed of sound. (p. 366)

GLOSSARY

This Glossary will help you to pronounce and understand the meanings of the vocabulary terms in this book. The page number at the end of the definition tells where the term first appears.

adapt (ə´dapt) To change in order to make suitable. (p. 75)

aerospace (âr´ō spās) The industry that builds planes and space vehicles. *See* **industry**. (p. 366)

agriculture (ag ri kul´ chər) The science and business of growing crops and raising animals. (p. 57)

alcade (al´cāde) A mayor. (p.177)

Allies (al´īz) Great Britain, France, China, and the Soviet Union–nations that fought against the Axis in World War II. *See* **Axis**. (p. 357)

alternative energy (ôl tûr´nə tiv en´ər gē) Energy, from sources other than coal, gas, or oil, that does not pollute. (p. 23)

amendment (ə mend´mənt) A formal change made according to official rules. (p. 343)

aqueduct (ak´wə dukt) A canal or pipe for bringing water from a faraway source. (p. 330)

aquifer (ak´wə fər) A layer of rock or gravel that traps water underground and supplies wells and springs. (p. 334)

archaeologist (ark ē ol´ə gəst) Someone who studies artifacts. (p. 96)

artifact (ärt´ə fakt) Some things left behind by the people of long ago. (p. 96)

astronaut (as´trə not) A person who is trained to fly a spacecraft. (p. 367)

Axis (ak´sis) Germany, Italy, and Japan–nations that fought against the Allies in World War II. *See* **Allies**. (p. 357)

baby boom (bā´bē büm) A growth in population that occurred between the late 1940s and early 1960s. (p. 365)

bay (bā) A part of an ocean or lake that is partly enclosed by land. (p. 63)

barrio (bär´ē ō) The Spanish word for neighborhood, a neighborhood where Mexican Americans live. (p. 318)

bill (bil) A proposal for a new law. (p. 448)

biotechnology (bī´ō tech nol´ə gē) Technology that uses living cells to create new drugs. (p. 404)

boycott (boi´kot) A refusal to do business with a company. (p. 396)

bribe (brīb) Money or gift that is given to someone, usually an official, to do something. (p. 341)

budget (buj´it) A plan for using money. (p. 447)

C

California banknotes (kal i fôr´nē ə bank nōts) What cattle hides were called because they were so valuable in California. (p. 206)

Californio (kal i fôr´nē ō) A Mexican person who lived in California. (p. 197)

campuses (kam´ pə səz) Areas where schools are located. (p. 390)

canal (kə´ nal) An inland waterway built by people for transportation or irrigation. (p. 329)

capital (kap´ə təl) A city that is a government center. (p. 250)

cash crop (kash krop) A crop that is grown to be sold. (p. 307)

Central Pacific Railroad (sen´trəl pə sif´ik rāl´rōd) One of the first railroads. (p. 289)

charter (chär´tər) A document that gives and explains certain rights and obligations. (p. 390)

Chinese Exclusion Act (chī nēz´ ek sklü´zhən akt) A law that kept out Chinese workers. (p. 298)

Pronunciation Key									
a	at	ē	me	ō	old	ū	use	ng	song
ā	ape	i	it	ô	fork	ü	rule	th	thin
ä	far	ī	ice	oi	oil	ů	pull	th	this
âr	care	îr	pierce	ou	out	ûr	turn	zh	measure
e	end	o	hot	u	up	hw	white	ə	about, taken, pencil, lemon, circus

citizen (sit´ə zən) A person who is born in a country or who has earned the right to become a member of that country by law. (p. 429)

city council (sit´ē koun´sil) The legislative branch of city government, a group of representatives that makes a city's laws and decides how it should spend its money. (p. 448)

civil rights (siv´əl rīts) The rights of all people to be treated equally under the law. (p. 393)

claim (klām) An individual's special mining area. (p. 237)

climate (klī´mət) The pattern of weather of a certain place over many years. (p. 31)

clipper ship (klip´ər ship) A fast sailing ship. (p. 230)

coast (kōst) The land next to an ocean. (p. 17)

Cold War (kōld wôr) The belief that the United States would be in a war against the Soviet Union. (p. 366)

colony (kol´ə nē) A place ruled by another country. (p. 135)

combine (kom´bīn) A farm machine that can cut and bind wheat into bushels at the same time. (p. 307)

communication (kə mû ni kā´shən) The exchange of information between people. (p. 281)

commuter (kə´mūt´ər) Someone who travels to a job. (p. 365)

competition (kom pi tish´ ən) An effort to win or gain something from others. (p. 323)

composer (kəm´pōs ər) A person who writes something, especially a musical work. (p. 411)

compromise (kom´prō mīz) An agreement in which each side gives up something. (p. 249)

conquistador (kon kēs´tə dôr) The Spanish word for the soldiers who seize land by force. (p. 135)

conservation (kon sər vā´shən) The protection and wise use of forests, rivers and other natural resources. (p. 22)

constitution (kon sti tü´shən) A plan of government. (p. 247)

convention (kən ven´shən) A formal meeting for a special purpose. (p. 247)

convert (kon´vərt) To change one's beliefs. (p. 163)

costs and benefits (kosts and ben´ə fits) The good and bad effects of an event, or decision. (p. 255)

county (cown´tē) One of the sections into which a state or country is divided. (p. 449)

cradle (krā´dəl) A mining method that used water and trays to sift gold out of dirt. (p. 238)

creation story (krē ā´shən stôr´ē) A story that tells how the Earth was made, and how animals came to look and act the way they do. (p. 123)

culture (kul´chər) A way of life a group of people share. (p. 37)

culture areas (kul´chər ār ē ə) Areas into which cultures are divided geographically. (p. 97)

cutaway diagram (kut´əwā dī´ə gram) A drawing that shows the inside and outside of an object at the same time. (p. 110)

D

dam (dam) A wall built across a river to create a reservoir. *See* **reservoir**. (p. 330)

defense industry (də fens´ in dəs´trē) The production of weapons and equipment to help protect the United States. (p. 366)

degree (di grē´) A unit for measuring distance on Earth's surface; also a unit for measuring temperature represented by the symbol °. (p. 18)

delegate (del´i git) A person chosen to represent others. (p. 247)

delta (del´ta) Land formed by soil and sand left behind by one or more rivers. (p. 57)

democracy (də mok´rə sē) A government that is run by the people who live under it. (p. 429)

demonstration (dem ən strā´shən) A large gathering of people who want to call attention to a problem. (p. 393)

deport (dē pôrt´) An action of the government of a country that forces people to leave that country. (p. 350)

derrick (der´ik) A tower used to support drilling machines. (p. 325)

dictionary (dik´ shən er´ē) A book that has words, and their meanings, arranged in alphabetical order. (p. 140)

digging (dig´ing) A name for the gold fields. (p. 237)

discrimination (di skrim ə nā´shən) An unfair difference in the way people are treated. (p. 298)

diseño (di sen´yō) A map showing a rancho's borders. (p. 199)

diverse (di vûrs´) Great difference, variety. (p. 37)

drought (drout) A long period with very little rain, or no rain at all. (p. 307)

Dust Bowl (dust bôl) A seven-year drought in an area in the Great Plains of the United States that turned the land into dust. *See* **drought**. (p. 348)

earthquake (ûrth´kwāk) A shaking of the earth. (p. 66)

economy (i kon´ə mē) The way a region uses or produces natural resources, goods, and services. (p. 113)

elect (ə´lekt) To choose by voting. (p. 430)

elevation (el ə vā´shən) How high a place is above the ocean, or the earth's surface. (p. 31)

empire (em´pīr) A large territory where different groups of people are ruled by a single country or ruler. (p. 135)

encyclopedia (en sī klə pē´dē ə) A book, or set of books, that has a great deal of information about many things. (p. 140)

engineer (en´jə nīr´) Someone who is skilled in designing and building things. (p. 215)

entrepreneur (äntrə prə nûr) A person who starts a business that provides a needed service. (p. 237)

environment (en vī´rən mənt) The surroundings in which people, plants, or animals live. (p. 16)

epidemic (ep i dem´ic) An outbreak of a disease that makes many people ill in an area in a short time. (p. 165)

erosion (i rō´zhən) A wearing away of Earth's surface. (p. 57)

erupt (i´rupt) To break out suddenly, or to release ash and liquid rock. (p. 49)

ethnic group (eth´nik grüp) A group of people whose ancestors come from the same country or area and/or who share the same culture. (p. 38)

executive branch (eg zek´y ə tiv branch) The branch of government that carries out laws. (p. 431)

expedition (ek spi dish´ən) A journey of exploration. (p. 135)

export (ek´sport) Something sold or traded to another country. (p. 206)

fault (fôlt) A crack in the ground caused by moving plates. *See* **plate tectonics**. (p. 66)

federal (fed´ər al) A system of government that shares power between local and national governments. (p. 430)

fertile (fur´təl) Able to produce abundant crops. (p. 56)

fiesta (fē es´tə) The Spanish word for a party. (p. 203)

financial (fī´nan shəl) Anything having to do with money. (p. 146)

Forty-Niner (for´tē nī´nər) A person who went to California in 1849 to find gold. (p. 231)

free trade (frē trād) A way of trading that does not use rules or extra costs to limit trade. (p. 407)

freeway (frē´wā) A fast road that has no toll, and more than two lanes. (p. 365)

galleon (gal´ē ən) A big, heavy ship built to carry goods. (p. 144)

game (gām) Wild animals that are hunted or caught for food. (p. 109)

geographers (jē og´rə fərs) People who study geography. (p. 16)

geothermal energy (jē ə thûr´məl en´ər gē) Power that comes from hot water or steam beneath the earth's surface. (p. 23)

glacier (glā´shər) Large sheets of thick ice. (p. 95)

Gold Rush (gôld rush) A rapid movement of people to California in search of gold. (p. 231)

granary (grān´ər ē) A building used for storing food. (p. 108)

Great Depression (grāt di presh´ən) A time of hardship in many countries, started in 1929. (p. 347)

grid (grid) A set of lines that cross each other on a map that help to determine the location of a place. (p. 18)

guide words (gīd wûrds) Words that appear at the top of each page of a dictionary, they are the first and last words on each page. (p. 140)

H

harbor (här bər) A sheltered place along a coast where boats can be docked. (p. 63)

hemisphere (hem´ə sfīr) One half of the earth or another sphere (p. 15)

heritage (her i tij) Something handed down from earlier generations or from the past; tradition. (p. 38)

hide (hīd) An animal skin. (p. 203)

hydraulic mining (hī dro´lik mī´ning) A process in which miners used hoses to shoot water at hillsides thought to have gold. (p. 259)

hydroelectric power (hī drô i lek´trik pou´ər) Electricity made from falling water. (p. 332)

I

Ice Age (īs āj) The period when temperatures were so cold for so long that glaciers formed on Earth's surface. (p. 95)

immigrant (im´i grənt) A person who comes to a new country to live. (p. 37)

import (im´pôrt) Something brought in from another country for sale or use. (p. 206)

industry (in´dus trē) All the businesses that make one kind of product or provide one kind of service. (p. 50)

initiative (i nish´ə tiv) The right of citizens to suggest laws and then vote on them. (p. 343)

Internet (in´tər net) A computer network that has information on many different subjects. (p. 140)

interstate highway (in´tər stāt hī´wā) A road with at least two lanes of traffic in each direction that connects two or more states. (p. 416)

invention (in ven´shən) A new idea or tool for doing something. (p. 307)

investor (in vest´ər) Someone who puts money into a business and expects a share of the profit. (p. 289)

irrigation (ir i gā´shən) The use of ditches or pipes to bring water to dry land. (p. 76)

isthmus (is´məs) A narrow strip of land with water on both sides. (p. 233)

judicial branch (jü dish´əl branch) The part of government that makes sure the laws are followed. (p. 431)

jury (jur´ē) A group of citizens in a court of law who decide if a person is innocent or guilty (p. 429)

kayak (kī´ak) Small boats made with seal skins. (p. 211)

keyword (kē wûrd) Word that you enter into a search engine that helps you find other information. (p. 408)

labor union (lā´bər ūn´yən) A group of workers who organize to make agreements with their employer. (p. 396)

land grant (land grant) Free land the Mexican government gave to Mexicans who settled in California. (p. 199)

land management (land man´əj mənt) Care of the land. (p. 109)

landmark (land´märk) An important building, structure, or place. (p. 422)

large scale map (lärj skāl map) A map that shows many details in a small area. (p. 216)

latitude (lat´i tüd) A measure of distance north or south of the equator on Earth. *See* **parallel**. (p. 18)

legislative branch (lej´is lā tiv branch) The branch of government that makes laws. (p. 431)

legislature (lej´is lā chər) A group of representatives who make laws. (p. 249)

levee (le´vē) An earth wall that farmers built to keep water from overflowing onto the land. (p. 308)

Liberty ships (lib´ər tē ships) Battleships built in California during World War II using a new, faster method. (p. 358)

longitude (lon´ji tüd) A measure of distance east or west of the prime meridian on Earth. *See* **meridian, prime meridian**. (p. 18)

long tom (long tom) A mining method that used a slide with a special container at the bottom to catch the gold. Dirt was shoveled in at the top and as water washed the dirt down the slide the gold was separated out. (p. 238)

Manifest Destiny (man´ə fest des´tə nē) The belief that the United States had the right to take over other countries' lands in North America. (p. 219)

map scale (map skāl) The measurement a map uses to indicate the real size of a place on Earth. (p. 216)

mayor (mā´ər) The head of the city government. *See* **alcalde**. (p. 448)

meridian (mə rid´ē ən) A line of longitude. *See* **longitude**. (p. 18)

Mexican American War (mek´si kən u mer´ə cən wôr) A war between Mexico and the United States for possession of Texas that spread to California. (p. 220)

Mexican War for Independence (mex i cən wär fôr in də pen dəns) The war that won Mexico's freedom from Spanish rule. (p. 196)

microchip (mī´krō chip) The small chip in computers that passes along information. (p. 462)

migrant workers (mī´grənt wur´kərs) People who move from place to place to harvest different crops as they ripen. (p. 58)

migration (mī grā´shən) A large movement of people, or animals, from one place to another. (p. 315)

mineral (min´ər əl) Something found in the earth that is not a plant or an animal (p. 21)

minimum wage (min´ə məm wāj) The lowest amount of money a business can pay its workers. (p. 345)

mission (mish´ən) A Spanish settlement in the Americas where priests taught Native Americans the Christian religion. (p. 155)

missionary (mish´ə ner ē) A person who teaches religious beliefs to others who have different beliefs. (p. 155)

mother lode (muth´ər lôd) A gold-rich area in the central Sierra Nevada foothills. (p. 237)

mountain man (moun tən man) A trapper who lived in the Rocky Mountains (p. 212)

mountain pass (moun´tən pas) A narrow gap between mountains. (p. 48)

mountain range (moun´tən rān gəs) A chain of mountains. (p. 17)

mutual aid society (mû´chü əl ād sə sī´i tē) A group in which the members help each other. (p. 318)

mutualista (mû chü ə lē´stə) Mexican mutual aid society. (p. 318)

nanotechnology (nanō tech nol´ə gē) Technology that uses atoms to make structures that are very small. (p. 404)

NAFTA (naf´ tə) A trade treaty in which the United States, Canada, and Mexico promise to cooperate in trading with one another. (p. 407)

natural resource (nach´ər əl rē´ sôrs) Something found in the environment that people can use. (p. 21)

needs (nēdz) The food, clothing, and shelter humans must have to live. (p. 113)

neophyte (nē´ō fīte) A new believer. (p. 166)

New Deal (nü dēl) A series of programs that put people to work during the Great Depression. *See* **Great Depression**. (p. 349)

news article (nüz är´ti kəl) A story based on facts about an event or events that happened. (p. 356)

nonrenewable resource (non ri nü´əbəl) Something that cannot be replaced, such as a fuel or mineral. (p. 21)

Northwest Passage (nôrth´west´ pas´ij) A sea route from Europe to Asia. (p. 143)

nugget (nug´ət) A small piece of metal. (p. 231)

Overland Mail Company (ōv ər´lənd māl kəm´pə nē) A mail company that used stagecoaches to carry mail across country. (p. 285)

Pacific Rim (pə sif´ik rim) All the countries that touch the Pacific Ocean. (p. 406)

panning (pa´ning) A process in which a miner scooped dirt into a shallow pan, filled the pan with water, and spilled out the water and dirt. Any heavy gold in the dirt would stay in the pan. (p. 238)

parallel (par´ə lel) Another name for a line of latitude. *See* **latitude**. (p. 18)

pelt (pelt) The skin of an animal with its fur still on it. (p. 211)

petroleum (pi trō´lē əm) Commonly called oil, it is formed into gasoline, kerosene, or oil for heating buildings (p. 21)

pioneers (pī´ə nērs) Early settlers of the United States; the first people to settle in a region. (p. 213)

pit house (pit hous) Homes built partly underground to keep them cool in hot weather and warm in cold weather. (p. 109)

placer gold (plās´ər gōld) Gold found on the banks of sandy streams. (p. 238)

plain (plān) A large area of nearly flat land. (p. 17)

plate (plāt) Large pieces of earth that make up the earth's surface and are constantly moving, causing earthquakes. (p. 66)

plateau (pla´tō) An area of high flat land. (p. 126)

pobladore (pō blä´dorā) A settler. (p. 176)

Pony Express (pō´nē eks pres´) A mail service that used riders on fast ponies to carry mail across country. (p. 286)

population (pop yə lā´shən) The number of people who live in a place or area. (p. 258)

population map (pop yə lā´shən map) A map that gives information about where people live in a particular region and how many people live there. (p. 252)

precipitation (pri sip i tā shən) The moisture that falls to the ground as rain, snow, sleet, or hail. (p. 32)

prejudice (pre´jü dəs) Hatred or unfair treatment of a particular group, such as members of a race or religion. (p. 319)

presidio (pri´sid´ē ō) A fort where Spanish soldiers lived. (p. 174)

primary source (prī mār ē sôrs) First hand accounts of events. (p. 68)

prime meridian (prīm mə rid´ē ən) The line of longitude, marked 0°, from which other meridians are numbered. (p. G9)

public education (pub´lik edū kā´shən) A system that allows people to attend school without having to pay for it. (p. 389)

pueblo (pweb´lô) A town that focused on farming. (p. 176)

R

railbed (rāl´bed) A flat, smooth surface on which railroad tracks are laid. (p. 296)

rain shadow (rān sha´dō) The side of a mountain that is usually dry because precipitation falls on the other side. (p. 32)

rancho (ran´chô) A ranch where cattle, horses, and other animals were raised. (p. 199)

recall (rē´kol) A process that allows citizens to vote someone out of office. (p. 343)

recruiter (rē´krü tər) Someone who finds workers for an employer. (p. 295)

recycle (rē sī ´ kəl) To use something over again, instead of throwing it away. (p. 22)

reference material (ref´ ər əns) A book, CD, or website that has facts about many subjects, arranged so that you can look them up. (p. 140)

referendum (ref´ər end əm) A process that allows citizens to vote on laws already passed by the legislature. (p. 343)

refine (rē´fīn) To improve or make pure. (p. 325)

reformer (ri form´ər) A person who wants to improve the way government is run. (p. 341)

refrigeration (ri frij´ə rā shən) The process of keeping food cool to preserve it. (p. 310)

refugee (ref yü´gē) Someone who flees unsafe conditions in his or her homeland. (p. 37)

region (rē ´jən) An area with common features that set it apart from other areas. (p. 16)

relative location (rel´ə tiv lō kā shən) Where a place is compared to one or more other places on earth. (p. 16)

religion (ri lij´ən) A set of beliefs. (p. 105)

relocation camp (rē lō´kā shən kamp) A camp where Japanese Americans were imprisoned during World War II. (p. 360)

renewable resource (ri nü´əbəl) Something that can be replaced. (p. 21)

representative (rep ri zen´tə tiv) A person who speaks for one or more people. (p. 178)

republic (ri pub´lik) A government in which people choose their own leaders to represent them. (p. 220)

reservation (res ûr vā´shən) Land set aside for Native Americans. (p. 257)

reservoir (rez´ər vwär) A natural or human-built lake used to store water. *See* **dam**. (p. 331)

resident (rez´ i dent) A person who lives in a certain place. (p. 432)

revolt (rē´vōlt) A violent attack against a government or other authority. (p. 167)

road map (rôd map) A map that shows roads. (p. 416)

rock art (rok ärt) pictures drawn or painted on rocks. (p. 102)

rodeo (rō´dē´ō) A roundup of cattle. (p. 205)

route (rüt) The course you take to get somewhere. (p. 416)

sacred (sā´krəd) Holy. (p. 155)

sea level (sē lev´əl) The level of the surface of the sea, an elevation of zero. (p. 31)

search engine (sûrch en´jən) A computer program that looks for information on the Internet. (p. 402)

secondary source (sek´ənd ā rē sôrs) Second hand accounts of events. (p. 68)

segregation (seg´ri gā shən) The practice of keeping groups of people apart from one another. (p. 393)

settlement (set´əl mənt) A new community. (p. 156)

shaman (shä mən) A religious leader and healer. (p. 105)

shares of stock (shârs of stok) A piece of a company that someone buys as an investment. (p. 347)

site (sīt) A collection of pages on the Internet. (p. 408)

sluice (slüs) A long trough that used water to flush away the dirt and leave the gold. (p. 238)

small scale map (smal skāl map) A map that shows few details but great area. (p. 216)

software (sôft´wâr) A program or set of instructions that tells a computer what to do. (p. 402)

source (sôrs) The place where a river begins. (p. 48)

Space Race (spās rās) The race between the United States and the Soviet Union to put a man on the moon. (p. 366)

specialist (spesh´ə ləst) Someone who focuses all their time on an activity they do well. (p. 113)

squatter (skwot´ər) A person who took the Californios' land because they thought California belonged to the U.S. (p. 258)

stagecoach (stāj´kōch´) A carriage pulled by horses. (p. 281)

stock market (stok mär´kət) Where shares of stock are bought and sold. (p. 347)

stock market crash (stok mär´kət krash) When the prices of many different shares becomes low. (p. 347)

strait (strāt) A narrow passage of water. (p. 136)

suburban (sub ûr´bən) A community near a large city. (p. 58)

suffrage (suf´rij) The right to vote. (p. 344)

superintendent (sü pər in ten´dənt) A person who directs or manages something. (p. 389)

sweat house (swet hous) A building where men and boys sat around an open fire until they sweated. (p. 127)

T

tallow (tal ō´) Boiled animal fat that was used to make soap and candles. (p. 205)

tax (taks) Money people pay to the government for public services. (p. 176)

technology (tek nol´ə jē) The use of skills, tools, and machines to meet people's needs; new method of doing something. (p. 76)

telegraph (tel´ə graf) A way of sending messages by sending an electrical code through a wire. (p. 284)

time line (tīm līn) A list that shows the order of important events. (p. 160)

tomol (tō´mōl) A kind of light canoe built by the Chumash Indians. (p. 106)

tourist (tur´ist) A person who is traveling for pleasure. (p. 50)

trade (trād) To exchange; the business of buying and selling goods. (p. 113)

trailblazer (trāl´blā zər) Someone who leads the way for others. (p. 213)

transcontinental (trans kon tə nen´təl) Crossing an entire continent. (p. 285)

transportation (trans pôr tā´shən) The movement of people and goods from one place to another. (p. 281)

trapper (trap´ər) Someone who traps, or catches, animals, such as beavers, for their fur. (p. 211)

treaty (trē´tē) An agreement to make peace. (p. 222)

Treaty of Guadalupe Hidalgo (trē´tē uv gwä dä lü´pa ē dälgō) The agreement that ended the war between Mexico and the United States. *See* **treaty**. (p. 162)

tribal government (trī´bəl guv´ər mənt) The government of a reservation. (p. 449)

tributary (trib´yə ter ē) A small river that flows into a larger river. (p. 48)

U

Union Pacific Railroad (ūn´yən pəs i´fik rāl´rōd) One of the first railroad companies. (p. 289)

urban (ûr´bən) A city and its surrounding areas. (p. 58)

URL (u r l) The address of a site on the Internet. (p. 409)

valley (val´ē) An area of low land between hills or mountains. (p. 55)

vaquero (va ke´rō) Spanish word for cowhand, or cowboy. (p. 205)

veto (vē´tō) The power of the executive branch to reject a bill passed by the legislature. (p. 441)

viceroy (vīs´roi) A ruler picked by a king. (p. 136)

Vietnam War (vē et näm´ wôr) A war (1954–1975) in which the United States fought on the side of South Vietnam in its fight against North Vietnam. (p. 397)

vigilante (vig i lan´tē) A person in a group that punished people who broke laws. (p. 258)

volcano (vol kā´nō) An opening in the earth through which liquified rock, and ash may pour out. (p. 49)

wagon train (wä gən trān) A group of people in covered wagons traveling together. (p. 213)

wants (wänts) Things humans want but do not need to survive. (p. 334)

water rights (wô´tər rīts) The right to use a source of water. (p. 334)

weir (wēr) A fence across a river used to catch fish. (p. 124)

Western Union Telegraph Company (west´ərn ūn´yən tel ə graf komp´ə nē) A company that owned many telegraph wires. (p. 284)

wickiup (wick´ē up) A bowl shaped hut built with willow frames and mats. (p. 127)

World War II (wûrld wär tü) A war between the Allies and the Axis powers that began in 1939. (p. 357)

World Wide Web (wûrld wīd web) A collection of information, programs, videos, songs and games on the Internet. (p. 408)

Index

This index lists many topics that appear in the book, along with the pages on which they are found. Page numbers after a *c* refer you to a chart or diagram, after a *g* refer you to a graph, after an *m* refer you to a map, after a *p* refer you to photographs or artwork.

B

★ Credits ★

Photography Credits: All photographs are by Macmillan/McGraw-Hill (MMH) and Ken Karp for MMH except as noted below:

Cover Photos: (t) Ron Watts/CORBIS; (b) Royalty-Free/CORBIS. Back Cover: (bkgd) M. Angelo/CORBIS; (inset) Tim Zurowski/CORBIS. Endpapers: (flag) Macmillan/McGraw-Hill; (seal) One Mile Up/Fotosearch, LLC.

i: Royalty-Free/CORBIS. iv-v: Greg Probst Photography. v: (t to b) David Muench/CORBIS; Galen Rowell/CORBIS. vi: Lawrence Migdale. vii: Courtesy of The Bancroft Library, University of California, Berkeley. viii: Dorling Kindersley. ix: The Granger Collection, New York. G2-G3: James Randklev/CORBIS. G3: Courtesy of Steve Cunha. G4: (cr) Douglas Slone/CORBIS; (br) Richard Nebesky/Lonely Planet Images. G5: (tr) Robert Landau/CORBIS; (cr) David Butow/CORBIS SABA; (br) Yann Arthus-Bertrand/CORBIS. G8: (c) Bryan Allen/CORBIS. **Unit 1** 2-3: Tony Dunn. 4: (l) The Granger Collection, New York; (r) Yale Collection of American Literature, Beinecke Rare Book and Manuscript Library. 5: David Hume Kennerly/Getty Images. 11: John Nordell/The Image Works. 12: (l) Phil Schermeister/CORBIS; (r) John Nordell/The Image Works. 13: (l) Craig K. Lorenz/Photo Researchers, Inc.; (r) Gibson Stock Photography. 14-15: Greg Probst Photography. 20-21: Galen Rowell/CORBIS. 21: Victoria Hurst/First Light Associated Photographers. 23: John Nordell/The Image Works. 24: Mark E. Gibson/CORBIS. 25: (tr) CORBIS; (cr) Kerrick James Photography/Getty Images. 26: (t) Mack Henley/Visuals Unlimited; (inset) Comstock Images/Alamy; (l) Ambient Images Inc./Alamy; (br) John Mock/Lonely Planet Images. 26-27: Dynamic Graphics Group/Creatas/Alamy. 27: Thomas Wiewandt; Visions of America/CORBIS. 30-31: David Muench/CORBIS. 31: Craig K. Lorenz/Photo Researchers, Inc. 33: Yale Collection of American Literature, Beinecke Rare Book and Manuscript Library. 34: Thomas Winz/Index Stock Imagery. 36: Joe Sohm/Alamy. 37: Gibson Stock Photography. 38: (bl) A. Ramey/Photo Edit; (bkgd) David Peevers/Lonely Planet Images. 39: (t) A. Ramey/Photo Edit; (br) Gibson Stock Photography. 40: Digital Vision/Getty Images. 44: (bl) Mike Chew/CORBIS; (bc) Lawrence Migdale for MMH; (br) Theo Allofs/Visuals Unlimited. 45: James Randklev/The Image Works. 46-47: Galen Rowell/CORBIS. 48: (bkgd) Charles Webber ©California Academy of Sciences; (inset) Galen Rowell/CORBIS. 49: James Randklev/Visions of America/CORBIS. 50: Mike Chew/CORBIS. 51: (tr) Courtesy of The Bancroft Library, University of California, Berkeley; (cr) Ansel Adams Publishing Rights Trust/CORBIS. 54-55: Charles O'Rear/CORBIS. 55: AGStockUSA, Inc./Alamy. 56: Courtesy of State Museum Resource Center, California State Parks. 56-57: Airphoto North America. 57: Richard Hamilton/CORBIS. 58: Lawrence Migdale for MMH. 59: Thor Swift/The Image Works. 60: (bl) Courtesy of Jorge Alvarado; (bc) Courtesy of Paris Davis; (br) Courtesy of Jenelle Schneider. 60-61: Thor Swift/The Image Works. 62-63: Gibson Stock Photography. 63: Theo Allofs/Visuals Unlimited. 64: Rick Doyle/CORBIS. 65: (tl) Cosmo Condina/Getty Images; (r) Jerry Alexander/Getty Images. 66: Brand X Pictures/Alamy. 67: Michael Newman/Photo Edit. 68: Catalog # 50/758 Courtesy, American Museum of Natural History, Division of Anthropology. 68-69: Joseph Sohm/Visions of America/CORBIS. 69: AP Photo/Kevork Djansezian. 70: Image Farm Inc./Alamy. 70-71: Pete Stone/CORBIS. 72-73: Bill Binzen/CORBIS. 74: Royalty-Free/CORBIS. 75: Jeff Lepore/Photo Researchers, Inc. 76: James Randklev/The Image Works. 77: Theo Allofs/CORBIS. 78: AP Photo/Kevork Djansezian. 83: (b) Richard Hewett. **Unit 2** 84-85: Private Collection, Index/Bridgeman Art Library. 86: (l) Elsie Allen and Finished Baby Basket, Photo by Robert Cooper. Pomo Basketmaking: A Supreme Art for the Weaver by Elsie Allen. Copyright ©1972 by Elsie Allen. Published by Naturegraph Publishers, Inc. All rights reserved; (c) Robert Holmes/CORBIS; (r) Courtesy of the San Diego Historical Society. 87: (l) North Wind/Nancy Carter/North Wind Picture Archives. 92: (bl) Christie's Images/CORBIS; (bc) Santa Barbara Museum of Natural History; (br) Dorling Kindersley. 93: Royalty-Free/CORBIS. 96: (tl) Lawrence Migdale; (tc) Peabody Museum, Harvard University Photo T5020; (tr) Felicia Martinez/Photo Edit; (b) Ruben G. Mendoza. 97: Christie's Images/CORBIS. 98: A. Ramey/Photo Edit. 99: Lawrence Migdale/Photo Researchers, Inc. 100: (tr) Courtesy of the Phoebe Apperson Hearst Museum of Anthropology and the Regents of the University of California-photographed by Therese Babineau, 1-198157; (r) Elsie Allen and Finished Baby Basket, Photo by Robert Cooper. Pomo Basketmaking: A Supreme Art for the Weaver by Elsie Allen. Copyright ©1972 by Elsie Allen. Published by Naturegraph Publishers, Inc. All rights reserved. 102: (tl) Catalog # 50/1584 Courtesy, American Museum of Natural History, Division of Anthropology; (bc) Tom Bean/CORBIS; (br) Catalog # 50/758 Courtesy, American Museum of Natural History, Division of Anthropology. 103: (tr) Catalog # 50.1/4253 Courtesy, American Museum of Natural History, Division of Anthropology; (c) Tom Vezo/Nature Picture Library; (br) Michael McFadden Photography. 105: Portland Art Museum, Portland, Oregon. Gift of Elizabeth Cole Butler. 106: (cw from top) Jim Sugar/CORBIS; Kennan Ward/CORBIS; Kennan Ward/CORBIS; Jim Sugar/CORBIS; Jim Sugar/CORBIS; Kennan Ward/CORBIS; Kennan Ward/CORBIS; Jim Sugar/CORBIS; Santa Barbara Museum of Natural History. 107: Bowers Museum of Cultural Art/CORBIS. 108: The Field Museum, CSA10372, Photographer John Hudson. 109: Charles Webber/California Academy of Sciences. 110: Catalog # 50.2/4670 Courtesy, American Museum of Natural History, Division of Anthropology. 111: Catalog # 50.2/928 Courtesy, American Museum of Natural History, Division of Anthropology. 112-113: Tom Bean/CORBIS. 113: Catalog # 50.2/3762 Courtesy, American Museum of Natural History, Division of Anthropology. 114: T. Kitchin & V. Hurst/NHPA. 115: (tl) Catalog # 50/2789 Courtesy, American Museum of Natural History, Division of Anthropology; (tr) Catalog # 50/2149 Courtesy, American Museum of Natural History, Division of Anthropology. 116: California Historical Society. 116-117: Gibson Stock Photography. 117: photos.com. 118: (t) Arizona State Museum, University of Arizona, photo Helga Teiwes – C-16742; (cr) Courtesy of the Phoebe Apperson Hearst Museum of Anthropology and the Regents of the University of California-photographed by Therese Babineau, 1-1730. 119: Dorling Kindersley. 120: Catalog # 50/3192 Courtesy, American Museum of Natural History, Division of Anthropology. 120-121: Tony Freeman/Photo Edit. 121: (tl) Courtesy of the Phoebe Apperson Hearst Museum of Anthropology and the Regents of the University of California, 15-20942; (tr) Marilyn "Angel" Wynn/Nativestock.com; (cl) Peabody Museum Harvard University Photo T5017; (cr) Courtesy of the Phoebe Apperson Hearst Museum of Anthropology and the Regents of the University of California-photographed by Therese Babineau, 1-211613a,b. 122: Royalty-Free/CORBIS. 123: (tr) Courtesy of the Phoebe Apperson Hearst Museum of Anthropology and the Regents of the University of California-photographed by Samuel Barrett and crew, 25-5798; (br) Royalty-Free/CORBIS. 124: (bl) Northwestern University Library, Edward S. Curtis's 'The North American Indian': the Photographic Images, 2001; (br) Kennan Ward/CORBIS. 125: (tl) Courtesy of The Bancroft Library, University of California, Berkeley; (br) Courtesy of the Phoebe Apperson Hearst Museum of Anthropology and the Regents of the University of California-photographed by Therese Babineau, 1-1420. 128: Catalog # 50/3433 Courtesy, American Museum of Natural History, Division of Anthropology. 132: Robert Holmes/CORBIS. 133: Archivo Iconografico, S.A./CORBIS. 134-135: Roy Ooms/Masterfile. 135: Library of Congress. 137: (r) David Muench/CORBIS; (b) Marilyn "Angel" Wynn/Nativestock.com. 138: Gary Crabbe/Enlightened Images. 139: Robert Holmes/CORBIS. 142: Tom W. Freeman 1992. 143: Mary Evans Picture Library. 145: (t to b) The Trustees of The British Museum; The Trustees of The British Museum; National Geographic Society. 146: Courtesy of the San Diego Historical Society. 147: (t) Zig Leszczynski/MaXx Images Inc.; (inset) Archivo Iconografico, S.A./CORBIS. 152: (l) Craig Lovell/CORBIS; (r) David Rickman. 153: Craig Lovell/CORBIS. 154: Dorothy Judd/California Academy of Sciences. 155: (tr) The Granger Collection, New York; (r) Historical Picture Archive/CORBIS. 157: (t) Tate Gallery, London/Art Resource, NY; (inset) The Granger Collection, New York. 158: (tl) Craig Lovell/CORBIS; (inset) Courtesy of the San Diego Historical Society. 161: Joseph Sohm; ChromoSohm Inc./CORBIS. 162: Smithsonian American Art Museum, Washington, D.C./Art Resource, NY. 163: Craig Lovell/CORBIS. 165: (bl) Catalog # 50/2468 Courtesy, American Museum of Natural History, Division of Anthropology; (br) Catalog # 50/2140 Courtesy, American Museum of Natural History, Division of Anthropology. 167: Courtesy of State Museum Resource Center, California State Parks. 169: N.Carter/North Wind Picture Archives. 170: (t) Robert Holmes/CORBIS; (cl) Lee

Foster/Lonely Planet Images; (br) Richard Cummins/CORBIS. 171: (tl) Gunter Marx Photography/CORBIS; (cr) Dr. Lloyd Glenn Ingles/California Academy of Sciences. 172-173: Peabody Museum Harvard University Photo 41-72-10/68. 173: Royalty-Free/CORBIS. 175: David Rickman. 176: Photograph courtesy of Ruth Wallach, USC. 183: (b) Hulton Getty/Archive Photos. **Unit 3** 184: Smithsonian American Art Museum, Washington, D.C./Art Resource, NY. 186: (c) The Granger Collection, New York; (r) Bettman/CORBIS. 187: (l) The Granger Collection, New York; (c) Security Pacific Collection/Los Angeles Public Library; (r) CORBIS. 192: The Granger Collection, New York. 194: (l) The Granger Collection, New York; (r) Brian A. Vikander/CORBIS. 195: Cindy Charles/Photo Edit. 196: Dagli Orti/National History Museum Mexico City/The Art Archive. 197: The Granger Collection, New York. 198: U.S. National Archives. 199: Courtesy Palo Alto Historical Association. 200: San Francisco History Center, San Francisco Public Library. 202: California Historical Society. 203: The Granger Collection, New York. 205: Courtesy of the Bancroft Library, University of California, Berkeley. 206: Library of Congress, Rare Book and Special Collections Division. 207: The Granger Collection, New York. 208: (tr) Sombrero, felt, wool, leather, 1810-1850, Museum of the American West collection, Autry National Center; (bl) Dave G. Houser/CORBIS. 209: (tl) Saddle, Main and Winchester Saddlery, rawhide, leather, wood, circa 1855, Museum of the American West collection, Autry National Center; (cl) Patrick Ward/CORBIS. 210-211: The Granger Collection, New York. 211: Clive Druett/Papilio/CORBIS. 213: Brian A. Vikander/CORBIS. 214: James L. Amos/CORBIS. 215: (tr) C Squared Studios/Photodisc/Getty Images; (inset) Bettmann/CORBIS; (r) The Granger Collection, New York. 218: Courtesy of the Bancroft Library, University of California, Berkeley. 219: Brooklym Museum of Art, New York, USA/Bridgeman Art Library. 220: (l) Bettmann/CORBIS; (r) Stockbyte Silver/Getty Images. 221: Cindy Charles/Photo Edit. 223: CORBIS. 224: (bl, bc) Courtesy of the Bancroft Library, University of California, Berkeley; (br) California Department of Parks and Recreation Photographic Archive/Tom Myers. 224-225: Courtesy of Franklin D. Roosevelt Library. 228: (c) Dirk Wiersma/Science Photo Library/Photo Researchers, Inc.; (r) California State Archives. 230: (b) Dave G. Houser/CORBIS; (inset) Oakland Museum of California, Prints and Photographs Fund. 231: Dirk Wiersma/Science Photo Library/Photo Researchers, Inc. 232: (tl) Museum of the City of New York/CORBIS; (tr) Courtesy of The Bancroft Library, University of California, Berkeley. 233: Courtesy of The Bancroft Library, University of California, Berkeley. 235: San Francisco and a forest of masts. 1979.90.141. Mystic Seaport. 236: Courtesy of The Bancroft Library, University of California, Berkeley. 237: Historical Society of Seattle/CORBIS. 238: Courtesy of the California History Room, California State Library, Sacramento, California. 239: Courtesy California State Library. 241: (bl) Courtesy of The Bancroft Library, University of California, Berkeley; (br) Courtesy of the Oakland Museum of California. 242: (bl) Courtesy Levi Strauss & Co. Archives; (bkgd) The Granger Collection, New York. 244: Courtesy Dorothy Sloan Books. 245: Library of Congress. 246: Stephen Saks Photography/Alamy. 247: Courtesy of The Bancroft Library, University of California, Berkeley. 248: Bettmann/CORBIS. 249: (tr) Image Farm Inc./Alamy; (inset) Courtesy of the Bancroft Library, University of California, Berkeley. 250: Gary Moon. 251: (tr) Image Farm Inc./Alamy; (inset) Security Pacific Collection/Los Angeles Public Library. 254: Library of Congress, Prints and Photographs Division [LC-USZC4-7421]. 255: Library of Congress, Prints and Photographs Division [LC-USZC4-5250]. 256: (tl) CORBIS; (b) Armed Forces History, Division of History of Technology, National Museum of American History; (br) CORBIS. 257: (tc) Courtesy of the California History Room, California State Library, Sacramento, California; (r) The Granger Collection, New York. 258: Seaver Center for Western History Research, Natural History Museum of Los Angeles County. 259: Library of Congress, Prints and Photographs Division [LC-USZ62-9889]. 261: Courtesy of the Bancroft Library, University of California, Berkeley. 267: (b) Cover background Archive Photos; portrait, detail of The Emigrant Train Bedding Down for the Night by Benjamin Reinhart in the Collection of The Corcoran Gallery of Art. **Unit 4** 268-269: The Granger Collection, New York. 270: (l) The Granger Collection, New York; (c) Courtesy Jack Kim; (r) Underwood & Underwood/CORBIS. 271: (l) Courtesy California Department of Parks and Recreation Photographic Archive 2005; (c) Hulton-Deutsch Collection/CORBIS; (r) Special Collections Department U.S.C Library. 276-277: David Pollack/K.J. Historical/CORBIS. 279: The J. Paul Getty Museum, Los Angeles, Carleton Watkins, Trestle on Central Pacific Railroad, 1887, albumen silver, 8 1/16 x 12 3/8 in. 280: Wells Fargo & Company. 281: Wells Fargo & Company. 283: (tl) Bettmann/CORBIS; (tc) CORBIS; (tr) St. Joseph Museum Inc., St. Joseph, Missouri; (br) The Granger Collection, New York. 284: (tr) Getty Images; (inset) Smithsonian photo by Alfred Harrell. 286: Union Pacific Historic Collection. 288: CORBIS. 289: Union Pacific Historic Collection. 290-291: Claver Carroll/Alamy. 291: The Granger Collection, New York. 294: Union Pacific Historic Collection. 295: Wolfgang Kaehler/CORBIS. 296: (tr) Courtesy of the Bancroft Library, University of California, Berkeley; (bl) General Collections, Library of Congress. 297: The J. Paul Getty Museum, Los Angeles, Carleton Watkins, Trestle on Central Pacific Railroad, 1887, albumen silver, 8 1/16 x 12 3/8 in. 300: (t) Gibson Stock Photography; (cl) Neil Lukas/Dorling Kindersley; (br) Phil Schermeister/CORBIS. 300-301: Eric Luse/San Francisco Chronicle. 301: Michael Maloney/San Francisco Chronicle. 304: New-York Historical Society, New York, USA/Bridgeman Art Library. 305: (bl) Phil Schermeister/CORBIS; (bc) Jim Cornfield/CORBIS. 306: CORBIS. 307: Courtesy of the Bancroft Library, University of California, Berkeley. 308: (tl) Orange Public Library, Orange, California; (tr) California State Railroad Museum. 309: (tr) Courtesy of the Riverside Municipal Museum, Riverside, CA #A572-2; (inset) AGStockUSA, Inc./Alamy; (br) Royalty-Free/CORBIS. 311: (r) Underwood & Underwood/CORBIS; (br) David Roseburg/CORBIS. 312: Tetra Images/Alamy. 314: Courtesy of State Museum Resource Center, California State Parks. 315: New-York Historical Society, New York, USA/Bridgeman Art Library. 317: Courtesy of State Museum Resource Center, California State Parks. 318: (bl) Bettmann/CORBIS; (br) Hulton-Deutsch Collection/CORBIS. 319: Anaheim Public Library Photograph Collection on Anaheim Local History. 320: (bl, br) Courtesy California Department of Parks and Recreation Photographic Archive, 2005. 322: Security Pacific Collection/Los Angeles Public Library. 323: P-1154, Eastman's Originals Collection 1997, Special Collections, University of California Library, Davis. 324: Pomona Public Library Special Collections - Courtesy of: Frashers Fotos/Tomesha. 325: Security Pacific Collection/Los Angeles Public Library. 326: (tr) Jim Cornfield/CORBIS; (bl) Bettmann/CORBIS; (br) Lorey Sebastian/Fox Searchlight/CORBIS. 327: Jim Cornfield/CORBIS. 328: Phil Schermeister/CORBIS. 329: Herald Examiner Collection/Los Angeles Public Library. 330: CORBIS. 332: Pascal Crapet/Getty Images. 334: Bureau of Reclamation. 335: Lady Philippa Scott/NHPA. 338: Courtesy of The Bancroft Library, University of California, Berkeley. 339: (bl) CORBIS; (bc) E.F. Joseph/Department of Defense. 340-341: CORBIS. 341: CORBIS. 342: Courtesy of The Bancroft Library, University of California, Berkeley. 343: (tl) California State Archives; (tr) Ann Johansson/CORBIS. 344: (tl) Bettmann/CORBIS; (inset) Security Pacific Collection/Los Angeles Public Library. 345: Courtesy of Bryn Mawr College Library. 346: American Stock/Getty Images. 347: C Squared Studios/Photodisc/Getty Images. 348: CORBIS. 349: (c) Bettmann/CORBIS; (br) Thomas Winz/Panoramic Images. 351: Special Collections Department U.S.C Library. 352-353: Ric Ergenbright/CORBIS. 354-355: Phil Schermeister/CORBIS. 355: Bettmann/CORBIS. 356: Bettmann/CORBIS. 357: Armed Forces History, Division of History of Technology, National Museum of American History. 358: (tl) The Granger Collection, New York; (tr) CORBIS. 359: E.F. Joseph/Department of Defense. 360: (bl) AP Photo/National Park Service; (inset) Ansel Adams/Library of Congress, Prints and Photographs Division [LC-USZC4-5549]. 361: Courtesy of National Archives. 363: CORBIS. 364: Courtesy The Multicultural Music and Art Foundation of Northridge. 365: Sheri Blaney/Index Stock Imagery. 366: Bettmann/CORBIS. 367: Bettmann/CORBIS. 368: Carphotos/Alamy. 369: (tr, cl) Bettmann/CORBIS; (inset) Petrified Collection/Getty Images; (br) Cooperphoto/CORBIS. 375: (bl) Courtesy of the Obata family. **Unit 5** 376-377: Rufus F. Folkks/CORBIS. 378: (l) Library of Congress, Prints and Photographs Division; (c) Courtesy of The Bancroft Library, University of California, Berkeley; (r) Najlah Feanny/CORBIS. 379: (l) Mark Ludak/The Image Works; (c) Marion Kalter/akg-images; (r) AP Photo. 386: (bl) Ric Ergenbright/CORBIS; (br) David J. & Janice L. Frent Collection/CORBIS. 388: Tom & Dee Ann McCarthy/CORBIS. 389: Ric Ergenbright/CORBIS. 390: John Elk III. 391: Royalty-Free/CORBIS. 392: AP Photo/Sakuma. 393: (tr) David J. & Janice L. Frent Collection/CORBIS; (br) Francis Miller/Time & Life Pictures/Getty Images. 394: (l to r) Herald Examiner Collection/Los Angeles Public Library; Bettmann/CORBIS; Shelley Gazin/CORBIS. 395: (tr) AP Photo; (bl) Christ Stewart/San Francisco Chronicle. 396: (tr) Arthur Schatz/Time & Life Pictures/Getty Images; (bl) Ed Young/CORBIS. 397: (t) Bettmann/CORBIS. 398: Bettmann/CORBIS. 399: Getty Images. 400: Brand X/First Light Associated Photographers. 401: A. Syred/Photo Researchers, Inc. 402: Bettmann/CORBIS. 403: (c) Edd Westmacott/Alamy; (r) HO/AFP/Getty Images. 404: (tr) Bruce Frisch/Photo Researchers, Inc.; (inset) The Craighead Group/Cornell University. 410: Richard Cummins/CORBIS. 411: Royalty-Free/CORBIS. 412: (tr) Christine Alicino; (bl) AP Photo/Eric Risberg; (br) Neville Elder/Corbis. 413: (tr) Christopher Felver/CORBIS; (inset) The Newark Museum/Art Resource, NY. 414: Robert Landau/CORBIS. 415: (tr) Nathan Benn/CORBIS; (br) Robert Landau/CORBIS. 418: Richard I'Anson/Lonely Planet Images. 419: Larry Downing/CORBIS. 420: (tr) Royalty-Free/CORBIS; (b) Macduff Everton/CORBIS. 421: (t) Van Hilversum/Alamy; (br) David Young-Wolff/Photo Edit. 422: (bl) Captain Heidi Tiura/Sanctuary Cruises; (br) Phil Schermeister/CORBIS. 426: (bl) William Whitehurst/CORBIS; (br) Gerald French/CORBIS. 427: Richard Cummins/CORBIS. 428-429: Royalty-Free/CORBIS. 429: (tr) Joseph Sohm/Visions of America/CORBIS; (bl) William Whitehurst/CORBIS. 430: CORBIS. 431: (tr) Brooks Kraft/CORBIS; (cr) Frederick M. Brown/Getty Images; (bl) Kat Wade/San Francisco Chronicle/CORBIS. 432: (tl) Karen Quincy Loberg/Ventura County Star/CORBIS; (r) Gene Blevins/CORBIS. 433: Norbert von der Groeben/The Image Works. 434: Joseph Sohm/Visions of America/CORBIS. 435: The Granger Collection, New York. 436: (bl) Courtesy of Shona Hemmady; (bc) Courtesy of Adrian Perez; (br) Courtesy of Arturo Silberstein. 436-437: Royalty-Free/CORBIS. 438: ART on FILE/CORBIS. 439: (tr) Robert Holmes/CORBIS; (bl) California State Archives. 444: (t) Gerald French/CORBIS; (l) John Elk III; (b) Jan Butchofsky-Houser/CORBIS. 445: (tl) Gibson Stock Photography; (r) Steven Hellon/California State History Museum. 446: Jan Butchofsky-Houser/CORBIS. 447: Kim Kulish/CORBIS. 448: Courtesy Office of Councilmember Nora Campos. 449: (t) Giulio Marcocchi/Getty Images; (br) Bob Rowan/Progressive Image/CORBIS. 451: AP Photo. 453: California State Archives.

R16: (t) California State Archives; (l) Art Wolfe/Getty Images; (r) California State Archives; (b) Royalty-Free/CORBIS. R17: (tl) Royalty-Free/CORBIS; (r) John Warden/Getty Images; (bl) Jules Frazier/Photodisc/Getty Images. R19: (tl) Jeff Kan Lee/The Press Democrat; (tr) Reuters/CORBIS; (c) Mark Wilson/Getty Images; (bl) Doug Menuez/CORBIS; (br) Bettmann/CORBIS. R20: (tl) Stephane Cardinale/People Avenue/CORBIS; (cr) Zack Seckler/CORBIS; (bl) BRIAN SNYDER/Reuters/Corbis; (br) JASON REED/Reuters/Corbis. R20-R21: MIKE BLAKE/Reuters/Corbis. R21: (tr) Reuters/CORBIS; (l) George Kruse/The Sun-Reporter; (r) RAY STUBBLEBINE/Reuters/Corbis; (bl) NASA; (br) Courtesy Gary Soto. R22: (tl) Tom W. Freeman 1992; (tr) Courtesy of the San Diego Historical Society; (bl) Bettmann/CORBIS; (br) The Granger Collection, New York. R23: (tl) California Historical Society, FN-13905; (tr) Kenneth James/CORBIS; (bl) The Granger Collection, New York; (bc) The Granger Collection, New York; (br) Doug Mills/Pool/Reuters/CORBIS.

Acknowledgments

Relation of the Voyage of Juan Rodriguez Cabrillo, 1542 – 1543, by The American Journeys Collection. Copyright © 2003 by The Wisconsin Historical Society. <http://content.wisconsinhistory.org/cgi-bin/docviewer.exe?CISOROOT=/aj&CISOPTR=1522> Used by Permission.

Lands of Promise and Despair: Chronicles of Early California, 1535-1846, by Rose Marie Beebe and Robert M. Senkewicz. Copyright © 2001 by Heyday Books. All Rights Reserved. Used by Permission.

Sir Francis Drake on the California Coast, by The American Journeys Collection. Copyright © 2003 by The Wisconsin Historical Society. <http://content.wisconsinhistory.org/cgi-bin/docviewer.exe?CISOROOT=/aj&CISOPTR=2351&CISOSHOW=2232> Used by Permission.

The Diary of Sebastian Vizcaino, 1602 – 1603, by The American Journeys Collection. Copyright © 2003 by The Wisconsin Historical Society. <http://content.wisconsinhistory.org/cgi-bin/docviewer.exe?CISOROOT=/aj&CISOPTR=1586> Used by Permission.

Fr. Junipero Serra, by the Historical Society of Southern California,1999. <http://www.socal-history.org/Biographies/serra.htm> Used by Permission.

Hispanics of Achievement: Junipero Serra, by Sean Dolan. Copyright © 1991 by Chelsea House Publishers. Used by Permission.

Junipero Serra, by Don DeNevi and Noel Francis Moholy. Copyright © 1985 by Harper and Row. All Rights Reserved. Used by Permission.

The Indian in the Closet, from "Southern California: An Island on the Land," by Carey McWilliams. Copyright © 1979 by Peregrine Smith. <http://cogweb.ucla.edu/Chumash/McWilliams.html> Used by Permission.

The Prideful Mission and the Little Town: Los Angeles, by Douglas Monroy. From Common-place: The Interactive Journal of Early American Life, Inc. <http://www.historycoop-erative.org/journals/cp/vol-03/no-04/los-angeles/index.html> Used by Permission.

The History of San Diego, by Richard F. Pourade. Copyright © 1960 by Union-Tribune Publishing Company, Copley Press. <http://www.sandiegohistory.org/books/pourade/explor-ers/explorerschapter10.htm> Used by Permission.

Cover permission for **Native Ways: California Indian Stories and Memories**, Edited by Malcolm Margolin and Yolanda Montijo. Copyright © 1995 by Heyday Books. All Rights Reserved.

Cover permission for **Cabrillo: First European Explorer of the California Coast**, Written and Illustrated by Nancy Lemke. Copyright © 1991 by Nancy Lemke. Cover image based on a statue at Cabrillo National Monument and painted by Salvador Bru. It appears courtesy of the National Park Service. Published by EZ Nature Books. All Rights Reserved.

Cover permission for **The California Missions**, by Ann Heinrichs. Copyright © 2002 by Compass Point Books. All Rights Reserved.

Rachel's Journal, by Marissa Moss. Copyright © 1998 Marissa Moss. Published by Harcourt Brace & Company. All Rights Reserved. Used by Permission.

Gold Fever, from California History Online <http://www.californiahistory.net> Used by Permission.

Polk: The Diary of a President, edited by Milo Quaife. Copyright © 1929 by Longmans, Green, and Co. All Rights Reserved. Used by Permission.

California: An Interpretive History, by James Rawls and Walton Bean. Copyright © 2003, 1998, 1993, 1988, 1983, 1978, 1973, 1968 by the McGraw-Hill Companies, Inc. All Rights Reserved. Used by Permission.

"More Like A Pig Than a Bear": Mariano Guadalupe Vallejo Is Taken Prisoner During the Bear Flag Revolt, 1846, from <http://historymatters.gmu.edu/d/6535/> Used by Permission.

San Pasqual, A Crack in the Hills, by Mary Rockwood Peet. Copyright © 1949 by The Highland Press. All Rights Reserved. Used by Permission.

What A Country, from New Perspectives on the West, Episode Two. Copyright © by the Public Broadcasting Society. <http://www.pbs.org/weta/thewest/program/episodes/two/> Used by Permission.

California: An Interpretive History, by James Rawls and Walton Bean. Copyright © 2003, 1998, 1993, 1988, 1983, 1978, 1973, 1968 by th McGraw-Hill Companies, Inc. All Rights Reserved. Used by Permission.

Discovery, from "The Gold Rush." The Public Broadcasting Society. <http://www.pbs.org/goldrush/discovery.html> Used by Permission.

California: An Interpretive History, by James Rawls and Walton Bean. Copyright © 2003, 1998, 1993, 1988, 1983, 1978, 1973, 1968 by th McGraw-Hill Companies, Inc. All Rights Reserved. Used by Permission.

Gold Dust, by Donald Dale Jackson. Copyright © 1980 by Alfred A. Knopf, Inc. All Rights Reserved. Used by Permission.

New Orleans to San Francisco in '49, transcribed by Russell Towle, February, 1995. From Oakland Museum of California <http://www.museumca.org/goldrush/tales.html> Used by Permission.

Boom Towns, from California History Online <http://www.californiahistory.net> Used by Permission.

A Letter from a Gold Miner, Placerville, California, October, 1850, from the Friends of the Huntington Library, 1944. Used by Permission.

Prospecting: Miners Working a Long Tom, from "Gold Rush! California's Untold Stories at the Oakland Museum." <http://www.museumca.org/goldrush/fever13-lo.html> Used by Permission.

Biddy Mason, by James Rawls. From California History Online <http://www.californiahistory.net> Used by Permission.

California: An Interpretive History, by James Rawls and Walton Bean. Copyright © 2003, 1998, 1993, 1988, 1983, 1978, 1973, 1968 by th McGraw-Hill Companies, Inc. All Rights Reserved. Used by Permission.

Cover permission for **Two Years Before the Mast: A Personal Narrative of Life at Sea**, Text by Richard Henry Dana, Jr. First published by Harper & Brothers 1840. Published in The Penguin American Library 1981. Reprinted in Penguin Classics 1986. Introduction and Notes Copyright © Viking Penguin Inc., 1981. All Rights Reserved.

Cover permission for **A Covered Wagon Girl: The Diary of Sallie Hester**, Edited by Christy Steele with Ann Hodgson. Published by Blue Earth Books. Copyright © 2000 by Capstone Press. All Rights Reserved.

Cover permission for **The Celebrated Jumping Frog of Calaveras County**, by Samuel L. Clemens. Copyright © 1965 Filter Press. All Rights Reserved.

Baseball Saved Us, Text by Ken Mochizuki. Illustrations by Dom Lee. Text Copyright © 1993 by Ken Mochizuki. Illustrations Copyright © 1993 by Dom Lee. Published by Lee and Low Books, Inc. All Rights Reserved. Used by Permission.

Golden Spike, by Robert M. Utley and Francis A. Ketterson, Jr. From Golden Spike National Historic Site <http://www.cr.nps.gov/history/online_books/hh/40/hh40s.htm> Used by Permission.

We were there, too! Young People in U.S. History, by Phillip Hoose. Copyright © 2001 by Farrar, Straus and Giroux. All Rights Reserved. Used by Permission.

The First Transcontinental Railroad, by John Debo Galloway. Copyright © 1950 by Simmons-Boardman. All Rights Reserved. Used by Permission.

Transcontinental Railroad, from the Public Broadcasting Society. <http://www.pbs.org/wgbh/amex/tcrr/peopleevents/p_cprr.html> Used by Permission.

The Human Meaning of Migration, from Digital History site: <http:// www.digitalhistory.uh.edu> Used by Permission.

We were there, too! Young People in U.S. History, by Phillip Hoose. Copyright © 2001 by Farrar, Straus and Giroux. All Rights Reserved. Used by Permission.

Gold Ridge: Luther Burbank's Experiment Farm, from Western Sonoma County Historical Society <http://www.wschs-grf.pon.net/bef.htm> Used by Permission.

Flower lady brings beauty, pleasure to work, by Sue Moncure. From University of Delaware <http://www.udel.edu/PR/UDaily/2005/dec/yang121404.html> Used by Permission.

Island: Poetry and History of Chinese Immigrants on Angel Island, 1910-1940, by Him Mark Lai, Genny Lin, and Judy Yung. Copyright © 1991 by the University of Washington Press. All Rights Reserved. Used by Permission.

Black Life in the Sacramento Valley 1919-1934, by Thomas C. Fleming. Copyright © 1999 by Thomas C. Fleming and Max Millard. Published by Boson Books. All Rights Reserved. Used by Permission.

Oranges for Health-California for Wealth, by James Rawls. From California History Online <http://www.californiahistory.net> Used by Permission.

Governor Hiram Johnson, by James Rawls. From California History Online <http://www.californiahistory.net> Used by Permission.

Rosie the Riveter, by by Redd Evans and John Jacob Loeb. Copyright © 1942 by John J. Loeb Company and Music Sales Corporation. All Rights Reserved. Used by Permission.

The Assignment I'll Never Forget: Migrant Mother, from Popular Photography, February, 1960. Used by Permission.

The Grapes of Wrath, by John Steinbeck. Copyright © 1939 by John Steinbeck. Published by Penguin Books. All Rights Reserved. Used by Permission.

Breaking the Sound Barrier, by Gen. Chuck Yeager (USAF, Retired). From Popular Mechanics, November, 1987. <http://www.popularmechanics.com/marketing/1100997.html> Used by Permission.

Cover permission for **Riding Freedom**, Text by Pam Mun_oz Ryan. Drawings by Brian Selznick. Text Copyright © 1998 by Pam Mun_oz Ryan. Drawings Copyright © 1998 by Brian Selznick. Published by Scholastic, Inc. All Rights Reserved.

Cover permission for **Nature Art with Chiura Obata**, Text by Michael Elsohn Ross. Illustrations by Wendy Smith. Text Copyright © 2000 by Michael Elsohn Ross. Illustrations Copyright © 2000 by Wendy Smith. Published by Carolrhoda Books, Inc. All Rights Reserved.

Cover permission for **The Children of Topaz**, by Michael O. Tunnell and George W. Chilcoat. Copyright © 1996 by Michael O. Tunnell and George W. Chilcoat. Published by Holiday House. All Rights Reserved.

The Upside Down Boy: El niño de cabeza, Text by Juan Felipe Herrera. Illustrations by Elizabeth Go_mez. Text Copyright © 2000 by Juan Felipe Herrera. Illustrations Copyright © 2000 by Elizabeth Go_mez. Published by Children's Book Press. All Rights Reserved. Used by Permission.

The Core Values of Cesar Chavez, from the Cesar E. Chavez Foundation. <http://chavezfoun-dation.org> Used by Permission.

Early Vision of Semple, Swett Realized in Broad, Firm, Educational System, by Will C. Wood. From the Virtual Museum of the City of San Francisco. <http://www.sfmuseum.org/hist3/schools/html> Used by Permission.

The Peaceful Warrior, by Martin Luther King, Jr. Copyright © 1968 by Martin Luther King, Jr. Published by Pocket Books. All Rights Reserved. Used by Permission.

Alcatraz Is Not An Island. From the Public Broadcasting Society website: <http://www.pbs.org/itvs/alcatrazisnotanisland/occupation.html> Used by Permission.

Dolores Huerta, from "California's Remarkable Women." California State Capitol Museum <http:// www.capitalmuseum.ca.gov/> Used by Permission.

A Sculptor's World, by Isamu Noguchi. Copyright © 1968 by Harper and Row. <http://www.noguchi.org/intextall.html>Used by Permission.

Noguchi East and West, by Dore Ashton. Copyright © 1992 by Dore Ashton. Published by Alfred A. Knopf. Used by Permission.

The Story of Cesar Chavez, from United Farm Workers. <http://www.ufw.org/cecstory.htm> Used by Permission.

S.F. police chief, aides step aside; Sanders on sick leave; others suspended, by Jaxon Van Derbeken, Rachel Gordon, Jim Herron Zamora. San Francisco Chronicle, March 4, 2003. <http://sfgate.com/cgi-bin/article.cgi?file=/chronicle/archive/2003/03/04/MN225639.DTL> Used by Permission.

Cover permission for **Farmworkers' Friend: The Story of César Chávez**, by David R. Collins. Text Copyright © 1996 by David R. Collins. Published by Carolrhoda Books, Inc. A Division of Lerner Publishing Group. All Rights Reserved.

Cover permission for **Steve Wozniak: A Wizard Named Woz**, by Rebecca Gold. Copyright © 1994 by Lerner Publications Company. All Rights Reserved.

Cover permission for **The Capital That Wouldn't Stay Put**, by June Oxford. Original Copyright © 1983 by June Oxford. Copyright © transferred 1995 to James Stevenson Publisher. All Rights Reserved.

California Framework

Historical and Social Sciences Analysis Skills

Chronological and Spatial Thinking

1. Students place key events and people of the historical era they are studying in a chronological sequence and within a spatial context; they interpret time lines.
2. Students correctly apply terms related to time, including *past, present, future, decade, century,* and *generation.*
3. Students explain how the present is connected to the past, identifying both similarities and differences between the two, and how some things change over time and some things stay the same.
4. Students use map and globe skills to determine the absolute locations of places and interpret information available through a map's or globe's legend, scale, and symbolic representations.
5. Students judge the significance of the relative location of a place (e.g., proximity to a harbor, on trade routes) and analyze how relative advantages or disadvantages can change over time.

Research, Evidence, and Point of View

1. Students differentiate between primary and secondary sources.
2. Students pose relevant questions about events they encounter in historical documents, eyewitness accounts, oral histories, letters, diaries, artifacts, photographs, maps, artworks, and architecture.
3. Students distinguish fact from fiction by comparing documentary sources on historical figures and events with fictionalized characters and events.

Historical Interpretation

1. Students summarize the key events of the era they are studying and explain the historical contexts of those events.
2. Students identify the human and physical characteristics of the places they are studying and explain how those features form the unique character of those places.
3. Students identify and interpret the multiple causes and effects of historical events.
4. Students conduct cost-benefit analyses of historical and current events.

CALIFORNIA FRAMEWORK

History–Social Science Content Standards
Grade 4 California: A Changing State

4.1 Students demonstrate an understanding of the physical and human geographic features that define places and regions in California.

1. Explain and use the coordinate grid system of latitude and longitude to determine the absolute locations of places in California and on Earth.
2. Distinguish between the North and South Poles; the equator and the prime meridian; the tropics; and the hemispheres, using coordinates to plot locations.
3. Identify the state capital and describe the various regions of California, including how their characteristics and physical environments (e.g., water, landforms, vegetation, climate) affect human activity.
4. Identify the locations of the Pacific Ocean, rivers, valleys, and mountain passes and explain their effects on the growth of towns.
5. Use maps, charts, and pictures to describe how communities in California vary in land use, vegetation, wildlife, climate, population density, architecture, services, and transportation.

4.2 Students describe the social, political, cultural, and economic life and interactions among people of California from the pre-Columbian societies to the Spanish mission and Mexican rancho periods.

1. Discuss the major nations of California Indians, including their geographic distribution, economic activities, legends, and religious beliefs; and describe how they depended on, adapted to, and modified the physical environment by cultivation of land and use of sea resources.
2. Identify the early land and sea routes to, and European settlements in, California with a focus on the exploration of the North Pacific (e.g., by Captain James Cook, Vitus Bering, Juan Cabrillo), noting especially the importance of mountains, deserts, ocean currents, and wind patterns.
3. Describe the Spanish exploration and colonization of California, including the relationships among soldiers, missionaries, and Indians (e.g., Juan Crespi, Junipero Serra, Gaspar de Portola).
4. Describe the mapping of, geographic basis of, and economic factors in the placement and function of the Spanish missions; and understand how the mission system expanded the influence of Spain and Catholicism throughout New Spain and Latin America.
5. Describe the daily lives of the people, native and nonnative, who occupied the presidios, missions, ranchos, and pueblos.
6. Discuss the role of the Franciscans in changing the economy of California from a hunter-gatherer economy to an agricultural economy.
7. Describe the effects of the Mexican War for Independence on Alta California, including its effects on the territorial boundaries of North America.
8. Discuss the period of Mexican rule in California and its attributes, including land grants, secularization of the missions, and the rise of the rancho economy.

4.3 Students explain the economic, social, and political life in California from the establishment of the Bear Flag Republic through the Mexican-American War, the Gold Rush, and the granting of statehood.

1. Identify the locations of Mexican settlements in California and those of other settlements, including Fort Ross and Sutter's Fort.

2. Compare how and why people traveled to California and the routes they traveled (e.g., James Beckwourth, John Bidwell, John C. Fremont, Pio Pico).

3. Analyze the effects of the Gold Rush on settlements, daily life, politics, and the physical environment (e.g., using biographies of John Sutter, Mariano Guadalupe Vallejo, Louise Clapp).

4. Study the lives of women who helped build early California (e.g., Biddy Mason).

5. Discuss how California became a state and how its new government differed from those during the Spanish and Mexican periods.

4.4 Students explain how California became an agricultural and industrial power, tracing the transformation of the California economy and its political and cultural development since the 1850s.

1. Understand the story and lasting influence of the Pony Express, Overland Mail Service, Western Union, and the building of the transcontinental railroad, including the contributions of Chinese workers to its construction.

2. Explain how the Gold Rush transformed the economy of California, including the types of products produced and consumed, changes in towns (e.g., Sacramento, San Francisco), and economic conflicts between diverse groups of people.

3. Discuss immigration and migration to California between 1850 and 1900, including the diverse composition of those who came; the countries of origin and their relative locations; and conflicts and accords among the diverse groups (e.g., the 1882 Chinese Exclusion Act).

4. Describe rapid American immigration, internal migration, settlement, and the growth of towns and cities (e.g., Los Angeles).

5. Discuss the effects of the Great Depression, the Dust Bowl, and World War II on California.

6. Describe the development and locations of new industries since the nineteenth century, such as the aerospace industry, electronics industry, large-scale commercial agriculture and irrigation projects, the oil and automobile industries, communications and defense industries, and important trade links with the Pacific Basin.

7. Trace the evolution of California's water system into a network of dams, aqueducts, and reservoirs.

8. Describe the history and development of California's public education system, including universities and community colleges.

9. Analyze the impact of twentieth-century Californians on the nation's artistic and cultural development, including the rise of the entertainment industry (e.g., Louis B. Mayer, Walt Disney, John Steinbeck, Ansel Adams, Dorothea Lange, John Wayne).

4.5 Students understand the structures, functions, and powers of the local, state, and federal governments as described in the U.S. Constitution.

1. Discuss what the U.S. Constitution is and why it is important (i.e., a written document that defines the structure and purpose of the U.S. government and describes the shared powers of federal, state, and local governments).

2. Understand the purpose of the California Constitution, its key principles, and its relationship to the U.S. Constitution.

3. Describe the similarities (e.g., written documents, rule of law, consent of the governed, three separate branches) and differences (e.g., scope of jurisdiction, limits on government powers, use of the military) among federal, state, and local governments.

4. Explain the structures and functions of state governments, including the roles and responsibilities of their elected officials.

5. Describe the components of California's governance structure (e.g., cities and towns, Indian rancherias and reservations, counties, school districts).

THE GREAT SEAL OF THE STATE OF
CALIFORNIA
EUREKA